CONSPIRACY WORLD

CONSPIRACY WORLD

A Truthteller's Compendium of Eye-Opening Revelations and Forbidden Knowledge

TEXE MARRS

RiverCrest Publishing
4819 R.O. Drive, Suite 102, Spicewood, TX 78669

ACKNOWLEDGEMENTS

Especially deserving mention for helping me to produce this book are the outstanding members of my publishing team: Michelle Hallmark, administrator; Sandra Myers, publishing specialist and art director; Jerry Barrett, computer and internet manager; Phyllis Weedon and Kami Snyder, customer service. In the shipping department, Rosario Velásquez, manager, and Nelson Sorto are to be thanked for their excellence.

And of course there is my precious wife, Wanda, my treasure and inspiration.

Conspiracy World: A Truthteller's Compendium of Eye-Opening Revelations and Forbidden Knowledge

Third Printing, 2020

All Scripture quotations are from the King James Version of the Holy Bible

Cover design: Sandra Myers and Texe Marrs

Printed in the United States of America

Library of Congress Catalog Card Number 2009909701

Categories:
1. Current Affairs
2. Politics and Government
3. Religion
4. Occult New Age
5. History

ISBN 978-1-930004-55-9

"Ye shall know the truth, and the truth shall make you free."

—John 8:32

Other Books By Texe Marrs

Mysterious Monuments: Encyclopedia of Secret Illuminati Designs, Masonic Architecture, and Occult Places

Codex Magica: Secret Signs, Mysterious Symbols and Hidden Codes of the Illuminati

Mystery Mark of the New Age: Satan's Design for World Domination

Days of Hunger, Days of Chaos

Project L.U.C.I.D.: The Beast 666 Universal Human Control System

Circle of Intrigue: The Hidden Inner Circle of the Global Illuminati Conspiracy

Dark Majesty: The Secret Brotherhood and the Magic of a Thousand Points of Light

Millennium: Peace, Promises, and the Day They Take Our Money Away

America Shattered

New Age Cults and Religions

Dark Secrets of the New Age

Other Books By RiverCrest Publishing

Synagogue of Satan, *by Andrew Carrington Hitchcock*

New Age Lies to Women, *by Wanda Marrs*

Letters on Freemasonry, *by John Quincy Adams*

For More Information

For a complete catalog of books, tapes, and videos about the Illuminati, secret societies, occultism, Bible prophecy, conspiracy and related topics, and for a free sample of Texe Marrs' informative newsletter, *Power of Prophecy*, please phone toll-free:

1-800-234-9673, or write to:
RiverCrest Publishing
4819 R.O. Drive, Suite 102
Spicewood, Texas 78669

For additional information we highly recommend the following websites:

www.powerofprophecy.com
www.conspiracyworld.com

Table of Contents

Introduction

Welcome to Conspiracy World

I must admit, I was lamentably late in discovering that virtually the entire world is an undiscovered labyrinth of conspiracy. For the first four decades of my life I was so busy going to school and college, serving the nation through a productive, full career in the U.S. Air Force, and then afterward, embarking on a career in high technology that I had little time for anything else. But, about a quarter of a century ago, I finally hit upon the field of *Conspiracy Science*.

Yes, I do view this important, life-changing area of knowledge a *science*. Perhaps it's the most vital of all sciences. It's certainly not *conspiracy theory* we're interested in. What is most essential is to meticulously investigate facts and discover facts that can be proven and demonstrated. Let the unlearned critic call me and you "conspiracy theorists," "kooks," "whackos," "wingnuts" or whatever other scathing, descriptive phrase they care to conjure up. *I really do not care. Not a whit.*

Scientific truth is its own reward, and as the old saying goes, *"Truth is often stranger than fiction."*

Frankly, I find that most people who scoff at the evidence you'll find in this immense volume of truthful information are, themselves, woefully ignorant on these subjects. Really, most people who dismiss conspiracy research turn out to be useless idiots whose imbecile, sponge-like brains are fed constantly at the public trough of propaganda and disinformation. These pitiful fools actually believe the silly nonsense they read in such garbage rags as *The New York Times*, *The Chicago Tribune*, *The Houston Chronicle*, *Newsweek*, or *Time*, and they are easily bamboozled by the fairy tales and myths woven by news anchors daily reading the teleprompter at *CBS*, *Fox*, and other TV networks.

These poor folks remind me of the biblical story of the pompous but ill-informed Roman Governor Pontius Pilate who, face to face with Jesus—who, literally was "The Way, the Truth, and the Life"—cynically asked Him, *"What is truth?"*

Sadly, the vast majority of critics of conspiracy research have been spoon-fed so much clap-trap and so many absurd, useless lies by the deceivers, they now cannot comprehend reality. Consequently, they are helpless and utterly unable to escape Big Brother's matrix. Like a fly caught in the spider's web, their destiny is fixed. Tragic, indeed. But there is hope for those entrapped individuals. If they want to really, really know the truth, it is available, though very hard to find. It requires maximum effort, but discovering truth can be highly rewarding.

Once I began my research and investigation into Conspiracy Science, I was hooked. Those of you who, like me, continually hunger for truth and light know of what I speak. What a joy it is to discover real, honest truth and to discard and pitch into the waste-bin the lies and unfactual trash piled and heaped upon mankind throughout the centuries by so many con-men, psychopaths, and dishonest manipulators of truth and history.

I sincerely hope you, a fellow truthseeker and conspiracy scientist, will be blessed by the fruits of my many years of labor. A treasure-trove of unusual information impacting your life and future, these articles come from over 20 years of my monthly newsletters. Yet, the subject matter is as timely as today's headlines—and vastly more truthful and significant.

In these pages you will discover, as advertised, a "Truthteller's Compendium of Eye-opening Revelations and Forbidden Knowledge." Christ Jesus surely stated the truth when He promised that, "He who seeks, shall find" and that "Ye shall know the truth and the truth shall make you free."

—Texe Marrs
Austin, Texas

A Postnote: I'm now working on a second volume of *Conspiracy World* which will focus exclusively on the important topic of conspiracy science as related to Israel, Judaism, the Jews, and Zionism. Please watch for its publication (It may be already in print by the time you read this). I promise: you will not be disappointed in the upcoming, second volume. It will be explosive and on-target!

Illuminati, Global Conspiracy, and Secret Societies

Legacy of the Illuminati...

Revolution of Blood

For fifteen years now I have diligently and meticulously studied and researched the Illuminati, taking careful note of their origins and history, doctrines, and objectives. In all my investigations, one, clear fact has stood out: The men of the Illuminati are the most bloodthirsty group of savages that has ever walked the earth. Far from being a cultured, refined, and sophisticated elite, the Illuminati have demonstrated over and over again their pagan instincts and their obsessive and remarkable bloodlust.

The ongoing revolution of the Illuminati—from the days of Spain's Loyola and the *Alumbrados* to Voltaire and Robespierre of the French Revolution, and on to Lenin and Trotsky of Bolshevik Soviet infamy and Mao and Pol Pot of Asian barbarism, a trail of terror and blood has been the identifying sign of these "enlightened" Luciferian man-gods.

Age of Terror

The prime legacy of the Illuminati these past 500 years has been their Revolution of Blood. It is significant that historians have branded the period of the French Revolution the *Age of Terror*, or simply as The Terror. Likewise, chroniclers of Leninism in Soviet Russia call the years 1917-1923 the time of the *Red Terror*.

It is with reason that in the Bible's book of *Isaiah*, God declares, *"All those who hate me love death."* Consider if you will Loyola, the Catholic hero and occult Illuminist who oversaw the torment and torture of thousands of Protestant and other innocents during the inquisition. The secret order he founded, the Jesuits, continues to this day to promote Communism, murder and suffering through its Liberation Theology in South and Central America.

Vladimir Lenin, Illuminist and bloodthirsty patron of the Communist Revolution, with his sister and doctor in August 1923. By this time, Lenin's mind was ravaged by syphilis and he was a raving maniac. Note the strange look in his eyes. Communist adorers in Russia built Lenin's mausoleum using the Babylonian temple in Pergamon (*Revelation*—"the seat where Satan dwells") as a prototype.

In France, in 1798, the Freemason Voltaire privately told his Jacobin Illuminati co-conspirators, *"Our real object is to crush the wretch."* The "wretch" to whom Voltaire referred was Jesus Christ. And so, a small band of determined plotters, organized by Adam Weishaupt, a Jesuit professor who has been called "a human devil," set out to destroy all organized religion, murder every minister and priest, dismantle civilization, and return mankind to a primitive, savage state.

In his classic textbook, *Memoirs Illustrating the History of Jacobinism*, describing the Illuminist plot in France, Abbe Barruel affirms that, "The grand object of this conspiracy was to overturn every altar where Christ was adored." Theirs, Barruel wrote, was an "unrelenting hatred for Christ and kings."

Liberty, Equality, Fraternity

The rallying cry and motto of the Illuminati in France was, *"Liberty, Equality, Fraternity!"* Seemingly worthy goals. But in reality, the actual meaning and operation of these three terms was diabolical.

The word *"Liberty,"* to Illuminism, means liberty of man *from* God, the liberty of man to do as he wants, when he wants, free of the shackles of the Christian religion. Rebellion and anarchy are to be used to achieve such liberty.

"Equality," meanwhile, implies that all authority is to be smashed and that no man should own more goods than his fellows. Man would have little or no property to tie him down, no family or children, no cities, no government. Instead, rewilded man would live pure in nature in a savage and primitive, yet exalted, state.

"Fraternity" means that all men are to be brothers, the artificial strictures of national borders, religions, and races, etc. obliterated.

To attain these goals of *Liberty, Equality, Fraternity,* a Masonic physician, Dr. Guillotine, invented a bloody, head-chopping blade machine, and heads began to roll. The King and the Queen were just two of thousands executed. Next, perceiving the guillotine as too cumbersome and slow—only one person at a time was beheaded—other killing methods were employed.

Christians and Churches Persecuted

Christians in towns and cities across France who refused to renounce Christ were bound hand and foot and loaded onto boats. The boats were pushed out into deep waters of rivers. Riflemen would then shoot holes in the boats. Plaintive screams and cries were heard as the vessels sank and helpless, bound Christians drowned.

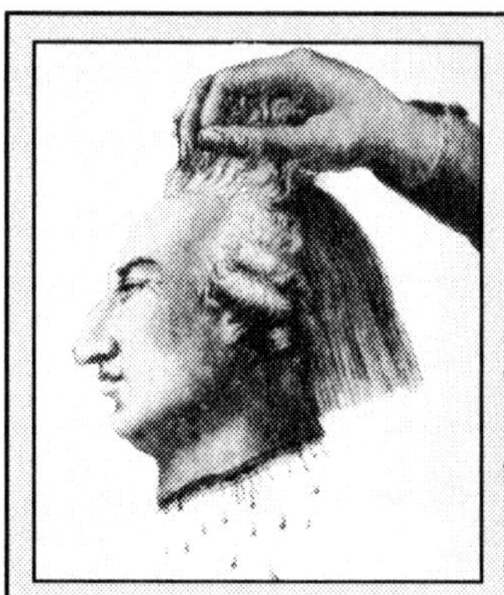

France's King Louis XVI was beheaded by Illuminati revolutionaries. The lies they told of him are still believed and taught by establishment historians.

Protestant ministers and Catholic priests alike had their eyes gouged out. Many were shot, others bayoneted, still others stomped to death or killed with the sword. Crazed rioters tore many to pieces. Some who renounced Christ were spared after being humiliated.

Inside churches, revolutionary mobs shattered stain glass windows, defecated on and destroyed pews, and threw down crosses and urinated on them. In some churches, naked women paraded inside as "Lady Liberty," proceeding to the altar where they were adored and pawed at by drunken revelers shouting obscenities at God. Pornographic art was displayed in galleries and in homes.

Across France, over three million people perished—many of whom were small merchants and shop owners, simple farmers, and God-fearing elderly persons. In some cases, entire towns were razed and destroyed.

Finally, the executors became the executed. Robespierre, chief of the Illuminati butchers, was,

Robespierre sent many innocent victims to the guillotine. But the devil is a fickle master and eventually Robespierre himself was beheaded.

in turn, himself dragged to the gallows and his head lopped off. It was the bloodthirsty feasting upon the bloodthirsty. Terror begetting terror.

When the Terror finally exhausted itself, the fake messiah, Napoleon, appeared on the scene. Many more died in the wars and famine that ensued after the crowning of the little Corsican dictator.

Of Barbarians and Devils

It was, however, in Russia and the Soviet republics that the Illuminati brought bloody terror to its ultimate peak in demonic perfection. As Donn de Grand Pré, in his sensational book, *Barbarians Inside the Gates*, reveals, the French and the Bolshevik (Communist) revolutions were funded, incited and supervised by "Jews who were not Jews," and aided and abetted by "Christians who were not Christians." Marx, whose literary works inspired the Russian Revolution and Terror, was a satanic Jew. Lenin, who led the bloody revolution in Russia, was married to a Jew, was himself Jewish. Trotsky, Lenin's deputy and co-barbarian, was also a secular Jew—he came from the Bronx, New York City, and his real name was Lev Bronstein. Almost all the Communist leadership were Jews.

Killing Rabbits, Executing People

In *Under the Sign of the Scorpion*, a stunning book published in Sweden and written by Juri Lina, the author uses freshly unearthed historical archives from Russia to finally explain the Red Terror. Lina notes that Lenin's own wife, Nadezhda Krupskaya, in her *Memoirs* (1932), describes how Lenin once rowed a boat out to a little island in the Yenisei River where many rabbits had migrated during the winter. For his own sick pleasure, the cruel Lenin clubbed so many rabbits to death with the butt of his rifle that the boat sank under the weight of all the dead bodies. Lenin became drunk with glee at the awful sight.

As dictator, Lenin adopted the merciless terror methods of France's Illuminati chief, Robespierre. To help in the killing, Lenin mobilized 1,400,000 Jews, putting many to work for the *Cheka* secret police. Lenin ordered the Cheka to *"execute weapons owners!"* They were also to kill as many students as possible, including every youth seen wearing a school cap.

Concentration camps were set up from which victims never emerged. Barges were used to drown people. Eyes of churchmen were poked out, tongues cut off, hands sawn off, heads drilled with dental tools—while screaming victims were still alive. Those nearby were forced to cut off the scalp and skull of victims and eat their brains; then, they, too, were executed. Whole families were arrested, mothers brutally raped and killed with children and fathers watching. Then all were grotesquely tortured and killed. The Volga and other rivers ran red with blood.

Churches almost everywhere were razed and bulldozed to ruins or converted to warehouses. A few were spared so the Communists could claim freedom of religion was being honored.

"Put more force into the terror!"

Lenin and Trotsky were, nevertheless, never satisfied. "Put more force into the terror," Lenin demanded. The Russian Jewish newspaper *Yevreyskaya Tribuna* (August 24, 1922), stated that

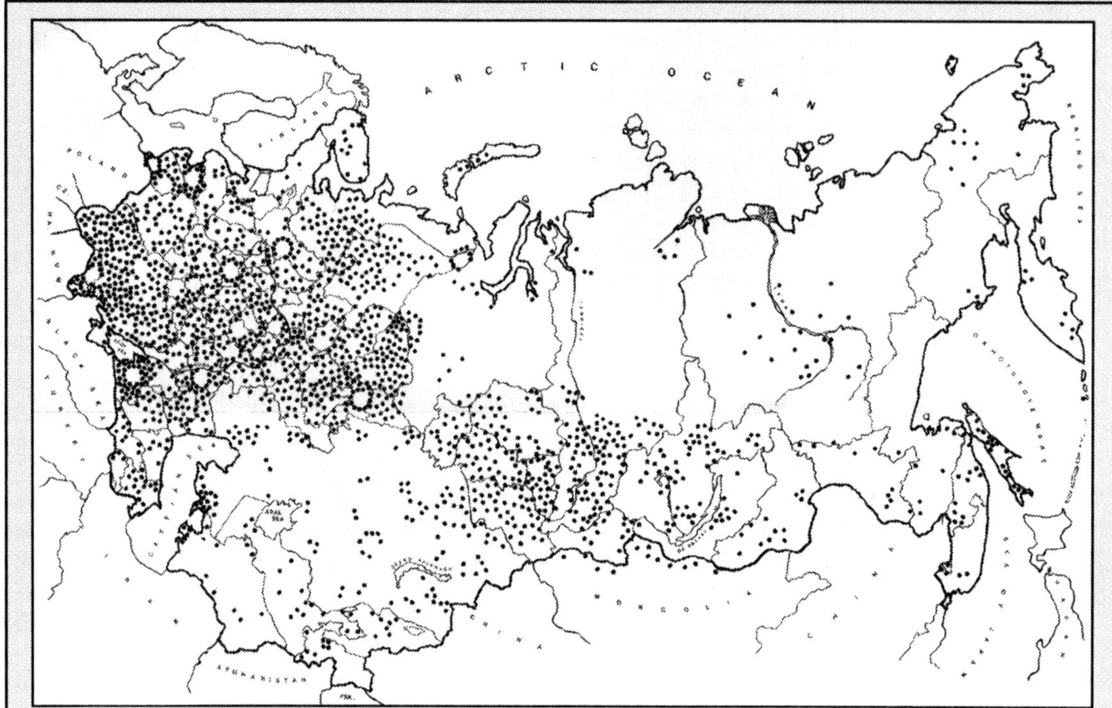

Soviet gulags: In this map of concentration camps and psychiatric prisons, each dot represents a prison camp built during the Soviet Russian regime. Satanic Illuminati Jews were the chief architects of this incredible and monstrous system of evil. Amazingly, Hitler used the Soviet gulag system as model for his own concentration camps, and the Nazis populated them primarily with innocent Jews, as well as Christian resisters.

Lenin had asked Russia's chief rabbis if they were satisfied with the particularly cruel executions meted out to Christian clergy and Christian followers.

Lina shows in his book how Lenin saw his Bolshevik Revolution as the mirror image of the French Revolution. Indeed, he was correct—both were products of Illuminist skullduggery. The French revolutionists wanted a One World Order with God dethroned. So did Lenin's Communist revolutionaries.

In August, 1923, with syphilis ravaging his mind, an ailing Vladimir Lenin sat on his balcony at Christmas and howled at the full moon like a wolf. A few weeks later, he was dead. But the Red Terror had only begun. Lenin's bloody successor, Josef Stalin, was at his bedside ready to assume Lenin's mantle as chief executioner. From 1923 to his own death in the 50s, Stalin saw to it that tens of millions more were purged, arrested, locked away in psychiatric hospitals and gulags, and tortured in KGB chambers of horror.

Where Next?

Stalin is now in Hell. So are Lenin, Mao, and Pol Pot, and, for that matter, Voltaire, Danton, and Robespierre. But the devils who possessed the dark hearts of these soulless human monsters survived, and now they take up residence in the bodies and minds of today's Illuminati.

As the world marches exuberantly onward we might well ponder when and where next these demon-infested men of the Illuminati will strike with their revolutionary fervor, wielding their bloody terror. Europe...Asia...the United States? Your hometown? Remember, we warned you in advance.

Rockefeller Money, the Illuminati, and the Breeding of the New "Super Man"

Anytime there's a global satanic event such as the upcoming Parliament of World Religions, you better believe the Illuminati are nearby, lurking in the background. In fact, my investigation reveals that it is *Illuminati money* that is behind the Parliament.

The main money sponsor of the Parliament is the *Institute for 21st Century Studies*, a Rockefeller-funded group based in Arlington, Virginia. Its executive director is Dr. Gerald O. Barney. This organization was a Club of Rome venture and grew out of the *Global 2000 Report* commissioned by President Jimmy Carter, himself a Rockefeller man. Carter was a member of both the Rockefeller-founded Trilateral Commission and the Council on Foreign Relations.

The Banking Elite Lurking Behind the Scenes

Members of the board of trustees for the Institute of 21st Century Studies include Dr. D. Jane Pratt, an officer of the World Bank who also serves as coordinator for the United Nations Environmental Program. Another trustee is Dr. Daniel A. Gomez-Ibañez, a director with the Wisconsin Power and Light Corporation (a company which has close ties with the Clinton administration). Gomez-Ibañez, a Hindu, is also the executive director of the Council for a Parliament of the World's Religions. He's the guy overseeing the satanic gala in Chicago.

Financial backing for this premier New Age organization, the Institute for 21st Century Studies, comes primarily from the Rockefeller Brothers Fund and the Rockefeller Foundation. Other money supporters include UNESCO, the World Bank, the United Nations, the World Council of Churches, and the Evangelical Lutheran Church.

In a recent brochure the Institute brags about its sponsorship of the Parliament of World Religions, asserting that, "At the 1993 Parliament, the spiritual leaders of the world will be invited to share the wisdom of their faith tradition on the critical issues of the 21st century."

A scary dimension of the Parliament of World Religions is that its location—Chicago—is not

John D. Rockefeller, Sr. (left), with the help of apostate Baptist minister, Frederick T. Gates (center), donated millions to fund a "scientific" project to create the new Super Man. At far right is the current czar of the Rockefeller clan, the fabulously wealthy banker and trilateralist, David Rockefeller.

by accident. Chicago has long been a hub of occult and Illuminati activity. Moreover, this sinister gathering of the globalist leaders of false, Luciferian religions and cults has been designed to create maximum psychological effect on the participants and the public at large through the mass media who will cover the event.

The Parliament is actually designed by alchemist mind control experts who intend to literally hypnotize the multitudes and bring them captive into a mental state of heightened occultic consciousness. Absurd though this may sound at first, let us closely examine a *special project* of the Illuminati that has been ongoing for more than a century. The relationship of the Parliament of World Religions to this special project will become self-evident. The Rockefeller connection will also become apparent.

Development of an Occult Magick Science

The Prison Fellowship ministry of Chuck Colson has announced that during the Parliament of World Religions this August in Chicago, Colson will be honored with the "John S. Templeton Prize for Progress in Religion," which includes a one million dollar award. The group also announced that the ceremony for this award will be held at the *Rockefeller Chapel* on the campus of the University of Chicago.

> ***The real goal, as we shall see, was to fund a type of occult magick science, to hasten the day when the whole world could be illumined and the New World Religion could be inaugurated.***

The Rockefeller Chapel? Yes, indeed. You see, it was John D. Rockefeller, Sr. who, in the late 19th century and at the turn of this century, gave millions of dollars to establish the University of Chicago as a prestigious institute of science. The real goal, as we shall see, was to fund a type of *occult magick science*, to hasten the day when the whole world could be illumined and the New Age World Religion could be inaugurated.

Rockefeller, Sr. was a philanthropist, but his money went for only one cause: to further the aims and objectives of the Secret Brotherhood—the Illuminati. To that end, he and his philanthropy director, Frederick T. Gates, set up the Rockefeller Institute for Medical Research. Gates had been a Baptist pastor, but, in 1911, he decided that the Bible was full of errors and that Jesus was not God. He also disavowed the traditional Christian belief that Jesus Christ was the founder of the Christian Church. These despicable, anti-Christian views were warmly received by John D. Rockefeller, Sr. who, nevertheless, remained a baptist until the day he died.

Rockefeller Money and the "Super Man" Aryan Race Theory

Working closely with the elder Rockefeller's young son, John D. Rockefeller, Jr., Gates used Rockefeller money to fund certain, very mysterious "scientific" programs at the University of Chicago, at Cold Spring Harbor Biological Laboratory in Long Island, New York, and elsewhere. The Illuminati doctrine heralded the coming of the illumined "Super Man," the "god man," who, as a result of evolutionary progress, would be endowed with a superior consciousness. It was the goal of Gates and young Rockefeller to use the Rockefeller fortune to develop and breed this new "Super Man."

Frederick Gates and his successors who wielded the Rockefeller purse were convinced that modern science could, through research in *genetics* and in *mind processes*, find the keys to evolutionary progress.

In 1933, the very year that Adolf Hitler became chancellor of Germany, the trustees and officers of the Rockefeller Foundation came up with a "new formula" for philanthropy. Instead of feeding the hungry and sheltering the homeless, they decided to spend their hundreds of millions of dollars on biological research and specifically a new area of study they called *"psychobiology."* According to the recorded minutes of their meeting held on April 11, 1933, the Rockefeller board members sought to develop a means of assuring "the control of human behavior."

In his book, *The Circuit Riders: Rockefeller Money and the Rise of Modern Science* (New York: W.W. Norton and Co., 1989)—written under the guidance of and through the "financial generosity" of the Rockefeller Foundation—Gerald Jonas points out that Jewish scientists were employed to do this research. According to Jonas, the scientists were directed to study certain "vital processes" of human animals and to "concern themselves with the rationalization of social control." (pp. 204-210)

A man named Warren Weaver was chosen by the Rockefeller combine to oversee this ambitious "psychobiology" experimental research project. In his annual report presented in 1934 to the Board of Trustees of the Rockefeller Foundation, Weaver wrote these revealing—and ominous—words about the Illuminati's plan to breed the Super Man:

> Can we develop so sound and extensive a genetics that we can hope to breed, in the future, superior men? Can we develop, before it is too late, a therapy for the whole hideous range of mental and physical disorders? Can we release psychology from its present confusion and ineffectiveness and shape it into a tool...Can we, in short, create a new science of Man? *(The Circuit Riders,* p. 210)

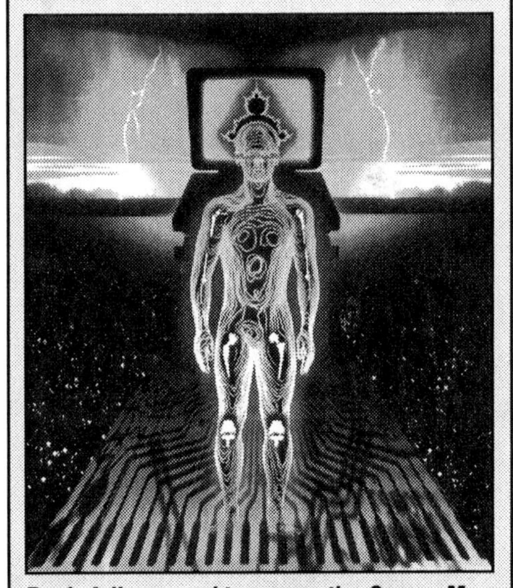

Rockefeller sought a genetic Super Man whose brain could be controlled.

Toward a New Millennium of Unharnessed Evil

Understood in context, then, Chicago's Parliament of the World's Religions is but a continuing chapter in the decades-old plan of the Rockefeller dynasty and the Illuminati hierarchy to so change and transform man that an entirely new creature will spring forth.

The new Super Man is depicted by advocates as a creature beyond good and evil, a divinely illuminated being whose superior mind is totally attuned to the desires and goals of Lucifer, the "light bearer."

Today, scientific laboratories and psychiatric think-tanks around the world, funded by Illuminati money, continue to work non-stop to devise psychological, occultic, and genetic engineering methods of improving biological man. Meanwhile, the Parliament of World Religions has been assigned the task of furthering man's spiritual consciousness.

Thus, evolutionary progress is now being fostered by the conspiratorial elite simultaneously on three different planes: mental, physical, and spiritual. And so the Great Work of the Illuminati, the illumination of mankind, continues its creepy advance as mankind moves, blissfully unaware, toward the dawn of a New Millennium of unharnessed evil.

The CFR Plot for the New Amero Currency, the Death of the Dollar, and the Impoverishment of the American People

Money, Alchemy, and Betrayal

"For the love of money is the root of all evil."

— *1 Timothy 6:10*

"From now on, depressions will be scientifically created."

— Congressman Charles A. Lindbergh, Sr.

In 1990, when I published my book, ***Millennium: Peace, Promises, and The Day They Take Our Money Away***, it created a sensation. In the book, I exposed the Illuminati elite's plan to destroy the American dollar and eventually replace the dollar and all national currencies with a new global unit, the phoenix. Of the Illuminati, I warned, "These are the men, despisers of America, who plot to take our money away and replace it with empty promises and deceitful lies."

The death of the dollar, I noted in *Millennium*, will signal a dramatic revolution in the everyday lives of American citizens, with financial misery, bankruptcy, and economic desperation stalking working men and women like some pale and apocalyptic death horse. I also named the Council on Foreign Relations (CFR) as the "kingpin" of the conspiracy against the dollar.

The Amero is on Drawing Board

Those who have read *Millennium* are not surprised, therefore, about new revelations that the CFR and its puppets in the Bush Administration now have on the drawing board a brand new currency, the *amero*. The amero is to replace the dollar upon the inauguration of the North American Union and the ending of U.S.A. sovereignty in 2010.

Eventually, of course, when the New World Order is fully realized, the phoenix will be required worldwide and all other currencies, national and regional, will be recalled. Until that bitter day of

As I reported in my eye-opening bestseller book, *Millennium: Peace, Promises, and the Day They Take Our Money Away*, the Illuminati elite eventually will replace the Amero, Euro, and other regional currencies with the *Phoenix*. Indeed, the influential *The Economist* financial magazine out of Great Britain had the audacity to picture the logo of the proposed new global currency on its cover with the feature article entitled, *"Get Ready for a World Currency."*

infamy, Europe will have its euro and the Americas will be saddled with the regional amero.

Love of Money is Root of all Evil

Why the emphasis by the Illuminati on money and currency? The love of money, the scriptures attest, is the root of all evil. After over 20 years of studying the men behind the global conspiracy and their aims, I have found this biblical principle most valid. True, the evil elitists also desire power, fame, sex, and other commodities, but above all, they lust after money. Indeed, they are persuaded that with enough money, they can buy all these other things.

That the Illuminati will scheme and murder—even commit genocide—to acquire more and more money is also a truism. Again, this is prophesied and explained in the scriptures, where James, the brother of Jesus, warned that in the last days the rich would gather for themselves heaps of gold, silver, and other treasures. Greedy and homicidal, they will not hesitate to defraud working men and women. These ordinary citizens who protest will be killed.

Paper Currency Not Real Money?

To fulfill their inordinate lust for filthy lucre, the rich have developed a banking and credit system that maximizes their return. A chief feature of this system is the employment of paper money. Of course, this is not real money; it is a pale substitute. Thomas Jefferson, one of our nation's most illustrious founders, scornfully noted this in a letter he wrote to a friend back in 1788. "Paper," said Jefferson, "is poverty." "It is only the ghost of money, and not money itself."

As a young child I readily discovered the wisdom of Jefferson's admonishment. Growing up in East Texas, a region passionately attached to the Confederacy during the War Between the States, a surprising number of Southern citizens kept their old worthless Confederate currency, somehow figuring that, someday, "The South Will Rise Again." The old Confederate dollars remain a mere museum novelty. The day General Robert E. Lee surrendered to Grant, the South's currency instantly became worthless, by Union fiat.

Lesson learned: Money is whatsoever value the government says it is. That and nothing more.

Magic in Currency Design

For some time now I have carefully investigated the design of currency, especially U.S. dollars of all denominations. I find that in every nation and society, the design of currency is of vast importance. It often has almost a magical connotation. Money reflects the spiritual understructure and the social aims of a nation's ruling class and can even reflect the prophetic goals of rulers, perhaps serving as a predictor of future events.

The design and art on its currency notes is often very revealing of a nation's culture and the aims and beliefs of its ruling elite. Above is a Mexican peso. Observe the grotesque image of the Aztec sun god emblazoned on this peso note and recall that it was this pagan sun god to whom the cannibalistic native Mexicans annually sacrificed tens of thousands of human beings. Meanwhile, the U.S. dollar also has a satanic image—the pyramid and all-seeing eye of the Egyptian version of the sun god. One can only imagine what hideous design the new amero currency will incorporate!

Dean Grace, a researcher and friend who has spent many years studying the symbology of the U.S. one dollar bill, emphasizes that such symbols as the pyramid, the all-seeing eye, and the eagle of the

Professor Robert Pastor, of American University in Washington, D.C., influential member of the Council on Foreign Relations, co-authored the CFR report, *Building a North American Community*, in which he proposed a currency unit called the amero to replace the U.S.A. and Canadian dollars and the Mexican peso.

Great Seal speak volumes about America's ruling elite and their conspiratorial aims. The color green has keen significance, and a message in occult numerology is also found in the art and design.

Meanwhile, the design of the Mexican peso also is of great interest because, apparently, the ruling elite of Mexico and the U.S.A. have every intention to soon replace both the peso and the dollar with the new currency, the amero. In March, 1995, in Waco, Texas, President George Bush, along with Mexico's President Fox and Canada's Prime Minister Martin, signed the *Security and Prosperity Partnership* (SPP) agreement. As conceived by the Illuminati's powerful organ, the Council on Foreign Relations, the SPP requires that by 2010, the three countries will be merged into one, the North American Union. Our Constitution is betrayed, American sovereignty is coming to an end, and our dollar will be replaced by the amero, much the same as happened in Europe with the European Union's euro currency.

To the Illuminati, it is essential that the art and the design of the *amero* reflect the New Reality—the fact that the U.S.A. is forever to be ended as a functioning, independent entity. The unique heritage, history, and culture of the United States must be obliterated for the psychological and emotional conquest of the citizens to be realized. The *amero* will thus be a brainwashing tool, a constant reminder carried in the pocket, wallet, and purse of every resident of the late, great U.S.A., that we are no longer special, no longer a proud and separate people. We shall henceforth be only a *regional entity*, a subverted and conquered *subdivision* of the reigning Big Brother *global colossus*. This is the true meaning of the North American Union and the amero currency.

A Financial Crash Ahead?

Today, economic conditions are being prepared for the dollar to be shredded and devalued in world markets. A financial crash of the dollar is inevitable. Saudi Arabia, Russia, China, Iran, Germany and others are already beginning to go to the euro and are about to leave the dollar in the dust. No longer is the dollar king of world currencies. It has already, in the past five years, lost much of its value, and today, the U.S.A. is the world's largest debtor nation. Our country is drowning in red ink.

By the time the Illuminati and its bankers are through draining the dollar of every last vestige of value, the American people will be impoverished and frightened. Then will come our President, our Fed Chairman, and our banking and corporate chieftains, to reassure us, to win us over to the New Reality. The North American Union and its amero—that and that alone, they shall say, will save us from economic depression and money chaos. The amero is our future, our only hope.

Without the amero, our esteemed leaders will caution, you will be decimated, reduced to misery. With it, and with SPP and the North American Union, you will be secure and prosperous. Yes, maybe your savings and pensions and your social security funds will be gone—poof! Vanished in thin air!—your wages diminished and your economy reduced to Third World status. But you will at least survive and will subsist, if at a more "sustainable" level. The Amero: Don't leave home without it!

So, say goodbye, George Washington, Ben Franklin, Andrew Jackson and the others whose somber and trusty faces now gaze upon us from America's historical currency notes. It's been a grand 225-year long experiment in freedom and liberty, hasn't it?

Pigs in the Parlor

"Give not that which is holy unto the dogs, neither cast your pearls before swine…"

— *Matthew 7:6*

This month, we're offering a dynamic new exposé audiotape, *Pigs in the Parlor*. This tape reveals the truth about the men who make up two of the most sinister organizations on planet earth: the *Trilateral Commission* and the *Council on Foreign Relations*.

The logos of both of these organizations speak louder than words. The Trilateral logo is an interlocking system of three arrows, each designed to suggest the number "6." Thus: 6-6-6. The shape and projectory of these arrows causes a triangle of three parts to be formed. In occult paganism, this represents the unholy trinity of deities worshipped in the ancient Mystery Religions. Note, also, that the arrows point to "the One," symbolically meaning that *all things* are to eventually come under the domination and control of the Secret Brotherhood and, eventually, its Antichrist leader.

Meanwhile, the Council on Foreign Relations has used a logo of a *rider on a white horse*. To understand the horrendous meaning of this curious logo, we need only turn to Revelation 6 of our Bibles. There, we discover that the first of the dreadful and bloody Four Horsemen of the Apocalypse is the rider on the white horse!

Money and World Control

Dig a little beneath the surface and one discovers that both the Trilateral Commission and the Council on Foreign Relations (CFR) are both controlled by the same, small inner circle of wealthy elitists. These men have a vise grip on the international banks and on our Federal Reserve.

Left: the Trilateral Commission logo, at right is the logo of the Council on Foreign Relations.

At any given moment in time they can simply give the order—and the whole world's economies will immediately plunge into devastating chaos.

To illustrate how money and world politics

are inseparably intertwined, consider these recent remarks by John Huddleston, chief of the budget and planning division of the International Monetary Fund (IMF). In Huddleston's book *Achieving Peace By the Year 2000*, published—note this!—by *One World Press*, he proclaims that "A true world government...is the logical outcome of present long-term trends and would provide many benefits."

Huddleston and the money men of the Trilateral Commission and CFR Commission, not only want us to enthusiastically accept a World Government—led by *them* of course—they also want us to accept the globalist propaganda now being pumped into our educational system. These sinister men want to make sure we get the message.

The meetings of the Council on Foreign Relations are held in their headquarters, the Harold Pratt House, at 58 East 68th Street in New York City.

Poison in our Schools

IMF official Huddleston suggests that to impress upon Americans that they are "world citizens" and to get across the message that nationalism and patriotism are dangerously outmoded, a *new curricula must be implemented at once in all schools and universities.* He writes:

> One effective way to do this is to institute compulsory classes at all levels of the education system in all countries. Such classes would...demonstrate the oneness of mankind...They would teach people to distinguish...nationalism which causes division and destruction.

Accept it...or Else!

How enlightening that this top muckety-muck of the international banking fraternity wants to mandatorily educate us all on the merits of World Government. Moreover, according to the Trilateral and CFR boys, we commoners are going to have to accept the inevitable...or else. John D. Rockefeller IV, the U.S. Senator from West Virginia who has been tapped for a future important role in the New World Order, put it this way in a key Trilateral Commission publication back in 1988: "The United States (people) will adjust to this different world . . . We have no choice."

Senator Rockefeller

Pigs In Our Parlor

It is accurate, I believe, to portray these greedy, would-be potentates as what they truly are: pigs in our parlor! I'm sure that, like me, you deeply love this country. You and I are proud to be Americans. But we are also sick and tired of this once great land being trashed and despoiled by rich elitists and their servants who have no respect for either God or for the greatness of the American heritage and tradition.

Do you agree with me that it's high time we shined some much needed light on these men and their filthy plot?

The Plot of the Council on Foreign Relations, the Trilateral Commission, the Bilderbergers, and Other Illuminati Cults

The Pigs Are *Still* in the Parlor

Some years ago I unmasked the nefarious plot of a dragon's nest of illuminist organizations, secret societies, and orders working to end America's long stretch of freedom and independence. I titled my Special Report, *"Pigs in the Parlor."* Well, guess what, dear friends? The pigs are still in the parlor, and now they're more swinish, more greedy, and more filthy and covered with mud than ever before.

I decided, therefore, that it is time to give you an update on the sinister schemes and covert activities of these groups that are so bent on unraveling America. Their objective, of course, is self-aggrandizement, the will and desire for money and for the power and authority money can buy.

The men and women comprising these elitist groups are globalists, that is, internationalists, and it can be said even of those who were born in the U.S.A., that they have no particular fondness or sentimental attachment to our once, great country. In fact, it seems they loathe and despise our nation's heritage and constitution. That is why they strive to end American sovereignty by forming a North American Union by 2010, followed by merger with Russia and Europe.

Four Pillars of the Illuminist Agenda

In my audiotape/CD exposé of the elitists and their exclusive, little "rich men's clubs," I document four principal objectives of these criminal politicians, corporate CEOs, and bankers. I call them the *"Four Pillars of the Illuminist Agenda."* They are:

1) Incite and oversee a disastrous "clash of civilizations," pitting religions, ethnic groups, and nation-states against one another;
2) End American sovereignty and merge the U.S.A. into regional and global systems of governance;
3) Transform the United States into a Third World culture, crushing America's middle class, collapsing its economy, and making its desperate citizens willingly subservient to illuminist leadership and solutions;
4) Establish a dictatorial, Masonic-inspired Zionist Global Empire

Alfred Lord Tennyson's poem, *Locksley Hall*, inspired illuminists with its vision of a "Federation of the World." U.S.A. President Harry S. Truman, shown here in 33rd degree Mason regalia, kept a copy of it in his wallet.

A Federation of the World

The Illuminati plot has been masterminded and executed over the years by a number of so-called illustrious "heroes." Their globalist philosophy was perhaps best expressed by 19th century British poet, Alfred Lord Tennyson, an occultist and Mason, whose revealing poem, *"Locksley Hall,"* epitomized the lofty aims of the elitist conspirators. President Harry Truman, a 33rd degree Mason, carried a typed copy of Tennyson's *"Locksley Hall"* in his wallet every day of his adult life and often pulled it out and read it to friends.

One of the more pungent stanzas in the prophetic, illuminist poem is this one:

"For I dipt into the future,
far as human eye could see,
Saw the vision of the world,
and all the wonder that would be;
Till the war-drum throbb'd no longer,
And the battle flags were furled
In the Parliament of man,
the Federation of the world."

David Rockefeller, Sr., who says he is a "Proud Internationalist," is shown here from my book, *Codex Magica*, giving a cabalistic hand sign.

New York's globalist banker, David Rockefeller, Sr., would no doubt appreciate the prophetic vision of fellow occultist Tennyson. In my audiotape/CD report, *The Pigs Are Still In the Parlor*, I quote Rockefeller as he proudly boasts of his many achievements in founding and/or leading the top illuminist groups in the world today, including the Council on Foreign Relations, the Society of the Americas, the Bilderbergers, and the Trilateral Commission. Admitting in his recent autobiography to being a "Proud Internationalist," Rockefeller noted that he has been accused by "conspiracy theorists" of "conspiring with others around the world to build a one-world political and economic system."

"If that's the charge," trumpeted the banking mogul, "I stand guilty, and I am proud of it."

The End of the Story

The globalist clock is ticking. It appears that we have little time left to prepare ourselves for the coming days of supreme treachery and betrayal by the illuminist traitors in our midst. Already they hold an iron leash around the neck of our federal government in Washington, D.C., and few of our 50 state capitals are immune from their leprous grip. More than ever, we must discover the truth and get all the facts out on the table. That's why I broadcast my revelations and offer them to you as *"The Pigs Are Still in the Parlor."*

However, please always remember the end of the story. You and I may confidently look to the future and know with certainty that past all the coming hours of turmoil and strife, the victory of God's people—those of us who believe in and trust Jesus our Lord—is assured. I invite you, dear friends, to take hold in your heart of this great prophecy as foretold in the Holy Scriptures:

> *"And the seventh angel sounded; and there were great voices in heaven, saying, THE KINGDOMS OF THIS WORLD ARE BECOME THE KINGDOMS OF OUR LORD, AND OF HIS CHRIST, AND HE SHALL REIGN FOREVER AND EVER." (Revelation 11:15)*

Solving the Riddle of the Council on Foreign Relations

Naked Man on a White Horse

"And he will be a wild man; his hand will be against every man, and every man's hand against him..."

—*Genesis 16:12*

"Let the Rider from the Secret Place come forth..."

The Great Invocation,
The Lucis Trust

Does a tiny logo, printed on the cover of each issue of the authoritative journal, *Foreign Affairs*, hold the key to the future of America and, indeed, of the entire world? Moreover, could this same mark, or symbol, reveal to the wise the mysterious power that energizes and motivates the deadly global cult that the Holy Bible refers to as the last days *Synagogue of Satan?*

Revelation 6 paints for us an ominous, grim picture of the last days. It describes four horses and riders, popularly known as the Four Horsemen of the Apocalypse, to arrive on the world scene. First comes the Rider of the White Horse. He has a bow in his hand, the means to make war; he is given a crown and he goes forth to conquer and to subjugate all the world.

The conquering hero on the white horse is swiftly followed by the frightening riders of the Red, the Black, and the Pale Horses. Each, in turn, brings in its wake bloodshed, famine, disaster, disease and death on a massive scale. By these catastrophes the whole earth is ravaged, and few survive.

The man who sits astride the white horse is an impressive figure. The people honor him as a leader and warrior. While he is capable of making war, he comes initially as a man of peace. Thus, he rides a white horse, the symbol of peace. He will, the world's population concludes, usher in an unprecedented era of global harmony and tranquillity.

> And I saw, and behold a white horse: and he that sat on him had a bow; and a crown was given unto him: and he went forth conquering, and to conquer.
>
> Revelation 6:2

But this conclusion is wrong. Instead, his arrival on the world stage presages the most devastating period in the annals of human history. Death, the feared Destroyer, is the

In this famous painting set in Egypt, the conqueror Napoleon, a Freemason and Illuminist, gives the Sign of Admiration of the sixth degree of the Masonic Lodge.

The official logo of the Council on Foreign Relations pictures a wild, naked man on a white horse flashing the 6-6-6 occult salute of the sixth degree of Freemasonry.

companion of the white horse rider, and a cloud of misery soon envelops all humanity.

From Caesar to Lenin—Heroes are Acclaimed

For centuries, men have eagerly awaited the emergence of this heroic figure atop the white horse. Julius Caesar, Charlemagne, Napoleon, Hitler, Lenin, and many others were once acclaimed as world heroes. Each attained only a partial measure of glory before the fire of their achievements flickered out and was extinguished.

Today, once again, nations and people everywhere hungrily long for and await the coming of a Great One, a figurative hero riding a white horse, to set things right. They believe that he and he alone will be able to bring peace to a war-torn, troubled world.

In Rio de Janeiro, Brazil, in 1992, world leaders from 120 nations assembled for the first Earth Summit. Fearing a looming environmental disaster such as global warming, they began their global conclave with a prayer. That prayer, *The Great Invocation*, was furnished the attendees by the Lucis Trust, a New York and Geneva-based occult organization with close ties to the United Nations. *The Great Invocation* literally invokes, or invites, the heroic Rider of the White Horse to come forth to take the reins of world government, to unite the nations and lead the New World Order. In unison, world leaders from the United States, Germany, Russia, Britain, France, China, and scores of other nations solemnly stood and cried out, *"Let the Rider from the Secret Place come forth..."*

The Council on Foreign Relations and its Logo

This brings us back once again to that curious logo, or mark, on the cover of *Foreign Affairs* journal, which is the official publication of the powerful elitist cult group, the Council on Foreign Relations (CFR). The CFR truly is the inner circle of the Illuminati conspiracy. Mostly Jewish, its 3,300 members are the *crème de la crème* of American politics, corporations, banking and finance. The Chairman of the Federal Reserve, the Secretary of the Treasury, the Secretary of State, and the CEOs of virtually the entire Fortune 500—they're all here, each serving as an obedient vassal to the Jewish elite who sit as the CFR's governing council.

This Jewish elite that rules the CFR agenda can, with certainty, be identified as the prophesied *Synagogue of Satan (Revelation 2:9)*, a sinister group covertly led by devils from the pit of hell which everywhere opposes and seeks the destruction of Christians and the end of liberty and freedom.

The logo of any group, organization, or corporation typifies and encapsulates the aims and goals of that group. This can easily be seen in the logo of the CFR, which consists of a blackened circle, and inside the circle, a naked man riding a white horse. The man's nakedness gives evidence he is a "Wild Man," a rebel; yet, by his demeanor and attitude, the Rider of the White Horse clearly is a determined warrior confident of his mission.

The white horse rider pictured on the CFR's official logo does not as yet have the crown that is to be given to him. But since 1921, the CFR has labored to manipulate and deceive the world and has now contrived conditions in the Mid-East for a climactic World War III that will accomplish this. Meanwhile, the United States, in its Great Seal, has the mighty eagle clutching the arrows in its talon, or claw, that are already being employed as armaments of a global war. The emergent leader of the Synagogue of Satan, this naked man on a white horse, possesses, then, the awesome military might of the world's only remaining superpower, the U.S.A. Everything is at the ready for a final, bloody struggle.

You Cannot Escape the Naked Man

On the CFR logo, below the naked rider on the white horse, is a motto, an inscription in Latin, *Ubique*. It's meaning is "Everywhere," or "We are everywhere." Implicit in this Latin word is the connotation of "Big Brother is watching you!" His all-seeing eye is pervasive. He reigns over all. He sees, he governs, and you cannot escape his global dominion.

The naked wild man holds forth his right arm and hand in an erect position, a salute toward the sky, the fingers cast in the recognizable Masonic gesture demonstrated by initiates of the 6th degree of Freemasonry. In the ceremony and ritual for the 6th degree, the initiate displays hand and body signs which compute to 6-6-6, the prophesied number of the beast *(Revelation 13)*. This is well-explained in my exposé book, *Codex Magica*.

The hand/arm salute of the CFR's naked man atop the white horse, in Masonic textbooks, is called the *"Sign of Admiration."* Its explanation is bound up in the ancient pagan temple rituals of Israel's apostate King Solomon. In reality, this sign is the occult salute of those who are of the Synagogue of Satan. The salute is made in honor of their leader and king, Lucifer, whom the Scriptures call, the "Prince of the Power of the Air."

Seething with Luciferian Energies

The late Manly P. Hall, 33°, officially declared by international Freemasonry as the Scottish Rite's greatest "Scholar of the 20th Century," revealed to his Masonic brethren the true, hidden meaning of the One who rides the White Horse. According to Hall, the works of the Mason, if exemplary and exceptional, may well earn him the status of godhood. Such men are rewarded by the Great Architect of the Universe (Lucifer) with superhuman wisdom and powers. Thus endowed, the exalted, divine Mason virtually seethes with "Luciferian energy;" Hall says he is a "dynamo" of action, a "Warrior on the block."

The dynamic leader endowed (possessed?) with this powerful Luciferian energy answers only to the one whom the prophet Daniel identified as the "God of

The Great Seal of the United States, printed on the one dollar bill, depicts an eagle clutching in its talon arrows with which to make war. Above the Eagle's head are stars mysteriously arranged to form a six-pointed Jewish Star of David—sign of the prophesied Synagogue of Satan.

The elite membership of the CFR includes the top movers and shakers of American politics and money including (from left to right) Ben Bernanke, Chairman of the Federal Reserve System; Henry Paulson, Secretary of the Treasury; Condi Rice, Secretary of State; David Rockefeller, New York City banker; and Bill Clinton, former President of the United States.

Forces." He is, indeed, a wild man, a warrior, and the Bible's prophecies describe him as such *(Genesis 16:1-12; Genesis 21:1-21; Galatians 4:29)*. He is, moreover, a soldier, a centurion of sorts, in the Legion of Satan. His religion, meanwhile, is Apostate Judaism, the religion practiced by all who comprise the Synagogue of Satan. It is these "wild men" of the Synagogue of Satan who dare to make war with the saints, to cast some into prison and to kill others.

Jesus—King of Kings and Lord of Lords

But in the end, a Greater One shall come, and Him they cannot withstand. This Greater One's name is Jesus. He, too, symbolically rides a white horse *(Revelation 19:11-16)*, and he has a name written, "King of Kings and Lord of Lords." He also has an Army, an Army that cannot be defeated. It is made up of the Overcomers. And with Him, with their King and Lord on the throne, they shall reign forever. The Kingdom which their leader establishes shall never fall. It is everlasting.

But as for the enemy, the unrighteous and damnable naked man on the white horse, he and his followers shall be forever humbled. Defeated, they shall be cast down into the lake of fire which is everlasting. This is the second death, and it is beyond our imagination in its horror.

Day of Decision

The warrior-lord, the Satan-led naked man on the white horse, is at your doorstep. He demands you serve him, his CFR elite and the Synagogue of Satan. He lies and offers you treasures and rewards here on earth if you will pledge to serve him and help him build his earthly kingdom.

The true and honorable King from heaven also implores you, *"Take up your cross, follow me. I am the Light of the World, the Lamb slain from the foundation of the world; yet, I live forevermore."*

Choose this day, dear friend, whom you will serve. But choose carefully. Your immortal life depends on it.

And if it seem evil unto you to serve the LORD, choose you this day whom ye will serve; whether the gods which your fathers served that were on the other side of the flood, or the gods of the Amorites, in whose land ye dwell: but as for me and my house, we will serve the LORD. (Joshua 24:15)

The Next President of the United States Will Be An Initiate of ...

The Order of Skull and Bones

"The gaunt, naked initiate, John Kerry, was lifted out of the coffin and his blindfold removed. As he blinked his eyes and gazed about the room, he was shocked at the scene. He saw before him members in skeleton suits, in red suits, in bloody, torn, scroungy garb, and in ghostly costumes. The heads of some were covered with black hoods. And he noticed that some wore sparsely cut, grayish robes with strange symbols inscribed thereon. He was then brought silently into the tower room before the mysterious hooded and crowned figure who sat regally on a throne. "Bow to the Master," the order came from attendants. But, who was the Master?, Kerry asked himself. Was this just an ordinary man, the human leader of Skull and Bones, or was this mysterious, hooded figure, in fact, the one whom men fear and quiver before? Could this be Lucifer himself, Prince of Darkness?"

Senator John Kerry, Democrat from Massachusetts, appears primed to win the nomination of his party as candidate for the high office of President of the United States. Can he defeat incumbent George W. Bush? The polls indicate the answer could be "yes." In head-to-head competition, voters surveyed now favor Kerry over Bush.

But oddly, no matter which man, Kerry or Bush, wins the electoral college and takes possession of the White House, one thing is for certain: The next President will be a member of one of the planet's most elitist and most exclusive secret societies, the Order of Skull and Bones.

Digging Up Bones

I am author of ***Dark Majesty***, only the second book ever to be published exposing the Luciferian goals and exclusive membership of Skull and Bones. I have also produced two audiotape investigative reports unmasking the Order, ***The Society of Skull and Bones—A Stunning Exposé,*** and the in-depth follow-up, ***Digging Deeper Into Skull and Bones***.

Standing before a U.S. flag displayed for propaganda effect, presidential candidate John Kerry gives the classic Communist, clenched fist salute.

As an outsider, only one other person on Earth knew more than I about this wicked and ambitious organization: my good friend and fellow conspiracy researcher, the late Dr. Antony Sutton. Sutton's classic book, *America's Secret Establishment: An Introduction to the Order of Skull & Bones*, predated my own book on this subject. Just before his death, the elderly, ailing, yet still brilliant Antony Sutton was kind enough to send me his entire set of extensive files on the Illuminati. It proved to be a treasure trove of detailed, revealing information. Antony Sutton encouraged me to keep moving forward in my work of shedding light on this dark and evil group and the shadowy elite behind it.

"I am old and in my 80s" Sutton wrote me, "and I have studied the conspirators and their crimes for many decades. Now, it's all up to you."

Antony Sutton, who became the avowed enemy of the Illuminati while a researcher at the Hoover Institute at Stanford University, was delighted at the publication of my seminal volume, *Dark Majesty*. My book touched on and amplified his own investigative work, but also brought forth even more shocking details and discoveries about the Order.

Before his passing, Sutton had seen the elevation of bonesman George Herbert Walker Bush (the elder) to the presidency. He also had observed the meteoric rise to political prominence of a young Arkansan, Yale Law School graduate William Jefferson Clinton, an ambitious initiate chosen by Skull and Bones patriarch Averell Harriman for future stardom. But Antony Sutton, if he were still with us, would be amazed at the sensational chain of events that have occurred in more recent years.

George W. Bush renders a familiar hand sign well-known to insiders.

From Elder Bush to Younger Bush and Kerry

For one thing, there was the surprising emergence of young George W. Bush from relative obscurity to become, first, Governor of Texas, and then, President of the world's sole remaining superpower nation. George W., of course, is a graduate of Yale and a bonesman, like his father and his grandfather before him.

As if that weren't enough to shake the cobwebs off the musty door of The Tomb, the Order of Skull and Bones' mausoleum-like residence just off the Yale campus in New Haven, Connecticut, there is also the matter of John Kerry. Kerry, as it turns out, is a brother of George W. Bush. Not a brother in the genetic realm, but a "brother" nevertheless in terms of each man's joint membership in the Skull and Bones.

In May, 1966, John Kerry lay nude in a coffin and bowed before the throne as fellow bonesmen, in strange garb and mouthing mysterious epithets, gathered about him. As a result of that satanic ritual, he became a "blood brother" to George W. Bush and to some 800 other bonesmen alumni. These 800 men now hold positions of exceeding power and influence in fields such as politics, banking, finance, and education. One is President of the U.S.A. Another, John Kerry, wants to succeed him.

Kerry's Concealed Jewish Heritage

John Kerry's real surname is, of course, not really Kerry. And he's neither of Irish heritage nor of Catholic religious persuasion. Those are mere fronts, deceptive facades created by his masters for public consumption. Both Kerry and Bush have their images created and molded by their Illuminati overlords, the better to deceive the masses.

The persona created by the Illuminati for bonesman initiate George W. Bush was that he would be an earthy, cowboy and boots Texas type. This was to be an image which, naturally, belied George's Kennebunkport, Maine, roots and his privileged Brahmin upbringing among the Wall

Street elite of his grandfather, Prescott Sheldon Bush.

Nobody much cares for a wealthy New Englander and Yale graduate who got to Yale by blood ties, not on merit, and who dodged military service, drank, and partied most of his life. So, young playboy George, who never worked a day in his life, was chosen to play the part of a Texan tycoon and to portray himself as a reformed, evangelical, born again Christian.

The Illuminati even brought imposter evangelist, 33rd degree Masonic brother Billy Graham, in on the deal. The propaganda script written by the Illuminati called for playboy George W. Bush to be turned around and "saved" personally by Billy Graham. It all "happened" when, while visiting the Bush family in their beachside mansion at Kennebunkport, Maine, evangelist Billy Graham took a walk with George along the beach by the sparkling ocean and prayed with him. That's the myth, and it sold good to the gullible Christian masses, who eagerly pulled the "correct" lever or marked the correct spot on the ballot for George W., "born again Christian," to be elected President of the U.S.A.

The propaganda script written by the Illuminati called for playboy George W. Bush to be turned around and "saved" personally by Billy Graham.

Kerry's Czechoslovakian and Wall Street Roots

Now comes bonesman John Kerry, whose real name is John Kohn, whose wealthy father, Richard Kohn, was a State Department big shot and whose Jewish grandfather, Fritz Kohn, originally came over to the U.S.A. from Czechoslovakia. Fritz Kohn set up shop with fellow Jews on Wall Street and soaked up a fortune ripping off hapless Gentile clients.

In Massachusetts, Jews are not as popular as Irish Catholics, so the name "Kerry" was assigned the Kohn tribe. For his entire life, John Kerry has pretended to be Irish and Catholic. It got him his U.S. Senator post some 19 years ago. Now he wants to be President, and rich Jews have billions to donate to Jewish and pro-Zionist candidates. So, in 2003, Kerry publicly announced that he had just made a startling genealogical discovery. "Yep, I'm Jewish," Kerry told the press. "I never would have thought it," he said. "Gee whiz."

This revealing picture in *Newsweek* magazine (Feb. 9, 2004, pg. 45) shows Senator John Kerry peering out from behind the curtains. It's concealed message, understood by insiders: "Our Illuminati bonesman initiate John Kerry, adeptly hides his secret from the gullible, deceived masses."

The Heinz Ketchup Heiress and Hadassah

My investigation shows that Teresa Heinz, the wife of John Kerry, is also Jewish. Heir to the billion dollar Heinz ketchup and foods dynasty, Teresa is active in Jewish and Israeli causes. She's chair of Hadassah, the national Jewish women's organization. Kerry's brother is also now out of the closet as a Jew, and regularly attends worship at a Jewish synagogue. He evidently dropped the Kerry family pretense of being "Irish Catholic."

For some reason, the Illuminati has decided that it is time. Time for many formerly hidden Jews to come out of the closet. A few years ago, Madeleine Albright, Clinton's Secretary of State, surprisingly "discovered" she was a Czech Jew. General Wesley Clark, another Democrat, also made the same discovery just this year. Clark now says his father's real name was "Kanne," Jewish. The General even bragged to a Jewish group of millionaires whom he auditioned with that, "My Jewish father came from a long line of Rabbis."

General Wesley Clark discovered that his real surname is the Jewish "Kanne." Clark recently boasted to a Jewish audience: "My Jewish father came from a long line of Rabbis."

Jewish Conspirators in the White House

Yes, it does seem a certainty that whether Bush or Kerry, our next President will be a bonesman. He may be a Jew, too, and his vice President may be a Jew. Two Jews who once claimed to be Gentiles!

So what's the big deal? Why does it matter? Well, you history buffs may recall that in 1917, two closet Jews named Lenin and Trotsky vaulted to the leadership of the Russian Empire, an empire then among the world's greatest superpowers. They and their Jewish henchmen went on to imprison, torture, and kill some 66 million Christians and other "enemies" of Jewish Zionism. The Soviet gulags, run by Jewish commandants, dwarfed the Nazi concentration camps in size and deadliness.

Could it happen again, this time in America? You better believe it can! We should not forget that, at their occultic initiation, the rich young men tapped to become bonesmen by the Order are cautioned by their mysterious, hooded leader that they, bonesmen, are to reign as gods on earth, the Chosen Ones. They are also told they must never forget that, *"All those creatures outside the Order are barbarians, vandals, and gentiles."*

O LORD, how long shall I cry, and thou wilt not hear! even cry out unto thee of violence, and thou wilt not save! Why dost thou shew me iniquity, and cause me to behold grievance? for spoiling and violence are before me: and there are that raise up strife and contention. Therefore the law is slacked, and judgment doth never go forth: for the wicked doth compass about the righteous; therefore wrong judgment proceedeth.

Yet I will rejoice in the LORD, I will joy in the God of my salvation The LORD God is my strength, and he will make my feet like hinds' feet, and he will make me to walk upon mine high places. (Habakkuk 1:2-4. 3:18,19)

Barack Obama, Mysterious Monuments, and the Second Coming of Osiris...

Black Pharaoh

"There is scarcely a king (or would-be-king) in a hundred who would not, if he could, follow the example of Pharaoh—get first all the people's money, then all their lands, and then make them and all their children slaves forever."
— Thomas Jefferson
Writings of Thomas Jefferson

What is the significance of the mysterious pyramids, obelisks, and other Egyptian architecture and monuments rising across America? Will Barack Obama become America's first "Pharaoh?" Could the intuitively intelligent Senator from Illinois be destined to become the second coming of Osiris, the Egyptian Sun God? It was Osiris, the ancients believed, whose spirit was reincarnated in the person of the Pharaoh. Honored as the Lord of the Underworld, the divine Osiris is the very same deity depicted on America's one-dollar bill—as the All-Seeing Eye in the capstone hovering over the Novus Ordo Seclorum pyramid.

Obama is "The One"

Commentators have noted the stunning messianic tone to Barack Obama's presidential campaign. His followers reverently speak of Obama as *"The One;"* they print impressive eye-catching posters of their candidate's handsome face, glowing, surrounded by radiant sun rays. They boast of Obama's extraordinary oratory skills and point to his uncanny ability to inspire the masses.

In all these things and more, the countenance and leadership qualities of Barack Obama seem to be amazingly reminiscent of those attributed to Egypt's ages-old Sun god. Egypt, of course, is situated geographically in north Africa. Obama's roots, meanwhile, can be traced to three continents. His birth to a white mother was in America; he was raised as a boy in Indonesia, in Asia; but his biological father, a black man, came from Kenya, in Africa.

Obama & Osiris: Fascinating Parallels

The Egyptian deity Osiris was usually depicted as black, but sometimes, in his guise as god of agriculture and vegetation, as green in color. Obama is ideologically a doctrinaire environmentalist and is portrayed by Democrats as the ecologically correct "Green" candidate.

Osiris had many titles, including *"The Great Word."* He was said to be endowed with "the creative power of speech." Likewise, Obama's creative power of speech has enabled him to draw huge, cheering crowds of 75,000 in Portland, Oregon, and some 200,000 in Berlin, Germany.

Osiris was proclaimed to be the *"World Teacher,"* a great, traveling teacher-god who "civilized the world." Barack Obama's recent travels to Israel and to Europe were, indeed, remarkable. In Berlin, he declared, "This is our moment...This is our time." We have it in our power, he assured the masses watching on television around the globe, to *"remake the world."*

Osiris was deemed to be a "living god," for his spirit entered into the body and soul of the living Pharaoh, leader of the people. As a man-god, the Pharaoh taught the people the proper form of worship. He consolidated and unified the diverse religious sects of Egypt and established himself as the incarnation of Osiris, "God above the gods."

It perhaps deserves noting that in his Berlin "New World Order" speech, Senator Obama spoke of the necessity of uniting the three major world religions—Christianity, Judaism, and Islam.

Osiris required sacrifice of the people and made slaves of millions. Barack Obama, in his speeches, has warned, "sacrifice will be required."

Osiris united all races and ethnic groups. Obama, in his Berlin address, urged that the barriers between ethnic groups, tribes, and races be dissolved. Immigrants, he said, must be welcomed by all nation-states. Obama also announced that he considers himself a citizen not only of the United States, but *"a citizen of the world."*

Osiris was a god of peace but also of war. Obama has called for uniting the nations of Europe side-by-side with the United States in a perpetuation of the ongoing bogus "War on Terror." Far from being a peacemaker, in Berlin, Obama made a clarion call for intensification of global conflict, with the pretense of this being a holy war against the remnants of the dreaded Osama Bin Laden and his rag-tag band of fanatical Moslem separatists and zealots.

Enthusiastic crowds follow Obama.

Obama, then, portrays himself as a type of priest for the whole world and all its populace. Like the ancient Pharaohs, whom he emulates, he is the One who promises to bring peace, prosperity, and plenty—*new life*—to the land. But, at the same time, he threatens his rebellious enemies with ruthless and imminent military destruction. Osiris, after all, was known as the "Avenger."

Obama & Israel

Obama's promises to Israel are especially significant. While in Israel, he met with Prime Minister Olmert, Netanyahu, Barak, and other militant Jews and publicly pledged his loyalty to the nation of Israel. He fawningly declared Jerusalem to be their inviolable capital, laying waste to Palestinian and Arab claims to the city. Obama wore the heinous "skull cap" on his head and prayed at the wailing wall on the Temple Mount, a clear mark of his spiritual and political unity with Jewish cabalistic ambitions to reign over a reconstructed, "Israeli-triumphant" Middle East.

Obama threatened the potential enemies of Israel—for example, Syria and Iran—with destruction and promised his Jewish hosts that Iran would never be permitted to develop nuclear weapons. This in spite of the fact that an aggressive, ever saber-rattling Israeli military force bristles with over 400 nuclear bombs and missiles, courtesy of the U.S.A.

Israel Prophesied to Become "Sodom and Egypt"

But, exactly what connection does Barack Obama's alliance with Israel have to do with the modern-day revival of the spirit of Osiris, the Egyptian Sun God? Chiefly this—that the prophecies of the Holy Bible plainly and unmistakably identify Israel spiritually as latter-day *"Sodom and Egypt."* That's right. *Revelation 11:8* minces no words, painting Jerusalem (thus Israel) as the Great City, Mystery Babylon, the endtimes, demonic headquarters of the whole world. It is in Israel's prophetic

role of Mystery Babylon that she not only slays the faithful witnesses of God, but then celebrates their blood being shed by a global orgy of gift-giving.

Israel has now become spiritual Sodom and Egypt. That is God's judgement and decree. And his judgement and decree will stand, though Barack Obama and all the denizens of Hell vainly attempt to overturn it.

Barack Obama, Osiris, and Change: Divining the Future

Could Barack Obama, as President of the United States, become the reincarnated Osiris (Satan)? Will he take the reins of a Police State erected by his corrupt predecessors, Bush and Clinton, and make himself like unto a Pharaoh?

Is that the promised change we can expect? Is this why many new pyramids have risen in both Israel and throughout the United States? I do not say this is so. Time will tell. But given the calamitous times in which we live and the striking similarities between the two, Osiris and Barack Obama, should we not carefully watch…and pray?

The Bible says that God's Chosen—that is all who trust in Christ Jesus—will not be taken by surprise. In due time we will know. Of that you can be sure.

Divine Goddess of Europe and the Tower of Babel

After the publication of my book, *Mysterious Monuments*, can anyone seriously doubt the mushrooming explosion of an Architectural Colossus across America and the world?

Across the Atlantic, in Brussels, Belgium, in front of the European Union Building, stands a strange, yet revealing monument. It is a statue of a modern-day goddess, holding high the symbol of the Euro in her hand. Below her, cowering in a supine, slave position are the figures of a man and woman. These represent the people of Europe, the Divine Woman's admiring subjects, vassals of the New World Order.

Also in Europe, amazingly built in the shape of an unfinished "Tower of Babel," is the new European Parliament building. Arching up toward the sky and surrounded by occultic arches, triangles, circles, and domes, its architectural message is undeniable. The Illuminati elite are determined to do what their forebearers in ancient Babylon failed to do—complete the satanic kingdom for planet earth.

Phallic Architecture and Sex Monuments of the Illuminati

Baal's Shaft and Cleopatra's Needle

The wizards of Madison Avenue and Hollywood use sex and perversion to subconsciously manipulate peoples' minds. Results in the marketplace tell us that sex sells, especially when presented in a psychically powerful subliminal or symbolic format.

However, how many know that the Illuminati elite also use sexual symbology and sexual archetypes on an even grander scale to accomplish their dictatorial, utopian power schemes? This is being done via the powerful, transformative means of architecture. Across the planet, the elite have crisscrossed and interlaced the world with a network of phallic and other sexual monuments, statues and buildings. These objects are hidden in plain sight.

Careful investigation proves conclusively that the men and women of the Illuminati and its secret societies are active participants in a gigantic, global-wide religious sex cult. Illuminati architects are regularly commissioned to erect phallic obelisks and towers and mammary-breast domed buildings, which serve as cultic idols of worship. These strange, monumental idols celebrate the ancient, pagan Mystery Religions to which the modern Illuminists subscribe.

To an Illuminati Mystery religionist, the phallically designed Washington Monument—which is, in reality, an Egyptian obelisk—is held in the greatest esteem as an object of religious veneration and sexual desire. Christians have the cross, the Illuminists the phallic obelisk!

My video, *Baal's Shaft & Cleopatra's Needle*, is the first and only video that dares to tackle this eye-opening topic. In it, you will discover why the unusually shaped architectural towers and buildings in Barcelona, Spain have earned for that city the dubious title of "Phallic Capital of the World." Noteworthy, too, is Florida's new state capitol building, recently acclaimed by architects as "The Most Phallic Building in the U.S.A."

Also unmasked: the bizarre Egyptian and Babylonian religious doctrines which underlie America's thousands of obelisk monuments, the tallest of which is the Washington Monument, the gargantuan idol secretly designed by Masonic architects to commemorate the number of the Beast, 666.

From Calcutta to Jerusalem, and from Bangkok to Rio de Janeiro, sexual monuments of the most obscene and grotesque nature dominate the landscape. Yet, few observers comprehend the hidden doctrine and meaning behind their erection and use.

This exciting video is available from *Power of Prophecy*. Please phone 1-800-234-9673.

Why, for example, are four cities—Paris, Rome, London, and New York—each adorned by a towering Egyptian obelisk? Why are the Egyptian obelisks in London and New York both named *"Cleopatra's Needle?"* Why, also, are obelisks around the world often referred to as *"Baal's Shaft?"*

In ancient Egypt, in Babylon and in classical Greece and Rome, sexual salons and temples flourished, places where holy priestesses (prostitutes) and priest-sodomites were ritually "yoked" with devoted believers. In these religions, sexual intercourse in a mysterious, esoteric, religious setting was considered highly desirable as a pathway to initiation, self-divinity, and spiritual advancement.

In India, even today the practice of tantric sexual ritual continues. Everywhere we discover sexual motifs in temple art and Hindu architecture, with the male and female sex organs venerated.

Deeply concealed in Mystery symbols, coded language and theatrical guises, this same sexual worship is at the center of modern Masonic ritual in the U.S.A., Europe, and around the world. Sexual ritual is also a feature of the orgiastic ceremonies at California's annual Bohemian Grove conclave and of the occult rituals engaged in by initiates of Yale University's elitist Order of Skull & Bones.

African herms.

Because of structures like the newly erected Agbar Tower (above), Barcelona, Spain is jokingly referred to as the "Phallic Capital of the World."

The *Light of Truth Universal Shrine,* Yogaville, India, is designed as a many-breasted goddess dome.

The tomb of our nation's first President, George Washington, at historic Mt. Vernon is designed as an Egyptian queen's palace, with 2 obelisks at the entrance. In illuminism this symbolically represents death and resurrection (the two phallic obelisks and the womb of the Great Goddess.).

The "Vigiland Monolith" phallic monument is visited each year by millions of tourists in Oslo, Norway.

Newly built state capitol building in Florida chosen by a poll as America's "Most Phallic Building."

I highly recommend you order your copy of my video, *Baal's Shaft & Cleopatra's Needle* video right away. Please know that while the subject is admittedly coarse and recommended for mature audiences only, the video does not present unwholesome scenes—sexual activity, etc. The topic is dramatic enough, and we do not want to offend anyone. Still, the awful truth of the Illuminati's darkest secrets deserve to be known. As the Apostle Paul wrote, *"For we are not ignorant of the devices of the devil."*

Believe me, in viewing *Baal's Shaft & Cleopatra's Needle*, you will see just how amazing—and how decadent and depraved—the Illuminati Mystery religion really is. I promise: Never again will you view much of the world's most acclaimed architecture and monuments in exactly the same way.

> "I have heard much of the nefarious and dangerous plan and doctrines of the Illuminati. It was not my intention to doubt that the doctrines of the Illuminati and the principles of Jacobinism had not spread in the United States. On the contrary, no one is more satisfied of this fact than I am."
>
> —George Washington
> *The Writings of George Washington*

Phallic Monuments and Mystery Architecture Provide Shocking Proof

The Illuminati Are Obsessed With Sex

"The word "obelisk" literally means 'Baal's Shaft' or Baal's organ of reproduction. This should be especially shocking when we realize that we have a gigantic obelisk in our nation's capital known as the Washington Monument."

—Dr. Cathy Burns
Masonic and Occult Symbols Illustrated

My explosive video, ***Baal's Shaft & Cleopatra's Needle***, appears to have really shocked those who have so far seen it. Viewers report surprise that the Illuminati elite and their secret societies are able to plant and display so much architecture of a vulgar and offensive sexual nature out in the open, in plain sight.

My in-depth investigation finds that the Illuminati constitutes the world's most obsessed sex cult. Architects and builders of the Illuminati and its secret societies have proven their devotion to Satan's kingdom by honoring and revering the Mystery gods and goddesses and are ever busy creating new sex idols devoted to "sacred" demons.

Secret society rituals, symbols, logos, art and architecture is saturated with covert sexism and rakish debauchery. Take, for example, the Masonic Lodge's square and compass logo. Arthur

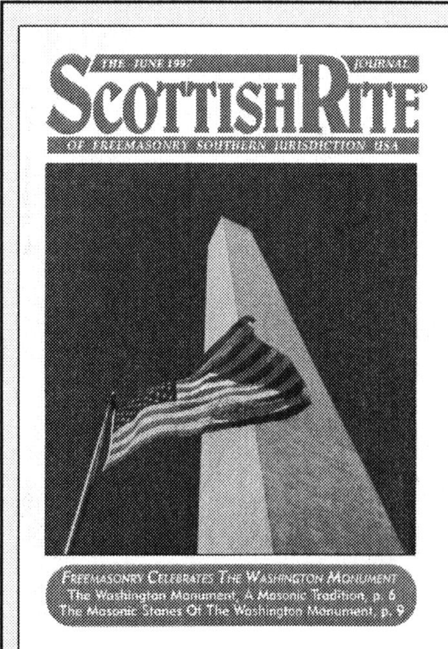

This issue of *Scottish Rite Journal* (June 1997) featured the Washington Monument, calling it "A Masonic Tradition." the 6,666 inch tall structure, an Egyptian-styled obelisk, symbolizes the erect phallus of Osiris, the sun god whose eye hovers over the pyramid on the one dollar bill.

Masonic Sex Perverts: The symbols of the Masonic Lodge are permeated with sexual meaning. The "Tubal Cane" pin worn by some Masons symbolizes the male genitals (tubal=two balls; cane=male phallus). The familiar Masonic square and compass represents the male mounting the female in the sex act. The "G" within stands for the "Holy Fire," the act of sexual regeneration.

To commemorate the 40th anniversary of U.S. Forces landing on D-Day at Normandy Beach (France) during World War II, President Ronald Reagan gave a talk to this group on June 6, 1984, at the D-Day Memorial. Note the clearly phallic design of the Memorial.

The phallic image is unmistakable in the design of the Barsana Dham Temple outside of Austin. The Hindu guru who leads the community associated with this temple was recently indicted for the sexual crime of "indecency with a child." (*Austin American-Statesman*, Sept 28, 2008)

Waite, 33°, in *Mysteries of Magic*, confides that this symbol represents "heavenly fire"—code words for the sexual act between male and female. Albert Pike, 33°, formerly Sovereign Grand Commander of Scottish Rite Freemasonry, agrees with Waite, pointing out the sexual significance of the symbol as pertaining to the "generative principle" (sexual intercourse).

Pyramids, Obelisks, Circles, and the Yin/Yang

The ancient pyramid is seen by Illuminati as a structure in which the sun's rays—the "holy fire" (semen) of Osiris the Egyptian sun god—illuminate the outer structure, then enter within the pyramid's walls. The interior is envisioned to be the womb and vagina of the goddess, Isis. The word "pyramid" literally means "amid the pyre, or fire."

The obelisk, a heathen idol common in towns and cities across America, is said to be the phallus of Osiris. Not by coincidence, the largest obelisk in the world, the Washington Monument, stands erect in Washington, D.C., our nation's capital.

The point within the circle ⊙ is a symbol adopted by Bavarian occultist Adam Weishaupt, the founder (May 1, 1776) of the original Order of the Illuminati. The point is considered to be the phallus, or penis, of the Mystery god, the circle the goddess' vagina (see "Point Within A Circle," *Short Talk Bulletin*, Masonic Services Association, p. 4).

The yin/yang symbol ☯ is similarly a sign of sexual activity. Yang represents the male (sun) principal, yin the female (moon) principle.

Jewish Cabalism and Sexual Symbology

The Jews' cabalistic six-pointed star ✡ is yet another covert, symbolic representation of the generative act. It is a combination of the male phallus (triangle pointed up) entering and conjoining the female vagina (triangle pointed downward).

Moreover, the number 666 is hermetically coded into this symbol (the star has six points, six lines, and a six-sided hexagon within). Both the Rothschilds and the chief rabbis insisted that this

The eye-catching theme of the sensual, bare-breasted Goddess of Liberty leading the charge was popular in paintings and art of the Illuminati-inspired French and American Revolutions.

star be the dominant feature on Israel's national flag.

The Jews' Talmud, their most holy book, and the Jewish Cabala are full of sexual content. Given their embrace of satanic sexual symbology, it is thus no accident that the Jews today are the masterminds and distributors of the vast majority of pornography found over the internet and in movies. Israel leads the world today in sex trafficking and sexual slavery.

President Nixon Called Them Filthy & "Faggoty"

Hindu tantric ritual and the rites of secret societies such as the O.T.O. *(Ordo Templi Orientis)* and the Order of Skull & Bones are also devoted to sexual acts and depravities. Alex Jones, in his video exposé, *Dark Secrets of the Bohemian Grove*, demonstrates that this elite secret society group is consumed by sexual imagery. A disgusted President Richard Nixon, in now released White House tape recordings, is overheard criticizing the Bohemian Grove conclave which he attended as one of the most sexually filthy and "faggoty" (homosexual) affairs he had ever witnessed.

Richard M. Nixon

Pagan sexual symbols abound in Illuminati art, architecture and monuments, a repulsive situation in a country like America, long presumed to be a "Christian Nation." The elite delight in their ability to deceive the masses, who foolishly discount the multitude of graphic evidences that surround them. Sex is, of course, a primal urge basic to all humans, and Satan pulls out all stops to use this psychological instinct in drawing in and seducing gullible initiates of the various secret societies.

Succumbing to the Devil's Cheap Thrills

Fortunately, the Apostle Paul, in the New Testament, declared that alert Christians *"are not ignorant of the devices of the devil" (II Corinthians 2:11).* In the end, we can conclude that the Illuminati, smugly thinking themselves to be wise, cosmopolitan and superior to the rest of us, are only deceiving themselves. Instead of the pure and undefiled religion of Jesus Christ, the elite dupes have settled for a lesser bowl of rough porridge. Consumed and titillated by visions of sexual hedonism, they have succumbed to the Devil's cheap thrills. In so doing, they have chosen squalid, fleshly depravity and have voluntarily forsaken the eternal gifts and exceptional joy and happiness tendered to men through Jesus, and made available by His grace and love. I truly and sincerely pity the Illuminati. What a waste of human dignity. What a waste of human life.

World-Famous Christian Leaders Linked With Sinister Groups

The Illuminati Build Tower of Infamy

"And they said one to another...Come, let us build a city and a tower, whose top may reach unto heaven..."

— *Genesis 11:3-4*

In his revealing book, *Out of Control*, distributed privately among the elite of the Bilderbergers, Council on Foreign Relations, Trilateral Commission and other groups, Zbigniew Brzezinski, Rockefeller operative and former National Security Advisor to President Jimmy Carter, declared that the New World Order cannot be built on a foundation of politics and economics alone. To truly establish ironclad global control over all peoples and nations, Brzezinski explained that the elite must also use the religious element.

Likewise, at his State of the World Forum in San Francisco, former Soviet President, Mikhail Gorbachev, advocated the setting up of a United Nations of Religions organization. Indeed, the establishment of just such an antichrist, global religious order was the goal of the hundreds of Christian, Jewish, Muslim, Buddhist, Hindu, African Tribalist, and other religious leaders who met a few years ago in Chicago for the World's Parliament of Religions.

Since the end of World War II, the Illuminati have recognized that if their cherished aim of total dictatorial lordship over mankind is to be realized, the spiritual need in man must be channeled and directed. It is not enough to control a man's body and to micro-manage his social and economic environments. Nor is it sufficient to be able to brainwash and hypnotize men's minds. The very souls of men must be molded like some type of psychic clay.

Astonishingly, the Holy Bible prophesied this very thing: That, in the last day, Satan's wicked empire, Mystery, Babylon the Great, would carry on trade and commerce across the globe. All manner of merchandise will be traded and sold, including the "souls of men!" *(Revelation 18:13)*

Worship the Ultimate Aphrodisiac

Worship, to the elite, is the ultimate aphrodisiac. More than money, more than political power, Satan desires that man adore and worship him. He wants to replace the God in the heavens as the object of man's veneration. He lusts to sit on the throne of heavenly and earthly power. As the deceitful Angel of Darkness himself once boasted, "I will exalt my throne above the stars of God...I will be like the Most High" *(Isaiah 14:13-14)*. With this objective in mind—the chaining of men's souls to Lucifer's grotesque desire to replace God, to be God—the Illuminati, agents of Satan on earth, have worked now for half a century. Their disciples, communists Marx, Lenin, and Mao, scornfully taught that religion is the opiate of the people.

Agreeing with this principle, the satanic elite intend to feed the people intoxicating, soul-

Zbigniew Brzezinski, former National Security Advisor and Trilateral Commission insider, advised his Illuminati superiors that the New World Order can be established only be employing religion as a key weapon of global influence.

Joseph Smith, (right) founder of the 15 million member strong Mormon religion, patterned his new religion on the rituals and symbols of Zionist Freemasonry.

C. I. Scofield, (right) the corrupt lawyer whose "Scofield Bible" became a huge international "Christian classic," was paid handsomely by wealthy New York Jews for his service to the Illuminati. Thanks to the Scofield Bible, generations of Christians have been trained up and indoctrinated as unholy Judaizers and Zionists.

numbing, religious opium on a gargantuan scale, in the form of fake religions. In other words: satanic religion.

Religious Puppets of the Illuminati

To capture and manipulate the souls of men, the satanic agents have actually bought and sold Christian pretenders—religious puppets—whom they have installed as leaders of scores of ministries, mega-churches, seminaries, Bible colleges and other religious organizations and institutions.

The Illuminati overseers have raised up and trained their loyal religious disciples to pretend to be Christians and even to feign an intense love of Christ. These false ministers and lying prophets are con artists persuasively speaking to audiences in what appears to be sincere and biblical lingo, all the better to deceive, if it were possible, even the very elect *(Matthew 24:20)*. While they come as angels of light and ministers of righteousness, inside, these deceitful servants of evil are ravenous wolves.

Secret Societies and Elite Orders Fund Religious Corruption

Illuminati minions of Satan have founded many of the world's largest and best known ministries and groups. The wealthy elite have given their religious puppets the funding and the means to crank up many new religious groups and get them going. In fact, entire new denominations and religions have been founded and are today huge in size, thanks to covert Illuminati assistance.

It is well known that wealthy Illuminati chieftains Henry Luce (Order of Skull & Bones patriarch and head of the Time-Life empire) and William Randolph Hearst (Hearst newspapers) puffed up and made evangelist Billy Graham a "star." Knights of Malta magnate, J. Peter Grace (W.R. Grace and Co. Chemicals) and his cronies, such as Ted Turner (CNN), were the prime movers behind Pat Robertson's Christian Broadcasting Network apparatus. Other Illuminati helped set up the Crouches and their Trinity Broadcasting Network.

The Rockefellers and the heirs to the Firestone and other fortunes funded Alcoholics Anonymous. An Orthodox Jewish billionaire from Canada and the corrupt but fabulously wealthy Riady family from Indonesia secretly funded both televangelist Morris Cerullo's TV broadcast and Jim and Tammy Faye Bakker's PTL Network. The Rockefellers also ponied up millions for the work of the apostate Jesus Seminar scholars and the heretical World Council of Churches organization.

The Vatican's secret societies also were instrumental in furthering the charismatic movement. Rick Joyner, one of the popular charismatic "Kansas City Prophets," was even initiated into the

Vatican's mysteriously evil order, the Knights of Malta. Meanwhile, CIA operative Reverend Sun Myung Moon has spread millions of bucks among his favorite evangelical Christian stooges, ranging from Tim and Bev La Haye (author of the book, *Left Behind*) to the Crystal Cathedral's positive-thinking guru Dr. Robert Schuller and Christian pop singer Pat Boone.

Schuller also was rewarded with big bucks by his Illuminati pal, the late Communist-puppet oilman, Armand Hammer (Occidental Oil Corp). Meanwhile, James Dobson's Focus on the Family moved into a luxurious new Colorado facility a few years ago, paid for by a curiously secret Roman Catholic foundation. All this and more I explain and document in my explosive video and DVD *Tower of Infamy*.

Zionists and Masons Help Build Tower of Infamy

Zionist sources tied to the Illuminati richly rewarded puppet Jerry Falwell with the gift of a multimillion dollar executive jet and set up crooked lawyer C.I. Scofield as a "Bible scholar," a hoax of the century if there ever was one! Zionist Masons helped organize the heretical Jehovah's Witnesses religion. Mormonism's founder Joseph Smith also organized that false religion on the basis of Freemasonry's rituals and symbols.

In sum, the Christian establishment is not Christian at all. It and its leaders are bought and paid for by the Illuminati. It is an integral and inseparable part of the worldwide Luciferian network of evil: The Tower of Infamy. Now, do you understand why today we have hundreds of new false New Age Bible versions? Can you see why heresies and atrocities abound and proliferate within the so-called Christian world?

A Faithful Remnant Remains

Thank God, there is still in existence a tiny but faithful remnant of true Christian believers. Though few in number, true Christian believers cannot be deceived for long. They miraculously are able to spiritually recognize each other. Gifted with discernment, they know the genuine from the counterfeit. The remnant is hardy and tough. They refuse to bow down to Baal.

I long ago gave my heart and life over to be a part of the remnant. I pray you have done the same. If not, may I beseech and implore you to make this vital and everlasting decision today, before it is too late?

Yes, trust in Christ alone and join us. Be assured: We of the remnant will never, never, never give up. Praise God, with Him as our companion and strength, we shall overcome the evildoers:

> *"And they overcame him (the Devil, Satan) by the blood of the lamb and by the word of their testimony and they loved not their lives unto the death." (Revelation 12:11)*

All these strange, revealing logos have Illuminati links. They demonstrate the amazing extent to which the secret societies have infiltrated and now virtually control the entire Christian Establishment.

Devil Companies, Devil Products, Devil Logos?

What messages are some of the world's top corporations sending with their choices for names of products and companies? In my book, ***Project LUCID***, I uncover the curious, occultic overtones of the *Lucent Technologies*' logo—a fiery red circle. The name "Lucent" is itself questionable. Some say it stands for Lucifer's Enterprises. Of course, the corporation's spokesmen vociferously deny it.

Lucent Technologies is touting its newest software innovation, brand-named *"Inferno."* Inferno! What message is this mega-giant company—formerly known as AT&T's Bell Labs—trying to send us?

A ministry friend from Columbus, Ohio, recently decided to check out the Lucent web site on the internet and was shocked by what he found. Here's his report:

> "The Lucent Technologies web site pictures a whirlpool of fire that is vivid red. Also, the buttons are not only red, but they are moving like flames. If you go to the *Inferno* bulletin board on Lucent's site, you can also view this. I am certain that the Lord led me to this file because it was no longer available the following day. Either I was somehow enabled to access a classified file or it was pulled by Lucent. This file should leave no doubt—except to the most blind among us—that Lucent Technologies is the most blatantly evil company in the world."

Running with the Devil

Well, Lucent may or may not be an evil firm, but if so, it sure has a lot of company. Consider, for example, *Reebok International*, the athletic footwear company. Reebok recently gave one of its lines of women's running shoes the telling name, *Incubus*. In medieval magic and lore, the incubus is a demon that has sex with women while they sleep!

In *U.S. News and World Report* (March 3, 1997), it was reported that some 53,000 pairs of the Incubus line of shoes had, so far, been shipped to retailers. But a Reebok spokesman insisted that the company was surprised when the occultic meaning of the name Incubus was first brought to management's attention. "We had no idea," said the spokesman.

Lucifer Manufacturing

Then there's *Honeywell*, the Minnesota-based computer giant. Honeywell has some of its Christian employees upset because the corporation is reportedly pushing a pro-homosexual philosophy. All workers are required to attend "Diversity Training" seminars during which the virtues of the gay lifestyle are extolled and praised.

Honeywell has, for years, had a subsidiary company based in Europe named—believe it or not—*Lucifer Manufacturing!* That's right, *Lucifer*. Probably just another embarrassing surprise, right? Are we to believe that Honeywell's top executives had no idea who Lucifer is?

Honeywell works closely with *Oracle*, a software corporation active in Big Brother technologies. Together, Honeywell and Oracle produce computerized control systems for the New World Order, including scanning equipment for security operations. Honeywell's global division has especially found success selling Honeywell's "Smart Distributed System," which, like Superman's fabled x-ray vision, can literally see through materials.

Recently, a friend of the ministry e-mailed me a Honeywell press release in which the giant corporation announced that its *Lucifer* subsidiary has now been sold to another large corporation, Parker-Hannifin.

Lucifer Lighting

Not to be outdone, a U.S.A. company in San Antonio also goes by the name of Lucifer: *Lucifer Lighting Co.* A friend sent me one of this company's sale brochures. The brochure advertises that the firm makes and sells such products as Lucifer light strips and Lucifer halogen lights. Now please, tell me: What corporate CEO in his right mind would name a light company "Lucifer?"

666 Company Linked with Microsoft?

Now let us leave Lucifer and take a look at what's going on at *Microsoft*, the world's largest software corporation. Microsoft has recently announced it's gone into business with Apple Computers, one of the top makers of personal and networking computers. According to *Fortune* magazine, billionaire Bill Gates, founder of Microsoft, is the richest man in the U.S.A. Gates was an attendee and a key player at Soviet Communist Mikhail Gorbachev's *State of the World Forum* in San Francisco recently.

Cooperating with Apple, Gates and his Microsoft Corporation will gain significant new inroads into the computer market. Microsoft's global software and internet superiority will intensify. But, have Bill Gates and Microsoft linked up with a devilish company in Apple?

Consider Apple's choice for its corporate symbol? The company's logo is an apple that has had a bite taken out of it. To many occult insiders, this signifies that the eating of the forbidden fruit (symbolically, the apple) by Adam and Eve in the Garden of Eden was a *good* thing. Occultists and New Agers teach that taking a bite out of the apple gave the first two humans knowledge, or gnosis, putting them on the path to self-divinity and godhood.

Apple Computers was co-founded in the 70s by Stephen Jobs, a weird, New Age guru-type, and Steven Wozniak, also an advocate of the Aquarian Age culture. When entrepreneurs Jobs and Wozniak first marketed their earliest, crude personal computer, they put a price tag of $666 on the product. 666! Coincidental—or on purpose? You decide.

Proctor & Gamble's Old Man in the Moon

We receive mail from time to time asking us if *Proctor & Gamble* (P&G), the maker of many well-known soap and detergent products, is a satanic organization. Inquirers frequently call our attention to P&G's curious logo.

In fact, I have no evidence whatsoever that Proctor & Gamble is linked with satanism. The constant rumor that the president of this huge company once went on a major TV talk show and professed to being a member of the Church of Satan has definitely been proven to be false. The company believes that rumor was begun by corporate competitors.

Strangely, however, Proctor & Gamble has for years stubbornly refused to toss out its logo of an old man in the moon surrounded by 13 stars. Some people suspect that the stars represent the occultic number 13, and the belief is that they were arranged to roughly appear as a 6, the number of the beast of *Revelation 13*. What seem to be two horns come out of the old man's head.

The Old Proctor & Gamble logo.

Proctor & Gamble vigorously denies the accusations, contending that the horns are merely curls of hair. And the 13 stars? According to Proctor & Gamble, they represent the original 13 colonies of the U.S.A. The man in the moon, a company spokesman claims, also honors the original colonies.

In 1992, Proctor & Gamble decided to slightly revise its bizarre and troublesome logo. A corporate spokesman announced that the curls (or horns?) were being softened artistically. Other minor changes were also made, ostensibly to alleviate concerns. But rumors and questions still remain.

In any case, soap-maker Proctor & Gamble has filed lawsuits against several people believed to be responsible for spreading the allegations of devilism. But, in at least one of the lawsuits, the company raised eyebrows when the news came out that Proctor & Gamble was seeking exactly $66,600 in damages!

What we see in many of today's company logos and emblems is no doubt a prime manifestation of spiritual wickedness in high places.

Of Pyramids, Eyes, Serpents, Eggs, and Crosses

Everywhere one turns, the corporate logos seem to be sending us messages. Internet provider *America On-Line* has for its logo a pyramid with an all-seeing eye inside. CBS-TV also uses the enigmatic all-seeing eye for its symbol. Meanwhile, *Intel's* computer chips, including the company's top-selling Pentium chip, come with the company's celebrated symbol, which suspiciously resembles the ancient occultic symbol of eternity, the *oroboros*, a serpent biting its own tail.

The Saturn automobile folks proudly display their red-colored logo in TV ads and billboards, with its double lines looking suspiciously like crossed horns. Nabisco's long-standing logo has what seems to be a stylistic, multibar cross affixed to an egg-shaped emblem. Is Nabisco's logo a Masonic phallic symbol of fertility?

The *Shell Oil* logo appears to be the golden shell of Aphrodite, the goddess who, pagan legend says, rose from the sea (see *Revelation 13:1* for details). Meanwhile, *Texaco Oil* displays the Egyptian tau cross in a black and red coloration.

Disney has been much in the news lately. Christians are not at all happy with what they say is the smutty, anti-Bible direction the company is now taking with its movies, television shows, and CD albums. Is Disney's hostility to traditional Christian values reflected in its corporate logo? Carefully examine the Disney logo pictured here. Can you find what are alleged to be three 6s (666) concealed?

WALT DISNEY

Does the Walt Disney corporate logo conceal three cleverly disguised "6s"—thus, 666?

Just a Coincidence?

Are the shapes of these logos just coincidences? The corporations mentioned above, and others who have adopted equally

Corporate Triangle Logos—A Sign of Illuminati Influence?

The above logos are trademarked by the corporations concerned.

questionable marks and logos, would almost certainly deny that their logos are either pagan, occultic, or New Age. It may be that the corporate leadership is, in fact, innocently unaware of the esoteric, sometimes hidden, meanings of these symbols. Moreover, it must be admitted that a given symbol can have a multiplicity of meanings. Therefore, we make no railing accusations against these companies and their products.

But regardless, we do know for sure that Satan, the temporal "god of this world" *(II Corinthians 4:4)*, can be expected to plant his symbols of evil throughout the globe in the last days. He is the father of liars, the blasphemous one, the dragon and serpent. I am convinced that Satan and his agents are very busy these days, conditioning men's minds and programming their senses with stunningly effective visual magic and sorcery.

Our argument, our battle, is not with the corporations of this world. Our struggle is with higher powers. Our holy campaign is against "spiritual wickedness in high places." What we see in many of today's company logos and emblems is no doubt a prime manifestation of spiritual wickedness in high places.

Thank God, He is able and willing to guide us into knowledge and wisdom as we expose today's multiplying, visible manifestations of evil. Only He can protect us from their hypnotic, mind-control effects. To paraphrase one corporation's catchy advertising slogan, it can be said of Jesus—"Don't leave home without Him." He is powerful, and He is the ultimate in personal security in these deceit-filled last days. A symbol is a mere representation, or shadow, of something. But Christ Jesus is real. He is beyond symbolism. He gloriously lives, and He reigns.

And the Lord shall deliver me from every evil work, and will preserve me unto His heavenly kingdom: to whom be glory for ever and ever. Amen. (II Timothy 4:18)

Architectural Secrets of the Rothschilds, Rockefellers, Vanderbilts, Astors, DuPonts, and Other Storied Bloodlines of the Illuminati

Where the Rich and Famous Dwell

"I have been insane on the subject of money-making all my life."
—Cornelius "Commodore" Vanderbilt
Fortune's Children

"But God said unto him, Thou fool, this night thy soul shall be required of thee; then whose shall those things be?"
—Jesus Christ
Luke 12:20-21

In his classic novel, *The Great Gatsby*, acclaimed writer F. Scott Fitzgerald examined the wildly reckless, yet oddly foreboding lifestyle of the superwealthy, America's monied class. In the novel, observing the depraved and unethical character of the superwealthy, one, less financially endowed character confided, "The rich are different than you and me."

Is this true? Are the rich—the monied blood dynasties and financial titans of this world—*different* than you and me? The answer, if we judge these sinister and calculating men solely on the basis of their fabulous dwellings—their palatial estates and luxuriously appointed mansions—is...*yes!*

I believe that in a decadent material world, where men and women are unfairly judged on how much money they possess, what kind of expensive auto they drive (or are chauffeured in!), and how huge and magnificent is their dwelling place, we can, with clarity, conclude that the rich are far, far different than you and me.

I know, I know—an egalitarian might object, pointing out the Jeffersonian credo that "All men are created equal." However, look around—you and I know that is not so, certainly not in regard to wealth and prosperity. Sadly but surely, as George Orwell, of *1984* fame, suggested in his insightful essay, *Animal Farm*, "Everyone is born equal, but some are born more equal than others."

Habitats Brimming with Luciferian Energy

Considering their dwelling places, the rich are definitely in a far different league. But the estates and mansions of the wealthy Illuminati elite are different in ways other than measured by their huge size, ritzy décor, sprawling grounds, and price tag. As I illustrate quite vividly in ***Where the Rich and Famous Dwell***, my video documentary, the dwellings of the rich are brimming with Luciferian energy. Look closely at the ominously dark architectural features of their habitats and you'll discover strange things—beasts in stone, occult designs, wicked furniture appointments, and pagan works of art.

Cornelius "Commodore" Vanderbilt, and the Biltmore Estate, decorated with demonic gargoyles.

Since it is true that in an immoral, Christless world, men and women are judged by the things with which they surround themselves and by where and how they live, the conclusion is inescapable: *The Illuminati are soul-possessed human devils!*

The decadent lifestyles, unethical business practices, and raw personal character of the wealthy elite are mirrored in their dwellings. Consider, for example, Cornelius Vanderbilt, who manipulated the stock market and unscrupulously heaped for himself a staggering fortune. Vanderbilt admitted to associates that for as long as he could remember he had been obsessed with making money—"I have been insane on the subject of money-making all my life."

Gargoyles, Horned Devils, Ancient Gods, and Phallic Signs

The Vanderbilt Dynasty's fabulous Biltmore Estate no doubt reflects this money mania, and it also reflects the fact that, according to his biographers, Vanderbilt never made a single business decision until he first consulted with demon spirits. Featured in the video *Where the Rich and Famous Dwell*, the Vanderbilts' Biltmore Estate openly displays gargoyles and horned devils in stone, paintings of ancient Mystery Religion gods and goddesses, and witchcraft furnishings.

At the Rockefellers' Kykuit estate you'll find a statue of a nude goddess, sculptures of Greek deities, zodiac signs in mosaic, and an Egyptian obelisk. The gravesite of the wealthy dynasty's founding father, oil magnate John D. Rockefeller, is shown to be a towering Egyptian obelisk, a phallic sign of the Illuminati's core doctrine of reincarnation.

> ***Can the minds and souls of these men remain free of demonic influence when their household are so thoroughly immersed in satanic architectural decadance?***

Also in *Where the Rich and Famous Dwell*, you'll visit the Rothschild's ornate Waddesdon Manor in England, where America's richest billionaire, Warren Buffett, and California Governor—the *"Chosen Disciple"*—Arnold Schwarzenegger recently met with Lord Jacob Rothschild. The architecture of Waddesdon Manor is highlighted by a striking fountain in the gardens with statuary of a gigantic vicious serpent terrorizing hapless victims.

Ca'd'Zan, (below) the opulent home of John Ringling, founder of Ringling Brothers and Barnum & Bailey Circus. Ringling, a 33° Mason, placed a horned devil on the exterior of his Florida home.

The family of New York illuminist John Jacob Astor (above, in costume for a party) adopted as his family crest the crowned dragon-serpent.

On the grounds of the DuPont mansion we find a great owl and skull & bones design carefully grafted into the landscape while, parked outside the chauffeurs' garage, we observe luxurious Rolls Royce automobiles.

Astor Court, home of John Jacob Astor, boldly shows forth the Astor family crest—a crowned dragon serpent. Hmmm. Doesn't the Bible describe the devil as both a serpent and a dragon?

At the Getty estate, meanwhile, we discover the statue of a devilish faun resting on a rock in the pool, and, nearby, a statue of the Greek deity Hermes, "Messenger of the Gods." Inside, painted on a wall mural, is the hideous image of a man's decapitated head, hanging from a cord on the ceiling.

The sumptuous Sarasota, Florida, estate of John Ringling, of Ringling Brothers and Barnum & Bailey Circus fame, startles with its horned devil in stone on the exterior façade. A fountain honoring the Roman/Greek sea beast god, Poseidon, or Neptune, sits outside the entrance to the Ringling Art Museum.

Then there's the Hearst Castle in the hills of San Simeon, California, with its "insane abundance," and my video also takes viewers to the "Disneyland" castles of Bavaria's King Ludwig the Mad. Previewed as well is the library of Wall Street titan J.P. Morgan, furnished with marble, bronze, and walnut, not to mention the Zodiac signs and occult pieces of art.

Lives of the Elite Saturated in Occultism

These are just a few of the many breathtaking examples of the dwelling places of the Illuminati rich and famous showcased in my eye-opening video. It is undeniably true that the lives of the elite are saturated in occultism. Surely, the mansions and castles in which they and their families dwell have become the habitats of devils. Can the minds and souls of these men remain free of demonic influence when their households are so thoroughly immersed in satanic architectural decadence?

You Can't Take It With You

Some years ago, the Broadway play, *You Can't Take it With You*, captivated audiences. James Stewart starred in the movie of the same name. In the scriptures, the Apostle Paul states much the same principle, reminding us all that no matter how rich and how many possessions we acquire, these insanely abundant things will do us not one iota of good when we depart this earth.

The Apostle James issued a notable fiery warning to men who gain their great wealth and build their immense fortunes on the backs and misery of those whom they oppress. "Ye have heaped treasure together for the last days," he admonished, "Behold, the hire of the labourers…which is of you kept back by fraud, crieth: and the cries of them…are entered into the ears of the Lord." *(James 5:4)*

It was, however, Christ Jesus whose life and example as an humble man lights our path today. The Lord possessed not even a foxhole in which he could lay his head. "Take heed," Christ warned, that worldly riches and things not be your downfall. In His parable of the greedy rich man who foolishly built up his vast estate, drank wine and pleasured in his great possessions, the Lord said: "Thou fool, this night thy soul shall be required of thee: Then whose shall these things be?…So is he that layeth up treasure for himself, and is not rich toward God."

Doesn't that say it all? The Illuminati are, indeed, fabulously, insanely, rich. Their dwellings provide them lifestyles of abundance you and I as ordinary people can scarcely imagine. But Jesus lays down the ultimate guidestone by which all men, on that great day coming, will be measured.

Who is the man who is *"rich toward God?"* He it is who shall be rewarded. He it is who shall receive the Kingdom and be made joyous by the presence of His Glory. Truly, as this same Jesus promised, "In my Father's house are many mansions." What mortal man—even a Rothschild or a Rockefeller—can top the incalculable treasure that awaits the redeemed child and servant of God?

At left: The DuPont Mansion. Notice the great owl and the Skull & Bones design. Inset are the chauffeur's garage with its Rolls-Royce automobiles, and also Alfred DuPont.

At right: John D. Rockefeller, shown with his telling grave marker, the obelisk.

Secret Signs, Mysterious Symbols, and Hidden Codes of the Illuminati

Codex Magica

"...binding myself under no less penalty than that of having my breast torn open, my heart plucked out and placed on the highest pinnacle of the temple, there to be devoured by the vultures of the air."

—Oath taken by Second Degree Freemasons
Duncan's Masonic Ritual and Monitor

They each took a solemn oath never to reveal the innermost secrets of The Order. They have labored for centuries, even millennia, to hide their sick, murderous deeds. They have their own strange, diabolical language. Their language, in reality, is a type of *hidden code*, cloaked in enigmatic body gestures, hand signs, handshakes, tokens, grips, and symbols.

Up to now, no one had been able to unravel the true meaning of this fiercely guarded, *hidden code* of deception. Their leaders laughed at the feeble attempts of many who tried.

They won't be laughing anymore. My blockbuster book, ***Codex Magica***, smashes down the doors of secrecy and deceit. Now, with ***Codex Magica*** in hand, you can crack the Illuminati code wide open! These evil men—and not a few women—have plundered the earth and despoiled America for far too long.

Incredible Revelations

The incredible revelations in this monumental book stagger the imagination. Awesome in scope, ***Codex Magica*** contains over 1,000 actual photographs and illustrations. You'll see with your own eyes the world's leading politicians, financiers, and celebrities—including America's richest and most powerful—caught in the act as they perform occult magic.

Once you understand their covert signals and coded picture messages, your world will never be the same. Destiny will be made manifest. You will know the truth about the Illuminati and their astonishing plan to control and manipulate. Everything will become clear. The Emperor will wear no clothes.

I must admit, I love exposing the Illuminati elite. I especially relish tearing off the sinister masks which they wear while wickedly deceiving the ignorant masses. The exposure and outing of these reprehensible disciples of destruction is way past due.

Codex Magica **is the first to expose how the Illuminati patterns its secret signs, mysterious symbols, and hidden codes after those found in the Mystery Religions of the ancients.**

Secret Signs and Symbols Have Ancient Origins

Why did I author and publish *Codex Magica*? *Codex Magica* is an encyclopedic book that incorporates many years of in-depth scholarly research. It took five full years for me to produce the final manuscript. Almost twenty years ago, while working on what proved to be my #1 national bestselling book, *Dark Secrets of the New Age*, I discovered an interesting phenomenon. The break-through came as I was investigating the literature, art, and archaeology of the ancient Mystery Religions of Babylon, Egypt, Rome, Greece, Asia Minor, Central and South America. I was drawn to the manner in which the ancient deities were depicted in art and stone displaying mysterious body gestures and hand signs. My study of the magical rituals of the Mystery Religions was also enlightening. It revealed how very influential these symbols and hieroglyphic marks were to Satan's High Priests of old.

Then came my eye-opening discovery. I realized that these same mysterious, but distinctive, hand signs, handshakes, gestures, marks and symbols are being employed today by powerful politicians, financiers, bankers, and celebrities. *The power elite of the Illuminati around the globe are imitating the ancients.*

Here is indisputable proof that the prophecies of the Bible are assuredly being fulfilled. *"Mystery, Babylon the Great, Mother of harlots and abominations of the earth,"* is alive. The wicked religion and political system of the alluring Woman, drunken with the blood of the saints and of the martyrs of Jesus, can be seen in the secret signs, mysterious symbols and hidden codes of today's Illuminati conspirators.

Cracking the Illuminati Code

Codex Magica is the first book ever to crack the Illuminati code. It is a fully documented, authoritative reference source, as you'll see from its lengthy index and footnotes sections. Now they won't be able to dodge and duck, because, in addition to my exclusive investigative materials, *Codex Magica* also heavily quotes and relies on the Illuminati's own, most touted textbooks and manuals.

That's why, in the pages of *Codex Magica*, you'll find references to *Coil's Masonic Encyclopedia; Mackey's Encyclopedia of Freemasonry; Duncan's Masonic Ritual and Monitor; Richardson's Monitor of Freemasonry;* Pike's *Morals and Dogma*; Blavatsky's *The Secret Doctrine*; Crowley's *Book of the Law*; LaVey's *Satan Speaks*; Spence's *The Encyclopedia of the Occult*, Hutchens' *A Bridge to Light*; Raleigh's *Occult Geometry*; Robinson's *Born in Blood*; Zain's *Ancient Masonry*; Huston's *Mastering Witchcraft*; Hall's *The Secret Teachings of All Ages*; and hundreds of others.

Discover in *Codex Magica* a comparison of the hidden language of the Illuminati to the hand signs and grips illustrated in Masonic encyclopedias and the textbooks of secret societies.

Codex Magica proves the megalomania of the Illuminati and exposes their dangerous psychopathic behavior. It opens up the identity of the bloodthirsty god whom the Freemasons and others worship under such mysterious pseudonyms as "Mahabone," "Abaddon," and "Jahbuhlun."

A Shocking Collection of Names

In *Codex Magica*, you'll discover the biggest and most shocking collection of names and pictures of Illuminists and Illuminati sympathizers ever found in one volume, from Lord Rothschild and Arnold Schwarzenegger to Hillary Clinton, John Kerry and Jacques Chirac.

You'll be amazed to see pictures of a *Seinfeld* TV show character clearly giving the sign of *El Diablo* and a *Star Trek* star displaying the Jewish cabalistic sign of "shin," disguised as the enigmatic sign of the mythical "Vulcan" race. You'll know why Pat Robertson is pictured giving a Masonic hand sign on the cover of *Time* magazine. You'll also learn why the oval office of the White House displays two different Great Seals of the United States, each having an Eagle facing in the opposite direction!

Mr. Spock gives the "shin" sign.

Other riddles are also unraveled, including the surprising, true meaning of the pyramid and the all-seeing eye on our dollar bill; the mystery of the Oroboros serpent biting its own tail; the secret worship by the elite of Baphomet, the horned goat-god idol; the awful truth about the Jewish Cabala; the inside story of Masonic witchcraft; and the telling sign of the devil's claw given by Illuminists.

You'll also find proof that the notorious *Priory of Sion* secret society written about by Dan Brown in his bestselling novel, *The DaVinci Code*, is now active in America, and much, much more.

The Illuminati...An Overpowering Threat

Codex Magica is an overwhelming 624 pages long and is a large format production with many illustrations and photos. The evidence amassed in this book is breathtaking and convincing. Anyone who dares to open up and examine even a tiny portion of this encyclopedic work will, I believe, be forced to concede that: (1) Yes, there is an Illuminati conspiracy; (2) The elite corps of this gargantuan conspiracy do, in fact, covertly communicate in their own sinister language of hand signs, handshakes, body gestures, and symbols; (3) The elitists of the Illuminati are today an overpowering threat and force for evil in America and the whole world; and (4) The insidious, ages-old Plan of the Illuminati is a clear and present danger to our liberties, our lives, our eternal souls. They must be stopped, and soon, before it's too late.

Illuminati Magicians Delighted at Stupidity of Those Who Employ...

Satan's "El Diablo" Hand Sign

"People that are Christians now, but were satanists, recognized President Clinton's signal at his inauguration as a sign of Satan. That seems fairly cut and dried, and it is. Clinton communicated what he wanted to the people to whom he wanted to communicate. The whole affair with him flashing the satanic hand signal took only a couple of seconds."

—Fritz Springmeier
Bloodlines of the Illuminati

"A symbol veils or hides a secret, and it is that which veils mysterious forces. These energies when released can have a potent effect."

—Foster Bailey, 33°
The Spirit of Freemasonry

Manuela, now 23, was first introduced to vampirism and the Goth lifestyle at age 16, when she ran away to London and met up with a secret colony of blood drinking satanists in that city's north side. Soon, she hooked up with lover Daniel Ruda, another would-be vampire and satanist. The two got married in a satanic ceremony and went to live in Germany, taking up the dark Goth lifestyle there.

Manuela and Daniel Ruda and their many Goth friends gave the *El Diablo* hand sign back and forth as a sign of recognition. It was a sign indicating their love and worship of their Master, Lucifer. It also signified their hatred of everything good.

They killed for Satan! **Manuela and Daniel Ruda (embracing—below, left) sacrificed a friend to the devil, stabbing him 66 times. Then, they drank his blood.**

On July 6, 2001, Manuela and Daniel followed what they claim was their Master's order to *"kill, sacrifice, bring souls!"* The chosen victim, Frank Hackert, 33, *"suffered well,"* bragged Manuela. After inviting the unsuspecting Hackert to their apartment for a satanic party, she and her vampire husband, Daniel, pitilessly stabbed the hapless

Hackert a grand total of *66* times on that *6th* day of the month (666). They then cut a satanic pentagram (5-point inverted star) in his chest and drank his blood from a bowl on an altar topped with skulls. Afterwards, the two satanic killers celebrated by enjoying sex together as they lay in a silk-lined oak coffin.

Three versions of the *"El Diablo,"* the sign of Satan, the horned god. The hand sign at right is also the deaf's gesture, or signing, for "I love you," a fact which has many people confused.

Hand Sign The Devil's Calling Card

Strangely, family members and friends not involved in satanism and vampirism say they did not realize that the hand sign was the devil's calling card. "I thought it was just a fun thing, you know, sorta the kind of cool way kids show they are having an awesome time at a heavy metal concert," said a cousin.

Manuela's mother says she was, however, increasingly disturbed over her daughter's lifestyle. Especially when Manuela had two teeth removed and had metal vampire fangs implanted. She was also taken aback by her daughter's tattoo—an upside down cross on her scalp. But the hand sign? "Well," she said, "I thought it was like the sign the deaf give, meaning, I love you."

"I often heard Manuela say she was not of this world and was a satanic vampire," recounted her mother, "but I figured it was just so much silly talk. Just another way of living. After all, not every Goth vampire ends up sacrificing victims to Satan."

In the end, it was Manuela's mom who turned the couple in to the police. She was alarmed after her daughter wrote her a letter confessing the crime and showing no remorse whatsoever. Manuela even told her mother she looked forward to serving Satan, her Lord, in hell.

Back to Babylon

In ***Codex Magica***, my mammoth exposé book of the Illuminati and their occultic sub-elements, I fully explore the use by Manuela, Daniel, and other occultists of the sign and symbol of *El Diablo*. It is wildly popular today among legions of depraved men and women, including top Illuminati initiates, and has been now for almost half a century.

Also called *Il Cornuto* and *Diabolicus*, the employment by the elite of the hand sign of the horned devil can actually be tracked all the way back to Babylon. On the great wall of Babylon, adjacent to Ishtar's Gate, was a mosaic image of a horned bull, representing the sun god. The horns were symbolic of the Babylonian god's power over the hearts of men.

Later, in Imperial Rome, Caesar's military legions and millions of common people worshipped the sun god, Mithras. Mithraic initiates were baptized in the blood of a horned bull, slain and sacrificed by temple priests.

The Knights Templar, predecessor to today Scottish Rite Freemasons, worshiped the grotesque horned goat-god, Baphomet. It is believed that many Illuminists continue to sacrifice to this unspeakable deity to this very day.

Reportedly, the Illuminati take great delight in seeing the masses adopt their ancient symbol of satanic worship on such a vast scale. How easy it has been for the elite to persuade the stupid and gullible to enter into satanic bondage. In giving the El Diablo, that is exactly the message the giver is signalling the devil: *"I'm yours forever, Satan, heart and soul I'm yours!"*

I Love You, Devil?

The *"El Diablo"* hand sign often is confused with the deaf's signing of the phrase, "I love you." While at first this appears an odd resemblance, we register an "ahh, I get it!" emotion when we discover that the person who popularized the hand sign system for the deaf, Helen Keller, was herself an occultist and Theosophist. Did Keller purposely intend the deaf's "I love you" sign to be such a remarkable imitation of the classic sign of Satan? Was Keller saying, basically, "I love you, Devil?"

Then, we have the confusion of the El Diablo hand sign with the University of Texas "hook 'em horns" sign. Texas' mascot is the longhorn steer and it is only natural that the horns sign be employed by the student body, alumni, and fans of that great institution.

When Jenna Bush, the daughter of President George W. Bush, gave the horns sign at the 2004 presidential inauguration, it shocked the world. Most viewers of international TV did not know that Jenna is a recent graduate of the University of Texas. However, at that same inaugural gala, the President also was photographed giving the sign, and so was the other Bush daughter. Not only that, but the First Lady, Laura, and even the President's mother, Barbara Bush, got into the mix. They, too, were seen giving the sign.

However, the inauguration of President George W. Bush was not the first which had featured the giving of the *El Diablo* sign. President Bill Clinton also did it at his first inaugural, and, in *Codex Magica*, you'll see a shocking example of the El Diablo sign of Satan given at the inauguration of George Washington, our nation's very first President!

A22 San Francisco Chronicle

Karla LaVey held the hand of a wax statue of her father, Anton LaVey, who died last week in San Francisco of heart disease

Satanist's Daughter To Keep the 'Faith'

High priest of the Church of Satan, Anton LaVey, was honored upon his death in this article in the *San Francisco Chronicle*. In the picture, LaVey is giving the "El Diablo" hand sign while, on the wall, is the "Baphomet" version of the satanic pentagram star. Was it mere coincidence that on the very day that this wicked satanist died in California, across the sea, in England, Illuminati chief Lord Edmond de Rothschild also passed away?

President George W. Bush is very adept at giving the sign.

Marion Berry, then Mayor of the nation's capital, Washington, D.C. Later arrested for cocaine possession, Mayor Berry once remarked, "Outside of the killings, Washington has one of the lowest crime rates in the country."

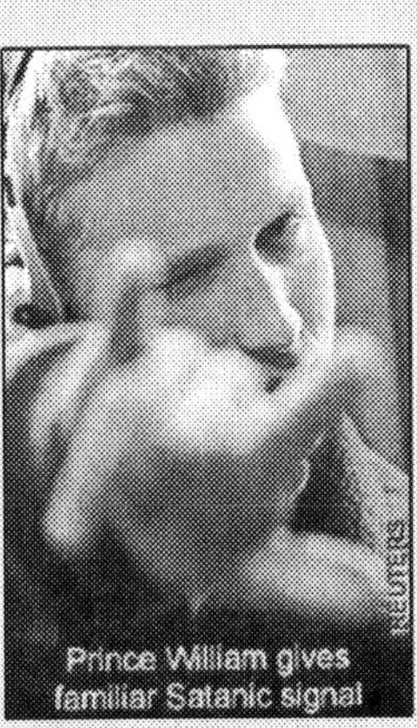

Prince William of Britain's royal family.

President Bill Clinton is often seen flashing the horned devil sign.

Actress Meryl Streep gives the sign of the Devil just over the head of "Angels in America" director, Mike Nichols. In 2004, the HBO series "Angels in America" was aired. It was possibly the most evil TV program ever broadcast. The director and actress were given "Golden Globe" awards, indicating how hateful Hollywood and the TV networks have become. The series depicted angels having sex with homosexuals and blasphemously mocked God. It praised communist spies like Ethel Rosenberg. (Photo: *Newsweek*, November 17, 2003)

Entertainer Michael Jackson sends a message to his fans.

Watch Those Hands! Actor Jason Alexander ("George" in Seinfeld TV series) performs a cabala ritual in plain sight of a vast audience. To the uninitiated and ignorant millions of people who read TV Guide and see this cover, Jason Alexander appears to be merely hamming it up. Little do they know of the deeper occult meaning. For example, we find Jason's left and right hands giving the *"El Diablo"* satanic hand sign. His arms—one pointing up, the other down—indicate the dualistic (marriage of opposites, or reconciliation), cabalistic magical philosophy "As Above, So Below" (The devil goat *Baphomet* performs the same sign). We also note the three triangles presented by Jason's legs and arms.

Partying, Drinking, Rebellion, Or...?

With the rapid rise in popularity of the *El Diablo* sign among rock music fans, many people seem to be blissfully unaware of the satanic background and dark history of this sign. To some, giving the sign more likely indicates eagerness and gusto for fun, partying, drinking, and rebellion.

I leave it to you, the reader, to decide which of the persons shown here and in my book, *Codex Magica*, rendering the *El Diablo* sign, are paying homage to Satan and which are employing it for some other purpose. I have my own opinion, what's yours? For example, in *Codex Magica* you'll discover former President Bill Clinton, entertainer Michael Jackson, and Italian Prime Minister Silvio Berlusconi all giving the sign. Are they telling us they are Texas Longhorns fans...or that they love Satan?

Judging the Evidence

A final word: Even if you and I are willing to allow that the giving of this sign by some is not intentionally satanic, we cannot dismiss the evidence that many, if not most, who employ the sign are, in fact, knowingly honoring Satan, the rebellious dark angel. The case of the vampire satanists who stabbed a victim 66 times and drank his blood undeniably stamps the El Diablo hand sign given by the murderers as intensely satanic in nature.

Neither can the pictures in *Codex Magica* of a Hindu sect member, a witch, and of Anton LaVey, High Priest of Satan, giving the sign be disputed or explained away.

As for top-ranked Christian evangelists pictured in *Codex Magica* giving what appears to be the *El Diablo* sign, are these men servants of the One, True God as revealed in the Holy Bible, or do they cryptically serve His adversary, Lucifer? Judging from their hand gestures, what do you say?

Sinister Illuminati Signs and Symbols

Writing me from Morristown, New Jersey, Stephen, a perceptive friend of *Power of Prophecy*, stated, "I no longer see the world in quite the same way ever since I read ***Codex Magica.*"** Many people have told me that after *Codex Magica* had alerted them to the secret, black magical rituals of the Illuminati, they began to discover these extraordinary rites everywhere. In fact, Illuminist symbology saturates our culture. For example, Stephen cited a recent cover of *Business Weekly* magazine, which shows *MTV* CEO Judy McGrath making a double "X" sign. Also, he recently found a picture of U-2 rock star Bono giving the "V" sign and pictures of Jewish tombstones carved with the "shin" of Kabbalism as well as the triangle symbol.

As Judy, a ministry friend from Idaho, puts it, *"No area of our lives is untouched. We are immersed in satanic Illuminati symbology from dusk to dawn."*

On the following page, I reprint just a few of the many fascinating pictures and images ministry friends have sent me in the few months since ***Codex Magica*** was released. It is evident the mind of the average American is bombarded with literally hundreds, sometimes thousands, of dangerous signs, marks, and symbols each and every day. You can't escape them.

Our society is embroidered by these symbols of evil. They are everywhere, on TV, in magazines, on billboards, and in our newspapers. Even at church and in retail establishments. But sadly, most people are ignorant and unaware of the ever-present assault on our senses by the Illuminist disciples of deception.

Codex Magica is, indeed, opening the eyes of thousands of men and women. They are now acutely aware of the magnitude of the Illuminati conspiracy and, truly, they never again will see the world in quite the same way. This may well be a profound fulfillment of the prophetic Word of God. *Daniel 12:10*, for example, declares that, at the *"time of the end...the wicked shall do wickedly: and none of the wicked shall understand; but the wise shall understand."*

In his revealing 1970 book, *Between Two Ages: America's Role in the Technetronic Era*, Zbigniew Brzezinski, Rockefeller associate and director of the Illuminati's Trilateral Commission, looked forward to the time a few decades ahead (our time now!) when Big Brother would be capable of *"effectively exploiting the latest communications techniques to manipulate emotions and control reason."*

This is exactly why we are now seeing everywhere an explosion of psychologically mesmerizing symbols, marks, numbers, and signs. For Satan's mind control specialists—those devils in the hidden realm as well as human disciples operating here on earth in Big Brother's mental health laboratories—symbols and signs are occult technological tools used to alchemically program and take captive mens' minds. They are a form of magical code that enters our brain's visual cortex, conditioning, shaping, and molding men into globalist zombies readied for exploitation by elite controllers.

Brzezinksi well knew the end result of alchemical programming through the proliferation of carefully crafted demonic symbols and images. This, he noted, will lead to a technetronic era in which *"human beings become increasingly manipulatable and malleable."*

In his brilliant book, *Secret Societies and Psychological Warfare*, Michael Hoffman II analyzes the impact of all this ritual magic being shoveled into our brains. He describes it as *"the immersion of mankind into the computer-generated cryptosphere."* Frighteningly, Hoffman warns that the net effect of ritual Illuminati magic could well be *"the spiritual and mental deaths of the animated corpses of the masses of the walking dead of America."*

Do you want to escape the mental prison in which so many now find themselves captive? Jesus our Lord told us to pray that we would be accounted worthy to escape the tribulation of the last days. So prayer is essential and is of the first priority. I also highly recommend to you my massively researched book, ***Codex Magica***. Knowledge is vital in this age of deceit, and ***Codex Magica*** will arm you accordingly. Please remember, the Word of God wisely reminds us that, *"without knowledge, the people perish."*

Millennium Shocker!—Illuminati Black Mass Set For Great Pyramid

"Why do the heathen rage, and the people imagine a vain thing? The kings of the earth set themselves, and the rulers take counsel together, against the Lord, and against His anointed..."

— *Psalms 2:1,2*

"Egypt plans to crown the Great Pyramid," said the headline in the *Philadelphia Inquirer* newspaper (November 22, 1998). "It has long been missing its stone top. A millennium ceremony will highlight the installation."

The newspaper article, datelined Cairo, Egypt, and written by Vijay Joshi of the *Associated Press*, went on to explain: "For ages the Great Pyramid has been without its apex, the pointy stone top that completes its triangular shape. Now Egypt plans to make the pharaoric structure whole again by affixing a gold-encased capstone—if only for one night—to celebrate the advent of the third millennium on December 31, 1999, says the pyramid's custodian, Zahi Hawass."

Hawass, Aiwass, and The Great Pyramid

The custodian's name immediately grabbed my attention: *Zahi Hawass*. The man's name is Hawass! I had recently seen this same man, Zahi Hawass, on TV's *The Discovery Channel* as he was interviewed for a program on the mysteries of the 13-story tall Great Pyramid. Hawass is both custodian and curator of the huge, Egyptian stone monolith.

Strange and bizarre is the fact that the name, *Hawass*, is remarkably similar to *Aiwass*, the name of the devil who mentored and taught Aleister Crowley, the notorious British satanist, the mysteries of Egyptian magick and occultism. Other sources use the spelling *Aiwaz* for this demon from hell who assisted Crowley.

Aleister Crowley, who pridefully called himself the "wickedest man on Earth," claimed that his devil spirit guide, Aiwass, told him that the year 2000 A.D. would see the arrival of the Beast and signal the triumph of the occult Illuminati.

Crowley claimed that his 1904 book, *The Book of the Law*, was dictated to him word-for-word by Aiwass. It was this same devil spirit, Aiwass, who boasted to Crowley that the 1990s would end in tumult and chaos, leading to the domination of planet Earth by satanic Illuminati chieftains.

Fascinating is the fact that Crowley divulged to his most intimate associates that the name of his spirit guide, Aiwass, is a corrupt derivative of the name of the great Egyptian sun god, *Horus*. In other words, Aiwass and Horus are the same.

The eye inside the sunlit capstone of the pyramid on the U.S. one dollar bill is that of Horus, the Egyptian sun god. Horus represents the coming Son of Perdition who will lead the nations into a Luciferian New World Order (Novus Ordo Seclorum).

The Illuminati plot thickens when, on our U.S. dollar bill, we discover the mysterious image of the Egyptian pyramid with the revealing Latin inscription below, *Novus Ordo Seclorum* (In English, *New World Order*). Suspended above the pyramid is the structure's capstone, sun rays blazing and glowing around it. Inside the capstone is the cryptic, all-seeing eye of Horus, the Egyptian sun god, son of Osiris, whom all occult Masons revere as the "Great Architect of the Universe."

All of this is, of course, the Devil's Masquerade. In fact, Lucifer is the incarnation of Osiris, and Horus represents Satan's antichrist, 666, the chosen man whom Lucifer will possess and who shall reign over a short-lived, coming world kingdom.

Invocation to Lucifer

According to the *Associated Press* item, custodian Hawass is proposing that the entry into the pyramid's inner sanctum be closed forever to prevent it from being damaged by tourists. "Why do you want to visit a tomb?," he asks. Good question. In fact, there is a very special reason why Hawass desires the King's tomb, or chamber, deep inside the pyramid's structure, be closed to tourists.

The creme of the Illuminati, the men of the Inner Circle, will be conducting a black mass inside the King's chamber. The grotesque ceremony, these men believe, will culminate in a visit by their glowing Masonic god of light and magic, Lucifer himself, at exactly the stroke of midnight, December 31, 1999.

To insure the comfort of the congregating VIPs, custodian Hawass has installed a new ventilation system for the cramped room and a new lighting system for the once dark passageways that lead to it. To accomplish this renovation work, Hawass temporarily closed the pyramid's interior beginning in 1998 for almost a year and only opened it again February of 1999.

Pomp and Revelry

While Lucifer is being invoked deep inside the massive stone structure, on the grounds just outside the Great Pyramid there will be a festive, official celebration open to the public. Mr. Hawass declares that, "The official millennium ceremony will mirror the pomp and revelry that must have accompanied the installation of the pyramid's builder, Pharaoh Cheops, in a celebration about 4,600 years ago."

The A.D. 2000 extravaganza, involving a cast of thousands, will be telecast live to a world audience. As midnight arrives, cameras will capture images of tens of thousands of revelers and

Inside the King's chamber of the Great Pyramid, at exactly midnight, December 31, 1999, Lucifer is expected to appear to his chief disciples on Earth—the wicked men of the Illuminati. He will inaugurate the Solar Age, also known as the New Age.

mystery religion worshippers from around the globe, most dressed in ancient Egyptian costume and carrying religious idols and tiny statues of ancient Egyptian deities.

The deluded, decadent people of the world watching on TV will, indeed, envision a gala millennium spectacular. But hidden from view, yet another spectacle—one of consummate evil—will be taking place. In the Great Pyramid's secluded King's chamber, Lucifer will be privately communing with his chief human disciples and energizing their Great Work of establishing his antichrist kingdom on this planet *(Revelation 17 and 18)*.

The Devil's Masquerade

If you have read my book, *Circle of Intrigue*, you are fully aware of the sinister aims and activities of these men who comprise the Inner Circle of the Illuminati conspiracy. Unfortunately, the ordinary man or woman in America is totally oblivious to the existence of a conspiratorial elite group of wickeds. Nor can they possibly imagine the depraved nature of the black ceremony that will be taking place inside the pyramid.

The masses are ignorant, unseeing, and unknowing, because the Illuminati uses magick and illusion to mask its true purpose and cleverly conceals its blasphemous activities. As Robert Wilson writes in his occult novel, *Masks of the Illuminati*:

> "Don't believe the human eye in sunlight or in shade.
> The puppet show of sight and sense is the Devil's Masquerade."

UPDATE: This article was published just prior to the dawning of the 21st century. In fact, the gala outside the Pyramid and secret ceremony inside the Great Pyramid were held just as scheduled. But the plan to crown the Pyramid with its capstone was shelved after millions of Islamic demonstrators publicly protested. The Egyptian government, fearing the angry and aroused Moslems who constitute a majority of Egyptian citizens, put off their plan.

A Massive Golden Pyramid for Elvis

In a press release from Memphis, Tennessee, it was reported that "A Golden Pyramid is going up for Elvis." A phone call from a Memphis area pastor to Texe at the ministry confirmed that the spectacular new 32-story structure can already be seen at a distance against the outline of the city.

Meanwhile, news reports tout that "Elvis Presley is about to be promoted from The King to the Pharaoh of Rock'n'Roll."

"The Memphis pyramid will be one huge monument to American music," says David Less, vice president of The Pyramid Companies. "Memphis is the logical spot," he added, "because it's where Elvis lived and where rock'n'roll was born. Coincidentally, it was also the name of the ancient capital of Egypt."

"Elvis is alive, but God is Dead."

The Great American Pyramid is to be an $80 million tourist attraction. It is to house a 22,000 seat arena and an American Music Awards Hall of Fame. A 52-acre amusement park is also planned. Towering 321 feet above the ground, the golden sheath of external skin will "glisten like the sun" says the Pyramid's promoters. They note, too, that it is modeled after the magnificent Great Pyramids of Cheops in Egypt.

The Memphis Pyramid is scheduled to open in May 1991. Memphis city fathers believe it will be universally recognized as "The Eighth Wonder of the World."

How fitting that a golden, sun-like monument for Elvis be erected in the form of an Egyptian Pyramid.

The Egyptians were taught by the Babylonians to worship the Sun God and the Goddess. Our Bible tells us that in the last days there will be a world-wide revival of this Mystery Babylon religious idolatry. Rock'n'roll music is a major contributor to this present-day awakening of the decadent Mystery Babylon system, and Elvis is famed for spreading the shame of this perverse style of sensuous music.

Pastor Mike Tuminello, the dedicated man of God who first reported to us the building of this Pyramid for Elvis, believes that this pagan monument will no doubt create a horrible local breeding ground for demonic influences. Dedicated to fighting the growth of such terrible influence. Mike noted that the New Agers in his city have already begun to promote "pyramidal powers." "In Memphis," Mike sighed, "Elvis is alive, but God is dead."

"In Memphis, Elvis is alive, but God is dead."

An artist's conception of the Great American Pyramid.

It is a sign of the times that the people of today's America are increasingly allying themselves with the Mystery Babylon religion of ancient Egypt and forfeiting the covering of Biblical Christianity. Memphis is not alone in its modern-day worship of Baal. Throughout the U.S.A. men and women have opted to worship the idols of money, sexual vulgarity, rock music, and New Age spirituality. Elvis is alive in New York, Los Angeles, Dallas, Charlotte, Orlando and in every city and town in America, while, to many, God is in fact "dead."

But God is *not* dead. *He* is *alive*, and His call for righteousness echoes and reverberates across the American landscape. Someday—I believe very soon—Satan's "pyramid powers" will fail. The Truth of God's Word will be made manifest to the world. Of that glorious day we can be sure.

We encourage Christians in Memphis and everywhere to pray that God will put up a shield of protection around those who remain earnest contenders for the faith. And we ask Christians everywhere to pray that Pastor Tuminello and other Christians in Memphis will, in the midst of this evil temple and its works, reach many with the wonderful truth and saving grace of Jesus and His Word.

UPDATE: The Great American Pyramid is today open and in use for various athletic and entertainment purposes by Memphis' citizens. It opened to great controversy, and rumors continue to swirl with many believing it contains hidden chambers and passageways where occult rituals are conducted.

Pyramids of Mystery, Temples of Blood

The Sun at Midnight

> "The Ministry of Truth…was startlingly different from any other structure in sight. It was an enormous pyramidal structure of glittering white concrete, soaring up, terrace after terrace, three hundred meters into the air."
>
> —George Orwell
> *1984*

Throughout the ages the pyramid, symbolizing esoteric knowledge and occult initiation, has remained an object of mystery and awe. It has also often proven to be a grim place—a satanic temple—of death, blood, and human sacrifice.

In George Orwell's frighteningly prophetic novel, *1984*, the bureaucratic apparatus of Big Brother's dictator is housed in white buildings shaped as pyramids. In one such building, government agents are kept busy torturing and brainwashing imprisoned dissidents considered disloyal to Big Brother and his rule.

In fact, as I reveal in my video documentary, *The Sun at Midnight*, in this, the twenty-first century, governments continue to build pyramidal buildings which are used for the most brutal and insidious of governmental crimes and atrocities.

It is undeniable that the pyramid is a chosen and favored architectural design of the end-times New World Order. World-acclaimed architects are today being inspired by ancient devils to design modern pyramids across the face of planet earth.

A stunning 21st Century pyramid rises out of the desert sands. The pyramid, located in Dubai, has been aptly named "Ziggurat."

At left, Architect I.M. Pei looks over a scale model of his mind-boggling crystal pyramid at the Louvre Museum, Paris, France.

Below: Overview of the pyramid-shaped building of the new U.S. Mint complex in Fort Worth, Texas.

At left: A mysterious black hand and finger point to this pyramid at Felicity, California, claimed to be the "Center of the World."

I have discovered that there are deeply coded Illuminist messages incorporated and imbedded in the architectural specifications of these many new pyramids. Satanic leaders are well aware of the Luciferian intent of the pyramids and this is why this design is so immensely popular among the wealthy, elite builders of today's Illuminati global network.

The Secret Doctrine of the Pyramid involves the initiation of all humanity into the coming prisoner matrix of the New World Order. Its design also inspires the devotion of Illuminists because the pyramid contains within its sun-bright walls the womb of the goddess. Its exterior pictures in symbolic art the phallus of the Mystery Religion god whom they devoutly worship. All this I explain in my eye-opening video.

Always, Satan's deceived and foolish people are building, ever building, seeking to erect a new Paradise, a gulag Kingdom, here on planet earth. Illuminist architecture, including the pyramid, is the chief visible evidence of the cold, cruel Kingdom of Evil they are laboring to build.

This *Architectural Colossus* of the Illuminati reflects their demonic spiritual goals. As occurred in ancient Babylon so long ago, rebellious human agents of perdition continue to this day to build towers to reach to the heavens. Their goal, of course, is to overthrow God and establish their own *Novus Ordo Seclorum*. Their building project on the plains of Shinar—the ill-fated Tower of

Babel—proved a colossal failure. The Holy Scriptures prophesy that the same bleak destiny awaits this more recent, extravagant effort.

The Illuminists boast that their Great Teacher is coming. They ardently are building a Kingdom for his foul pleasure. But, alas, as the Scriptures so eloquently pre-announce, the Illuminists have tragically lain the wrong foundation for their new architectural wonders. The only sure foundation being Jesus Christ, the cornerstone and creator of that perfect Temple miraculously being built today without human hands, a marvelous, eternal work, indeed, that shall never wobble, decay, ruin, or fall.

"And he that sat upon the throne said, Behold, I make all things new...He that overcometh shall inherit all things; and I will be his God, and he shall be my son." (Revelation 21:5, 7) 

At left: Rothschild's unholy legacy in the Holy Land is this Masonic memorial in Eilat, Israel.

Below: The design of this newly built Catholic Church in Poland has a stylistic all-seeing eye and six sun rays.

At far left: A building crane puts the finishing touch on the towering, new pyramid in Pyongyang in communist North Korea. Also shown: Statue of North Korean strong man Kim Jong-Il.

Mysterious Monument Enshroud the World With Magic and Seduction

Mysterious Monuments

"Architecture remained a chosen instrument for the perpetuation of The Grand Design—the building of the perfect world."

—Manly P. Hall, 33°
The Secret Destiny of America

Are the Illuminati elite erecting an *Architectural Colossus* of heart-stopping cosmic significance in our very midst? When decoded, does this strangely curious, symbolic architecture reveal the malignant intentions of the Illuminati to destroy America and set up in the wake of its ashes an illuminist, Big Brother "Utopia?"

Can we, in fact, discover our amazing future by deciphering the secret, hidden meanings of the many mysterious monuments and buildings now rising across the globe?

Picture this scene: An unsuspecting visitor to the nation of France passes near a Catholic chapel in the tiny village of Rennes-le-Chateau. Desiring to go in and worship God, he immediately realizes something, somehow, is horribly askew. A sign over the entrance reads, *"This Place is Terrible!"* Then, inside, he encounters a frightening sight: A menacing, black devil figure, bearded and with horns. Cringing with fear, he asks himself, *"Is this Satan?"*

The hideous idol carries a basket containing two small dragons. What exactly is happening? Is this for real? Is this a Christian church, or is it, instead, an occult den of iniquity?

American Beauty?—The Beast, the Serpent, and the Naked Woman

Now let us move a little closer to home, back to the United States of America. Every citizen, it seems, wishes at one time or another to tour our nation's illustrious capital, Washington, D.C., with its rich store of history and tradition. Having been taught practically from birth that ours is a Christian nation, founded on biblical values, what might the visitor discover in his brief tour of this great city on the Potomac River?

Starting first at the Library of Congress, our visitor comes upon a scene that sets his mind a'roaring. His eyes behold the great Fountain. What is that he sees? Could it be? Yes, it is—a hideous, green, horned beast rising from the waters of chaos. The beast is surrounded by demonic dolphins and other sea creatures. A vicious sea-spitting serpent is his companion. To

North American Union Pyramids, erected in Princeton, West Virginia, in 1995—ten years before President George W. Bush signed a pact with the leaders of Mexico and Canada to forge a North American Union. Notice there are three pyramids and three flags—those of Mexico, the U.S.A., and Canada.

his right there is a wild and tempestuous naked woman in stone, a sea nymphet astride a horse, a horse driven stark, raving mad.

Who, or what, wonders our visitor, does this beast and his companions represent? What is this monstrosity doing poised at the entrance to one of America's most magnificent buildings, the Library of Congress, said to house the "collective wisdom" of the people of the United States, acknowledged widely as the world's only remaining superpower?

Mysterious Monuments—Rise of the Architectural Colossus

That beast and fountain, incidentally, are pictured on the cover of my book, *Mysterious Monuments—Encyclopedia of Secret Illuminati Designs, Masonic Architecture, and Occult Places*. In its 624 pages you will also find pictured the black, horned devil from the chapel at Rennes-le-Chateau, France. Indeed, in *Mysterious Monuments* you will view many mind-boggling things. Lavishly illustrated with 875 pictures, this thoroughly documented, encyclopedia of knowledge reveals the most awesome of occult secrets and gives evidence galore of the amazing spectacle being steadily built all around us.

Based on over two decades of intense investigation, *Mysterious Monuments* is a massively documented book as large and thick as the phone book of America's largest metropolises. It shows with remarkable clarity that a sinister and curious Architectural Colossus—a countless array of mysterious monuments and buildings secretly veiled in magical code, numerology, and symbol—is exploding across every continent on earth. This spellbinding Architectural Colossus is visible proof that Satan's last days "New Order of the Ages" is rising from the flames like a phoenix serpent, ominously spreading its wings across the expanse of the planet.

The United States of America is at the heart of this incredible surge, but the hell-driven inventors of evil are erecting monuments, towers, and talismanic architecture in every nation on earth. In some cases, entire new cities of Illuminati mystery architecture are rising.

The Grand Design of Illuminist Architecture

Mysterious Monuments breathtakingly demonstrates that a *Grand Design* exists and that the Illuminati elite are working a Master Plan to seduce men's minds and catapult humanity into a manifest New Age of deviltry and witchcraft. Here is graphic evidence that you and I—and especially the doubters and skeptics—can witness with our own eyes, irrefutable evidence in the tangible form of stone, paint, brick, mortar, glass, and steel. The devil's Architectural Colossus can be seen and touched. It is real. No wonder the scriptures reveal the shocking truth that until the moment Christ Jesus returns, Satan reigns as "god of this world" *(II Corinthians 4:4)*.

Yes, that's right. Until our Saviour returns and casts the Evil One and his dark angels and human disciples into the fiery pit of hell, Satan is god and ruler of this corrupt planet. What's more, as god, he is entitled to build whatever monuments, statues, buildings, and cities he wishes so that all the world's wicked inhabitants may worship and honor him. *Mysterious Monuments* is the first book ever to reveal that Satan is now building what, for him, is to ominously become the "perfect world," the ideal world, an illuminist utopia of consummate evil and debauchery, chock-full of prophetically designed architecture.

Architecture the Chosen Instrument in Building the New World Order

Manly P. Hall, 33°, acclaimed as the twentieth century's greatest Masonic scholar, wrote in his book, *The Secret Destiny of America*, that architecture plays a key role in the alchemy of human control. Indeed, says Hall, as far as the secret societies and their hidden lord are concerned, architecture is *"the chosen instrument for the perpetuation of the Grand Design—the building of the perfect world."*

Mysterious Monuments opens up all the fantastic secrets of this diabolically orchestrated Grand Design and uncovers the hideous details of the Illuminati's Orwellian "perfect world" that is now being created and threatens to overwhelm us.

Inspired by otherworldly dreams and visions, the Illuminati are globally creating a serpentine New Earth being readied for habitation by hordes of demonic invaders. Satanic architecture and Masonic monuments are an occultic type of "gospel in stone." The colossal, new architecture is built symbolically according to witchcraft and occult ritual and is being used to seduce and program peoples' minds; in effect—to seize and possess human souls.

Architecture is Power, Prophecy and Destiny

But never forget that God, too, has a Plan—one much greater and far more powerful than that of the Adversary. That majestic, Holy Plan is revealed in my new book. Awesome events are definitely on the horizon. The Glory of the Kingdom cannot be denied.

The return of Christ is surely at hand as hell and earth are being joined in unholy matrimony. *Mysterious Monuments* presents the undeniable, thrilling truth that architecture is much more than a collection of statues, monuments, and buildings made of stone, brick, mortar, wood, steel, and glass. Architecture is power. It has become the chief vehicle of satanic treachery on this planet and is thus endowed with all the trappings of prophetic destiny.

Darth Vader is a gargoyle at the National Cathedral.

Below: erotic 555-foot tall Sex Goddess statue proposed by a well-known architect for Houston, Texas, called "The Spirit of Houston."

The Illuminati Are Preparing the Earth for the Coming Dragons of Wisdom

Architectural Colossus

"A symbol veils or hides a secret, and it is that which veils mysterious forces. These energies when released can have a potent force."

—Foster Bailey, 33°
The Spirit of Freemasonry

Wasn't it fascinating that Senator Barack Obama's acceptance speech at the Democrat Party's National Convention in Denver was delivered from a raised podium in the midst of an elaborate, columned stage resembling an ancient Greek temple? What exactly was the meaning behind this Grecian symbolism? Did it have any connection to the many Greek temples found throughout America, designed and built by Illuminati builders and architects?

Take, for example, Nashville, Tennessee's fabulous Parthenon, recreated on the exact model of the famous Greek temple of the goddess Athena, now in ruins on the Acropolis in Athens. Or consider the New York Stock Exchange building on Wall Street, yet another Greek temple which comes complete with ornate Corinthian columns and a sculpture in stone of the Great Goddess outstretching her arms to embrace the masses.

These architectural edifices do, indeed, embody mysterious and potent spiritual forces. What's more, in their symbology is incorporated a mysterious Grand Design. Manly P. Hall, 33°, in his revealing volume, *The Secret Destiny of America*, writes that this Grand Design will eventually result in the "illumination" of a small cadre of superior godlike human elite and the regeneration on planet earth of a long-lost Golden Age of prosperity and perfection. Architecture, says Hall, is "the chosen instrument of the Grand Design."

We further learn from studying occult and Masonic texts that the Illuminati builders and architects hold to the belief that their occultly-designed, symbolical monuments, buildings, and statues are intended to serve as a habitat for strange cosmological gods and entities expected to arrive on planet earth at an appointed future time of destiny.

In my groundbreaking video, *Planet X: Red Star on A Collision Course With Earth*, I examine this odd ancient belief system which prevails among the world's elite. I reveal, for example, how Freemasonry's highest initiates are convinced that powerful, divine spirit entities, led by a dark, serpent or dragon warrior-lord leader are expected to arrive from the dog-star Sirius. Amazingly, this Masonic legend seems to be a fulfillment of *Revelation 9:11* which speaks of 200 million devils being unleashed from the Pit in the last days. Their leader is identified as a demonic entity named *Abaddon*, or *Apollyon*.

In sum, the *Architectural Colossus* now exploding across the face of planet earth is to serve as the headquarters, habitat, and kingdom of devils! The Illuminati are merely an advance corps of front men. They are visionary builders of palaces uniquely fit for habitation by their potentate, the Prince of the Power of the Air, and his legions of spiritual intelligences (demons).

The arrival on earth of this serpent or dragon leader from his starry abode is to be celebrated by a sacrificial Death Festival, a momentous age of war, famine, and devastation of humanity during which some six billion humans are slain. There will be blood. The earth shall be baptized in it. That, too, is discovered in the Grand Design—mass sacrifice, capped by a supposedly glorious new Grecian Golden Age of rule by the spiritual "Giants" (see *Genesis 6*).

I encourage each of you to obtain my video, entitled *Architectural Colossus: Mysterious Monuments Enshroud the World With Magic and Seduction.* This video, along with my earlier *Planet X* video documentary and the CD/audiotape report, *The Secret Doctrine Behind Planet X—Return of the Serpents of Wisdom*, carefully lays out this sinister doctrine and plan of the Illuminati elite and its secret societies.

The scriptures tell us that virtually every person on earth will fall prey to this inhuman plot. Having rejected the Truth that can set men free, most will, instead, believe the Lie and be damned. They will not escape the Strong Delusion to come upon the whole world *(II Thessalonians 2).*

You and I, however, can know what is coming and prepare. The Word of God provides the way. My videos merely reflect the magnificence of God's prophetic Word while exposing the Adversary's foul plan, a plan foretold long ago:

> *"And they worshipped the dragon which gave power unto the beast: and they worshipped the beast, saying, Who is like unto the beast? Who is able to make war with him?...If any man have an ear, let him hear. He that leadeth into captivity shall go into captivity..." (Revelation 13: 4, 9, 10)*

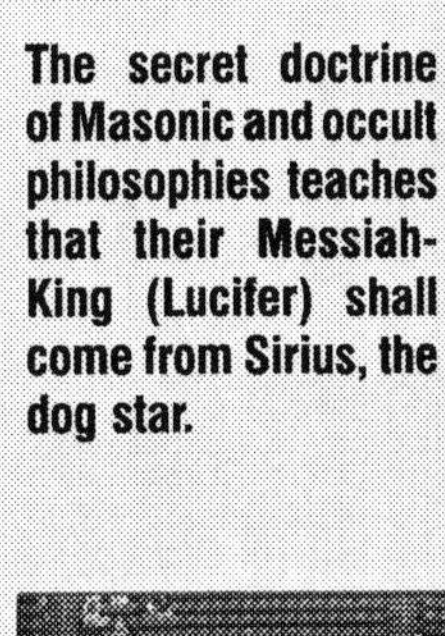

The secret doctrine of Masonic and occult philosophies teaches that their Messiah-King (Lucifer) shall come from Sirius, the dog star.

Above: Wall Street's New York Stock Exchange building honors the ancient goddess.

Left: The backdrop of Barack Obama's acceptance speech at the Democratic National Convention was modeled after an ancient greek temple.

Close Encounters With Unexpected Evil

Face to Face With the Devil

"And we know that we are of God, and the whole world lieth in wickedness."
— *1 John 5:10*

You don't see them, not unless you know what to look for. But they see you. They're always there, standing, perching, sitting, crouching, hiding, always watching, observing, sometimes grinning, certainly leering. I call them beasts: *Stony beasts*.

The Bible speaks of them as "idols" and warns that while they may consist of mere stone, marble, plaster, or wood, they nevertheless have supernatural powers of hideously strange nature. To deny this is to risk falling victim to their foul and overwhelmingly repugnant grip.

Their universal existence, often in the most unexpected places, is no accident. It was planned long ago that they would be there. But even after you discover their presence, these menacing, grotesque, supernatural entities refuse to budge. They seem to be carefully obeying the orders of someone, somewhere who sent them forth to be advance agents of some mysterious, dark force. In accomplishing this mission, they are unusually successful, hugely so, harbingers as they are of a cruel and evil agenda which, some horrible day surprisingly soon, will be fully realized.

Can Devils Inhabit Material Objects?

In my video documentary, *Face to Face With the Devil: Close Encounters With Unexpected Evil,* I investigate the presence and meaning of these incredible creations of hell. I show just how amazingly prevalent they are in our everyday lives. They are, in fact, *devils incarnate*, for the Scriptures clearly tell us that spirit entities (demons, or devils) surprisingly do inhabit material substances.

Chicago's downtown is populated by hosts of stony beasts. This one is found along Lakeshore Drive.

The unwitting and unlearned in these things may imagine that an idol fabricated to represent the real Satan (*aka* the Devil) is just another inanimate object, even if it is an ugly and repulsive object. But the human imagination is often deceived. The devil and his demon cohorts have the power to literally enter and possess an unregenerated, that is, unsaved, person's brain and mind. From that point on, the devil (or, demon) is a type of "walk-in," possessing and directing the physical human entity.

Foreign spiritual entities are also able to supernaturally co-exist within many other material items, ranging from satanic paintings to voodoo dolls, witchcraft trinkets, charms, and talismans, and including ungodly designed furnishings and décor and malevolently wicked, symbolic jewelry and clothing.

Just as an invisible cyberforce (artificial intelligence) animates and operates advanced robots

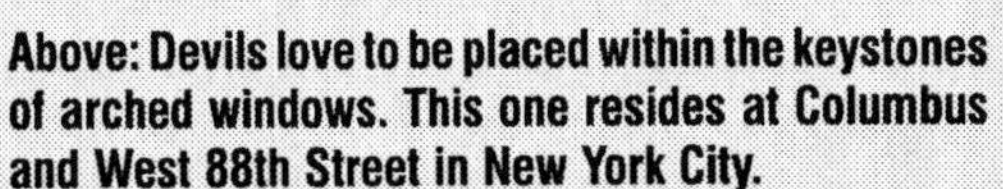

Right: Horned Celtic god from Germany.

Above: Devils love to be placed within the keystones of arched windows. This one resides at Columbus and West 88th Street in New York City.

Above, middle: The Devil, in his guise as the horned god Pan, plays his flute in this statue in Indianapolis, Indiana.

Right: This bust of a bearded and horned devil is found at the building in Hollywood which housed the Motion Picture Producers of America.

and other computerized electromechanical gadgets and machines, invisible spiritual entities likewise are able to inhabit, activate, and energize (e.g. "possess") organic materials. Advanced technology is, therefore, often indistinguishable from psychic and spiritual phenomena.

I have heard of voodoo dolls, occult books and figurines, and other satanic artifacts (including album covers of satanic, heavy metal, rock 'n' roll music groups) literally screaming and crying out when thrown into the fires. No wonder, then, that the early Christian Church gathered up pagan and witchcraft books and materials (curious arts) and cast them into the burning flames:

> *"Many of them also which used curious arts brought their books together, and burned them before all men: and they counted the price of them and found it fifty thousand pieces of silver. So mightily grew the word of God and prevailed." (Acts 19:19-20)*

The Scriptures sagely warn that it is an abomination to worship idols or even to possess witchcraft occult materials. Indeed, keeping such in one's home leads to a dreadful curse.

The Magical Power of Demonic Idols

Now, you may deem all this so much superstitious mumbo-jumbo. Modern-day men and women, after all, consider themselves too sophisticated and cosmopolitan to buy into such talk of demon-possessed idols and artifacts. But hardened Satan worshippers, including the initiates of the Illuminati secret societies, strongly believe in the magical powers of demonic-possessed idols and artifacts. They are convinced that idols of stone, wood, plaster, or other materials are, in essence, *alive!*

Occult doctrine teaches that devils inhabit and animate these things. That is why more and more idols are built, displayed, adored and secretly venerated. Every statue of a devil is, in the reckoning of Illuminists, a potential or real *god*, and collectively these devil figures represent the supreme God of the Illuminati; that is, Satan.

So obsessed are the Illuminati elite—the rich and famous of this world—with devil idols that they have caused them to be built and put up in places of honor in countless locations across this planet. You'll be shocked and flabbergasted, in viewing my video *Face to Face With the Devil*, to find them on the exterior and interior of cathedrals and churches, and on the facades of banks, museums, civic auditoriums, and government buildings. Devils in stone are discovered on arches of doorways and window ledges at the headquarters of *Fortune 500* corporations, on cruise ships and in the galleys of the billionaires' yachts. They're festooned on the exterior of majestic movie theatres and department stores and over the doors of public park restrooms.

Mormon (LDS) temples and churches often use occult symbology in their architecture. This Sun Stone, from the original Mormon Temple, Nauvoo, Illinois, was the brainchild of Church founder, Joseph Smith, a Masonic initiate and occult conjurer.

Ignorance Leads to Danger

Devils, devils, devils, everywhere, yet few are aware of them at all. It is as if a great black curtain has been pulled over most peoples' eyes. They either don't see the great multitude of devils in their midst, or they simply *don't want* to see them. Reality, apparently, intrudes violently on most peoples' comfort zones.

But, why remain unaware? Ignorance leads to danger. Once you view my newest video, your awareness will increase a thousand-fold. Your eyes will be opened to the horrible truth—and to the *reason* why I have produced such a mind-numbing documentary exposé. The prudent, wise person realizes that the whole earth lies in wickedness and is under the control of the Wicked One. This planet is temporarily his fiefdom and kingdom, and his loyal, if sometimes ignorant, human subjects honor Satan everywhere with idols of stone, marble, alabaster, metal, plaster, and wood.

You've Got to Serve Someone

Now, the Good News! If you are born again through faith in Jesus Christ, you are not subject to Satan's authority. Jesus rightly said that His Kingdom was not of this earth; therefore, you are immune from Satan's devices. God has erected a hedge of protection around each and every citizen of His Kingdom. Right where you are, you are surrounded by God's love and sheltered by innumerable numbers of victoriously powerful, protecting angels. This being so, these idols of wickedness neither speak to you nor command your obedience. They exist as mute, dumb idols, worthless hunks of matter fit only for eventual destruction.

I must sadly report, however, that if you are not a citizen of Christ's holy realm you are in dire jeopardy. You have no legal right to complain of Satan's many idols that decorate and populate the landscape. He is your master, so get used to it. You are, then, faced with a prickly, momentous choice: Either believe in Jesus and be rescued, or bow down to the Evil One and simply resolve to learn to love Big Brother.

> *"And the rest of the men which were not killed by these plagues yet repented not of the works of their hands, that they should not worship devils, and idols of gold, and silver, and brass, and stone, and of wood..." (Revelation 9:20)*

Government Coverups and Big Brother Police State

Federal Gestapo Shamelessly Targets Good Americans

"When the righteous are in authority, the people rejoice: but when the wicked beareth rule, the people mourn."

— *Proverbs 29:2*

It is a truism that, *"He whom the federal 'gods' intend to destroy, they first seek to smear and slander."* Big Brother's Gestapo forces have now made Texe Marrs and the ministry a key target. The elite in the Shadow Government who secretly rule America have been stung by the documented revelations in my latest books, *Circle of Intrigue* and *Project L.U.C.I.D.* Now, they're striking back.

A prime example is the events behind a recent, blazing headline in a major New York newspaper: *"Fridge Repairman Armed for a Revolution."* The sensational article reported that the apartment of Davaughn Roper, a 25-year old refrigerator repairman, had been raided by a SWAT team made up of federal Bureau of Alcohol, Tobacco, and Firearms *(BATF)* agents and New York Police Department (NYPD) marksmen and detectives. Inside the man's apartment, said a BATF spokesperson, was found a "vast arsenal of assault weapons and ammunition."

According to the feds, Roper was stockpiling weapons to defend himself against a group called the "Illuminati." The newspaper described the Illuminati as a fictitious, "mythical group of super rich elite who want to take over the world."

Radical, Right-Wing Literature Found?

A BATF spokesman alleged that Mr. Roper not only had this "vast arsenal of assault weapons and ammunition" he was stockpiling, but he also possessed "radical, right-wing, militia-type literature," including a book by Texe Marrs. As the newspaper account had it:

> Also taken into evidence by police during the search of Roper's apartment were videos and literature supporting his ideology, including a book by Texe Marrs entitled, *Circle of Intrigue.* The 14-chapter book describes the "Inner Circle" of the Illuminati as a group who aim to defeat God and who will not stop until every man, woman and child bow down before them.

Cocaine, Cash, and the Swastika

The fear-mongering article also quoted a BATF spokesman who declared that Mr. Roper had "29

NEW YORK POST

HOME DELIVERY 1-800-940-7678 CALL TODAY!

S.I. conspiracy buff stashed vast arsenal: cops

By the time the case got to court, the BATF's report of a "vast arsenal of assault weapons and ammunition" had shrunk to only a few rifles, shotguns, and revolvers and a meager quantity of ammunition. So much for the credibility of the new, federal Gestapo.

envelopes stuffed with cocaine" in his residence, along with a "substantial amount of cash." The suspect, the BATF spokesperson suggested, was selling cocaine and using the profits to buy his "huge stock of dangerous assault weapons."

Other mainstream newspapers quickly picked up the story and even magnified certain details. *The New York Post* (Aug. 31, 1996) claimed that Roper had admitted that he "sold drugs to buy weapons so he could fight the New World Order."

The New York Post also reported, in ominous tones, that the book found in Roper's apartment, Texe Marrs' *Circle of Intrigue*, "features a swastika on its cover." This, the newspaper suggested, might make Roper a cog in a national, militia-type, neo-Nazi conspiracy.

The New York Post ended its exposé by quoting a U.S. Attorney who warned that the suspect taken into custody, Davaughn Roper, could "face up to 20 years in prison if convicted."

Next, the infamous establishment mouthpiece, *The New York Times*, picked up the story and ran with it, further embellishing the supposed "facts." The *Times* article scoffed at the suspect's belief in the existence of an Illuminati. Reporter Clifford Kraus termed it an "imaginary" conspiracy. *The Times* article also quoted a BATF agent who warned readers that the man in custody, Mr. Roper, is "a fanatic and dangerous."

Interestingly, however, contradicting the BATF was a NYPD spokesman who explained that, "All the weapons Roper was stockpiling were for his personal protection."

"There is no conspiracy by others that we are aware of," said the NYPD detective.

Hindu Neighbor Reports Suspicious Activity

The New York Times also interviewed a Hindu man named Ravinder Singh—thought to be an illegal immigrant—who described his neighbor, Mr. Roper, as "a quiet, very secretive man." The Hindu neighbor confessed that, while he did not know Roper personally, he was concerned because, "so many people were seen visiting his apartment." *The New York Times* implied that perhaps these visitors were buying cocaine from Mr. Roper and that, maybe, he had something to hide.

Like the other establishment newspapers, *The New York Times* eagerly labeled Mr. Roper's belief in a globalist conspiracy as a pure "concoction."

An Open and Shut Case?

So there you have it: According to the federal BATF and their liberal associates in the media, it's an open and shut case. A poor, uneducated, foolish and dangerous, conspiracy fanatic—obviously a right-wing, neo-Nazi, militia-type—stockpiles a vast arsenal of deadly assault weapons. The man is bent on arming himself to fight a nonexistent "Illuminati" elite and is inspired to action by a radical, anti-government book by Texe Marrs—an evil book which seems to praise Adolf Hitler and death by picturing the dreaded, Nazi swastika on its cover.

Then...A Stunning Retraction!

But the saga doesn't end yet. The very day after these sensational headlines were splattered across the front page, a later edition of another establishment newspaper, *The New York Daily News*, published a stunning retraction! Buried, unfortunately, in the back pages of the *Daily News* was this report:

(1) New York's federal prosecutor, Bernadette Miragliotta, admitted that there was no cocaine, in fact, there were no drugs of any kind, seized from Roper's apartment. The BATF had made up this story out of thin air. The feds used the media to sensationalize the story, grab headlines, and frighten the masses into believing that a dangerous, neo-Nazi, right-wing conspiracy exists, threatening everyone's security.

(2) The federal prosecutor, Ms. Miragliotta, also admitted that no radical literature was found in the accused man's apartment. As *The New York Daily News* reported: "The arrest complaint made no mention of any seized drugs or radical literature."

(3) The BATF's much ballyhooed claim of discovering a "vast arsenal of assault weapons" also proved false. The prosecutor stated that Mr. Roper had a grand total of five rifles, two shotguns, and two handguns. There were *no* grenades, *no* bombs, *no* machine guns, *no* assault weapons, *no* "vast arsenal." Just some hunting rifles and shotguns and two revolvers—about the same number of firearms an average Texan, Montanan, Nebraskan, or Mississippian might have in their home.

The fed's inflated count of "thousands of rounds of ammunition" also inexplicably shrank. In court, the feds alleged that "about 300 rounds" were seized.

(4) Mr. Roper was charged only with a single count of possessing what the BATF claims is a shotgun with a barrel too short. Interestingly, this is the same, farcical violation the BATF charged Randy Weaver with at Ruby Ridge.

(5) The attorney for Mr. Davaughn Roper told the court that his client is "a gainfully employed" man with no criminal record whatsoever, not even a traffic citation! Roper, is, moreover, a military veteran who served with distinction for six years in the U.S. Navy. He is not a member of a militia, he is opposed to drugs, and he possesses no right-wing, radical literature.

Why are the elite so determined to smear and discredit Texe Marrs' thoroughly documented book, *Circle of Intrigue*? Is it because this powerful book unmasks the vast globalist, conspiracy for a dictatorial New World Order?

Goal: To Arouse Fear and Incite Hatred

In other words, the BATF and its cohorts in slander, the New York establishment media, flat-out lied about Mr. Davaughn Roper! The BATF planted false stories in the press, alleging Roper to be a cocaine dealer and a dangerous revolutionary—all the better to arouse fear and incite public hatred against this man and against anyone who dares to defy the New World Order. Mr. Roper is the victim of a shameless, Big Brother con job and a media hoax.

What was Mr. Roper's real "offense?" In New York City, a seedy metropolis teeming with crime, he simply had a tiny collection of guns to protect himself. That and the fact that he read pro-Christian literature, like my book, *Circle of Intrigue*, evidently made Mr. Roper a "politically incorrect" non-person. This is why he became a handy target of the fascist, BATF Gestapo police: a trophy victim.

Incredibly, the feds are more than willing to lie or to manufacture and illegally plant concocted evidence. They'll stop at nothing to libel, slander, and falsely accuse good, loyal, patriotic citizens.

They'll stop at nothing to attain their filthy goals of robbing the citizenry—you and me!—of our constitutional rights.

My Book is Pro-America

The feds and the media know that my book, *Circle of Intrigue*, is anything but neo-Nazi, "militia-type, radical literature." Indeed, the book exposes the revival of fascism in America in high places. That, I believe, is exactly why the feds were so eager to include my name and the title of one of my bestselling books in their libelous report to the media.

My books, such as *Circle of Intrigue*, *Big Sister is Watching You*, and *Project L.U.C.I.D.*, tell the absolute truth about the evil powers of intimidation. It documents the crimes and schemes of the black-hooded, jackbooted thugs of the BATF and many other federal Gestapo, alphabet agencies. This hidden elite constitute the true Nazis. In fact, as fascists, they are worse than Nazis. They are "CommuNazis!"

"The problem is that God is gone from government."
—Officer Jack McLamb

"God is Gone From Government"

Once upon a time, America had law enforcement of which it could be proud. No more. Today, the BATF, CIA, FBI and other federal bureaucracies continue to drag the good name of law enforcement through the gutter. As my friend, Officer Jack McLamb, said in a radio interview, "The scum of law enforcement has risen to the top."

"The problem," says McLamb, "is that God is gone from government."

Jack McLamb knows what he's talking about. Jack is the most decorated police officer in the history of the Phoenix, Arizona, police department. Currently retired, the man is a genuine hero, and he's on a campaign to clean up our crooked police systems and restore the integrity of law enforcement.

Friends, it is high time that we, too, like Officer Jack McLamb, stood up to and unmasked the rotten apples in federal and local law enforcement. Shamelessly, the police associations now endorse New World Order puppet, President Bill Clinton. The federal Gestapo are manufacturing tainted evidence and railroading good American citizens—men and women guilty of no crimes—into jail cells. Meanwhile, real criminals—murderers, dope dealers, rapists, and savings and loan thieves, go free, their crimes often covered up by the authorities.

Yes, Jack McLamb is right. The problem is that, "God is gone from government." And until there is repentance at the highest levels of the government bureaucracy, He's not coming back, either.

Illuminati Elite and New Agers Eagerly Anticipate the Coming of...

The Man of Sin

"And they worshipped the dragon which gave power unto the beast: and they worshipped the beast, saying, Who is like unto the beast? Who is able to make war with him?"

— *Revelation 13:4*

"How long do we have before the coming of antichrist and the horrors of his reign as the prophesied 'Man of Sin'?" That is a question I am often asked. I do recognize what a tremendously important question this is. In an attempt to answer it, we must turn first to the prophetic Scriptures. What does God's Word say about the coming of antichrist? After that and only after that we turn to the occult world. What do the Illuminati elite have planned? What is their timetable?

The Scriptures tell us that before the Man of Sin bursts on the scene, there will first be a great "falling away" from the truth (II Thes. 2). Jesus indicated that few would believe the truth. Our Saviour rhetorically asked, "When the Son of Man (Christ) returns, will He find faith on planet earth?"

Certainly there has recently been a remarkable falling away from the truth. My video, *Tower of Infamy*, documents that the strong delusion has hit. I am at a loss to name more than a few Christian leaders alive today who still cling tenaciously and earnestly to the True Faith, to that old-fashioned Gospel of the Cross.

John Negroponte, brutal Jewish thug responsible for mass killings in Central America, is now America's Gestapo SS Chief and spy Czar.

The proliferation of tainted, false Bible Versions is only one indication of how far people have fallen from the ancient landmarks of the Faith. Everywhere, the minds of men and women are fastened on the path to riches and prosperity, but almost no one is in the least concerned with storing up treasures in heaven. Stand up for Jesus as exclusively the Way, the Truth, and the Life today, and watch out! You can expect to be battered, bashed, and called despicable names. They'll quickly label you as "judgmental," "bigoted," "negative," "close-minded," "ignorant," and worse.

So yes, many of the prophetic signs warning of

the emergence of the Man of Sin are seen today. That includes the prophecies of Revelation 13, the capability of governments to require every man, woman, and child to take the mark, the name, or the number of the beast (666) in order to buy and sell. Big Brother's cousins—computers, biochips, and other high technologies—are harbingers of the prophesied global economic control system.

The Son of Hell Is Coming

We see, then, that the Bible's prophecies alert us that the time of the Man of Sin is close at hand. Next, we look at the plans of the leaders of the occult world, and what do we find? It is an alarming fact that everywhere I investigate today, I discover that the Illuminati elite are ecstatic. These self proclaimed, enlightened "god-men" are in an intensive state of perpetual anticipation. THE ELITE ARE PERSUADED THAT THEIR GREAT KING—THE SON OF HELL—IS ON THE VERY THRESHOLD OF SEIZING ALL POWER ON PLANET EARTH.

Michael Chertoff, evil Zionist neocon Bush has appointed as America's head of Homeland Security.

Perhaps, "seize" is not the proper word. The Illuminati are convinced their occult king will not have to force anyone to accept his rule. They believe the majority of people will voluntarily clamor and demand that the Man of Sin be exalted as global emperor. He will be loved by the masses and considered a type of spiritual Messiah and Lord.

The Coming One—Cosmic Christ and New Age Avatar

Not too long ago I received in the mail a booklet from World Goodwill, an international organization headquartered in London, New York, and Geneva, Switzerland. The booklet, entitled *The Coming One*, announced the supposed good news that, finally, the One whom all the world awaits is coming soon. Every eye is to behold Him, and all men shall be affected:

> "Right down the ages, in many world cycles and in many countries (and today in all countries), great points of tension have occurred which have been characterized by a hopeful sense of expectancy. Some one is expected and His coming is anticipated...
>
> For decades the reappearance of the Christ, the Avatar, has been anticipated...not only by the Christian faithful, but by those (Hindus and Buddhists) who look for Maitreya and for the Boddhisattva as well as those (Moslems) who expect the Imam Mahdi... They look for a Savior."

Please notice that the elite who run the World Goodwill organization expect not Jesus, but another Christ figure. They look for a Savior who will represent not only apostate Christians, but also Hindus, Buddhists, Moslems, and those of every other faith, and no faith! This is the God of AA's 12 Steps Program—A Higher Power who loves humanity. Yes, He will be a Cosmic Christ who loves and is loved by all and acceptable to all. He comes, therefore, as an Angel of Light.

Are Bush and Sharon initiates of a dark secret society founded in 37 A.D., almost 2000 years ago?

This illustration from *Mackey's Encyclopedia of Freemasonry* dates the founding by Jews of the Royal Order of the Freemasons in Palestine at Anno Lucis 4037, or 37 AD.

This scene is set at the White House in March, 2001, with Israeli Prime Minister Ariel Sharon and President George W. Bush both presenting mirror-image descending (female, delta, or vulva) triangles. Two triangles joined together constitute a Jewish Star of David. For added subliminal power, the room was arranged so that the bust of Lincoln was directly behind Sharon. The message: In bludgeoning hapless Palestinians and denying them their own state, Sharon is simply being Lincolnesque. After all, Lincoln put down the Southern insurrection, right? (Photo and article: *USA Today*, March 21, 2001, p. 13A)

Crises to be Created

The World Goodwill booklet says this "extraordinary" man will "inaugurate a new era in the destinies of humanity." The expected Savior is said to be coming at a time when "evil is rampant" in the world. But not to fear: We are told that the extraordinary Avatar and Leader realizes it will be necessary to "create crises in order to bring to an end the old and the undesirable and make way for new and more desirable forms."

Sounds to me like Freemasonry's "Ordo Ab Chao," doesn't it?

Of course, the stubborn Christian who refuses to discard the unacceptable "old and undesirable" orthodoxy, who refuses to make way for the new and more desirable New Age forms of spirituality and culture will be among those whose old ways—even whose very existence—shall be brought to an end.

If necessary, crises will be contrived so that opportunities will arise for the Man of Sin to throw off and remove the vestiges of old-fashioned, obsolete Christianity and replace them with a new spirituality more to the liking of He and His Father in Hell.

Remember, the Man of Sin will "create crises," that is, invent pretexts to deal with we who adamantly refuse to be rehabilitated and transformed into New Age creatures.

Isn't this really the reason for Bush's global series of wars and rumblings to make the world safe for "democracy?" Isn't it why legislatures everywhere are quickly passing draconian "hate crime" laws designed to shut true Christians mouths and extinguish forever the cries of those who resolutely demand the right to free speech, freedom of religion, the right to privacy, and the right to be free of heavy-handed Big Brother government intrusion?

Love Big Brother or Else

Either you love Big Brother, or Big Brother will silence you, that's the message of today. And to insure the message is heard, President Bush now has installed two murderous Jewish thugs in high places. The two will be steadily watching us. They are to be given 250 billion dollars per year to develop an iron-tight Police State and to perfect and continue the Gulag prison camps in which many of us will be incarcerated.

The names of Mr. Bush's two sadistic Jewish disciples from hell are John Negroponte and Michael Chertoff. Negroponte is America's newly appointed Intelligence Czar. Chertoff, meanwhile, takes over as the new chief of Homeland Security.

Negroponte and Chertoff are cunning, treacherous men whose souls are possessed by darkness. They are ice-cold, Luciferian politicians with no respect for either human rights or for God in Heaven.

Negroponte and Chertoff are to Bush as Beria and Kaganovich were to Stalin.

Don't Be Deceived

My friends, I am persuaded that George W. Bush has made a confidential pact with the devil. Forget this man's pious exterior. Do not be deceived by the compromised evangelical leaders who sing Bush's praises. Don't be fooled by his puny tears and his protestations of how much he cares for the soldiers in Iraq and Afghanistan who are shedding their blood and losing their limbs in a useless and arbitrary war whose twin goals are oil riches and Israeli territorial conquest.

It tears at my stomach and brings me profound sorrow to say it. But I must. George W. Bush is a hard-hearted, calculating killer who merely pretends to be a Christian. Believe it and be prepared for the worse. As World Goodwill trumpets in their booklet, the time is at hand, the Coming One will soon be at the threshold of global power, and everything is changing.

Does AT&T's New Baby Have Horns?

Human Slavery in the Technetronics Age

The men who comprise the Inner Circle of the Illuminati have a global plan. In implementing this plan, they appear to have the full cooperation of the planet's largest and most powerful high tech corporations. The world's premier telecommunications combine, of course, is that giant of giants, AT&T. Recently, it was announced that AT&T is splitting into three separate companies. One of the three—the company formerly known as Bell Laboratories—has been freshly renamed *Lucent Technologies*.

Does the name *Lucent* have any link to the name *Lucifer*? In the Bible, Lucifer is bequeathed the title, the "son of the morning." He is said to often come disguised as an "angel of light." He was anciently worshipped by pagans as "the Sun God, the Illumined One, the God of Light."

Modern-day New Age groups continue this ancient glorification of Lucifer. One prominent New Age organization is the *Lucis Trust*. Its late founder, Alice Bailey, hailed the horned one as "bringer of light," the "shining one." He is, she trumpeted, the "Illuminator" of mankind.

Lucent Means "Glowing With Light"

Now read carefully the accompanying article (see page 2), published in *U.S.A. Today*, February 6, 1996, entitled, "AT&T Names the Baby: Lucent." Note especially AT&T's possibly revealing statement that the name for its spin-off corporation, *Lucent*, means "glowing with light."

The logo for the new corporation is a rough-edged, red-colored *circle*. My latest book exposing the Illuminati, *Circle of Intrigue*, sheds light on the true and concealed meaning of the fiery, serpentine circle. Among the sources quoted in my book is Hislop's classic treatise, *The Two Babylons*. Hislop wrote: "In ancient Babylon, the King...a type of Antichrist... was acclaimed to be the Sun-god...the *Illuminator* of the material world...the *enlightener* of the souls of men." (p. 224, *Circle of Intrigue*)

To occultists, the circle represents their satanic deity, the great and fearsome Solar Serpent. The fiery, red sun, or circle, is his image. Scriptures reveal him as the "great *red* dragon" and his global system as the scarlet (*red*-colored) beast *(Revelation 12:3 and 17:3-5)*. How interesting that the logo for Lucent Technologies is a *red* circle.

Just as intriguing, in the *U.S.A. Today* article, we read: "AT&T hopes the name and logo—a simple red circle—will illuminate awareness."

A Coincidence?

Perhaps AT&T's unfortunate choice of name *(Lucent = Lucifer?)* for its new, baby bell spin-off, is simply a coincidence. Without definitive proof we cannot, with certainty, attribute evil intent. It could also be that the eyebrow-raising and occult-infused language and terminology used by AT&T and quoted in the *U.S.A. Today* article—phrases like "illuminate awareness" and "glowing with

AT&T names the baby: Lucent

By Melanie Wells
USA TODAY

The company without a name finally got one.

AT&T will call the equipment company being created in the three-way split of the telecommunications giant Lucent Technologies.

Lucent? The name means glowing with light, or clear — even though it has little to do with what the company sells — telephone equipment.

AT&T named the company Monday in a Securities and Exchange Commission filing. It plans to offer Lucent shares in an initial public offering this spring.

AT&T hopes the name and logo — a simple, red circle — will illuminate awareness.

"There are a lot of new names in particular markets that are hitting right now; they'll have to buy their way in," says telecommunications analyst Jeffrey Kagan.

Industry experts say more than $100 million in advertising and marketing dollars will be spent to support the brand awareness push. Ads from agency McCann-Erickson will begin airing after Lucent's IPO.

Lucent was one of 700 names suggested by company employees and identity consultant Landor Associates. Among other contenders: American Bell Labs and AGB — short for telephone creator Alexander Graham Bell.

There's no consensus among brand experts, however. "My only doubt is it's a soft name; you want to look for it on supermarket shelves among the soaps," says Alan Brew, corporate identity specialist at Addison, Seefeld and Brew.

Says New England Consulting Group's Gary Stibel: "Initially, most people will think it sounds cute and not very good, but from a marketing standpoint it has potential."

▶ Lucent IPO, 6B

AT&T employees with banner reflecting new name and logo for Bell Labs. Corporate spokesmen dubbed the new logo symbol the "innovation ring." The red circle was said to "illustrate movement and energy" and to represent "glowing with light."

At left, in this *U.S.A. Today* (February 6, 1996) article, AT&T says Bell Laboratories' new name and logo "will illuminate awareness."

light"—are also incidental. But combined with AT&T's choice for a logo of the fiery-red circle so prevalent and prominent in pagan and other dark cultures, these things do, indeed, arouse inquiry and suspicion.

As if to emphasize this point, just days before I received the *U.S.A. Today* announcement, I received a phone call from an AT&T manager who is a Christian. He expressed horror that his company had done such a thing. Rejecting AT&T's assertion otherwise, this man flatly stated: "Many company employees suspect a Luciferian meaning to the chosen name, Lucent."

The caller also emphasized his belief in a connection between the curious circle logo adopted for Lucent Technologies and the occultic goals of the Illuminati as revealed in my book, *Circle of Intrigue.*

A Brave New Technetronic World

Today, we have the mark of the beast identification system being constructed practically before our eyes. Meanwhile, under the watchful supervision of the Illuminati, all the world's military intelligence, spy, and police agencies are laboring furiously to invent ever more effective electronic, high tech shackles. The intent of the controllers is to force us, as slaves, into a Brave New Technetronic World. Their projected target date is the year 2000.

Suddenly, the planet's premier telecommunications company creates a research and development spin-off named Lucent Technologies. Will the innovative brains at the venerable company known historically as Bell Laboratories, but now dubbed Lucent, be active in carrying out Big Brother's unholy mission of technetronic control?

Will Lucent's world-class scientists and engineers be at the forefront in the development of advanced tools of human control which I have categorized as "black science?" Will Lucent Technologies assist in inventing the wiretap equipment, microchips, spy and surveillance systems, artificial intelligence, virtual reality, robotic controls, and other devices which shall usher in the final and ultimate Age of Technetronics? Will Lucent play a key role in instituting new, high tech equipment and methods which will make possible the grim, financial control system prophesied in God's Holy Bible?:

> *...that no man might buy or sell, save he that had the mark, or the name of the beast, or the number of his name. (Revelation 13:17)*

To Devour the Whole Earth

What once was inconceivable has now entered the realm of possibility—even the *circle* of reality. Lucent, as well as thousands of other high tech research corporations and centers, is briskly pushing us—every last one of us—into that brutal and frightening era in which the final, crushing blows will be delivered to man by his controllers.

> ***Yes, the prophesied, last days Beast is slouching toward Jerusalem. He is, moreover, setting up his heinous and intrusive technological systems around the globe, filling up every nook and cranny with his high tech eyes and ears, and his bloody hands.***

The Bible prophet, Daniel, was shown a vision of this very age—the Age of Technetronics and human slavery. Daniel's vision foresaw four beast kingdoms that would rule the earth in historical succession. Now we are seeing and experiencing the momentous emergence of the last and final kingdom, or global authority, on planet earth—that of the Fourth Beast Kingdom. Yes, the prophesied, last days Beast is slouching toward Jerusalem. He is, moreover, setting up his heinous and intrusive technological systems around the globe, filling up every nook and cranny with his high tech eyes and ears, and his bloody hands. Very soon, the citizens of the U.S.A. and, indeed, the whole earth will begin to shake and quiver before the unstoppable onslaught of his unbridled, technological fury:

> *Thus he said, The fourth beast shall be the fourth kingdom upon earth, which shall be diverse from all kingdoms, and shall devour the whole earth, and shall tread it down, and break it in pieces. (Daniel 7:23)*

"Watch ye, therefore..."

Are you ready for the rapid-coming arrival of the Fourth Beast and his dark, technological marvels? Is your life in order? Are you trusting only in the Lamb of God for your protection and sustenance? Be alert, be sober, be vigilant, the prophetic scriptures warn: *"Watch ye therefore: for ye know not when the master of the house cometh...Lest coming suddenly he find you sleeping." (Mark 13:35-36)*

America in Grave Danger

The Foreigners In Our Midst

America's so-called "War on Terrorism" is a cruel and sick joke! Why do I say this? Because, while a pitifully small contingent of U.S. troops and air power are striking at hundreds of would-be terrorists 10,000 miles away in remote Afghanistan, literally *tens of thousands*—that's right, *thousands* of potential terrorists—may be operating right here in our midst.

"We Have Met the Enemy—And He Is Us!"

Our President, George W. Bush, has warned that any nation that harbors, financially aids or gives comfort of any kind to terrorists makes itself our enemy. By that definition, then, America is its *own* worst enemy. A deranged and confused America is, in fact, at this very moment harboring, funding, aiding, abetting, and comforting many of the world's most ruthless terrorists. As a character in the popular cartoon, *Pogo*, once exclaimed, "We have met the enemy—and he is us!"

Consider these shocking facts and statistics:

- The U.S. Immigration and Naturalization (INS) admits there are seven million illegal immigrants now inside our borders. But some authorities warn there may be up to 25 million illegal aliens in the U.S.A.
- The INS does not have any way to make sure foreign "tourists" visiting the U.S.A. go home after their visas expire. The INS does not keep statistics nor does the agency report the names of illegal aliens to law enforcement authorities.
- Annually, the U.S. Armed Forces train over 100,000 foreign troops—Turkish, Syrian, Lebanese, Chinese, Malaysian, Indonesian, Moroccan, Saudi Arabian etc.—on U.S. soil. At Fort Polk, Louisiana; Fort Drum, New York; and other posts, the foreign marauders are taught how to attack American towns, break into peoples homes, confiscate weapons, and commit a variety of acts of terror.
- According to the FAA, eighty percent of airport screeners—the people charged with finding terrorist bombs and weapons before they are taken aboard U.S. airlines—are non-citizen foreigners. Many are Arabs! Most of the airlines' food service and janitorial employees are also non-citizens.
- In Sacramento, California, 75,000 Ukrainian immigrants crowd public facilities. Most are on welfare, and many are illegals. In Los Angeles and San Diego, most of the residents are foreigners—many are illegal aliens, including Arabs, Red Chinese, Mexicans, etc. California is now an "alien nation!" The corrupt, pro-diversity INS laughs and says, "So What?!"
- In New York City, the majority of the cab drivers are Russian Jews. Few have legal status in the U.S.A. The INS doesn't care. Neither does Mayor Rudy Giuliani.

Americans Told to "Shut Up and Take It!"

Do these statistics and facts disturb you? They do me! Indeed, a Gallup Poll shows that a vast majority of U.S. citizens are alarmed. They want the open and free influx of illegals to stop, pronto! But our politicians, Democrat and Republican, say, "No Way!"

To citizens who complain about America being taken over by illegal foreigners, our politicians say, "Go to Hell. We're going to keep our borders open and the illegals coming in droves."

"Shut up, Americans," say President George W. Bush and his New World Order pals in Congress. *"Welcome to the New World Order!"*

State Tax Money Goes to Educate Terrorists and Other Aliens

Our State universities and colleges are now clogged with foreign students. At the University of Texas, foreigners from Moslem countries like Saudi Arabia, Pakistan, Qatar, and Yemen are learning aerospace engineering. Why? So they can use their knowledge to make weapons of mass destruction and use them against Americans, their teachers?

This Moslem crowd at this rally in Pakistan shouted, "Death to America." Soon, such rallies may begin right here, in America. Our nation is now populated by six million legal resident Moslems—and untold millions of illegal alien Moslems.

At U.C.L.A. and the University of California (Berkley), foreign Moslem students are being taught molecular biology. Why? So they can construct anthrax, smallpox and other bioterror weapons for use against us, their benefactors? They are also majoring in nuclear physics and engineering. These Moslems will thus be able to make nuclear bombs and kill millions of Christian Americans.

You don't believe me? Check it out. I investigated and found, for example, that at the state taxpayer funded University of Texas, where I once taught, an astonishing 93% of the advanced graduate students are not Texans. They're not American. They are foreigners: 93%.

I also discovered that an eye-opening 85%—yes, 85%!—of married student housing is now occupied by foreign students. American taxpayers paid millions to build these residential units. Now, Israelis, Chinese and others live in them.

The same is true for State-supported universities in Florida, Georgia, Virginia, Oregon, Washington, and every other state. American universities are training future terrorists on how to use computer viruses to destroy our computers, how to build nuclear weapons, how to demolish buildings, how to kill people with diseases, and more.

Harvard Paid to Teach Moslem Garbage

At Harvard University in Massachusetts, Osama Bin Laden's oil-rich family has donated four million dollars. The catch: To get the tainted money, Harvard had to agree to teach their students "Islamic law." *The Wall Street Journal* (September 19, 2001) quoted Robert Clark, the Harvard Law School Dean, boasting of how wonderful it is now to teach "mutual understanding" and help U.S. students learn about Mohammed and Allah's legal system. Sure.

Mexico's President Vicente Fox just got his nation to change its laws. Mexicans in the U.S.A. can now *simultaneously* be citizens of both countries. That's great, says Leticia Quezada, a Mexican school board member in Los Angeles. "I have become a United States citizen," explained Ms. Quezada, "but it's sort of an intellectual commitment, whereas emotionally I'm Mexican. I want to be Mexican." (*Middle American News*, p.5, September 2001).

So she wants to be Mexican, while plundering the prosperity she enjoys here in the U.S.A. Well, I have some advice for you, Ms. Quezada. If you want to be Mexican, go back to Mexico! Leave us alone—and take your foreign socialist culture with you!

Nations like Israel, Czechoslovakia, and many others have joined the bandwagon. They're telling their people to live in America and prosper financially while becoming *dual* citizens. In Israel, the despicable authorities will allow any Jew—even murderers and rapists—to immigrate. Now, such criminals are coming here to the U.S.A.—and the INS is letting them in.

Criminal Psychotics Allowed in U.S.A. by Corrupt INS

One such foreign monster, a Muslim Croatian, was legally branded a criminal psychotic by his native country, Croatia. The INS saw that as no problem, and our Embassy abroad gave the wacko a visa. He was the crazy who cut the throat of the Greyhound bus driver, hijacked the bus, and killed five passengers by running the bus off the road.

In Sacramento, another criminal psychotic, a Ukrainian, went on a rampage, killing most of his family and threatening townspeople. Meanwhile, in Indianapolis and Atlanta, hundreds of Third World immigrant women and children have been discovered by police locked up and imprisoned, used as sex slaves. Their captors were themselves illegal immigrants.

President Bush Says, "We Want More Aliens in the U.S.A.!"

The incredible irony is that President Bush, his Republican cohorts in Congress, and the Democrats, too, are in favor of *expanding* the huge and gaping loopholes now existing in our immigration laws. No one in Washington, D.C. is serious about *excluding* potential terrorists from our shores. They all favor bringing in more and more foreigners, to open up borders, promote "free trade," and usher in the globalist paradise of the New World Order.

Illegal immigrants are not being tracked down. No law enforcement agency cares a whit. No police checks are made. Racial profiling is called bad, though we are told that all nineteen of the September 11th hijackers were of one race, one religion. Our borders are open sieves.

America is the worst promoter of terrorism in the world. Foreign terrorists live side-by-side with Americans, enjoying our prosperity, *hating* our country and despising our Lord, Jesus Christ.

Time **recently published this disgusting ad, offensive to every Christian, in its magazine. The caption blasphemously declared, "God, Allah, Krishna, Waheguru, Jehovah bless America." Also in the ad, Time's editors stated: "America's diversity is united under one ideal." Really? What ideal would that be?—that America is united under a multitude of false gods?**

Foreigners Favored by Affirmative Action Laws

In most states, cities, and towns in the U.S.A., affirmative action laws and regulations actually require that foreigners—even illegal aliens—be hired for jobs in preference to U.S. citizens. Why? Because the illegal aliens and the non-English speakers are classified as "minorities."

Thanks to this cockeyed rule, State universities, government agencies, and other employers are now packed to the brim with foreign workers who can't even speak English. Call most federal offices in Washington, D.C. and many city offices throughout the U.S.A. and often a person with a heavy foreign accent answers the phone. I tried to communicate with one such federal employee—an IRS receptionist—and gave up when she couldn't understand one iota of what I was saying.

Hospitals Packed With Foreigners

And, of course, there are the hospitals and medical clinics—populated now with incompetent, foreign-trained, alien doctors and nurses. Many are Islamic, and some no doubt are glad to see Christian patients suffer and die.

Please don't tell me I don't know what I'm talking about. My 52 year-old brother, Troy, died after being referred by his family physician to a Pakistani doctor, a supposed heart specialist in Houston, Texas. The Pakistani quack looked at my brother's chart and told him, "No problem. You are healthy." The Pakistani doctor told my brother that his family physician, an American citizen, had erred in his earlier diagnosis.

My brother left the Pakistani's office without medication or treatment, satisfied that he was fit and healthy. One week later, he was dead—of a heart attack. The county coroner who did the autopsy was horrified at the incompetence of this foreign Muslim quack. How many other Americans have died at the hands of these inept, alien medical "specialists?"

We will have no security, no safety, in our homes, and in our communities as long as our multicultural nation is under this staggering assault from within. Why wage war overseas when the real enemy is here, now, among us?

No Security, No Safety

My friends, we will have no security, no safety, in our homes and in our communities as long as our multicultural nation is under this staggering assault from within. Why wage war overseas when the real enemy is here, now, among us?

Up to 25 million foreigners live as our "neighbors." Many are sympathetic to terrorist causes. Tens of thousands of non-citizen and other alien terrorists—no one really knows how many—may now be operating within our borders, organized in cells, preparing bombs, bacteria, and viruses, plotting our destruction. And no one is doing anything about it. How many illegal aliens do you see being deported today? That's right, almost none!

In fact, our politicians want it this way. Their "War on Terrorism" is a joke. They're laughing at you and at me. They've got the vast majority of us brainwashed into believing they're sincere. In reality, they surrendered up this nation to the foreign invaders a long time ago. Yes, the leadership of America is, finally, united. *United behind our conquerors: The foreigners in our midst.*

The Plot to Dissolve the United States and Establish a North American Union

The Murder of America

"There appears to be no evidence that the American people themselves are even aware of the catastrophic events soon to overtake them."

—Steve LeFemine,
Independent candidate for Congress

"Our worst fears confirmed! We are suffering a *coup d'etat* in America. It is in the final stages of completion...the program to abrogate American Sovereignty...May God have mercy on America."

—Lawrence Patterson
Criminal Politics (May-June 2006)

The evidence is overwhelming. There is absolutely a wicked and devastating plot and conspiracy to overthrow America. The traitors are now confident they will soon wash over 225 years of American tradition and history down a sinkhole. If their foul plan succeeds, the vision we as patriots once had of a strong, prosperous nation of liberty, freedom and prosperity will soon vanish beneath a cavernous cesspool of forgotten dreams.

Over the years I have personally withstood a torrent of abuse and ridicule over my assertion that a small clique of traitorously evil men and women were plotting to bring down the walls of history. Still, I soldiered on, enduring the cruel arrows of ignorant and malicious critics. I refused to play along and keep quiet, and I have done my best to expose their heinous plot to shutdown the fabled American experiment in freedom and self-government.

Among the evil culprits I fingered over the years were such anti-American globalist groups as the Council on Foreign Relations (CFR), the Trilateral Commission, the Freemasons and the Bilderbergers. All play important roles in the on-going conspiracy. But behind them all is the satanic influence and power of Zionists. Zionists, in fact, are the real, but, so often, unheralded authors of the globalist plot.

This is the Council on Foreign Relations document requiring President Bush and the U.S. Congress to dissolve the United States as an independent nation and allow Mexican illegal aliens free access to America's land and resources.

Stepping Out Of the Shadows

Bush, Mexico's President Fox, and Canadian Prime Minister Martin relax and chat just after signing a new, CFR-prepared pact designed to dissolve the United States as a separate and independent nation. President Bush and congressional leaders are now pushing for amnesty and full citizenship for all Mexican illegals in the U.S.A. That is only one of scores of changes that must take place by the year 2010, according to the CFR agenda.

Now, finally, this traitorous clique of elitists has stepped out of the shadows into the light. No longer need they fear public disapproval. So effective has been their psychological brainwashing campaign and their dumbing down of the citizenry, the arrogant plotters believe they can finally come out and defiantly show themselves. Evidently, they think that no one is able to stop or even delay their bold plot to murder—yes, murder—America.

The CFR has even published its despicable plan in a book, entitled *Building A North American Community*. Authored by three elite members of the New York-based organization, the book calls for the ending of American sovereignty and the overthrow of the American Constitution and government.

The CFR's membership of 4,275 conspirators, backed by the organization's predominantly Zionist Jew leadership, demands that, by the year 2010, America as we once knew it will no longer exist. By that date, the Illuminati intends that the following be achieved:

1. A new currency, called the *Amero*, replace the dollar.
2. All borders between Mexico, the U.S.A., and Canada be erased and the Border Patrol retired.
3. A North American Parliament Group, composed of Mexican politicians and U.S. quislings, take over legislative authority, superseding our own Senate and House.
4. A North American Judicial Council, or Tribunal, take over the judicial function and demote the U.S. Supreme Court to an advisory only role.
5. A joint Executive Authority be set up, possibly with its capitol in Mexico City or Toronto, to dictate to U.S. citizens the terms of surrender.
6. The 106 million citizens of Mexico be given full rights by the defunct U.S.A. and be allowed to enter our territory, re-conquer and seize whatever lands and property they wish within the once sovereign U.S.A.
7. The Bill of Rights be abolished and a new North American "Declaration of Rights" be drawn up. It will comprise a shrunken list of abridged, government granted privileges more suitable to the changed times.
8. Over 100 million Mexicans living South of the Border, plus 20 million more Mexicans now residing illegally in the U.S.A., will be awarded full social security and medicare benefits and have full job, voting and other rights granted to them. American taxpayers will foot the bill.
9. Mexican workers will be given affirmative action and preferential job quotas. Millions of Anglo-Americans will lose their jobs.
10. Hispanic-owned corporations will be favored with government grants and contracts. The economies of Mexico, the former U.S.A., and Canada will be totally merged and a 4-football

fields wide NAFTA super highway is already being built. Thousands of air-polluting Mexican trucks and vehicles will rumble up I-35 and disperse to the various states.

11. The 50 existing American states will be formally dissolved and the former U.S.A. will be divided into ten weakened administrative regions. Some will have Mexican leaders appointed over the local, formerly American citizens.
12. Spanish and English will both be recognized as joint official languages. Mexican textbooks critical of United States history and disrespectful of American "gringo" traditions will be required in all North American schools.
13. The North American Union will join the European Community and the ASEAN (Asian) Union as the three major subdivisions of the planned global governance system, as envisioned by Rockefeller's Trilateral Commission.

This is Nothing Short of Treason!

As shocking as the CFR plot is, equally upsetting is that President George Bush, Mexican President Vicente Fox, and Canadian Prime Minister Paul Martin met in Waco, Texas, March 23, 2005, and signed a secret pact called the *Security and Prosperity Partnership*. That pact, prepared by CFR and Bilderberg administrators, sets forth step-by-step what each nation must do to insure the new, merged slave "nation," the North American Union, is fully operational by the year 2010.

Forget about the fact that the U.S. Constitution requires the President to submit treaties such as this to the Senate for a vote. Imperial dictator Bush knows that no U.S. Senator dare utter one word of protest against the CFR Plot. That would be the kiss of death for his or her senatorial career.

Having disposed of American sovereignty, the "New World Order" forged by Bush and Gorbachev in the 80s and cemented by traitorous Clinton-Bush, Democrat-Republican alliances will finally become a reality. The fly in the ointment, of course, will be the small contingent of true American patriots that remain. This is why the Bush Administration recently gave Halliburton a $385 million contract to build new detention camps. It is also why NSA computers have all our names tagged in its "dissident" database list. If necessary, they will get rid of us—permanently.

Masonic handshake: Mexican President Vicente Fox shares a Masonic handshake with Canadian Prime Minister Paul Martin as U.S. President George Bush looks on. The three met in Waco, Texas in 2005 and jointly signed a pact requiring the United States to be dismantled as an independent nation and integrated into a CFR-planned North American Union.

American military forces will enforce the New World Order. Mexican and other foreign officers will no doubt be given high military commands to guard against mutiny by angry U.S. soldiers.

A few rogue nations—Venezuela, Cuba, etc.—must be dealt with. The hapless Islamic masses will not be a major problem. They are to be enslaved and/or killed off, just as is happening now in Iraq and Afghanistan. Their oil resources will be expropriated.

The Zionist Connection: The CFR is Dominated by Jews

The *Zionist Connection* is the sinewy thread that ties this entire, vast, traitorous enterprise together. The Bush Administration is only a puppet operation. The Council on Foreign Relations has among its leading members such Zionist fanatics and servants as Vice President Dick Cheney, Secretary of State Condi Rice, and Secretary of Defense Donald Rumsfeld. In all, over *seventy percent* of the membership of the CFR is Jewish!

Also on the CFR's rolls: Ben Bernanke, Chairman of the Federal Reserve; Robert Rubin, Clinton's former Secretary of the Treasury; and Madeleine Albright, Clinton's former Secretary of State. *Every one of these persons is a Jew and a Zionist Agent.* Their first allegiance is to the Jewish World Authority.

Ben Bernanke

Here are some other top Jewish names that dominate the CFR. Indeed, the CFR is nothing more than America's premier Zionist Secret Society, a traitorous front for global Jewish interests and headquarters for the furtherance of the Zionist plot for a global Jewish Utopia: Carla Hills, Henry Bienen, Kenneth Duberstein, Martin Feldman, Richard Salomon, Bart Friedman, Maurice Greenberg, Morton Janklow, Ira Lipman, Seymour Sternberg, Frank Wisner, Michael Moscow, Roger Altman, Jessica Einhorn, David Greenberg, Louis Perlmutter, Joshua Steiner, Anita Wien, Douglas Schoen, Malcolm Weiner, Charles Schumer, Nancy Soderberg, Peter Tannoff, Abraham Lowenthal, Marc Thiessen, Daniel Yergin, Douglas Feith, Richard Perle, Carl Gershman, Peter Rosenblatt, Joseph Lieberman, Mortimer Zuckerman.

All of those listed are CFR Jews. All are globalists. As CFR conspirators and associates, all, in my opinion, are deceitful traitors, guilty of treason, enemies of the Constitution of the United States of America. They deserve to be arrested, indicted, and, if found guilty by a jury of 12 honest American Patriots, sent to prison or executed.

The Trap Has Been Set

Dear friends, the trap has been set. The media are not on our side. Neither are the leaders of the Christian religious establishment. They are owned by Jewish Wall Street corporate interests. Neither can we count on either of the two major political parties to rescue us. The Congress and the State Capital delegations are packed with CFR traitors who have already sold out the American Republic for a pot of porridge. Today in America, we have the best politicians and clergy that money can buy!

Please, I encourage you: Call today and order the audiotape/CD special report I have released revealing the facts you need to know to understand and survive the horrible crisis now facing us all: *The Murder of America—The Council on Foreign Relations Plot to Dissolve the United States and Establish a North American Union.*

Be aware of the facts, and remember, though the storm clouds gather and the twilight hour is at hand, there is One who is able to lift us up and bring the Adversary to heel. We can cast out fear and face the future with zest and confidence. Jesus, you may recall, said it simply and powerfully: *"Only believe."*

The Beast 666 Universal Human Control System

Project L.U.C.I.D. is Here!

Texe Marrs has received astonishing evidence of an incredible, new "Beast 666 Universal Human Control System." Officially called L.U.C.I.D., this grotesque system of universal slavery is—even as you read this—being implemented by federal and international intelligence and police agencies. The new Beast 666 system will mandate that every man, woman, and child on planet Earth be issued a high tech, "Smart," I.D. card, called a *Universal Biometrics Card.*

This I.D. card allows the New World Order's police state to track and link every man, woman, and child on planet Earth. Our activities are to be monitored 24 hours a day, seven days a week, by federal Gestapo agencies—the FBI, IRS, BATF, CIA, DIA, DEA, NSA, U.S. Treasury Service, and Department of Justice. International police and intelligence agencies are linked with the Beast 666 system, to include America's Big Brother-enforcing CIA, the vicious Russian KGB, the devious and wicked British Intelligence Service, and Israel's terroristic Mossad spy organization.

No Privacy With the Orwellian "Beast I.D." System

The computerized *Universal Biometrics Card* guarantees the control and surveillance of every living human being. The card contains templates, or samples, of the "individual's DNA genotype" and his or her "human leukocyte antigen." The artificial intelligence software and special sensors loaded into the card implement a number of other identification methods, including the capture of such human features as profile and facial photos, fingerprints, footprints, and iris scans of the eye.

A computerized, pen-like, fiber-optic and laser camera will be used at I.D. card issuing centers to be set up around the world. All citizens will be ordered to report to these centers and "volunteer" their bodies to the camera devices so that the I.D. card can instantly be manufactured and issued. Babies born in the future will immediately be entered into the system at hospitals and other birthing centers.

Massive, Global Computer System Established

Sophisticated, international, computerized, telecommunications and intelligence gathering centers have already been established in preparation for the issuance of the new, human control cards. The world's most advanced super computers are being utilized.

All spy information acquired on humans, plus the data from their *Universal Biometrics Card,* is fed into the gigantic network, which is called the *Universal Computerized Identification Clearinghouse Resource Center.*

This center is the very heart of the evil L.U.C.I.D., or Beast 666 Universal Human Control System. *L.U.C.I.D.*, reports one reliable source, is an interactive and instantaneous tracking system

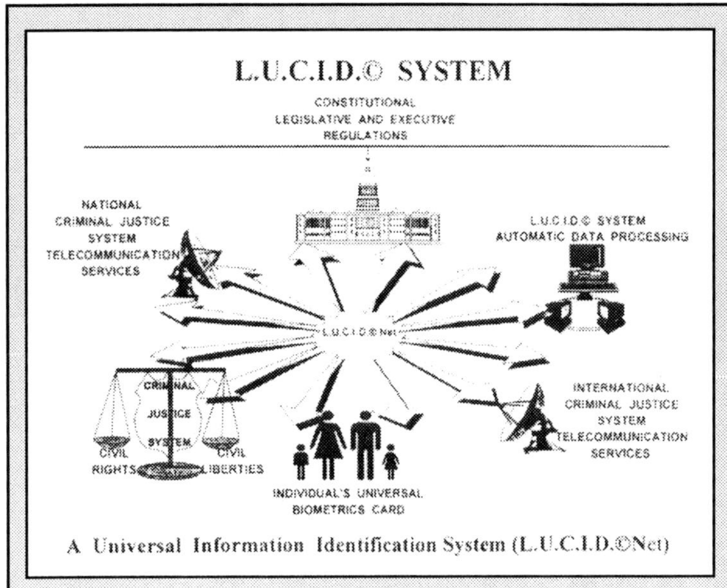

Startling information about the *L.U.C.I.D.* police state system was recently published in *The Narc Officer*, an authoritative journal for narcotics law enforcement officers. Included was this shocking chart depicting how a typical family—husband, wife, and two kids—is to be minutely controlled by computerized Universal Biometrics I.D. Cards linked with the global net.

of all living beings on Earth. It is designed so that no one can escape its clutches. No one!

Gestapo Agencies to Arrest Anti-Government Suspects

Federal and international Gestapo agencies will use the instantaneous information maintained on file at the Beast Universal Computer Center at Fort Meade, Maryland, to trace, investigate, monitor, spy on, arrest, and incarcerate "resisters." Resisters are categorized as: "Any and all persons who protest or oppose the Illuminati's fascist agenda for the New World Order."

Recently enacted, so-called "anti-terrorist" legislation, plus the Omnibus Anti-Crime Bill of 1994, are the catalysts which make possible the immediate arrest and imprisonment of any and all persons suspected of being a "terrorist." These persons are deemed as "risks to internal security." Significantly, the arrest of a targeted Christian or other citizen will take place whether or not that person has actually committed a criminal act. "Thought crimes" alone provide justification for the arrest of dissidents. Arrests of targeted citizens are to be euphemistically called "preventive detention."

Homes and Other Private Property to be Seized

The person's home, auto, bank account, and other property shall be seized. This will be accomplished under existing forfeiture laws, originally designed to stop drug dealers and kingpins, but now being used across America by Gestapo police to harass and bankrupt private citizens opposed to Big Brother government's criminal activities. These forfeiture laws are conveniently used by federal agencies and local law enforcement authorities throughout the 50 states to grab the property of people not guilty of any crime. No court order, no warrant is needed. Recently, treasonous federal courts have ripped to shreds over 200 years of American constitutional law, ruling that "a person's property has no constitutional rights."

Processing Centers...or Concentration Camps?

Individuals who have been arrested and their property seized and sold at auction will then be transported with other dissidents by truck, bus, and air to a FEMA-managed, regional *Federal Prison Transfer Center* for proper "categorization" and "disposition." Entire families are to be disposed of in this manner. Neighbors and the local communities will be given the excuse that the surviving spouses and children of those arrested are being "assisted" by the government.

Final disposition, when deemed appropriate, will be made at a regional *Processing and Detention Center*. The Nazis called such centers *concentration camps!* At these "Centers," methods and techniques of interrogation, torture, and final disposition honed and developed by the CIA through its Operation Phoenix program are to be used on victimized citizens.

During the Vietnam conflict, the federal government's Top Secret *Operation Phoenix* program was responsible for the arrest, incarceration, torture, and murder of over 50,000 innocent civilians. The CIA and U.S. Army Special Forces acclaimed it a success and a model and prototype for future "human pacification programs."

"For Your Own Protection and Safety"

Preliminary information on *Project L.U.C.I.D.* is even now being disseminated to federal law enforcement agencies. Managers of these agencies will be briefed on how to use propaganda and cleverly respond to public and local press inquiries, so that the awful truth will not become known until it is too late. For example, government PR experts will reassure the frightened and startled masses that, "All constitutional protections remain in place."

The White House spin doctors will, of course, soothingly reassure worried citizens that the new system is designed to "protect them" from savage acts by international and domestic terrorists, such as allegedly occurred in the Oklahoma City and New York's World Trade Center bombings. The public is to be conned into believing that, "*L.U.C.I.D.* is for your own good, and anyone who says differently is either a conspiracy nut or a dangerous, anti-government protester."

God Warned This Day Would Come!

The Bible predicted that an end-times Beast 666 Universal Human Control System would be used to control and enslave humanity: "That no man might buy or sell, save he that had the mark, or the name of the beast, or the number of his name" *(Revelation 13:17)*. Thus, we knew it was coming. Now, finally, it's here, just as was prophesied!

Project L.U.C.I.D. is being implemented at the direction of the *Inner Circle* of the Illuminati. Using the global internet, the system has been developed and is being installed by international corporations, working jointly with United Nations consultants and U.S. intelligence and law enforcement personnel. *Project L.U.C.I.D.* is Satan's diabolical, end-times system of total and absolute human control. It will put mankind under direct subjection to the Antichrist and his jackbooted, Gestapo-thug storm troopers. Every government on Earth will cooperate to oppress its citizens. *There will be nowhere to hide!*

Purging and Cleansing of "Enemies of the State"

The purging and cleansing of planet Earth is at hand. The Beast intends to be rid of such dynamic "enemies of the state" as Christian Bible-believers, American patriots, and flag-waving nationalists. Every nation on Earth will join in this campaign to eradicate the "human vermin and diseased human rats" who, it is said, now infect the wounded, sacred body of Mother Earth.

Project L.U.C.I.D. is vividly bringing to pass *Daniel 7:25* which reveals that the Beast:

> *"...shall speak great words against the Most High, and shall wear out the saints of the most High, and think to change times and laws: and they shall be given into his hand until a time and times and the dividing of time."*

This frightening development in human control signals the rapid, breathtaking emergence of the end-times Beast. His universal system is described by the Bible as "dreadful and terrible." The awesome power of the Beast is such that he "devoured and brake in pieces, and stamped the residue" of the saints with his feet *(Daniel 7:7)*.

"The Wise Shall Understand"

Why do I publish these astonishing facts about *Project L.U.C.I.D.*—facts which, admittedly, are both alarming and stupefying, though absolutely true? My friends, it is our duty to warn those who dwell in unbelief that the time is upon us. Some will wisely understand and prepare by taking shelter in Jesus Christ. He alone provides help and protection.

Regrettably, the vast majority will shun this knowledge. Many will be apathetic. Others, frightened and scared, will desperately seek to deny these staggering facts. But, this, too, was prophesied in God's Word. Only the chosen, the wise—those who know and believe in our Lord Jesus Christ—will understand, and this is as it should be. For we read that in the final, momentous days:

> *"Many shall be purified, and made white, and tried; but the wicked shall do wickedly: and none of the wicked shall understand; but the wise shall understand." (Daniel 12:10)*

The insider information we have obtained on *L.U.C.I.D.*© is tremendously important, unbelievably vital, and earthshaking. So much so, that I have produced a special book exposing this monstrous project and warning of its deadly implications for Christian believers and American patriots. Order your personal copy of this investigative book, *Project L.U.C.I.D.: The Beast 666 Universal Human Control System,* by calling our order line, toll free, at 1-800-234-9673.

Are Labor Unions Selling Out?

The Secret Brotherhood has taken dead aim at American workers. Through financial fast-dealing and corporate disloyalty to America, jobs and factories are being shifted overseas. The impoverishment of the American worker is a chief goal of the elite. And now comes the North American Free Trade Agreement to hasten the process.

Ironically, most labor unions have been keeping strangely quiet about this hemorrhaging of jobs and the traitorous and unAmerican acts of their corporate overlords. Wanna know why?

In a July 10, 1992 letter to a constituent, Bill Clinton's new Secretary of the Treasury, Lloyd Bentsen, then a U.S. Senator, admitted that he attended the secretive *Bilderbergers* conclave in Evian, France, the previous May. In his letter, Bentsen stated that among the other participants were Jack Sheinkman, president of the Amalgamated Clothing and Textile Workers Union, and Lynn Williams, head of the United Steelworkers of America.

Now perhaps we can better understand why America's textile and steel industries are practically insolvent and why foreign nations are benefitting from the misery of workers laid off here at home. Are our union leaders now conspiring against American workers? Obviously, things have changed very little in the labor unions since the corrupt days of Jimmy Hoffa.

Project L.U.C.I.D. Thunders Ahead

"And when these things begin to come to pass, then look up, and lift up your heads; for your redemption draweth nigh."

— *Luke 21:28*

The shadow government's sinister plan to minutely control our daily lives via a global, beast computer network has recently made astonishing advances. The high tech noose is quickly being tightened around the necks of the citizenry.

President Bill Clinton announced last October 10th that the government wants every home in the United States to have a computer and be linked on the internet. Trumpeting a new, $500 million government initiative to launch this idea, Clinton made it seem a noble thing as he remarked, "Let us reach for a goal in the 21st century of every home connected to the internet, and let us be brought closer together as a community through that connection."

The Cyclops Eye of Big Brother

Brought closer, indeed! The goal is to bind us all together as 21st century slaves under the watchful, electronic, cyclops eye of Big Brother. *Project L.U.C.I.D.* thunders ahead!

The National Security Agency (NSA) has now established a consortium of computer hardware and software corporations to further develop this unified control. Under the system about to be launched, no individual in the world will be able to access a computer without his or her *Universal Biometrics I.D. Card.*

Big Brother wants to keep all patriots, nationalists, constitutionalists, fundamentalist Christians, and other supposed "discontents" off the internet. Working the internet and getting their message out exposing the New World Order will no longer be allowed.

The scheme to require the Universal Biometrics I.D. Card for computer access was first revealed in an article in *The European* newspaper (29 Aug.-4 Sept. 1996, pg. 21). The article explained that *Acorn Computer Group*, based in England; *Oracle Software*, a California software giant; and *Things That Think*, a Massachusetts-based, high technology research and development outfit, are working on this project, along with "40 other companies representing a cross-section of the world's business community."

The people behind this massive development project envision that soon, every home will become a "cyberhome." Neal Gershenfeld, speaking for the consortium of companies, put it this way: "In the not so distant future, intelligence will be imbedded throughout the home and the people who live there."

"The intelligence," says Gershenfeld, "will be in the objects and devices that inhabit the home."

Just as revealed in Texe Marrs' book, *Project L.U.C.I.D.*, big brother government and huge corporations are working furiously to implement Project L.U.C.I.D.

But the master control unit, the article notes, is the home computer, tied in with a global link. Every home and apartment will have a central computer, and nothing will happen in a home unless the owner first gets the O.K. to use the home's intelligent objects by inserting a smart card, the Universal Biometrics I.D. Card, into a special I.D. reader device connected to the computer.

Unless you have and use the Universal Biometrics I.D. Card, your garage door and front door won't open. Your lights will not go on. Your heating and air conditioning will remain off. Your cookstove will not light up and be operative. Your commodes won't flush. *Without your Universal Biometrics I.D. Card, you'll be rendered virtually homeless!*

Digitizing Your Billfold

Another element of the overall plan is to "digitize your billfold." This feature is explained in a syndicated article (Sept. 23, 1996), published recently in newspapers in Austin, Texas; Seattle, Washington; and other cities. The article, entitled "Microsoft Wants to Digitize Your Billfold," reports that:

> "Microsoft is leading an initiative to marry the personal computer with so-called "smart cards." A smart card is essentially a computer chip imbedded in plastic that people can carry in their wallets. Among other purposes, the devices can be programmed to store an individual's medical information or as a substitute for cash.
>
> Along with Hewlett-Packard Co. and several European computer hardware companies, Microsoft said last week it is developing technical standards that would allow smart cards and personal computers to interact, regardless of the manufacturer...
>
> Consumers could access their checking accounts over the internet and replenish their smart cards electronically, then carry the cards to retailers to make purchases."

In other words, very soon *you won't be able to buy or sell* unless you use your specially numbered, computerized I.D. card. This will put *L.U.C.I.D.* into full operation and enable the Beast of Bible prophecy (Revelation 13) to insure that "no man might buy or sell, save he that had the mark, or the name of the beast, or the number of his name" (666).

When will this incredible event occur? Microsoft, the titanic corporation founded by Bill Gates, the man reported to be America's richest billionaire, is aiming this system at us right now. Microsoft's chief executive, Mr. Gates, probably received his fire-hot marching orders to get this system up and running during his attendance at Mikhail Gorbachev's illuministic *State of the World Forum* in San Francisco last year. Prady Misra, Microsoft's product manager in the internet division, assures us that, "the day is very near" when all personal computers will have smart card readers built right into the machine to enable their use over the internet.

"The readers can be built for less than $30," says Blair Dillaway, manager for Microsoft's smart card project.

Meanwhile, another consortium company, Hewlett-Packard, announced that it will provide smart card readers for personal computers using Microsoft's *Windows* software, the universal standard.

TVs and Computers to Wed

A third industry giant, Oracle Software Corp., is working on the *Network Computer*. This will be a marriage of your home TV with the worldwide web, or internet.

In this setup, your TV will become the computer and your remote control will give you the means to work the system. Of course, you will not be able to gain access or get your TV to operate at all until you insert into the Network Computer's accessory device your personal Universal Biometrics I.D. Card.

Oracle's founder, billionaire Larry Ellison, is the present darling of the Illuminati crowd. When President Clinton traveled to California last October, news reporters observed Ellison climbing into the back seat of Clinton's presidential limo. "I was explaining to him how the Network Computer will operate," said Ellison.

Oracle was the company chosen two years ago by the National Security Agency, the CIA, and the U.S. State Department, to develop a national I.D. card control system for Mexico. Every citizen of Mexico was issued a high tech I.D. card, ostensibly for voter registration purposes.

Actually, this was part of the Illuminati's campaign, explained in my book, *Project L.U.C.I.D.*, to require every man, woman, and child on Earth to soon be issued the Universal Biometrics I.D. Card.

A Huge, New Bureaucracy is Set Up

To insure that all goes well and the behemoth *Project L.U.C.I.D.* is fully implemented, last July 15th President Clinton signed an executive order (No. 13010, Federal Register, July 17, 1996, Vol. 61, No. 138, pp. 37345-37350) setting up a monstrously huge federal bureaucracy to oversee and direct all high tech, citizen control operations and systems.

The executive order established the *"President's Commission on Critical Infrastructure Protection."* Its membership includes top-level officials from the Treasury, Justice, Defense, Commerce, Energy, and Transportation Departments.

Meanwhile, a global police organization called the *"Infrastructure Protection Task Force"* (IPTF) was also established. Made up of FEMA, the FBI, the CIA, and the NSA, the IPTF will use its considerable police, law enforcement, and intelligence authority to whip the citizenry into line. The internet and all individual computers will be monitored and censored to make sure that no "cyber terrorists" can thwart or prevent *Project L.U.C.I.D.*

What we intend to do, says Dan Gelber, a counsel to the Senate Committee on cyberspace chaired by CFR's Senator William Roth (R-Del.), is to "create a culture of security."

"We also need international cooperation in law enforcement," says Gelber, adding, "This is a borderless problem."

Global Cyber-Cops

To police Big Brother's invasive *Project L.U.C.I.D.* and enforce the planned, total security state they are now erecting, the government is setting up a *Global Cyber-Cops Corps*. We must have the means to prevent cyber terrorist attacks on our computer systems, CIA Director John Deutsch explained recently (*Parade* magazine, Sept. 29, 1996).

"The danger of cyber terrorist attacks on the worldwide net," Deutsch warns, "is second only to that posed by nuclear arms and other weapons of mass destruction."

Robots in Rebellion

So the *Project L.U.C.I.D.* train continues its thunderous and inexorable journey toward the dawning of the New Millennium. And to make sure it arrives on time, with all its Orwellian potential intact, the global superpower government has formed an unheralded, but massive, police and intelligence apparatus. The elite fear that some Americans will revolt once they realize what is in store for them. They suspect that, regardless of the wave of pro-government propaganda being spewed out by the media, millions will, nevertheless, refuse to voluntarily enter the high tech, silicon cages being built for them.

To the tyrannical slave masters of the global plantation, you and I—constitutional proponents of the old order—are the new, designated enemy. They fear we may become, in their warped view, thinking robots in rebellion—"cyber terrorists" who decide to "just say no" to *L.U.C.I.D.*, to its I.D. card, and the implantable chip. We the citizens must be stopped, whatever the cost. The elite have determined that if the slouching Beast is to ever reach Jerusalem, *Project L.U.C.I.D.* must be implemented.

Gorbachev Picked to Lead International Green Cross

The citizens of Russia have firmly rejected their once "great" comrade leader, Mikhail Gorbachev. But no problem—Gorby's superiors in the Secret Brotherhood have found another top position for their faithful servant. At the Earth Summit, the great environmental devilfest held in Rio de Janeiro, Brazil, last June, the elitists chose Gorbachev to head-up a new worldwide group to be known as the International Green Cross.

According to a recent World Goodwill newsletter (1992, No. 4), it was Gorbachev himself who, in 1990 at Moscow's Global Forum, first suggested the creation of an International Green Cross. Such a group, said Gorbachev, is needed to protect the environment and save the earth. Mocking the sacrifice of Jesus on the cross, in a statement that was as blasphemous as it was cunning, Gorbachev lamented "the crucifixion of Mother Earth" by those who would pollute her.

The World Goodwill newsletter, pompously claiming that the spiritual welfare of Mother Earth is at stake, explained that, "The aim of the International Green Cross is to come to the aid of nature in the same way the Red Cross comes to the aid of human victims in war and disaster."

This coming April, 1993, in Kyoto, Japan, Mikhail Gorbachev, the first president of this new Illuminati environmental organization, will convene with other disciples of the Secret Brotherhood to "draft the International Green Cross's charter, structure, and organizational plans."

Is it mere coincidence that one of the major religious symbols of the Knights Templar, the precursor to today's Illuminati, was an occultic cross?

The Illuminati Council on Foreign Relations Builds a Global Spirituality

Occult Theocracy

Occult Theocracy: definition. 1. Ancient Myth. A mingling of various deities or divine attributes into one personality; also a mixture of different deities.
—*Murray New English Dictionary*

Having temporarily failed to usher in its new global order by military force, the Illuminati has now decided to unleash a far greater power in pursuit of its wicked, dictatorial goals: The power of *Global Spirituality*.

To achieve this, the Illuminati's premier political and economic organ, the socialistic, pro-Zionist *Council on Foreign Relations* (CFR), has elevated to membership two key operatives, two men who are at the helm of America's most influential Christian evangelical groups. I refer to Pastor Rick Warren, Saddleback Community Church in California, and Dr. Richard Land, reigning religious potentate and poobah of the massive Southern Baptist Convention.

In this issue of their influential journal, the Council on Foreign Relations announced its intention of using their chosen puppet leaders in the evangelical community to bring about their scheme of a united global order and an Occult Theocracy.

For the first time in the almost 100-year history of the CFR, evangelical leaders have been elevated to elite status as members of the exclusive globalist secret society. Their charge is to bring over 100 million Americans who are thought to be religious conservatives into the fold of the Illuminati and into the Big Tent of the emerging Zionist Global Order.

Rick Warren, called "America's Pastor" by the Illuminist-controlled media, has over 100,000 churches and pastors signed up in allegiance to his New Age Purpose-Driven Movement. Richard Land, meanwhile, is heard on over 600 radio stations and is a featured speaker at Southern Baptist conclaves.

Rick Warren—CFR Puppet, "America's Pastor"

The CFR elite have assigned their religious stooge, Mr. Warren, the task of bringing Africa and many of the world's Muslims into the fold of Illuminism. Warren was recently trained by the CFR's neocon Jews in residence at the Bush White House and was sent forth to Syria where he cuddled up with that nation's Moslem brotherhood and leadership.

Warren was also chosen by Jewish Zionist billionaire Rupert Murdoch to be given a full hour of praise in a special report entitled, *"Can Rick Warren Change the World?"* This video documentary, aired on Murdoch's neocon Jew network, Fox-TV News, was a puff piece lauding Warren's ministry and especially his propagandistic African crusades.

The Illuminati's Council on Foreign Relations has enlisted the services of evangelicals, Pastor Rick Warren (left) and Richard Land (right), to marshall tens of millions of evangelical Christians in a global crusade to convert humanity to the New Global Spirituality.

Meanwhile, the Jewish-controlled media colluded to make Rick Warren's New Age classic book, *The Purpose Driven Life*, a #1 New York Times bestseller.

SBC's Richard Land a Devoted Environmentalist

Dr. Richard Land, President of the Southern Baptists' Ethics and Religious Liberty Commission, was chosen by the CFR elite for promotion after he proved to the Illuminati his base loyalty in two very key areas: (1) Zionism; and (2) Environmentalism. Richard Land, supposedly a religious conservative, strangely is a globalist associate of Jim Wallis, liberal darling and head of the Masonic-oriented *Sojourners* group.

Land is also an ardent Zionist and is joint backer with Falwell, Hagee, Vines and others, of Jewish and Israeli racist supremacism. He is the evangelicals' leading point man on environmentalism. Land essentially teaches that Jesus died on the cross to save Mother Earth *and* to save human souls. Land says that the Great Commission includes the preaching of environmentalism just as much as it does the traditional *John 3:16* message.

The Illuminists love it when their Mother Earth Gospel is promoted by a neocon backer and Zionist advocate, Richard Land, who sits at the helm of power in the 16-million strong Baptist empire. At this time, Dr. Land, like some others whom the CFR has recruited, still preaches Jesus. But over time, it is expected that he and the SBC will moderate these exclusivist views to accommodate the new and approved CFR spiritual model of *Unity and Diversity*, a model that holds that Jesus is only one of many religious ways.

The Illuminati's CFR elite, with help from global servants like Warren and Land, has crafted a new gospel, a Global Spirituality. The new versions of the Bible are now quickly incorporating this new gospel message into their latest printings. Rick Warren uses quotes from these new versions, including the New Century Version and The Message, in his Purpose-Driven books.

Everything is God: Core Teaching of the Global Spirituality

The new gospel of CFR and its evangelical associates holds that *"All Things Are One."* Therefore, the Lord's Prayer, as quoted from the New Age Bible version, *The Message*, as found in Rick Warren's books, uses the well-known occultic phrase, *"as above, so below."* In the King James, we find a quite different rendition, the wording, *"Thy Kingdom come. Thy Will be done in earth, as it is in heaven."*

Every student of the occult instantly recognizes the motto, "as above, so below." This ancient occult formulation, taught from the days of the Egyptian/Greek god, Hermes, brings with it the doctrine that all things are One, that there is no God outside of us, that heaven and earth are now and have always been a unity, and that we, ourselves, are collectively "God." The earth is God, the stars are God, nature is God. All is One. All is Divine.

Of course, this is pantheism; it is classic Hinduism and New Age. This new gospel is of paramount significance to the Illuminati for it dethrones the external God. The new theology unites all deities and faiths. It refutes any conception of a separate heaven and hell. It sacrilizes and deifies planet earth, and it enthrones Man as God incarnate.

It is essentially the old lie spoken of in the Bible's book of Genesis, in which Lucifer promised a rebellious Adam and Eve, "Ye shall be as gods." It is the lie prophesied in 2 Thes. 2 to come to fullness in these last days, the lie in which the whole world will believe and be damned. It is the lie which is described by the Apostle Paul as the Strong Delusion. This lie represents the Great Apostasy, the falling away that was prophesied.

Occult Theocracy—The Mingling of Deities

Shortly after the turn of the twentieth century, Britain's Lady Queensborough authored a wonderfully descriptive book that unmasked this perennially deceptive philosophy. She called it *"Occult Theocracy,"* which she defined as a Luciferian combining, or mingling, of secret society and ancient religious dogma to produce a deadly ecumenical mixture that presents itself as a great and global danger.

Now come the new evangelicals, chosen as 21st century prophets of the Council on Foreign Relations, apostles of the gospel of *Global Spirituality*, in new shiny garb, fervently preaching this same, incredible, occult doctrine: As Above, So Below.

This Mystery Religion doctrine, "As Above, So Below," and its goal of the setting up of an Occult Theocracy is expressed symbolically (see *Codex Magica*) as the Masonic Lodge's black and white tiled floor and as Masonry's double-headed eagle; it can be seen in the form of the Roman religion's god, the two-faced Janus, as the Oriental Tao's yin and yang, and as the Jews' six-pointed Star of David, composed of two superimposed triangles. It represents the defiant threat of Lucifer who arrogantly boasted, "I will ascend into heaven, I will exalt my throne above the stars of God." *(Isaiah 14:13)*

Their Destiny is the Pit of Hell

Let the wicked rulers of the Illuminati and its Council on Foreign Relations who plot in secret take heed, and let their globalist religious puppets, Rick Warren, Richard Land and others take note. When Lucifer had finished making that idle boast, after he had blasphemously declared, *"As Above, So Below,"* Isaiah, a mighty Prophet of God, immediately pronounced judgment on the Wicked One: *"Yet thou shalt be brought down to hell, to the sides of the pit."*

And so it shall be for all who join themselves together as partakers of the ongoing Occult Theocracy. These disciples of evil will be recompensed for their unholy rebellion against God and against His anointed. *"For God shall bring every work into judgment, with every secret thing, whether it be good, or whether it be evil." (Ecclesiastes 12:14)*

The prime directive, or teaching, of the Illuminati's new Global Spirituality is expressed in these four symbols.

Of Presidents, Prisoners of War, and Beasts

If anyone still has lingering doubts that there has long been a sinister conspiracy by wealthy elitists and their political appointees, the ongoing U.S. Senate investigation into the POW/MIA scandal should easily resolve them.

Colonel Philip Corso (U.S. Army-retired), a former intelligence officer and high-ranking White House aide to then President Dwight Eisenhower, testified to a Senate Committee (November 9, 1992) that at the end of the Korean War in 1953, "at least two trainloads" of American prisoners of war were not repatriated. Instead, they were clandestinely shipped to Siberia by the North Koreans at the request of Kremlin dictator Josef Stalin.

Evidently, President Eisenhower was well aware that these hapless men would become tortured slaves for the rest of their natural lives. Eisenhower also knew that these POWs would suffer in the bitter cold of Siberian wastelands and that they would literally be worked to death in gulag slave camps. But, said Corso, the president and the intelligence community decided to do nothing—nothing that is except to lie to the American people and cover-up the truth about the fate of these men.

Censorship and Lies an Official Policy

"Censorship was part of the policy," Colonel Corso testified. "It was the system."

Corso also reminded the Senate panel that he had given this same testimony to Congress in the 1960s. At the time, the appropriate congressmen decided to continue the cover-up. So his testimony, some 30 years ago, was classified secret and all documentation and proof has been locked up ever since.

A smiling President Dwight D. Eisenhower (left) did not utter even a whimper of protest when communist butcher Josef Stalin (right) had two trainloads of U.S. prisoners of war transported to Siberia in 1953.

Our Smiling, Golfing President

In the 1950s President Dwight D. Eisenhower was lionized by the media establishment. He was lauded for ending the Korean War and "bringing the boys home." He was held up to millions of school children as a paragon of honesty. Now we know the hideous truth: Eisenhower was, in reality, a vacuous, deceitful, smiling monster—a beast who served the Secret Brotherhood and its Council on Foreign Relations with untiring fervor and devotion.

As president, Eisenhower frequently sunned himself, strutting up and down the links of the ritziest golf courses in the country. While he lived in the lap of luxury at the White House, dining on fancy delicacies served up by his taxpayer-salaried chef, over in Siberia, thousands of abandoned American fighting men were consuming roach-infested brine and watered-down soup. While here in the U.S.A. Eisenhower daily enjoyed the adulation of an admiring public, our forgotten POWs were receiving daily beatings and enduring other deprivations and horrors.

Why Were They Abandoned?

In my exposé book *Dark Majesty*, I reveal the astonishing truth about why our POWs and MIAs were shamelessly abandoned. It is undeniable that from Woodrow Wilson to George Bush and Bill Clinton, this once great nation has been held captive by forces alien both to God and to freedom and liberty.

From Roosevelt to Eisenhower, Kennedy, Nixon, Bush, and Clinton, rigged elections have given us presidents who were adulterers, crooks, and liars.

But the current prisoner of war scandal is, in my opinion, the ultimate in evil. Who can possibly justify the antichrist, Judas-like behavior of high-level freemason Harry Truman, and such sinister

While here in the U.S.A. Eisenhower daily enjoyed the adulation of an admiring public, our forgotten POWs were receiving daily beatings and enduring other deprivations and horrors.

men as Dwight Eisenhower and Richard Nixon? Following World War II, the Korean conflict, and the Vietnam war, these scheming politicians gave up our men in uniform to foreign butchers and slave lords—a fate worse than death—then calmly and deliberately lied to the people of America, claiming that all the POWs were home again and safe.

Are You Sick at Heart?

My fellow Americans, are you, like me, sick at heart from the excess of monstrous lies and deceptions that have been fed to us over these past decades by the Illuminati-led, beast politicians who have ruled and continue to rule over us? Would you agree with me that it's time for all of us, as Christian Americans and as God-fearing, patriotic citizens who love this country, to rise up and put an end to the long-running charade of the Secret Brotherhood?

Then I implore you: support our work with your prayers and, yes, with your finances. I need you and you need *Power of Prophecy*. Together we can tear down the wall of lies and fabrications that now separate us from our government.

Together, we can restore the honor of our nation's cherished Constitution. Together, we can unmask the monsters and beasts in our midst—whether they be greedy bankers or cunning politicians. And together, we can overcome this vast, dark conspiracy and present danger now confronting us on every side.

Please, time is fast running out. Let me hear from you today.

Secretary of Commerce Ron Brown and Former CIA Director William Colby

Mysterious Deaths Leave Unanswered Questions

"Some men are of so cruel a nature as to take a delight in killing men more than you should try to kill a bird."

— Thomas Hobbes, in the year 1671

Was the recent airplane crash of Secretary of Commerce Ron Brown an accident? And what about the mysterious drowning of former CIA director William Colby? Do we have reason to suspect foul play in these tragic mishaps?

To plumb the answers to these intriguing questions, it is necessary to examine the circumstances surrounding the lives—and the deaths—of these two, high-ranking Washington, D.C. bureaucrats.

At the time his U.S. Air Force T-43 (modified Boeing 737) slammed into a mountain in Croatia, Ron Brown was in dire political and legal hot water. A special prosecutor looking into allegations that Brown had taken $700,000 in bribes from Vietnamese officials, was, reportedly, on the verge of issuing a criminal, grand jury indictment. The evidence indicates that Ron Brown and his mentor, President Bill Clinton, had privately told Vietnam's Communist overlords that the White House would re-establish diplomatic and trade relationships between the United States and Vietnam in exchange for a $700,000, *under-the-table* bribe.

Presumably, the graft money was paid and went into secret bank accounts controlled by Clinton and Brown. President Clinton then promptly opened relations with Hanoi, unconscionably going back on his '92 campaign promise he would not do so until the still missing POWs and MIAs were accounted for.

San Francisco Chronicle

COMMERCE CHIEF LOST IN CRASH

Ron Brown, 32 others feared dead in Croatia

Top Executives From 2 Bay Firms Missing

This makes the airplane crash resulting in Ron Brown's demise—and the deaths of 34 others—much more incidental. If Secretary Brown, under indictment, were to squeal and turn state's evidence against Clinton, the President's hopes for another four years in office would go up in flames. *Ron Brown had to go!*

Not surprisingly, within 48 hours after Brown's death, the independent special prosecutor announced he was discontinuing

CAMBY, BRYANT JUMP INTO THE NBA

GWYNN TARGETS BATTING RECORD

AL STATISTICS

USA TODAY

GUURMET GROCERS GRAB MORE OF MARKET

MICHAEL JORDAN'S MOTHER SHARES PARENTING TIPS

TUESDAY

NEWSLINE

WALL STREET:

WAR ON DRUGS:

INDIANA BASKETBALL:

Ex-CIA chief missing, search resumes

Gas prices spark U.S. oil sale

the bribery investigation and turning over all his files on the case to Attorney General Janet Reno.

Meanwhile, strange and quirky facts about the crash haunt the families of survivors. For example, why did the top executive at Dyncorp, reputedly a CIA proprietary corporation, decide *not* to make the plane trip with Brown and the others, canceling at the very last moment? Did he get the word from his CIA buddies about the impending "accident?"

Why was the Air Force lieutenant-colonel in charge of this aircraft at its home base in Germany inexplicably fired and removed from his position five days before the ill-fated flight? Did Niko Junic, 46, the Croatian aircraft maintenance chief responsible for checking the T-43's navigational aids at Dubrovnik's Cilipi Airport, really commit suicide immediately after the crash, as alleged by U.S. and Croatian officials...or was he murdered? Why did the Croatian government at first report that a flight recorder "black box" had been found in the wreckage, then later retract this statement?

Why did the doomed aircraft veer so dramatically off-course? Were the instruments tampered with before take-off? And why did the U.S. government take so long to respond to the crash, dashing any prospects of saving the lives of dying victims at the crash site? Why, too, did the U.S. government initially *lie* and claim the airplane went down under dangerous and hazardous weather conditions when, in fact, the weather was not even a major factor and many other aircraft took off and landed safely at this airport during the same time frame?

The Puzzling Case of CIA Director William Colby

Then, there is the puzzling case of *William Colby*. Colby, the former top official at the CIA, was pulled from the waters of a Maryland river after being reported missing. The authorities want us to believe that this 76 year-old man left his dinner in the kitchen, his computer screen and radio on, and his door unlocked, and just strolled out to take a quick canoe ride down the white, rocky waters of the storm-swollen river adjacent to his residence. Authorities also claim that Colby "forgot" to wear his life preserver.

Even the establishment-oriented *U.S.A. Today* has questions about the official account of Colby's death. In its April 30, 1996 edition, the newspaper noted: "He is the second ex-CIA official to disappear. In 1978, a sloop belonging to retired deputy director John Paisley was found empty. A body—four inches shorter than his—was quickly cremated, leading to speculation."

My sources inform me that William Colby was about to "spill the beans" about the CIA's deadly *"Operation Phoenix."* Colby, as head of the spy agency's Saigon office during the Vietnam war years, personally directed Operation Phoenix. It was a sinister, Top Secret, occult project that resulted in some 50,000 civilian men and women rounded up and taken to concentration camps, where they were brutally tortured and murdered.

Was William Colby working at his computer on his Saigon memoirs when he suddenly "decided" to take a fatal canoe ride? Was his intent to expose the CIA's Operation Phoenix as the experimental prototype for the Concentration Camp Program in America planned for the late 1990s? Did Colby die because he knew too much about both the past...*and* the future?

Blood Money and the Making of Human Cyberslaves

Is the corporate world actively involved in helping Big Brother government enslave mankind through the forging of a global, high tech order? My shocking, new exposé book, *Project L.U.C.I.D.*, contains an important chapter entitled, *"Blood Money: Corporate Profiteering and The Making of Human Cyberslaves."* The staggering information revealed in that chapter demonstrates just how far corporate, or commercial, Mystery Babylon (Revelation 18), is willing to go in building the silicon cages into which all of us are to be herded like so many chattel cattle.

"A Chip Behind Everyone's Ear"

Consider, for example, what Ronald Kane, vice president of Cubic Corporation, a top maker of high tech control systems, had to say recently about the profit potential of the implantable biochip. "If we had our way," Kane remarked, "we'd implant a chip behind everyone's ear in the maternity ward."

Today, the making of human cyberslaves is a highly profitable enterprise. The business of creating human cyberslaves translates into big, big money. Trillions of dollars are at stake for able corporations supplying government with computerized, smart I.D. cards, iris-scanning devices, DNA blood analysis equipment, fingerprint digitization video displays, and other forms of human control technology.

Stock market *(Nasdaq)* records indicate how very lucrative the making of silicon cages can be. Recently, the stock of one tiny company, Comparator, shot up an astounding 2,900 percent in just three days. This occurred after the company's CEO announced that Comparator had invented an advanced type of portable, biometric, fingerprint identification device.

Satan certainly seems to be inspiring the work and activities of the world's largest, high tech corporations. As the Apostle Paul wisely stated in the Scriptures, "For the love of money is the root of all evil" *(I Timothy 6:10)*. From the look of things, if enough money were to exchange hands, most of America's giant, multinational corporations would, today, eagerly compete to build better and more modern concentration camps and more efficient guillotines. In other words, these greedy, corporate chieftains have no scruples about making blood money.

Lucent Technologies Revisited

Some corporations seem to take strange delight in their provocative activities. Take *Lucent Technologies*, for instance. In a recent edition of our newsletter, I asked of this AT&T spinoff corporation: "Does AT&T's new, baby Bell have horns?" In announcing the creation of Lucent earlier this year, AT&T unveiled the new corporation's mysterious logo: a rough-edged, red-colored circle. In response, I noted:

> To occultists, the circle represents their Satanic deity, the great and fearsome Solar Serpent. The fiery, red, sun orb, or circle, is his image. Scriptures reveal him as the "great red dragon" and his global system as the scarlet (*red*-colored) beast *(Revelation 12:3 and 17:3-5)*. How interesting that the logo for Lucent Technologies is a *red* circle.

Of course, AT&T's choice of a rough, esoteric-looking, red circle for the corporate image of its bright, new spinoff, *Lucent Technologies*, could have been purely coincidental. Surely, the influential, unselfish bigwigs who are leading this behemoth, multinational organization into the brave New World of the 21st century had no malevolent intent, right? And the gentleman who works in management at AT&T and wrote me of his belief that the name Lucent *(Luc ent)* stands for *Luc*ifer's *Ent*erprises—surely, he must be way off? Right?

Well, maybe. And then again, maybe not.

Lucid, Lucent, Inferno: Hellish Similarities?

It deserves mention that the name *Lucent* is remarkable in its similarity to *Lucid*, or *L.U.C.I.D.*, which, I am convinced, means *Luc*ifer's I.D. system.

But what really set my adrenaline flowing is the report just released by Lucent Technologies touting its latest innovation, a revolutionary, new "network operating system and programming environment." The name for this new Lucent product staggered my imagination: *Inferno*. Yes, *Inferno*.

What's more, the logo for this highly advertised product, *Inferno*, is the name "Inferno," decorated in fiery, brimstone-like, edged type and surrounded by bellowing smoke!

Then I looked at the top of Lucent's publicity release and discovered this quote, from Dante's classic work, *The Inferno*:

> Day was departing, and the darkening air
> Called all earth's creatures to their
> evening quiet
> While I alone was preparing as
> though for war...
> *The Inferno of Dante, Canto II*

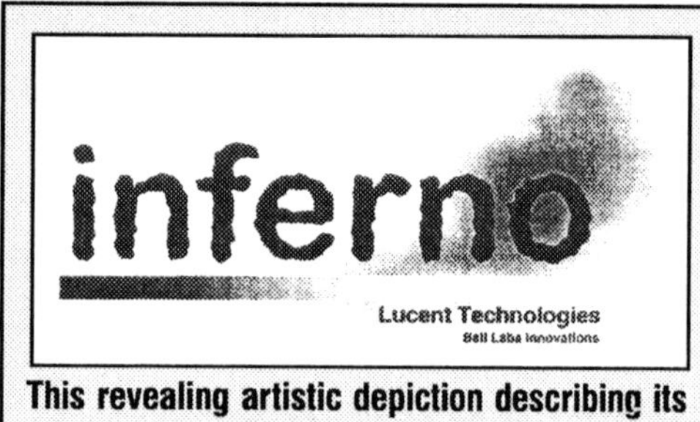

This revealing artistic depiction describing its new, Inferno software system, is from Lucent Technologies' own press release.

Dante's enduring work, *The Inferno*, was a tale of hell and of Lucifer! Thus, I asked myself, "Is Lucent not announcing that its new, global-wide internet connection product is of hellish, Luciferian origins?"

An Electronic Tower of Babel?

It was Lucifer, the master of hell, who, through his human servant, Babylon's Nimrod, defied God and sought to create a New World Order by building a colossal Tower of Babel. Nimrod's mighty efforts were ruined, however, when God confounded the builders by causing them to babble incoherently in different languages. Chaos ensued.

How spellbinding it was to also read, in Lucent's press release for Inferno, a promotional quote by Peter Bernstein, president of Infonautics Consulting, who praised Lucent's software product with these words: "*Inferno* is designed to take the chaos out of the electronic Tower of Babel."

I delved further into the Inferno materials and next discovered the statement by Lucent that, "*Inferno* (internet/computer) applications are written in a new language called Limbo which was designed specifically for the Inferno environment."

Limbo? Isn't that a word, like "purgatory," meaning to be suspended in a lower compartment of hell, awaiting judgment or punishment?

I also discovered that the "communications protocols" designed into Lucent's Inferno software are called styx. Now, in pagan mythologies and religion, styx is a synonym for the fiery, brimstone underworld region where devils reside. In other words: *hell*!

Above: Lucent Technologies chose this bold, red, rough-edged circular symbol for its highly publicized, new corporate logo.

Left: The red-colored symbol on this New Age book, The Tao of Leadership, is strikingly similar to Lucent's new corporate logo.

Right: The Oroboros, or serpent biting its own tail, is an occultic symbol of reincarnation and Lucifer's eternal reign.

Left: This symbol, remarkably similar to Lucent's logo, is found in a recent edition of *Gnosis* (Spring 1996), an occultic magazine of the Hermetic tradition.

Lucent Offices at 666 Fifth Avenue!

I've noted that AT&T's Lucent Technologies has adopted as its logo the fiery, red circle. We've also analyzed the name *Lucent* itself. Is there an even stranger coincidence indicating this corporation's connection with the Beast, 666, and the globo-cop computer system, *L.U.C.I.D.?* Indeed, there is!

Crain's (formally, *Crain's New York Business*) is one of America's most influential and respected business publications. It is eagerly read by New Yorkers and the Wall Street crowd. In *Crain's* July 1-7 issue, on page one, we find this staggering bit of information, repeated here exactly as it was printed:

> Lucent Technologies, the $21 billion former equipment division of AT&T, is cruising Manhattan for space. The company has already signed a lease for 40,000 square feet at 666 Fifth Ave.

What kind of mind-warping coincidence is this?...Lucent Technologies, the company with the red, circle logo, the company with the amazing, new, internet software called Inferno, is moving into offices at *666 Fifth Avenue!* The number 666, we know from the book of *Revelation*, identifies the Beast. The number "five" (as in Fifth) is the number of the dead in occult and Masonic numerology. So, once again, I ask: Are all these things mere coincidences?...Or, is this evidence that Lucent Technologies is, indeed, an Illuminati proprietary group?

A Brave New Technetronic World

Today, we have the Mark of the Beast identification system being constructed practically before our eyes. Meanwhile, under the watchful supervision of the Illuminati, all the world's military, intelligence, spy, and police agencies are laboring furiously to invent ever more effective, electronic, high tech shackles. The intent of the controllers is to force us, as slaves, into a Brave New Technetronic World.

Could it be that the men who are the brains behind Lucent and other corporations have no conception of how their creative "children"—products like Lucent's *Inferno, Limbo*, etc.—fit in to the end-time scenario? Without definitive and irrefutable proof, I am not ready to label these men as willing and knowing agents of the Evil One. Still, Satan is more than capable of using even the most sincere of unwitting dupes and stooges to do his dirty work here on Earth. Incalculable damage can be done with the control products produced by the brilliant, but spiritually unaware, men who roam the halls and corridors of the world's premier, high technology establishments and laboratories.

"Watch ye, therefore..."

The vast majority are fast asleep as monumental disaster gallops furiously toward us. What about you? Are you awake? Are *you* ready for the rapid-coming arrival of the Beast of Revelation and his dark, technological marvels? Are you at present a cyberslave of the Adversary or a bondservant of the Almighty God? Is your life in order? Are you trusting only in the Lamb of God for your protection and sustenance? Be alert, be sober, be vigilant, the prophetic scriptures warn: *"Watch ye therefore: for ye know not when the master of the house cometh...Lest coming suddenly he find you sleeping" (Mark 13:35-36).*

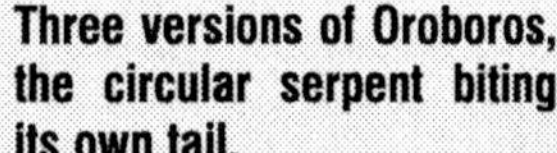
Three versions of Oroboros, the circular serpent biting its own tail.

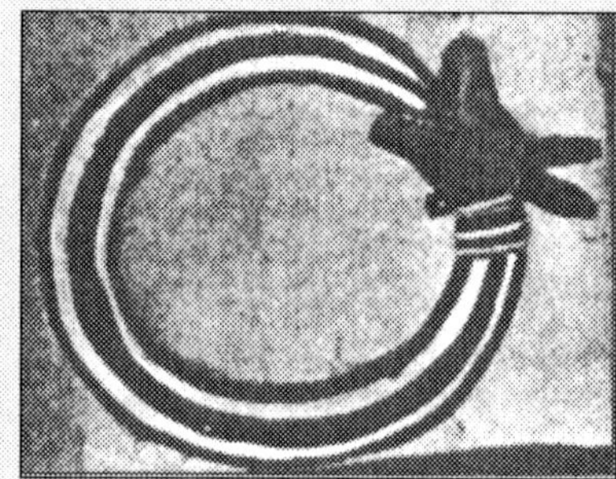

Above left: This version is from Atlanta Fugiens, by Michael Maier, 1618.

Above right: This version of Oroboros is from Dahomey, West Africa.

Left: An early, hand-painted Masonic apron depicts many occult symbols, including the serpent Oroboros, the skull and bones, pentacle stars, the pyramids, the mallet, and the X.

"Like a savage bunch of crazed banshees, the Nightstalkers attacked the children with demonic glee."

The Bizarre Deaths of the Waco Branch Davidians

It is with a mixture of both sorrow and tear-stained anger that I present this information to you, my good friends and partners of *Power of Prophecy*. Those federal officials and agents guilty of the sickening bloodshed at Waco must be punished by State of Texas law enforcement and courts. We must cry out until they are. Until justice is done, we must never forget the admonition of *Isaiah 59:14: "And judgment is turned away backward, and justice standeth afar off: for truth is fallen in the street, and equity cannot enter."*

"Torch the Mother f...rs. Do it today!" That was the direct order given Janet Reno's Justice Department by Hillary Rodham Clinton from the East Wing of the White House. And so, on the morning of April 19, the day beginning the witches' annual High Holy Days, on the 51st day of the siege, the combined forces of the FBI's and the Army's dreaded Delta Force Nightstalkers lit into the beleaguered men, women, and children held up inside their Branch Davidian church/home just outside Waco, Texas.

They ran wild, ravaging and slaughtering. Then, besotted by blood, their satanic lust and fury to kill satiated, the FBI and U.S. Army Nightstalker mass murderers took a few moments to stalk their lifeless prey, walking to and forth in the burning rubble, casting their jerky, nervous eyes to and fro over the smoldering ruins and the burnt and mutilated corpses of their seventy-six victims. Like cannibalistic savages, some took pictures of each other while pridefully holding in their hands the charred heads of their victims.

Gruesome Chain of Events

Power of Prophecy has received shocking information revealing some of the gruesome chain of events that transpired that awful, fateful day in Waco, Texas. We have learned, for example, that the initial, unlawful BATF attack on the innocent Branch Davidians was carried out not because of any crime that David Koresh or others had committed, but because of Koresh's bold claim that he was the "King of the Jews!"

Leaders of powerful Jewish organizations with ties to the Clintons, the BATF, and the FBI were enraged by Koresh's teachings that he was the new King David. They had learned from Israel's Mossad spy agency that Koresh had spent months in Jerusalem seeking to recruit Israelis into his pseudo-Jewish religious sect. And when they were told by informants that Koresh and his people were flying an Israeli Star of David flag over their residence and church in Waco, they went ballistic.

The Jewish lobbyists called on their inside contact in the White House, Hillary Rodham Clinton. Hillary is herself Jewish—her grandmother, Della Rosenberg, spoke Yiddish to Hillary as a little girl, as reported in August 1999 in Forward, the influential Jewish newspaper. Hillary rapidly put things in motion, working at first through her BATF underlings at the Treasury Department, then later through her puppet at the Justice Department, Web Hubbell, Janet Reno's corrupt deputy.

A Diabolical, Wicked Scheme

The plot, from the very beginning, was to use violent force, complete with helicopter machine gun fire, in a surprise attack against the Branch Davidians. This failed.

Hillary and her witchcraft lesbo associates then devised a more diabolical, wicked scheme. They would lay siege to the Branch Davidian residence, conveniently keeping the inept, and otherwise friendly, liberal media some three miles away. Then, on the 51st day of the siege (in occult numerology, 5+1=6, the untripled number of the beast), which would fall on April 19th, the beginning of the witches' High Holy Days, the men, women, and children inside were to be offered up in a fiery holocaust as innocent, burned victims to the witches' horned god, Pan, whom the ancient pagans called Marduk, or Malek, and to the witchcraft Goddess, Hecate, also revered as Athena and simply as the "Crone."

Hillary Clinton reportedly gave the order to "torch" the people at Waco. Hillary is shown here hob-nobbing in 1995 at the White House with Colombian narcotics drug kingpin, Jorge Cabrera. A year later, Cabrera was sentenced to 19 years in prison after being convicted of transporting three tons of cocaine into the United States.

Shameless Sexual Crimes of Federal Agents

During the 51-day siege, the FBI perverts camped outside the Branch Davidian church/home were told to be "as bad as you wanna be." Almost on a daily basis, they would come close to the Branch Davidian compound, so close they could see frightened men, women, and children watching from the windows.

The drunken, sadistic FBI would shamelessly drop their pants and underwear and, with gales of satanic laughter, grab and fondle their naked genitals, shoot their fingers, and moon the watching Branch Davidians.

At night, the FBI and Delta Force personnel loudly played over a P.A. system horrible, pre-taped recordings of howling, crying and moaning sounds of baby humans and animals—rabbits, cats and dogs—being slaughtered and sacrificed. This was intended to arouse and please demon spirits of hell, while also terrifying the helpless Branch Davidian men, women and children inside.

On one occasion, the FBI took the dead body of a hapless Branch Davidian they had machine gunned when they caught him just outside the church/home building. They mutilated it, then draped the desecrated body over a fence in plain view of the compound's inhabitants.

The FBI and Delta Force's Nightstalker team also had their tanks and armored personnel carriers run over and demolish the childrens' bicycles and toys just outside the buildings. They shot the kids' pets and animals and threw the carcasses near the walls of the compound, taunting and scaring children and parents alike. These things were all part of what the feds called "psyops," or "psychological operations."

The Bloodthirsty Raid Begins

After 51 days of the most excruciating, diabolic torment, and within hours of receiving Hillary Clinton's angry order to *"Torch the mother f....rs. Do it today!"*, the FBI's murderous, misnamed "hostage rescue team" and the Delta Force "Nightstalker" thugs put on their gas masks, outfitted themselves with armaments, riot gear and black face, and prepared to charge the residence. First, however, they lobbed in salvos of CS gas canisters, to incapacitate their targeted victims.

The so-called federal "counterterrorist" brigade then rushed the back of the residence, carrying with them 50 cal. machine guns, laser devices, and new high tech *Star Wars*-type weapons. One particularly violent and bloodthirsty agent actually carried in a huge, sharp sword, which he planned to use to cut off the heads and limbs of chosen victims.

Breaking through easily, thanks to the U.S. Army tanks and APCs that knocked down and collapsed walls, like a crazed bunch of banshees the Nightstalkers—this is the name the U.S. Army proudly dubs its Delta Force warriors—attacked the children, men, and women. Many victims were murdered as they lay curled up in a fetal position, heaving from the devastating effects of the poisonous gas.

Withdrawing from the compound, having massacred an untold number, the next step was to do as Hillary ordered—*torch the whole complex and leave it in ashes,* all the way down to concrete and dirt. After tanks and APCs crunched holes in the complex—to allow oxygen and air in and hasten the fire's work—dozens of fire-starter grenades were lobbed in. Explosions rocked the buildings as grenades set off fire after fire.

Attempts to Escape Thwarted by Machine Gunfire

People inside who were still alive strived to escape the burning flames and caving-in walls and floors. But when, after great effort, some did manage to exit, jumping out windows and through holes and cracks, they were met just outside by a withering blizzard of machine gun fire *directed at them* by the federal killers. Frightened and confused, most dashed back into the fiery chaos, quickly perishing.

Thankfully, a few nevertheless did make it through the deadly gauntlet of machine gun fire. Met by federal agents, they were handcuffed, and arrested, in anticipation of a show trial later that would portray the federal killers as heroes.

Federal Judge Was a 33rd Degree Mason

Later, survivors were tried and convicted of bogus crimes of which they were not guilty by corrupt Justice Department prosecutors and a fixed, mock court, presided over by a federal judge who wore a 33rd degree Masonic Lodge ring on his hand each day in the courtroom.

What We Must Do Now

And that's the way it was, April 19, 1993 at Waco, Texas—a black, black day that will live forever in infamy. Now, it is your duty—and mine—to labor to insure that this kind of atrocity does not soon happen again.

Time is short. Please make copies of this article, and pass it on to others after you have read it. Please—blow the trumpet; be a watchman: *"But if the watchman see the sword come, and blow not the trumpet, and the people be not warned; if the sword come and take any person from among them...his blood will I require at the watchman's hand." (Ezekiel 33:6)*

Oklahoma City: Things Just Don't Add Up

As additional evidence—evidence censored or blacked out by the major news media—pours in about the Oklahoma City bombing, it becomes more and more clear that things just don't add up. It is indisputable that both the federal government and the controlled media are colluding in a massive coverup of the truth. The federal Gestapo (the FBI, CIA, BATF, and their allies) are spreading lies and disinformation on an unheralded scale.

Here are just a few of the more significant discrepancies demonstrating that things just don't add up about the Oklahoma City incident:

1. Timothy McVeigh, accused of the bombing, wrote very literate—but thoroughly left-wing, socialist-oriented letters to the editor of a New York State newspaper. Why, then, do the White House and the media gleefully accuse him of being a "right-wing" terrorist?

2. McVeigh is said to be intelligent enough to build an elaborate bomb. He even taught himself how to program computers. His high school teachers say he was an excellent student. He won the army's Bronze Star in the Persian Gulf conflict and quickly earned sergeant (E-5) rank. So why, then, was he supposedly so stupid he drove off in a car with *no license plate* after just blowing up a federal building?

3. If McVeigh had just murdered almost 200 people in the bomb blast, why did he meekly submit to being arrested by the lone highway patrolman who stopped him and his vehicle on an Oklahoma freeway? Reportedly, he had a gun in his possession. If McVeigh is the monster the government makes him out to be, why didn't he use it?

4. Also, it's claimed that McVeigh was stopped for speeding 81 mph while driving the car that had no license plates. Would an intelligent man who wanted to quietly escape and avoid being noticed by the cops be blaring down the road at 81 mph?

5. McVeigh had no prior criminal or arrest record, and his U.S. Army record was immaculate. His hometown priest, high school teachers, and friends expressed shock that he was charged with this crime.

From his picture, he appears clean-cut and alert and not a troublemaker—no drugs, long unkempt hair, tattoos, etc. Definitely not a Klansman, a neo-Nazi, or a Manson type. Is this a profile of the kind of guy who would plot and carry out such a heinous crime?

6. When he was first arrested, the FBI announced that McVeigh had signed for the Ryder rental truck that carried the bomb in his own name. But just hours later, the feds changed their story and claimed that McVeigh had used an alias. Which is the truth?

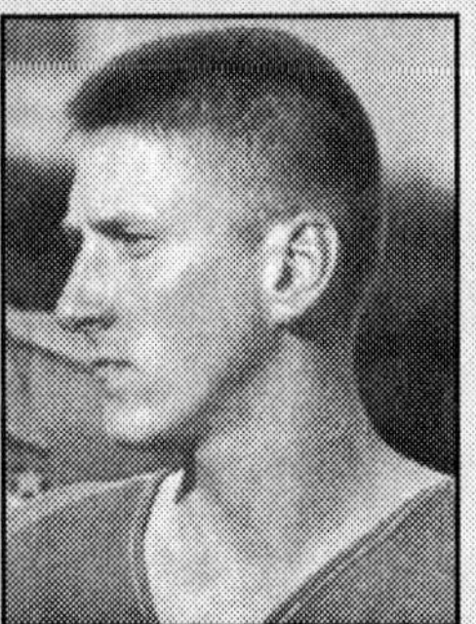

Robert Rodriguez (center), the undercover BATF agent who tried to get bosses to call off the Waco Raid, was made scapegoat. He is now suing the BATF. In this photo, run in *Soldier of Fortune* magazine's June 1995 issue, Rodriguez is escorted as a witness into the Branch Davidian trial in San Antonio by case agent Davy Aguilera (left) and an unidentified agent (at right) who reportedly sat in the press section with a burp gun under his coat. Note the amazing resemblance of the unidentified agent at right to Tim McVeigh and of the agent at left to John Doe #2.

7. Also consider this: as any frequent traveler knows, you can't rent a truck or auto from an agency like Ryder unless you do present a valid driver's license and ID. Again, this puts into question the FBI's assertion that McVeigh used an alias.

Curiously, the Ryder agency also provided the truck used by the World Trade Center bombers. Could Ryder be a CIA front operation?

Revealing is the fact that motel operators in Kansas and Oklahoma, where McVeigh had stayed overnight, stated that McVeigh had rented their rooms *under his own name* presenting his Arizona driver's license.

8. Two attorneys from Houston, Texas mysteriously showed up in Oklahoma City shortly after his arrest claiming to represent Mr. McVeigh. They said the defendant's family had asked them to take the case. But McVeigh denied it and sent a letter to the federal judge in the case insisting that these two men were *not* his attorneys. (This fits the CIA pattern in which hapless patsies are assigned CIA-related attorneys—who promptly sell them down the river!)

9. Meanwhile, the court-appointed attorney of Terry Nichols, the second man charged in the bombing, complained to the Court that the FBI and BATF had forced his client, Nichols, to submit to "counseling" by an unidentified, government "psychologist." Again, this fits a definite federal pattern: federal defendants in sensitive cases are given "counseling" and other "treatment" (i.e. administered mind-control drugs or Project Monarch programming) by CIA or FBI-controlled psychiatrists, psychologists, and physicians.

10. The FBI claims that according to Michael Fortier, a friend of McVeigh's from Arizona, the two men had visited Oklahoma City a few days *before* the bombing. The two are said to have walked and cased the building, floor by floor, talking with personnel working in the various federal offices. They supposedly asked how many BATF agents were in the building, where the BATF offices were located, and whether or not the BATF agents were armed. According to the FBI, to allay suspicions, McVeigh and Fortier told everyone in the various federal offices visited that they were job applicants, and the two filled out applications for federal positions.

This report by the FBI is patently ridiculous. It's full of holes. Would a man who intends to bomb a building in a few days be so ignorant as to walk around asking probing questions to its occupants? Wouldn't he be afraid of being later identified?

Furthermore, for federal jobs there is only one personnel office that processes job applications. It's impossible to go from office to office filling out job application forms.

Finally—and most crucial—if McVeigh did case the building and knew the exact location of the BATF offices, *why, then, did he park his truck with the bomb in it on the opposite side of the building?*

If, as the government claims, McVeigh bombed the Oklahoma City facility because he was so outraged over what the BATF did at Waco, why didn't he park the truck bomb on the BATF side of the building? Besides, the BATF offices were on the *ninth floor!* An intelligent bomber would easily have realized the impossibility of his explosive device reaching as high up as the ninth floor—on the opposite side of the building! *This makes no sense.*

11. The FBI now also claims that Michael Fortier admits that McVeigh "told him in advance of his intentions to bomb the building." Yet earlier, May 8 on CNN news, Fortier stated: "I do not believe Tim McVeigh blew up any building in Oklahoma. There's nothing for me to look back on and say, 'Yeah, that might have been. I should have seen it'... There's nothing like that."

It is very likely that the FBI has trumped up false drug and gun charges against Michael Fortier and threatened him: "If you don't cooperate with us in getting McVeigh convicted" (in other words, lie!), *"you'll* be indicted yourself on separate charges." Could it be that the FBI released the bogus account of Fortier's "confession" to friendly news sources to frighten and persuade him to play along with the concocted myth?

They Must Think We're Stupid

President Bill Clinton, Attorney General Janet Reno, and FBI Director Louis Freeh are lying to us. The coverup is on and the fix is in. They must think the average, patriotic American Christian is really stupid. Well, too bad for them—we're not. What they want us to believe just doesn't add up, and we are on to their diabolical methods of propaganda and disinformation.

I encourage you, my friends, do not allow yourselves to be intimidated by the government. The Bible says we are not to fear what man can do to us. *God is still on the throne in Heaven.* He judges the hearts and actions of all of us here below. I have been told by reliable sources that even now, the FBI and CIA are seeking ways to "get Texe Marrs." Nevertheless, I will not stop telling you the truth. So please, pray for my protection. Prayer accomplishes marvelous things!

Our Mission

Remember: Those who did this horrible deed in Oklahoma City will someday be punished for their awful crimes. It is not our task to exact revenge but, rather, we are commanded to expose and reprove the works of darkness (Ephesians 5:11). God knows how to punish the wicked. As His obedient servants here on Earth, our mission is to speak and broadcast the truth with boldness. Let us pray and work until Jesus returns. Make no mistake: He will reward each of us for our faithfulness to His righteous cause.

> *Now the Lord is that Spirit: and where the Spirit of the Lord is, there is liberty (II Corinthians 3:17).*

> *And shall not God avenge his own elect, which cry day and night unto him...? I tell you that he will avenge them speedily. Nevertheless, when the Son of man cometh, shall he find faith on the earth? (Luke 18:7-8)*

Surviving Mother Told to "Shut Up!"

You'll recall Edye Smith—she was the young, red-haired mother who lost not one, but *two* precious children in the tragic Oklahoma City bombing. Here is a grieving mother whose little babies were savagely taken away from her by the unconscionable and despicable act of deviant criminals. On May 23, 1995, the day an implosion collapsed the leftover hulk of the cratered Oklahoma City federal building, a *CNN* on-the-scene TV reporter, Gary Tuchman, stuck a microphone in the face of a grieving Edye Smith, who bravely stood on the sidewalk watching the building fall into a heap of rubble. He asked her to comment on what this event meant to her. *Significantly, this was on live TV, therefore, could not be edited.* Here, verbatim, is the incredible exchange between CNN correspondent Tuchman and surviving mother, Edye Smith:

> ***Gary Tuchman:*** Edye, at this point you're very busy. You've been talking to people like us, you've been talking to police officials, you've been with your family. But in the next couple of months, when things start to get quieter here in Oklahoma City, do you think it will begin getting tougher for you?
>
> ***Edye Smith:*** Yeah, but I don't think things are going to start getting very quiet, you know? There's a—there are a lot of questions that have been left unanswered, a lot of questions we don't have answers for. We're being told to keep our mouths shut, not talk about it, don't ask those questions, and I think things are going to get a lot busier.
>
> ***Gary Tuchman:*** What kind of questions have people been telling you to keep your mouth shut about?
>
> ***Edye Smith:*** Well, we've—just from the very beginning, we, along with hundreds and thousands of other people, want to know just—and we just innocently ask questions, you know—where was ATF? All 15 or 17 of their employees survived, and they live—they're on the ninth floor. They were the target of this explosion, and where were they? Did they have a warning sign? I mean, did they think it might be a bad day to go in the office? They had an option to not go to work that day, and my kids didn't get that option, nobody else in the building got that option. And we're just asking questions, we're not making accusations. We just want to know, and they're telling us "Keep your mouth shut, don't talk about it."

Edye Smith (left) and her two sons, Chase, 3, and Colton, 2. She was told by the feds to "Keep your mouth shut, don't talk about it."

Tuchman, seeming to be more than a little surprised and frightened over what Edye Smith had just said, quickly broke off the conversation at that point. But it was too late, the truth was out. Millions had heard the soft-spoken mother of two small victims of the bombing complain that the vulgar, gestapo-like law enforcement agents of our own federal government were ordering her to *"keep your mouth shut"... or else!*

Is this any way to treat a grieving mother who has recently suffered such an unimaginable loss? Would the jack-booted thugs of even Hitler and Stalin have committed such heinous and immoral acts against the wounded mother of two little babies killed? CNN repeatedly ran the news segment throughout the rest of the day showing the building coming down. Edye Smith was also shown, standing there watching. *But, not surprisingly, her testimony of abuse by government agents was never again broadcast by CNN.* This revealing news footage apparently went into one of George Orwell's *(1984)* black holes. Apparently, the joint coverup by the federal government and major news media requires the silencing of Edye Smith and anyone else who dares to ask embarrassing questions.

Two Bomb Explosions

There is definitive, irrefutable proof that there were, in fact, two separate bomb explosions in Oklahoma City the morning of April 19, 1995—the second following the first by 10 full seconds. I actually have in my files copies of two, perfectly matching *seismograph reports* showing two bomb blasts—one released by Dr. Charles Mankin, director of the University of Oklahoma's Geological Survey, the other from the Omniplex, an Oklahoma City science museum. Dr. Mankin insists there were two, separate and distinct explosions, 10 seconds apart, just as the seismograph reports prove.

Why do *CBS, ABC, NBC, CNN, the Washington Post, the New York Times, USA Today*, and the *Associated Press* all uniformly refuse to acknowledge this astonishing, documented information? Dr. Mankin is himself perplexed. He notes: "The news media even reported two bomb blasts initially, but later changed their story." Mankin further reveals:

> The seismograph evidence is that there were two bomb blasts. The second blast could not have been a wave caused by the building collapsing. They were two explosions and both are comparable. The second wave was definitely a second event (bomb blast) given the oscillations, amplitude, duration, and wave form.

Adding to the seismograph evidence is the statement of retired Air Force Brigadier-General Benton K. Partin. Partin was the Air Force's top munitions design expert. He spent 25 years researching, designing, developing, and testing bombs and weapons. He was commander of the Air Force's Armament Technology Laboratory, worked closely with the Ballistics Research Laboratory, and was the first chairman of the Department of Defense's Joint Service Air Munitions Requirements and Development Committee.

Few people in the world are as qualified as General Partin to comment on the characteristics of bombs and on the mechanics and effects of bomb blasts. Given this unassailable fact, it is a real eye-opener to discover that General Partin dismisses outright the government's absurd report that a fertilizer and oil bomb alone caused the damage in Oklahoma City:

> When I first saw the picture of the truck bomb's asymmetrical damage to the federal building in Oklahoma, my immediate reaction was that the pattern of damage would have been technically impossible without supplementary demolition charges at some of the reinforced concrete column bases inside the building—a standard demolition technique.

Air Force General Partin explains that, "reinforced concrete targets in large buildings are hard targets to blast." He adds: "I know of no way possible to reproduce the apparent building damage through simply a truck bomb parked outside... The evidence indicates that there was an inside bomb effort." "To hell with the truth" is the government's telling response.

The North American Union by 2010 Will Only Whet Their Appetites

The Coming Merger of the United States and Russia

"Lenin said that national oppression and national borders will be abolished under socialism...and under socialism the interests of nationalities will be fused into a single whole."

—Josef Stalin (June 27, 1937)

"The Ford Foundation's personnel are continuing to operate under directives from the White House to so alter life in America as to make possible a comfortable merger with the Soviet Union."

—H. Rowan Gaither, President
The Ford Foundation (1953)

In 1972, while a student at Park University where I graduated *Summa Cum Laude* with a degree in political science, I authored a 46-page report entitled, *Will the U.S.S.R. (Soviet Union) Survive Until 1984?* In that exhaustive study, I built upon the work of a courageous Russian dissident, Andrei Amilryk, who earlier had covertly published a monograph by that same name.

My learned prediction—and Amilryk's—was that the Soviet Union, in its form as a Communist Empire, would, indeed, implode by 1984, and that a new system of economics and government would emerge from the resulting chaos. The Soviet Union and its so-called "Bolshevist Paradise," I concluded, was in its latter stages, being hopelessly enfeebled by bureaucratic rigidity and internal decay, fueled by socialist incompetence, and suffering from myopic stupidity on the part of a brutal satanic leadership.

My professors at Park University were shocked over what I wrote in that report.

Remember now, this was in 1972, and virtually no one at the time agreed with my assessment. Richard Nixon was in the Oval Office at the time, cutting deals with the Kremlin's unyielding dictator, Leonid Brezhnev. Henry Kissinger, Nixon's Secretary of State, was quietly spreading the word to favored media representatives that the Soviet juggernaut was invincible and growing ever stronger, and that it was therefore necessary for the United States to make certain "concessions" to the Communist monoliths. For one thing, Kissinger insisted, the West must give in to Soviet demands that Eastern Europe (Poland, Hungary, Czechoslovakia, Romania, and all the other satellite nations of the Soviet gulag empire) remain firmly in the Soviet camp, ostensibly forever more.

In *Whole Earth Review*, a popular New Age magazine, the editors endorsed creation of AmerRuss.

Obviously, Mr. Kissinger was, at heart, an avid admirer of the Kremlin's oppressive system of totalitarian slavery. Being a Zionist Jew, he no doubt knew that from the days of Lenin and Trotsky, a small cabal of demon-led Zionist Jews secretly controlled the Moscow regime; they alone, though assisted by Stalin, were responsible for the savage repression, torture and murder over the years of some 66 million innocent victims, most of whom were Christians.

Kissinger, then, had no qualms about the Communists retaining power in Moscow. In fact, the German-born Kissinger, a Rockefeller and Rothschild associate and CFR disciple of long-standing, during his stint as head of America's foreign policy corps, aided Mao Tse Tung and the Communists in Red China in their bid to stay in power. He also turned South Vietnam over to the Communists of North Vietnam.

Objective: Synthesis of Communism and Capitalism

Kissinger well knew that the real goal of the Illuminati was not to totally crush and defeat socialism/communism. No, the real objective has always been to merge communism with capitalism. This is the Hegelian dialectic in operation—the synthesis of opposites, Marxist communism first competing with, then synthesizing and integrating with the capitalism of the west.

The final product would be *neo-fascism*, a form of governance and control that also can be described as CommuNazism.

Today, however, in this age of Big Brother doublespeak, the Jewish neocons who run the U.S.A., Europe, and Russia and tell Bush and Putin what to do, prefer the high-sounding title of *Democracy*. The Bush neocon lie, therefore, is that by invading without cause previously independent "rogue" nations like Afghanistan, Iraq, Iran, and Syria, why, we are just helping to spread "Democracy" across the globe.

Iron Curtain Falls—Right on Schedule

Exactly as I predicted, and on schedule, the Iron Curtain had a resounding fall in the 1980s. Russia's Gorbachev and America's Reagan joined hands in forging a New World Order. The synthesis began to take shape. Now, fast-forward.

As I have reported on the pages of *Power of Prophecy* newsletter, the U.S.A., Mexico, and Canada are this moment in the throes of being merged into one large union. Everything will change—our culture, our way of life, our government. America has already been conquered from within by Judas Goat traitors, with the active assistance of corrupt men like Bush, Cheney, Clinton, Guiliani, O'Reilly, Limbaugh, Murdoch, *et al.* The invasion of the foreigners—what I call the "Invasion of the Liberty Snatchers"—is in its most active stage.

But, if you think that the North American Union (NAU) will be the last word of the Illuminati on our fate, think again! Recently, this May, our esteemed President, Mr. Bush, went over to Europe and signed yet another unconstitutional pseudo-treaty, this time with Mr. Solar Deity himself, Javier Solana, head of the European Union (EEU). Bush committed the U.S. to increasingly draconian socialistic regulations and laws, with the intent of complete merger with the EEU sometime in the not so distant future.

AmerRuss Union Planned by Elite

That merger, however, will have to wait. First there's the NAU deal to be consummated in 2010, followed swiftly by—get this, dear friends—a pending merger with Russia. Yes, Russia! They don't have a name for this atrocity yet, so let's just call it *AmerRuss*.

You may find all this hard to believe; after all, who could imagine that the once proud United States of America would ever be merged with the Eurasian power that is Russia. But, just watch and see. First, they will build a gigantic tunnel under the frozen sea from the Siberian coast over to Alaska. Then, certain Alaskan islands and territories will be given to Russia as a "love offering." Next on the docket: the U.S.A. will offer to buy Siberia (a ploy to raise American consciousness).

Russian legislator Vladimir Zhirnovsky warned, "There has long been a hidden agenda to merge America and Russia under the New World Order."

Finally comes the "The Merger." *AmerRuss* becomes a bitter, mindboggling reality, as a braindead, Mexicanized North American Union population sits idly by, its drug and pleasure intoxicated inhabitants oblivious of their pending euthanasia.

Everything is in Place

Regrettably, everything is already in place for the eventual *AmerRuss Union*. Russian President Vladimir Putin is putting on a show right now, making like Russia is America's 21st century enemy and might just reignite the Cold War. Sure...like, baloney! The truth is that Zionist Jews own the governments of both America and Russia, lock, stock, and barrel. America's oil corporations are the brokers for Russia's vast store of petroleum and gas. Meanwhile, Zionist bankers today dictate the value of the Russian ruble currency and they preside over Moscow's stock and commodity markets. Any animosity of Putin's toward the U.S.A. is just showboating, reminiscent of the days of CFR lackeys Lenin and Trotsky, when U.S.A. President Woodrow Wilson's Administration secretly aided the Bolshevik Jewish Communists in their monstrous and bloody campaign of Red Terror and conquest of the hapless Russian Gentile majority.

> *Zionist Jews now occupy and are the hidden dictators of Israel, the United States, and Russia alike.*

I repeat: Zionist Jews now occupy and are the hidden dictators of Israel, the United States, and Russia alike. Don't think otherwise or you'll end up totally confused about today's geopolitical equation. As Vladimir Zhirinovsky, controversial member of the Russian Parliament and himself a Jew, revealed at a United Nations press conference (November 9, 1994), *"There has long been a hidden agenda to merge America and Russia under the New World Order."*

The Master Plan

So here's the disgusting Master Plan. First, the U.S., Mexico, and Canada become the North American Union: Then, all nations of the Americas, Central, South and North, are brought together

> **The invasion of the foreigners—what I call the "Invasion of the Liberty Snatchers"—is in its most active stage.**
>
> **—Texe Marrs**

as One. Simultaneously, *AmerRuss* is set up, followed by merger of all these entities with the European Union. Meanwhile, a Greater Israel Empire of the Middle East and Africa will be formed, giving the Jews dominance of the vast stores of oil, gold, diamonds, platinum, and other minerals and natural resources in these two troubled regions.

Finally, the Asian component will be dealt with as China and India are empowered by the elite to run roughshod over the Pacific and Near Eastern regions. Finally, *ordo ab chao* will have been achieved, and the CFR's naked man on the white horse will assume the throne of global leadership.

Bible Prophecies Fulfilled to the Max

What I can say with absolute confidence is that *Revelation 13, 17*, and *18* will be fulfilled to the maximum. As we read in *Revelation 17:12-14*, the leaders of all the world's nations, consumed with evildoing, conspire together with the Beast. *"These have one mind, and shall give their power and strength unto the beast."*

Rest assured, God is superintending all events and these pro-Zionist wicked rulers, blinded by greed, are ignorantly laboring hard to achieve their ultimate pitiful destiny—the Pit of Hell. They and their minions are endeavoring to build up the global colossus the Bible calls *Mystery Babylon*, a colossus which shall go down to ignominious defeat in a single hour. God's justice shall prevail and it will be swift.

That's right, in one tiny hour, the efforts of the Illuminati for over 6,000 years will come to naught, to which I say, *"Farewell, wicked Illuminati and Synagogue of Satan, and good riddance!"*

> *"Therefore shall her plagues come in one day, death and mourning, and famine: and she shall be utterly burned with fire: for strong is the Lord God who judges her." (Revelation 18:8)*

> *And the ten horns which thou sawest are ten kings, which have received no kingdom as yet; but receive power as kings one hour with the beast. These have one mind, and shall give their power and strength unto the beast. These shall make war with the Lamb, and the Lamb shall overcome them: for he is Lord of lords, and King of kings: and they that are with him are called, and chosen, and faithful. (Revelation 17:12-14)*

What Will Happen When They Occupy America?

United Nations "Peacekeepers" Raise Hell

"And they worshipped the dragon which gave power unto the beast: and they worshipped the beast, saying, Who is like unto the beast? who is able to make war with him?"

— *Revelation 13:4*

Now it can be told. The United Nations forces are not "peacekeepers" as they are claimed to be. Instead, the blue-helmeted troops of the UN are proven to be sinister, war-waging hellraisers. The evidence is accumulating that the UN and its subsidiary NATO soldiers rank with Hitler's SS Gestapo, Stalin's Red Army, Gorbachev's *Spetznatz* (Special Forces), and Pol Pot's *Khmer Rouge* as this century's most brutal and bloody occupation forces.

The UN forces are regrettably buttressed by American military units, money, and military high technology. With U.S. assistance, they are plundering, raping, and murdering people at an alarming pace. The goal of the UN overlords is not to bring forth peace out of chaos but to install Communist, pro-New World Order regimes in every nation on Earth. Any national leader who opposes this UN scheme is immediately targeted for destruction, and his country's citizens are scheduled for genocidal massacre.

The controlled media—*CBS, ABC, NBC, CNN, The New York Times, The Washington Post, etc.*—are doing their best to coverup and conceal the atrocities of the UN peacekeeper forces. Most Republicans and Democrats in Congress remain silent.

Meanwhile, the Christian establishment—James Dobson's *Focus on the Family*, Pat Robertson's *The 700 Club* and others—are not interested in exposing the United Nations' horrors. Indeed, some Christian groups, such as Chuck Colson's *Prison Fellowship*, are actually affiliated with the UN and are officially accredited as UN NGOs (United Nations non-governmental organizations).

Peace Tools: Roasting, Worms, and Vomit

Surprisingly, I credit the ultra-liberal, alternative

press for first going to bat against the UN terror. Following their lead are several patriotic groups. As a result, the grim facts of UN crimes are now laid bare for all to see.

One of the liberal publications exposing the UN is New York's *Village Voice* newspaper, which reported the following in its June 24, 1997 edition:

> Two United Nations soldiers from Belgium will stand trial in their own country beginning next Monday on charges of roasting a live Somali child over an open fire during "peacekeeping" operations...A third Belgian soldier will stand trial for forcing another Somali child to drink salt water, vomit, and worms.

The *Village Voice* article was accompanied by shocking photographs documenting these and other gruesome crimes against human beings. Court affidavits indicate that many additional crimes have been committed by this same, UN, military unit from Belgium, as well as by UN troops from Canada, Italy, Turkey, Germany, and the United States.

Sent to strife-torn countries such as Bulgaria, Albania, Serbia, Bosnia, and Burundi, UN forces engaged themselves in harsh genocide and acts of terror. Crimes committed include padlocking young boys in metal containers left outside in the scorching sun until they died from the heat. UN troops have also urinated on suspects, applied electrodes to victims' genitals, burned the soles of prisoners' feet with hot irons, and stripped flesh away from peoples' bodies with razor wire while those tortured screamed in agony.

Proud of Their Evil Works

The UN peacekeepers have appeared rather proud of their foul deeds. Canadian troops took pictures of each other tormenting and slaying a captured Somali (African) youth. They sent the photos back home to friends.

One photo pictured elite paratroopers grinning as they stood beside the lifeless, blood-spattered torso of a teenager who had been beaten with a metal pipe, wooden baton, fists, and boots. The teen's feet were burned with cigarettes.

The White House and its UN cohorts portray their global peacekeeping forces as imbued with humanitarian goodness. When then President George Bush first sent U.S. troops into Somalia under the UN insignia, the public was told that this was *"Operation Restore Hope."* We're going there to feed a suffering people, said the President, and to bring peace and an end to chaos. We were portrayed by the media as the good guys, saviors of humanity.

Evidently, the Somalia people knew better. When UN Secretary-General Boutros Boutros-Ghali subsequently visited the capital city of Mogadishu in 1992, the people rioted. Angrily, they stoned his armor-plated, luxury limousine, hurled epithets at Butros-Ghali, and tried to kill him.

Then, in October, 1993, 18 U.S. Army rangers were killed in a pitched battle with civilian militias in the streets of Mogadishu. An unruly mob spit on and disfigured the bodies of their former tormentors. They dragged the dead soldiers' corpses through the streets, creating a grim display for the controlled world press.

The American public was crushed. How could this be, many asked? We spend billions of dollars to send our elite troops there on a UN peace mission to feed these people, and they hate and fight us. Why? The answer was never forthcoming. The truth was censored out.

Making War and Exalting Communism

The fact is, from Burma and Rwanda to Peru and Haiti, UN peacekeepers are now busy making war on local leaders and their followers. Entire populations are being subjected to illegal, house to house searches. Suspects are rounded up and routinely tortured and abused. Young girls are often molested and raped.

Communist chieftains are being exalted and installed in power while opposing locals are tracked down and hunted like wild beasts. The UN forces constantly stir up one faction against another, such as in Rwanda (Africa), where successive genocidal massacres occurred among rival Hutu and Tutsi tribesmen.

Libya, the Sudan, Iran, Iraq—wherever there are holdouts to the New World Order, leaders are being threatened: "Comply, or else—you're next!"

Once employed, the lawless troops of the United Nations move against the local people of invaded countries with supreme arrogance and consuming bloodlust. In Somalia, enlisted Italian soldiers of the UN kidnapped a pretty girl off the street, tied her to the front of an armored personnel carrier, and raped her. Their officers looked on. One Italian battalion commander, who happened to be a pedophile, ordered his troops to strip and hold down a young Somali, 13-year old boy. After the youth was sexually abused and sodomized, the Italian UN officer strangled him to death.

"They are Just Niggers Anyway"

One Italian paratrooper, justifying these vile acts, was quoted as saying, "What's the big deal? They are just niggers anyway." Could the troops of Italy's late Fascist Dictator, Mussolini, been any more cruel, savage, and callous than these 1990s Italian forces under UN command?

Putting it another way, columnist Joseph Farah, writing in the patriotic magazine, *Media Bypass* (August 1997), posed this question: "Do you think the Somali people will ever forget the lessons they learned from their (UN) saviors?"

Some U.S. Soldiers Are Disturbed

Some U.S. soldiers, airmen, sailors, and marines are extremely disturbed over what is happening. But increasingly, American servicemen who oppose integration into UN peacekeeping operations are being persecuted and rooted out. They are being told they are "no longer fit" for military duty in this New Age of global unity and UN hegemony.

Here is the testimony of just one career soldier, stationed overseas, upset and concerned over this revolting turn of events. His testimony was recently published by Officer Jack McLamb in his excellent newsletter, *Aid & Abet* (May 1997):

> The political climate being what it is, I trust you will keep my identity confidential… Many soldiers feel something is wrong with some of our missions and some of the things we are commanded to do… Soldiers can't serve under the United Nations without violating our national oath…
>
> American soldiers and the soldiers of other nations have been used to take guns and freedom away from poor black, Asian, and Hispanic people who need their guns to try to retain their freedoms by fighting against Communist renegade leaders in their own nations.
>
> The people of Somalia were a prime example. Going in, we were not aware that they were fighting to resist the barbaric, UN/US-backed Communist war lords. Some of us lost good friends in that "peace enforcement" effort against the poor Somali people. Many of them now detest us, for good cause. In Haiti, we accomplished the same, installing a Marxist dictator…

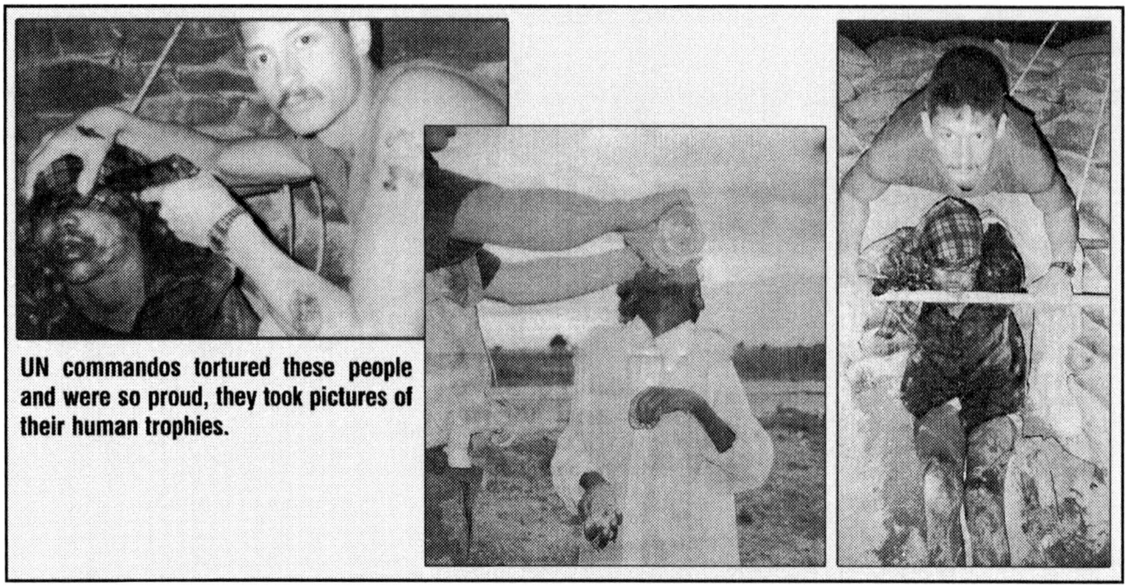

UN commandos tortured these people and were so proud, they took pictures of their human trophies.

When we inquire of our military superiors why, we get no logical answer. World peace under UN Communism is a fraud. Our military leaders go about bewildered, but undaunted. One wonders if they understand these geo-political machinations.
We have been instructed that any U.S. military individuals or groups that espouse or publish patriotic causes, or who help to expose constitutional violations and government conspiracies, will be considered "subversives." It will do our careers severe damage to get involved or even to express interest. Having a leftist world view is beneficial at promotion time.

We see this more and more, and discuss it quietly, but it does seem the day will come when we will all have to decide whom and what we shall serve.

America Not Immune From UN Atrocities

In his thought-provoking essay, the soldier who wrote these words went on to warn readers that it is not only the impoverished people in Third World countries like Somalia, Guatemala, and Cambodia who are at risk. A pretext will someday soon be created so that the people of America will, themselves, fall under the crushing jackboots of the UN oppressors. Remember—the rampaging UN forces do not have a Constitution, law, or military code of conduct to restrain their lecherous acts of murder, rape, and torture.

Many U.S. troops, ignorant of the big picture, will simply follow orders. Germany's common soldiers did the same in the 30s and 40s when they obeyed their Nazi superiors. Later, they obeyed their Communist bosses in East Germany by shooting unarmed civilians attempting to bridge the Berlin Wall.

In the view of cold-eyed UN soldiers, you and I are just objects. In the eyes of the UN's bureaucrats and the Illuminati elite who covertly run the United Nations behind the scenes, we who continue to stubbornly love our country, proudly salute its flag, and endeavor to uphold the Constitution of the United States, are worse then mere objects. As Joseph Farah ominously notes, to them, "We're all just niggers anyway, right?"

The United Nations Plan to Make "Nature Worship" a State Religion

The Treaty From Hell

> "Treaties made, or which shall be made, under the Authority of the United States shall be the Supreme Law of the land; and the Judges in every state shall be bound, thereby, any Thing in the Constitution or Laws of any State to the Contrary notwithstanding."
>
> —*Article VI, Constitution of the United States of America*

Most Americans are of the erroneous impression that the U.S. Constitution *guarantees* them certain rights, such as freedom of speech, freedom of religion, right to protection of property, and, if indicted by grand jury, right to a fair and impartial trial by a jury of your peers. The awful truth, however—unknown to the masses—is that our founding fathers buried within the body of the Constitution a most disingenuous and diabolical escape clause, a ticking time bomb. These men, the majority of whom were Masons or Illuminists, *inserted one, brief, seemingly insignificant provision.* This little known provision could, in light of current events, soon prove to be the utter undoing and voiding of every inalienable right, every freedom, and every vestige of liberty we once were privileged to enjoy as Americans.

Tricked by Masonic Founding Fathers?

What Washington, Franklin, Jefferson, Hancock, and other founders did was to specify in Article VI of the Constitution that *any and all treaties entered into by the U.S.A. and foreign countries have precedence and authority over every article, jot, tittle, and iota of the Constitution.* In other words, our Masonic forefathers masterfully tricked the citizenry into believing a lie—that the government would forever guarantee the rights of free citizens. In fact, these men made sure that dictatorial, ungodly, and savage breaches and violations could craftily be written later into law simply by the ruse of treaties.

Treaties, then, are *the* Supreme Law of the Land. A treaty, says Article VI of the Constitution, is of *greater authority* than the basic Constitution itself and all of its provisions. Moreover, every judge in the United States, from Supreme Court justices to local, municipal traffic court magistrates, is legally bound to enforce treaties and favor them over all other laws. As the wording in Article VI puts it, the

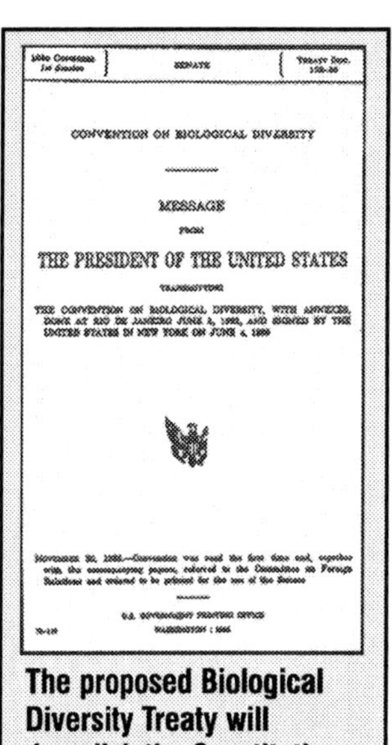
SENATE

CONVENTION ON BIOLOGICAL DIVERSITY

MESSAGE

FROM

THE PRESIDENT OF THE UNITED STATES

The proposed Biological Diversity Treaty will demolish the Constitution.

provisions of a treaty, however satanic, disgusting, and mean-spirited they may be, shall ever be enforced, *"any Thing in the Constitution or Laws of any State to the Contrary notwithstanding."*

I know this sounds preposterous—and it is. But it's also fact. A treaty made with, say, corrupt politicians down in Mexico, with Jesuit "Father" Aristide over in Haiti, with commie boss Boris Yeltsin in Russia, or with some Islamic Arab sheik from Kuwait, *immediately* becomes the Supreme Law of the United States of America. Every provision therein must be complied with by residents of every town, city, and village throughout the U.S.A.

How does *that* make you feel, fellow Americans? Do you feel secure?

Treaties become the Supreme Law when approved by the U.S. Senate and the President. That's it. No majority vote by the citizenry needed or requested. Just two-thirds of the corrupt politicians who sit in the U.S. Senate plus the rubber-stamp approval of the one man who resides at 1600 Pennsylvania Avenue—that's all it takes for Big Brother government to dramatically transform our lives in almost unlimited ways.

Court Precedent Elevates Treaties Over the Constitution

In sum, our most cherished constitutional rights may quickly and without public debate be legally abolished by a scheming, wicked president and a passel of graft-taking politicians in Washington, D.C. Together, these traitors are free to draw up a diabolical treaty with any Third World, puppet government, tin-horn prime minister on the face of planet Earth.

If you don't believe this is possible, I heartily recommend you go to a law library and read up on the following Supreme Court cases. *Yes, read for yourself—and then weep:*

U.S. v. Thompson, 258 F. 257, E.D. Ark. (1919)

U.S. v. Samples, 258 F. 479, W.D. Mo. (1919)

Missouri v. Holland, 252 U.S. 416, 434, 40 S. Ct. 382, 284 (1920). Also see U.S. v. Selkirk (1919); U.S. v. Rockefeller (1919); and U.S. v. Lumpkin (1921).

Cerritos Gun Club v. Hall, 96 F. 2d 620 (9th Cir., 1938)

Bailey v. Holland, 126 F. 2d 317 (4th Cir., 1942)

U.S. v. Jin Fuey Moy, 241 U.S. 394, 36 S. Ct. 658 (1916)

Stutz v. Bureau of Narcotics, 56 F. Supp. 810, 813 (N.D. Cal., 1944)

Balfour, Guthries & Co. v. United States, 90 F. Supp. 831 (N.D. Cal., 1950)

Lowell H. Becraft, Jr., a highly regarded attorney from Alabama, has carefully researched court precedents relating to the chilling, abusive power of the federal government based on treaties. He warns:

> It's easy to imagine what may be on the minds of a multitude of federal agencies: the pursuit of more power which is otherwise prohibited by the Constitution. Based on the Supreme Court's blessing of treaty-based powers, the federales could theoretically feign a "treaty" with tiny Guam to secure huge municipal power over virtually any subject

> formerly reserved "to the States respectively or the people" by the 10th Amendment. (*Anti-Shyster* magazine, Vol. 4, No. 4, 1994)

Who can doubt that, at this very moment, Attorney-General Janet Reno and her mentors, Bill and Hillary Clinton, are working on a slew of sickening schemes which can be put into action by simple treaty. All that's needed, they must reason, is to grease the palms of a cooperative Mexican, Haitian, Pakistan, or other decadent foreign politician, many of whom are already secretly in the employ of the CIA.

Universal healthcare—Hillary's failed, socialist medical scheme—may soon be resurrected and put into effect—by treaty. Ownership of firearms by the citizenry could be banned and outlawed—by treaty. Ammunition could be confiscated; patriot newsletters closed down; resisting Christian churches raided; homosexual rights extended, and government-funded abortions required—all enacted into *Supreme Law* by simple treaty. The desires and wishes of the suffering electorate notwithstanding.

It's Here!—The Treaty From Hell

Indeed, the Clinton administration has *already sent* to the U.S. Senate for ratification the most astonishing, most heinous treaty ever devised by the sinful hearts of evil men. It's call the *Convention on Biological Diversity*, and if this document is voted into law, you can kiss 220 years of American freedom and justice goodbye forever.

When I first obtained and read this Biological Diversity Treaty, I could scarcely believe my eyes. My heart pounded. That night, I was gripped by fearsome nightmares. My friends, listen to me: This is unquestionably the *Treaty From Hell*. How a president of the United States could have the audacity to actually propose the adoption of this treaty beggars the imagination. Bill Clinton and his co-president, Hillary Rodham Clinton, have to be demon possessed, period!

The treaty itself is vaguely and fuzzily worded. In effect, it gives the Clinton administration's environmental crazies a blank check to rewrite and override the Constitution. It enables the United States and every other nation on earth to change and revise all existing laws to conform to *ten United Nations objectives*.

Drafted by World's Leading Occultists

The world's slimiest occultists first put this piece of trash together at Rio de Janeiro's Earth Summit in 1992. Maurice Strong, the Illuminati baron whose daring exploits I exposed in my book, *Dark Majesty,* is the chief, conspiratorial plotter behind it. Strong, the chairman of the United Nations Environmental Program, is tied in with the notorious elitists who run the Trilateral Commission, the CFR, the World Economics Forum, and the Bilderbergers.

Here is a sampling of the malignant UN objectives that are to be accomplished under this treaty:

> First, it proposes "to make nature worship a state religion."
>
> Second, "people will be classified as the enemy," menaces to society. Populations must be reduced to save the planet!
>
> Third, entire land areas of the United States will be "made void of human presence" to create huge, unpopulated, environmental "biospheres." The people who now live in these vast regions will be driven off their land. Their homes, farms, and ranches will be

confiscated. This is necessary, say treaty sponsors, to protect fungi, plants, bugs, birds, and other endangered species.

Fourth, all passenger motor vehicles will be prohibited because, supposedly, they "pollute" the environment. All home air conditioning systems must be inactivated because they use too much energy and theoretically release ozone-destroying pollutants into the atmosphere.

Fifth, a global environmental tax will be levied on richer nations, such as the U.S.A. and Canada, so that citizens of these countries can pay for damage they've supposedly done to Mother Earth over the decades and centuries past.

Sixth, a world government authority will be set up to enforce the treaty.

Seventh, citizens anywhere in the world who fight the system will be arrested and punished by international courts.

Illuminati's Bureaucrats to Rule Over Us

This is only a brief overview of the tremendous horrors to ensue once this monstrous treaty is enacted. Thousands of bureaucratic regulations based on the *Treaty From Hell* will forever supersede and take the place of our U.S. Constitution. Moreover, the treaty will render obsolete most state and local laws and ordinances. The Bill of Rights will be history—trashed and forgotten. The radiant fullness of the New World Order will finally be ushered in. Christians and patriots who dissent will be crushed and discarded. A sun-lit New Age will miraculously be at hand. The ages-old dream of Lucifer and his Secret Brotherhood will be realized. All because of the passage of this one, monumental, but deceitfully innocent, treaty—the *Convention on Biological Diversity.*

It Can't Happen... Can It?

"But," say scoffers, "surely these horrors will not come to pass. Why, they could never succeed in getting such an evil treaty passed by the U.S. Senate."

To these uninformed citizens, I say, WAKE UP! Just this year, the Republicans and Democrats, working *together* in Congress, slam-dunked on us the GATT bill, complete with its provision for a dictatorial World Trade Organization. Senator Bob Dole and the boys also gave us the Brady Gun Control Act, and they backed President Clinton 100% in doling out some $40 billion to the international bankers during the recent Mexican peso financial crisis. When the American people complained, our controlled leaders hollered, "Shut up, and take it!"

Keep in mind, too, that the controlled, liberal media is populated by a host of environmental wackos. They're thrilled to promote the politically correct agenda of the biodiversity conspiracy. CBS, NBC, ABC, CNN, and the rest of the media will never tell Americans the awful facts about this treaty. *They don't want the public to know what is about to happen.* Instead, the masses are to be propagandized and made to believe that this treaty is just another, wholesome tool to help America clean up its suffering, at risk environment. It's something good, we'll all be told, like recycling and saving the bald eagle from extinction. *A mass media blackout of the true facts regarding the Biological Diversity Treaty is already in operation.*

My friends, if the truth is to be told, it is you and I who must do the telling. The sooner the better!

Our National Parks Now Belong to the United Nations

Across this great land, our national parks, wildlands, forests, and lakes are being turned over to UN control. Joseph Urso, Jr., a friend of the ministry who hails from Knoxville, Tennessee, recently sent me a photograph of the entrance sign of the Great Smoky Mountains National Park. Notice the telling phrase on the sign: "AN INTERNATIONAL BIOSPHERE RESERVE."

This means that, under the United Nations Biodiversity Treaty, a precious resource—owned by American citizens for over 200 years—has been turned over to the UN's bureaucrats for control. Yes, you and I will continue to pay taxes for the maintenance and upkeep of the Great Smoky Mountains National Park. But we no longer own it. Now, the UN has ultimate jurisdiction. This alone is startling evidence that the once independent nation-state known as the United States of America is going out with a whimper and not a bang. Our sovereignty is coming to an end.

As a consequence, across the U.S.A., our parks and wilderness areas are slowly being closed to the public. Roads inside the parks are being grazed over. Mountain passes and hiking paths are being blockaded. "No fishing," "No hunting," "No trespassing" signs are being erected everywhere on public lands. Entrance fees are being jacked up 100%, even 500% higher, to keep American families out of their own lands.

The UN and its elitist masters don't want you on their property! And in case you do "trespass" and enter forbidden areas of these pristine UN lands, you might just be shot. U.S. Fish and Wildlife Service agents and park personnel are now taught to love nature's Mother Earth and to despise and loathe human beings. They are being given firearms and instructed to use them. Meanwhile, foreign immigrants from India, China, Pakistan, Bulgaria, Russia and other nations are being recruited for this national park service police duty because, unlike U.S. nationals, non-English speaking foreigners will not hesitate to carry out orders and shoot American citizen "intruders."

But even if you are not shot or arrested, there is still a possibility of being bitten—or eaten! As my friend, Joseph Urso, Jr., points out, the feds have been reintroducing vicious wolves into Yellowstone National Park and into Great Smoky Mountains National Park. The idea is to put the lives of park visitors in jeopardy and to frighten tourists away.

Environmental groups, of course, are overjoyed that the UN is taking over our parks and forests and putting the screws to the people. Such organizations as the Nature Conservancy and the National Wildlife Federation are funded and controlled by Rockefeller monied interests. The leaders of these organizations hate human beings and believe that the takeover of our parklands and heritage sites by the UN is the paying of homage to their pagan nature goddess, "Mother Earth."

In protest, I have registered a complaint with U.S. Senator Jesse Helms of North Carolina. Helms, a Republican, is Chairman of the Senate Foreign Relations Committee. As Chairman, he has the power to put a stop to all this nonsense. What's more, the Great Smoky Mountains National Park lies partly inside Helm's home state, North Carolina, as well as in neighboring Tennessee.

My answer from Senator Helms came in March when he and his committee warmly embraced and voted for President Clinton's choice, Madeleine Albright, to become Secretary of State. Albright, a Marxist, is an avid supporter of the UN's Biodiversity Treaty. She endorses the unconstitutional giving away of American sovereignty over its lands and natural resources.

Some may be surprised that Jesse Helms would commit this act of high treason. They are puzzled that the Senator, who is so warmly supported by the Christian Coalition and other conservative groups, would conspire with Bill Clinton, the UN, and the Illuminati elite to give away our birthright and heritage to New World Order forces.

As happens with all Masons, the occultic, 33° ritual brings on possession of the celebrant by devils.

Ever since Jesse Helms was elevated to the 33° of Freemasonry, bowing his knee before the black stone altar of the false gods Jahbuhlun, Mahabone, and Abaddon, he has digressed in his strong support of American sovereignty. As happens with all Masons, the occultic, 33° ritual brings on possession of the celebrant by devils.

In fact, Jesse Helms can't help himself. Like Judas Iscariot, he is taken captive by alien forces. Helms has been neutralized, and our historic, great nation is laid low before vile, global forces—forces intent on America's unconditional surrender to the Illuminati's antichrist, United Nations establishment.

We should all oppose violence. But when the American populace—or at least the few who still care and are not dumbed-down—realize that this country's national treasures and heritage have been given away for a mess of globalist porridge, intense anger will result.

No doubt, the elite are preparing for just such an eventuality. If Joe and Jane American discover that Yellowstone, Big Bend, Sequoia, Rocky Mountain, Great Smoky, Yosemite, and the other national parks and monuments are under UN jurisdiction and control, the government fully expects a counter-revolutionary explosion.

That's why the UN is bringing in foreign troops and training them—at Fort Polk, Louisiana, and other military bases—to assault U.S.A. cities and towns. That's why the Universal Beast 666 Computer Control System, *Project L.U.C.I.D.,* is being implemented. It is why the White House is making a priority the passage by Congress of totalitarian, gun control legislation and supposed "anti-terrorist" acts. It is why our Armed Forces are now earnestly training to quell a domestic insurrection by militias and patriots. The elite know what's just ahead. They are preparing to deal with the resisters and dissidents—in other words, the old-fashioned, solid American patriots and Christians who still refuse to bow to the gods of the New World Order.

Unmasking President George W. Bush and His Merry Band of Homoerotic Thugs

White House Bordello

"The smell of sulfur (from hell) still lingers in this place after President George W. Bush spoke at this podium yesterday, the 19th of September."

— Hugo Chavez, President of Venezuela
Speech at the United Nations (2006)

"Come out of her, my people, that ye be not partakers of her sins, and that ye receive not of her plagues."

— *Revelation 18:4*

Ted Haggard, pastor of the 140,000-member New Life Church in Colorado Springs and head of the 30-million strong National Association of Evangelicals, after being outed as a crystal meth snorting sodomite guilty of paying male prostitutes for sex and drugs, reluctantly admitted, *"I am a deceiver and a liar."*

Now, isn't it way past time that yet another high profile sodomite, a cocaine abuser shamelessly guilty of hiring male prostitutes to service him, also finally step forward and admit, *"I too, am a deceiver and a liar?"*

I'm referring, of course, to George W. Bush, current occupant of the nation's #1 political job, the presidency. This may be quite a shock to some readers, but most folks in the Washington, D.C. beltway already know what I'm going to reveal here. Yes, they know that George W. is a bisexual and a procurer of male prostitutes.

Many insiders snicker and laugh ha, ha, ha, at brain-dead Christian evangelicals who actually believe that George W. is a God-fearing heterosexual, born again Christian. As David Kuo, former top White House adviser in the Bush Administration, reveals in his new book, *Tempting Fate*, the Bush White House team sneers and jokes about the evangelicals so easily deceived by the President. Kuo presents evidence that the Bush people view Christian evangelical leaders and their flocks as ridiculous, silly, nuts, even insane. To the Bush people, Christianity is a farce and Christians are easily duped idiots.

George W. Bush's Tarnished Reputation

George W. Bush, as many Texas politicos could easily tell you, had quite a reputation back in the Lone Star State for both his sexual misconduct and for his snorting of loads of white powder (cocaine) up his nose. The man never held a real job; he shirked his Air National Guard duties, having joined the Guard in the first place only to evade serving in Vietnam. Bill Clinton dodged

Left: President Bush raised eye-brows at a White House press conference by kissing homosexual prostitute Jeff Gannon on top of his head. Gannon was issued press credentials by Karl Rove at Bush's request and attended the sessions.

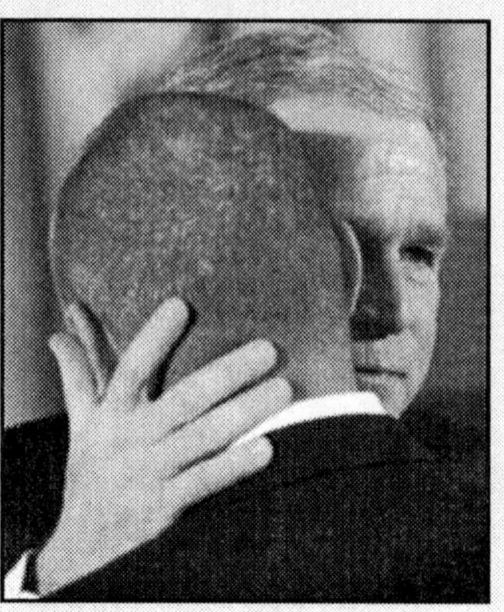

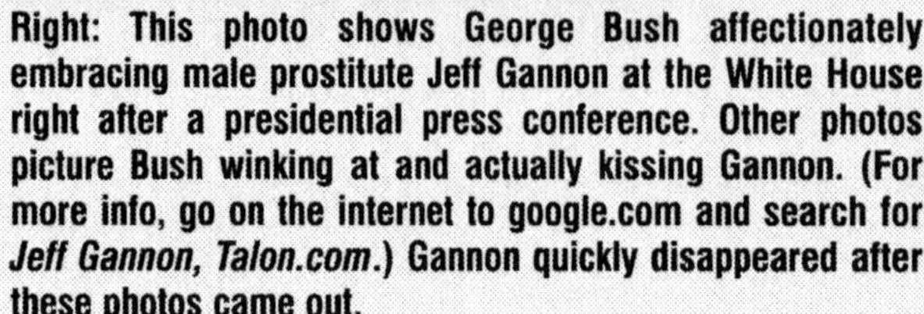

Right: This photo shows George Bush affectionately embracing male prostitute Jeff Gannon at the White House right after a presidential press conference. Other photos picture Bush winking at and actually kissing Gannon. (For more info, go on the internet to google.com and search for *Jeff Gannon, Talon.com*.) Gannon quickly disappeared after these photos came out.

military service, too, by running off and hiding in England, but Bush hid in plain sight, in an Air National Guard uniform. It's great to have friends in high places to help out in time of need, isn't it?

Bush and Clinton are alike in one other aspect as well. Both used the White House as a Whore House. Bill did sexual things with cigars with a young intern, while George had his muscular, boy-man homosexual lover, Jeff Gannon, stay over many a night in the White House. He and young Jeff Gannon weren't discussing foreign policy and affairs of state all those times in the wee hours of the morning in the presidential bedrooms, I assure you.

Fabulous, Gorgeous, Queer

Since assuming the presidency, George W. has surrounded himself with gay men. The White House is jokingly referred to as the "Pink House" by the Gay Community. First, there's Karl Rove, Bush's campaign chief. Rove's father was gay, and Rove himself is a queer. According to Fox-TV News, Karl Rove smiled knowingly when a Fox-TV reporter asked him about the special nickname his pal, the President, lovingly has for him.

President Bush calls me "Turdblossom," Rove said. Why "Turdblossom?"—Please, let's not go there.

George W. Bush often commends male visitors to the White House for their "fabulous" clothing. He told the Canadian Prime Minister that his young, male press advisor was "gorgeous." Bush appointed Ken Mehlman, a Jewish homosexual, as the Chairman of the Republican National Committee. Think of it—a homo as titular head of the entire Republican Party!

Bush also named his gay roommate at Yale University, Tennessee's Victor Ashe, Ambassador to Poland. As Global AIDS Coordinator, another Ambassador-rank position, Bush chose homosexual activist Mark R. Dybul. Secretary of State Condi Rice administered the oath of office to the new appointee, recognizing Dybul's gay lover and live-in partner, Jason. Condi, a reputed lesbian dominatrix, even permitted the Ambassador's homo partner, Jason, to hold the Bible upon which Dybul laid his hand while taking the oath of office.

President Bush has more homosexuals in his Administration than Bill Clinton, and he's more

At Yale University, student George W. Bush roomed with his homosexual pal, Victor Ashe. Later, as President of the United States, Bush appointed his old friend Ashe Ambassador to Poland.

Secretary of State Condi Rice swears in sodomite Mark R. Dybul as Bush's Global AIDS Coordinator. First Lady Laura Bush looks on and Dybul's gay partner, Jason, holds the Bible.

than accommodated their "special needs." For example, Bush appointed a queer to be the new Ambassador to Romania, then approved the man's sodomite lover to fly off with him in a U.S. aircraft to Bucharest, the capital of that nation, where the gay Ambassador and his lover now contently shack-up together in an embassy-leased mansion, at U.S. taxpayers' expense. The two sodomites even attend official functions together. I wonder what the leaders and citizens of Romania think about that?

Homosexuals Love Bush's Supreme Court Nominees

Bush's biggest coup was his choice to be the new Chief Justice of the U.S. Supreme Court. John Roberts, a gay judge, is not only queer himself, but he's the infamous attorney who represented the entire homosexual community of America in the notorious, landmark court case, Romer v. Evans (1996), in which all state laws forbidding acts of sodomy were declared unconstitutional.

The depraved Judge Roberts is so fanatical in his support of sodomy and gay rights he even fought the case for his limp-wristed buddies on a pro bono basis—he didn't even charge the queer groups a dime for his services. Now that's real devotion to a cause, however corrupt.

So, thanks to our "born again Christian President," George W. Bush, we have sitting at the helm of the U.S. Supreme Court one of the most highly acclaimed gay rights attorneys in the world. Whoop-te-do!

What's more, so enamored of Bush and slavish to his every need are evangelical leaders like Pastor Ted Haggard, James Dobson, Pat Robertson, and Jerry Falwell that they ended up enthusiastically throwing their full support for John Roberts' confirmation by the Senate. So, gays owe a great debt of gratitude to the Dobson-Falwell crowd, as well as to George W. Bush, for this generous favor.

When just a few, old-line conservatives complained about Judge Roberts' devoted, pro bono work on behalf of the gay rights movement, Jerry Falwell, always a boot kisser to Republican presidents, jumped in to defend Bush's pro-gay choice. Gay rights, said Falwell, *"is not a liberal or conservative value. It's an American value that I would think that we pretty much all agree on."* Uh, hold on there, Jerry. Not "all" of us agree on that. In fact, I suspect there are at least several

Convicted criminal, Lewis "Scooter" Libby, is also a pornographic novelist. Where have all the family values gone?

thousand readers of *Power of Prophecy* newsletter who believe sodomy and its cousin, pedophilia, are both a sin and a crime.

Steamy Lesbian Sex and the Infamous Bear Novel

And there's more. George W. Bush was the first President to have formal public meetings in the Oval Office with the Log Cabin Republicans group—a merry band of GOP queers into politics. He chose for his running mate Vice President Dick Cheney, whose wife, Lynn, authored several novels with what have been called *"steamy lesbian sex scenes."* Fitting since, as it turns out in real life, the Cheneys' daughter is a full-scale lesbian political activist.

Cheney for four years was served by his Chief of Staff, an odd fella named Lewis "Scooter" Libby. Libby, who has been indicted by a federal grand jury for intelligence crimes, is reputed to be an Israeli secret agent. Libby, or "Scooter" as Cheney and neocon friends so lovingly call him, also is a novelist. In one of his fiction books, he has an account of a caged bear being sexually tormented by human sex fiends with sticks. (Incredible? Yes, but also sickeningly true).

Israel's President Rapes Ten Aides

Bush and Cheney are, as we all know, huge backers of Israel and are extremely supportive of Israeli politicians. Is it not significant, then, that Israel's President, Moshe Katsov, is now under investigation in that country for raping and sexually molesting ten young staffers? The crimes of Katsov, the sex-fiend President of Israel, are perhaps exceeded only by those of Bush and his homoerotic cohorts.

Consider the sexual sadism practiced at Abu Ghraib prison. Video films of Iraqi male, nude prisoners showed many being victimized in acts of brutal sodomy. Naked Iraqi males—many whom later were found to be innocent—were stacked in pyramids, their sexual organs revealed.

Evidence shows that top Bush White House and Pentagon officials, including Secretary of State Rumsfeld, privately viewed these obscene, monstrous movies, no doubt for their own, wicked pleasures. Apparently, Bush, Cheney, Rumsfeld, and all the other Bush Administration perverts get a real rise out of viewing young men screaming in agony as they are ritualistically tortured and sexually abused by sodomite creeps. Shades of the abominable activities of France's notorious sadist, the Marquis de Sade.

Seymour Hersh, acclaimed New York writer who uncovered the My Lai, Vietnam atrocities decades ago, reports that inside the Pentagon's inner sanctum, kept hidden by Bush people

Defrocked Congressman Mark Foley, poster boy for rampant homosexuality of Republicans and Democrats alike in Washington, DC.

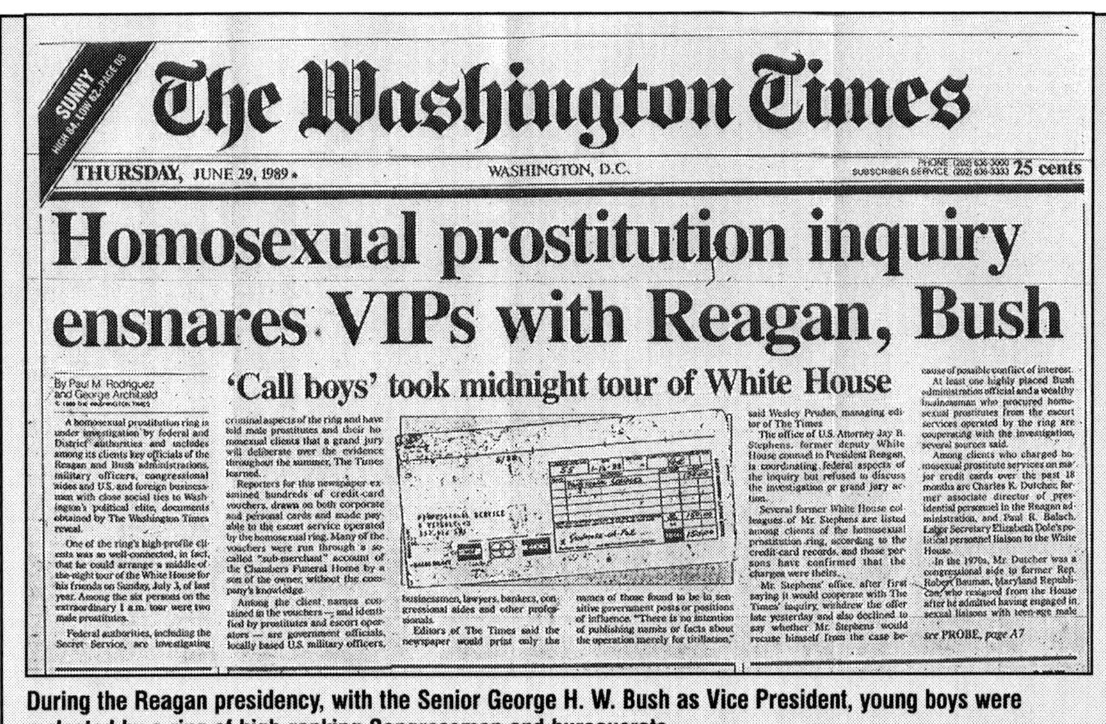

SUNNY HIGH 84, LOW 62 — PAGE D6

The Washington Times

THURSDAY, JUNE 29, 1989 • WASHINGTON, D.C. • 25 cents

Homosexual prostitution inquiry ensnares VIPs with Reagan, Bush

'Call boys' took midnight tour of White House

By Paul M. Rodriguez and George Archibald

A homosexual prostitution ring is under investigation by federal and District authorities and includes among its clients key officials of the Reagan and Bush administrations, military officers, congressional aides and U.S. and foreign businessmen with close social ties to Washington's political elite, documents obtained by The Washington Times reveal.

One of the ring's high-profile clients was so well-connected, in fact, that he could arrange a middle-of-the-night tour of the White House for his friends on Sunday, July 3, of last year. Among the six persons on the extraordinary 1 a.m. tour were two male prostitutes.

Federal authorities, including the Secret Service, are investigating criminal aspects of the ring and have told male prostitutes and their homosexual clients that a grand jury will deliberate over the evidence throughout the summer, The Times learned.

Reporters for this newspaper examined hundreds of credit-card vouchers, drawn on both corporate and personal cards and made payable to the escort service operated by the homosexual ring. Many of the vouchers were run through a so-called "sub-merchant" account of the Chambers Funeral Home by a son of the owner, without the company's knowledge.

Among the client names contained in the vouchers — and identified by prostitutes and escort operators — are government officials, locally based U.S. military officers, businessmen, lawyers, bankers, congressional aides and other professionals.

Editors of The Times said the newspaper would print only the names of those found to be in sensitive government posts or positions of influence. "There is no intention of publishing names or facts about the operation merely for titillation," said Wesley Pruden, managing editor of The Times.

The office of U.S. Attorney Jay B. Stephens, former deputy White House counsel to President Reagan, is coordinating federal aspects of the inquiry but refused to discuss the investigation or grand jury action.

Several former White House colleagues of Mr. Stephens are listed among clients of the homosexual prostitution ring, according to the credit-card records, and those persons have confirmed that the charges were theirs.

Mr. Stephens' office, after first saying it would cooperate with The Times' inquiry, withdrew the offer late yesterday and also declined to say whether Mr. Stephens would recuse himself from the case because of possible conflict of interest.

At least one highly placed Bush administration official and a wealthy businessman who procured homosexual prostitutes from the escort services operated by the ring are cooperating with the investigation, several sources said.

Among clients who charged homosexual prostitute services on major credit cards over the past 18 months are Charles K. Dutcher, former associate director of presidential personnel in the Reagan administration, and Paul R. Balach, Labor Secretary Elizabeth Dole's political personnel liaison to the White House.

In the 1970s, Mr. Dutcher was a congressional aide to former Rep. Robert Bauman, Maryland Republican, who resigned from the House after he admitted having engaged in sexual liaisons with teen-age male

see PROBE, page A7

During the Reagan presidency, with the Senior George H. W. Bush as Vice President, young boys were molested by a ring of high-ranking Congressmen and bureaucrats.

from view by ordinary Americans, are horrific videos that beggar the imagination. They include grim scenes of U.S. CIA and military interrogators raping and sodomizing Iraqi children. Hersh has seen them and says the *"soundtrack of the shrieking boys"* and hearing their mothers, forced to watch, crying out for mercy, made him sick to his stomach.

Bush is a sick, sick man, indeed. Lenin, Trotsky, Stalin, and Beria don't have a thing on this man. Bush and his coterie of homoerotic thugs are craftier and more sinister than anything the brutal Soviet system ever produced. And coincidentally, Lenin and the boys in Russia were all Jews, and they were all homosexuals to boot. *Just like Bush and his neocons.*

Crushing the Testicles of Little Boys

Once we peer within, we find worse and worse elitist Bush perversion down deep inside the White House rabbit hole. In a debate in Chicago with Notre Dame professor and scholar Doug Cassel, Bush Justice Department attorney John Yoo argued that President George Bush has the full legal authority to sexually torture anyone suspected of being a terrorist. According to Yoo, if Bush

> *According to Yoo, if Bush desires, he can even order the sexual torture of infants. He can, for example, order interrogators to crush the testicles of a person's child, to get the parent to "confess."*

desires, he can even order the sexual torture of infants. He can, for example, order interrogators to crush the testicles of a person's child, to get the parent to "confess." It was Yoo who authored Bush's misnamed *Patriot Act* legislation, authorizing the torture, the suspension of constitutional rights for suspects, and the imprisoning of "potential" criminals at U.S.-run gulag camps.

Extending outside the White House, we find even more evidence of the sicko regime: GOP Congressmen Mark Foley, Dennis Hastert, Jim Kolbe, and a slew of others, including Governors,

Senators, and Judges. Homoerotic thugs all, and not a few pedophile predators among them. The evil goes back all the way to the Lyndon B. Johnson and the Reagan Administrations. Many of President Ronald "Hollywood" Reagan's White House pals were also sodomites.

Jewish Talmud Approves Pedophilia

That most of the Bush queer battalion are Jews is not a surprise. The *Jewish Talmud*, the rabbis' most holy book, officially endorses pedophile acts by homosexual fiends. The Talmud says that sex with a girl under three years of age, or a minor boy under nine, is permissible. It's not even a "sexual connection," say the rabbis.

Evidently, evangelicals like TBN's Paul Crouch (who gave $425,000 to hush-up his homosexual lover from writing a tell-all exposé of he and Paul's sodomite affair) and the NAE's gay deceiver, Ted Haggard, for years either winked at the White House Bordello, or just avoided the issue.

So, apparently, did Dobson, Falwell, Hagee, Graham, Warren, Hybels, Schuller and all the other evangelical fakesters. For this crowd, it's the old monkey's routine of *"see, hear, say nothing."*

The Best Little Whorehouse in Texas **is named as a favorite by Laura Bush.**

Laura Bush's Revealing Choice

First Lady Laura Bush has surely known about her hubby, George's, sexual infatuation with male prostitute Jeff Gannon. And she must at least suspect the grotesque goings-on of the strange men who carry on their sick and sordid behavior inside the secure work areas of the White House Bordello.

A hint of her sure knowledge came a couple of years ago when officials of the Texas Library Association asked Mrs. Bush to identify a single play or book that the First Lady personally enjoyed and was representative of what Laura considered "the best that Texas authors and playwrights had to offer." Madam Bush's revealing choice: *"The Best Little Whorehouse in Texas."*

Could it be that the best little whorehouse in Texas is actually a bordello, an exclusive yet seedy establishment located not in Texas but in Washington, D.C., a giant, white Greco-Roman mansion sitting behind a handsome wrought iron-fence at 1600 Pennsylvania Avenue?

Masonic Lodge and Freemasonry

The Masonic Plan for America

Is there in existence a small core of hidden leaders of international Freemasonry? Are these men involved in an ongoing world conspiracy destined to bring planet earth to a chaotic, end-times climax? Is America destined to play the key role in this conspiratorial scenario?

Very few people know that there is, in fact, a disciplined, yet corrupt, covert elite controlling all Masonic lodges worldwide. In the Scottish Rite—the largest Mother Lodge of Freemasonry with some 4 million initiates—the 33° is said to be the highest degree, or rank, possible. But in fact, a select few of those who reach this lofty status are chosen for even higher honors.

Some Christian researchers have noted that this chosen cadre proceed past the 33°, being initiated through the secretive Palladium Rite into a fervent worship and adoration of Lucifer himself, the concealed Great Architect of the Masonic Lodge.

The average Mason has no idea that he is merely a pawn and a stooge, manipulated like so much putty by an Illuminati leadership devoted to Lucifer, the Lodge's infernal, supreme deity. Few Masons understand the occult meaning of the esoteric symbols and ceremonial rituals encountered during their lodge meetings. And they have no knowledge whatsoever that there exists a secret agenda by satanic forces within their own organizations. The Luciferian overlords deceptively call this agenda "God's Plan."

In the September 1950 edition of *The New Age*, the official publication of "The Supreme Council 33°" of Scottish Rite Freemasonry, Mason brother C. William Smith briefly outlined "God's Plan in America." Evidently, back in 1950 the Masonic hierarchy felt they could safely release this information to the general membership. But since that time, the lodge's Luciferian overlords have been more discreet. Disclosures such as this are rarely, if ever, made today.

Following this article we reprint significant passages from what international Freemasonry called "God's Plan in America," as found in *The New Age* journal of September 1950. As you read these passages, keep in mind that the "God" of the Masonic order is Lucifer. So in effect, this is the devil's plan for America.

Freemasonry: Aryan Race Superiority for the Novus Ordo Seclorum

Please note several, important facts about the so-called "God's Plan in America" as revealed in Freemasonry's premier publication. First, it is a racist Plan. According to the Lodge, only the Nordic peoples—the white-skinned Anglo-Saxons—possess "The Great Light." Masonic doctrine teaches that it is the Nordic race alone which has been chosen by "God" "to unfold the New Age of the world—a 'Novus Ordo Seclorum.' "

Second, the Masonic Plan announces that the Nordic race is destined to become the "*sixth Aryan Civilization*," a beautiful race of people of "wonderful fragrance." Readers will recall that

Nazi fuhrer Adolf Hitler also spoke of the superior Aryan race chosen by Providence to rule the world. His book, *Mein Kampf (My Struggle)*, prophesied the ascension of this Aryan super race to the heights of world power. In other words, the Great Light given to Freemasonry is the very same light which illuminated the poisonous mind of Nazi Germany's Adolf Hitler.

Christian Sect Hated by Masonry

Third, carefully consider the frequent use by the Masonic author of the term "*sectarianism*." Presumably, Masons are taught to "love God but hate sectarianism." We are further told that "God's Plan" is a nonsectarian plan. So what is *sectarianism*?

Sectarianism is simply the belief that one's faith has an exclusive corner on the Truth and that all others are false. In fact, Christianity is deemed by Freemasonry to be a *sect*, and Christians who believe in Jesus alone are said by Masons to be *sectarian*. Since it is revealed that their Masonic "God" hates sectarianism, in effect, *Freemasonry's elite is admitting that they hate Jesus Christ*. That is why the Masonic institution freely accepts Buddhists, Moslems, Zoroastrians, Voodooists, and even Satanists into its fraternal chambers. All are welcomed so long as each agrees that his particular religion is not exclusive. That would be sectarianism.

However, Jesus Christ testified that He alone is the one true God, that He alone is "The Way, The Truth, and The Life." Therefore, all those who believe in Him as Lord refuse to give glory to any other deity. Every true Christian, in the strictest Masonic view, is therefore, necessarily hated and despised as a *divisive, sectarian believer.*

Plot Against Our Public Schools

Finally, observe from the passages in *The New Age* article Freemasonry's evil plot to use the public schools of America to foster Satan's foul Plan. The Palladin masters of the Masonic Order proudly boast that their great God and King *(Lucifer!)* "has chosen the great American schools to pave the way for the new race, the new religion, and the new civilization that is taking place in America."

The diabolical, racist Plan of international Freemasonry is that America's youth are to be steadily propagandized and indoctrinated to accept and embrace *Novus Ordo Seclorem*—the New World Order. Regrettably, over the last few decades the Masonic Order, working with other interests such as the antichrist ACLU, has been able to successfully remove Jesus Christ, the Ten Commandments, and prayer from school classrooms. That has been the Masonic plot—to make public schools *nonsectarian*; that is, *nonChristian!*

Devoid of the teaching of Christian values, our children are sitting ducks for New Age and occult philosophies introduced into the classroom. These ungodly, oriental and pagan philosophies now rampant in our school classrooms are the direct result of Freemasonry influence.

Birthday of a New World Is At Hand

This, then, is the Luciferian Plan of the Masonic Order—a Plan to "begin the world all over again"—to "reinvent America" as Bill Clinton, a Masonic brother, puts it.

The Plan was designed to seduce the minds of a generation of school children. Now, the Masonic seduction of the innocents is almost complete. As C. William Smith exclaims in his revealing Masonic article, "The birthday of a New World is at hand."

The True God is Still on the Throne

Will international Freemasonry prevail in its heinous scheme to conquer and subdue the American people and the world? Possibly. But again, maybe not. I am encouraged by the fact that grass roots

American patriots are more than ever awakening to the truth. I am further emboldened by the power of prayer.

Let us always remember that it is God who is in charge of this universe, not His pitiful, defeated foe, Lucifer. The Masonic Plan for America's demise and the end of the Christian Church may well just crumble into dust. One thing we can know for sure is that our God is still on the throne—and always shall be. His Kingdom is everlasting, and we who know Him shall reign with Him as His obedient servants forever and ever. The Bible records our destiny, for it is written of Jesus our Lord:

> *"And there was given unto Him dominion, and glory, and a Kingdom, that all people, nations, and languages, should serve him: his dominion is an everlasting dominion, which shall not pass away, and his kingdom that which shall not be destroyed" (Daniel 7:14).*

God's Plan In America

(Note: This revealing article was originally published in *The New Age*, the official publication of international Freemasonry, September 1950. It was authored by Masonic scholar C. William Smith.)

God's plan is dedicated to the unification of all races, religions and creeds. This plan, dedicated to the new order of things, is to make all things new—a new nation, a new race, a new civilization and a new religion, a nonsectarian religion that has already been recognized and called the religion of "The Great Light."

Looking back into history, we can easily see that the Guiding Hand of Providence has chosen the Nordic people to bring in and unfold the new order of the world. Records clearly show that 95 percent of the colonists were Nordics—Anglo-Saxons.

Providence has chosen the Nordics because the Nordics have prepared themselves and have chosen God...The Nordics are God's chosen people always looking for more light on the mission of life...

Just as Providence has chosen the Jewish race—the Children of Israel—to bring into the world righteousness by carrying the "Ten Commandments" which emphasize "Remember the Sabbath Day and keep it holy," so also Providence has chosen the Nordic race to unfold the "New Age" of the world—a Novus Ordo Seclorum."

One of the first of the Nordics to reach the New World was the Viking, Leif Ericsson. He sailed from Norway to bring to his people in Ireland a new message, the message of the Christian God. But Providence moves in a mysterious way His wonders to perform, and so Leif the Lucky was sent by Providence to the New World. From the abundance of grapes found there Leif Ericsson called the place Vinland.

It is easy to sense that Leif Ericsson was sent by the Guiding Hand of Providence to bring the Norse spirit of the "All-Father" to the shores of the New World.

The Nordics are the highest branch of the fifth Aryan Civilization. The Latins are of the fourth Aryan Civilization, and the American race will be the sixth Aryan Civilization. This new and great civilization is like an American Beauty rosebud, ready to open and send its wonderful fragrance to all the world.

George Washington, Thomas Jefferson, Benjamin Franklin, John Adams, Thomas Paine and many others of the founders of the new nation in the New World were Nordics.

Thomas Paine, the spark plug of the American Revolution, loved God but hated sectarianism. In "These Are the Times," he wrote: "We have it in our power to begin the world all over again! A situation similar to the present hath not happened since the days of Noah, till now. The birthday of a New World is at hand."

As stated before, God's Plan in America is a nonsectarian plan. Our Constitution is nonsectarian. Our great American Public Schools—God's chosen schools—are nonsectarian. The Great Spirit behind this great nation is nonsectarian.

Our great American Public Schools have never taken away from any child the freedom of will, freedom of spirit or freedom of mind. That is the divine reason that Great God our King has chosen the great American Public Schools to pave the way for the new race, the new religion and the new civilization that is taking place in America.

Any mother, father or guardian who is responsible for the taking away of freedom of mind, freedom of will or freedom of spirit is the lowest criminal on this earth, because they take away from that child the God-given right to become a part of God's great plan in America for the dawn of the New Age of the world.

A "Gentler and Kinder" World—According to Freemasonry

In *Dark Majesty* I prove and document that President George Bush's phrase, "A Thousand Points of Light," is of occultic, Masonic origins. Interestingly, another of the president's more famous phrases—a "kinder and gentler" America—is also of Masonic origins.

This phrase was first spoken by George Bush at the Republican Party National Convention in New Orleans in 1988. But on page 396 of his acclaimed book, *Freemasonry in American History*, Masonic authority Allen E. Roberts credits a Mason brother, Joseph Fort Newton, with coming up with this phrase. Newton, a dentist who wrote one of the bestselling Masonic books ever published, *The Builders* (1946), is quoted as saying: "Freemasonry's dignity and its spirituality…permit me to join hands with my (Masonic) Brethren everywhere…to make a *gentler and kinder* world." (Evidently, all that George Bush did was to transpose the two words, kinder and gentler.)

It was Newton's claim that Masonry, by showing man that he is divine, would bring "beauty" to this "gentler and kinder world."

The majority of people are being sucked in by this grand vision of a "gentler and kinder" world that is planned for us. But for you who read my newsletter and understand what this actually means, it's going to be a bitter pill to swallow.

For example, in the revealing book *Masonic Harvest*, by noted Masonic Lodge author Carl H. Claudy (published by The Temple Publishers, Washington, D.C.), we are told of how all things here on earth will end:

> How will it end?…If we keep our Masonic philosophy within the framework of Freemasonry—which means within the Fatherhood of God and the brotherhood of man—it will probably round itself out in a vision of a universal religion, which will embrace all creeds, a universal government, which will embrace all humanity; and a universal knowledge, which will make all mankind kin, thus outlawing war, eliminating the criminal and bringing about the Utopia in which…all men are happy.

Joseph Fort Newton, a Mason who predicted a coming age when the world would be a "gentler and kinder" place. In *The Builders*, Newton also wrote: "Here lies the great secret of Masonry—that it makes a man aware of that divinity within him" (p. 293).

This, then is the picture of the coming great society once the

Secret Brotherhood establishes final, iron-clad control. We shall all be happy and the world will be a gentler and kinder place.

But of course, the "criminals" will first have to be eliminated. And I think I know just who the criminals are, according to Freemasonry. They include anyone who opposes this coming Utopia in which Christianity and American patriotism are to be totally extinguished.

Yes, the "criminals" include men and women like you and me who refuse to sit idly by and remain "happy" and contented as a Council of Wise Persons presides over a totalitarian World Government based on Luciferian principles.

The Golden Serpents of Freemasonry

In my book *Dark Majesty*, I closely examine the religion of the Illuminati. Meanwhile, in *New Age Cults and Religions*, I unmask the occult underpinnings of Freemasonry. Not surprisingly, the doctrine and rituals of the Illuminati are identical to those of Freemasonry.

The Illuminati and Masonic faith is, at its core, the worship of Lucifer, the serpent. This is a religion that comes complete with a false "Christ," an occult ritual (initiation by degrees), and church sanctuaries—known as temples and lodges to Freemasons and the men of the secret societies.

Washington, D.C.'s ornate, Egyptian-style House of the Temple is the seat, or headquarters, of the Scottish Rite, the world's largest Masonic organization. It is here that the ceremony and ritual is conducted for all Masons receiving the exalted 33°. It is here, at the black altar, that the 33° candidate comes, kneels, drinks wine from a human skull, and kisses a false "holy book."

Moreover, it is also here, in the Temple Room of Freemasonry's most revered sanctuary, that you will find the two, huge, fiery golden serpents on the wall behind the altar. This is a dead giveaway of the satanic goals of the international Masonic brotherhood.

For confirmation we simply need turn to the Bible. In *Revelation 12:9* we read: *"And the great dragon was cast out, that old serpent, called the Devil, and Satan, which deceiveth the whole world..."*

Freemasonry Wages War Against the Truth

The Grand Sovereign Commander and other Masonic overlords are going all out to wage a public relations war against their critics. In the process, they are making malicious and misleading attacks on good Christians.

You see, the Masonic big-wigs are worried. June of 1993 in Houston, the nation's largest protestant denomination, the Southern Baptist Convention (SBC), is going to vote on whether Freemasonry is compatible with Christianity. This is due to the efforts of dedicated Baptist men like Dr. James L. Holly, a medical doctor from Beaumont, Texas, who has courageously stood up to the most ungodly and hostile attacks imaginable.

Holly, who has been labeled a "vicious liar" by angry Freemason officials, is rightly insisting that Southern Baptists once and for all do what's right and exclude the dark evils of Freemasonry from their churches.

The Plot: Pack the Southern Baptist Convention

Freemasonry's overlords are now calling for Masons everywhere who are Baptists to pack the convention hall in Houston this June and vote down the proposed resolution (See the Feb. 1993 issue of *Scottish Rite Journal.*) They are also asking Masons to send a barrage of letters to the leaders of the SBC asserting that there is no conflict between the Lodge and their faith.

But any true Christian who has studied Masonry knows that this is a bald lie. Sadly, many sincere men have been deceived into joining the Lodge, unwittingly entering into its Luciferian rituals and dogma. Indeed, in the very issue of the *Scottish Rite Journal* that seeks to portray Freemasonry in a favorable light, supporters of the Lodge blatantly reveal the ungodly nature of their sect.

The February 1993 edition of *Scottish Rite Journal* calls on Masons to wage a public relations war on critics. To impress Southern Baptists, the front cover pictures two officials of Baylor University, a baptist school, both of whom are 33° Masons. What the magazine fails to say is that one of the men, Dr. Herbert Reynolds (right), President of Baylor, is a theological liberal who calls himself a "moderate" but has often bitterly attacked the Biblical conservatives within the Southern Baptist ranks.

Masons Refuse the Name of Jesus

Norman Vincent Peale, himself a 33° Mason, brags in one article about the wonderful tolerance of Freemasonry. Peale explains that

"Freemasonry does not promote any one religious creed." Instead, he writes, all Masons simply believe in "the Deity."

Well, Mr. Peale, "the Deity" has a name—the name you stubbornly and arrogantly refuse to acknowledge in your article. His name is Jesus Christ; He alone is Lord of Lords. There are no other deities, except false ones, and the Bible clearly teaches that Jesus is the name above every other name. Every Mason of every creed or of no creed will, to their regret, someday discover the astonishing Truth and testimony of God's Word:

> *Wherefore God hath highly exalted Him, and given Him a name which is above every name: That at the name of Jesus every knee should bow...And that every tongue should confess that Jesus Christ is Lord, to the glory of God the Father. (Philippians 2:9-11)*

Any organization which denies this basic Truth is not of God. That is why Freemasonry must be exposed for the lying monstrosity that it is.

Freemasonry Worships False Gods

The Masonic Lodge lies to its own members by claiming that its rituals are compatible with Christianity. Yet, it also tells them that, in the Masonic Lodge ritual, they can freely worship at the altar of the *god of their choice*. William Hinton, a former Grand Commander of Freemasonry, in an article entitled "Freemasonry, Politics, and Religion," seeks to assure his readers that:

> In regard to religion, one should know that upon the world wide altars of Masonic Lodges may be found the holy writings of at least five major world religions: Judaism, Christianity, Islam, Buddhism, and Confucianism.

Mr. Hinton, in his blindness, reveals exactly the reason why the Masonic Lodge is in league with the devil. Would a Christian organization place on its altar the scriptures of Buddhism, a religion that teaches reincarnation, or the "holy book" of a satanic religion such as Hinduism, with its worship of serpents and cows and its three million false gods and demon spirits?

Masonic Serpent Worship and The Egyptian Book of the Dead

Christians who have honestly studied the Lodge know why, in its ceremony for the 32nd degree, Freemasonry uses for its holy book *The Egyptian Book of the Dead.* We also know why, in the Scottish Rite's own textbook, *A Bridge to Light*, the author makes the grotesque claim that the Holy spirit is nothing more or less than the Serpent!

Masons, please understand: *Freemasonry is a death trap. But belief in Jesus Christ leads to life everlasting.* My hope for all Masons is that you will awaken to God's Truth before it's too late. I pray that this very day you will call on the name of Jesus and put aside the harmful and destructive dogma of the Lodge.

Appeal to Christian Believers

Christian Friends, let us not allow the hellish minions of Freemasonry to succeed. I highly encourage readers of this newsletter to take a stand for righteousness. Let us bravely suffer the persecution and anger that will come our way by publicly renouncing the deceit, treachery, and hidden evils of Freemasonry. We must do our utmost to shed needed light on one of Satan's darkest and most extraordinary cults—Freemasonry—and are a testimony to the revealed Truth of God's Word.

Nation's Sixth President Opposed Masonic Lodge

John Quincy Adams and Freemasonry

"Freemasonry is deceptive and fraudulent...Its promise is light—its performance is darkness"

— John Quincy Adams

The question of Freemasonry and the controversy over its character—whether the fraternity is good or evil—has long been a feature of American life. Since the earliest days of the American republic, politicians, clergymen, and ordinary citizens alike have engaged in vigorous debate and investigation into the virtue, purposes, and meaning of the Masonic Lodge.

For John Quincy Adams, writer, poet, faithful husband, patriot, former Ambassador and Secretary of State, and sixth President of the United States, there was no question. The dispute was firmly settled in his mind. The teachings and practices of Freemasonry, Adams asserted, are detrimental, noxious, and unfortunate. John Quincy Adams was persuaded that the Lodges were a bane to society, evil and Luciferian.

So convinced was Adams of the devilish and negative effects of Freemasonry in the affairs of men that the former President of the United States helped to found the Anti-Mason Political Party. In 1830, he was elected to the U.S. House of Representatives on the Anti-Mason Party ticket. For years Adams carried on an active and heated literary and speaking campaign against Freemasonry. The classic book we have just reprinted, *Letters on Freemasonry*, contains important correspondence written by John Quincy Adams on the controversial subject of Freemasonry.

John Quincy Adams was possibly America's most intelligent President. He spoke and wrote seven languages by age 10 and knew Shakespeare and the classics. Adams saw it as his Christian duty to oppose and unmask Freemasonry.

A Sterling Place in History

A brief biographical sketch of John Quincy Adams is in order. His illustrious father, of course, was John Adams, one of America's most famous and revered founding fathers. While the fortunes of history favored his courageous father, the son, John Quincy also successfully carved out for himself a sterling place in history. As a precocious young man, he traveled and lived years in Europe with his parents and relatives. By age 10 he was already reading Shakespeare and took up a formal education at the distinguished Passy Academy near Paris, France. He went on to master Latin, Greek, French, Dutch, and Spanish languages and studied law. He graduated from Harvard University in 1787 second in his class, with high honors.

After serving in succession as Minister to Great Britain, U.S. Senator, and Secretary of State, Adams ascended to the presidency of the U.S. following the election of 1824. Among his achievements as chief executive were extended roadways and the construction of the Chesapeake and Ohio Canal. Earlier, as Secretary of State he helped formulate the Monroe Doctrine, and as an U.S. Representative, Adams was responsible for the founding of the Smithsonian Institution.

John Quincy Adams was neither a social backslapper nor a "smooth operator" type of politician. He was known as quiet, sober, plainspoken, and serious, and he was dedicated to the improvement of his country.

Interestingly, Adams recognized and was keenly aware of his uncompromising nature and less than charismatic personality. He wrote in his diary, "I am a man of reserved, cold, austere, and forbidding manners...My political adversaries say gloomy and unsocial."

Adams lamented this "defect in my character" and remarked "I have not the pliability to reform it."

"I never was and never shall be what is commonly termed a popular man," Adams concluded. "I have no powers of fascination; none of the honey..."

Perhaps he had no fascination and honey to attract and influence people, but what John Quincy Adams did have was considerable. He had the respect of his peers, and he earned the admiration of the people. Adams was strong in opinion, single-minded, determined, honest and highly intelligent. Though he checked his temper, he did not hesitate to stand up for what he perceived as injustice, unrighteousness, and wrongdoing.

Adams never quit fighting for the abolition of slavery. In 1841, in the Amistad case, he argued successfully before the Supreme Court to win freedom for black slaves who had engaged in a mutiny against oppressive white slavemasters aboard the Spanish ship Amistad.

"A Devout Christian"

No doubt it was his sense of duty as a Christian which so compelled Adams to fiercely battle against injustice and prejudice and to support freedom, liberty, and human rights. The authors of *The Complete Book of the Presidents* note that John Quincy Adams was a devout Christian. They add:

> "He attended church regularly and often worshipped twice on Sunday. All his life before retiring each night, he recited...prayer...In the morning he invariably read several chapters of the Bible before starting his day."

Adams occasionally wrote of his faith, testifying: "I have at all times been a sincere believer in the existence of a Supreme Creator of the world...and of the divine mission of the Crucified Saviour, proclaiming...'Thou shalt love thy neighbor as thyself.'"

On his deathbed on February 23, 1848, realizing his grave condition following a massive stroke, Adams simply said, "This is the end of earth. I am content," and he gave his last breath.

Intense Desire to Expose the Masonic Lodge

It was, I am convinced, his strong Christian faith and religious convictions, as well as his thirst for justice and his common sense, that ignited the intense desire in Adams not only to expose the falsehoods inherent in Freemasonry, but also his desire to discourage men of good will from joining or participating in what he clearly saw as an unethical, unscriptural, and unholy secret society.

If he needed any additional justification, it was the tragic murder of Captain William Morgan in the state of New York in the year 1826 that further heightened Adams' sense of urgency to warn

Today, the Masonic Lodges boast of many famous leaders who have been Masons. They claim George Washington as one of their own and point to this famous painting depicting our first President as Worshipful Master of his Lodge. In fact, Washington was a dedicated Freemason.

of the dangers of the Masonic Lodge. Morgan, an ex-Mason, had revealed some of the secrets of the Masons—oaths, handshakes and ritual trappings, etc. In retaliation, he was ritually murdered in a particularly gruesome manner, and his lifeless, mutilated body abandoned in a lake.

The facts of Morgan's murder were subsequently covered up by lawful authorities, reputed themselves to be Masons. When evidence ensued that the Masonic Society had assisted the culprits responsible for Morgan's death to elude capture and escape punishment, the event caused a national scandal. Newspapers and periodicals across America—especially those whose publishers and editors were not Masonic initiates and supporters—carried all the gory details of the Morgan affair. Politicians were forced to take sides; some went so far as to found the Anti-Mason political party to elect candidates and enact legislation to overturn what many feared and suspected was the undue influence of the Lodge throughout government and society.

Adams was instrumental in founding this Anti-Mason Party. But politics was only one arena of life in which Adams overtly took on his Masonic opponents. For him this was a holy cause.

John Quincy Adams set out to investigate and learn all he could about Freemasonry, and in the backwaters of the Morgan affair, there were many former Masons who had renounced their involvement and were willing to share their knowledge.

Membership in Lodges Eroding

The significance of John Quincy Adams' campaign in opposition to Freemasonry is vital. Indeed, the debate regarding the merits—and demerits—of the secret society continues to this day. From its high point in 1959, the number of Master Masons has continued to slide, even though the general male population of the United States has rapidly grown. According to the Masonic Services Association, in 1959 there were 4,103,161 Master Masons in lodges in the U.S.A. By 1997 that number sank to just 2,021,909—and indications are that membership continues to erode.

Why I Oppose The Lodge

It is very possible that the more recent ferocious opposition to the Masonic Lodge in the 1990s is at least partly responsible for this dramatic drop. If so, admitting my own bias, I am glad. I count myself as one of those who oppose Freemasonry.

My reasons are many, though they center mainly on my informed conviction that the Masonic Lodge is unChristian, generally amoral, and decidedly *un*wholesome. Indeed, I view today's Freemasonry as a loathsome leftover of the old pagan religions and an sad reminder that a virulent form of occultism and Egyptianism lingers on within the boundaries of these United States.

I readily admit the Lodge is responsible for some worthy humanitarian endeavors, and there are some good men who are Masons. Nevertheless, its origins, nature, rituals, and practices negate whatever noteworthy attributes there are pertaining to Lodge membership.

Masonry Radically Anti-Christian

If Masonry was a negative force detrimental to the spiritual welfare of men in the day of Adams, it is much more so today. Following the great U.S. Civil War (1861-1865), a man named Albert Pike became Sovereign Grand Commander of Scottish Rite Freemasonry. Pike overhauled and revised the lodge rituals, implementing a 33 degree system of initiations that is far more radically anti-Christian and pagan than was previously in place.

Moreover, more recent Masonic leadership has continued to promote a universal theology and other distasteful aspects of Freemasonry which fall, in my opinion, on the dark side.

Tremendous research in this matter by authoritative researchers Ralph Epperson, John Ankerberg, James Wardner, Ed Decker, Bill Schnoebelen, Cathy Burns, Reginald Haupt, James Holly, Jim Shaw, Tom McKenney, Jack Harris, E.M. Storms, and by many others confirms my own findings. Thus, the warnings of John Quincy Adams, if anything, strike with greater clarity and impact today than they did upon their first publication in the nineteenth century.

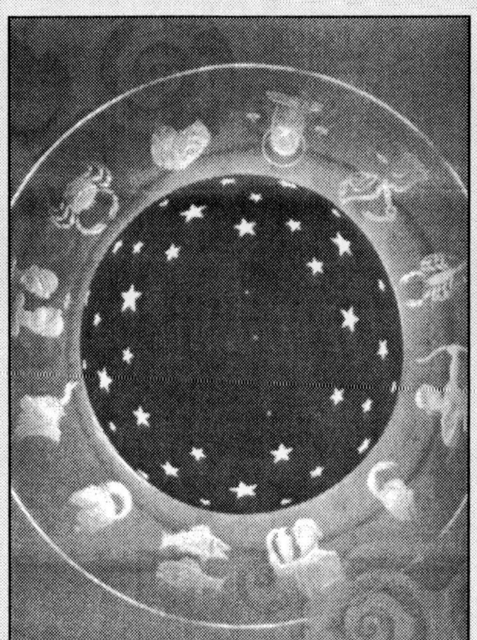

This Masonic Zodiac decorates the interior of the Federal Reserve Board Building in Washington, D.C. If the Nation had heeded the advice of President John Quincy Adams, Freemasonry would not have gained the foothold it has today in American government.

With this in mind, I consider the writing of John Quincy Adams in the insightful volume, *Letters on Freemasonry*, remarkably current and a godsend. I heartily recommend this book to every thinking and caring man and woman on earth—and especially to the men who frequent the Masonic Lodge.

Let them read what one of our nation's most excellent leaders and builders had to say about the Lodge. Then may they well compare the teachings, rituals, and symbols found behind the Lodge's closed doors to the open doctrines and marvelous principles prescribed and contained in God's Holy Word, the Bible.

I believe that, having done so, no true Christian, no earnest seeker of religious truth, will continue in the Masonic Lodge. Surely, a Christian can be a Mason, but if the truth of Christ lies within his heart, that man will not for long *remain* a Mason.

Masons at the U.S. Capitol

On September 18, 1993 in Washington, D.C., Freemasons, accompanied by members of the U.S. Congress, gathered in the rain to re-enact the ritualistic laying of the cornerstone of the U.S. Capitol building. Masonic Grand Masters from all 50 states were on hand. In a pagan, fertility ceremony reminiscent of the original affair held 200 years ago, a new cornerstone was laid. According to press reports, the cornerstone was first "anointed with corn, the symbol of plenty; wine, the symbol of refreshment; and oil, the symbol of joy and happiness."

No wonder our Congress is so daffy. Its members can't help themselves. Their foundation—their very cornerstone—is of Luciferian origins.

Pope Paul VI: "The Smoke of Satan Has Entered the Very Sanctuary of St. Peter's Cathedral."

The Pope, the Devil, and the Masonic Lodge

"And they worshipped the dragon which gave power unto the beast: and they worshipped the beast, saying, Who is like unto the beast? who is able to make war with him?"

—*Revelation 13:4*

Blatant Satan worship is now rampant within the Catholic Church. High-ranking churchmen are guilty of this heinous crime against God. According to one reliable source, the smoke of Satan has entered the very sanctuary of St. Peter's Cathedral in the Vatican. Mind-boggling though it may be, priests and bishops alike are known to have taken contract oaths to serve the devil, signed in their own blood!

These amazing facts about devil worship inside the Vatican and its subsidiaries have come not from hostile Protestant critics of Roman Catholicism, but from top-ranking Catholic prelates themselves. Evidently, this awful malignancy is so far advanced that Satanism has reached the papacy itself and has seriously affected the rank and file of nuns and priests in the U.S.A. and throughout the globe. Untold numbers of outright Satan worshippers are now masquerading as Catholic clergy while secretly paying homage to Lucifer.

"Lucifer is Enthroned"

Catholic scholar Dr. Malachi Martin, formerly a Jesuit professor at Georgetown University and a confidant of Vatican insiders, flatly declared in a recent New York City interview: *"Yes, it's true. Lucifer is enthroned in the Catholic Church."*

Martin was also interviewed by *The Fatima Crusader*, a well-known Catholic publication. He repeated his allegations, and expressed his dismay and distress that the Catholic institution of which he is a part has grown so decadent and morally reprobate since the Vatican II conference of the 60s. The contention that there are Satanists in Rome is "completely correct" said Martin, adding:

> Anybody who is acquainted with the state of affairs in the Vatican in the last 35 years is well aware that the prince of darkness has and still has his surrogates in the court of St. Peter in Rome.

Blood Oaths and Blasphemous Rituals

Malachi Martin is a very traditional Catholic. Author of *Hostage to the Devil* and numerous other books, his acclaimed *Keys of This Blood*, published some five years ago, was a strong, apologetics volume supporting the papacy of the current Pope, John Paul II. But now, Martin has doubts. He cannot understand why this Pope allows such evil to exist and even prosper within the church.

It has gotten so bad, Dr. Martin contends, that in one shocking incident, high-ranking churchmen actually took oaths signed with their own blood and participated in "meticulously enacted rituals that blaspheme and devilishly mimic the holy sacrifice of the mass."

Treachery Inside the Sanctuary

If Dr. Malachi Martin was the only authority sounding the alarm about devil worship in the Catholic Church, the whole affair would simply be dismissed as the outrageous accusations of a single cleric. But as far back as 1976, Pope Paul VI shocked a papal audience by confiding that, "The smoke of Satan has entered the very sanctuary of St. Peter's Cathedral." The Pontiff went on to explain that he had knowledge of a midnight hour, Black Satanic Mass having been conducted at the altar of St. Peter's, on the exact spot where the Pope himself regularly says mass.

Secret Involvement Exposed

Already reeling from Martin's accusations and stung by the memorable revelations of a previous pontiff, the Catholic hierarchy was further set back on its combined heels in Rome last November. With thousands in attendance at Rome's Fatima 2000 International Congress on World Peace, a respected Archbishop, Emmanuel Milingo, strode to the podium. The crowd gasped as they heard Milingo solemnly affirm that members of the Catholic Church hierarchy are secretly involved in the darkest kinds of formal Satan worship.

Archbishop Milingo, an exorcist, is author of a bestselling book exposing the occult, *Face to Face With the Devil.* In his speech, Milingo called Satan worship the "Third dimension of Evil," and explained:

> Now, the third dimension (of evil) is the most dangerous. It is subtle and the most terrible…I could not believe when I discovered this third dimension of evil. The third dimension is people who follow instructions in satanic sects…
>
> Now with this third dimension, I'm sorry to say, our church belongs to it. I'm very sorry, I could not understand myself, and even now I don't understand. But the only consolation I have is that, well, Judas Iscariot was one. Together with Jesus three years, he never changed. Then I understand that the third dimension of evil existed not only now, but it existed even then. Because nothing could change the heart of Judas Iscariot—nothing.

Devil Protected by Catholic Authorities

Archbishop Milingo went on to make an accusation which sent hurricane force shockwaves throughout the Catholic community. According to Milingo, the devil is actually protected by the Catholic Church:

Archbishop Emmanuel Milingo stunned an international audience of bishops, priests, nuns, and laity in Rome by exposing Satanic worship by the Catholic hierarchy.

> The devil in the Catholic Church is so protected now that he is like an animal protected by the government; put on a

> game preserve that outlaws anyone, especially hunters, from trying to capture or kill it. The devil within the Church today is actually protected by certain Church authorities from the official devil hunter in the Church—the exorcist. So much so that the exorcist today is forbidden to attack the devil. The devil is so protected that the one who is the hunter, the exorcist, is forbidden to do his job.

In a subsequent interview, the courageous archbishop stated: "Certainly, there are priests and bishops alike who are followers of Satan." When asked whether cardinals or even the Pope himself were guilty of this repulsive heresy, Milingo responded that, because he is an archbishop, he does not feel it is proper for him to name or comment about superior officials. The archbishop's silence, of course, spoke volumes.

Catholicism and the Ravages of Freemasonry

Satan worship apparently has mushroomed in recent years as Catholic cardinals, bishops, and priests have joined the Masonic Lodge in record numbers. Until the papacy of today's Pope John Paul II, membership by Catholics in any kind of Masonic order was an excommunicable offense. Now, however, it is commonplace. Indeed, in 1980, New York's Terrance Cooke, one of America's most powerful Catholic cardinals, addressed a gathering of 3,000 Masons. Cardinal Cooke electrified the assemblage when he said that, as friends, Masons and Catholics should recognize each other.

Refraining from mentioning the name of Jesus—the name despised by many Masons and prohibited inside their lodges—Cardinal Cooke bowed to Masonry's worst heresy by remarking, "I know of your firm belief in the Supreme Being, the Great Architect of the Universe, and of the holy writings appropriate to the religion of your members, and I salute you for your loyalty to these ancient values."

Cardinal Cooke's words were obviously well chosen and imbued with hidden meaning. In fact, the Masonic Lodge's "Supreme Architect of the Universe" is none other than *Lucifer*, who cloaks himself in Masonic literature with the names of such deities as Zoroaster, Shiva, Abaddon, and in other Masonic pagan-god disguises. As for the "holy writings" of Freemasonry, these have their origins in the Roman mystery religions, in 19th century occultism, and in Egyptianism/Babylonianism. Such are the "ancient values" of the satanic Masonic Lodge.

In late 1996 the Vatican put on sale this commemorative coin with a portrait of Pope John Paul II. Observers were taken aback at the coin's Caesarean Empire features. Note the ancient Roman lettering style. The three stars at bottom have exactly six points, or rays: thus, signifying an unholy trinity of 6-6-6.

Catholic insiders say that Pope John Paul II, shown here with his ally, Communist New Ager Mikhail Gorbachev, has done nothing to stop the rising tide of satan worship.

Satanism in Methodist, Episcopal, and Mormon Churches

In my special edition audiotape, *Satan Worship in the Vatican Exposed*, I explore further the overwhelming evidence of devil worship by the Catholic hierarchy. Authoritative quotes and documentation are given. I also tie the aging Pope John Paul II to this horror.

We must remember, however, that Satanism is not only practiced by Catholic clergy. This wickedness is found in some of today's Methodist and Charismatic churches, and especially in Episcopal and Anglican churches. Two years ago, the Mormon Church hierarchy even went public, admitting that satanic rituals had been secretly conducted by some church elders.

Meanwhile, members of the Masonic Lodge, including pastors and denominational leaders, continue to dominate the Southern Baptist Convention.

Contrary to what some believe, the devil is not a "Catholic." Indeed, he is remarkably tolerant of all false religion, and he is known to be pleasingly nondenominational in his approach to religion. Satan is proud to be an ecumenical being. "Any faith but Jesus and His Word, the King James Bible," is the devil's handy motto.

The Power of Prophecy

These revelations of devil worship inside churches which claim to be "Christian" should not surprise us. The power of Bible prophecy is thereby made manifest. The books of *Daniel* and *Revelation* describe the Antichrist as a man who appears as a lamb but has horns. He ordains amongst his flock men and women who are unrepentant murderers, liars, fornicators, pedophiles and adulterers. Daniel says that the devil's Antichrist shall speak "dark sentences" and shall worship a god his fathers knew not.

Thus we understand why Satan worship is so fervently and irreverently practiced in the very seat of Rome, inside the profane temple the popes built—the temple known as St. Peter's Cathedral, which has the Egyptian sun god obelisk on display in its front courtyard.

Yes, 666 is rising fast. The Pope, his Vatican, and its hierarchy are preparing the way for the corrupt Beast. They, as well as their non-Catholic helpers, are opening a creaking doorway to the Ultimate Evil. May God have mercy on their souls.

The Trail of Two Serpents

This revealing photo of Catholic Cardinal Myroslav Ivan Lubachivsky, of the Ukraine, appeared in the magazine *Inside the Vatican* (1997), in an article entitled, "The Princes of the Church." Observe the cardinal's unusual staff, with its vile phoenix serpents facing each other and its Maltese Cross at the apex. This same imagery—the dual phoenix serpent—is found on the wall behind the black stone altar inside the sanctuary of Freemasonry's House of the Temple in Washington, D.C.

In Pergamos, where *Revelation* says that "Satan's seat" was, the sun deity was worshipped in the form of "Aesculapius, the man-instructing serpent." His seed, the son (or Antichrist), was the devil's spitting image—an incarnation, as depicted in the illustration, at left, from Hislop's classic book, *The Two Babylons*.

According to Hislop, the mysterious symbol of the dual serpent was brought from Pergamos to Rome, where Satan began to be worshipped by the Pope and the Catholic hierarchy. Satan worship can thus be traced from Babylon, to Pergamos, to Rome.

Freemasonry Unmasked in the Vatican

Over the years a growing number of Catholic publications have exposed the hidden connections within the Vatican of high-level agents of Satan's secret society, Freemasonry. The infamous, P2 "Black Lodge" scandal involving the head of the Vatican bank is one of many which have been uncovered. Now comes documentation of even greater involvement in Masonic evildoing by the Catholic hierarchy.

The Catholic publication, *Sangre de Cristo Newsnotes*, reports that, upon arriving in Rome for duty as Mexico's ambassador to the Vatican, Enrique Olivares Santana, a militant Mason, immediately felt right at home. Why? Because, "Within the eight city blocks that make up the Vatican State, no fewer than four Scottish Rite Freemason Lodges are functioning."

Sangre de Cristo Newsnotes also discloses that, "Many of the highest Vatican officials are Masons, and in certain countries where the church is not allowed to operate, it is the lodges that carry on Vatican affairs, clandestinely."

Meanwhile, the respected Catholic news magazine, *30 Days* (Issue No. 9, 1993), says that Italian prosecutors have contacted the Vatican "in their search for information on the alleged Masonic membership of prelates." The sought for information is needed to help the Italian government unravel Mafia connections inside the Catholic church hierarchy.

Purportedly, two recent popes, John XXIII and Paul VI, were initiated into the mysteries of the Masonic brotherhood. John XXIII, pontiff during the 60s who was responsible for the decadence of Vatican II, was also a high-level Rosicrucian initiate.

Ironically, until our generation, the Catholic Church seemed to be an implacable foe of international Freemasonry. For decades, while Southern Baptist, Presbyterian, Methodist, Episcopal and other Protestant denominations were eagerly embracing this Luciferian cult and all its horrors, the popes were fiercely and bravely denouncing the evil Masonic Lodge and all for which it stands. But times have changed. Today, thousands of Catholic priests have been initiated into the inner sanctum of Freemasonry.

Yet, Manly P. Hall, 33°, the man whom Masonic authorities have revered as "one of our greatest Masonic scholars of the 20th century," admitted that the Lodges are not Christian. He wrote: "The true Mason is not creed-bound. He realizes with the divine illumination of his lodge that as a Mason his religion must be universal: Christ, Buddha, or Mohammed, the name means little...All Masons know that all religions are but one story." (*The Lost Keys of Freemasonry,* 1976, p. 65).

The Apostle Paul warned: "But though we, or an angel from heaven, preach any other gospel unto you than that which we have preached unto you, let him be accursed."

Unmasking the Sexual Perversions of the Illuminati

Two on a Saddle

"Who will rise up for me against the evil doers? or who will stand up for me against the workers of iniquity?"

—*Psalm 94:16*

Serial killers, government tyrants, academic liberals, Catholic priests, politicians, Mormon Church higher-ups, Jewish rabbis, environmental extremists, communists, religious heretics, mass murderers, occultists, spies, and the Illuminati share something hideous and grotesque in common. Almost all are homosexual. Worse, most of the sick-minded men who comprise these demented social groups are not only homosexual, they practice the most kinky and perverted forms of sexual licentiousness—pedophilia, satanic bondage, physical torture, bisexuality, transvestitism, and even bestiality.

If you doubt this, I invite you to consider the wicked lives of some of these moral degenerates—men like Lenin, Mussolini, Hitler, Marx, Jim Jones, Albert Kinsey, Michael Jackson, Jacques DeMolay, Bill Clinton, Jim Bakker, Jimmy Swaggert, Mick Jagger, Aleister Crowley, Hubert Humphrey, Paul Tsongas, Martin Luther King, Mario Cuomo, Rudy Giuliani, Jeffrey Dahmer, Richard Speck, and John Wayne Gacy.

Homosexuality in the Mystery Religions

In the ancient pagan Mystery Religions, homosexuality and pedophilia were popularized. Worshippers of Baal erected shrines and temples of male prostitution *(I Kings 14)*. Roman Emperors Nero, Caligula, and Commodus engaged in incest, sex with boys, bondage, and a variety of evil crimes. So, too, did those in Pharaoh's court. Alexander the Great was a homosexual who loved little boys.

Two versions of the official seal of the Knights Templars, precursors of the Freemasons. Note that in the version at right, the two riders carry a shield. But, in the other version of the seal (left), one's shield is gone and the knight has placed his hand in a most sensitive area of his body.

When the Spanish Conquistadors conquered Central America and the Yucatan in Mexico, they found that most native Indian priests were sodomites.

In their pagan temples were sacred statues depicting gay sex acts. In Babylon, people sacrificed and prayed to gods and goddesses requesting sexual favors and carnal pleasures.

The Knights Templar and Baphomet

In the 14th century, a Catholic band of crusaders known as the Order of Knights Templar grew in power and riches. They and their leader, their Sovereign Grand Master, Frenchman Jacques DeMolay, built temples and tabernacles of worship. Only Knights Templar initiates could enter therein. Soon, reports spread of the grotesque and unseemly mode of worship of these depraved men. Their secret religion was based on worship of an androgynous (1/2 male, 1/2 female) satanic goat god named *Baphomet.*

Baphomet, the half male, half female goat god of the Knights Templar, was revived by Eliphas Levi, the infamous 19th century Freemason and magician and reportedly is worshipped today by homosexual cults.

In the Knights Templar rituals, a crucifix of Jesus was reviled and urinated on, and homosexual orgies were rumored. Strangely, the seal, or coat of arms, of the Order depicted two knights riding on one horse! Was this an emblem of their homosexual passion or, as the Templars protested, a statement of their "brotherly love?"

When the rumors and gossip of their antichrist activities reached a feverish pitch, the Kings of continental Europe were forced to move against the Order. Their Sovereign Grand Master, DeMolay, was tried, convicted and burned at the stake, their temples shut down. Amazingly, the Knights Templar survived, hiding out in Scotland and underground in Europe. Then, in the 1800s, they made a startling comeback in the new form of Freemasonry! Today, the Masonic youth group is even named the *DeMolays.* Bill Clinton, as a teenager, was a member of this organization.

Jaques DeMolay

Communists, Homosexuality, and Perversion

Communism, as propounded by satanist Karl Marx, was an offshoot of Templarism. As Jüri Lina documents in his sensational book, *Under the Sign of the Scorpion,* Vladimir Lenin, the communist monster who founded the bloody communist regime in Soviet Russia, frequented brothels and maintained three mistresses.

Laventi Beria, Stalin's decadent Chief of Secret Police, a man who arrested, tortured, imprisoned, and executed some 20 million innocent victims in Russia, was truly a heinous sex criminal. Beria would have his chauffeur drive him around Moscow in a limo evenings searching for a young girl or boy out walking alone. Then, Beria would order his security police to grab and kidnap the hapless youth. What horrible fate transpired to such victims I do not wish to recount here. Obviously, Stalin knew of Beria's evil criminality and had no objections.

Religious Sodomites are Legion

Religious fakes who are sodomites predominate. Jim Bakker, PTL televangelist disgraced and defrocked for sexually abusing church secretary Jessica Hahn, reportedly actually preferred young

Religious charlatans often turn out to be sex perverts. (From left to right: Joseph Smith, Jim Bakker, and Jimmy Swaggart)

boys. He frequently had young homo staffers go swimming nude with he and his top aides. Like Bakker, Assembly of God television preacher Jimmy Swaggert also was a sexual deviant—reportedly into porno literature, trampy prostitutes, etc. He stayed away from real sex with real women—desired bizarre acts.

Satan loves to debauch religious charlatans. A headline in *The Houston Chronicle* newspaper, page one of its May 9, 1999 issue, trumpeted, *"Mormons Caught up in Wave of Pedophile Accusations."* In fact, *Power of Prophecy* has received startling information about satanic rituals and pedophile Mormon elders in the so-called Church of Jesus Christ of Latter Day Saints (LDS). No Wonder! Joseph Smith and Brigham Young, Mormon founders, took numerous wives, and Smith was an occultist and sexual pervert of the highest order, as even many of his biographers confess. (See next article—Part 2 of *Two On a Saddle*.)

"Mormons Caught Up In Wave of Pedophile Accusations"
—Headline, *The Houston Chronicle*
(May 9, 1999)

Sordid Priests, Cult Gurus, Politicians, Masons, and Serial Killers Populate Homosexual Ranks

Two on a Saddle (Part II)

Legions of Catholic priests are now recognized as plunderers of little boys. It is estimated that at least 80 percent of all Catholic priests are queers, and most nuns are lesbians! Father Ritter, the priest who founded Covenant House, a New York City shelter, to "help" homeless teens, was discovered to be molesting his charges. At Boys Town, the famous Catholic boys' orphanage founded by Father Flanagan (played by actor Spencer Tracy in the classic movie), a scandal recently broke when it got out that little boys were being passed around by priests to local gay politicians.

Some orphans from Omaha's Boys Town were even flown to Washington, D.C. for sex parties with top-level Republican Party chieftains. You can read about this in John DeCamp's shocking exposé, *The Franklin Cover-up*.

Religious cultist Jim Jones, who, the controlled news media alleged, induced hundreds of his followers to commit mass suicide in Guyana by drinking poisoned Kool-Aid (actually, most were murdered—but that's another story) was both a Communist and a vile homosexual. Jim Jones was also a leading Democratic Party boss in California and a loyal initiate of the Masonic Lodge. The filthy Reverend Jones had his choice of boys, girls, and grown-ups among his "congregation" as sex partners.

David Koresh of Branch Davidian infamy had a taste for young girls and other men's wives, claiming that, as the Messiah, he had a perfect right. Strangely, Koresh was murdered at the behest of Janet Reno, a butch lesbian; FBI Director Louis Freeh, a member of the reportedly homosexual-oriented *Opus Dei* Catholic secret society; and Hillary Clinton, a flaming, lesbian activist.

Bill Clinton and other Homosexual Masons

President Bill Clinton became famous for the Monica Lewinsky affair. But actually, Bill Clinton never had conventional sexual relations with the young Jewish woman. Clinton enjoys kinky perversion and it is well known in some circles that old Bill is bisexual. Indeed, Clinton is a woman-hater, and documented evidence proves he has brutally raped at least two women.

Albert Pike

One report says that Bill Clinton and a former pal, Arkansas Governor, Winthrop Rockefeller, had a fling. Winthrop, of the monied Rockefeller family, was well known as a homosexual. It is also possible that Clinton was himself abused and molested as a youthful member of the Masonic Lodge's DeMolay organization.

Albert Pike, the 19th century occultist who, as Masonry's Sovereign Grand Commander, created its rituals for the 33 degrees of the craft, was himself a notorious sodomite.

"Cuomo the Homo"

Political networks of both political parties are eaten up by gay men. Former New York Governor Mario Cuomo, a Democrat, has been labeled "Cuomo the Homo." New York's former Mayor, Rudy Giuliani, a Republican, has been known to dress up as a woman transvestite.

The Mayor also carried on an open affair with a female assistant. And when Giuliani and his wife separated, the Mayor moved in with two gay male friends. He now resides in the Manhattan apartment the gay couple share.

New York's Mayor Rudolph Giuliani performed on stage as "Rudia," transvestite, at the annual Inner Circle banquet for the elite. Giuliani now lives in an apartment with two homosexual men but has a female lover. Time magazine named Giuliani its "Person of the Year" for 2001.

Indeed, according to *The New York Times*, the Mayor actually performed in female attire, posing as "Rudia the Transvestite" at a nightclub. The occasion: The annual "Inner Circle" show.

The late Senator and Vice-President Hubert Humphrey often frolicked about nude in the YMCA swimming pool in Minneapolis. President Lyndon B. Johnson skinny-dipped with male friends, including evangelist Billy Graham and his Vice President, Hubert. In fact, the "Y" is a popular meeting place for homo politicians and religious bigwigs. The gay disco group, *The Village People*, in coded language revealed such wicked goings on in their national hit record tune, *Y-M-C-A*!

The Republicans even have a sodomite lobby group, which calls itself the Log Cabin Republicans. Senator Bob Dole heavily pandered to these "conservative" queers during his presidential campaign.

A "butch" type homosexual shows off at a "Gay Pride" demonstration. Reportedly, Congressman Gary Condit also wears leather and homo-fascist garb when in bed in threesomes with men and women.

Gary Condit, Satanism, and Homosexuality

The Democrats don't need an exclusive special homo group. Almost all active Democratic Party political professionals are bisexual and gay. Those who aren't are into other weird, abnormal sexual behavior—satanic sex bondage rituals, etc.

Congressman Gary Condit, suspected of having something to do with the disappearance of intern Chandra Levy, is reputedly known in the Washington, D.C. gay community as a bisexual into major sexual deviance. Condit reportedly dresses up in leather and chains, practices satanic bondage, and has had multiple male sex partners. Condit, an owner of a Harley Davidson motorcycle, is also a regular at Hell's Angels biker parties, especially when "butch" male homo bikers are throwing a shindig. Yet, Condit enjoys degrading and despoiling young women, too. Clintonesque, isn't he?

Remember Senator Paul Tsongas, the Massachusetts Democrat who ran for President and was so beloved by the media? Well, as *The Washington Post* newspaper (2/4/92) noted, the gay Mr. Tsongas had quite a stable of homo pals. He was noted for lustfully staring at young men's bodies, and the newspaper remarked that, "No one sat around the pool when Paul Tsongas was there."

Massachusetts Democrat Congressman Barney Frank (whom a

Texas Republican congressman once called "Barney Fag") and his live-in male lover were discovered several years ago running a homosexual prostitution ring out of Frank's home. An attempt in the House of Representatives to censor Frank for his criminal misconduct fell flat when Republican leader Newt Gingrich came to his rescue. House Speaker Gingrich later resigned after it was about to come out that he was cheating on his wife with a female member of his own congressional staff. Gingrich warmly praised homosexuals in Congress for their "courage in running for office."

Homosexuality A "Wonderful Thing"—Al Gore

Former Vice President Al Gore and his wife, Tipper, also were big backers of queers and sodomites. In June 2000, Al and Tipper threw a party in their home for 150 brazen homos. Gore gushingly told the group, "It's a wonderful thing to do what you are doing... It's an outgrowth of the way you live your entire lives."

Say what, Al? Are you kidding us? Homos are the ominous bringers of AIDS, a variety of other sexual diseases, wide-ranging child abuse and molestation, and sundry other evils—and you say that's a *"wonderful thing?"*

Recently, some 600 homosexual congressmen and politicians threw another wild party, this time inside a certain federal building in Washington, D.C. Security guards were led to vomit at what they saw going on inside and even outside, on the grounds. You may be interested in knowing that among the "proud" sponsors of this disgusting homo-sex gala were wealthy corporations such as American Airlines, Snapple beverages, Miller Lite beer, Starbucks coffee, and Ben and Jerry's ice cream.

Gay Jews and Hollywood

Jewish rabbis and intellectuals are into homosexuality in a big way. James Klugman, British Communist Party leader; U.S. Supreme Court Justice Stephen Breyer; wealthy socialist Victor Rothschild; and British economist John Maynard Keynes come to mind. The ADL, ACLU, and Southern Poverty Law Center are Jewish organizations noted both for their antichrist liberal views and the perverted sexual orientation of some of their leaders.

Jewish rabbis are frequently in the news, with charges of child molestation highlighted. Meanwhile, Jews virtually run the entire international porn industry. Even *Jerusalem World Report*, a prominent Jewish publication, has admitted that the kingpins of the "ecstasy" drug trade are Jews based in Israel.

Michael Eisner, a Jew and head of Disney Corporation, is actively pushing the gay agenda, as are most other Hollywood moguls—almost all of whom are Jewish. Sodomite Tom Schumaker was chosen by Disney to be executive producer of the kids movie, *The Lion King*. Homosexual singer Elton John was chosen to do the music score for the movie. Schumaker brags that Disney is actively recruiting homosexuals and that already, "There are a lot of gay people at every level" in the company.

Actress Sharon Stone said she relished her role in one film as a masculine lesbian lover.

Hollywood has long been much more gay than traditional America has known. The Christ-hating Jews that run the movie industry have always gotten their kicks from secretly pushing homosexual actors and actresses into leading roles as "romantic" leads. Katherine Hepburn was a lesbian deceptively dressed up as a lover of men like Spencer Tracy. Lesbian actress Marlene Dietrich pranced about in male suits with pants and yet the movie audiences were led to believe she was "All Woman." Male stars like comedian Danny Kaye and British actor Laurence Olivier were lovers, and comedian Jack Benny was queer as a three-dollar bill.

Pedophile Criminals Evade Punishment

In places like Hollywood and San Francisco, homosexual crime is rampant and never do the police intervene. Pedophile black singer Michael Jackson molests little boys and jokes are made—but no arrest. Little boys are molested at gay masquerade balls, and police look the other way. Corrupt Congressmen back in Washington know, but they are too busy running their own sex rings to care. Washington, D.C. is a place where homosexual masked men and women cavort in secret places—mansions, federal building auditoriums, military installations, and so forth.

Heavy metal rock music stars are predominantly homosexual. That's the reason for the leather garb, the satanic tattoos, the long hair, and the transvestite make-up and appearance. Perhaps the top rock idol of all time, Mick Jagger of the *Rolling Stones* group, is a sick bisexual. In her autobiography, Marianne Faithful wrote that, while in bed with her, Mick Jagger said, *"If Keith (a member of his band) were here right now, I'd lick him all over."*

And some Christian parents allow their kids to listen to the music of these addle-brained homo sickos!

Singer/entertainer Michael Jackson reportedly molested little boys, then paid their parents hush money. Police and law enforcement looked the other way.

Moral reprobate Mick Jagger, initiated into the Rock'n'Roll Hall of Fame, has talked openly about how much he enjoys performing sex acts on other men.

Serial Killers are Homosexuals

However, if you really want to know to what depths of degradation the homosexual lifestyle takes people, all you need to do is study the inner lives of the world's most dangerous criminals—serial killers. In his book, *Violence and Homosexuality*, Dr. Paul Cameron noted that the top serial killers were all homosexual:

> "The nexus between homosexuality and violence is notorious. We have motorcycle gangs, black leather boys and rough trade addicted to chains, torture, slaves, and sadism. Hitler rose on the backs of 'Storm Troopers' led from the top by a gang of homosexuals headed by Ernst Roehm."

According to the Associated Press, as reported in *Christian News* newspaper (July 23, 2001 p. 3), the seven worst serial killers in the U.S.A. were all homosexual deviates:

- Donald Harvey - 37 murders
- John Wayne Gacy - 33 murders
- Patrick Kearney - 32 murders
- Bruce Davis - 28 murders
- Dean Corll, Elmer Wayne Henley, and David Owen Brooks - 27 murders

The monstrous conduct of these homo killers is almost beyond belief. John Wayne Gacy, the sadistic torturer and raper of 33 boys, dressed up as a circus clown to attract victims. "A clown can get away with murder," Gacy once boasted.

Houston Chronicle

Mormons caught up in wave of pedophile accusations

Church deals with abuse cases without reporting them, critics say

Catholic priests are not the only religious leaders molesting children today, as evidenced by this newspaper headline in the *Houston Chronicle*.

Jeffrey Dahmer, who was a satanist and a cannibal, homosexually raped and killed 17 boys and young men after slipping "knockout" pills in their drinks. He attempted to keep some alive as sex zombies, but they, too, died from his fiendish brain operations.

Why is it the controlled mass media never tells America these savage serial murderers are always homosexuals? Why do CBS, ABC, NBC, and all the others cover-up and consistently paint gays as gentle, loving, caring, and compassionate humanitarians? Is it not because most of the TV and news executives and broadcasters are themselves homosexual, bisexual perverts and weirdos?

The case of homo serial killer Andrew Cunanan is interesting in that most of Cunanan's victims were themselves gay men. Among the five men he killed in a cross-country spree was wealthy fashion designer Gianni Versace. *Time* magazine (April 5, 1999) commented that Cunanan was "a gregarious, wildly clever mythomaniac and petty thief in the kinky gay netherworld of alcohol, drugs, prostitution, and sadomasochism." Andrew Cunanan's torrent of death ended in 1997 in Miami Beach with the demon-possessed homosexual taking his own life.

Reliable sources tell us that Andrew Cunanan's rage was triggered when he was horribly abused at a Chicago mansion during a homo-satanic ritual at a gay "masquerade ball." Cunanan, a handsome but confused young man in his 20s, had been used as a sexual gigolo by an inner circle of rich, gay Illuminati adepts—he was passed around and used up like a mildewed sack of potatoes. Gianni Versace, a billionaire who had singer Elton John as one of the frequent live-ins at his luxurious residence, was reputed to be a figure in this inner circle of Illuminist homosexuals.

Why are homosexuals almost uniformly so corrupt, evil, and wicked? The truth is that such men (and women) have spiritually been turned over to Satan. The scriptures declare that the grievous and damaging sin of homosexuality leads one straight to a reprobate mind. The world applauds and rewards the homosexual, but God brands this conduct as "vile," "unclean," "unnatural" *(Romans 1:24-32)* and an "abomination" *(Leviticus 18:22; Deuteronomy 23:17-18; I Kings 14:24).*

Then Arkansas Governor Bill Clinton and U.S. Senator Paul Tsongas (D-Mass) were Democratic presidential candidates in 1992. Like many other Democratic politicians, both were bisexual.

Thomas Jefferson—"Castrate Homosexuals!"

Thomas Jefferson, one of our nation's illustrious founders, was not, history records, a strong biblical Christian. Yet, as Governor of Virginia, in 1779 Jefferson introduced bills to punish homosexual sodomy with the penalty being banishment and castration. There is no record that anyone at the time accused Mr. Jefferson of bigotry or hatred. Americans back then were a great degree wiser than they are today.

Today, no politician, no king, no man admired by the public dares to declare the homosexual what he is: a "sinful reprobate." If they were to do so, their heads would, figuratively, be immediately lopped off by the media, and their careers and reputations destroyed. However, the biblical Christian has no option but to tell the truth—that homosexuality is a vile abomination, for God Almighty has declared it. And who among all the world's powerful and famous can reasonably criticize *His* commandments? Who is so foolish as to even attempt to annul *His* decision?

Zionist Secret Society Conducts Luciferian Rituals Deep in Cave Under City of Jerusalem

Masonic Jews Plot to Control World

Now the lid is blown off the forbidden, secret powderkeg of the Masonic Jews who run Israel and, by extension, the United States and the world. Unbeknownst to either the Israeli elite or to America's pro-Israel cabal in Washington, D.C., for over six years I have conducted an intensive investigation of Jewish Masonic influence. I have released three bombshell videos unmasking my grotesque discoveries in this area, *Masonic Lodge Over Jerusalem, Thunder Over Zion,* and *Cauldron of Abaddon.*

Illuministic Communism the Goal

The goal of the Jewish Masonic elite is to establish dictatorial Illuministic Communism and to enslave all of mankind under the thumb of a Jewish master race led by a world messiah who is to rule from Jerusalem.

An essential element in this grandiose plan is the Masonic plot to blow up and destroy Islam's golden-domed monument now sitting on the Temple Mount in Jerusalem, despised by Orthodox Jewish rabbis and the secularist Masonic Illuminists alike.

On the heap of its ruins, the Masons intend to build a Jewish Masonic temple where they and their satanically energized messiah shall worship and pay homage to the Egyptian double-headed eagle deity, Mammon-Ra, the god of money and prosperity *(Daniel 11:37-39).*

The Jews are beset with an unbridled ambition—a consuming desire to acquire global power and establish once and for all their long-delayed Zionist Kingdom on planet earth.

Freemasonry is Jewish Magic

One of the unheralded and least known facts about Freemasonry and the Masonic Lodge is its Jewish origins and nature. The religion of Judaism, based on the Babylonian Talmud, and the Jewish Cabala (or, Kabala), an alchemical system of magic and deviltry, form the basis for the Scottish Rite's 33 ritual degree ceremonies.

Thus, *The Jewish Tribune* of New York, on October 28, 1927, stated; *"Masonry is based on Judaism. Eliminate the teachings of Judaism from the Masonic Ritual and what is left?"*

The well known rabbi, Isaac Wise, was emphatic when he concluded: *"Freemasonry is a Jewish establishment, whose history, grades, official appointments, passwords, and explanations are Jewish from beginning to end."*

In the classic treatise of the Masons, *Morals and Dogma*, authored by the late Sovereign Grand Commander of the Scottish Rite, Albert Pike, we discover the revelation that the Jewish cabala is the very basis of Masonic practice and ritual and that the cabalistic "Theology of the Sephiroth" is at the root of all Masonic knowledge. This, admits Pike, is *"high magic,"* the *"Sacerdotal Art,"* and the *"Royal Art."*

The Jewish cabalistic nature of Masonry is demonstrated by the Lodge's odd view of evil. Pike writes: *"The true name of Satan, the Kabalists say, is that of Yahweh reversed; for Satan is not a black god, but the negation of God...For the Initiates, this is not a Person, but a Force, created for good, but which may serve for evil. It is the instrument of Liberty and Free Will."*

As for Lucifer, the alternate name for the Devil, the former Sovereign Grand Commander frankly admits that he, Lucifer, is a good angel, and a divine god worthy of our esteemed worship. *"Doubt it not!,"* Pike commands.

Intimating that the antichrist, the one whom the Bible warns shall have the unholy, combined triple number 666, is the one whom the Masons (Jews) await and shall recognize as their Messiah, Pike cryptically refers to the *"Triple Secret of the Great Work."*

Of course, he adds. *"Masonry...conceals its secrets from all except the Adepts and Sages, and uses false explanations and misinterpretations of its symbols to mislead."*

Having studied the dark recesses of occultism and satanism for nearly two decades and having produced and authored dozens of books and videos on this foul subject, I can assure you that Masonry, which, as Pike, Wise, and others assure us, is nothing more than pure Jewish cabalism, is rife with sorcery and witchcraft.

The idolatrous image of the double-headed eagle—shown here on the cover of Albert Pike's classic text, *Morals and Dogma*—is a much-treasured symbol of Jewish Masons. It represents the Babylonian god of money and forces, Mammon-Ra, as well as the Hegelian dialectical process practiced by the Jewish elite. This same symbol is the "Masonic Jewel" awarded high-level Masons initiated into the 33rd degree.

It is of great interest that in the book of *Revelation, chapter 18, verse 23*, we are told that the bloody and wicked, last days "Great City," *Mystery Babylon* (Jerusalem!—see *Revelation 11:8*), shall constitute a vast Empire of Evil that is to compass the whole earth. Its octopus-like tentacles spread via its control of money, banking, and commerce. Its rich men are secretly also sorcerers who merchandise both products and the souls of men: "*... for your merchants were the great men of the earth; for by your sorceries were all the nations deceived.*"

When we survey the traditions of the Masonic sect, we see sorcery and witchcraft in abundance. We view their unmitigated worship of Mammon, their god. We also see how the Masonic Lodge is pleased to welcome in its ranks not only Jews but Gentiles, even apostate Moslems, Buddhists, and men of every religion...and no religion. Yet, Jews remain "first among equals," to use George Orwell's phrase from *Animal Farm*. They are the "Princes of Masonry" (*Morals and Dogma*, p. 819).

"Masons of Peace"

In *The Jerusalem Post* (November 1994) was an advertisement placed by "The Grand Lodge of the State of Israel." The display ad was addressed "To the Masons of Peace," and listed: *"The Honorable Yitzak Rabin, Prime Minister of Israel," "His Majesty, King Hussein of Jordan,"* and *"The Honorable Bill Clinton, President of the United States."*

The ad closed with these fascinating words: *"With warm fraternal congratulations on the signing of the peace agreement between Israel and Jordan."* Signed—*Ephraim Fuchs, President of the Israel Order of Masons."*

In his remarks graveside at the funeral service in Israel for the assassinated Israeli Prime Minister Rabin, President Bill Clinton, wearing a Jewish yarmulke, a skull cap, referred to the slain Rabin as "Our elder brother." Of course, he was referring to the Brotherhood of the Lodge.

King Hussein, a Moslem, was also present to honor his fallen Masonic elder brother. Later, shortly after the death of this same Jordanian King Hussein, Israeli Prime Minister Ehud Barak traveled to Amman, Jordan, where he met with Hussein's successor, King Abdullah II. An *Associated Press* photo of Barak and the King clearly shows a Masonic handshake being exchanged.

The Grand Lodge of the State of Israel
of Ancient Free and Accepted Masons

To the Masons of Peace

The Honorable **Yitzhak Rabin,** Prime Minister of Israel
His Majesty **King Hussein** of Jordan
The Honorable **Bill Clinton,** President of the United States

With warm fraternal congratulations
on the signing of the peace agreement
between Israel and Jordan

Ephraim Fuchs
President of the Israel Order of Masons

This display ad was run in *The Jerusalem Post* newspaper in November, 1994.

Jordan's King Abdullah II gives his "brother," then Israeli Prime Minister Ehud Barak, a Masonic hand-shake at their meeting in Amman, Jordan, in August, 2000.

Masons: Masters of Israel and the World

The rise of Masons to political power in Israel dates back to 1948 and to Israel's founding as a modern-day nation. David Ben-Gurion, its first Prime Minister, was both a Mason and an avowed Marxist-Leninist and Communist. Since that time, every single Prime Minister has been a high-level Mason, including Golda Meier, who was a member of the women's organization, the Co-Masons.

In 1993 in Jerusalem, a celebration of political Masons was held. According to the respected Italian newspaper *La Republica* (October 1993), in an article entitled, "Israel: There is a Pact Between Politicians and Masons," the ceremony was attended by the Mayor of Jerusalem, Teddy Kollek, as well as by the Ashkenazi Chief Rabbi, Israel Meier Lau. Kollek told the gathered Masons, *"You do a great honor to Jerusalem. This is natural, considering that King Solomon was the great builder of the temple, which is at the roots of the Masonic idea, and that his workmen were the first Masons."*

At that same ceremony, sponsored by the "Grand Lodge of the State of Israel," Rabbi Lau stated that, *"The principles of Freemasonry are all contained in the Book of Books of the Jewish people."*

It is presumed that Rabbi Lau was referring to the pornographic and racist Jewish (Babylonian) Talmud, which is, in fact, their chief law book and guide for living. I have a picture of this same Chief Rabbi, Meier Lau, giving a cabalistic Masonic hand signal to Egyptian President Hosni Mubarak, at a meeting in Cairo, Egypt, in 1998.

Former Prime Minister Benjamin Netanyahu has publicly stated (see the Israeli publication *Shishi*, Spring 1994) that he was initiated into the Masonic Lodge while in the United States. The *La Republica* newspaper stated that Prime Minister Yitzak Rabin was active in Masonry and estimated there are 4,000 Israeli Freemasons, divided into 76 lodges. Most Israeli judges and religious figures are Masons. Rothschild-supported Hebrew University in Israel has erected an Egyptian obelisk, symbol of Freemasonry, in its courtyard, and inside the new Israeli Supreme Court building is a law library architecturally designed in the shape of an Egyptian pyramid.

The B'nai B'rith Lodge of New York is affiliated with Israel's lodges and so is the hate-mongering ADL and ACLU, not to mention almost every top investment magnate on Wall Street in New York. Truly, the Holy Bible is proven true in its prophecy of great "merchants" who, in the last days, deceive the world through their commercial trade *and* their *sorcery*.

The Planned Jewish "Temple of all Religions"

In my video, *Masonic Lodge Over Jerusalem*, I reveal the secret rituals conducted by Jewish Masons deep in a cave under the city of Jerusalem. I also expose the sordid plot of these men to utterly destroy and remove from the Temple mount both the Islamic Mosque of Omar and the Golden-domed structure known as the "Dome of the Rock." These two Islamic religious edifices will be brought down by Israeli defense forces—by missiles, sapper bombs, laser bursts, or other means. Naturally, this atrocity will be done in the chaotic midst of an ongoing war, and the disaster will be scandalously blamed on the Arabs. It will be said that an errant Arab missile or bomb is responsible.

Then shall come a prophesied *(II Thes. 2)* Masonic Temple of All Religions to be built on the very spot from where the debris and ashes of the Moslem structures were bulldozed off and cleared.

Through its golden portals shall pass the New Zionist Messiah, King of Planet Earth. Before its evil altar he shall announce to all the world, via television, that their Universal Savior has finally come, a man knowledgeable of "the Holy Kabbalah, the exclusive heritage of the people of Israel" (*Morals and Dogma*, page 839).

The Jews to Become Christ and God Collectively

The Zionist Messiah will confide that it is God's Chosen People, the Jews, who collectively are "Christ." According to the Kabbala and the Zohar, the Jews created "God" in their image and, in turn, this "God" of the Jews is the reflected image of divine man (the Jews) himself, for Jews are said to be "partakers of the *Divine Nature*."

This, then, is the ages-old, two-fold goal and final secret mystery of the Masons: First, through the worship of Mammon-Ra, god of forces (Daniel 11:39) and of money and riches, is to come the synthesis of all religions, superintended by a Jewish Messiah. Then will come *a Jewish Utopia: World Government, of the Jews, by the Jews, and for the Jews, forever and ever. Amen.*

A Resounding Surprise

But regardless of their plots and their Grand Scheme, the Lord of Hosts, our Savior Jesus Christ, true God of the Universe, has a resounding surprise in store for these Masonic criminals. The scriptures describe these evil men as *"natural brute beasts made to be taken and destroyed" (II Peter 2:12)*. Their fate is clear. The scriptures say their plots shall utterly fail, their Empire shall be dissolved, their covenant and agreement with hell disannulled, and they "shall utterly perish in their own corruption."

Oh, what a glorious hour that shall be when an angel from heaven cries mightily with a strong voice, saying, *"Babylon the Great is fallen, is fallen and is become the habitation of devils, and the hold of every foul spirit, and a cage of every unclean and hateful bird...For in one hour so great riches is come to nought..." (Revelation 18: 2,17)*

UFOs, Aliens, Extraterrestrials, and Space

Bible Prophecy and the Astonishing Truth About UFOs and Alien Abductions

Project Abaddon

UFOs—is there a colossal conspiracy and cover up? The Pentagon, the CIA, and the FBI refuse to divulge Top Secret documents about UFO investigations. Why? For years we have been bombarded with sensational reports of mysterious UFO sightings and alarming alien abductions. Hundreds of documented and reliable UFO incidents are on record, being reported by experienced U.S. Air Force and commercial airline pilots, NASA astronauts, engineers, scientists, even a former president of the United States.

Unquestionably, something is going on—something both ominous and frightening. Something which—very, very soon—may totally and dramatically change our lives. It might even end this world as we know it. That is why it is important that we discover now the astonishing truth about the greatest of all puzzles and deceptions—the manipulation of mankind by the dark forces behind the invasion of Unidentified Flying Objects (UFOs)!

World Unity and UFOs

"I often wonder how quickly the peoples of the world would unite if we were threatened by an alien invasion," pondered (then) President Ronald Reagan in a major speech to the United Nations General Assembly. How eye-opening that the President of the United States would make such a comment to representatives of the 176 nations comprising this globalist organization.

President Reagan is not the only world leader to voice such a concern. Russia's communist party chief Mikhail Gorbachev stated much the same thing. What if hostile UFO aliens were to attack mankind on a mission to conquer and destroy? Would mankind unite to stave off defeat by a dreaded, common foe? Humanity was, of course, once united in a vain attempt to build the Tower of Babel. But God thwarted that evil effort. Could a UFO threat fuel yet another attempt to unite all men and nations?

The Planned Invasion is Now in Progress

In fact, as I demonstrate in my investigative audiotape report, *Project Abaddon*, there is planned an invasion of this planet by evil aliens and "extraterrestrials" bent on our destruction. Indeed, this invasion and attack has been proceeding now for many years—at least since 1947. In recent years, the scope and breadth of the UFO assault has expanded by exponential proportions. Thus, we are literally plagued today with UFO sightings, including reported cases of alien abduction and vile experimentation on human beings in the chambers of mysterious spacecraft.

Believable Reports and Questionable Theories

Many influential and fully believable authorities claim to have observed UFOs.

General Nathan Twining, respected, former Chief of Staff of the U.S. Air Force, once stated: "The UFO phenomenon is something real and not imaginary or fictitious."

Former President Jimmy Carter testified to seeing what he believes was a UFO. "It seemed to move toward us," the President recalled, "then return, then depart. It was bluish, reddish, and luminous."

Who's behind the UFO phenomenon? Some say that UFO alien beings are for real, that they are physical entities from another planet or from a nearby star system. They claim further that the government is covering up their existence. Some say that the U.S. government is even cooperating with interplanetary, UFO alien civilizations, *allowing* citizens to be kidnapped, to have genetic experimentation conducted on their human bodies, etc.

These theorists suggest that when President Ronald Reagan gave his now famous speech at the UN in which he mentioned a "what if" situation in the event UFOs were to launch an invasion against the planet, he was revealing an actual, future event that is to occur. A carefully contrived and stage-managed event. This, they say, is to be a dramatic, heart-stopping episode in which UFOs will be observed *en masse* in our skies, followed by our government leaders announcing that, to meet the demands of the superior, technologically advanced UFO forces, they, our leaders, have agreed to establish the New World Order, including a World Government.

Following the "surrender" to the UFOs, all the world's religions would promptly be merged, and all national borders erased. Global unity, as in Babylon, would finally be established. Naturally, the conspiring UFO commanders and Earth leaders would tell us that this is for our own good—that the UFO aliens simply are forcing us to do what is in our own self interest.

My own extensive research and investigation only partially confirms and corroborates these theories. However, it is a fact that the U.S. government knows much more than it is revealing to us about UFOs. The CIA, the FBI, and other government spy and police agencies, under the cloak of a "Top Secret" security classification, refuse to divulge what we, as citizens, have the right to know about the UFO visitors.

Secret CIA Projects

We are also not being fully informed about what our own government has been doing. We are kept in the dark about secret CIA scientific projects, for example, which apparently are related to the UFO phenomenon. I refer here to the CIA's highly classified *MK-Ultra* project, which involves the training and indoctrination of selected, multiple-personality assassins.

These are not only people whose minds are programmed to kill, but also include a number of human subjects who, under the influence of chemical agents administered by the CIA and after repeated torture and hypnotic brainwashing sessions, are given selective, implanted "memories"—memories which include intense recall of UFO sightings and abduction experiences.

Fantastic reports are coming out of South Texas, Mexico, and Latin America about "La Chupacabra," The Goatsucker, a beast that's been attacking livestock and drinking their blood. Many believe the beast is a UFO alien-human experiment gone wrong.

It can also be proven that CIA medical doctors employed by the U.S. government are implanting in the brains and ears of selected subjects high technology devices and, possibly, microchips. Reportedly, such devices—directly or indirectly—stimulate brain centers, fostering mental imagery of UFOs.

Conclusions: The Relevance of Bible Prophecy

What are my conclusions about UFOs? As I explain in

great detail in my CDs and audiotapes, I am convinced that mankind is now confronted with a combination of human connivery and plotting, and satanic, otherworldly mischief. Bible prophecy forewarned us of this very thing.

It is interesting and informative that so many UFO reports describe encounters with figures from ancient Babylon, such as the goddesses Ishtar and Ashtar. In *Communion*, his #1 *New York Times* bestselling book, Whitley Streiber describes, for example, how he was abducted by a triangle-shaped, crystal-like UFO spacecraft. While on board, he was hypnotically and physically restrained and forced to participate in a sacred sexual ritual which, he believes, was some kind of mystical, religious initiation.

Streiber further reports that the female alien who seduced him appeared to be Ishtar, the ancient, Babylonian Mother Goddess, also called Ashtar. Amazingly, the Bible, in Revelation 17, prophesies that a world-wide religious system of evil deception will take shape in the last days, to be known as "Mystery, Babylon the Great, The Mother of Harlots."

Bible prophecy thus has much to offer us in our quest to understand why the UFOs are here and why their occupants are so keenly interested in the human population. What we discover is that, just as God's Word explains, Satan has always operated on two fronts simultaneously—through human agents but also through the spiritually powerful, supernatural realm. That is why I have entitled my CD and audiotape reports *Project Abaddon*, because the Bible reveals, in *Revelation 9*, that in the last days a special type of demon power will be unleashed on the earth. This power will involve the assault on human beings by what appears to be spacecraft or vehicles, with "wings" and with "breastplates of iron."

The wicked entities who control these craft, the Bible says, use them to *hurt and torment* the helpless people of planet earth. But more frightening than this is the *identity* of the *leader* of these hostile and cruel, non-human entities. He is the dark angel whose realm is the "bottomless pit." God's Word reveals that he is the one whose "name in the Hebrew tongue is *Abaddon*, but in the Greek tongue hath his name *Apollyon*." You and I, as Christians, know him by yet another name: *Satan*, or *Lucifer*.

The Apostle Paul identified the evil, malicious angel, Lucifer, as "prince of the power of the air." How appropriate a title for the one who, today, works with the aid of both human conspirators and demon spirits to deceive through the magical and black imagery of UFOs and aliens!

No wonder the Bible warns us, "Be sober, be vigilant; because your adversary the devil, as a roaring lion, walketh about, seeking whom he may devour."

A Satanic Failure, A Godly Triumph

But the UFO plot of Satan and his agents will eventually fail. Satan's doom is sealed, for God was first victorious eons ago, when the devil foolishly rebelled and he and his dark angels were cast down in disgrace from God's presence. As *Revelation 22:12,16* majestically puts it, Jesus is coming again to deal Satan the final, eternally condemning blow and to reward His saints who persevere against the tricks and deceptions of the devil: *"And, behold, I come quickly; and my reward is with me, to give every man according as his work shall be . . . I Jesus have sent mine angel to testify unto you these things in the churches. I am the root and the offspring of David, and the bright and morning star."*

All who believe and trust in Christ have nothing to fear from either UFO aliens or from government co-conspirators. Quite the opposite—we who know Christ as Lord are the overcomers, forever and ever. Amen.

Strange Mysteries, Oddities, and Monstrosities of the U.S. Space Program

Leviathan in Space

Q*uestion*: Is the devil orchestrating the U.S. space program? *Power of Prophecy* Ministries is releasing its newest video (and DVD disk) this month which presents a mountain of evidence indicating that the answer to this provocative question just might be...*yes!*

We know, of course, that the Holy Bible identifies Satan, or Lucifer, as the false deity worshipped by the ancients (and by many today) as the "star god" who fights against God's people from the heavenlies. The Apostle Paul, therefore, accurately identified Lucifer as *"the prince of the power of the air."* In *Isaiah 14:12-15* we find the judgement of Lucifer, the fallen angel, who arrogantly boasted that he would someday defeat and take the place of the Most High God:

> *"For thou hast said in thine heart, I will ascend into heaven, I will exalt my throne above the stars of God: I will sit also upon the mount of the congregation, in the sides of the north:*
>
> *I will ascend above the heights of the clouds; I will be like the most High.*
>
> *Yet thou shalt be brought down to hell, to the sides of the pit."*

The Real Space Race

We used to think that the Soviet Empire and the United States were competitors in a great space race. But, in fact, the real space race was the one going on out of human sight, in the realm and dimension from which Lucifer continues to wage futile warfare against God, His holy angels, and His people here on earth.

The amazing events involving our U.S. space program chronicled in *Leviathan in Space* demonstrate just how much the devil so desperately wants to win this space race, this war against God's Kingdom. NASA's organization and agenda are horribly permeated with Luciferian artifacts and activities. We point, for example, to striking evidence of Masonic occultism and to magician astronauts. Also, we, regrettably, must bring to light the dark history of NASA's chief founders.

Jack Parsons, genius inventor of solid fuels used for spacecraft, was high priest of the O.T.O., a satanic church. NASA honored Parsons by naming a crater after him on the dark side of the moon.

The power of NASA's occultic origins is seen in the life of John ("Jack") Parsons, the scientist who helped found JPL Labs in Pasadena, California, and the genius who invented the solid fuel technology that

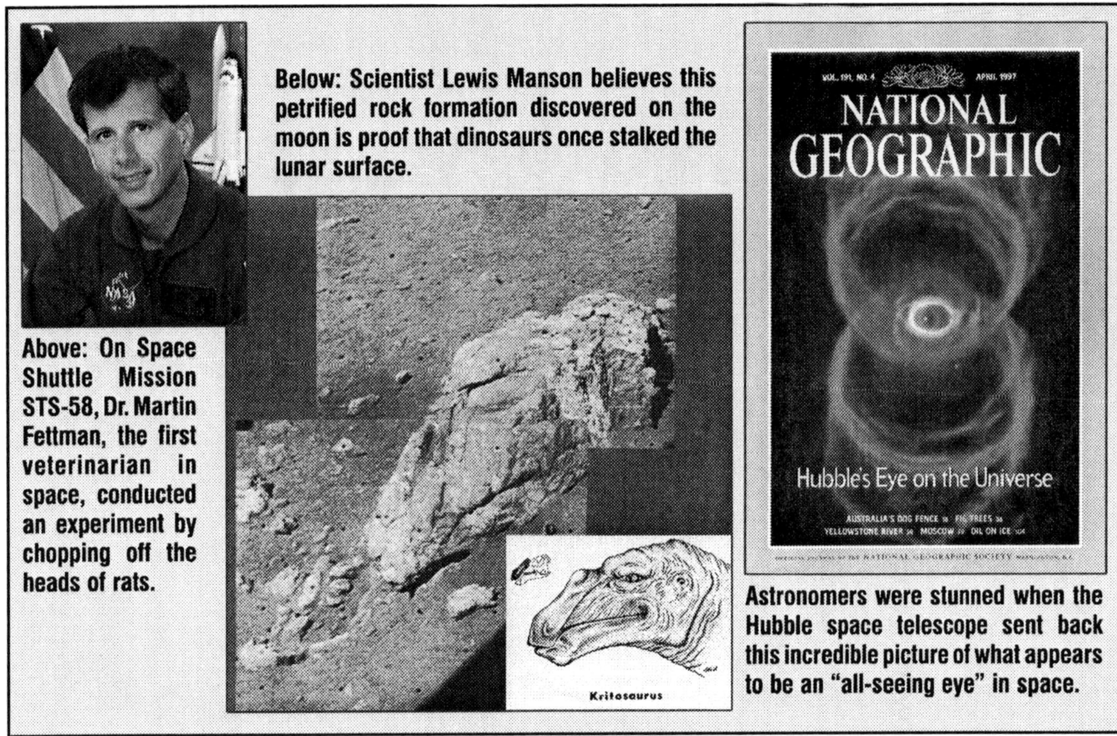

Below: Scientist Lewis Manson believes this petrified rock formation discovered on the moon is proof that dinosaurs once stalked the lunar surface.

Above: On Space Shuttle Mission STS-58, Dr. Martin Fettman, the first veterinarian in space, conducted an experiment by chopping off the heads of rats.

Astronomers were stunned when the Hubble space telescope sent back this incredible picture of what appears to be an "all-seeing eye" in space.

made the space shots possible. The memory of Parsons is so well regarded by NASA that the agency has named a lunar area after him. Yet, as proven in a revealing book, *Sex and Rockets: The Occult World of Jack Parsons,* Parsons is outed as a sexual pervert who headed the American branch of satanist Aleister Crowley's notorious secret society, the O.T.O.

The Serpent's Seed, Nazis, and "Strong Powers"

On Halloween night, 1968, Jack Parsons and a woman disciple conducted a black magic satanic sex ritual called *"Babalon working"* in a vain attempt to invoke the Antichrist and produce a "man-child," a serpent seed offspring. Shortly afterward, Parsons was killed in what was claimed to be an accidental explosion in his home laboratory. The FBI quickly moved in and mysteriously seized all his records and notes.

However, perhaps the most famous and respected of NASA's space scientists was the late Werner von Braun. Von Braun had been a top leader in Adolf Hitler's Nazi rocket program and was brought to the U.S. after World War II. Possibly, Dr. Von Braun recognized the powers of hell that energized the space race. He is quoted once as ominously warning, "We find ourselves faced by strong powers whose base of operations is at present unknown to us."

The Masonic Lodge and Magical Rituals

My video, *Leviathan In Space*, also documents an extensive Freemasonry influence and exposes various magical rituals connected to NASA operations. Take occult numerology, for example. Is it strange to you that the *planned* launch of Apollo 13—note the supernatural number of witchcraft, 13—was set for exactly 13:13 military time on April 11th? Apollo, of course, is a name of the pagan sun god. The Bible, in *Revelation 9:11*, identifies *Apollyon* (Apollo + On, another name of the chief Egyptian god) as the devil.

In the year 2000, the Scottish Rite, the largest masonic sect, formally established Tranquility Lodge #2000, a Masonic Lodge, on the moon.

Oddities and Weirdness in Space

Over and over, *Leviathan in Space* documents oddities and weirdness pointing to Satan having a field day in plotting out NASA's space activities. Examples include:

- The strange face of a beast discovered in space by the Hubble space telescope.
- The "Chandra" X-ray laboratory telescope (Chandra is Hebrew for "star").
- The stunning image of an all-seeing eye sent back from space by a NASA telescope. *National Geographic* magazine called it *"The Eye On The Universe."*
- What appear to be frightening creatures seen in space.
- Spiders, bees, and rats sent aloft in space on NASA craft. Astonishing is the incredible NASA report that a number of the rats were beheaded in space by an astronaut who used a specially built *miniature guillotine* to off the hapless critters' heads!
- Actual film footage of what appear to be UFOs and strange lights active around NASA spacecraft.

Houston Chronicle

Challenger explodes

Space shuttle falls into ocean; crew's fate uncertain

Some allege that the explosions of the Challenger and other spacecraft were deliberate plots, even occult sacrifices.

Dinosaurs On the Moon?

And there is more I've discovered in this space theater of the bizarre. For example, the video examines mind-boggling fossil evidence of dinosaurs who once roamed the moon's surface.

Then there are the reports of the murder of some astronauts, especially one astronaut who had threatened to blow the whistle on NASA's ineptness and treachery. Is there also an ongoing coverup of the Challenger and Columbia space shuttle blow-ups and destruction?

Hoaxes and Scams

Finally, in the video I discuss the claims by some very intelligent researchers that man never went to the moon—that it was all a hoax! Some even call it *"Moongate."* Did astronauts Buzz Aldrin (33rd degree Mason) and Neil Armstrong in 1969 *really* walk on the lunar surface, or was it all a giant, criminal scam—perhaps the greatest scam of all time?

In my fascinating video, I mention also the provocative Hollywood movie, *Capricorn One*. This movie's plot depicted a staged spaceshot hoax with astronauts being forced to cooperate or be killed. Oddly enough, actor O.J. Simpson played the starring role of an astronaut in the movie. *Capricorn* just happens to be the astrological sign of the horned goat (Satan?) in the Zodiac.

Dark Red Star on a Collision Course with Earth

Planet X

"But in those days, after that tribulation, the sun shall be darkened, and the moon shall not give her light. And the stars of heaven shall fall, and the powers that are in heaven shall be shaken. And then shall they see the son of man coming in the clouds with great power and glory."

—*Mark 13:24-26*

A catastrophe ominously looms on the horizon. Planet X, a huge planetary body, or star, is headed our way. Described as a great "Red Star," the path of this approaching, heavenly object puts it on a potential, head-to-head collision course with our planet, Earth.

If you haven't heretofore heard of the mysterious and deadly Planet X—so-called because it is said to be a newly discovered yet ancient *tenth* planet for our solar system—believe me, you will eventually .

Smashing Into Earth

Doomsayers say it is only a matter of time before a star, like Planet X, or a meteor, or other wandering object smashes into Earth's orbit. One book published predicts Planet X will blindside the Earth soon, causing untold chaos, with the Earth literally tilting on its axis. The ensuing upheaval will spawn horrific hurricanes and unparalleled tornadoes, floods, and volcanic blowouts, and leave other planetary calamities in its wake.

Many pseudo-astronomers and perennial astronomical doomsayers point to Zechariah Sitchin's works in which the British scientist/author alleges that a planet named *"Nibiru,"* which travels an orbit from the other side of Pluto to earth on a 3,600 year cycle, causes manifold disasters each time it makes a pass. They say this is now the time for Nibiru to return.

Some cite other names for Planet X, including *"Wormwood."* This is prophetic since the Holy Bible does, in fact, prophesy catastrophic earth changes to occur due to a star by this name:

And the third angel sounded, and there fell a great star from heaven, burning as it were a lamp...And the name of the star is called Wormwood...and many men died..." (Revelation 8:10-11)

Some maintain the shattering specter will occur in the fateful year 2012 (the last year on the Mayan calendar), or even 2078. Others claim it could be thousands or even millions of years before the tenth planet orbits near Earth once again.

Surprisingly, a number of professional astronomers at the world's top observatories share the

The myths of the pagan religions of Sumeria, Babylon, and Egypt often told of lizard-like, reptilian ancient astronauts visiting earth, mating with women, and worshipped by ancient mankind as powerful gods and goddesses. Now, many New Age teachers and occultists are gladfully and expectantly proclaiming the soon return of these strange hybrid "dieties."

view that there is a tenth planet out in space. Scientific reports conclude that the gravitational pull of this tenth planet, a planet not now observable by most telescopes, is already disturbing the heavens and causing what the astronomers call "perturbation."

Planet X and The Secret Doctrine

Significantly, Freemasonry and the occult world have long awaited the arrival of Planet X. The occultists, in their Secret Doctrine, teach that the ancients once worshipped gods and deities, mighty men of renown, who came to Earth from the heavens, from a planet star called *Sirius*.

The Egyptians knew this star, Sirius, as Dogon, the "Dog Star" and worshipped it under its guise as Anubis, the jackal-headed god. From its name were also derived the names of the chief deities of the Egyptian religion and culture, Osiris (Lord of the underworld) and Isis (the star goddess).

Noah and The Giants

Amazingly, the Holy Bible, in *Genesis 6*, describes an early time in the days of Noah when these star gods—in reality, Satan and the fallen angels, the Nephilim—committed the abomination of mating with the daughters of men, producing hideous hybrid. These supernatural offspring the Bible calls "giants." It was because of the unimaginable wickedness and sin of these hybrid man/beast "giants" that God decided to cause a flood to overflow the earth and destroy them all. Only Noah, whose blood and DNA were unpolluted, and his family survived the great flood.

Yet, for whatever reason, God permitted a small number of the Nephilim to appear again years after the Noahic flood, and in Deuteronomy these monstrous, half-human creatures are called the Anakim, or Rephaim (literally—the *"Congregation of the Dead!"*)

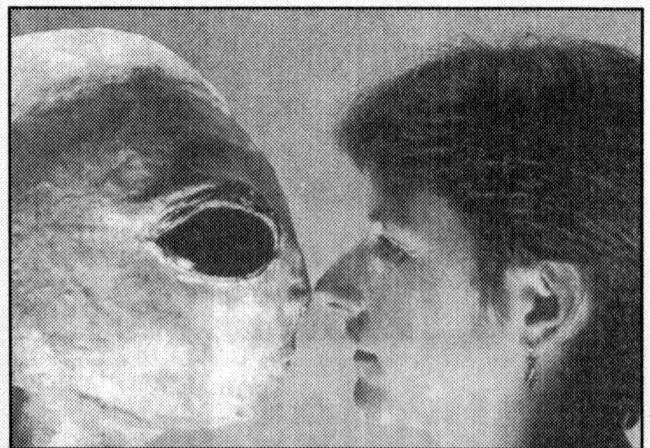

Increasingly, we are being inundated with tales and accounts of UFO abductions, alleging that men and women are being taken into spacecraft and sexually used to create human/extraterrestrial hybrid beings. Does this have some connection to the *Genesis, Chapter 6* account?

What's more, the Scriptures prophesy the return of these satanic mighty men, these evil "giants," in the last days. Yet, not as gods, but as devils! In *Matthew 24:37-39*, Jesus warned that as it was in the days of Noah, so shall it be when Christ comes once again. Moreover, the return out of the abyss of these "stars" fallen from heaven shall be accompanied by incredible, mind-boggling signs in the heavens. As for Earth, the prophet Isaiah prophesied that mountains shall fall down and the planet will *"reel to and fro like a drunkard."*

Worse, even as one tragedy after another exacts its bloody toll on humanity, the Bible tells of the powerful beings who shall be unleashed from the bottomless pit and come abroad to torment men and women. Described with frightening impact in *Revelation 9*, these entities have a Star, or "King," over them, "which is the angel of the bottomless pit." Indeed, *Satan* himself shall be the leader of these "fallen ones."

Now, as we near that ominous, prophesied Last Day signaling our Lord's coming, false religions such as Mormonism and Scientology, and Illuministic secret societies such as Freemasonry, the O.T.O., The Priory of Sion, and the Order of the Solar Temple, loudly and cheerfully are proclaiming the return of their star gods, to accompany the approach of the Sirian-related, star planet Nibiru, more better known as Planet X.

Extraterrestrials Among Us—The Dark Truth

This, then, is the great Hidden Secret behind the heralded coming again of Planet X and its star gods and goddesses.

The movie moguls are telling us that interplanetary creators of humankind, our saviors and overlords, are soon to descend. As depicted in a score of UFO accounts, sci-fi stories, and blockbuster movies such as *ET—The Extraterrestrial, Close Encounters of the Third Kind, Star Wars*, the *Jedi* sagas, and so many more, these supernatural beings love us and wish to guide us peacefully into a New Age of intergalactic harmony.

This teaching is at the very core of the Secret Doctrine of Helena Blavatsky's *Theosophy*, of L. Ron Hubbard's *Scientology*, and of Freemasonry's *Sirius* mystery teachings. But as I show on my startling video, the events surrounding the return of *Planet X—The Dark Red Star on a Collision Course with Earth*, are much, much more unsettling than what the expectant world has been duped into accepting as fact.

The ancient and hideously marred Secret Doctrine taught by the occult world and by Freemasonry and other satanic sects tells of the return of supernatural "giants" from outer space accompanying the cyclical return of the mysterious Planet X.

The truth, my friends, isn't *"out there somewhere,"* as they proclaim on the popular TV series, *The X-Files*. It's found only in the prophetic pages of the Holy Bible. Isn't it time therefore, that Christians asked, what does *God* have to say about the tumultuous coming of Planet X?

Magic, Alchemy, and the Illuminati Conquest of Outer Space

"The Eagle Has Landed"

"Though thou exalt thyself as the eagle, and though thou set thy nest among the stars, thence will I bring thee down, saith the Lord."

— *Obadiah 4*

"Hoodwink (definition)… the secrecy, silence, and darkness in which the mysteries of our masonic art should be preserved from the unhallowed gaze of the profane."

— Dr. Albert Mackey 33°
Encyclopedia of Freemasonry

"Magnificent Achievement," blared the headline in the *Chicago Tribune* newspaper. "Bravo!," trumpeted *The London Guardian.*

The year was 1969. In what appeared to most eyes as the most monumental and technologically incredible feat in human history, man had walked on the moon. Blasting from earth into space, NASA's *Apollo 11* craft, carrying aloft three heroic astronauts, sat down on the moon's dusty surface. A breathless and ecstatic audience numbering in the billions were glued to their TV sets and radios. Then, they heard those historic words from the astronauts, "THE EAGLE HAS LANDED!"

Shortly thereafter, these same throngs of well-wishers saw Commander Neil Armstrong step out into the lunar environment and state the historic phrase, "One small step for man. One giant leap for mankind."

A Clarion Call to Global Unity

A fitting and politically correct epitaph to a remarkable journey, was it not? A clarion call to global unity. No acknowledgement to the United States of America, the great nation that made it all possible. No patriotic mention of the military veterans who, over the centuries, fought and died to keep our nation strong and free. No thanks was given to suffering taxpayers whose dollars had paid for the nonessential, but propagandist, moon shot. And certainly, no honor was given, nor homage paid, to Jesus Christ, by whose love, ransom and sacrifice on the cross the whole world has been set free.

No, the Illuminati script called only for a nebulous acclaim for the human collective, of the "giant leap for mankind."

A Strange Ritual and Secret Ceremony

True, a small replica of our proud U.S. flag was dutifully carted off the Eagle lander and posted for all to see. But, then, a strange ritual of an entirely different sort, of a dark and ominous character, took place at Tranquillity Base on the moon. It was not beamed to the earth via television, for this ritual was carefully crafted beforehand as a secret ceremony, to be hidden and seen only by the eyes of the adepts of the Illuminati and its Masonic fraternity.

Astronaut Edwin "Buzz" Aldrin took this Masonic flag to the moon on Apollo 11 in 1969 and conducted a secret ritual.

CURRENT INTEREST

Apollo II Display

On the 25th anniversary of man's first walk on the lunar surface and man's second walk by Col. Edwin E. "Buzz" Aldrin, Jr., 33°, Valley of Los Angeles, California, another Scottish Rite Freemason close to this historic event visited the House of the Temple to view a featured display dedicated to Apollo 11 and the first moon landing. Ill.·. Kenneth S. Kleinknecht, 33°, Manager for the Command and Service Modules for the Apollo Space Program in 1969 and a Brother of Sov.·. Gr.·. Cmdr.·. C. Fred Kleinknecht, 33°, was pleased to view a timely display of Apollo 11 artifacts. Arranged by the newly appointed Museum Curator and Collections Manager of The Supreme Council, 33°, Kimberly K. Sprow, the display is located in the Atrium of the House of the Temple and consists of original photos and documents from the Apollo 11 mission.

Included is a Scottish Rite flag sewn by Inge Baum, Librarian of The Supreme Council, 33°, at the time of the moon landing. The flag was carried by astronaut and Brother Aldrin, then a 32° Scottish Rite Mason, Valley of Houston, Texas, during his historic moonwalk.

The featured display is typical of the timely and changing exhibits which make repeated visits to the House of the Temple always interesting and informative.

On July 20, 1994, the 25th anniversary of the Apollo 11 moon landing, Ill.·. Kenneth S. Kleinknecht, 33°, Manager for the Command and Service Modules for the Apollo Space Program in 1969, visited a featured display of Apollo 11 artifacts in the House of the Temple in Washington, DC.

SCOTTISH RITE JOURNAL OCTOBER 1994 37

Right: This page 37 from *Scottish Rite Journal* (October 1994), the official publication of the Masonic Lodge, shows Kenneth Kleinknecht, 33°, NASA's Apollo Program Manager, behind a featured display of Apollo 11 artifacts. The accompanying article discusses the Scottish Rite flag carried by Masonic astronaut "Buzz" Aldrin to the moon.

Astronaut Neil Armstrong carefully took out his Masonic apron and held it up for the cameras over his space suit as if to cover his genitals area—the power center, or dynamo, of Luciferian energy in Masonic ritual. Today, a photograph of Armstrong holding his occultic apron hangs on a wall at the House of the Temple, the sanctuary of the Scottish Rite, in Washington, D.C.

Next, brother Edwin "Buzz" Aldrin, at the time a 32° Masonic initiate, planted on the moon's surface the *real flag* intended for honor, the flag the Apollo 11 had carried in its storage compartment, the flag with the Scottish Rite's emblem of deep and mysterious spirituality, the double-headed eagle.

The Phoenix Bird—The Doubleheaded Eagle

This, then, was the esoteric, but hidden and encoded meaning of the name "Eagle" for the lander. The cabalistic ritual script called for elevated man, initiated god-man, to "ride" the black phoenix bird, the "Eagle," to glory, upward toward the sun. God-man was to make his nest among the stars which decorate the black-garbed night, amidst the day-time canopy of the blue sky (the blue lodge).

And so, following their occultly prescribed pagan psychodrama ritual to the letter, the astronauts claimed the moon for their Sovereign, whom they, the Masons, majestically address as *The Great Architect of the Universe,* known more simply as *The Builder*.

Just as Christopher Columbus, Hernando DeSoto, Ferdinand Magellan and all the great explorers had planted their flag and had claimed the land and territory they had discovered to be the legal possession of their respective monarch and country, the astronauts declared the celestial body of the moon to be the property of their own Noble and of his fiefdom. In their warped minds, the moon belongs to Lucifer, with title held by his high servant and potentate, the Sovereign Grand Commander, Supreme Mother Council, 33°.

NASA Manager a Mason

Meanwhile, back on earth, overseeing all, was Mr. Kenneth S. Kleinknecht, Manager for the Apollo Space Program. Mr. Kleinknecht, now retired, is a 33rd degree Mason and, not coincidentally, is the brother of C. Fred Kleinknecht, the current Sovereign Grand Commander and titular head of all Scottish Rite Masons throughout the world.

The incredible and unheralded saga of Apollo 11, the moonwalk by the astronauts, their bizarre occult ritual, and the ownership of the Moon by the Masonic Order, are among the many mind-boggling revelations found in my two-hour video, *"The Eagle has Landed!"—Magic, Alchemy, and The Illuminati Conquest of Outer Space.*

Perhaps the most astonishing discovery revealed in this video is the fact that NASA's space program has from the start been founded on the principles of Masonic alchemy and the magic of the mystery religions of the ancients. The prophet Daniel told us that the last day's world ruler, the antichrist king, would be mighty, *"And through his policy also he shall cause craft to prosper..." Craft, as in witchcraft!*

Nazis, Magic and Witchcraft

The earliest beginnings of the U.S. space program involved the secretive OSS/CIA project, *Operation Paperclip*, in which Nazi rocket scientists like Werner Von Braun were brought from war-torn Germany to America and given responsibility for development of space vehicles. The Freemasons were then put in charge of the newly created space agency, and magic and witchcraft were integrated and wedded with the newest advances in technology.

This is the official logo, or emblem, of the tragic Space Shuttle Columbia mission during which seven astronauts recently lost their lives. It contains a number of esoteric symbols and messages, including representations of a phallic obelisk passing through a feminine circle shooting a star upward toward the heavens. Also, note the geographic nations map overseen by a sun symbol.

Virtually everything that NASA does is permeated with magic and alchemy. Moreover, the real purpose of NASA is contained in another matrix, hidden from the public at large. This process involves the creation of Satanic ritual magic enabling the Illuminati elite to acquire and accumulate power even as the mind-controlled and manipulated masses are pushed into ever increasing states of altered consciousness.

As occultist Antero Alli comments in his book, *All Rites Reversed*, *"The most mysterious and fascinating areas of ritual work involve those triggering mechanisms producing altered states of consciousness."*

One is reminded also of the statement by Professor John Wu of Auburn University, *"The truth is to know that everything is an illusion."*

Theater and Hoodwink

In essence, the widely publicized successful flights and missions—and even the staggering tragedies such as the fate of the crews of the ill-fated *Challenger* and *Columbia* space shuttles—are masterfully scripted theatrical productions. It is all *Grand Theater*, hoodwink, in which some rather harmless rites are made public to deceive and charm the profane masses; while others, more sublime and evil, are concealed and known only to the elite.

Dr. Robert Anton Wilson, a well-known but unfortunately rabid anti-Christian writer on occult magic and conspiracy, touches on this when he wryly remarks, *"Theater is, and has always been, magic."*

My thorough investigation detailed in my video, *"The Eagle Has Landed!,"* cuts through this magic and slices into reality. It is time for the fog to be dispelled and the truth to become known about NASA, the U.S. space program, and the Illuminati. After all, our Lord Jesus promised us, *"Ye shall know the truth, and the truth shall make you free."*

The Pope, Catholicism, and the Vatican

The Seduction of Christianity and the Triumph of Rome

Vatican Rising!

You would think that the Vatican today would be reeling, with all the unseemly revelations about pedophile priests, lesbian nuns, witchcraft teachings advocated by cardinals, and so forth. But, not so. Indeed, contrary to what you might expect, the Papacy and the Catholic Church have never had it so good. That's what I report in my shocker video documentary, *Vatican Rising!*

In fact, as I detail in my new video exposé, Rome is unexpectedly experiencing a huge comeback that is shaking the Protestant establishment—or what's left of it—to its roots.

Billy Graham "At Home in Catholic Church"

Vatican Rising! documents, for example, the almost total collapse of the historic Protestant doctrinal positions. Nearly every evangelical and fundamentalist leader on earth has, in recent years, gone over to the Catholic side. Billy Graham is quoted in the video as sharing with CNN host Larry King the revelation that he is now "at home in the Catholic Church." Evangelist Graham, on CNN's international broadcast, also praises the Pope as, *"The moral voice of the 20th Century."*

Televangelist Jack Van Impe, once upon a time Pastor Jerry Falwell's sidekick and nationally known as a fundamentalist Baptist crusader, says all that is far, far behind him now. Now that he's discovered the *"spiritual riches"* that are found only in Roman Catholicism and in the Papacy.

Though beset by revelations about pedophile priests molesting little boys and other woes, Pope John Paul II never had it so good. As one ex-Protestant leader recently remarked, "Martin Luther is dead. Long live the Pope!"

On my video you'll see Jack Van Impe and his wife and co-host, Rexella, gush with fulsome praise for the Pope and for Rome's priests. Van Impe exhorts Catholics to obey their black-robed, white-collar spiritual superiors in the Church.

He excitedly exclaims: *"You Catholic people, listen to your priests...Thank God for these Catholic leaders."*

"The Catholic Doctrines Are Right On"

According to TBN's Jack Van Impe, the Vatican's doctrines are wonderfully correct: *"I believe in this book,"* Van Impe tells the TV audience, holding high the New Catholic Catechism. *"The Catholic doctrines are right on,"* he adds.

Prophecy author Hal Lindsey agrees with Trinity Broadcasting founder Paul Crouch that the Pope is a man of faith.

Who turned Van Impe around to the Papacy's way of thinking? Why, it was the Pope himself, Van Impe reveals: *"Pope John Paul II has given me real direction in my life." "He is a giant of the faith,"* says Van Impe.

Note please, that it isn't Jesus Christ or His Word that really motivates Van Impe. Instead, it's the Pope, he reports, who has given him *"real direction"* in his life.

In *Vatican Rising!* you'll see other ex-Protestants, too, grovel as they speak in admiring tones about the Pope and the Catholic institutions. In one conversation, prophecy teacher Hal Lindsey and TBN founder Paul Crouch agree that, *"The Pope is a man of faith."*

And Hal Lindsey explains how much he has recently learned from the visitations of Mother Mary: *"In my work,"* Lindsey tells Crouch, *"I brought in the prophecies of Mary at Fatima."*

"We Are A Team"

Meanwhile, in the video, at New Orleans' massive Superdome, tens of thousands of Pentecostals and other charismatics are seen speaking in tongues, cheering and roaring their approval as keynote speaker, Catholic priest Tom Forrest, head of the Vatican's tongues-speaking department, leads the throng in a rallying cry worthy of a Super Bowl halftime show: *"We are a team!"* Forrest bellows. The crowd goes wild.

Yes, virtually the entire list of top-rank evangelical, charismatic, mainline denomination, and other Christians have gone over to the Vatican's side. James Dobson, Jerry Falwell, Pat Robertson, Vinson Synan, David Allen Lewis, James Bakker, Ralph Reed, Chuck Colson, George W. Bush—you name 'em and they are now servants of the Pope.

We're the Holdouts

The only Protestants remaining are just a few, old-time, King-James-believing Christians like Texe Marrs and the subscribers to *Power of Prophecy* newsletter. We're the hold-outs.

That's why the "Christian" establishment hates and despises us so ferociously. We refuse to give in. We refuse to kowtow to the purple bedecked Pope and his black robe dressed bevy of homosexual priests and lesbian nuns.

When Vatican official, Catholic priest, Tom Forrest, hollered out, "We are a team!" the Charismatic throng at the New Orleans Superdome went wild with ecstasy.

Increasingly, we are the minority. But, just where is the Pope and his cardinals and bishops taking the others—the Billy Grahams, Paul Crouches, Van Impes, Robertsons, Colsons and their millions of deluded followers?

Sadly, these multitudes are now all holding on fast to the Pope's sweaty hand. He is their spiritual guide, their last days guru. As Van Impe reveals, the Catholic Pope is the one giving the apostates *"real direction."* He's taking them all somewhere very, very fast. But just where is the Pope of Rome taking all his newfound disciples?

Lightning Bolt Strikes Basilica; Devils Mock Pope

Heaven's Fury, or Hell's Presence?

Is God angry at Pope John Paul II and the scarlet and black-robed cardinals of the Catholic Church from around the globe who bow their will to that of the Roman Pontiff? Has the Almighty now opened up the abyss to allow mocking devils of blasphemy and cunning to come forth, occupy the Vatican, and take possession of *their property*—the "Holy Father" and the corrupt priests who slavishly serve him?

Stunning new evidence provides the answers, and here, for the first time, is revealed the awful, even horrifying true story of how the leaders of the world's largest false church—one billion adherents strong—have fallen under the sly grip of devils.

A Train of Hellish Events

The train of incredible hellish events which have led to the current pitiful situation began, I believe, on June 29, 1995, at the Vatican City in Rome. Pope John Paul II and the visiting head of the Orthodox Church stood side by side in harmony on the balcony of the massive Basilica of St. Peter, waving to throngs of admirers who stood below, mingled together around the Egyptian obelisk monument erected in St. Peter's square facing the great basilica. *Orthodox Life (Vol. 45, 1995)*, an official journal published by the Holy Trinity Monastery of the Orthodox Church, chronicled the event:

> John Paul II, head of the Roman Catholic Church, and Patriarch Bartholomew, symbolic head of Orthodox Christians, together, on Thursday, June 29, from the balcony of the basilica of St. Peter, blessed their faithful all over the world. They addressed a common appeal for the reunification of the Christian churches, separated for 1,000 years. The two religious leaders came to participate at a mass in the Vatican, where they undertook to redouble their ecumenical efforts…
>
> In an atmosphere charged with intensity… ambassadors credited to the

Across the world, spurred by the example of their Pope, interfaith worship services are being conducted in Catholic Church sanctuaries. Here we see Moslem Sheikh Safdar Razi at the pulpit of St. Mary's Cathedral in Austin, Texas. Sitting behind him is Catholic Bishop Gregory Aymond and two other Islamic clerics. The caption for this photo in the *Austin American-Statesman* newspaper (Jan 21, 2002, page B-1) read: *"Two Faiths United."*

> Holy See, members of the Sacred College, and numerous high officials of the Vatican, the Pope, and the Patriarch each in their turn spoke...to express their intention to 'dispel' the misunderstandings which have separated Christians... since the 11th century...
>
> The Patriarch underlined "that today, happily... we have arrived at a maturity." The Pope, in turn, suggested that papal authority would have to be supreme in a unified Church because Christ had given Saint Peter, the first pope, free power to rule the flock on earth.

Lightning Strikes!

So here we have the supreme leaders of the Catholic and Orthodox churches joining ecumenical hands, standing on a balcony as thousands cheer. Then, says *Orthodox Life*, lightning struck. Literally—

> Patriarch Bartholomew then asked Christians to pray and fast to oppose the power of the Devil and to drive out demons. At that exact moment, all the faithful were startled by a lightning bolt which struck the basilica, followed by a violent summer storm.

Was it mere coincidence that the lightning bolt struck just as Bartholomew asked the audience to oppose the power of the Devil and drive out demons? Can Satan cast out Satan? Was it God who sent the lightning and the violent rain, or was it the Devil?

Pope Fails to Exorcise Mocking Demons

Perhaps the answer was revealed in September, 2000 when Catholic sources (*The Record*, Louisville Diocese, Louisville, Kentucky; also see *Christianity Today*, November 13, 2000) revealed that Pope John Paul II, said to be the vicar of Christ on earth, dramatically failed in a personal attempt to cast demons out of a girl.

The 19-year-old girl had flown into a rage during a general audience with the Pontiff inside the Vatican on September 13. She began screaming insults at him, her voice said to be deep, raspy, masculine and cavernous. When security personnel tried to restrain the girl, she displayed superhuman strength in resisting them.

The Pope then personally intervened. He spent a half hour praying over the girl, hugging her, and ordering the demons to leave. The Pope even promised to celebrate a mass especially for her the next day. All to no avail.

The Pope also had the official Catholic exorcist of Rome, priest Gabrielle Amorth, perform repeated exorcism rituals to cast the demons out of the young lady. One ritual lasted two hours. But priest Amorth reported to the Pope that he, too, was unsuccessful.

Chillingly, the priest stated that during his exorcism, one demon inside the girl mocked the Pope, saying, "Not even your church head can send me away!"

In contrast, Jesus told his disciples, *"And these signs shall follow them that believe: In my name shall they cast out devils..." (Luke 16:17)*

What, then, does their utter inability to order the demons out of this possessed girl tell us about the Pope and his priests?

Mother Theresa Demon-Possessed?

On September 5, 2001 came an equally shocking revelation. The Archbishop of Calcutta (India), Henry D'Couzas, admitted that in 1997, just prior to her death at age 87, the world's most famous

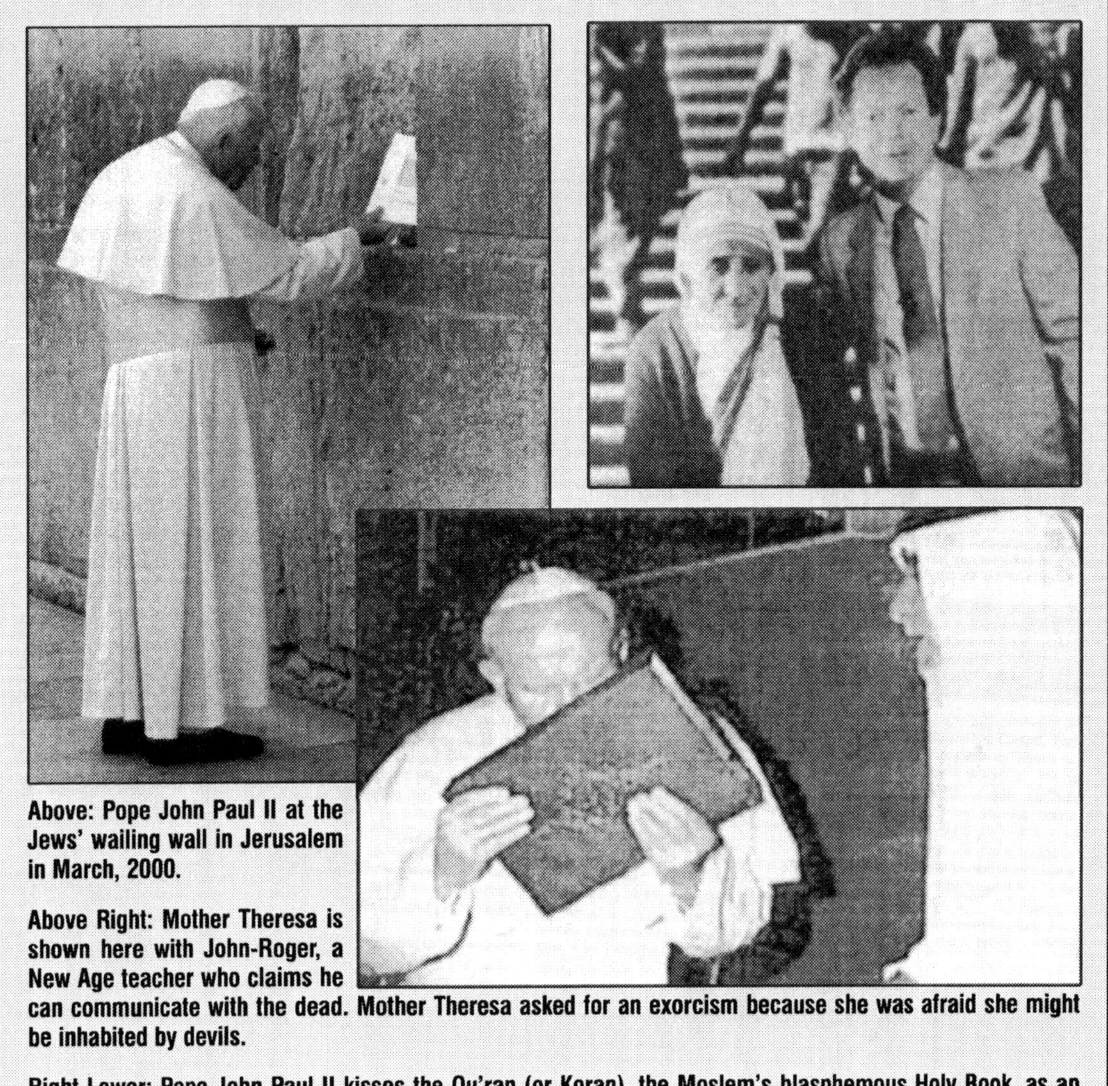

Above: Pope John Paul II at the Jews' wailing wall in Jerusalem in March, 2000.

Above Right: Mother Theresa is shown here with John-Roger, a New Age teacher who claims he can communicate with the dead. Mother Theresa asked for an exorcism because she was afraid she might be inhabited by devils.

Right Lower: Pope John Paul II kisses the Qu'ran (or Koran), the Moslem's blasphemous Holy Book, as an Islamic clergyman from Iraq looks on.

nun, the almost universally admired Mother Theresa, had an exorcism performed on her to cast out devils. The exorcism took place, said the Archbishop, in a hospital, at the request of Mother Theresa. She had been having trouble sleeping, he said, and was afraid she was possessed. (See *The Fayetteville Observer*, Sept. 6, 2001; and *The Gospel Catholic*, Raleigh, NC 27012). If Mother Theresa was, in fact, possessed by devils, that would explain why she had repeatedly told Hindus they did not need to convert to Jesus to go to heaven. Their own Hindu gods and goddesses were sufficient.

Once, when asked why God allowed so much human pain and suffering on planet earth, Mother Theresa sarcastically replied that when she eventually died and went to heaven, the first thing she was going to say to God was, "You've got a lot of explaining to do."

Doctrines of Devils Attract Devils

Why did God allow these frightful demonic events to occur? Why are devils now attacking and mocking the Pope and those closest to him in the Catholic Church? When we examine the actions of this Pope and of his associates, the answers become clear. The Pope himself has attracted to his person legions of demons because he and his Vatican colleagues have rejected Christ's doctrines, found in the Holy Bible, and instead have adopted doctrines of devils. Here are only a few recent examples:

1) **Kissing the Moslem's Holy Book:** In January 2000 at the end of an audience with Patriarch Raphael I of Iraq, the Pope bowed to the Muslim holy book, the Qu'ran, presented to him by the visiting delegation, and kissed it as a sign of respect. This is the same Islamic Holy Book that instructs Moslems to "fight and kill the infidels (Christians) wherever you find them."

2) **Heaven is for All Good People!** In December 2000, the Pope issued a Vatican pronouncement that *"Heaven is open to all as long as they are good."* It is not necessary, the Pope added, for the person to believe in Christ, and he/she may be of another, non-Christian religion. The Pope insisted that, *"All of the just on earth, including those who ignore Christ, are called upon to build the Kingdom of God."* Interesting. But also a stunning whopper of a lie! The Apostle John said, "The whole world lieth in wickedness." This means that all who reject Christ are helping to build the wicked kingdom of Satan. Jesus stated, *"I am the Way, The Truth, and The Life."* Jesus is our salvation, not the Jewish rabbis, not Islam's Mohammed, not the Hindu's Krishna. Jesus Christ is Lord.

   And He, Jesus, said that no one is good or just. No one is righteous in themselves. Instead, a man must be born again in spirit and in truth to enter the Kingdom of Heaven (John 3:3).

3) **Heaven and Hell Not Places:** In 1999, Pope John Paul II pleased the devils when he publicly revised and "modernized" the Bible's ages-old definition of "Heaven." Heaven, the Pope explained, "is not a physical place." And Hell? Well, according to the Vatican, Hell is not a physical place either. It's simply a temporary "separation from God," chosen by those who choose not to be good.

4) **Yoked with Unbelievers:** In January, 2002, the Pope again met at Assisi, Italy with leaders of other religions, Including the Hindus, Moslems, Jains, Zoroastrians, Jews, and Buddhists. He encouraged all to work together in harmony for world peace. The Pontiff assured the satanic servants assembled together that, "We have in common worship of the one true God."

   Evidently, the Pope overlooked the fact that Hindus worship some three million deities, and that Buddhists and Shintos pray to their dead ancestors. The Pope also must have forgotten the primary law embodied in the first of God's Ten Commandments: *"Thou shalt have no other gods before me."*

5) **Jewish False Messiah:** Also in January, 2002, the Vatican issued an important new doctrinal encyclical that explicitly states, "The Jewish wait for the Messiah is not in vain."

   The new doctrinal statement is an eye-opener since, indeed, the Jews do wait for their messiah, the Antichrist, in vain. The true Messiah has *already come!* His name: Jesus! But this same Jesus prophesied that while he, as Christ and Messiah, came in the name of the Lord, someday, *another would come in his own name*. Jesus warned that when this false imposter comes, the Jews would tragically believe in him, the imposter, as Messiah! In other words, contrary to the Pope's soothing lies, the one on whom the Jews now anxiously wait is none other than Antichrist, the Son of Perdition *(II Thes. 2).*

"I Beheld Lucifer"

And what about that lightning bolt, accompanied by a violent rain that jarred the faithful on June 29th, 1995, heralding the approaching of the New Millennium when it struck St. Peter's Basilica, the very headquarters of world-wide Roman Catholicism? Was it a sign sent by an angry God? Was it the work of the Devil? Or, was the lightning strike simply a coincidental natural phenomenon?

Frankly, I do not know the answer. But I do remember Jesus' breathtaking description in the gospel of Luke of Satan being cast down: *"I beheld Satan as lightning fall from heaven."*

My mind also races to *Revelation 13:12-18*, where we are told of the miraculous evil power to be given the second beast "whom all the world shall worship" except those whose names are written in Christ Jesus' book of Life: *"And he doeth great wonders, so that he maketh fire come down from heaven on the earth in the sight of men."*

> *Did Satan, in the form of a fiery bolt of lightning, come down from heaven on the earth in the sight of men?*

Could it be that on June 29, 1995, the Catholic Pope and the Orthodox Patriarch, together representing false Christiandom, along with their devoted audience, were on hand at the Vatican, witnesses to that amazing moment when Satan was cast down to earth *like fire and lightning from heaven?* Did Satan, in the form of a fiery bolt of lightning, come down from heaven on the earth in the sight of men?

Out of The Bottomless Pit

Could it also be that at that exact moment, on that same fateful day, June 29, countless devils, locked up for millennia in the abyss, were released, coming forth with fury, prepared for the coming great and final conflict?

> *And the fifth angel sounded, and I saw a star fall from heaven unto the earth: and to him was given the key of the bottomless pit.*
>
> *And he opened the bottomless pit; and there arose a smoke out of the pit, as the smoke of a great furnace; and the sun and the air were darkened by reason of the smoke of the pit.*
>
> *And there came out of the smoke locusts upon the earth: and unto them was given power, as the scorpions of the earth have power....*
>
> *And they had a king over them, which is the angel of the bottomless pit, whose name in the Hebrew tongue is Abaddon, but in the Greek tongue hath his name Apollyon. (Revelation 9:1-11)*

AA: The Jesuit Connection

Did the Jesuits secretly found Alcoholics Anonymous? In a previous newsletter I wrote that a Catholic priest was instrumental in the founding of Alcoholics Anonymous (AA). As you'll discover below, that priest was a member of the Jesuit Order, long suspected of being implicated in Marxist-Communist schemes and other radical movements.

The two men most often credited as founders of AA and its 12-step programs are Bill Wilson and Bob Smith. Wilson was a con man and a disgraced stockbroker from New York City; Smith was a medical doctor from Akron, Ohio. Both were drunks, and both were life-long New Age occultists who eagerly took part in such abominations as séances, spirit channeling, and psychedelic drugs (LSD). Both men enthusiastically promoted Christian Science and New Thought teachings (*New Age*—see my book, *New Age Cults and Religions*).

In 1939, when AA first burst prominently upon the public scene, there was not a single Catholic member in the organization. Then along came Ed Dowling, a St. Louis, Missouri, Jesuit priest who was publisher of an influential Roman Catholic publication. Dowling recognized that AA's 12-step program and techniques were remarkably similar to those of the late Ignatius of Loyola.

"Saint" Ignatius of Loyola had given the Catholic Church the "gift" of an Eastern mystical form of meditation that he chose to call the "Spiritual Exercises." This occult meditation—similar to Hindu guru Maharishi Mahesh Yogi's *Transcendental Meditation*—is widely used today by Catholic priests around the globe, especially those of the Jesuit Order.

Meeting privately with AA founder Bill Wilson, Jesuit priest Dowling agreed to promote AA to Catholics worldwide. Financial help from Catholic sources quickly followed, and AA was on its way as a Catholic-supported institution.

Saint Ignatius of Loyola had given the Catholic Church the "gift" of an Eastern mystical form of meditation—similar to Hindu guru Maharishi Mahesh Yogi's Transcendental Meditation—that is called the "Spiritual Exercises."

To "sweeten the deal" and make AA's universalist, "God as you understand Him" doctrine more palatable to the Catholic hierarchy, in 1947 Bill Wilson began taking instructions in the Catholic faith. His personal tutor was Monsignor Fulton J. Sheen, one of the best known Catholic priests in America.

Favorable reports of Bill Wilson's conversion to Roman Catholicism caused Catholic priests everywhere to embrace local AA groups. AA's membership soared. By 1955, approximately one-third of the members of AA were Catholic.

Bill Wilson (top) and Bob Smith, co-founders of Alcoholics Anonymous

A rare picture of Jesuit priest Ed Dowling.

But his supposed conversion was all a sham. Within a year, Bill Wilson quietly dropped out of his Catholic instructional classes. Confirming his New Age inclinations, he confided to friends that he could accept the "mystical aspects" of Catholicism, but didn't want to be bothered with all the rest of the dogma.

No doubt, Wilson's conversion to Catholicism was engineered by the astute Jesuit Priest Ed Dowling. Later, Dowling was honored by Wilson as the keynote speaker at an international AA convention held in St. Louis. His address was warmly received by attendees because he affirmed for them that his New Age beliefs were perfectly compatible with AA's.

For example, referring to psychiatrist Freud's theory that man's subconscious mind has a moral element called the "id," Dowling told the conventioneers that God is merely a part of one's subconscious mind:

> "My trying to understand God reminds me of a definition of psychiatry…It is the id… The id is…God."

Then Dowling got a round of applause when he told the crowd, "We are three things, I think—alcoholics, alcoholics anonymous, and agnostic." Later in his talk, Dowling repeated: "We are all agnostic."

Note: AA gives Jesuit priest Ed Dowling credit for his "contributions" in its official and unoffical propaganda. For example, see the books: *Alcoholics Anonymous Comes of Age*, by Bill Wilson; *AA's Godparents*, by Igor Sikorsky, Jr.; *AA: The Way it Began*, by Bill Pittman; and *AA: The Story*, by Ernest Kurtz.

Mother Mary Warns: "Lucifer Controls the Vatican!"

The Mary apparitions appearing around the globe are spouting some very strange things. One of these "Marys," who appeared in Germany, reportedly told Catholic faithful that, soon, she would give each of them a *mark* in their forehead, indicating her ownership of their souls.

Now comes the eye-popping report from a Catholic ministry in Bayside, New York, that Mary is warning that Lucifer himself is in control of Rome! The well-known Catholic group, Our Lady of the Roses, claims that for some years now, Mary has been regularly appearing in Bayside, New York to a New Jersey housewife, Veronica Luekens. According to Veronica, Mary is announcing important prophetic messages and making proclamations.

In their June 1994 *Rose Notes*, the international newsletter published by Our Lady of the Roses, we are informed of a rather startling message given Mrs. Luekens by Mary:

> The message of Sept. 7, 1978 clearly states that Lucifer entered the Vatican in 1972, and has since controlled the state of affairs in Rome.

Does this mean that the current pontiff, Pope John Paul II, is in the grip of Satan? Well, almost. *Rose Notes* reports that Jesus appeared to Virginia and explained the situation this way:

> In the message of Oct. 2, 1989, Our Lord said that he is not holding Pope John Paul II responsible for the present turmoil and confusion, because, as he said, he (the Pope) is under the domination of his bishops and cardinals, especially in Rome.

Mary is speaking to people today, says the Catholic group in New York that put up this billboard.

Interestingly, in his provocative book, *Keys of This Blood*, Malachi Martin, a respected Catholic theologian and former Jesuit Professor, makes similar claims. Quoting unnamed Vatican insiders, he writes that during the 1970s, "the smoke of Satan entered the sanctuary of St. Peter's Cathedral in Rome."

Veronica Luekens, Mother Mary's Bayside, New York messenger to humanity, says that Mary is appealing to Catholics everywhere to pray to her as our intercessor and to say the rosary. Only in this way can the faithful forestall the disasters to come upon the earth due to Lucifer's evil plot against Rome.

Meanwhile, Malachi Martin assures us that a New World Order led by the Pontiff is at hand. Soon, Martin believes, Mary will give mankind a sign in the heavens. Then, the Pope of Rome will take his rightful place on earth as victorious Vicar of Christ. He will assume leadership of the New World Order and usher mankind into a glorious Golden Age.

True Christians will take note of God's Word and beware. Our holy Saviour and guide is not Mary but Jesus. In fact, it is He alone to whom we have the privilege to communicate directly, without an intercessor: *"For there is one God, and one mediator between God and men, the man Christ Jesus" (I Timothy 2:5).*

Apostate Israelites Worship the Queen of Heaven

As for the word that thou hast spoken unto us in the name of the LORD, we will not hearken unto thee.

But we will certainly do whatsoever thing goeth forth out of our own mouth, to burn incense unto the queen of heaven, and to pour out drink offerings unto her, as we have done, we, and our fathers, our kings, and our princes, in the cities of Judah, and in the streets of Jerusalem: for then had we plenty of victuals, and were well, and saw no evil.

But since we left off to burn incense to the queen of heaven, and to pour out drink offerings unto her, we have wanted all things, and have been consumed by the sword and by the famine.

And when we burned incense to the queen of heaven, and poured out drink offerings unto her, did we make her cakes to worship her, and pour out drink offerings unto her, without our men?

Then Jeremiah said unto all the people, to the men, and to the women, and to all the people which had given him that answer, saying,

The incense that ye burned in the cities of Judah, and in the streets of Jerusalem, ye, and your fathers, your kings, and your princes, and the people of the land, did not the LORD remember them, and came it not into his mind?

So that the LORD could no longer bear, because of the evil of your doings, and because of the abominations which ye have committed; therefore is your land a desolation, and an astonishment, and a curse, without an inhabitant, as at this day.

Because ye have burned incense, and because ye have sinned against the LORD, and have not obeyed the voice of the LORD, nor walked in his law, nor in his statutes, nor in his testimonies; therefore this evil is happened unto you, as at this day. (Jeremiah 44:16-23)

Pope Approves Voodoo and Other False Religions

"Now the Spirit speaketh expressly that in the latter times some shall depart from the faith, giving heed to seducing spirits and doctrines of devils."

—*I Timothy 4:1-2*

"When thou art come into the land which the Lord thy God giveth thee, thou shalt not learn to do after the abominations of those nations."

—*Deuteronomy 18:9*

Pope John Paul II has again sent bizarre messages to the Catholic faithful. In 1986 in Assisi, Italy, the Pope joined in a circle to pray and meditate with snake handlers from Togo, shamans and tribal witchdoctors from West Africa, Hindu gurus from India, Buddhist monks from Thailand, and liberal protestant clergymen from Great Britain. Many devoted Catholics were stunned and scandalized, especially since the Pope also announced in Assisi that there are "many paths to God."

Now, he's reaffirmed that same message. This time by inviting world religious leaders to meet for a second time in Assisi to pray for peace in Eastern Europe.

On January 9-10, 1993, the Pope again hosted the Dalai Lama of Tibetan Buddhism and representatives of many other false and ungodly religions. It was an incredible sight to see these weird persons, "holy books" in hand, all standing serenely, side-by-side with the Pope.

Pope Endorses Voodoo Magic and Ritual

But amazingly, as if to underscore his message of unity with false satanic religion, the very next month, this February, the Pope met in Africa with voodoo believers and sorcerers. Here, as reported in the New Orleans *Times Picayune* newspaper and in other daily newspapers across the U.S.A., is the *Associated Press* account of the Pope's visit to the country of Benin, in Africa:

At Assisi, Italy, Pope John Paul II met with the Dalai Lama of Tibetan Buddhism and other false religionists.

'Pope Meets With Voodoo Believers'

Cotonou, Benin (AP)—Pope John Paul II on Thursday sought common ground with the believers in voodoo, suggesting they would not betray their traditional faith by converting to Christianity.

On the second day of his 10th African pilgrimage, the pope held a dramatic and emotional meeting with the priests of the vodun, as the ancestral gods are known in the Fon language.

Voodoo worshipers believe in one God but also in the lesser deities. Snakes and fetishes are important in their rituals.

The pope told the voodooists that just as they draw on their ancestors for their religion, so do Christians revere their "ancestors in the faith, from the Apostles to the missionaries."

The "ancestors" of missionaries had their own faiths before converting and lost nothing by becoming Christians, he said.

Voodoo priests at the meeting warmly welcomed the pontiff.

"I have never seen God, but today when I have seen the pope, I recognize that I have seen the good God, who prays for all the voduns," said Sossa Guedehoungue, head of Benin's vodun community. He wore a wooden crown painted gold, a long pink robe and thick-framed eyeglasses.

Voodoo leader Senou Zannou gave a formal speech in which he announced his son was becoming a Roman Catholic priest. But he also offered a defense of his faith.

"God knows that the vodun has nothing to do with the devil or Satan," he said.

Africans passing from Benin into slavery brought vodun worship to Haiti and Brazil, where it mixed with Catholicism and came to be called voodoo.

Earlier, on the first full day of his journey, the pope led an open-air Mass before 15,000 people in Parakou, about 235 miles north of Cotonou. He urged religious communities working in Africa to strive to incorporate African cultural expressions into Roman Catholic worship.'

What Does the Bible Say?

The Pope appears to be wonderfully tolerant in accepting voodoo and Eastern religions as true pathways to God. But what does the Bible say about such things? In *II Corinthians 6:14-15* we read:

> *"Be ye not unequally yoked together with unbelievers: for what fellowship hath righteousness with unrighteousness? and what communion hath light with darkness? And what concord hath Christ with Belial? or what part hath he that believeth with an infidel?"*

The whole testimony of the Bible is that consorting with such hellish works is, in fact, the same as being in league with the devil. For example, consider the voodoo practice of calling up the spirits. The Bible warns against communicating with familiar spirits and ancestors from the dead. This is called an "abomination" by God (see *Deut. 18:10-14; I Sam. 28:1-25; Isaiah 8:19; I Chron. 10:13-14; Micah 5:12-15; Acts 16:16-18).*

The same harsh warnings are made in the Scriptures against involvement in or acceptance of idol worship, enchantments, shamanism, magic, wizardry, charms, and other elements of voodoo religion (see *Lev. 19:26; Jer. 27:8-9; Daniel 1:20; Rev. 21:8; Gal. 5:19-21; II Kings 17:17;* and *Deut. 18:10-12*).

The Bible sums up our individual responsibility by commanding us, in a very powerful way: "And have no fellowship with the unfruitful works of darkness, but rather reprove them" *(Ephesians 5:11).*

Whom Shall We Choose?

The Bible says we are to have *no* spiritual fellowship with the false cults. The Pope says we can.

In voodoo rituals the "spirits" possess worshipers, causing them to thrash about wildly, roll their eyes, and speak strange tongues in a trance. Magical symbols, totem poles, and idols are used.

Voodoo priests claim they can bless or curse followers. Dolls are used either to heal or to torment victims.

So then the question becomes: *Whom* shall we choose to be our inerrant guide—the God of Heaven, author of His perfect and inspired Bible, or the Pope, a man born in original sin like all of us and a vessel of clay? If we answer that the Pope *must* be right for he is God's vicar on earth, we commit a grave error. No man is above God nor superior to His Holy Word.

I am convinced from the mail I receive that many Catholics are themselves heartsick about the direction this Pope has taken their church. They cannot go along with voodoo magic and devilish Eastern religions. These good people have been taught to respect and revere their "Holy Father" in Rome, but they are shocked at what they see happening within the Catholic establishment. With sincere, broken hearts and often in tears, they phone and write me, asking, "Texe, what are we to do?"

"What Are We to Do?"

In fairness, it should be said that Pope John Paul II has also done much to deserve merit. For example, whereas Billy Graham has compromised and refused to publicly take a pro-life stand, the Pope has repeatedly and courageously labeled abortion as just what it is: "Violence and murder against the unborn."

Moreover, Pope John Paul II has refused to give in to demands by liberal clergy to ordain women priests. And in Africa, the Pope boldly stood up to Moslem dictators in the countries he visited, chastising them for their persecution of native Christian believers.

Anyone who has followed my ministry for any length of time knows full well that I have never picked on any one church or denominational group. Without a doubt, God's people can be found in many different churches and even outside our traditional churches.

But, sadly, the doctrines of devils and the spirit of evil and compromise are easily found today in almost every denomination—among Baptists, Methodists, Presbyterians, Assemblies of God, Episcopals, Charismatics, and yes, in the Catholic Church. In all these church groups can be found leaders who have either compromised or have abandoned the Bible and the true faith altogether.

I plead with all those who are torn by loyalty to one man or to a particular church to set aside the inventions of men, and instead, put Jesus Christ and His Word first in their lives. The coming of the Lord is drawing near. Now is not the time for compromise. This day, this very moment, each of us must choose *whom* we will serve.

Bible Prophecy

The World's Greatest Positive Thinker

He was and is the world's greatest Possibility Thinker. His Positive Thinking abilities are magnificent. He knows how to make the most terrific Positive Affirmations and Positive Confessions, and he always refrains from negative thoughts. He is the ultimate in Positive Consciousness.

Of whom do I speak? Why Lucifer, of course. Lucifer is without equal in the realm of Positive Thinking. He is *"the World's Greatest Positive Thinker!"*

Lucifer made the greatest, most Positive Confession I the history of angels and men when he pompously declared:

> *"I will ascend into heaven, I will exalt my throne above the stars of God: I will sit also upon the mount of congregation, in the sides of the north: I will ascend above the heights of the clouds; I will be like the Most High" (Isaiah 14:13-14).*

I will...I will...I will...I will...I will. Now that's a Positive Thinker!

Lucifer also demonstrated his Positive Thinking abilities in the Garden of Eden when he craftily told Eve, "Yea, hath God said, Ye shall not eat of every tree of the garden?" thus did Lucifer mock the Word of God, for the Lord had made the "negative" statement to Adam and Eve that if they ate of the forbidden fruit, they would die.

Lucifer, however, was in a more Positive Thinking frame of mind. "Ye shall not eat of every tree of the garden?" Thus did Lucifer mock the Word of God, for the Lord had made the "negative" statement to Adam and Eve that if they ate of the forbidden fruit, they would die.

Lucifer, however, was in a more Positive Thinking frame of mind. "Ye shall not surely die," he said through the serpent.

Throughout heavenly and human history, Lucifer has proven his incomparable Positive Thinking and Possibility Thinking capabilities. He though positively of the possibility that he could defeat Michael and his archangels and dethrone God. Later, he positively convinced the people of Shinar, in Babylon, that they could build a Tower to Heaven. He next instructed Pharaoh to "think positive" and keep the Israelites in captivity. He even tried out his positive thinking talents on Jesus, promising Christ that all the kingdoms of earth would be His if Jesus would fall down and worship him.

Lucifer is a *persistent* Positive Thinker, too. Bible prophecy tells us that someday he will once again attempt to overthrow God. However, yet again, Lucifer will fail. Armageddon will ensue and Lucifer will be cast into the fiery pit *(See Rev. 19)*.

Yes, folks, there is no equal to loser Lucifer. Yet, he easily deserves the hard-earned title of *"The World's Greatest Positive Thinker."*

The Invention of the Gospel of Positive Thinking

Meet Lucifer, The World's Greatest Positive Thinker

The terms "positive" and "negative" are not found at all in the Bible, but the New Age, the occult and witchcraft have been teaching the positive/negative gospel for almost a century. Hitler, too, promoted what he called a "Positive Christianity."

Today the Gospel of Positive Thinking has frighteningly swept into the church in a big way. The Gospel of Positive Thinking goes by many names; Positive Confession, Positive Affirmations, the Prosperity Gospel, Seed Faith, Possibility Thinking, and Self-esteem. It uses as its tools such unholy techniques as visualization, Eastern forms of meditation, reprogramming one's mind to erase negative thoughts, etc. All of these techniques, like the Gospel of Positive Thinking itself, began first in the occult and New Age communities. Then they were adopted by "Christian" leaders who brought the occult right into the church. Satan did not counterfeit the Gospel of Positive Thinking. He invented it!

It was Jesus Himself who told us that Satan is the Father of Lies. He is not always a counterfeiter, but is often the originator of much evil.

Positive or Negative—All Things Work Together for our Good

The Positive Thinking teacher's claim that through the exercise of our own minds and imaginations, we can have whatever we want. Worse, they say that anyone can do it. You don't have to be a Christian. These mind powers are neutral, they say. Even the occultists can use their positive thinking powers to manipulate this neutral force *to get what they want.*

This is contrary to God's Word. The Bible instructs us to *go directly to Jesus* for all our needs, not to depend on a mind-altering technique. We are to be obedient to God and walk in His Will, "casting down imaginations, and every high thing that exalteth itself against the knowledge of God..." *(2 Cor. 10:5).* However, only those who belong to Jesus will have their prayer answered. The only exception is a prayer of salvation. God hears the repentant sinner.

God's servants well know that everything works together for good for those who love the Lord. But not everything that happens is positive and good. For example, the Apostle Paul did not enjoy the luxuries of life and live sumptuously in comfort and good health because of his Positive Thinking and Positive Confession visualization abilities. In 2 Corinthians 11:24-29 we discover many horribly negative things happened to this great man of God:

> *"Of the Jews five times received I forty stripes save one. Thrice I was beaten with rods, once was I stoned, thrice I suffered shipwreck, a night and a day I have been in the deep; In journeyings often, in perils of waters, in perils of robbers, in perils by mine own countrymen, in perils by the heathen, in perils in the city, in perils in the wilderness, in perils in the sea, in perils among false brethren; In weariness and painfulness, in watchings often, in hunger and thirst, in fasting often, in cold and nakedness. Besides those things that are without, that which cometh upon me daily, the care of all the churches. Who is weak, and I am not weak? Who is offended, and I burn not?"*

Moreover, Paul suffered a "thorn in the flesh," some problem or temptation which the messenger of Satan (a demonic entity) used to buffet and punish him *(2 Cor. 12:7-8).* "For this thing

I besought the Lord thrice that it might depart from me," Paul wrote. But it was God's will that Paul continue to be plagued:

> *"And he said unto me, My grace is sufficient for thee: for my strength is made perfect in weakness. Most gladly therefore will I rather glory in my infirmities, that the power of Christ may rest upon me. Therefore I take pleasure in infirmities, in reproaches, in necessities, in persecutions in distresses for Christ's sake: for when I am weak, then am I strong" (2 Cor. 12:9-10)*

To hear today's Positive Thinking advocates tell it, Paul's afflictions were a result of his negative thoughts! No, my friends, they were not Paul's fault, but were by design of God, for Paul's benefit. God knows how to send adversity our way to strengthen us.

God has provided a way to meet all our needs according to His perfect will, but not because we want this or that and think positive about it. God's way is describe in His Word:

> *"...in everything by prayer and supplication with thanksgiving let your requests be made known unto God" (Philippians 4:6).*

Faith

The Positive Thinking advocates falsely claim that theirs is a "Faith" teaching. But what is Faith? Simply this: knowing and trusting, without wavering, that God loves us and that His will is always superior to our own. Faith is praying and asking Almighty, omnipotent God, believing He will answer when He wants and how He wants, and that His answer will always be correct regardless of whether it matches up our own desires and expectations.

Our faith resides in God, not in the power of our own mind and our own fertile imaginations (see *Romans 1:21; 2 Cor. 10:5; Genesis 8:21; Jeremiah 18:12* and *Luke 1:51*).

My friends, we must ask God to take complete control of our lives. In meekness, we yield to him and in so doing, we receive His inestimable blessings and guidance. "Humble yourselves in the sight of the Lord, and He shall lift you up" *(James 4:10)*.

How much greater than our own Positive Thinking ability is the strength and power of God! How much wiser is *His* plan for our lives! Therefore, James instructs us not to vainly declare and positively affirm: I will do this or that:

> *"Whereas ye know not what shall be on the tomorrow. For what is your life? It is even a vapour, that appeareth for a little time, and then vanisheth away. For that ye ought to say, If the Lord will, we shall live, and do this, or that" (James 4:14-15).*

The Most Powerful Negative Confessions on Earth

Now, let's talk about the most powerful negative confession on earth. Did you know that the greatest miracle on earth occurs *only* after we have sincerely made what false teachers call a "negative confession?" That's right. Here it is: "Father, I have sinned and need you, my Saviour, to wash away my sins. I can not do it. Only you can save me. Please come into my heart and make me whole. I totally commit my life to you. In Jesus name. Amen."

Some may call this negative. Not me. Could anything be more positive and magnificent than this sinner's prayer? Let the devil's folks have their so-called Gospel of Positive Thinking. I'll take God's plain, unvarnished word. How about you?

There can be no Zion without a King, and there is...

No King But King Jesus

"For thine is the kingdom, and the power, and the glory, for ever. Amen."
—*Matthew 6:13*

I am constantly amazed at the gross spiritual apathy and blasphemy of men and women, supposedly "Christians," who possess a woeful ignorance of the true meaning of the Kingdom of God.

As shocking as it may seem, millions of people who consider themselves perfectly knowledgeable of the prophetic scriptures are today working earnestly in a misguided effort to help Satan and the Beast of Revelation establish their latter days global kingdom.

Disgustingly, these millions of "evangelical" and "fundamentalist" Christians actually believe that in helping Satan and the Beast set up their bloody kingdom on earth, they are, in reality, serving God.

Their callous disregard for scriptural integrity brings graphically to mind our Lord's dire warning that as the end of time draws near, the religious of this world will kill true Christians and think they do God service *(John 16:2)*.

A Satanic Emblem for Israel's Kingdom

Some years ago, while attending a prophecy conference in Florida, I encountered a sincere but deluded woman proudly wearing a necklace bearing the so-called Jewish Star of David, the six-pointed star. She had no idea that this star secretly represents the number 666, that occultists universally call it the hexagram, and that satanists regularly use the six-pointed star in their satanic rituals and invocations.

This same woman gushingly told me she was a "lover of the nation-state of Israel." She bragged of giving large sums of money to a militant Jewish group in Jerusalem that has as its goal the blowing up of the Islamic mosque and the setting up of a new temple for the Jews atop its ruins.

The Jewish Star of David secretly honors Lucifer under the disguise of Remphan, the ancient Egyptian "Star" god. In Acts 7:39-43 the blessed martyr Stephen blasted the Jews, prophetically declaring, "Yea, ye took up the tabernacle of Moloch and the star of your god Remphan, figures which ye made to worship them: and I will carry you away beyond Babylon."

"But," I inquired of the woman, "are you not aware of *II Thessalonians 2*, which prophesies that the Antichrist, the Son of Perdition, shall show himself in such a temple, and blasphemously declare that he is above God?"

"Well, yes," she offered. "But isn't that a good thing? That would hasten the coming of the Kingdom of the Jews, wouldn't it?"

"The Kingdom of the Jews?," I repeated, almost incredulous.

"Oh sure," she excitedly exclaimed. "That is what the *Scofield Bible*, which my husband and I love, says. The Jews shall reign over all the earth. They are God's Chosen. In helping them to rebuild their great temple, I am helping to usher in the Kingdom of the Jews."

"My dear Sister," I confided, "You cannot serve God and the Devil at one and the same time. You cannot, on the one hand, help Jews, who despise our Saviour, Jesus Christ, rebuild their blasphemous temple in which they intend to carry out animal sacrifices. This would be mocking the once and for all sacrifice of Jesus on the cross. Do you really believe that in doing that, you are serving God?"

But, she objected, "in helping the Jews rise to power, I *am* serving God!"

"You cannot give money to help build Satan's kingdom," I explained, "and in doing so, please our Lord God. If the Zionist Jews are doggedly determined to mock and disrespect the truth, why should you, a Christian, help make that come to fruition?"

"Moreover," I concluded, "Are you not aware that it was Jesus Himself who prophesied that the Jewish Temple would be destroyed, stone by stone. And it was destroyed, by the Romans in 70 AD. You, therefore, are working to *undo* what God *has done*. Are you more wise than God?

You cannot help Jews, who despise our Saviour, Jesus Christ, rebuild their temple in which they intend to carry out animal sacrifices. This would be mocking the once and for all sacrifice of Jesus on the cross.

"But," she again protested, "God needs a place to live. He needs an earthly temple. And he needs a Holy City, Jerusalem, a capital for the Jewish Kingdom!"

Earthly Jerusalem vs. New Jerusalem

I had no more time to spare. If I did, I would have informed this poor creature that God has no need of a temple built with human hands. I would have patiently explained to her that, in any event, God considers the earthly Jerusalem, the intended world capital of the Jews, so wicked He compares it to *"Sodom and Egypt" (Revelation 11:8).*

I would also liked to have brought to her attention the prophetic fact that earthly Jerusalem is a doomed city in bondage to Satan *(Galatians 4:25-26).* But, thank God, our Lord Jesus has prepared for His bride, the Christian Church, a fabulous New Jerusalem:

> *"And I John saw the holy city, New Jerusalem, coming down from heaven, prepared as a bride adorned for her husband." (Revelation 21:2)*

However, I suspected that this unfortunate woman was not interested in the heavenly *New Jerusalem* of scripture. She was far too enamored of the earthly city of Jerusalem, site of what she was sure was going to be a *global empire* to be presided over by the worldly leaders and rabbis of the Jewish race she so devoutly idealized.

How sad and tragic. Like so many Christians, this pitiful lady had bought into the monstrous heresies first brought into the Church by Cyrus Scofield, a corrupt, crooked lawyer funded by Zionist Jews from New York City in the late 19th century. Scofield's heresies promoting a Jewish kingdom and an earthly Zionist New World Order to be ruled over by a god-like Jewish race, without any Christian gentiles around to mess things up, soon became fashionable among some

Cyrus I. Scofield and his heretical "Bible" continue today to be idolized by Southern Baptist leaders, pentecostal and charismatic teachers, and millions of deceived evangelicals. In fact, as documented in Joseph Canfield's stunning exposé book, *The Incredible Scofield and His Book* (available through the ministry for $25, plus shipping), Mr. Scofield was a crooked, adulterous lawyer who abandoned his wife and was paid handsomely by New York Jewish plotters to betray the Christian faith. Scofield planted "Judaizer seeds" in his Bible commentaries denying Christ's heavenly kingdom, whereas Jesus had proclaimed to Pilate, "My kingdom is not of this world" (John 18:36). Scofield and his Talmudic Jewish mentors conceived of a coming worldly kingdom led by powerful Jews who would reign over inferior Gentiles for a thousand years. Jewish rabbis everywhere must be laughing hysterically that the preposterous Scofield scam has worked out so beautifully over the years.

apostate denominations, especially among the Southern Baptists and their heavily Masonic Lodge membership.

Of course, the confused, but sincere woman wearing the hideous six-pointed star that day down in Florida had little knowledge of this Zionist plot by Scofield and his Jewish cohorts. She was a victim of some modern-day charlatan, perhaps a Hal Lindsey, Jack Van Impe, Pat Robertson, Jerry Falwell, or Billy Graham, who had infused her with the Jewish fables against which the Apostle Paul long ago warned us to avoid *(see Titus 1:14)*.

Money for the Master Race

For years, she and others have been taught that the Jews are the *Master Race*, that Christ-rejecting Jews, by virtue of their blood and fleshly race, are "God's Chosen" people. The deceived multitudes are, after all, constantly surrounded by the smooth words of Zionist fanatics like San Antonio's John Hagee and *Left Behind's* Tim LaHaye telling them that the Jews comprise a *"holy nation,"* that if they give money to the Jews to go toward their worldly kingdom, God will prosper them and that someday, after Christian gentiles are raptured up, the ruling Jews can get on with building their long-sought earthly Kingdom.

Jesus Not Our King in Heaven

As one pro-Zionist "Christian" publication recently explained it, Jesus Christ is *not* our King in heaven, he's only the groom of the church. According to the Scofield-inspired crowd, Jesus has been demoted. He's up in Heaven today wandering around in a Jewish human body without a throne, waiting for a second opportunity to someday be King of the Jews.

The Kingdom of God, say the Judaizers and Zionists, is not in heaven, nor is it in the hearts of men and women who have faith in Jesus their Lord. The Kingdom is the property exclusively of the Jews right here on earth!

According to the Scofield-inspired crowd, Jesus has been demoted. He's up in Heaven today wandering around in a Jewish human body without a throne, waiting for a second opportunity to someday be King of the Jews.

This, then, is the final landing point of the heretical, satanic journey and amusement ride on which the Zionist schemers are enthusiastically jockeying the Christian masses. Jesus, who was killed by the Jews after he told Pilate, "My kingdom is not of this world," is once again humiliated and degraded. Rejected almost two thousand years ago as King of the Jews, He is today rejected by Zionists and Judaizers as a heavenly Monarch as well. His heavenly crown is ripped from His brow. He is barred from the heavenly throne.

While Jesus is demoted and shunted aside, a mere human race, the Jews, are spiritually and materially enthroned and exalted. Soon, we are told, the Jews shall have the kingdom for which they have lusted throughout the centuries since before the days of John the Baptist. Of course, to guarantee this earthly kingdom, the Gentile Christians are first to be raptured and out of the way. Only then, say the Judaizers, can the racially blessed and God-favored Jews rise to the pinnacle of universal power. It is supposedly the destiny of the Jews to be god-men and rulers of planet earth.

The Kingdom Reserved for the Overcomers

Well, I have news for these Zionist and Judaizer schemers and plotters. Under the authority of God's majestic and incomparable Word, we can with assurance confidently proclaim that Zion is the destination and home only of born again Christian believers, people saved through faith in Jesus and not as a result of their flesh and blood or by accident of their national origins.

The prophecies of God clearly tell us that it is not just Jews who shall inherit the Kingdom and have power over the nations, but whoseoever believeth on the name of Jesus, for He has overcome the world, and we are of Him:

> *"And he that overcometh, and keepeth my works unto the end, to him will I give power over the nations." (Revelation 2:26)*

The Kingdom of our Lord Jesus is not a future Kingdom, and He is not interested in sitting on an earthly throne in Jerusalem. Indeed, God scathingly identifies wicked, earthly Jerusalem as the "Great City, Babylon" *(Revelation 18)*. He also brands this filthy city of earthly Jerusalem as "Sodom and Egypt" *(Revelation 11:8)*.

No, Jesus' Kingdom is not future. It is not limited to earthly habitation. It is alive. It is eternal. It exists now. Our Father in Heaven has declared His Majesty, and who is able to deny Jesus His deserved crown and Kingdom?

> *"But unto the Son He saith, THY THRONE, O GOD, IS FOR EVER AND EVER." (Hebrews 1:8)*

The Apostle Paul told us that *all who trust in Jesus as Lord are already entered into His Kingdom. We are even now "situated in heavenly places" (see Col. 1:13; I Thes. 2:12; Hebrews 12:22)*. Friends, would you then trade in your heavenly and joyous abode for a man-made residence here on this tumultuous, depraved planet earth? Well, count me out! My calling, destiny and hope is to reside in glory with Christ Jesus, not to remain here, on this doomed, miserable pile of dirt and rocks called planet earth. If the Jews and their Judaizer associates want it that bad, let them have this planet.

No Zion Without King Jesus

The true Kingdom of Zion is, in fact, the New Jerusalem, a heavenly city and habitat built by God without human hands. What's more, citizenship in Zion is based not on race and blood. A person must be *chosen* by the King of Zion and must be *born again* into this Kingdom *(John 3:3)*. Citizenship in this marvelous Kingdom is the privilege of believers.

The wonderful thing is that there can be no Zion without a King. And the Word of God trumpets the indisputable Truth: *There is No King but King Jesus!*

Bible Prophecies Foretell Use of Laser Death Rays and Nuclear Weapons

Does the Bible warn us of the effects of nuclear weapons and laser death rays to be unleashed in the last days? A compelling case can be made that the Bible does, indeed, prophesy the employment of these deadly weapons of horror.

For example, Zephaniah described the great day of the Lord as "a day of wasteness and desolation, a day of darkness and gloominess, a day of clouds and thick darkness" *(Zephaniah 1:15).*

Isaiah prophesied that, in the latter days, cities would be totally destroyed, "even to the dust," following a blast of "heat with the shadow of a cloud" *(Isaiah 25:5, 12).*

The prophecies of Zephaniah and Isaiah paint a picture of the reality of a future nuclear holocaust. Isaiah also tells future generations of the suddenness of nuclear strikes. The blast, he says, will be upon its victims quickly and without warning: "It shall be at an instant suddenly" *(Isaiah 29:5).*

In his book, *Hiroshima*, noted author John Hersey described the torrid aftereffects of the atomic blast on hapless human victims in imperialistic Japan:

> Their faces were wholly burned, their eye sockets were hollow, the fluid from their melted eyes had run down their cheeks.

In *Zechariah 14:12* we find a chilling prophecy that matches almost word for word Hersey's description of nuclear effects on the bodies of victims:

> *And this shall be the plague wherewith the Lord will smite all the people that have fought against Jerusalem; Their flesh shall consume away while they stand upon their feet, and their eyes shall consume away in their holes, and their tongue shall consume away in their mouth.*

There are many, many other Bible

prophecies which seem to apply to the heat and raging infernos generated by nuclear blasts, to space weapons and missiles, and to the great destruction to come following a world nuclear conflict:

Your country is desolate, your cities are burned with fire (Isaiah 1:7).

For then shall be great tribulation, such as was not since the beginning of the world to this time, no, nor ever shall be (Matthew 24:21).

And I will shew wonders in the heavens and in the earth, blood, and fire, and pillars of smoke (Joel 2:30).

But the same day that Lot went out of Sodom it rained fire and brimstone from heaven, and destroyed them all. Even thus shall it be in the day when the Son of man is revealed (Luke 17:29-30).

Therefore the inhabitants of the earth are burned, and few men left (Isaiah 24:6).

And I will kindle a fire in his cities, and it shall devour all round about him (Jeremiah 50:32).

The mountains shall be thrown down, and the steep places shall fall, and every wall shall fall to the ground (Ezekiel 38:20).

These prophetic images rival any description of the effects of nuclear weapons found in military textbooks. Such references are not about a war of swords and lances or of hand-to-hand combat. It seems clear that the prophets of old were describing futuristic weaponry—as revealed to them by God.

Bible prophecy also forecasts the latter-day use of laser ray weapons. In my book, *Mega Forces*, I cite eight different prophetic passages in the Bible dealing with laser death rays, including the frightening prophecy of soldiers being *instantly blinded* in battle.

Amazingly, in a recent associated press newspaper story (*The Advocate*, Baton Rouge, LA, May 22, 1995, p. 12c), it was reported from Washington, D.C. that, "Human rights groups are criticizing the Pentagon for developing laser weapons with the potential to *blind* enemy soldiers, arguing they could open a new, more inhumane kind of arms race."

Then, in March, 1996, came the startling news report that President Bill Clinton had ordered the Pentagon to give these horrible weapons to the nation of Israel for its use against its foes, in event of a future conflict.

Believe me, that future war will come. And soon. The Bible prophesies these cruel weapons will be used in the last days, and they will.

The World is More Queer Than Most People Think

"Woe unto them that seek deep to hide their counsel from the Lord, and their works are in the dark, and they say, Who seeth us? and who knoweth us?"
—*Isaiah 29:15*

"The world is very queer, indeed," said one famous physicist to another. "Yes, and more queer than you or I think it queer," responded the second.

These men were talking about the odd and often confusing science of physics, the building blocks of the universe, acknowledging that no matter how much they investigated, they still could not unravel the essential mysteries of life, the planetary system, and the creation. Scholars affirm that what is considered "scientific fact" today will no doubt be frowned upon as "juvenile fantasy" or as "uninformed theory" some 25 years from now.

There's the "World's Truth," and Then There's Truth

The principle, interestingly, is the same in the arcane field of human affairs. Most people go about their life falsely believing they know the "truth." The majority delude themselves into imagining they are above being duped and deceived.

"We are too bright," they boast, "too with it," "too sharp."

"No one can fool me," says the average man or woman on the street. "I know what's going on."

Invariably, the masses, in fact, are duped. Dumbed down. Ignorant. Blinded. Incapable of understanding even the most rudimentary facts about true history or the way the world really works. Most absolutely trust the silly, tainted info they garner from the mass media and from our corrupted educational system.

Regrettably, the average American is a drone clone. His or her mind is weighed down with useless, so-called "truth." Such is the state of the *"Borg,"* the universal, programmed mind of the masses.

God's People to Know

The Holy Bible, of course, prophesied this pitiful state of affairs. *Daniel 12:10* tells us that in the last days none of the wicked will understand. But, said the messenger from Heaven: "The wise *shall* understand."

Indeed, God makes it possible for *His* people—not the millions who *say* they are Christians, but only the few who really are!—to understand things that the ignorant masses are quite sure just cannot be so. The multitudes, blissfully uninformed, do not even consider that the world is queer. They are mere robots, programmed by unseen powers to think and act. Most are like biomechanical automatons, meat machines that are devoid of the spiritual power and supernatural understanding necessary to understand the great events of yesterday. Unable, moreover, to decipher or conceive of the terrors which their elite controllers have programmed for them, coming up soon, just over the horizon.

But, unlike the deceived multitudes, the few who are God's elect will not be long deceived. They will understand. They will *know*, even if the jaded and unperceiving world scorns and heaps ridicule on them for the very knowledge they possess. True Christians persevere because they *know*. God sends them the information they need in His timing. And so, they know.

In my voluminous files are incredible portions of knowledge that God has thankfully sent my way. So Much information that, at present, I have but little opportunity to pass it on to you, my dear friends. But, in God's good time, I shall do so. He knew that I would. That's why He gave it to me.

Most of the materials in my *Secret Files* flies in the face of what the world thinks to be true. Some of the facts and knowledge buried deep in my files would appear at first glance to be incredible, even outrageous and absurd. Still, it is factual. Indeed, I have discovered through my investigations that the world is much more queer than the masses could even imagine it to be.

The Establishment of Israel

Take, for example, the establishment of the tiny nation-state of Israel in 1948. History books point out that his top advisors were bewildered over why President Harry Truman, refusing all their advice, would direct our United Nations representative to vote yes on the Israel question and to accord diplomatic recognition to the new, fledgling Jewish state.

Ted Hall as he looked when he worked on the top secret Manhattan Project creating the atomic bomb. Hall was part of a network of traitorous, Jewish Communist spies who gave away our nation's nuclear secrets to Russia.

Documents in my files, however, reveal what happened. Harry Truman was a 33rd degree Mason. Jewish Zionist billionaires, fellow Masons, secretly gave Truman *two million dollars in cash*, in a suitcase, aboard his whistle-stop campaign train. In return he gave them a nation, Israel. Money talks.

Those who romantically think of Harry S. Truman as honest and loaded with integrity will, naturally, get hot behind the collar and scream "No!, No!" at me for divulging this unheralded fact. But, in time, I will reveal even more details about Mr. Truman's dishonest and treacherous dealings, including his sell-out to his Communist pals in the federal government, but also his selection for political office in the first place by Kansas City gangsters tied to the lower echelon of the Illuminati.

The Stealing of the Atomic Bomb

Then there's the matter of *who* stole the plans for the atomic bomb and gave them first to Communist Russia, then to Israel, and on to China. Was it the Rosenbergs? Were quisling, turncoat U.S. traitors behind this perfidy and outrage?

Ted Hall, an American Jew living in England and now suffering from Parkinson's disease and kidney cancer, could tell you. It was, in fact, Mr. Hall, a Harvard University physicist recruited in 1944 by the U.S.A. to work on the top secret Manhattan Project, who gave his Red Communist buddies a detailed diagram of the nuclear bomb. The Russian KGB spy agency was very pleased at the efforts of their young associate.

Oppenheimer, also Jewish and the chief of the Los Alamos Manhattan Project, was also a Communist sympathizer, as well as a devotee of the Hindu scriptures, the *Bhagavad Gita.* He was aware of Hall's notorious deceit.

Later, American Jewish scientists in charge of our nation's atomic secrets criminally passed on the bomb technology to Israel's Prime Minister Ben Gurion. That nation created its present-days arsenal of some 400 nuclcar bombs using America's stolen secrets.

But the thefts didn't stop there. The Israel Mossad spy agency went on to give the Red Chinese the filched American secrets of A-bomb construction. Unknown to the American public at large, Israel and Red China have for decades been cooperating. Socialists and Communists help each other, and Israel has since its inception been a Socialist State.

Bush, Robertson, and China: The Treachery Continues Unabated

Before we throw too many stones at Israel, however, we should turn our attention back to the U.S., where we find several culprits equally guilty of treachery in handing over America's most precious secrets to Red China. First, there's President Bill Clinton, who willingly gave the Chinese free entry to our advanced nuclear and missle technology—in Department of Energy labs and through aerospace corporations like Loral, headed by Jewish billionaire Mr. Schwarz.

Pat Robertson meets with Red Chinese Premier Zhu Rongji in 1998. The 700 Club host has invested millions of dollars in Red China and supports its policy of forced abortions, all the time pretending to be "pro-life."

President George W. Bush had his little "show tilt" with the Red Chinese in the Hainan U.S. spy plane incident. But if you think for a moment that Bush is not a long time crony and pal of the Chinese dictators, well, think again. George W.'s brother Neil, is involved in a multimillion dollar project to build a luxurious $120 million country club for commie bureaucrats outside the capital city of Beijing.

Remember this Bush family connection someday when you read that the free nation of Taiwan (Nationalist China) has been sold down the river to Beijing. Believe me, this is in the works.

Pat Robertson is another of the Illuminati boys who have their greedy mitts in the Red Chinese arena. Robertson, unbeknownst to the Christian world, is a wealthy billionaire whose father, an influential U.S. Senator, was Chairman of the Senate Banking and Currency Committee.

Robertson has invested ten million dollars in the Red Chinese company Zhaodaola, the Asian tiger's equivalent of our Internet's *Yahoo* Corporation.

Robertson has assured Chinese Premier Zhu Rongji he'll back the reds politically, too. So, Pat told viewers of TV's *The 700 Club* they needed to back free trade between the U.S. and China. Then, this April, 2001, Pat Roberston told his audience that the United States should get off Red China's back and quit bitching about the Communists' depopulation policy of only one child per family and forced abortions.

"They've got 1.2 billion people," Pat complained. "If every family over there was allowed to have three or four children the population would be completely unsustainable" (*U.S. News and World Report,* April 30, 2001, p. 29).

Robertson also launched an attack on China's suffering and beleaguered Christians, severing ties with China's underground churches and recognizing only Beijing government-approved "churches." That bit of satanic treachery must have pleased the red butchers of Tiananmen Square immensely.

Jesse Jackson: Government Flunkie?

Was Jesse Jackson chosen by the Illuminati to replace Martin Luther King as the premier black spokesman? I have evidence that's the case. The plan was for the FBI to assassinate King, then promote Jackson as the only suitable replacement. Satchels-full of secret money went into Jackson's coffers to assure that Jesse Jackson had the financial wherewithal to be MLK's successor.

As part of the plot, the Hollywood myth was created that Jesse was right there, an anguished victim, by his side when King was shot, even got blood on his hands and shirt. Jackson would come out a media hero. And that is exactly what happened.

By the way, information in my files indicates that Martin Luther King, whom all the world now lionizes as a paragon of integrity, loved to have sordid sex with multiple white women—did so the very night before he was assassinated. King enjoyed slapping women around, and—get this!—he was a bisexual who actually favored men over women in bed!

Martin Luther King was a creation of the Communist Party U.S.A., but he ran afoul of the FBI's Director J. Edgar Hoover. Hoover had his FBI agents wiretap King's hotel rooms and get dirt. Hoover personally picked Jackson to replace King, and young Jesse was duly trained to be a government toady and Illuminati errand boy. That's why today the IRS lets Jackson and his crooked 501(c)3 nonprofit organization get away with payoffs to mistresses and other assorted mischief.

Odd, Strange, Queer...and True

These are just a few of the fascinating sidenotes to real world history. Things you *won't* read in a newspaper or school textbook or hear about on the Discovery Channel or on the Public Broadcasting System (PBS). After all, these are like, well, like "Alice in Wonderland!" Crazy. Insane. Mind-boggling and weird. If these things are true, and they are, then the world of human affairs is immeasurably more odd and strange than the majority envisions.

Well, dear friends, as you and I know, the world *is* queer; indeed, more queer than almost anyone—except the biblical Christian—could *ever* imagine.

Isn't it fascinating that the rulers of humanity really believe they can get away with these secret things, that no one will ever find out? They are confident that the masses are too dumbed down and mind-controlled to even suspect their evildoings.

But we who follow Christ do know. In any event, God knows. The day is coming, the scriptures say, when the Lord will bring all things into judgement: *"In the day when God shall judge the secrets of men by Jesus Christ" (Romans 2:16).* What a fine and wonderful day of Truth that will be!

> *"For God shall bring every work into judgement, with every secret thing, whether it be good, or whether it be evil" (Ecclesiastes 12:14)*

Blood, Empire, and the Coming Purification of Planet Earth

Hidden Prophecies in the Book of Esther

"Wherein the king granted the Jews...to destroy, to slay, and to cause to perish, all the power of the people...both little ones and women and to take the spoil of them for a prey."

—*Esther 8:11*

"Then said Esther...let it be granted to the Jews...and let Haman's ten sons be hanged upon the gallows. And the King commanded it so to be done..."

—*Esther 9:13*

Could the chilling account of the catastrophe, bloodshed, and treachery soon to befall America be concealed in the pages of a misunderstood and little suspected book of the Holy Bible? Could the riddle of modern-day Israel and the quest for global empire by its proxy, the United States, be solved simply by our heeding the prophetic warnings given in that unheralded Old Testament text?

The answer to both questions is, *Yes!* In the little book of *Esther*, I am convinced, are incredible prophetic keys of astonishing importance. For some inexplicable reason, God has hidden and imbedded these stunning prophetic truths in *Esther*. But beware: He who does not have eyes to see and ears to hear will be confused and will not understand; but the wise shall understand. Ask the average undiscerning Pastor or Christian what is the true meaning of Esther and he or she will

Understand the Bible's Book of Esther and you will have a step-by-step guide to exactly what is to happen prophetically to America and Israel.

surely say that Esther is simply a tale of how Jews faithful to God were saved from their enemies by the heroine Esther and her brave cousin, Mordecai. This is the Zionist and Judaizer version and interpretation.

In fact, God is neither named nor even mentioned in the entire text of the book of Esther! This is not a book about God but about the criminal acts of the Jewish people in rebellion against God.

God has shown me the little-known prophecies that are revealed in *Esther*. As it turns out, these prophecies are profound. Understand *Esther* and you will have a step-by-step guide to exactly what is to happen prophetically to America and Israel.

The Star Goddess and The God of War

First, it is necessary to realize that the name Esther stands for Star, or the *Star Goddess*. In Babylonia/Sumeria/Persia she was known as the goddess *Astara, Astar, Ishtar* or *Ashtar*. In Germania, her name was *Ostara*. In Greece, the people called her *Astarte*. In Babylon, she was called the Triple Goddess and her holy number was 666!

In the Bible, this Esther is seen to be a Jewish concubine, who became Queen of Persia by virtue of her great beauty, allure, and sexual charms. Esther won a contest to be the new Queen after the real Queen, Vashti, was ousted. It seems that Vashti was an upstanding moral woman who refused to parade around nude and show her body off to the drunken guests at one of the King's brawling parties. That angered King Ahasuerus who was advised by his Court that an example must be made of Vashti, else more women might follow her virtuous example!

Now the glamorous Esther had a sly and shadowy cousin named Mordecai who cunningly advised and guided her. The name Mordecai literally means *I am Marduk;* Marduk was the great god of the Persians who was worshipped as Mars, sixth planet from the sun, god of war, ritual sacrifice and fire, also known as *Merodach*.

The Jewish duo of Esther, the Queen, and her conniving cousin, Mordecai, thus represents the idolatrous Persian deities, Ashtar, the Mother Goddess, and Marduk, the God.

Haman's Plot to Kill the Jews

In the biblical story, the Jews who live in Persia are threatened by a Gentile named Haman, who happens to be Grand Vizier, or Governor, for the Persian King, Ahasuerus. Haman is concerned because the Jews are haughty and refuse to fit in with the Persian culture. Haman is also angered by Esther's cousin, Mordecai. Mordecai looks down on Haman. Mordecai thinks he's racially superior to Haman. Haman, you see, is a member of the Agagite tribe that Israel, generations before, had defeated.

Haman persuades King Ahasuerus that the Jews, being hostile and untrustworthy and hating everyone but their own race, should be put to death, and so the agreeable King allows Haman to cast lots *(pur)* to find an appropriate date for the killing of the nation's entire Jewish population.

Esther's Bloody Revenge

Mordecai, a hanger-on around the Palace grounds, found out about Haman's plot and got Queen Esther to intervene. Esther put on perfume and made herself up beautifully. So taken with her was the King (remember the parallel story of King Herod and Salome?) that he told the sexy and gorgeous Esther that she can ask for anything in the kingdom she wants and it will be given to her.

To make a long story short, with the King's permission, Esther overturned Haman's edict to kill all the Jews. In its place, she got the dumbed-down King to go along with Esther's revengeful, bloodthirsty scheme, which involved:

1. The hanging on the gallows of Haman, enemy of the Jews.

2. The double hanging on the gallows of Haman's ten sons, none of whom, so far as we can tell from reading the scriptures, were guilty of any crimes.

3. A license for the Jews to slaughter anyone whom they saw fit to murder anywhere in the Kingdom. Through this edict, a license to kill, tens of thousands of men, women, and even children were monstrously put to death simply because a Jew gave the word.
4. The massacre of many of the workers on the Palace staff just for good measure.

5. The taking of all the goods and properties owned by the dead victims.

According to the Bible's book of *Esther*, many people in the Kingdom converted to the Jews' religion (Babylonian Talmudism) so fearful were they of the murderous and vicious spirit of the unleashed Jews. Interesting, too, is that harlot Queen Esther also maneuvered things so that her wily cousin, Mordecai, became Grand Vizier in place of the dead Haman. And so, he and Esther apparently ran things their way in the Kingdom with the stupid and drunken King Ahasuerus being figuratively led around by the nose.

Festival of Purim Commemorates Bloodshed

Today, in Jewish synagogues and meeting houses throughout the world, on a given day each spring, the high holy day festival of *Purim* is celebrated in honor of Queen Esther's bloody accomplishments. During the festivities, Jewish children are given little triangle-shaped cookies which they eagerly bite into, imagining they are symbolically chomping off the head of their enemy, Haman.

The chief rabbis choose a living human "Haman" that all Jews can revile and hate on Purim. Twice, Saddam Hussein was chosen as the designated "Haman" for a given year.

> *Nowhere in the Bible do we find God ordaining this wicked festival, Purim, as one of His designated Holy Days.*

I have much documentation in my files that, during the celebration of Purim, the liquor flows inside the synagogues, and parties go on and on, punctuated by dancing, drinking, costumes, and unrivalled reveling. Sexual orgies are commonplace, and worse things occur. There is evidence that Gentile children are kidnapped and ritually sacrificed, this being practiced by certain, especially evil Kabbalistic Jewish sects.

Purim Ordained by Jews, Not God

Now, get this! Nowhere in the Bible do we find God ordaining this wicked festival, Purim, as one of His designated Holy Days. In fact, in the book of *Esther*, it makes clear that it is the Jews

Saddam Hussein was twice named "Haman of the Year" by rabbis.

themselves who ordained this day and who now require its unholy celebration.

In truth, Purim is nothing less nor more than the hideous commemoration of the vile and fulsome hatred of Gentiles by the Jews. After all, the Jews' own Holy Book, the Talmud, declares that Gentiles are but goyim (cattle) and are worthy of death. The arrogant and wicked Talmud, meanwhile, praises the Jewish race as so holy, pure, and great that even God and His angels are inferior to the intellect and wisdom of the top rabbis!

There is nothing in the Christian religion to compare with the murderous Jewish festival of Purim. Christ Jesus taught us to love our enemies and pray for them, not slaughter them and take their goods and property for spoil! Christians celebrate the birth of Jesus and His Resurrection, but we have no Purim, nor could we. The very thought of such a thing is alien to the Christian spirit.

Purim Plot Lives

Now the facts I recount here about Esther, Mordecai, and the bloodlust and treachery of these cruel people are true. But there's more. Within the book of Esther is God's hidden prophetic journal for what is soon to transpire for Christians everywhere on earth, if the Zionist zealots get their way.

You will be shocked to discover that there is, on earth today, a real-life Queen Esther. There also *does* exist, today, an actual plot to massacre and put to death, by genocidal acts, everyone on earth who refuses to go along with the Plan for a Jewish Kingdom on Earth. And there *is* a modern-day King Ahasuerus and his minister, Mordecai, scheming and conniving to bring the entire globe under the tight-fisted control of the mysterious Queen Esther and her Jewish conspirators.

Who will be the next designated "Haman" whose head is to be bitten off by the Jewish rebels against Christ Jesus and His people? Is it *you*? Is it *me*? Will we be cruelly sacrificed by the Zionist overlords as victims simply because of our faith in Christ Jesus? And when will the taking of Christian victims begin?

(NOTE: Texe Marrs has prepared an unparalleled two-part audiotape or CD series entitled, *Hidden Prophecies In The Book of Esther—Blood, Empire and The Coming Purification of Planet Earth.* The set ($12.00 plus $5 s&h; 2 hours; on CD or tape) is available from *Power of Prophecy, 1708 Patterson Road, Austin, Texas 78733, or phone toll free 1-800-234-9673.*)

Jewish Sanhedrin Honors George W. Bush as Chief Prince of Meshech and Tubal

Gog, Magog, and the Scroll of Bush

"And the word of the Lord came unto me, saying, Son of man, set thy face against Gog, the land of Magog, the chief prince of Meshech and Tubal, and prophesy against him, And say, Thus saith the Lord God; Behold, I am against thee, O Gog, the chief prince of Meshech and Tubal."

—*Ezekiel 38:1-3*

"And I will send a fire on Magog, and among them that dwell carelessly in the isles: and they shall know that I am the Lord."

—*Ezekiel 39:6*

An historic event occurred in Jerusalem this January, an event chronicled widely in Israel's newspapers but omitted entirely by America's Zionist controlled and owned press. President George W. Bush, visiting the nation of Israel, was presented with a rabbinical decree, the *Scroll of Bush*. The Scroll declared that he, Bush, is none other than the prophesied Gog, of the land of Magog; that is, Chief Prince of Meshech and Tubal.

Even as America's economic crisis grew deeper, with hundreds of thousands losing their homes due to mortgage foreclosures, the U.S. stock market sliding south, the U.S. dollar sinking like a rock against foreign currencies, and labor statistics showing unemployment rising as more and more American workers are laid off and manufacturing sent overseas, our President George W. Bush embarked on Air Force One on an eight day trip to Israel.

Yes, like bloody Roman Emperor Nero, who reportedly fiddled while Rome burned, a callous and indifferent George Bush left a desperate country and people gasping for breath to go to the Middle East and consult with his superiors—Zionist rabbinical overlords.

28 TEVET, 5768 • JANUARY 6, 2008

IN THE NAME OF THE *LORD*, ETERNAL GOD

TO THE HONORABLE MR. GEORGE W. BUSH,
PRESIDENT OF THE UNITED STATES OF AMERICA,

WHO COMES SEEKING THE PRESENCE OF THE MOST HIGH GOD, TO JERUSALEM, CITY OF GOD, DIVINELY CHOSEN SITE OF THE HOLY TEMPLE, ETERNAL CAPITAL OF OUR LAND, "THE JOY OF THE ENTIRE EARTH (PSALMS 48:3)," MAY IT BE REBUILT AND ESTABLISHED SPEEDILY AND IN OUR DAYS, AMEN!

ESTEEMED MR. GEORGE W. BUSH, THE CHIEF PRINCE OF MESHECH AND TUBAL (EZEKIEL 38:1), LEADER OF THE WEST!

UPON YOUR ARRIVAL IN JERUSALEM YOU HAVE THE ABILITY TO MAKE A DECLARATION, AS DID CYRUS, KING OF PERSIA – WHOSE MEMORY IS HONORED – WHO IN THE YEAR 538 BCE RETURNED THE EXILED NATIONS TO THEIR LANDS AND RECOGNIZED THE FULL RIGHT OF THE JEWISH PEOPLE TO REESTABLISH THEIR HOLY TEMPLE, THE "HOUSE OF PRAYER FOR ALL NATIONS" (ISAIAH 56:7), AND CALLED UPON THEM TO RETURN TO THEIR LAND.

AND IN THE MANNER OF LORD JAMES BALFOUR OF ENGLAND, WHO IN 1917, CALLED UPON THE JEWS TO REESTABLISH A NATIONAL HOMELAND IN THE LAND OF ISRAEL.

AND THUS IF YOU TRULY DESIRE PEACE AND BENEVOLENCE, AND YOU WOULD BE COUNTED IN THE COMPANY OF THE TRULY RIGHTEOUS, WE CALL UPON YOU TO DECLARE TO ALL THE WORLD:

THE LAND OF ISRAEL WAS BEQUEATHED TO THE NATION OF ISRAEL BY THE CREATOR OF THE WORLD. NEITHER COULD I, AS A SON OF MY FAITH, NOR THE MUSLIMS ACCORDING TO THEIR FAITH, EVER TAKE AWAY EVEN THE SLIGHTEST GRAIN FROM THE ETERNAL'S GIFT, WHICH HE GAVE TO HIS PEOPLE ISRAEL, THE ETERNAL PEOPLE. THUS I CALL

The Scroll of Bush identifying the U. S. President as the "esteemed Mr. George W. Bush, the Chief Prince of Meshech and Tubal *(Ezekial 38:1)* Leader of the West!"

Arriving on 666, a Prophetically Appropriate Date

He arrived in Jerusalem 1/09/08, numerically translated in occult numerology as *666*. On 1/11 (the 11th of January), he and Israeli Prime Minister Olmert, along with former British Prime Minister Tony Blair, were taken down into the earth, inside Zedekiah's Cave, for a clandestine ritual and black mass conducted by the Grand Master of Israel's Freemasons. The same day, Bush visited Yad Vashem, Israel's version of the Holocaust Museum, where he stayed exactly 90 minutes, a number again translating into <u>*666*</u>.

While in Jerusalem, President Bush and Prime Minister Olmert met with the press and referred to several key dates approaching. March 20th would signal the Jewish holy day of *Purim*, commemorating the mass murder and genocide by the Jews of more than 75,000 Gentile "enemies" of Persia (Iran) in the days of the Jews' Queen Esther. On May 8, Israel celebrates its 60th anniversary. Finally, President Bush predicted that by the end of his term in 2009 (2x9=18, translating again, into that number *666*), there will be a peace treaty between the Palestinians and the Israelis. The treaty will insure that the Palestinians will forever be squeezed into their pitiful, apartheid, poverty-stricken ghettos, while the victorious Jews enjoy the fruits of their crimes, luxuriously living in an enlarged, Greater Israel.

But those things were not the most significant that happened during Bush's historic visit. No, that occurred on the third day when, at a banquet, President Bush was presented with the *Scroll of Bush*, a document made out on ancient parchment and signed by the three most spiritually prominent Jews on planet earth:

- Rabbi Adan Steinzaltz, High Priest of the Sanhedrin
- Rabbi Chaim Reichman, Chief Rabbi of the Holy Temple
- Dr. Gadi Schel, Chief Representative of The New Jewish Congress

The Scroll of Bush, the first page of which is pictured here, pompously claims to be promulgated, *"In the Name of the Lord, Eternal God."* Of course, this is not Jesus Christ, since the Jews hate and despise Jesus Christ and brand him an illegitimate bastard and blasphemer in their Judaic Holy Law, the Talmud. Jesus himself said their "Lord" is, in fact, the Devil!

Bush Identified as Chief Prince of Meshech and Tubal

The Scroll goes on to address Bush as, "The Honorable Mr. George W. Bush, President of the

United States of America." Then, however, in a most shocking and prophetic manner, the Scroll of Bush, a document representing the entire Jewish nation both in Israel and dispersed throughout the world, a document composed by and authenticated by the highest religious rabbis on the planet, addressed Bush by yet another title:

> "Esteemed Mr. George W. Bush, the Chief Prince of Meshech and Tubal (*Ezekiel 38:1*), Leader of the West!"

President George W. Bush toasts Israeli Prime Minister Olmert during a visit to Jerusalem where Bush was presented the Scroll of Bush honoring him as Chief Prince of Meshech and Tubal; That makes Bush "Gog, of the land of Magog."

Oh my, oh my. This is an occult mystery of tremendous prophetic significance, one so incredibly deep and so stunningly revealing that I am offering to my friends an exhaustive 60-minute audiotape/CD investigative report, *Gog, Magog, and the Scroll of Bush*, carefully and fully explaining what all this means.

There can be no doubt that President Bush knows exactly why he holds the satanic title of "Gog, of the land of Magog," also known as Chief Prince of Meshech and Tubal. The "Leader of the West," as the Rabbis also put it, shall be incarnated and possessed by Satan himself in the last days. The Scriptures say he, as Chief Prince, "*shall go out to deceive the nations which are in the four corners of the earth, Gog and Magog, to gather them together to battle: the number of whom is as the sand of the sea*" (*Revelation 20:7-8*).

"Magog" of Skull and Bones

Decades ago, as George Bush, Sr., lay naked in a coffin, inside the bowels of the Tomb, the macabre, mausoleum residence of the Order of Skull and Bones, located next to the old town cemetery in New Haven, Connecticut, his fellows performed a hellish death ritual and raised George from his sarcophagus. They gave him, as they do all initiates, a new name. Hence more, George Herbert Walker Bush would secretly be known by the Brotherhood as "Magog."

Now, on a mission for his infernal Lord Lucifer, comes President George W. Bush, son of the bonesman named "Magog," to Jerusalem, Israel. There, the chief religious officials—including the High Priest of the reconvened Sanhedrin, the same devilish body that so long ago commanded that Jesus our Lord be tortured and crucified on a primitive wooden cross—recognized and honored Mr. Bush as Gog, of the land of Magog, Chief Prince of Meshech and Tubal *(Ezekiel 38:1).*

The Unwise Haven't a Clue

Imagine: Three hundred million people residing in the U.S.A. and only a few—the wise who believe and honor the word of God and the Lord's prophetic scriptures—are able to understand the profound nature of such a cardinal event. Of course, the rabbis and the Masons of Israel, disciples of Satan—they know. But America's Senators and Congressmen, America's TV news celebrities, America's radio talk show personalities, and the dumbed-down, Christ-rejecting masses—they haven't a clue.

The wise and informed, however, understand and shall be rewarded. But the careless and wicked shall perish in their ignorance and stupidity. Such is truth. Such is prophecy.

Deceptive Cults and Unholy Religions

Evil Rampant Throughout Planet Earth Until Jesus' Return

Is Satan "god" of This World?

Who is ruler of this present Earth? Who is the presiding monarch of our planet and its 200-plus nation-states? Is it the Lord Almighty, whose magnificent name is Jesus, or is it Satan who, in our day and age, rules over the affairs of men?

To those unfamiliar with Scripture, it seems unfathomable—even preposterous—to admit that Satan, that wicked and monstrous creature of hell, is god of this world. But, in fact, this is exactly what the Holy Bible teaches.

Though ignorant, unsaved men and women everywhere believe themselves to be masters of their own destiny, in truth they serve a god. His name is Satan. They may scoff or ridicule the notion. But again, I assert: Every person alive today on planet Earth who does not have Jesus is under bondage to the Evil One. Their deity and master is Lucifer—god of this world.

Satan Given Temporary Throne

Our Father in Heaven, God over all, has given Satan his temporary throne and endowed him with miraculous, if limited, powers. In the wilderness, Jesus was tested and offered the kingdoms of this world if He would bow down and worship Satan. Our Lord refused, rebuking the Adversary for his blasphemy. But Christ did not deny that these worldly kingdoms were Satan's to give.

Later, Jesus told Pilate, "My Kingdom is not of this world" *(John 18:36)*. The Lord declared to His disciples, "I have chosen you out of the world" *(John 15:19)* and encouraged them by proclaiming that He, Jesus, had overcome the world. Moreover, the Apostle John instructed fellow Christians: "Ye are of God, little children, and have overcome them: because greater is He (God's Holy Spirit) that is in you, than he (Satan) that is in the world" *(I John 4:4)*.

True Christian Not of This World

And thus we come to a mind-boggling and wonderful discovery: The man or woman who is of God is not of this world. He or she is not subservient to Satan nor under the influence of the devil's dark angels.

The man and woman of God is free, having obtained liberty through Christ Jesus and having become a pilgrim and alien, passing through, but not of this world. The Christian's glorious home and eternal abode is Heaven, where born again Christians shall live joyously with Christ forevermore.

What, then, of the unsaved person, the man or woman who knows not God? Again, we come to a shocking discovery: The lost person belongs, body and soul, to Satan. He or she is attached to this perishing, feudal world of which the devil is temporarily lord of the manor and possessor.

Yes, Satan is king of the unsaved world. And there is but one avenue of escape from the horrendous clutches of the one whom the Apostle Paul called the "god of this world" *(II Corinthians*

4:3-4). Only a person with a repentant heart who cries out to Jesus as Lord and Saviour can escape the ravages of this present-day world.

Lunatics in Charge of Planet

And what a sickeningly wild and desperately craven world this has become! The lunatics are now in charge of the asylum. Earth is turned into a nightmare as Satan furiously charges about, angry that his time is short and seeking whom he may devour. The ravages of the Evil One have made Earth into a fearful world, a dim place with no prospects and no future. Someday—I believe very soon—a new world is coming, with a victorious Jesus to reign as King and Overseer (see *II Peter 3:13* and *Revelation 21*). But until He comes, things will only wax worse and worse (*II Timothy 3:13*).

> ***The signs of Jesus' coming are clearly at hand. As in Noah's day, the world is filled with wickedness, and man, without God, does not cease to continuously produce evil works.***

How long will it be before Christ returns? I set no dates, but the signs of His coming are clearly at hand. As in Noah's day, the world is filled with wickedness, and man, without God, does not cease to continuously produce evil works. Consider please, the following, prime examples of these evil works, and witness the Earth's gathering darkness. Then, decide for yourself how close we are to the end.

A Pedophile Priest Victim Help Line

In Dublin, Ireland, the Catholic Church recently opened a special telephone help line for victims of child abuse by the clergy. The line went into operation after countless instances of rape and molestation by pedophile Catholic priests. The latest reported in Ireland was a 71-year old pedophile priest who sexually molested at least 74 children during his 36 year pastorate. (*New York Daily News*, July 27, 1997)

Billy Graham lobbied Congress for Red China, among other atrocities.

Billy Graham Does Political Favor for President Clinton

In the U.S.A., the world's most beloved evangelist, Billy Graham, has assured passage of a shaky congressional bill conferring "Most Favored Nation" trade status for Communist Red China by writing a letter strongly supporting the bill. Hesitant legislators on the fence quickly caved in to White House demands and voted for the bill after receiving Billy Graham's politically charged letter. (*Reuters*, June 23, 1997)

This same Billy Graham is the man who once raved about butcher Mao Tse Tung's sayings, favorably comparing them to the Ten Commandments. Graham also once complimented a gulag-ridden Soviet Russia during the dark era for its "freedom of religion," and he called North Korea's vicious, bloody dictator, the late Kim Il Sung, a "great leader."

Now Billy Graham aids the Illuminati agenda as he seeks to gain financial advantage for a barbaric Red China. Red China's leadership slaughtered thousands in Tiananmen Square and, even now, persecutes and locks many Christian Chinese up in filthy jail cells.

Dr. Hedy Fry, shown here with local drag queen and transvestite, Ruby Stone, celebrates her election as a member of Canada's Parliament.

Billy Graham has long been a water carrier and an errand boy for the Rockefellers, the Presidents, and other political and financial bigwigs. His recent scam, helping Communist China at President Clinton's behest, is just the latest in a string of political favors that Graham has tendered his influential and powerful friends in high places.

The unseemly behavior—and the political and moral compromises—of the world's most famous "evangelist" is one signal that the great falling away from the Truth foretold in Bible prophecy is underway (*II Thess. 2*).

Drag Queen and Politician Celebrate Together

In Vancouver, Canada, at the fancy and luxurious Vancouver Hotel, member of parliament Dr. Hedy Fry celebrated her election victory to the Canadian Parliament. Fry, a close friend and supporter of Prime Minister Jean Chretian, enjoyed a toast with a wide assortment of corporate bosses, abortionists, one worlders, gun controllers, labor leaders, environmental activists, and feminists. Also invited to the gala affair was a Fry associate, the local drag queen and transvestite homosexual, Ruby Stone. (*Westender*, June 5, 1997)

Hong Kong Handed Over to Communists

Great Britain has willingly turned over a thriving and democratic Hong Kong to slavery under Red Chinese tyranny. To tumultuous applause by the world's media, a treasonous Prince Charles, the royal monarch who rates Mohammed on a par with Jesus and whose adulterous affair with a married woman broke up his own marriage, gave a little farewell speech at Hong Kong's harbor. Then the New Age prince sailed off into the sunset aboard his royal yacht. Within hours, four thousand Red Chinese Army troops marched into the city as the bulk of its citizenry quaked behind closed doors. (*Reuters*, June 17, 1997)

Notorious Abortionist Honored

In Texas, Republican Governor George W. Bush, the son of former U.S. President George Bush, honored a baby-killing abortionist with a highway designation. Bush, who, like his father, is a member of the satanic secret society known as the Order of Skull & Bones, signed into law a House bill which names a section of State Highway 35 near Houston the "John B. Coleman Memorial Highway."

According to the National Coalition for Life, Dr. Coleman was named in 1991 by the *Houston Post* newspaper as one of the state's 12 most sued doctors. The newspaper noted that there is a "long list of malpractice suits against Coleman involving botched abortions and deaths."

Governor Bush, elected to office while proclaiming himself a "pro-life" candidate, is a front-runner for the Republican Party's nomination for the presidency of the U.S. for the next election campaign.

Pro-Homosexual Bishop Chosen

In Philadelphia, the conference of the Episcopal Church U.S.A. (2.5 million members) chose as its

In Amsterdam, thirty thousand demonstrators demanding more jobs protested the economic mire of Europe.

presiding bishop Frank Griswold III. Griswold promptly announced that he is a keen supporter of the gay and lesbian agenda. The new Episcopal Church head said he wants his denomination to okay same sex marriages and ordain homosexual clergymen. (*USA Today*, July 22, 1997)

Demonstrators Protest—Want Jobs

Thirty thousand protesters in Amsterdam, the Netherlands, were brutally suppressed by riot police during a demonstration against the plans by European politicians to unite all of Europe under a common economy, currency, and government.

Amazingly, they were not rioting for the cause of national sovereignty. The demonstrators believe a United States of Europe to be a good idea. They were angry, however, that the economic unity movement by corporate chieftains had already thrown millions of people out of jobs. Theirs was a protest for money and for more jobs.

The enraged European demonstrators threw stones, broke windows of buildings, and caused property damage, shouting slogans in Dutch, German, and Italian. But in the U.S.A., a dumbed-down citizenry continues to sit quietly, like sheep to be slaughtered, as this country's politicians herd the people into the NAFTA/WTO sheep pen. (*The Columbus Dispatch*, June 15, 1997)

The People Love Their Crooked, Immoral Politicians

President Clinton is by now fully exposed as being under the money-grubbing influence of seedy billionaires from Asia. Meanwhile, both political parties are proven guilty of accepting payoffs from Communist overlords in China. Clinton is also unmasked as a sexual harasser of Paula Jones and other women and is laughingly viewed by even his friends and supporters as a "liar par excellence."

Though scandal after scandal rocks the White House, Gallup, Roper, Harris, and other pollsters report that the President's approval ratings are up—way up. The people love and adore this man. Bill Clinton feels their pain. Clinton is just like the vast majority of the people of America. He reflects *their* values and morals. They deserve him, and vice versa.

A Superhero for the Millennium

Clinton is the acknowledged hero of the pot smoking, heroin and cocaine shooting-up, MTV Baby Boomer generation. But for the X'er generation and especially the under 14-year old crowd, a new superhero has emerged on the scene: *Spawn.*

Spawn, a warrior from hell, is the new superhero for the under 14 year old and the X generation.

A modern-day comic book legend, Spawn is the younger generation's version of the superhero. He's a hip counterpart to obsolete, traditional heros like The Lone Ranger, Roy Rogers,

Superman, and Captain Marvel. *Spawn*, you see, is qualitatively different than his older models. They were pictured as the epitome of wholesomeness and decency. But this new superhero, *Spawn*, is a war-like killer from hell.

Here's, how entertainment reporter Rene Rodriguez, in the *Miami Herald* (August 1, 1997), describes *Spawn*: "*Spawn* is a minion of the devil. His face is so horribly burned, he'd give Marilyn Manson nightmares. He lives in dark, shadowy alleys among rats and bums. He wears a crimson cape. He bleeds green goo. He can make deadly chains pop out of his rib cage. And he's the good guy."

Spawn is further described as "dark, moody, and extremely gory." That's why the movie is "an instant smash," says Rodriguez. The plot of the movie has a murdered man going to hell, but asking Satan to be allowed to come back to Earth to exact revenge. Satan makes a covenant with the man, who becomes *Spawn*. The devil allows the "superhero" to return to Earth to do his deeds, but *Spawn* agrees to return to hell afterward to lead hell's army against humanity in the apocalyptic battle of Armageddon.

The rock generation finds *Spawn* to their liking. "*Spawn*," writes David Ramsey of KMLE-FM rock radio in Phoenix, Arizona, "is a superhero for the Millennium."

Christians Long for a Better World

Considering the above scenes of a depraved world gone mad, Christians could well conclude that the planet has become a vile, buzzing mess of confusion and chaos. That may be so, but I believe this remarkable outgrowth of darkness has also, strangely enough, brought tremendous clarity to our present-day situation. Now we see the world for what it really is: A fiefdom and the province of its cunning master and overlord, Satan.

As Christians, we yearn for a better world where righteousness and sanity prevail, where goodness is supreme, and where mercy and kindness are in abundance.

As Christians, we yearn for a better world where righteousness and sanity prevail, where goodness is supreme, and where mercy and kindness are in abundance.

As Christians, we have come to loathe and despise this present-day world with its chaotic wickedness and treacherous immorality. *We know without a doubt that this is not our home.* We refuse to bow down to its "god." We reject its compromises and its "fabulous" new superheroes. We long for our *true home*—the gleaming and joyful Kingdom where our glorious King Jesus triumphantly sits on the regal throne.

Yes, we acknowledge that Satan is god of this corrupt and transient world. But he is not *our* god. He has none of us. He's a defeated and pitiful tyrant whose time is swiftly drawing to a close. Soon, Lucifer's pathetic, confused world shall be no more. As men and women of God, we pray for that day to come soon. And so it is today, that true Christians everywhere view this wicked world with sadness, and plaintively cry out, *"Please, come quickly, Lord Jesus!"*

How The Illuminati Secretly Funds Christian Heresy

On the surface, it seems like a benign, helpful, possibly Christian organization. It's membership ranges in the millions, and there are chapters and spin-off groups in almost every country of the globe. Practically every Christian leader, from Billy Graham to James Dobson, enthusiastically supports it. Moreover, books touting its methods as miraculous are currently all the rage in both secular and Christian bookstores. What, then, could possibly be wrong with *Alcoholics Anonymous (AA)* and other 12-step recovery groups?

The answer may just startle and surprise you. You see, AA is not, as many erroneously believe, a Christian organization founded by Christians and based on Biblical principles. Not hardly. After thoroughly investigating AA for a number of years, I have decided that now is the time to publish *the truth*—the whole truth—about an organization so corrupt, so demonic, and yet so seductive and beguiling, that it defies belief and shocks the imagination.

On close examination, AA proves to be a classic example of how *the Illuminati* has secretly funded and set up a network of ungodly groups worldwide, each designed to do its part in deluding the masses and moving the world steadily toward the New World Order.

A Secret Project of The Order?

Alcoholics Anonymous was and is a highly classified secret project of the elite. Its origins are traced back decades to a group whose headquarters in Oxford, England, worked hand-in-glove with the bloody Heinrich Himmler, head of Germany's Nazi death camps.

In America two men who were into spiritualism—communicating with spirits from the dead—are credited with officially beginning the organization now known as AA. These men—one a flim-flam stock broker, the other a defrocked Catholic priest—were deeply into druid witchcraft, satanic symbols and rituals, and also were heavy users of LSD and other mind altering, illegal drugs.

But the most telling part of this story is *how* these two decadent con men were supported and sponsored behind the scenes by certain well-heeled rich men whom we

Well-connected decadent founders of Alcoholics Anonymous, Dr. Bob and Bill W.

now know were involved in the conspiracy to establish a one world government and religion.

One of these wealthy elitists was the money man for AA. He saw to it that AA's founders got all the seed money that was required for their little endeavor.

Another wealthy benefactor made sure that AA and its corrupt founders got all the publicity needed for the organization to rapidly take-off and win quick acceptance by the masses. This man controlled the number one media outlet in the U.S.A., and his media coverage and key support caused AA's membership, then meager and disappointing, to explode.

Blotting Out the Name of Jesus

The awful facts about this occult backing for AA provide us with a clear understanding of just why this group's literature and its 12-step program cleverly blot out the name of Jesus. No, you won't find the name of Jesus in the 12-steps. Instead you'll find mention of a vague "higher power." You'll also discover in the 12-steps an invitation to worship *"God as you understand Him,"* not God as He is revealed in the Holy Bible.

> *No, you won't find the name of Jesus in the 12-steps.*

AA is the perfect unity world religion. In fact, New Age leaders have called AA the perfect religion for the 21st century. In AA, members worship a multitude of gods and goddesses. Some people—a diminishing number—call Jesus their "higher power," but they are prohibited from standing and professing His name because others in the group are simultaneously using the same hazy term, "higher power," to refer to their Hindu god Krishna, to Buddha, to the goddess Kwan Yin, to the New Age god "within," or even to the devil.

Yes, even a devil worshipper can enthusiastically participate in AA. So while a "Christian" at an AA meeting prays silently to "Jesus," standing next to him could very likely be a man or woman fervently invoking the name of "Satan."

> *Yes, even a devil worshipper can enthusiastically participate in AA.*

What blasphemy, what horror for a Christian to commune and spiritually fellowship with those who are honoring and praying to devils!

Does our Bible not warn us about becoming spiritually yoked with unbelievers? Does it not tell us that if we refuse to confess Jesus here on earth He will not confess us to His Father in heaven?

Are we not given the admonition in scripture that we cannot, we must not, sup at the same table with devils? Aren't Krishna, Buddha, and all other false gods in reality nothing more than devils? Is it not blasphemy to give these false gods and idols equal status with the one, true God?

No wonder the elite wanted the AA experiment to succeed! This is heresy and world unity at its best. AA is without a doubt a cardinal achievement of the wealthy men who comprise the Illuminati. In this one organization alone is found the complete embryo of, and the gel solution for, the coming One World Religion.

Beware of the "Bible Code"

A book written by a New Age-oriented Jew named Michael Drosnin has been making quite a stir in both the secular and Christian communities. In *The Bible Code*, published by major New York publisher Simon & Schuster, Drosnin claims to have used an advanced computer to discover coded, hidden prophecies in the scriptures. Because of its dramatic, futuristic content, the book has gripped the public's imagination. It is currently on the *USA Today* and *New York Times* bestseller lists.

Drosnin says that by analyzing biblical passages, using computer methodology and acrostics (letter-searching in sequences), he is able to find stunning information that would have predicted in advance such historical events as the Persian Gulf War and the assassination of Israeli Prime Minister Yitzhak Rabin.

Using the same methodology, Michael Drosnin says he has found prophecies which dramatically point to future, potential calamities such as giant earthquakes and a nuclear conflict which will lead to the "end of the world."

Playing the Odds

As readers will remember, I reported on the study by Professor Eliyahu Rips and other mathematicians at Hebrew University in Israel which claimed to have found the actual names of 20th century persons sequentially coded within the lettering of passages of the *Torah* (the first five books of the Old Testament). Statistically, the odds of this happening by chance were stated to be "one in 50,000,000,000,000,000."

It appeared from the results of this study that only a divine intelligence (God) could have created such a coding system. But significantly, the Hebrew University study did not make any outlandish predictions about future events, nor did it comment about past events. Nevertheless, it was the Rips study that seemed to ignite a spate of new books about hidden codes in the Bible. Drosnin's books and others similar to it attempt to titillate the public with scary prophecies which are claimed to have been encoded and concealed by a divine intelligence in the Bible text.

Is the Bible Code Scientific?... Is it Scriptural?

The question is: Are the books by people like Drosnin on target? Are they scientifically valid? More important, are the contents and suppositions in these books *scriptural?* Is it feasible that there are, indeed, coded, concealed prophecies contained in the Bible? Can any corporation or organization, or any man or woman with an advanced computer, ferret out and discover such hidden prophecies?

Is God's prophetic Word open only to the computer literate? In sum, are these books by the decoders valid, or just a bunch of ridiculous, sensationalist hooey?

To answer these pertinent questions, we turn not to a computer program, or to mathematicians or scientists, but to the Bible. *What does God say in His Word?*

In *II Peter 1:19-21* the Word of God cautions that "no prophecy of the Scripture is of any private interpretation." In other words, prophecy is not the private province of any person by virtue of a special and unique method of interpretation.

Every Christian alive today is privileged to read the same prophetic scriptures, from Genesis to Revelation. Understanding comes from reading the plain and clear prophecies in the written Word of God, the King James Bible. The individual Christian is led to understanding by the Holy Spirit:

> *For the prophecy came not in old time by the will of man: but holy men of God spake as they were moved by the Holy Ghost. (II Peter 1:21)*

Thus, we can know for sure that Drosnin and all others who claim that a computer or an acrostic analysis system can be used to render a "private interpretation" of prophecy are sadly mistaken. The Holy Spirit doesn't need a computer or lettering game to impart the clear, unvarnished prophetic Word to true believers.

Prophecy Revealed to God's Chosen

Further, the Bible states that God does nothing except He reveals it first to His servants, the prophets (*Amos 3:7*). Is Michael Drosnin a "servant" and "prophet" of God? By his own admission, he is

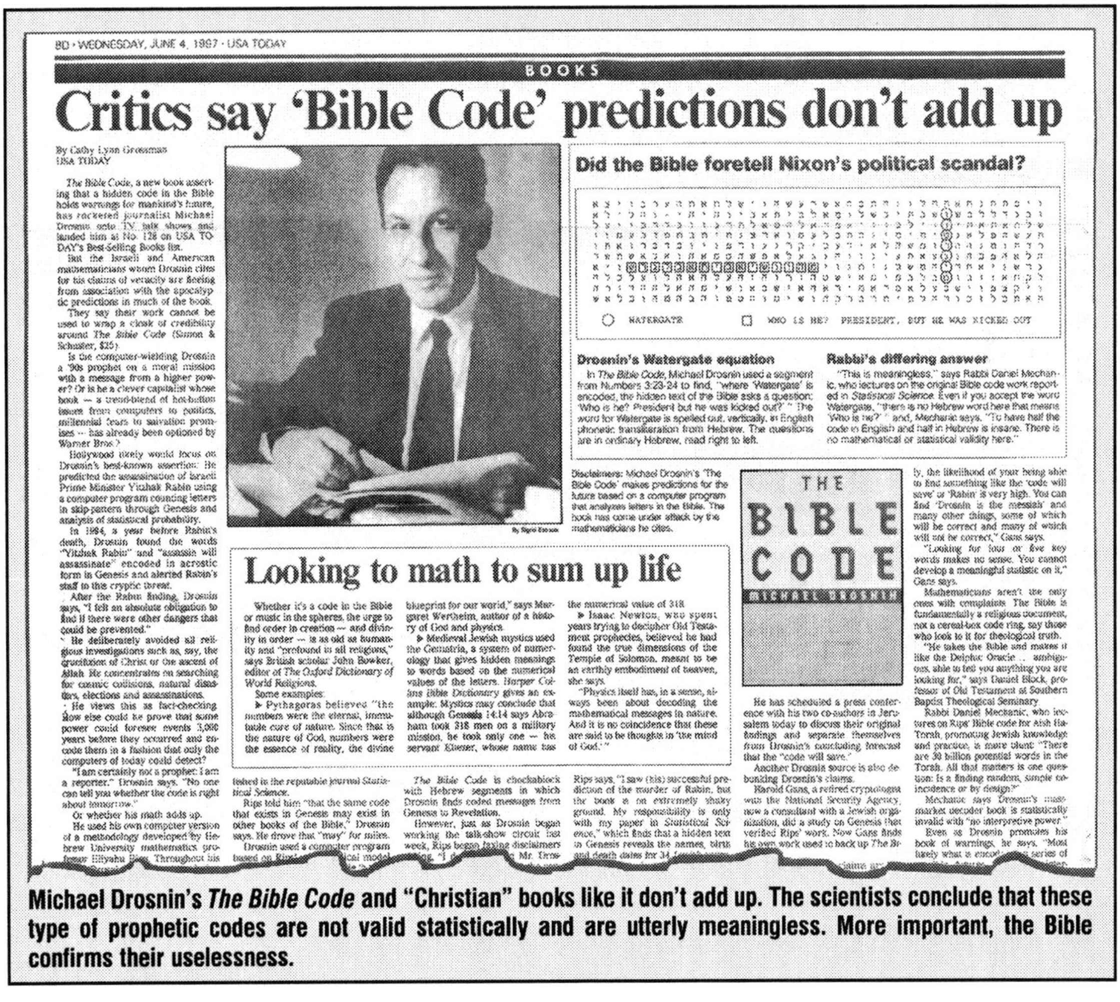

8D · WEDNESDAY, JUNE 4, 1997 · USA TODAY

BOOKS

Critics say 'Bible Code' predictions don't add up

By Cathy Lynn Grossman
USA TODAY

The Bible Code, a new book asserting that a hidden code in the Bible holds warnings for mankind's future, has rocketed journalist Michael Drosnin onto TV talk shows and landed him at No. 128 on USA TODAY's Best-Selling Books list.

But the Israeli and American mathematicians whom Drosnin cites for his claims of veracity are fleeing from association with the apocalyptic predictions in much of the book.

They say their work cannot be used to wrap a cloak of credibility around *The Bible Code* (Simon & Schuster, $25).

Is the computer-wielding Drosnin a '90s prophet on a moral mission with a message from a higher power? Or is he a clever capitalist whose book — a trend-blend of hot-button issues from computers to politics, millennial fears to salvation promises — has already been optioned by Warner Bros.?

Hollywood likely would focus on Drosnin's best-known assertion: He predicted the assassination of Israeli Prime Minister Yitzhak Rabin using a computer program counting letters in skip-pattern through Genesis and analysis of statistical probability.

In 1994, a year before Rabin's death, Drosnin found the words "Yitzhak Rabin" and "assassin will assassinate" encoded in acrostic form in Genesis and alerted Rabin's staff to the cryptic threat.

After the Rabin finding, Drosnin says, "I felt an absolute obligation to find if there were other dangers that could be prevented."

He deliberately avoided all religious investigations such as, say, the crucifixion of Christ or the ascent of Allah. He concentrates on searching for cosmic collisions, natural disasters, elections and assassinations.

He views this as fact-checking. How else could he prove that some power could foresee events 3,000 years before they occurred and encode them in a fashion that only the computers of today could detect?

"I am certainly not a prophet. I am a reporter," Drosnin says. "No one can tell you whether the code is right about tomorrow."

Or whether his math adds up.

He used his own computer version of a methodology developed by Hebrew University mathematics professor Eliyahu Rips. Throughout his

lished in the reputable journal *Statistical Science*.

Rips told him "that the same code that exists in Genesis may exist in other books of the Bible," Drosnin says. He drove that "may" for miles.

Drosnin used a computer program based on Rips' ... ical model

The Bible Code is chockablock with Hebrew segments in which Drosnin finds coded messages from Genesis to Revelation.

However, just as Drosnin began working the talk-show circuit last week, Rips began faxing disclaimers ... Mr. Dros-

Rips says, "I saw (his) successful prediction of the murder of Rabin, but the book is on extremely shaky ground. My responsibility is only with my paper in *Statistical Science*," which finds that a hidden text in Genesis reveals the names, birth and death dates for 34 ...

He has scheduled a press conference with his two co-authors in Jerusalem today to discuss their original findings and separate themselves from Drosnin's concluding forecast that the "code will save."

Another Drosnin source is also debunking Drosnin's claims.

Harold Gans, a retired cryptologist with the National Security Agency, now a consultant with a Jewish organization, did a study on Genesis that verified Rips' work. Now Gans finds his own work used to back up *The Bi*...

...ly, the likelihood of your being able to find something like the 'code will save' or 'Rabin' is very high. You can find 'Drosnin is the messiah' and many other things, some of which will be correct and many of which will not be correct," Gans says.

"Looking for four or five key words makes no sense. You cannot develop a meaningful statistic on it," Gans says.

Mathematicians aren't the only ones with complaints. The Bible is fundamentally a religious document, not a cereal-box code ring, say those who look to it for theological truth.

"He takes the Bible and makes it like the Delphic Oracle ... ambiguous, able to tell you anything you are looking for," says Daniel Block, professor of Old Testament at Southern Baptist Theological Seminary.

Rabbi Daniel Mechanic, who lectures on Rips' Bible code for Aish HaTorah, promoting Jewish knowledge and practice, is more blunt: "There are 30 billion potential words in the Torah. All that matters is one question: Is a finding random, simple coincidence or by design?"

Mechanic says Drosnin's mass-market decoder book is statistically invalid with "no interpretive power."

Even as Drosnin promotes his book of warnings, he says, "Most likely what is encod... series of

Disclaimers: Michael Drosnin's 'The Bible Code' makes predictions for the future based on a computer program that analyzes letters in the Bible. The book has come under attack by the mathematicians he cites.

THE BIBLE CODE
MICHAEL DROSNIN

Did the Bible foretell Nixon's political scandal?

○ WATERGATE □ WHO IS HE? PRESIDENT, BUT HE WAS KICKED OUT

Drosnin's Watergate equation

In *The Bible Code*, Michael Drosnin used a segment from Numbers 3:23-24 to find, "where 'Watergate' is encoded, the hidden text of the Bible asks a question: 'Who is he? President but he was kicked out?' " The word for Watergate is spelled out, vertically, in English phonetic transliteration from Hebrew. The questions are in ordinary Hebrew, read right to left.

Rabbi's differing answer

"This is meaningless," says Rabbi Daniel Mechanic, who lectures on the original Bible code work reported in *Statistical Science*. Even if you accept the word Watergate, "there is no Hebrew word here that means 'Who is he?' " and, Mechanic says, "To have half the code in English and half in Hebrew is insane. There is no mathematical or statistical validity here."

Looking to math to sum up life

Whether it's a code in the Bible or music in the spheres, the urge to find order in creation — and divinity in order — is as old as humanity and "profound in all religions," says British scholar John Bowker, editor of *The Oxford Dictionary of World Religions*.

Some examples:

▶ Pythagoras believed "the numbers were the eternal, immutable core of nature. Since that is the nature of God, numbers were the essence of reality, the divine blueprint for our world," says Margaret Wertheim, author of a history of God and physics.

▶ Medieval Jewish mystics used the Gematria, a system of numerology that gives hidden meanings to words based on the numerical values of the letters. *Harper Collins Bible Dictionary* gives an example: Mystics may conclude that although Genesis 14:14 says Abraham took 318 men on a military mission, he took only one — his servant Eliezer, whose name has the numerical value of 318.

▶ Isaac Newton, who spent years trying to decipher Old Testament prophecies, believed he had found the true dimensions of the Temple of Solomon, meant to be an earthly embodiment of heaven, she says.

"Physics itself has, in a sense, always been about decoding the mathematical messages in nature. And it is no coincidence that these are said to be thoughts in 'the mind of God.' "

Michael Drosnin's *The Bible Code* and "Christian" books like it don't add up. The scientists conclude that these type of prophetic codes are not valid statistically and are utterly meaningless. More important, the Bible confirms their uselessness.

not. In his book, *The Bible Code*, Drosnin confesses that he is not religious. He does not even believe in a personal God! According to Drosnin, it is not God the Father but some sort of New Age intelligence force that encoded these supposed prophesies in the Bible—a force Drosnin occasionally labels as "it" or a "friend."

Drosnin's man-made coding system is not revealed to him by God because "the natural (unsaved) man receiveth not the things of the Spirit of God: for they are foolishness unto him; neither can he know them, because they are spiritually discerned" *(I Corinthians 2:14).*

There's yet another way we can know that Drosnin and his "Code" are frauds. The whole purpose of Bible prophecy is to foresage and chronicle the coming of Jesus Christ in majesty and power. But interestingly, Drosnin's book does not give positive mention of Jesus Christ as a key figure in the prophetic drama. He is totally forgotten. In contrast *Revelation 19:10* tells us that the revelation of Jesus Christ is the very "Spirit of Prophecy."

The Bible Code is Inaccurate

Yet another truth detection principle we can use to evaluate Drosnin's theoretical "Bible Code" is to analyze and judge its accuracy. I have found that, on rare occasions, false prophets—from astrologers to psychics and now the decoders—are sometimes uncannily accurate. But the test of a true prophet of the Lord is that he or she is always 100% correct. This is an iron-clad criterion (see *Deut. 18*), and Elijah, Jeremiah, and others were always right in their prophetic vision. In Old Testament days, the prophets of Israel who erred in even one small aspect of their prophecy were stoned to death by the outraged religious people who recognized these men as deceivers.

Does Drosnin's method produce 100% accuracy as required by the scriptures? Not on your life. For example, Drosnin says that the key year 1996 was encoded in the Bible as the year for such

> ***The Bible Code will inject only confusion into the world and will not lend to our understanding.***

staggering events as an "atomic war;" the Israeli takeover of "Amman, Jordan;" and a "holocaust of Israel" to occur. Naturally, none of these prophesied events occurred in 1996.

Drosnin cleverly attempts to divert the reader's attention from this grievous error by contending that the word "delayed" was also encoded in the Bible text. Moreover, Drosnin suggests that we, as human beings, can reverse "God's" plan. He says we possess the power to change the future, to affect and influence prophetic events according to our own, collective wills. Drosnin explains that the prophecies only warn of what could happen if man doesn't voluntarily change his ways.

If Drosnin is right, then it is man, and not God, who holds the keys to man's and the cosmos' future. God has programmed events that will occur only if man chooses to allow them. But, does this arrogant form of man-centered theology line up with the Word of God?

Our Futures Determined by God Alone

Drosnin and the decoders are again proven dead wrong. *Daniel (9:26-27 and 11:36)* tells us that the prophecies are "determined" by God, and are unchangable by man. Jesus declared, "I have told you before" *(Matthew 24:25* and *John 14:29).* The Scriptures advise us that God knew and planned the end from the very beginning. Man has no absolute, minute knowledge of the final timetable. Jesus said that only our Father in Heaven knows the day and the hour of Jesus' return and the end *(Matthew 24:35-36).*

A wise and omniscient God has determined our future, and that of the Earth, in advance. *He* is master of time and events. *We* are not. *The Bible Code* is demonstrated to be pure malarkey. It will inject only confusion into the world and will not lend to our understanding.

Scientists Say Drosnin's Work is Flawed

We must wisely judge things like this on whether they conform to Scripture. But, in Drosnin's case, it seems that even the scientists have concluded that the "code" is just a giant, silly, unscientific hoax. Hebrew University Professor Eliyahu Rips, who authored the original study of a possible hidden code has been faxing letters warning people about Drosnin's work. Rips, an Orthodox Jew who professes a belief in God, emphatically states: "I do not support Mr. Drosnin's work on the codes, nor the conclusions he derives…the book is on extremely shaky ground.

Rabbi Daniel Mechanic, a noted Professor of the Torah in Israel, agrees. He says that Drosnin's mass-market decoder book is statistically invalid with "no interpretive power."

Meanwhile, Harold Gans, a retired cryptologist with the National Security Agency, told *U.S.A. Today* (June 4, 1997, p. 8D), that, "Mr. Drosnin's claims are unreliable." Gans warns that, using such unreliable methods, you can find all kinds of nonsensical, so-called "hidden messages" in the scriptures. You can even find "Drosnin is the Messiah" if you acrostically search long enough! "It makes no sense and you cannot develop a meaningful statistic on it," Gans insists.

Truth Not Proven by Man's Science

Thus, some noted Rabbis and most scientists agree that Drosnin's prophetic code is all wet. But, as Christians, we do not need either the Rabbis nor the scientists to inform us. In my newsletter and books, I occasionally cite a scientific study, like the Hebrew University study of coded names in the Bible, which seems to confirm what we Christians already know by faith—that the Bible could only have been written by God.

Science is not, however, the determiner of what is Truth. Science is a body of ever changing theories and cannot be safely used to predict the future. Science is a dismal teacher and has always been so. It was, after all, the scientists who once taught that the Earth is flat and who confidently declared that, "Man will never fly." Then came Christopher Columbus, and the Wright Brothers and Kitty Hawk.

How to Know Bible Prophecy

Christian friends, don't look for the future to be revealed by unsaved, ungodly authors or by a computer program. You may just as well use tea leaves, the entrails of animals, or a Ouija board. All such methods are about equally predictive—and equally flawed. But if you really share with me a love of Bible prophecy, please read and study God's Word. It's all there, in plain King James English. And if you have a passionate heart for truth and ears to hear, the Holy Spirit will instruct your understanding. Then, and only then, will you know of things to come, including the good news of the second coming of our precious Lord and Saviour, Jesus Christ:

> *Now we have received, not the spirit of the world, but the Spirit which is of God; that we might know the things that are freely given to us of God. Which things also we speak, not in the words which man's wisdom teacheth, but which the Holy ghost teacheth... For who hath known the mind of the Lord, that he may instruct him? But we have the mind of Christ (I Corinthians 2:12-16).*

UFO Cults Multiply in End-Time

The 39 men and women found dead in a mass suicide at a luxury estate in Rancho Santa Fe, California, in March were only the first victims of many more to come. That is my evaluation after assessing the grim situation now facing us caused by the public's unearthly fascination with antichrist UFO religious cults.

Since the beginning of this ministry I have sought to warn people of the coming disaster. Unfortunately, the media's soft-core, politically correct, "tolerant" reporting of the New Age cult known as Heaven's Gate will only insure a continuation of the suicides and the madness.

In my book, *Mystery Mark of the New Age*, I reported on the astonishing occult connection of UFOlogy and alien abductions. My book was the first to disclose that the ritualistic Mark of the Beast was literally being given to some of the men and women who claimed to have been abducted by extraterrestrials.

UFOlogy: A New Age Religion and Theology

"UFO cults and societies" was also one of the categories explored in my later book, *New Age Cults and Religions*, in which I stated:

> Unlike the old days when UFOs and flying saucers were considered mechanical objects...today's UFO cults and societies are promoting a religion and a theology...this religion and theology is classic *New Age*. (page 321)

In *New Age Cults and Religions* I quoted New Age psychic and spirit channeler Brad Steiger, well known in UFOlogy circles, who contends that UFO aliens are the "Herald of the New Age," bringing mankind hope through a "space age theology." Steiger also stated his belief that: "The UFO contactees may be evolving prototypes of a future evangelism."

UFO messengers, Steiger added, offer humanity a unique "blending of technology and traditional religious concepts."

Fast forward with me now to 1997, as cult leader Marshall Applewhite leads his deluded flock of true believers into what they imagined to be a fantastic adventure from death to new life as UFO explorers. Applewhite convinced his followers that the Hale-Bopp comet was the sign for which they had long waited—a grand opportunity to poison and kill their physical bodies—which they called their "shells" or "containers." Passing into spirit, the 39

This supposed 'Member of the Kingdom of Heaven' was displayed on the internet Web site of the Heaven's Gate UFO group.

FREE

UT's Penders turns down Rutgers job

Finding the perfect prom dress

76

Austin American-Statesman

Dozens found dead in home

At least 39 men die in apparent suicide, police say

After gorging on growth, city choking on the bill

The week following the Heaven's Gate suicides, this picture of the cult's leader made the cover of both *Newsweek* and *Time* magazines. On March 27, 1997, newspapers across America carried ghastly headlines similar to the one at right.

fully expected to then hook up with a UFO mother ship parked nearby in rugged mountainous terrain.

A Devil-Possessed Homosexual Pervert

Applewhite was verifiably a devil-possessed homosexual pervert. A former music professor, he had been fired from his college teaching position after he was discovered to be having homosexual relations with a male student. Voluntarily admitted to a mental hospital in Houston, Texas, he met up there with yet another disciple of Satan, nurse Bonnie Lu Nettles. She promptly introduced Applewhite to such standard New Age philosophies as reincarnation and planetary astrology.

The rest is history. Cruel, murderous history. And though Applewhite's UFO teachings led to the barbaric deaths of 39 people, the media practically painted a smiling happy face on the carnage through their biased reporting. If this had been a "fundamentalist Christian" group, the media would have had a field day blasting away at the "evil and dangerous Christian fanatics." But since it was a group of dazed-over, laid-back, cosmic-oriented New Agers that was involved in the Rancho Santa Fe incident, the media treated the affair with kid gloves.

Marshall Applewhite was often pictured as a loving, kind, and tenderhearted man, oozing with genuine concern for humanity. Even the surviving parents of his dead followers were sucked into a bewildering tolerance for this man's supernatural hocus-pocus. Nancie Brown, mother of one of the men found dead in the mansion, was quoted by *The New York Times* as being satisfied that her son was "calm, rational, and quite happy" during his years with the cult. As for her son's suicide, the intellectual mother expressed her pleasure that the group members "cared very deeply for each other" and that they "died contentedly."

Nichelle Nichols, the actress who played Lt. Uhura on the original "Star Trek" TV series, lost her brother, Thomas, to the cult. His body, too, was found at the estate. Yet, Nichols praised the dead Applewhite and his followers. "They lived with dignity," a tolerant and broad-minded Nichelle Nichols assured a CNN-TV audience. "They were great with their neighbors. They were kind to people."

Funny, but isn't that the kind of things once said about serial murderers like Ted Bundy and Jeffrey Dahmer? After all, before their exposure, they, too, were described as kind, soft-spoken, and calm. And what of Pastor Jim Jones, of Guyana mass suicide infamy? Didn't First Lady Rosalyn Carter once meet with Jim Jones in California and applaud him as a great humanitarian? Didn't the mayor of San Francisco give the demented Pastor Jones a civic award for his stalwart efforts in promoting harmonious race relations?

Christians Not Easily Deceived

The world at large is easily fooled and deceived by the Applewhites and their deadly ilk. But not so the true Christian. We are, of course, branded by the media and our detractors as intolerant and bigoted, as harsh and overly judgmental. Why? Because we know and recognize evil, that's why, and because we do our utmost to caution and warn the deceived masses and the unwary, biblically ignorant multitudes to avoid it like the plague!

To a discerning Christian knowledgeable of the devil's wiles, the Heaven's Gate group had all the earmarks of a wicked, thoroughly blasphemous, deceptive, and, therefore, deadly antichrist cult. Consider, for example, these facts:

(1) Applewhite and most of his followers were sodomites and lesbians, guilty of lewd acts labeled an "abomination" by God. The cult's leaders eventually began to preach the avoidance of sex and some members even submitted to physical castration.

(2) The cult's members wore clothes colored black, a familiar satanic sign. Their unisex hairstyles were of the close-cropped, "buzz" variety, intended to destroy individuality and eliminate male/female differences.

(3) Families were split up, children were abandoned, and marriage was forbidden among group members. This was prophesied to occur in the last days (for example, see *I Timothy 4:3*).

(4) On nightstands and on tables near the bodies of the cultists were found framed pictures of aliens, with their traditional, almond-shaped eyes. Obviously demonic in appearance, these otherworldly UFO beings were said to be greatly admired and adored by the cult as highly evolved beings.

(5) Visitors to the cult's residence reported that members would frequently speak to imaginary beings and claimed to have communicated with the dead (prohibited by God—see *Deut. 18:10-12*).

(6) Cult leader Marshall Applewhite taught the group that *he* was "the Second Coming of Christ." He told them that he came from the same place Jesus came from and boasted he was able to teach them how to evolve and become higher-level "god" creatures. Jesus, indeed, prophesied that many deceivers would come in His name, claiming to be the Christ *(Matthew 24:5)*.

(7) The bodies of the 39 were shrouded in purple colored cloths. On their shoulders were triangle-shaped insignia. In the occult world, the triangle is a symbol of satan's counterfeit trinity. The color purple symbolizes his infernal and hellish majesty.

(8) It may not be incidental that exactly 39 cult members committed mass suicide in the

final, deadly ritual. Thirty-nine is a powerful number for occult numerologists. Masons know of the profoundly occult properties of the number 39, teaching that this number conceals many arcane and esoteric mysteries, including the hidden number of the Beast. (The famed novel, *The 39 Steps*, later made into a movie, was written by a high-level British Freemason.)

(9) The logo of the group known as "Heaven's Gate" is clearly satanic. Included is the symbol of the pyramid and, atop that, the letter "G" (denoting the Cosmic "God") as the capstone. The same letter "G" is prominently displayed in all Masonic temples and lodges.

"A Good Way to Get Rid of a Few Nuts"

Regardless of these obvious (to Christians) occultic characteristics, the media portrayed Applewhite and his cult as just another space-age oddity. CNN-TV founder Ted Turner was less charitable. He said that the mass suicide in California was "a good way to get rid of a few nuts."

"We've too many nuts running around anyway, right?" Turner rhetorically asked, adding, "At least they did it peacefully."

San Diego medical personnel loaded the bodies of Heaven's Gate cultists into a truck and took them to the morgue for autopsies.

Multimillionaire Ted Turner and his wife, actress Jane Fonda, are not only rabid abortionists, they are also prime backers of the United Nations plan for depopulation of the planet. The idea is to kill off billions of people to help protect Mother Earth's environment. Turner stated once that only 2% of the Earth's 5.8 billion inhabitants are worthy to live. The others—some 98%—must die, says Turner. (Presumably, he and Jane would be among the 2% fit to survive.)

Fanaticism...or Faith?

More generous, but no less devilish in his comments than Turner, was Don McLeese, the liberal columnist for the *Austin American-Statesman* daily newspaper. McLeese painted the UFO suicide cult as little different in their beliefs than Christians. "What some call fanaticism is faith to others," he remarked.

Heaven's Gate, McLeese wrote, was just another faith group, a worthy people who died for what they believed in. These people, he explained, seemed "like the most devout Christians." They were, he postulated, "almost saintly."

What Applewhite taught his religious faithful, McLeese suggested, "is suspiciously what you're likely to hear from the pulpit on Easter morning."

"As crazy as it seems for these 39 to follow a comet," McLeese suggests, "what about the three wise men who followed a star?"

McLeese's blasphemous comments are diabolically sinister, and they are lies. The Christian faith honors a live King, not a dead, false "christ" like Applewhite. And the wise men, through inspiration, followed a star to the Messiah. They did not commit suicide in a vain bid to achieve their own divinity as did the grotesquely deceived followers of Applewhite.

Repugnantly, McLeese goes on to claim that, like Applewhite's followers, Christians today are "stumbling around in the darkness hedging our bets on the world to come." They worship, he scornfully adds, "a man who was nailed to the cross as a criminal 2,000 years ago."

To McLeese, the teachings of Applewhite's UFO group are, therefore, not much different and no more outlandish than those of the followers of Christ Jesus. McLeese asks: "Wasn't Jesus himself derided as a lunatic, a heretic, the leader of a crazy cult?"

Don McLeese writes his column for a newspaper owned by the Gannett chain, a media conglomerate which owns dailies across America. His column (*Austin American-Statesman*, page B3, March 30, 1997) gives those of us who know and love our Saviour and Lord, Jesus Christ, a clear indication of just where Satan is taking the masses of humanity.

The Road to Hell Paved by Scribes

The road to hell is paved with the deluded scribblings of Christ-haters like Mr. McLeese (Jesus said, "Woe to the Scribes"). These foul disciples, with their poisonous pens, seek to use such tragedies as happened at Rancho Santa Fe, California, as an excuse to belittle and bash true biblical Christianity.

Mark my word, Christian friends, in coming months and years, men like Don McLeese will rue the day they chose to so viciously attack Christianity and demean our Lord. Men like Ted Turner will lament their inhumane and callous lack of compassion for the 39 souls lost and their pitiful assault on the unborn children through abortion. It could be that their loved ones will, themselves, fall prey to the UFO cults which, even as I write this, are mushrooming in number and strength.

The wicked who falsely accuse Christians shall fulfill to the iota Matthew 7, which warns men to exercise righteous judgment, lest they themselves be judged by the very same measure.

Momentous Troubles Ahead

The UFO cults and their twisted doctrines are not something to praise, laugh about, downplay, or disregard. Their proliferation is a cardinal sign of momentous troubles just ahead. God's judgment is soon to be unleashed on an unbelieving world. When it comes, my friends, pray that you will be accounted worthy to escape. Pray that, like Noah, the Lord will protect you and lift you up in His spiritual ark of protection on that glorious day when the Lord shall appear and we shall be lifted up and translated in the twinkling of an eye.

When Jesus comes, it won't be in a UFO, I assure you. And it will not be done in secret, either. Every eye will behold Him. The McLeeses, the Turners, the Applewhites will be judged according to their works. But as for the righteous, His blood has already miraculously made us whiter than snow, washed and clean, without spot or wrinkle. He has Himself prepared the Bride!

In coming days, as the UFO cults multiply and the ravages of *Project L.U.C.I.D.* and other latter day schemes coagulate, let each of us press forward toward our high calling. Let us pray fervently that the cultists and their media accomplices will repent and surrender to Christ. And let us exclaim with the saints of old, "Come quickly, Lord Jesus."

Mormon Temples of the Dead

"For if he that cometh preacheth another Jesus, whom we have not preached, or if ye receive another spirit, which ye have not received, or another gospel, which ye have not accepted, ye might well bear with him."

—*II Corinthians 11:4*

The Mormon Church, officially named the Church of Jesus Christ of Latter Day Saints (LDS), is growing. Mormonism is today some ten million strong. Luxurious, new Mormon temples and tabernacles are being erected across America and the world to accommodate the fantastic, upward spiral in numbers.

Amazingly, these increases are in spite of the fact that Mormonism is one of the most demonic and devil-infested religions on Earth. Moreover, the fabulous, new multimillion temples are being built not to house living worshippers of God, but primarily to baptize the dead. Mormonism is, in fact, a religion of, by, and for the dead.

Religion of Deceit

In recent years, Mormon leaders, including the church's modern-day, Salt Lake City, Utah "Prophet," Gordon B. Hinkley, have sought to align the LDS organization's public teachings and practices with those of politically correct, global ecumenicism. Outright signs and portents of latent Luciferianism have been muted and toned down to deceive ignorant, unknowing masses of outsiders.

But this cosmetic, snow-job campaign to clean up Mormonism's unsavory history and to conceal its awful record of spiritual deceit only goes so far. Surface only. The LDS church has never formally abandoned the rampant, pagan corruption hidden behind closed doors and known to its top-level leadership. Satan remains the reigning Prince and overseer of this massive, end-times beast church.

Gordon B. Hinkley is today the reigning "Prophet" of the Mormon (LDS) church. Mormon doctrine, in common with the Catholic Church's claims of the Pope, maintains that the teachings of its Prophet are infallible.

Satanism, Pedophilia, and Corruption

Power of Prophecy has, through careful investigation, determined that the evil practice of pedophilia is prevalent among Mormons. Some local Mormon Church leaders are known to have literally conducted black satanic worship services. Masonic-originated rituals are used to initiate tens of thousands of unknowing, deluded members

Just three of the many new Mormon (LDS) temples secretly used to baptize dead people: top—Anchorage, Alaska; middle—Mesa, Arizona; lower—Mexico City, Mexico. All Mormon temples are closed to the public.

who participate thinking they are involving themselves in holy ceremonies.

The official doctrines of the Mormon Church include the teaching that all human beings alive today once were spirit beings in another realm. The Mormon lie is that these pre-existing spirits were chosen to come to earth to "gain earthly experience and progress toward perfection." Once perfected, male humans become gods of their own planets somewhere out in celestial space.

The Mormon doctrine holds that Jesus is likewise only one of many thousands of planetary gods—and that the particular planet to which he is assigned just happens to be Earth.

As I document in my ground-breaking book, *New Age Cults and Religions*, Mormon founder Joseph Smith was a charlatan, con-man and occultist. A serial adulterer, he took a number of wives. Smith patterned his new Church after the Masonic Lodge, of which he was a member, incorporating Masonic rituals and symbols.

Desiring to have sex with as many women as possible, Joseph Smith and his Mormon men early on adopted the practice of polygamy. To justify themselves, they created the Mormon doctrine, still taught today, that Jesus, too, was a polygamist and was married to the sisters of Lazarus and also took Mary Magdalene as a wife.

God, too, has multiple wives—thousands of them, say the Mormons, and you, too, can have a harem of wives someday and be god of your own planet.

This is a sexually enhanced doctrine that, say, a Hugh Hefner of *Playboy* magazine or an Arab Sultan could really appreciate. Of course, a Mormon woman might be taken aback a bit—she is slated in the afterlife to become just a mere ornament. One of a multitude of wives subservient to her husband-god.

Government Friendly

The federal government, including Bill Clinton, loves the Mormon (LDS) church. Official church doctrine tells Mormons to obey the Feds in all things, and patriotic Mormons are often warned not to become involved with militias. Not submitting an IRS tax return can result in church punishment. The FBI, appreciative of Mormon support, recruits an inordinate number of its agents from the LDS church.

This Luciferian sun stone appeared on the first Mormon temple in Nauvoo, Illinois. Today, Salt Lake City temple architecture includes pentagrams, all-seeing eyes, and other Masonic-occult symbols.

Tombs for the Dead

Mormon temples have one major purpose: They are luxurious palaces—really, tombs—where the dead are baptized. It is the

Mormon objective that every person who has ever lived since the days of Adam and Eve be baptized by proxy. Thus, the keen interest by the Mormon Church in genealogy and the dead. Mormon temples are places for dead people.

A Seamless River of Apostasy

I prophesy that in coming years we will witness a coming together of all false religions. The Mormons, the Scientologists, the Catholics, the Jehovah's Witnesses, and all Mystery Babylon-based religious systems will flow almost seamlessly in a river of apostasy. They will be joined by Hinduism, Buddhism, and Eastern cults and by hundreds of lukewarm Protestant denominations and charismatic Word of Faith cults and churches. Truly, Satan is constructing his latter-days Church. Strangely, the name of Jesus—or rather, the lying spirit who masquerades as "Jesus"—will be exalted by the billions who make up this church's fervent membership

We Who Are Alive

Though they appear to be alive, the billions of worshippers in those united religious systems are dead. I call them *The Walking Dead.* And their Church I call, The *Church of the Living Dead.* In sharp contrast, Jesus our Lord taught, "God is not the God of the dead, but of the living." (*Matthew 22:32*). He commanded, "Follow me; and let the dead bury their dead." (*Matthew 8:22*).

Please, dear Christian believer. Have no fear. The real Jesus, who shed his blood at Calvary, but lives, knows these things. He has quickened you with His spirit. *You and He are Alive forevermore.* He is coming, and when he does, we shall be lifted up, and so we shall be with Him forever and ever. Praise the Living God. Amen.

Mormon Author Declares that Jesus Was a Polygamist With Many Wives and Children

The leaders of the *Promise Keepers* are convinced that the Mormon Church is just another Christian denomination. That's why the *Promise Keepers* organization has been warmly praised by the official Mormon leadership. James Dobson's *Focus on the Family*, Billy Graham's organization, and many others also work closely with the Mormon Church.

But, is the Mormon Church (officially, the *Church of Jesus Christ of Latter Day Saints*) really just another Christian denomination? Consider its doctrine, for example, that Jesus is only one of many planetary "gods." And its teaching that you, too—if you're a faithful Mormon—can become god of your own planet, complete with your own sizeable harem of wives.

Does that sound "Christian" to you? Do these strange doctrines line up with the Holy Bible?

Mormon doctrine also teaches that Jesus had multiple wives while on Earth. In fact, this very teaching is emphasized in a book written by Darrick T. Evenson and published by a Mormon (LDS) publishing house. Evenson is the guy who once tricked people into believing that he was a born-again, fundamentalist Christian by authoring the book, *Lord Maitreya—The New Age Christ Identified.* That book was written by Evenson under the pen name "Troy Lawrence." It was distributed by a Christian publisher who, apparently, was unaware that its author was a closet Mormon.

In his Mormon book, *The Gainsayers* (Horizon Publishers, Bountiful, Utah), Evenson lashes out at the beliefs of non-Mormon Christians and especially attacks the leaders of ministries that expose Mormonism. He brands such men "Antichrists."

Point-by-point he vainly seeks to "prove" that Mormonism is superior to true Christianity. *The Gainsayers* is published by the Mormon (LDS) press itself; so, in effect, it is an official statement of Mormon beliefs. According to Evenson, both the Bible and early Christians "taught that man can become a god." That's why, he writes, Mormons teach that man's destiny is to become a god. He even tells us that Jesus himself came to Earth as a "god-maker."

In *The Gainsayers*, readers are informed that it is not enough to believe just in Jesus Christ. According to Mormonism, a man or woman must also acknowledge Mormon founder Joseph Smith as God's prophet, or suffer damnation: "If one rejects the herald the King has sent (Joseph Smith), he likewise rejects the King that sent him."

Moreover, Evenson tells us that it's necessary that we believe in the *real* Jesus taught by Mormons. And who is this real Jesus as taught by the Mormons? Evenson assures us that "Jesus was a polygamist" whose many wives included, among others, Mary Magdalene; Mary, the sister of Lazarus; and a woman named Joanna. Jesus also "fathered a number of children" writes Evenson, and because Jesus had many wives, we now have a "Mother" in Heaven as well as a Father.

"Jesus" and His Sex Manual

The New Age continues to attempt to pervert True Christianity by merging its Truths with the lies of Satan. Their goal is an entire new form of Christianity with a polluted gospel as its sick foundation.

A gross and disgusting example of this is the New Age book Wanda and I discovered entitled, *A Spiritual Sex Manual.* Published by a group that calls itself "The Christ Foundation," the book is a sex manual that gives detailed instructions on how to do just about every imaginable carnal sex act. Only a foul demon spirit could have inspired the human authors and publishers to print this despicable book.

No doubt many with a New Age worldview and others who are skeptics of Biblical Christianity will love this book because it comes packaged with beautiful prose and messages of "love," "peace," and "wholeness." It is an expensively and spectacularly produced book, with romantically pink paper, beautiful illustrations of roses and so forth. Moreover—and this is the startling news—the publisher claims the book is personally written by Jesus himself. Jesus supposedly even signed the foreword of the book.

In *A Spiritual Sex Manual,* "Jesus" gives a glowing and approving account of his sexual affair with Mary Magdalene (they supposedly slipped away from the disciples into the nearby fields outside of Jerusalem). Then "he" goes on to detail various sex rituals and acts readers can practice and master for their physical enjoyment and spiritual growth.

This "Jesus" talks vaguely about "God's Plan for the Salvation of the World." He seems to be a wonderful teacher who simply wants men and women to enjoy sex as a loving and holy act, in or out of marriage. If a person has not discovered the real Jesus—the Jesus revealed in the Holy Bible—he or she could well be suckered in by this sex instructor imitation.

It may all sound preposterous, but even some who *claim* to be Christians could also be taken in by such a hideous book. How? Consider this: pastors and teachers across America are now telling their congregations to lay aside their doctrines, put down their Bibles, and *come together in unity* with all who profess a belief in Jesus. *World Unity,* they claim, can only be achieved if we will stop criticizing our brothers' doctrines and embrace "The Living Jesus" alone. Bible doctrines, they say, are divisive.

"As long as you profess a belief in Jesus, you're one of us," they graciously contend.

This teaching, though it appears to be open and broad-minded, is in fact a hideous distortion of the Truth. The *real*

For if he that cometh preacheth another Jesus, whom we have not preached, or if ye receive another spirit...ye might well bear with him (2 Cor. 11:4).

But though we, or an angel from heaven, preach any other gospel unto you than that which we have preached unto you, let him be accursed (Gal. 1:7).

Jesus is revealed through His Word. His doctrines are not onerous, limiting, and cruel. They are not legalistic. Rather, they insure our happiness and liberty. Obedience to them is uplifting. On the other hand, Paul warns us that rebellion "is as the sin of witchcraft."

However, beware the counterfeit Jesus! Satan is pleased with the opportunity to present to the world his own "Jesus." But he can only succeed in doing so if the Jesus revealed in the Bible is set aside—if doctrine is dismissed as "divisive," and if the historical Jesus is pronounced irrelevant to us today.

At left is the cover of the book, ***A Spiritual Sex Manual***, which claims that the signature above is actually that of Jesus.

Remember: There *is* "another Jesus" and "another gospel" (see *II Cor. 11:4* and *Gal. 1:6-8*). This counterfeit Jesus may seductively whisper in a married woman's ears: "go ahead, have an affair with that other man. What your husband doesn't know won't hurt him." He may then encourage the husband: "Take a drink, be one of the boys. Just *one* drink!" This false "Jesus" may speak persuasively to a pastor: "Preach the prosperity gospel to your people. Tell them there's no hell, no judgement. Go on—they'll love you for it! Your church will grow by leaps and bound."

When we receive such messages, we can know they're straight from the pit of hell. How? Simply because they conflict with the clear teachings of the Bible. Since they are totally opposite the doctrines of Christ and the apostles, we should cast them aside as lies and deceitful temptations.

Therein lies the potential of Satan to sweep in and take advantage. Once the Bible is shelved and its Godly doctrines are pushed aside for the sake of an illusory unity, Satan enters boldly. A spiritual sex manual by "Jesus?" Without the guidelines (e.g. *doctrines*) in the Bible, all is permissible.

The world is today being prepared to accept as Lord a lying demon spirit who masquerades as the real Jesus. Some are making contact with this demon through such dangerous techniques as Eastern-type meditation and visualization. Many do so in ignorance because they are listening to their pastors and to televangelists who are promoting a dangerous false unity. Instead, they should be obeying what the Bible says to do about the doctrines and teachings of Jesus.

Sadly, these multitudes are being set up to receive the Lie. The devil will surely accommodate them. Much like the glib announcer of a late night television talk show, the devil bellows to eagerly awaiting throngs of admirers: "He-e-e-e-re's Jesus!"

The King James Bible vs. The New Versions

Why New Bible Versions Are Dangerously Inaccurate

Many good people have written to ask why we take such a strong stand in support of the King James Bible. Many honestly do not know what's wrong with such versions as the NIV, the NAS, the RSV, the New King James, etc. They really desire to know the truth about the new versions. The fact is that the new versions have been proven to be grotesquely inaccurate and polluted. The many liberal "scholars" who worked on these versions were not led by God, but by a spirit of deception.

Significantly, all of the new versions are *copyrighted* by major book publishers out to make big bucks off a gullible Christian public. How can God's Word be copyrighted and become the property of a commercial publisher? In my view, all these new "Bibles" are disreputable, untrustworthy frauds and an offense to the truth.

Lucifer's Identity Erased by NIV Version

One of the deceptions common in some of the new versions is their failure to identify Lucifer as a name for Satan. For example, compare Isaiah 14:12 in the popular New International Version (NIV) with the more reliable King James Version (KJV):

KJV: "How art thou fallen from Heaven, O *Lucifer*, son of the morning!"

NIV: "How you have fallen from Heaven, O morning star, son of the dawn!"

The NIV mysteriously deletes the name *Lucifer!* This verse exposes "Lucifer" as a name for the devil. If you use the tainted NIV Bible, just try witnessing to an occultist who worships Lucifer. It's an impossibility. They'll laugh at you and mockingly suggest you show them in the Bible that Lucifer is evil, or that he's really the devil—and you won't be able to if you use the NIV.

The Blood of Jesus Omitted

This is only one of hundreds of verses the NIV and other new versions mangle, twist, and distort. For example, let's compare *Colossians 1:14* from the popular but polluted, New American Standard (NAS) version with the more accurate KJV:

KJV: "In whom we have redemption *through His blood*, even the forgiveness of sins."

NAS: "In whom we have redemption, the forgiveness of sins."

Craftily, the NAS leaves out the key phrase, *"through His blood."* This is a hideous and gaping omission. Satan must love a Bible version that erases a powerful and life-changing reference to the blood of Jesus Christ!

Shamefully, not only is the blood of Christ omitted by many of the newer versions, but the new versions also are disingenuous in wiping out references to the *saving power* of Jesus Christ. Take *John 6:47*, for instance:

KJV: "Verily, verily, I say unto you. He that believeth *on me* hath everlasting life."

NAS: "Truly, truly, I say to you, he who believes has eternal life."

He who believes *what?* Or in *whom?* The NAS has purposely omitted the One in whom a man or woman must believe to be saved. Jesus' powerful words, "He that believeth on me," have been butchered by this new, supposedly "better" version.

Purpose: To Sow Confusion and Chaos

The devil's purpose in publishing the new "Bibles" is to sow confusion and chaos, and to undermine people's faith that God is able to preserve His word. This vile objective is made crystal clear when we compare Zechariah 13:6 in the most popular versions with the KJV. Just see what evil mischief the devil does with his new versions:

KJV: "What are these wounds in thine *hands*?"

NIV: "What are these wounds on your *body*?"

NAS: "What are these wounds between your *arms*?"

RSV: "What are these wounds on your *back*?"

All scripture is given by inspiration of God, and is profitable for doctrine, for reproof, for correction, for instruction in righteousness (II Timothy 3:16)

God is *not* the author of confusion. He did not author these hideous new versions. All of them, without exception, are based primarily on the defective manuscript which was once used by the gnostics and pseudo-Christians of Alexandria, Egypt. Some versions, including the NIV, even use the discredited Dead Sea Scrolls. In contrast, the saints of the reformation used an early, more reliable manuscript called the *textus receptus* to publish the King James Version.

God's Word Under Attack

Only in our generation has God's word come under such vile attack. Many modern "scholars" do not care for the truth. Some of the same "theologians" who write books denouncing the virgin birth and rejecting the miracles of Christ sat on the committees that put out these new versions.

Many belong to the most liberal of denominations—groups that ordain homosexuals and lesbians, and promote abortion and socialism. No wonder these new Bibles are so slanted and biased!

So please, don't be deceived by the new versions. As Bible-believing Christians, let us never allow God's Word to be watered down or twisted. Remember, God Himself called us to "earnestly contend for the faith which was once delivered unto the saints" *(Jude 1:3).*

Strange Symbol Adorns New King James Version of the Bible

Mark of the Devil Discovered?

"And he causeth all, both small and great, rich and poor, free and bond, to receive a mark in their right hand, or in their foreheads: And that no man might buy or sell, save he that had the mark, or the name of the beast, or the number of his name."

—*Revelation 13:16-17*

In a startling video exposé of the *New King James Version (NKJV)* of the Bible, renowned researcher and Bible scholar Gail Riplinger discusses the triquetra logo found on each issue of the *NKJV*. She demonstrates that the *NKJV* logo is strikingly reminiscent of the symbol employed by pagans and occultists for their unholy, Luciferian trinity of deities. The same unified—yet three-part logo, or symbol—is also connected with the theology of top New Age leaders, and with the dark initiation rites of high-level Freemasonry.

The publisher of the *NKJV*, Thomas Nelson Publishing, may claim that their bible's logo represents the Holy Trinity of Father, Son, and Holy Spirit. But, if so, why is the same design found dominant in New Age and occult circles? Why does a revoltingly blasphemous Masonic ritual also employ the same symbol?

A Symbol of Freemasonry

We reproduce here an illustration from the classic Masonic text, *Duncan's Ritual of Freemasonry*, which shows how the cryptic "Three Times Three" handclasp is performed in the Royal Arch Degree by three "brothers" of the Lodge. Incredibly, it is during this grotesque ritual that the Masonic initiate learns the true name of the Masonic god, nebulously referred to by Masons as the "Grand Architect of the Universe."

In this secret ritual, however, the Masonic Lodge reveals that the actual name of their deity is *Jahbuhlun*. This repugnant name is obtained by combining the name of Jehovah, or Yahweh, with the names of the Philistine god, *Baal*, and the Egyptian god, *On*. (On is one of the several names of the great Egyptian sun god.) Thus, Jah-baal-on, or Jahbuhlun.

On page 225 in *Duncan's Ritual of Freemasonry* we find this illustration of the "Three Times Three." This symbol thus created in the performance of this degree's ritual is the same symbol used by New Age authority Marilyn Ferguson on the cover of her book, *The Aquarian Conspiracy*. The same symbol is used as the logo for the New King James bible.

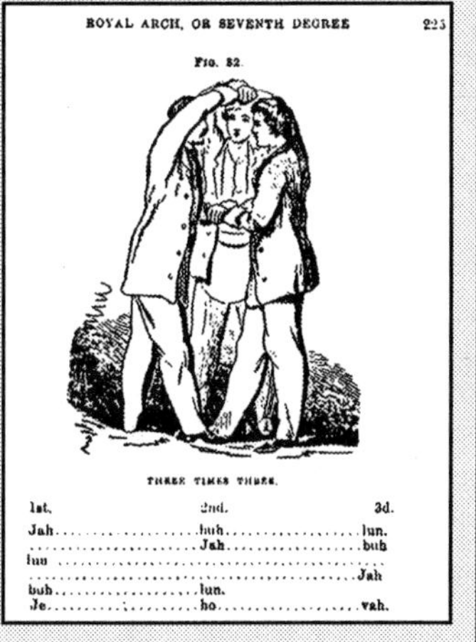

ROYAL ARCH, OR SEVENTH DEGREE 225

Fig. 32.

THREE TIMES THREE.

1st. ... 2nd. ... 3d.
Jah.................buh.................lun.
.......................Jah.................bub
lun ....
....Jah
bub.................lun.
Je.................ho.................vah.

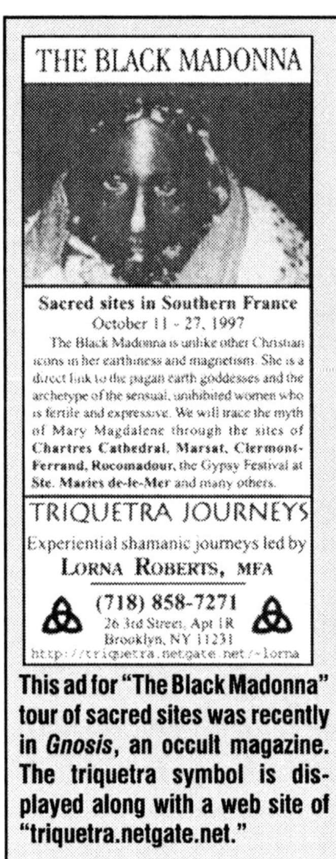

This ad for "The Black Madonna" tour of sacred sites was recently in *Gnosis*, an occult magazine. The triquetra symbol is displayed along with a web site of "triquetra.netgate.net."

Below: On the cover of Marilyn Ferguson's classic New Age bestseller is found the triquetra symbol. Inside the book the symbol is used repeatedly. Some have noted the striking resemblance to three 666s linked together. Is this the sign of the unholy trinity unified under the banner of Mystery, Babylon the Great?

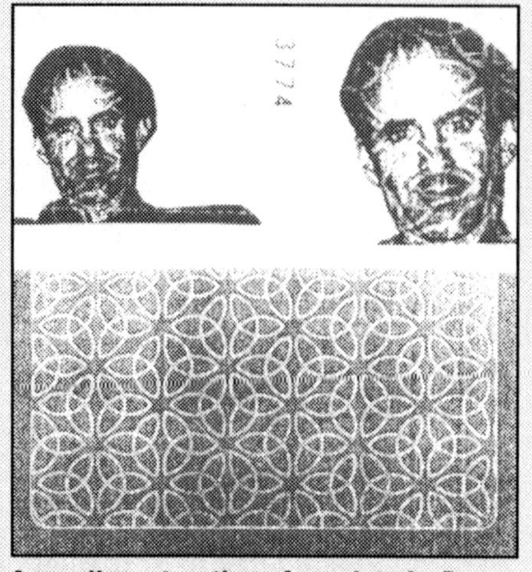

According to the *Associated Press*, MasterCard, Visa, Citibank, and Chase Manhattan Bank have teamed up to produce a new type of smart card. The electronic cash cards have a computer chip embedded in them. They are embossed with repeated triquetra symbols, arranged in circle patterns. Note the example here of a typical cardholder's face printed for I.D. purposes on the new smart card.

A Symbol of Occultism

Riplinger has brought to my attention that this same tri-part symbol is found concealed in the tail of the Green Dragon, illustrated in Harry E. Wedeck's occult classic volume, *Treasury of Witchcraft.*

The same symbol and logo can also be found on an album from Atlantic Records of heavy metal music by Led Zeppelin, the satanic rock group. Moreover, it is similar to the logo of the immense Krupp Works, the German manufacturing giant that was one of the most important producers for Adolf Hitler's Nazi war machine.

A Symbol of the Aquarian Conspirators

New Age leader Marilyn Ferguson, who wrote the million copy bestselling book, *The Aquarian Conspiracy*, included the triquetra symbol at the beginning of each chapter of her 447-page encyclopedia promoting New Age perversion. Indeed, the very cover of her book has this symbol prominently displayed against a stark, black background.

In her book, *The Aquarian Conspiracy*, Ferguson displays an arrogant, in-your-face attitude. She confidently discloses that yes, there *is* a global, New Age conspiracy. She gushingly reports that the goal of its leadership is to dramatically transform humanity and usher in a New Millennium of Oneness. Ferguson writes:

> A leaderless but powerful network is working to bring about radical change in the United States...This network is the *Aquarian Conspiracy*...
>
> There are legions of conspirators. They are in corporations, universities, and hospitals,

on the faculties of public schools, in state and federal agencies...and the White House staff. Whatever their station or sophistication, the conspirators are linked... (pp. 23-24)

A Symbol of the Black Madonna

In countless New Age magazines and books, one will find on prominent display the triquetra seal—the same logo that is used by Thomas Nelson Publishers as the dominant design to announce each copy of its false bible version.

In *Gnosis* magazine (Winter 1997, p. 10) I discovered an ad promoting a tour of "sacred sites in Southern France." Participants, the ad explained, will be taken to key places to honor and contemplate the Black Madonna, said to be "a direct link to the pagan Earth goddesses and the archetype of the sensual, uninhibited woman..."

A Symbol of High Tech Control

But perhaps the ultimate use of this strange, ancient symbol of foreboding evil is found on—of all places—a high tech smart card. Gail Riplinger sent me a prototype of a new smart card just unveiled by MasterCard, Visa, Citibank, and Chase Manhattan. I was utterly shocked to find the triquetra symbol emblazoned repeatedly on the card. As Gail told me in her letter, *"The latest smart card has the NKJV's logo all over the face of the plastic so that when a picture goes under it, you have 666 on your forehead."*

In other words, the image on the prototype smart card is that of a man, the bearer or holder of the card, who has this dreadful symbol splattered all over his face and head.

A Symbol of the Beast?

Gail Riplinger suggests that the design of the triquetra symbol on the smart card is alarmingly likened to that of three 6's linked together: 666! Could it be that this strange symbol is the prophesied Mark of the Beast, that terrifying seal someday to be given each person on Earth, in their forehead or right hand, as a sign of the Beast's unreserved ownership of the individual's body and soul?:

> *And the smoke of their torment ascendeth up for ever and ever: and they have no rest day nor night, who worship the beast and his image, and whosoever receiveth the mark of his name. (Revelation 14:11)*

The prophetic Word solemnly warns us not to receive the "mark of his name." And what is *his* name? We instantly recall that higher-level Masons worship a false god under the adulterous name, *Jahbuhlun*. And, as we have seen, the mark of Jahbuhlun is that of the triquetra, the same three-part symbol used by the publisher of the *NKJV* bible.

Therefore, I ask once again: Could it be that this symbol—the secretive sign of the Aquarian Conspirators; the symbol of the worshippers of the Black Madonna; the symbol plastered on the image of the face of holders of a coming, new universal smart card—is the very mark signifying the name of the beast?

A Sign From God

Frankly, I do not believe that in choosing this symbol for its bible version the publisher of the *NKJV* bible had any idea of the true meaning of its esoteric significance. But because this bible version, like so many others, is permeated with errors and omissions, I believe it possible that God saw to it that there would be a signal for true Christians—one glaringly printed on this false bible—warning us to reject the *NKJV*. God is faithful. He always gives His people the light of truth so that darkness can be avoided and rejected.

I believe, then, we are witnessing the hand of God, cautioning us to have nothing to do with the corrupt, new bible versions. As we have repeatedly stated, the authorized King James Version (KJV) remains the one, true, untarnished Bible. It is accurate and without mixture of error. No wonder, then, that so many deceivers today seek to cast doubt on the powerful, eternal Word of God contained in the *King James Bible*.

My friends, the real war in these last days is not in the field of economics. Our major enemy is not political. The greatest battle is not over the conspirators' scheme for the New World Order. What we are engaged in now is the epic contest of the ages. This is a struggle for the spiritual heart of mankind. I thank God that he has provided us with all the ammunition and answers we need to fight in this Holy War and prevail. The mighty weapons we require are found in ample supply in His Book, the majestic and incomparable King James Bible.

Co-Founder of New Bible Version Repents

> "For I testify unto every man that heareth the words of the prophecy of this book, If any man shall add unto these things, God shall add unto him the plagues that are written in this book: And if any man shall take away from the words of the book of this prophecy, God shall take away his part out of the book of life, and out of the holy city, and from the things which are written in this book."
>
> —*Revelation 22: 18-19*

Dr. Frank Logsdon could, with accuracy, be called "co-founder of the New American Standard Version (NASV) of the Bible." So important were his contributions that the publisher holding the copyright on this false Bible, the secretive Lochman Foundation, agreed to have Dr. Logsdon write the preface.

But thank God, Dr. Frank Logsdon, before his death, realized what a tragic mistake he had made.

After contemplating on the scary passage found in Revelation which sternly warns that is a person adds to or takes away from God's Word, that person's name will be blotted out and removed from the Book of Life of the Lamb, Logsdon was stricken in spirit.

Suffering pain and grief, Logsdon became consumed with the horror-filled conviction that, by cooperating in the NASV project, he might have forfeited his very salvation.

Beseeching God for forgiveness, Dr. Logsdon then wrote this poignant letter of atonement for his error. It is virtually a last testament:

> "I must under God renounce every attachment to the New American Standard Version... I'm afraid I'm in trouble with the Lord... We laid the groundwork; I wrote the format; I helped interview some of the translators; I sat with the translators; I wrote the preface... I'm in trouble; I can't refute these arguments; it's wrong; It's terribly wrong; it's frighteningly wrong... The Authorized Version (KJV) is absolutely correct."

God is merciful and just. Therefore, I believe that Dr. Logsdon is in heaven today in the arms of Christ Jesus. We read in *I John 1:9*, "If we confess our sins, he is faithful and just to forgive us our sins, and to cleanse us from all unrighteousness."

Let us continue to pray for the many others who continue to defile God's Word by promoting the false versions. May they, too, see the light just as Dr. Frank Logsdon did before his death.

Satan's New Age Goal of a One World Bible

"Lest Satan should get an advantage of us: for we are not ignorant of his devices."

—*II Corinthians 2:11*

In his haste and eagerness to defame Gail Riplinger and to derail her book, *New Age Bible Versions*, author Dave Hunt is making statements that even his most ardent supporters find utterly preposterous. In a harsh criticism of Riplinger's book, Hunt admits: *"I haven't read much of that book" (The Berean Call*, Sept. 1994). But curiously, immediately after confessing his ignorance of the overall contents of the book, Hunt goes right on to assert:

> What little I have read is full of errors both of logic and fact. The foundational premise stated on page 1—that the New Age movement has an "expressed goal of infiltrating the evangelical church and gradually changing the Bible to conform to its One World Religion"—is false. I've been exposing the New Age movement for at least 16 years and have never come across such a goal "expressed" by any leader, much less by the entire movement.

In sum, Dave Hunt aggressively denies that the New Age movement wants to change our Bible to promote a One World Religion. He contends that not even *one* New Age leader has *ever* expressed such a goal. Then, Hunt goes one giant step further: He suggests that Christians who make such claims are guilty of "fanning the flames of destructive extremism."

Dave Hunt's arrogance is monumental. But his ignorance of the goals of the New Age movement is even more monumental. His ignorance could have tragic, fatal results. What Hunt is doing is smearing some very dedicated Christians, unjustly accusing them of concocting myths and inventing lies. Meanwhile, the attempts to exonerate the New Age movement, holding its leaders blameless of their evil goals of infiltrating Christianity and developing a polluted Bible more to their liking.

One might justifiably ask: Is Dave Hunt a New Ager in disguise—an *Agent Provocateur?* Has he been commissioned by sinister forces to suck Christians in by first portraying himself as a New Age "expert," then intentionally wrecking opposition to New Age goals? Has Dave Hunt had a *paradigm shift?* Why else would a person make such ludicrous statements so totally opposite from the established facts?

***The Aquarian Gospel of Jesus the Christ* is only one of many counterfeit "Christian Bibles." The ultimate goal of Satan's New Age movement is to develop a unified One World Bible. The new Bible versions are a major step in that direction.**

In her book, *Toward a World Religion for the New Age*, former Christian missionary Lola Davis proposes a One World Bible be produced from the combined holy books, scriptures, and sacred teaching so all ancient and modern religions and sects.

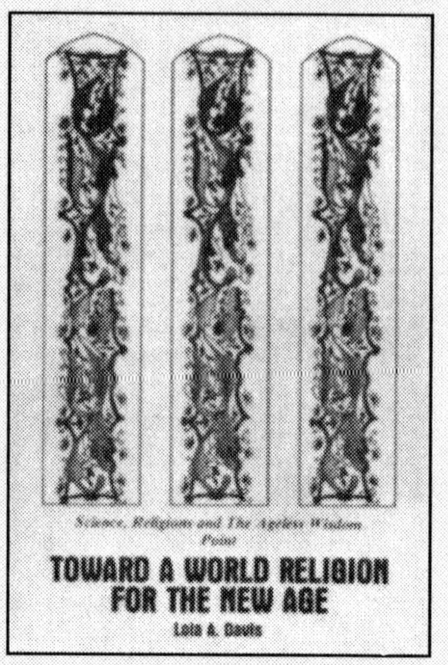

Frankly, I doubt if Hunt is a closet New Ager. I'll certainly give him the benefit of the doubt. His problem, most likely, is one of ignorance. He simply doesn't know. That, plus he is panic-stricken that he has been exposed as a promoter of the false, new Bible versions.

Could it be that Hunt's confusion over the goals of the New Age movement is caused by his criticism of the King James Bible, which, he claims, has errors and is "flawed" (see *The Berean Call,* Sept. 1992)? As Dr. Peter Ruckman, a stout defender of the King James Bible, once told me, "Texe, if a man messes with God's Book, God messes with his mind."

Whatever the reason, Dave Hunt's ignorance of the goals of the New Age movement is truly appalling. There exists a hideous gap in the man's research and knowledge. I do wish that Mr. Hunt had read my bestselling book, *Dark Secrets of the New Age*. In it, I quote a multitude of New Age leaders whose "expressed goal" is to infiltrate Christianity and develop a One World Bible. One of the chapters in my book is even entitled, *Unholy Bibles of the New Age*.

I also cover this same theme in such pivotal books as *Mystery Mark of the New Age, Ravaged by the New Age*, and *New Age Cults and Religions*. Taken together, these books include literally thousands of authoritative quotes by New Age leaders themselves.

Evidently, though he brags he has done 16 years of research into the goals of the New Age movement, Mr. Hunt evidently neglected to study the writings of literally scores of top New Age teachers—many of whom criticize and bash the King James Bible and openly state their goal of a *One World Bible*—a *common code* or *universal Scriptures*, for all the world's religions.

Here are just a few quotes by New Age teachers who've expressed a goal of merging Christianity in with a New World Religion and also have the goal of a unified Bible for the entire world:

> We need a religion to synthesize the world's religions...In this century religious data previously unavailable has been found or released. Among these are the Dead Sea Scrolls; the vast treasures of religious writings found in the Potola in Tibet; Christian writings deleted from the Bible during the 4th century; writings of Tellhard de Chardin; and previously carefully guarded knowledge of the Ancient Wisdom, including the writings of the Tibetan in the Alice Bailey books; writings of Mystics from various

religions; the materials offered by the Rosicrucians, and many books on Buddhism and Hindu philosophy and practices.

Also, we have gained much knowledge about human development, human states of consciousness, interpersonal relations, group functioning and educational methods. Some knowledge has resulted from research in the psychophysical and spiritual concomitants of meditation.

Probably, much of this knowledge could be advantageously used in synthesizing the major religions with a World Religion for the New Age.

—Lola Davis
Toward a World Religion for the New Age

Why should not Christians be glad to learn what God has wrought through Buddha and Zoraster—through the sages of China and the prophets of India and the prophets of Islam?

—Charles C. Bonney
Speech at the Parliament of the World's Religions (1993)

If the final planetary synthesis of the Eastern and Western spiritual traditions is to be realized, Eastern mysticism must be incorporated into traditional Christianity.

—Peter Roche de Coppens
The Meaning of Christ for Our Age

The Divine Plan will… be given out to mankind in the form of a Spiritual World Teaching… As concepts of the (New Age) world religion are scientifically validated, learned, and spread about, present religions will begin to make changes and evolve into centers for the world religion. From all archaeological archives…and the Illuminations of modern science and discovery…would develop a new "Bible" of a world religion which will be the basis of future education.

—Vera Alder
Humanity Comes of Age

Little by little, a planetary prayer book is being composed by an increasingly united humanity seeking its oneness.

—Robert Muller
The New Genesis

If you cleave only to the exact wording of a holy book which was released a guide for times past…you will not be growing in the way God wishes. Your interpretation of all holy books must be expanded…Some insist the Bible is a final work…To these ideas I say a resounding "No"…

—Virginia Essene
New Teachings for an Awakening Humanity

Contrary to Dave Hunt's assertions, it's plain to see that many, many New Age leaders have, indeed, expressed goals of polluting God's Word and developing a satanic One World Bible. What's more, New Age leaders are striving to infiltrate Christianity, and they are progressively establishing a New Age World Religion. As Salem Kirban, one of America's greatest prophecy teachers, explains in his excellent book, *The New Age Secret Plan for World Conquest*, "New Age leaders are already making plans for a New Age Bible." Its development, he notes, is part of the "strong delusion" prophesied in *II Thes. 2*. Kirban also writes:

> The New Age Bible will have a New Age Christ and his 12-person Spiritual Cabinet. It will contain the teachings of various mystics, Rosicrucians, Buddhist, and Hindu philosophies. It will encourage man to believe he is god.

Salem Kirban began his study of the New Age movement some three decades ago, long before people like Dave Hunt had even heard of the term "New Age." Kirban fully knows the New Age plan and he's been courageous in exposing it. How sad, then, that Hunt did not bother to read Kirban's fully documented book before making his own outrageous claims exonerating the New Age movement.

Indeed, if Dave Hunt had simply read Gail Riplinger's book he would have known of the sinister goals of the New Age movement. It's mind-boggling that Hunt could only quote from page 1 of her *New Age Bible Versions*. If he had read on to page 27, Hunt would have discovered a significant quote by New Age leader Helena Blavatsky, founder of Theosophy, revealing her delight that the King James Bible was being stripped of much of its powerful wording by new versions. Even before that, on page 11, is a telling quote from Lola Davis' book, *Toward a World Religion for the New Age*. And on page 30, Riplinger correctly quotes New Age teacher Vera Alder, who directly and unequivocally expresses that a primary New Age goal is to *"develop a new 'Bible' of a world religion."*

Unfortunately, it seems that Dave Hunt does not care for the truth. Worse, he has greatly assisted the implementation of Satan's New Age goals. Maybe it is because he is ignorant of the New Age devices of the devil. But unfortunately, in Dave Hunt's case, ignorance is not bliss. Many people are being misled, and the cause of Christ is being gravely compromised.

HOW ARE WE SAVED?		
KJV	NEW VERSIONS	NEW AGE/ HUMANISM
—	how hard it is	how hard it is
by grace	OMIT	OMIT
through his blood	OMIT	OMIT
the gospel of Christ	a gospel	a gospel
the door	a door	a door
the word	a message	a message
believe	obey	obey
faith	faithfulness	faithfulness
believe in him	believe	believe
Lord, Jesus	OMIT	OMIT

New Versions Remove Biblical Word "Virgin"

One of the unshakable truths of the Bible is that Jesus our Lord was born to a virgin. *Isaiah 7:14* proclaims: *"Behold, a virgin shall conceive, and bear a son, and shall call His name Immanuel."*

How glorious to realize that this Old Testament prophecy was fulfilled to the letter when our Saviour and King, Jesus Christ, was born to the Virgin Mary. *Matthew 1:22-23* records: "Now all this was done, that it might be fulfilled which was spoken of the Lord by the prophet, saying, Behold, a virgin shall be with child, and shall bring forth a son, and they shall call his name Emmanuel, which being interpreted is, God with us."

Over the years, thousands of Jews have accepted Jesus as Lord, seeing that His miraculous virgin birth, recorded in the New Testament, was amazingly—and accurately—prophesied centuries in advance by the Jewish prophet Isaiah.

But atheists, liberals, and other scoffers have long sought to discredit the Biblical account of this and other miracles of God. In their unbelief, they have laughed and, with sarcasm, exclaimed: "How can a baby be born to a virgin? Ridiculous!"

Jewish rabbis and teachers have particularly been critical. After all, if Jesus' birth is the fulfillment of Isaiah's prophecy in the Old Testament, this proves that Jesus is truly the Messiah. If He is Messiah, the Jews and Israel must acknowledge Him as Lord and King. This, they stubbornly refuse to do.

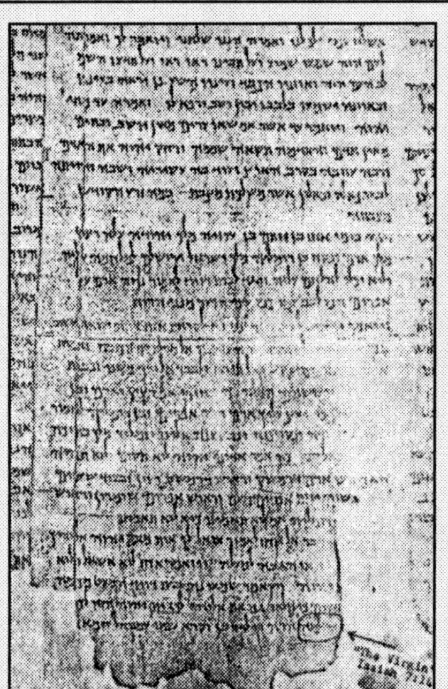

The oldest known manuscript of *Isaiah*, shown here, clearly uses the Hebrew word Almah (or Haalmah), which means "virgin."

Vicious Attacks on God's Word

As a result, over the years vicious attacks have been launched to discredit the virgin birth of Christ. These attacks have centered on the very Word of God. Satan and his human disciples reason that if they can cause the multitudes to doubt the Biblical account, they will win this ages-old battle to replace the truth with a lie.

More recently, Satan's followers decided that to demolish the gospel account, new Bible versions must be invented—diabolical versions which would veil and distort the true meaning of Jesus' *virgin* birth.

The first salvo against the miracle of the virgin birth of Christ Jesus came in the 60s from the hideous *Revised Standard Version* (RSV). In the RSV, put out by the apostate World Council of Churches, the word virgin—as accurately found in the 1611 King James Bible—was changed to "young maiden." The corrupted RSV was followed by still other false versions which reinterpreted the word virgin either as "young maiden," "young woman," or "young married woman."

Arno Froese Rejects "Virgin" Word

Now comes Arno Froese, the heretical prophecy teacher who publishes *Midnight Call.* Seeking to prove his assertion that the King James Bible (KJV) is flawed by "hundreds, if not thousands" of errors, Froese, in a letter dated December 22, 1994,writes that the word virgin in the King James Bible is incorrect and shouldn't be there:

> We see the KJV use the word "virgin" which is not to be found in the original Bible but it says "young woman."

Mr. Froese's statement that the word virgin "is not to be found in the original Bible" is odd to the extreme, especially in light of what he has also stated in his essay *"Which Bible?"* (August 15, 1994). In his essay, Mr. Froese asserts that the original Bible writings do not exist or, at least, he claims that no one knows where they are. He writes: "Unfortunately, none of the original writings are available."

Mr. Froese thus testifies that he has never seen, touched, read, or studied the "original writings." How, then, does he know that the word "virgin" is not in the original *if the original is not available for him to check and compare?*

In fact, Froese is mistaken. The original Word of God *does* exist, but in his ignorance he has rejected it. God's original Word has been faithfully passed down and preserved in the form of the Greek Received Text (New Testament) and the Hebrew Masoretic Text (Old Testament). Both of these wonderful and perfect Bible manuscripts were faithfully used by the King James translators in 1611. That is why these inspired men of God correctly chose the word "virgin" and rejected the gross and vulgar lie of the Bible scoffers.

Martin Luther's Scholarly Research

Martin Luther, the great Bible scholar and bold hero of the Protestant Reformation, had much to say on this vital subject. In his writings, he noted that the Hebrew word "Almah" in *Isaiah 7:14* could only mean "virgin:"

> "Behold," says Isaiah, "the virgin is with Child," etc. Here we have the word Almah, of which many others, and also I have written, that it means a virgin… If they make the claim that the Hebrew text does not state a virgin… the answer is easy from St. Matthew (1:22-23) and Luke (1:31), both of whom apply the passage in Isaiah to Mary and translate the word "Almah" virgin, whom we believe rather than the whole world. (Martin Luther, quoted by G. Stoeckhardt, *Der Prophet Jesaia*, Concordia Publishing House, 1902).

God's Word Stands

The manuscript evidence is irrefutable. Mary, a virgin, gave birth to the Son of God. God's Word stands! How pitiful and embarrassing, then, are the illogical and contradictory statements of the modern-day prophecy teachers who seek to defame God's King James Bible! I fervently hope that Mr. Froese believes Jesus was, indeed, born to a virgin. I assume he does. But, if so, why does he buy the lie of the liberals and Jews who vainly labor to mistranslate this word and wish to remove it entirely from God's Holy Bible?

Again, we see the tragic situation of those who reject God's promise of inerrancy, purity, and preservation of His precious Word. They accept, instead, the doctrines of devils. Let us earnestly pray for the new version heretics, including Arno Froese, to receive the light of God's truth.

Is the NIV Bible the Queer Version?

We offer through the ministry one of the most powerful books ever written, the 690-page *New Age Bible Versions*, by G. A. Riplinger. This book unmasks the occultic and anti-God origins of most of the new Bible versions, while demonstrating that the King James is truly God's inspired Word.

Now comes more graphic proof that the newer versions are dangerously tainted. Dr. Virginia Mollenkott, one of the supposed "scholars" who helped compose the New International Version, turns out to be a lesbian activist!

Ms. Mollenkott, an Episcopal who is a professor at William Paterson College in Wayne, New Jersey, has come out of the closet. She is now giving interviews bragging of her lesbian persuasion and admitting she has a female lover. Mollenkott even says that the Bible *approves* homosexual behavior, and she further claims that God knowingly created her as a lesbian, so it's not a sin. Sex outside of marriage, Mollenkott adds, is not prohibited by God's Word.

Pray tell, I wonder, how would this lesbian agitator and NIV translator interpret the Biblical story of Sodom and Gomorrah?

Feminist Mollenkott's contributions to the NIV translation were crucial. Undoubtedly, her work and views vastly affected the outcome of the final NIV edition.

Shouldn't Zondervan, the publisher of the NIV, also "come out of the closet" and admit that its twisted version is, in fact, a *"Queer Choice?"*

COMPARISON OF BIBLE VERSES

(Reference: *New Age Bible Versions*, by Gail Riplinger)

The "New Age" Christianity of the New Versions (NASB, NIV *et al.*)		First Century Christianity as Found in the King James Version
Then come, follow me	Mark 10:21	and come, take up the cross, and follow me
men	2 Pet. 1:21	holy men
heart	1 Pet. 1:22	pure heart
adequate	2 Tim 3:17	perfect
prosperity	Prov 21:21	righteousness
prosper	Jer 29:11	peace
godliness actually is a means of great gain	1 Tim 6:6	godliness with contentment is great gain
boast	Heb 3:6	rejoicing
be proud	2 Cor 1:14	your rejoicing
proud confidence	2 Cor 1:12	rejoicing
furthering the administration	1 Tim 1:4	godly edifying
You have made him a little lower than God	Ps 8:5	For thou hast made him a little lower than the angels
I retract	Job 42:6	I abhor myself
our humble state	Phil 3:21	our vile body
man shall not live on bread alone	Luke 4:4	That man shall not live by bread alone, but by every word of God
Salvation by works or faith in Jesus Christ?		
Children, how hard it is to enter the kingdom of God	Mark 10:24	Children, how hard is it for them that trust in riches to enter into the kingdom of God
By standing firm you will save yourself	Luke 21:19	In your patience possess ye your souls
obey	John 3:36	believeth
faithfulness	Gal 5:22 et al.	faith
OMIT	Rom. 11:6	But if it be of works, then is it no more grace
the gospel	Rom 1:16	the gospel of Christ
OMIT	Acts 8:37	I believe that Jesus Christ is the Son of God
In whom we have redemption	Col 1:14	In whom we have redemption through his blood
who believes	Mark 9:42	believe in me
he who believes has everlasting life	John 6:47	He that believeth on me hath everlasting life
calling on His name	Acts 22:16	calling on the name of the Lord
OMIT	1 John 5:13	and that ye may believe on the name of the Son of God
teaching	2 John 9b	doctrine of Christ
truth	1 Tim 2:7	truth in Christ
Neither is circumcision anything	Gal 6:15	For in Christ Jesus neither circumcision availeth any thing
I bow my knees before the Father	Eph 3:14	I bow my knees unto the Father of our Lord Jesus Christ
an heir of God	Gal 4:7	an heir of God through Christ
God who created all things	Eph 3:9	God, who created all things by Jesus Christ

False Teachers, Apostasy, and the Seduction of Christianity

"...and all the world wondered after the beast." (Revelation 13:8)

Rise of the Universally "Loved" New Jesus

"For the time will come when they will not endure sound doctrine; but after their own lusts shall they heap to themselves teachers, having itching ears; And they shall turn away their ears from the truth, and shall be turned unto fables."
—*II Timothy 4:3-4*

It was difficult for us to bear what we were seeing and hearing with our own eyes and ears. Recently, Wanda and I tuned in to TV's Trinity Broadcasting Network (TBN). A prosperity preacher named Rod Parsley was entertaining a huge crowd of thousands that filled an immense auditorium. In his smartly tailored suit, sweating profusely, his tie loosened, flailing away with both arms and working the crowd like a carnival pro, Parsley had these well-dressed people jumping up and down, shouting and hurrahing with all their might. The throng were exuberant and celebrating. They sure liked what Parsley had to say. It tickled their ears—and aroused their greed.

The Devil Stole Your Stuff

What we saw that night on TV was the most sickening staged performance we had ever witnessed occurring inside a church.

"The devil," Parsley boldly announced, "has taken your *stuff* and now you're going to get it back. We're going to kick the devil."

Suddenly, from the front of the auditorium two actors dressed in costumes like devils burst down the aisle and headed toward Parsley. The theatrical preacher militantly kicked his leg and shoes at them as if he were *Kung Fu* martial arts fighter. Soon, the two would-be imps were groveling in retreat. The crowd stood and cheered.

Then, Parsley ordered the two, defeated "devils" to bring out the "stuff." They slinked out behind a curtain and a moment later came back in, dragging along a whole wagonload of gaily wrapped gift packages. The two "devils" offered all the gifts to Parsley.

"Jesus Came to Get Your Stuff Back!"

Pastor Rod Parsley ran to the wagon and began grabbing the packages and tossing them into the audience. The people almost went wild with ecstasy as the sweaty-browed Parsley shouted, *"Jesus came and died on the cross to get back your stuff from the devil. Well, here it is!"*

It was a fascinating, if disgusting, spectacle. Of course, Parsley's weekly crowd-pleasing antics are only one of the many circus-like sideshows the world can view on the boob tube, especially on Paul and Jan Crouch's TBN network. Sometimes, the hoopla on Christian TV rivals the performances and extravaganzas staged by the Hulk Hogans of professional wrestling, and such entertaining events as rodeos, tractor pulls and stock car racing.

I doubt, however, that Hulk Hogan, the wrestler, takes himself seriously. Certainly, one's eternal destiny does not hinge on the results of a tractor pull or a tilt between two comedic wrestlers. But the Rod Parsleys of this world claim to bring men and women spiritual knowledge and spiritual truth. This is serious business of eternal significance.

The question, then, is: Did Jesus our Lord really come to earth and suffer unthinkable agony, being nailed to the hideous cross, so that you and I could get back our "stuff"—the material things which prosperity preachers contend the devil stole from us? Did Jesus really give Himself over to the Jews and to Pilate to painfully die at Calvary merely so that you and I could fatten our bank accounts, move into a fancier home, drive the newest auto, or shop for the coolest gadgets at the mall? Is *that* really what Christianity is all about?

Some say that as long as the name of Jesus is given credit or preached by a minister or evangelist all is well. If so, then Pastor Rod Parsley cannot be faulted. He did tell the thousands of people there live and watching on TV that it was Jesus who died on the cross so they could get more "stuff." He did preach the name of Jesus.

But, was what the popular teacher preached about Jesus *true*? Is this what Jesus meant when He commanded us to go and preach the Gospel to all nations, to every creature? Are we to assure lost souls that Jesus died on the cross so they can possess a bunch of earthly "stuff?"

Jesus, Jesus Everywhere...But No Real Jesus

Jesus this and Jesus that. Jesus, Jesus everywhere. But no Truth. That's the *New Spirituality* that has quickly grasped the jugular of the masses. What's more, according to Pope John Paul II, Billy Graham, Robert Schuller, and others, this new spirituality allows for a Jesus that enters the hearts of Christians, Buddhists, Moslems, and Hindus alike. As I previously documented in my newsletter, Billy Graham says that when people faithfully follow after the idols and gods of their own cultures, they already are saved and have "Jesus" within whether they know it or not.

Billy Graham's "Jesus" is incredibly broad-minded and flexible, isn't he?

Meanwhile, in New York City, a new Broadway play is under production, a play in which Jesus is depicted as a homosexual who lustily enjoys sex with John, Matthew, and other disciples. Yes, today's "Jesus" is, indeed, flexible and broad-minded.

Billy Graham's "Jesus" is flexible and nonjudgmental. Graham says that devout Buddhists, Moslems, Hindus, Jews, and nature worshippers already have Jesus within, whether they even know His name.

Who would have ever thought that Jesus would be so widely admired, loved, and accepted? Why, no one is opposed to Jesus anymore! I suspect that even the world's most despicable atheists could manufacture and concoct a mythical "Jesus" acceptable in doctrine and conduct to atheists everywhere.

The Pope Eyeing the World

In one edition of *Time* magazine (April 13, 1998), a rather odd picture of Pope John Paul II was published. The picture showed the Pontiff with his hands and fingers over his eyes. The caption read: *"The Pope keeps his eyes on the world."*

The picture and its captioned message were of great

symbolic significance. The Catholic establishment and its Pope are, indeed, eyeing the whole world.

In the year 2000, the Pope intends to dramatically usher in his new image of Jesus. The new Jesus of Catholicism is an ecumenical being. According to the Pope's own public statements and his *New Catechism*, the new Jesus allows Hindus, Moslems, and Jews, African tribalists, voodoo practitioners, and others to continue worshipping their own gods and idols. As the Pontiff explains it, all who follow after the "light" they have received—whether it be Christian or heathen light—are saved.

A few years ago during a visit to Israel, Russia's former Communist dictator Mikhail Gorbachev said that Jesus was "one of the world's most famous Socialists."

Amazingly, the *New Catechism* grants all men and women who worship *any* god full and unreserved membership in the Catholic Church. Thus, the devout Jew, Moslem, or Hindu, achieving salvation through good works, is automatically a bonafide member of the Roman Catholic Church—whether he or she knows it or not.

The Age of Jesus

Ours is truly the *Age of Jesus*. Long-haired, Christian rock music stars prance half-naked on stage, black Gospel singers jive and shake with the beat of the music, and inside the walls of fine, giant cathedrals and churches, millions of people are now laughing, roaring, creaming, rolling, rocking, swaying, jumping, cheerleading, marching, and mosh dancing to the name of "Jesus."

This modern-day "Jesus" is popular! No doubt, about that. Country music entertainers, pro football athletes, and championship boxers alike cheerfully give him glory and credit him with their successes and victories. Evangelists like Oral Roberts and Kenneth Copeland declare that if it weren't for Jesus, they couldn't afford those private executive jets and big mansions. "Jesus is the reason we're rich," they say.

Yes, the whole world is smiling and happy over what Jesus is doing in their lives—blessing them with money, power, fame, and worldly possessions. Not surprisingly, the new Jesus that has arisen is a sparkling creation. He's all loving, He never condemns, He's nonjudgmental, sends no one to hell, and wants everyone to be happy and rich, forever and ever. His followers even have the new "Bible" versions to describe His remarkable new features.

But Some are Sobbing

But, while most of the world loudly and openly trumpets the name of Jesus, hidden and secluded in their prayer closets and kneeling quietly beside their beds in the privacy of their homes are the broken-hearted, sobbing voices of true Christian believers. Blood-bought, born again Christian believers. *King James Bible* Christian believers. They number only a few and are despised by the majority of people. Aching inside and ashamed at what they see happening to the name of Jesus, their Lord and Saviour, these mournful Christian believers know that there is "another Jesus" *(II Corinthians 11:4)* and "another Gospel" *(Galatians 1)*.

They also remember the warning in *II Thessalonians 2* that the "strong delusion" is to overtake the whole world in the last days. Though they be few in number, with one voice this tiny cadre of dismayed, but trusting, Christians earnestly cry out and beg the real Jesus, God of all: *"Lord Jesus, please, come quickly."*

The Octopus Rises—in the Name of "Jesus"

I hereby prophesy that the name of "Jesus" will grow bigger and bigger in the coming months. You see, the octopus beast is now rising up from the sea *(Revelation 13:1)*; only, he doesn't look like a beast. Surprisingly, the beast doesn't appear to be a monster at all.

Slouching toward Jerusalem, intent on his prize, the beast of Revelation has not come breathing fire. He has no scales, no horns. Instead, he is a rewarder who bears gifts for all and promises universal prosperity and good times. He loves all mankind and touches everyone's life equally with his angels.

In the eyes of the vast multitude, the beast is not a villain. Shockingly, to the world he looks like—looks *just* like "Jesus!" Not, however, the Jesus of the Bible, but a Jesus of their own imaginations, of their own inventions. Yes, the representative of the dragon whom the whole world—except for a few blood-bought Christians—is destined to worship as their God and master appears to be "Jesus." The same "Jesus" they're regularly hearing about in their apostate churches, the same "Jesus" whose name is today a popular household word. The very same "Jesus" who is beloved by all, admired even by the worst heathens.

They Believe in Fables

Sadly, the Bible prophesies that in the last days, the masses will gladly accept and worship this god of New Age forces, this strange, other "Jesus." Loving and embracing the Lie, they are destined to reject the real Jesus, the one who died on the cross for their sins, the merciful Savior who pleads with them to take up the cross and follow Him.

The real Jesus of the Bible said we gain true prosperity by storing up treasures in heaven. He invites whosoever will to drink of His eternal living waters and be saved. But few want this kind of Jesus. This *real* Jesus they scorn and reject, accepting instead *another Jesus*, one more suitable to their modern tastes and lifestyles. Cavalierly tossing out the Truth, the masses entertain and rejoice in fables. This brings the Apostle Paul's prophecy in *II Timothy 4:3-4* to pass: *"And they shall turn their ears from the truth, and be turned unto fables."*

Friends, the counterfeit is at hand. What a deceiver he is, for he speaks like a lamb and comes in the form of "Jesus" *(Revelation 13:11).* But this universally acclaimed deity is "another Jesus," a false type of Christ whom the whole world has already begun to warmly embrace. Thus, we are witnessing today the remarkable fulfillment of prophecy. Now, more than ever, let us be sure of our salvation, and let us prepare ourselves and our families for the dreadful, near future sure to come.

> *"And then shall that wicked be revealed, whom the Lord shall consume with the spirit of His mouth, and shall destroy with the brightness of His coming.*
>
> *Even him, whose coming is after the working of Satan with all power and signs and lying wonders,*
>
> *And with all deceivableness of unrighteousness in them that perish; because they received not the love of the truth, that they might be saved.*
>
> *And for this cause God shall send them strong delusion, that they should believe a lie:*
>
> *That they all might be damned who believed not the truth, but had pleasure in unrighteousness." (II Thessalonians 2:8-12)*

Chuck Colson's Historic Secret Mission: Undo the Protestant Reformation

"And I saw one of his heads as it were wounded to death; and his deadly wound was healed: and all the world wondered after the beast."
—*Revelation 13:3*

If the courageous but bloodied Reformation saints profiled in *Foxe's Book of Martyrs* were on earth today, they would be aghast over Chuck Colson's newest project. He and a Catholic priest, "Father" Richard Neuhaus, have come up with a manifesto entitled *"Evangelicals and Catholics Together: The Christian Mission in the Third Millennium."* Colson and Neuhaus openly admit that they secretly worked for two years behind the scenes on this project. Their plan was to get the world's top evangelical and Catholic leaders to sign up and endorse the manifesto before expected opposition developed.

So far, over 50 famous evangelical leaders have signed the apostate document, including Pat Robertson of *The 700 Club*, Bill Seiple of *World Vision*, Bill Bright of *Campus Crusade for Christ*, J.I. Parker of *Christianity Today* magazine, and the two highest ranking bureaucrats of the massive *Southern Baptist Convention*, Larry Lewis, head of the *Home Missions Board*, and Richard Land, head of the *Christian Life Commission*. Also signing the manifest: a number of Roman Catholic cardinals, archbishops, bishops, and priests.

A Deceptive Unity

The manifesto of unity is cleverly and deceptively worded. Note, first, that Colson and Neuhaus disingenuously avoided the word "Protestant" in the title. They chose to emphasize "Evangelical" instead. In his acclaimed, mostly ghostwritten book, *The Body*, Colson had proposed that Protestants cease their attacks on Catholicism and join hands with Rome to fight the common enemy: the lack of morals and civility in society. In effect, he called for Protestantism to surrender.

Colson even criticized the use of the term "born again," explaining that his wife, a Catholic, and other Catholics were offended by the words "born again." Never mind that Jesus Himself told us in His Word, "Ye must be born again" to enter the Kingdom of Heaven (see *John 3:3*).

The Colson-Neuhaus manifesto of unity makes clear that "evangelicals" must never again seek to convert Catholics. Witnessing to Catholics must stop, period. Moreover, all who proselytized and witnessed to lost Catholics in the past must now repent (or do penance?) for their "sins." The manifesto reads: "We confess our sins against the unity that Christ intends."

"There are different ways of being a Christian," insists the manifesto. Really? The Bible says there is only *one* way.

According to Colson and Neuhaus, the fact that Protestant (oops, I means "evangelicals") and Catholics have been working arm in arm for years to fight such moral evils as abortion has now smoothed the way for the two factions to unite spiritually as well.

Fighting Evil is Not Enough

The truth is, however, that fighting abortion, or homosexuality, or corruption in government, or any number of evils in society is a good thing. I'm for uniting with anyone to support a clean and wholesome society and nation. But that doesn't make me a Christian. Indeed, being either "evangelical" or "Catholic" doesn't make a man a Christian. It is absurd—and unscriptural—to neglect to inform a lost person of Jesus' sacrifice and to let that person know that they must repent of their sins and be born again in spirit and in truth. Colson and his ecumenical associates do neglect the Gospel of Salvation in order to foster unity between man-made church denominations and institutions. This is the thing that is tragic.

Frankly, I care less whether a man or woman is a Catholic, a Protestant, a Baptist, a Seventh Day Adventist, or an Episcopalian. What I want to know is, does that person have Jesus in his heart? Is he born again? Does the person worship the true Jesus or, instead, does he give honor and reverence to "another Jesus" (II Cor 11:4), a false and counterfeit Jesus? Sadly, church pews today are full of confused and misled "Catholics," "Evangelicals: who have never had the amazing experience of being introduced to our wonderful redeemer and Lord. These masses are "Christians" in name only.

Chuck Colson has a hidden agenda—to undo the Protestant Reformation.

The Hidden Agenda of Chuck Colson

In my newsletter and on my radio program and tapes, I have repeatedly warned fellow Christians about the hidden agenda of Chuck Colson. I unmasked the fact that he had accepted over *one million dollars* from New Age, financial guru John Templeton, who gave Colson his "Prize for Progress in Religion." I also exposed the connections of Colson and his Prison Fellowship with the United Nations and with such liberal publications as *The Washington Post.*

As many of you know, when I unmasked Colson's willing and enthusiastic participation in the satanic Parliament of the World's Religions in Chicago in 1993, almost every "evangelical" and liberal magazine and ministry in Christendom came against me. I realize full well that Colson, who was convicted as a liar and perjurer in the Watergate scandal, has influential connections. He is supported by all the big name TV and radio personalities, from James Dobson to Pat Robertson.

Admittedly, in today's decadent Christian establishment, it's not popular to oppose Chuck Colson, a "Chosen One" of the Religious Right. Nevertheless, I will not shrink from my Christian duty and will continue to tell you the facts about the plots of Colson and his ungodly, Roman Catholic and "evangelical" associates. No doubt, the powers that be will viciously attack me for telling you the honest truth. But I don't answer to them. I answer only to my Lord and Saviour, whose Holy name is Jesus!

"Christian" Leaders Promote New Age's Earth Day

Christians need to embrace a *broader* sense of salvation: "salvation of humankind and salvation and redemption of *creation*." This is what Dr. Richard Land, executive director of the Southern Baptist Convention's Christian Life Commission, told ministers gathered in Nashville to promote global environmentalism. Land's remarks were reported in Virginia's Baptist newspaper *Religious Herald*. Apparently, Dr. Land is unaware that the true purpose of environmentalism is to promote the concept that the earth is Gaia, a living goddess, and that we must protect the environment in order to "save" our Mother Earth.

Land, amazingly known as one of the leading conservatives in the Southern Baptist Convention (SBC), is not only actively promoting the pagan doctrine of environmentalism, but he also recently sparked a controversy when he invited a pro-abortion advocate to speak at a major SBC conference. According to *The Baptist Standard*, by a narrow 12-11 vote, the board members of the denomination's Christian Life Commission directed Land not to invite pro-abortion advocates to speak at future meetings.

Dr. Richard Land

Apparently, Richard Land has bought much of the lie. Whereas Jesus told us in His Word that the *broad way leads to destruction* and the narrow way to God, Land remarked to the group in Nashville, "Our salvation history causes *too narrow* a focus for salvation."

What is necessary, he suggested, is that Christians must take on the burden of salvation for both people and the planet. "We should seek the salvation of earth itself. We must redeem not only mankind but the cosmos," he urged.

Land attempted to justify his unorthodox views by arguing that there is really no separation of heaven and earth. They are one. "A spatial concept of the world is needed," he remarked, "rather than a view that separates heaven from earth."

Even more scary were the speeches of other Southern Baptist leaders at the Nashville Earth Day conference. For example, Herbert Gabhart, chancellor of Belmont College, a Southern Baptist school, termed the focus on the environment "an inspired task of the new decade." However, "it may require sacrifice of some 'so-called rights,'" warned Gabhart.

Praise God, there are still a number of Southern Baptist pastors who are not falling for the New Age lies. I personally know many who are resisting the fast-growing apostasy in their ranks. Moreover, in fairness we should note that there are also Episcopal, Methodist, Catholic, Charismatic,

Pentecostal, Presbyterian, United Church of Christ, and other so-called "Christian" leaders caught up in New Ageism. Many of them are vigorously promoting the Earth religion.

Examples abound. Rev. Melvin West, in the *United Methodist Reporter*, called on all Methodists to take the lead in the environmental movement. He urged a new theology of "Earth-care," a theology needed, says West, because "We have focused on personal salvation to the neglect of society and the environment."

In agreement is Methodist Rev. Glenn Old, who is so hung up on the new earth and creation-centered theology he recently became president of Ted Turner's one world group, the Better World Society. Olds is also promoting the World Council of Churches' new eastern mysticism-oriented campaign to save the earth, represented by the Hindu symbol of the lotus blossom.

Meanwhile, Catholic priest Matthew Fox, in his new book, *The Coming of the Cosmic Christ*, cries out that "Mother Earth has been crucified and she must now be resurrected."

What a tragedy. Sadly, these men have forgotten the *Great Commission* of Christ. Instead of dedicating our efforts to reach people with a saving gospel, they want us to expend much of our energies on salvation for the earth!

This goes far beyond cleaning up the environment. It is the lie of Satan that Paul warned about in *Romans 1:18-25*—the worship of the creation instead of the creator.

My friends, did Jesus die on the cross for a rock in the sky called "Earth," for dirt? Or, rather, did He shed His precious blood so that the souls of men and women could be saved?

Does "the world" in John 3:16 mean that Jesus died for Mother Earth, or does it refer to living, breathing men and women in need of God's redemption? The New Age—and evidently Richard Land and those other Church leaders—believe their way. But true Biblical Christians know exactly for whom Jesus died—Us! We also realize that God loves us so much more than He does a transient planet made up of rock, clay, dirt and water.

We read in *II Peter 3:10, 13:*

> *But the day of the Lord will come as a thief in the night; in the which the heavens shall pass away with a great noise, and the elements shall melt with fervent heat, the earth also and the works that are therein shall be burned up...*
>
> *Nevertheless we, according to His promise, look for new heavens and a new earth, wherein dwelleth righteousness.*

God's Word is so marvelous. It reveals that this present earth will someday pass away, brilliantly exploding in a fury of fire. But the person who trusts in the Lord will live forever and ever, for all eternity!

Friends, I encourage each of you to invest your time, energy, and your fortunes in something more endurable and lasting than this fading and jaded planet Earth. Around the globe millions of people are actively meditating and working for the environmental salvation of planet earth. Yet, I pray that we who know Jesus as Lord will take the time on that day to speak to just *one* other person about *the only thing that really matters*—his or her individual salvation through Jesus Christ alone.

Yes, the pagan earthers are intent on deifying the material world. But "Greater is He that is in you than he who is in the world." While *they* celebrate their Earth Days, let us pledge ourselves anew to contend for the faith. Let us, then, continue our own eternal project of harvesting for our Lord. After all, one soul saved is worth the entire world.

Diabolical Activity Rampages Throughout Christian Establishment

Global Explosion of Religious Apostasy

Across America and the planet, we are now witnessing an unheralded explosion of the most virulent forms of religious apostasy. Incredibly, this is just as Jesus and the Bible's prophets foresaw. Yet, only those with eyes to see and ears to hear are even dimly aware of the rising tide of perverted spirituality. If you are one of the overcomers whom God has blessed with His precious gift of discernment, you will understand. You will recognize that what I reveal here is horribly sick and evil.

However, if you are not blessed with this gift of discernment, PLEASE DON'T READ ANY FURTHER. You will only get frustrated and mad. And you'll probably end up writing to Texe Marrs accusing me of being narrow-minded, intolerant and judgmental. You may even get so angry, you'll furiously brand me a tool of the devil, guilty of being an accuser of the brethren.

I'm used to this kind of response however, so if you do read the facts documented here, and it makes you see red, go ahead—feel free to write and blast me. I can take it. But, remember: What I say and present here is true. So, why attack the messenger?

Kenneth Hagin and the Spirit of the Serpent

I begin with a look at the man whom Word of Faith advocates and charismatics like Paul Crouch and Kenneth Copeland lionize and call "dad" and "papa"—Kenneth Hagin. I have a video of a series of "Holy Ghost" meetings evangelist Kenneth Hagin conducted in Chesterfield, Missouri in October, 1997. At one of these sessions, Satan was seen to manifest himself in the very body of Hagin. Hagin's tongue literally began sticking out and wiggling like a serpent's tongue.

The crowd, mesmerized by the evil display, groaned and virtually went insane as Hagin commenced to hiss like a serpent. Suddenly, many of the people began to slither down feet first out of their seats and onto the floor. Some were themselves hissing and wiggling their tongues.

Later, Hagin collapsed on stage, being proclaimed "drunk in the spirit." It took several men to hold him upright. Hagin's "name it and claim it" evangelist buddy, Kenneth Copeland, also got into the act.

Robert Schuller Assaults a Flight Attendant

In January 1998, the Associated Press and other news organizations reported that the Reverend Robert Schuller had been charged with the crime of physically assaulting an airline flight attendant. Reportedly, while the plane was aloft, Schuller became angry when the flight attendant refused to serve him some cheese. Schuller stood up and grabbed and shook the attendant by the shoulders. Later hauled into court, Schuller paid a $1,200 fine and apologized to the plane's crew and passengers. Asked by newspaper reporters about the incident, Schuller refused to acknowledge guilt, proclaiming "I have not broken even one of the Ten Commandments."

The devil at Robert Schuller's Crystal Cathedral? In January 1998, Schuller conducted an international conference of 2,200 church leaders at his Crystal Cathedral in Garden Grove, California. This picture of the assembled church leaders is from Schuller's own newsletter, *PowerLines* (April 1998). Curiously, in the picture, a rather unusual image can be found (blow-up, above). What is this? Does it not bear a striking resemblance to the image of Baphomet (top right), unmasked as the devil in Texe Marrs' book, *Mystery Mark of the New Age?*

Robert Schuller is pastor of California's Crystal Cathedral. He is financially backed by Australian media billionaire Rupert Murdoch, whose tabloids in Britain profit from their lurid, bare pictures of beautiful young women. Schuller has also been the recipient of money and influence from another Illuminati operative, the late Armand Hammer, a noted Marxist and Soviet bag man. It was Hammer who, years ago, arranged for the Communist hardliners in the Kremlin to broadcast Schuller's *Hour of Power* program on Russian television.

Jack Van Impe—A Puppet of the Pope

Jack Van Impe and his wife, Rexella, continue their propaganda campaign for Pope John Paul II. Van Impe's prophecy show is broadcast weekly over TBN's global and ecumenical TV network. On one segment, Van Impe said that he reads and loves everything that either the Pope or Billy Graham write. "The Pope is fulfilling what Christ told us to do," Van Impe added.

Jack Van Impe regularly quotes favorably from old Catholic books containing the discredited prophecies of now dead Catholic "prophets." He also quotes the Mary apparitions, expressing his and Rexella's conviction that "Mother Mary" is appearing everywhere with words of truth for mankind.

One of the most hideous things Jack Van Impe is doing is his rabid promotion of the *New Catholic Catechism*. This Vatican approved guidebook to the Catholic Church's official doctrines proclaims that Jews and Moslems do not need to convert to Jesus. It says that Mary and the saints are worthy of adoration and should be prayed to for intercession. The *Catechism* states that outside the Catholic Church "there is no salvation." The *Catechism* further explains that salvation and grace are not granted through faith, but also in exchange for good works and through use of the rosary and the sacraments.

These doctrines are clearly unscriptural. Yet, on one of his popular TV programs, Jack Van Impe held high a copy of the *New Catholic Catechism* and boldly announced, "This book contains the Gospel of Jesus Christ I believe in."

Falwell, The Christian Establishment, and the Moonies

Christian evangelical leaders are often paid by Reverend Moon to help give the cult leader an aura of respectability.

Reverend Sun Myung Moon claims to be the new Messiah, "come to earth to complete the mission that Jesus so miserably failed." Moon says that he and his wife are the "true parents for all humanity." Such blasphemy should draw scorn and ridicule from Christian leaders. Why, then, have Tim and Beverly LaHaye clandestinely accepted thousands of dollars from Moon's front organizations?

Why did Jerry Falwell's organization once pocket a stupendous $3.5 million "gift" from cultist Moon and continue to have scholarships to his Liberty University funded by Moon? Why too, did the Reverend Robert Schuller and the Christian Coalition's Ralph Reed accept handsome sums as honoraria in exchange for their celebrity attendance at Moonie social functions?

Tony Campolo Makes TV Host Sick

Tony Campolo is the acclaimed Christian author and college professor of religion who is widely quoted by the press as a strong supporter of his friend, Bill Clinton. Campolo believes in the "feminine side of Jesus." He says that homosexuals shacking up together is okay. When asked if two homosexuals having sex is acceptable from a biblical standpoint, Campolo retorted that he doesn't see anything wrong with the two "cuddling together" in bed.

Christian evangelicals devoid of discernment love Tony Campolo. But surprisingly, some unsaved nonbelievers can see right through the man's Christian pretense. Last year, Campolo was a guest on ABC TV's *Politically Incorrect* program. Questioned time and again about his Christian faith, Campolo pandered to the liberal audience, even making vulgar sexual comments.

At one point, the host, a secular Jew, Bill Maher, stopped Campolo for a commercial and said, "We're going to take a break because the religious guy's getting dirty."

From Serpents to Sound Bites

America's churches now are experiencing the hissing of the serpent. Spiritual atrocities have become commonplace. One of the world's best known "Christian" TV personalities angrily assaults a flight attendant and then brags, "I have not broken even one of the Ten Commandments." Another TV star, a so-called "prophecy teacher," warmly embraces the Pope's unholy doctrines and quotes "Mother Mary." Some of the biggest names in Christendom stuff their bulging pockets with cash from a depraved, satanically led blasphemer and false Messiah, Reverend Moon. Meanwhile, a Christian author and pal of President Bill Clinton's is castigated on TV by a secular Jew for his dirty talk!

My friends, I don't make these things up. I wish I did because my heart is at the breaking point. Just imagine what many lost people who need Jesus are saying today about Christianity. Because of the unconscionable acts of these reprobates, Jesus and His Church are being given a bad name. That is tragic and sad. So very sad.

How much worse can things get? Is this, indeed, that time of wickedness of which the Apostle Paul prophesied? He warned us that lawlessness, deceit, and falsehoods—even spread by supposedly Christian teachers—would result in a tragic "Falling Away" from the faith *(II Thessalonians 2:3).* This Falling Away, prophesied in the scriptures, would condition the world for the ascension to power of the *Son of Perdition*, or Antichrist. It would also enable the "Strong Delusion" to overwhelm the multitudes of people everywhere on earth.

My friends, we must rebuke these deceitful teachers and ministers of unrighteousness. Let us also pray for them, in the sincere hope that some might cast off their lies and falsehoods and return to the true faith.

Equally important, now is the time for all of us who love Jesus and hold His Word in awe to raise our voices in unison and shout to these false ministers; "Enough is enough. You cannot serve two masters. Choose this day whom you will serve: Christ *or* Satan."

Has the Entire Christian Establishment Finally Just...

Gone Berserk?

"Preach the word; be instant in season, out of season; reprove, rebuke, exhort with all long sufferings and doctrine. For the time will come when they will not endure sound doctrine; but after their own lusts shall they heap to themselves teachers, having itching ears; and they shall turn away their ears from the truth, and shall be turned into fables."

—*II Timothy 4:2-4*

Who but devils can deny that the Christian establishment is desperately sick? Every true Bible-believing Christian has to be filled with disgust and horror at what passes for "Christianity" today. To prove my point, please allow me to examine just a few examples of how the so-called "Christian" establishment and its leaders have *"Gone Berserk."*

Masonic Lodge Has Death Grip on Baptists

First, there is the matter of the vile, pagan cult of Freemasonry that almost has the entire Southern Baptist denomination in its death grip. Most Baptist pastors (and Methodist, and Presbyterian, and Episcopal pastors) are Masons.

As a result, the Devil has achieved a slick and sleazy pathway into the lives of millions of Southern Baptist churchgoers.

Most Southern Baptist seminaries and colleges are likewise controlled by Masons. Take, for example, Baylor University, Texas' premier Baptist institution. Baylor has always had a 33rd degree Mason at its helm. Baylor President Herbert Reynolds is a 33rd degree Scottish Rite Mason—meaning he has lain in a coffin and drank from a human skull, among other atrocities. He's also a licensed psychologist.

Reynolds angrily attacks Christians who oppose the lodge as "demagogues," and he actually branded one young Baylor student as "an aberrant individual with an unhealthy obsession" simply because the student questioned a Christian leader being a Mason.

Billy Graham says he is "comfortable" with the beliefs and teachings of Jews and Mormons.

Jesus in Everyone, Even Unsaved Prostitutes?

Then there's Tony Campolo, the bestselling "Christian" writer and professor of Bible at Eastern College in Pennsylvania. Campolo, who once wrote me a letter complaining because I exposed some of his activities, served as one of President Bill Clinton's spiritual counselors during the Monica Lewinsky affair. Campolo believes that homosexuals can live together and even go to bed together and "cuddle" without breaking God's laws. Anyway, all homosexuals have Christ within, he says, because all people do!

As Professor Campolo enthusiastically told a huge group of teenagers brought together by local churches during a visit to New Zealand, *"Jesus is everywhere and in everyone. When you go out there today and you witness to a prostitute, the Jesus in you will be witnessing to the Jesus that is already in her."*

One wonders if this is the kind of sordid advice Campolo offered Mr. Clinton. Did President Bill Clinton have the impression that the "Jesus" in him was simply ministering to the "Jesus" that was inside of Monica Lewinsky when they did what they did inside the oval office at the White House?

The Reverend Henry Lyons, president of the National Baptist Convention (8.2 million members—mostly black) was one of the many black Christian leaders who stood by Bill Clinton all the way. Even after Clinton's exposure as a liar, crook, perjurer, adulterer, and serial rapist, Lyons told an audience of 10,000 black pastors and laymen: *"We love him... We thank God for him... We're going to stand by him."*

Within months after making this statement, Reverend Lyons was himself exposed as having provided a mistress and lover a hefty sum embezzled from the Baptist denomination's bank accounts. Lyons and his lover spent thousands partying and jet-setting around the country. (Reminds one of the Reverend Jesse Jackson, yet another black "minister of God," doesn't it?)

We also have Benjamin Chavis, ordained a minister in the United Church of Christ. Chavis, a hater of white people in my opinion, left his position as head of the NAACP after his own hijinx with women and money. He went on to join the Nation of Islam—the Black Muslim sect headed by Minister Louis Farrakhan.

"I am affirming that the God who called me into the Christian church is the same God who is calling me into the Nation of Islam," Chavis said to a group in Chicago.

Resurrection A Myth?

Don't think, however, that the apostasy is only black in color. White leaders are just as evil and reprobate. Take, for instance, Dr. Martin Marty, a top leader of the Evangelical Lutheran Church in America. At Concordia Seminary in St. Louis, Marty reiterated his belief that the resurrection of Christ is pure myth. Nor can Christians who die expect someday to be resurrected, said Dr. Marty: "Resurrection does not mean that God will have to go hunting for our parts or ashes and reconstitute our body," he remarked, "nor does it mean", said the theologian, "that Jesus himself rose bodily."

Jerry Falwell, the one-time head of the now defunct Moral Majority and founder of Liberty University, may believe in the resurrection, but it is strange that he has been associated with Korean cult guru, Reverend Sun Myung Moon, leader of the "Moonies." Falwell has been paid huge sums for attending Moonie events.

So have Pat Boone, Beverly LaHaye, Robert Schuller, Gary Bauer, Ralph Reed, and other Christian establishment leaders. All of these people were handsomely paid $80,000 to $150,000 apiece for their attendance at a 1996 Moonie-sponsored Family Federation for World Peace event.

Reverend Moon teaches that Jesus failed in his mission and that he, Moon, is the true Messiah. Moon teaches, too, that men are to become gods, but only if they accept the true gospel of Moon's "godism" doctrine.

Being an ecumenicist, it is not surprising that Robert Schuller would accept tainted money from

Reverend Moon. Schuller has declared, "That's what sets me apart from the fundamentalists who are trying to convert everybody to how they believe."

Billy Graham is "Comfortable" With False Religions

Billy Graham was on the *Larry King Show* (CNN) in 1997 and what he said was right in line with Schuller's teachings. Asked what he thought of Mormonism, Catholicism, and other such faiths, Graham responded, "Oh, I think I have a wonderful relationship with them.

Billy Graham was especially commendatory of Catholicism. He explained, "I am very comfortable with the Vatican. I have been to see the Pope several times. He and I agree on almost everything."

"Well," said King, "are you comfortable with Judaism?"

"Very comfortable," answered Graham. "I depend on a Jewish rabbi, Rabbi Tannenbaum in New York, constantly, theologically and spiritually in every way."

Now, since the Bible clearly states that a man who does not have Jesus does not have God the Father either, one is puzzled to figure out just what an unsaved man, Jewish Rabbi Tannenbaum, has to offer a supposed Christian evangelist like Billy Graham in the way of spiritual advice.

Possibly the advice given Graham by a Jewish Rabbi is similar to the spiritual advice that Episcopal Bishop John Shelby Spong would give. Bishop Spong rejects the virgin birth, the resurrection, and ascension of Jesus and favors ordaining homosexuals. Bishop Spong even claims that the Apostle Paul was a homosexual. The Episcopal hierarchy loves the guy, and certainly men like Billy Graham and Schuller would *never, but never*, criticize a fellow "Christian" leader. They're way above that.

Charismania, The Knights of Malta, and "God's Bartender"

In Florida, Steve Hill, the man responsible for inspiring the charismatic "Brownsville Revival," was forced recently to make a stunning confession. He told the *Pensacola News Journal* that he had lied when he claimed to huge audiences that he was a former drug junkie and ex-convict. Hill says he did it to make a bigger impression on audiences, because Christians love to see how the miraculous powers of God can reform the worst sinners.

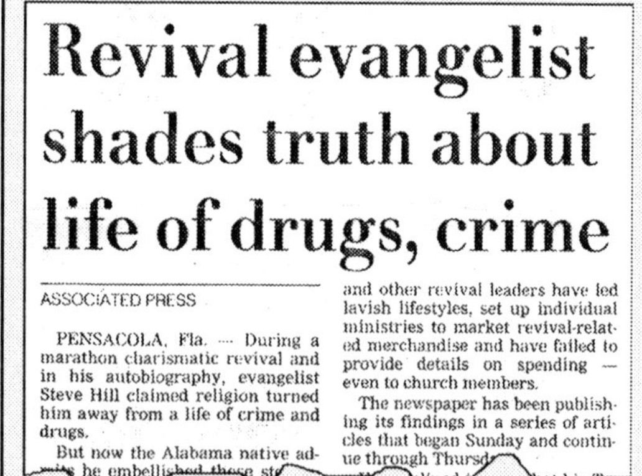

Revival evangelist shades truth about life of drugs, crime

ASSOCIATED PRESS

PENSACOLA, Fla. — During a marathon charismatic revival and in his autobiography, evangelist Steve Hill claimed religion turned him away from a life of crime and drugs.

But now the Alabama native ad-

and other revival leaders have led lavish lifestyles, set up individual ministries to market revival-related merchandise and have failed to provide details on spending — even to church members.

The newspaper has been publishing its findings in a series of articles that began Sunday and continue through Thursd

Fellow Charismatic, prophet Rick Joyner, is also in the news. He recently boasted of being initiated into the mysterious Catholic secret society, the Knights of Malta. When people complain, Joyner's supporters point out that famous Christian writer C.S. Lewis was very pro-Catholic, charismatic faith healer Benny Hinn is a great admirer of the Pope, and Chuck Colson (*Prison Fellowship*) and James Dobson (*Focus on the Family*) recently made pilgrimages to see the Pope at the Vatican.

Power of Prophecy recently heard from New Zealand that Rodney Howard-Browne, the man who calls himself "God's Bartender," for helping audiences go into drunken-like holy laughing hysteria, held crusades to giant crowds. He and his entourage stayed in thousand-dollar-a-night suites at the Hyatt Regency Hotel in Perth.

Reportedly, Mr. Howard-Browne left New Zealand with over a million dollars in his pocket. (People sure do shell out bucks when they're deliriously happy, laughing like loons, and out of their minds, don't they?)

New Bibles for New Age Christians

Rick Joyner, who claims to be a prophet, has joined the Catholic order known as The Knights of Malta.

In London, England, publisher Hodden E. Stoughton has released a new Bible called the *Couples Devotional Bible*. Using the NIV version, the commentary includes discussions about female and male orgasm, male sex fantasies, and other sexual topics. Steve Jenkins, a spokesman for the Church of England, says its about time that the church help couples improve their sex lives.

Not any better is a new version of the New Testament just out from Oxford University Press and now available in the United States. The editors of *The New Testament and Psalms: An Inclusive Version* boast that their bible meets the objections of Jews who despise the King James Version. The new Oxford inclusive edition deletes all negative and disparaging remarks about the Jews. For example, the passages in which the Jewish mob insisted that Pilate crucify Jesus and let Barabbas go free. Those passages were deemed "too anti-Semitic" and had to go. Also, the new version eliminates references to "God the Father" (too sexist). Meanwhile, Jesus is no longer referred to as the "Son of Man," but simply as "the Human One."

More Abominations...

Would you agree with me that these are all prime examples of a prideful and arrogant world stained with sin, calling itself "Christian" while going just plain berserk? If your blood hasn't boiled over up to this point with righteous indignation, I now offer up this final, savage news item, coming to us from Sweden.

Stockholm, Sweden this year hosted the *"Europride"* festival, a week-long exhibition that drew some 20,000 people to the Swedish capital, which bills itself as the "Culture Capital of Europe."

As examples of European culture on exhibit, there was a revised model of Leonardo da Vinci's famous painting, *The Last Supper*, in which the twelve apostles are now depicted as leather and chain wearing, gay transvestites. In another exhibit, Jesus' mother, Mary, was shown off as a lesbian, and in yet another, our Lord and Savior, Jesus, was portrayed as a homosexual with vivid makeup, rouge and lipstick, wearing black stiletto heels.

Swedish artist Elizabeth Ohlson, mastermind of the cultural exhibition, said she did it all because she is a Christian. "My aim," she explained, "is to show a loving God. One who loves, above all."

Cruel Acts to Receive Their Just Due

I am almost too pained to write of these cruel acts of devils and men, so daringly do they blaspheme our precious Lord and Savior. But I know that such as do these things are doomed to perdition. As Paul wrote in Galatians, those who bring a perverted gospel are *accursed* by God and damned to perdition, to an eternal, burning hell.

Yes, it's true. These men and women have "gone berserk." But on judgement day, there will be no plea of "innocent by reason of insanity" accepted. On that day, all men shall receive their just due. Until that great day, let us, as true God-fearing believers, not grow weary in fighting these present-day evils which confront us at every turn. Even though the larger Christian establishment goes berserk, let us, the faithful remnant, continue to worship God with a sound mind and with all respect. He deserves nothing less.

Startling Evidence Proves That...

God Punishes Evildoers

"Thou art righteous, O Lord... because Thou hast judged thus."
—*Revelation 16:5-6*

Does God judge the nations? Will He judge our political and religious leaders? Will He judge those who reject His rule and who laugh at, spit upon, and mistreat His people? Will the Almighty be your judge? Equally important: Does God, judging all things, generously reward the righteous while punishing evildoers?

Almost 2000 years ago the Jews rejected Jesus, The Messiah, and sought to kill Him. Because of their unbelief and their grievous sin, in 70 AD—just as was prophesied in advance by Christ—Roman troops under Titus invaded Israel and utterly ravaged the temple. The city of Jerusalem was demolished, and tens of thousands of Jews were banished. God's judgement had fallen on Israel.

This cataclysmic event is recorded in history. But, does God still judge today? In his thought-provoking book offered by this ministry, *God's Final Warning to America*, John McTernan documents that, in fact, many modern-day wars, famines, plagues, earthquakes, volcanos, floods, and other calamities are judgements from God.

Earthquakes in Assisi Italy

From Assisi, Italy, has come astonishing proof that God is judging men today for their evil and wicked ways. On September 26, 1997, two damaging earthquakes struck central Italy. Ten people were killed, dozens injured and about 12,000 were left homeless. The human toll was heavy, but the Catholic Church and the Italian government were especially concerned about the problems wreaked on the Basilica of St. Francis in Assisi.

The historic church at Assisi, with its renowned frescos and renaissance paintings, suffered monumental damage. Debris and rubble poured down from the roof and ceiling onto the altar area below, crushing two Franciscan monks and leaving the

Austin American-Statesman

More damage in Italy as earth rumbles again

By Daniel J. Wakin
Associated Press

ASSISI, Italy — Central Italy quivered and shook again on Friday, as earthquakes injured 20 people and inflicted more damage on the famed Basilica of St. Francis of Assisi and other buildings hit by temblors a week ago.

The earthquakes sowed panic in people still alarmed by the earlier shocks. Many residents once again fled homes and offices for the safety of open areas.

"What is this mystery of the earth moving? Can't it stay still?" asked the Rev. Pasquale Magro, head of the basilica's museum.

The epicenter of Friday's most powerful, 4.8 magnitude quake

ghost town. Its several thousand residents, along with up to 42,000 others in the regions of Umbria and Marche, have been sleeping outside in tents, campers and cars.

Diana Gandolfini, 50, sitting in front of a camper in an encampment near Serravalle, said she had left her home for good. "I won't go back after all that fear," she said.

About 20 people suffered minor injuries from falling debris in Friday's quake and a series of aftershocks that followed. A temblor with a magnitude of 3.5 struck at 1:04 p.m. and another almost as strong about 40 minutes later. In Foligno, the epicenter of last week's quake, a woman with a history of heart trouble died after Friday's temblor.

treasured frescoes were destroyed. In all, 11 people died in last week's double quake.

Magro said the basilica's damaged ceiling survived the new shocks. But more stones fell from the south facade, and showers of plaster rained down inside the cathedral.

Small cracks opened up in asphalt of the main plaza next to the lower church.

Technicians have been cataloging pieces of frescoes that fell last week and experts are studying ways to reinforce the basilica's structure.

Italy's civil defense chief, Nicola Barberi, said the strength of last week's temblors caught authorities by surprise. He said the after-

Austin American-Statesman

Shaken, Assisi is silent on St. Francis' name day

■ After a third earthquake and aftershocks, there are none of the usual festivities

By Vera Haller
The Washington Post

ASSISI, Italy — The small Umbrian hill town where St. Francis founded his religious order in the 13th century is usually a hub of ac-

tained by the basilica of St. Francis. Huge chunks of the vaulted ceiling in the basilica's upper sanctuary collapsed on Sept. 26, killing four people inside, including two Franciscan friars. Its renowned frescoes, including a cycle of 28 paintings depicting the life of St. Francis by the Renaissance master Giotto, were damaged.

"It's a disaster. Parts of the frescoes are irreparable. There aren't just chunks of plaster, but tiny, tiny fragments which will be almost impossible to piece together.

quick escape if another one hits," MacDermid said.

Armida Frappini, a woman in her seventies, said she was the only person remaining in her building of the five families who lived there. She had brought a folding chair to the sidewalk to watch what little activity was going on in the street. "They (the other people in her building) have cars and can leave. I don't, so I have to stay. There is not even a church open, only one small chapel way up the hill where one can go to Mass."

sanctuary a wreck. A Vatican spokesman estimated that the monetary damages added up in the millions of dollars. Pope John Paul II immediately appealed to Catholic faithful to donate money to a special fund set up to rebuild the Basilica and have it ready for use by the dawning of the year 2000, the advent of the New Millennium.

Was the earthquake that collapsed the roof and ceiling of the Basilica of St. Francis in Assisi just a random, natural occurrence? Or, could it be that this devastating blow was dealt by the very hand of God? Well, consider this: In 1986, the Pope invited leaders of all the world's false religions to come to Assisi, Italy for an unholy ecumenical conference. The Pontiff had chosen the site of Assisi because it was from here that St. Francis' ungodly, creation-centered, nature gospel had gone forth.

A dust cloud fills the altar area of the Basilica of St. Francis in Assisi, Italy, after an earthquake. Earlier, the Pope allowed the Dalai Lama to install an idol of Buddha on this very altar.

With the Pope in Assisi were Islamic muftis, Hindu gurus, Jewish rabbis, Protestant leaders, and Buddhist monks. During the conference, the Pope and local Catholic authorities invited the Dalai Lama, the living "god man" of Tibetan Buddhism, and his monks to conduct a Buddhist worship service. That satanically energized service was held at the Basilica of St. Francis in Assisi. There, on the church's massive medieval altar, the Dalai Lama placed hideously evil idols and charms, including a statue of Buddha.

History is replete with the miserable fate of men and nations who callously and unwisely scorned God and rejected His righteousness.

Did God rain down destruction on this notorious Basilica as a sign of His anger and displeasure over the sacrilege and blasphemy that occurred inside its ornate walls? I believe the answer is yes. History shows us that Sodom and Gomorrah were destroyed by fire, Rome by vandals and Huns, Jerusalem by the might of Roman military power, and now the Basilica in Assisi by earthquake. Surely, God will judge the heathen in these last days just as He has always judged sin.

Porno Peddler Larry Flynt is Judged

History is replete with the miserable fate of men and nations who callously and unwisely scorned God and rejected His righteousness. Take Larry Flynt, for example, the publisher of the pornographic magazine, *Hustler*. Flynt mocked God, claiming to be a born again Christian, but continuing to print and distribute his smut. Soon, a would-be assassin planted a bullet in his spine, paralyzing Flynt for life.

High Priest of Satan Dies

Anton LaVey blasphemed God and founded his filthy Church of Satan on June 6, 1966 (the 6th

Porno peddler Larry Flynt.

month, the 6th day of 66.) A crowd of Hollywood elite soon flocked to his church, including buxom actress Jayne Mansfield and singer-entertainer Sammy Davis, Jr. But eventually, membership in his diabolical cult evaporated. Then, on Halloween of last year, the very day when witches and satanists believe the ghouls and spirits come up out of their graves, Anton LaVey died.

News reports said that in the months prior to his passing, Anton LaVey was plagued with depression. Some suggested LaVey had committed suicide. Did the Devil send his spirits out to collect his human disciple that ominous Halloween night? Was this a judgement from God to recompense LaVey for this sick man's overflowing cup of wickedness?

Interestingly, *Time* magazine noted that on the very night LaVey died, a prominent Rothschild of the Illuminati Dynasty family also passed away in Europe.

Lenin and Trotsky: A Cruel Fate

Vladimir Lenin despised God, and after taking power in Russia in 1917, he and his Communist regime fiercely persecuted Bible believers. But by 1923, just six years later, the hero of the Bolshevik revolution sat wide-eyed and mute in a wheelchair, paralyzed and in a catatonic state. Many suspect that his successor, the monstrous Josef Stalin, had Lenin's own doctor inject him with poisonous mind and nerve-destroying chemicals.

In 1924, a year and some months after being confined to a wheelchair, Lenin died, surely being transported to Hell to receive his just reward prepared for him beforehand by devils.

Stalin also took care of another of his archrivals, Lenin's chief comrade, Leon Trotsky. Fearing Stalin's envious wrath, after Lenin's death Trotsky fled the country of Russia and went all the way to Mexico to hide. But the secret police of the butcher of Moscow tracked Trotsky down and murdered him with an axe blow to the head.

Three Communists—one fate? Lenin (left) and Trotsky (center)massacred millions of innocent people; Clinton has encouraged the massacre of millions of innocent babies through grotesque abortions. Pray for President Clinton, that the miserable fate of Lenin and Trotsky does not befall him.

Herod Devoured by Worms

The Bible tells us also of King Herod, whose oratory so inspired the Christ-rejecting multitudes. On one speaking occasion, when the adoring crowd acclaimed him a god, Herod's pride soared. At that very moment, God's judgement fell and worms inwardly devoured Herod's body. Stricken, he fell dead. It is a frightful thing to fall into the hands of an angry God!

America to be Judged

Today, Herod, Hitler, Stalin, LaVey, and all the other infamous men of history who died having mocked and rejected God's Truth are in torment in hell. Jesus Christ is their judge, and His judgement is just and right.

But God judges nations as well as people. America has forgotten God, and the Lord has repeatedly sent dire warnings. In recent years, from Florida, Texas and the Midwest, to the East Coast and the Pacific Ocean, America has been battered by tornados, hurricanes, volcanic eruptions, and floods. Is God not sending us a message?

For example, consider California. First, God sent earthquakes to the Golden State. There was no repentance. Now, He has sent El Niño to savage California. This is a state made infamous by Hollywood's vulgarity and by San Francisco's homosexual barbarity. If its citizens continue to wallow in the mire, what will come next for California?

> *"For the land is defiled; therefore I visit the punishment of it's iniquity upon it, and the land vomits out it's inhabitants..." (Leviticus 18:24-25)*

"Neither Repented They..."

Not just California is at risk. Already, the AIDS plague has devastated the homosexual populations of Los Angeles, San Francisco, New York, Houston, and Atlanta. Still, the people persist in their grotesque works:

> *"And the rest of the men which were not killed by these plagues yet repented not... Neither repented they of their murders, nor of their sorceries, nor of their fornication, nor of their thefts." (Revelation 9:20-21)*

The Wicked Have Their Reward

Some may protest: "But Texe Marrs, *not all* evildoers are punished. Many of God's people suffer, and multitudes of true Christians are poor and downtrodden. Meanwhile, many of the rich are rewarded. Why are the wicked and deceitful allowed to heap to themselves great wealth?"

In the Bible, the Apostle James addressed this very question *(James 2:5-7)* when He wrote:

> *"Hearken my beloved brethren, Hath not God chosen the poor of this world, rich in faith, and heirs of the kingdom which he hath promised to them that love him?... Do not rich men oppress you, and draw you before the judgement seats? Do not they blaspheme that worthy name (Jesus) by the which ye are called?"*

James then declared God's judgment on these wicked rich:

> *"Go to now, ye rich men, weep and howl for your miseries that shall come upon you." (James 5:1)*

Remember also the story that Jesus our Lord told us of Lazarus and the rich man. The faithful Lazarus, a diseased beggar, went on to his reward in heaven. However, upon dying, the unbelieving, corruptly immoral and uncaring rich man went on to his reward in hell where he suffered the pain of fire and the horror of eternal thirst.

Jesus said of the wicked, "They have their reward," while his message to the saints was: "But lay up for yourselves treasures in heaven."

Yes, the unrepentant rich and powerful who make merchandise of men's souls *(Revelation 18:13)* are sometimes at license today to partake of the lusts of the flesh. But the Bible warns that even if they escape God's harsh judgement on this side of the veil, afterwards, their ominous and frightening fate awaits them *(Hebrews 9:27)*.

Judgement Day is Coming

The inescapable truth is that God is merciful and tender. He is a rewarder of those who love Him and who respect His Word. He is quick to forgive and to blot from His memory forever the sins of the saints.

To His beloved, the Lord bequeaths the untold treasures of the Kingdom.

But for those who, in their vile conduct, display mockery and contempt for God, and especially for those who would harm and martyr God's children, *Judgement Day lies dead ahead.*

Mark this, my friends: Wicked men and women, as well as evildoer nations, are drawn to judgement like a moth to a flame:

> *"...Behold, the Lord cometh with ten thousands of His saints, to execute judgement upon all, and to convince all that are ungodly among them of their ungodly deeds which they have ungodly committed, and of all their hard speeches which ungodly sinners have spoken against Him." (Jude, vs.14-15)*

> *"For the wages of sin is death; but the gift of God is eternal life through Jesus Christ our Lord." (Romans 6:23)*

Judgement day is coming.

Listen to me, then, you who are sinners against the Truth and who defiantly seek to harm the people of God: Your riches, your earthly wisdom, cannot save you in the coming time of trial. Are you ready for His coming? Are you prepared to die? Have you repented, surrendered your will, and been saved by the Blood of the Lamb?

If your answer is no, I beg you: Turn back now and believe in Him. Judgement is even now at your very doorstep.

> *"Behold, I stand at the door, and knock: if any man hear my voice, and open the door, I will come in to him, and will sup with him, and he with me. (Revelation 3:20)*

Top Christian Leaders Abandon Truth

Christianity Afflicted With Doctrines of Devils

Please answer this question: Who are the most wicked and evil men in the world today?

If, in pondering an answer, your mind quickly considers the long list of global politicians, bankers, and corporate chieftains involved in the conspiracy for a New World Order, that's understandable. Barack Obama, Dick Cheney, George W. Bush, Bill Clinton, Baron Jacob Rothschild, Ted Turner—certainly, these and similar men are to be found in the "foul and mischievous scoundrel" category. But none of them are as evil or as sinister as the men I'm about to describe to you now.

Perhaps you have fingered the serial killers as the most evil—bloodthirsty, psychopathic murderers like Charles Manson and Richard Speck. Well, wrong again. These men are not the worst. They kill the body, but not the soul.

Men of Religion More Dangerous

You see, the devil achieves much, much more through *men of religion* than he does through politicians, financiers, or even the most grim of the serial killers. And the most carnage, the most damage, is caused by men who claim to be *Christian* religious leaders.

Satan's chief objective has always been to introduce doctrines of devils *inside* the Christian church. This is how he best gains and harvests souls for destruction—through a false "Christian" establishment.

Yes, the most cunning and wicked men on Earth are those schemers and fakers who *pretend* to be Christians. These men are apostate shysters, appearing to be holy. They aspire to and achieve top positions within the Christian community and then craftily sabotage and ravage men's souls by introducing *doctrines of devils* into the Body of Christ.

Men of Great Fame and Renown

Highly acclaimed and respected by the world—and raved about and praised by other diabolical deceivers inside the church—these are often men of great fame and renown. Their names are quickly recognized. They are universally adored by the craven, ignorant, and unscriptural masses

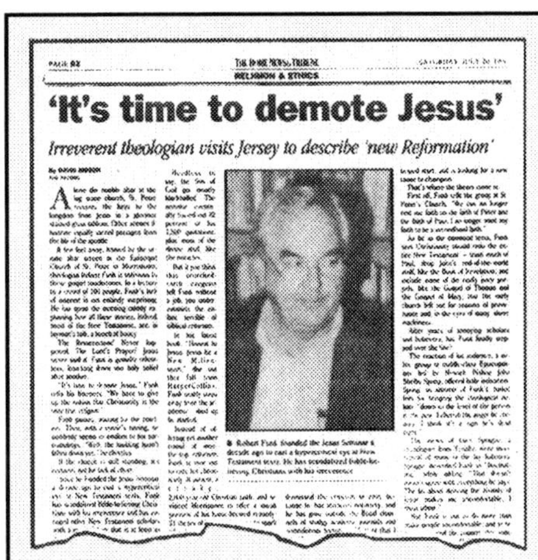

RELIGION & ETHICS

'It's time to demote Jesus'

Irreverent theologian visits Jersey to describe 'new Reformation'

Professor Robert Funk and the scholars of the Jesus Seminar say "It's time to demote Jesus."

who inhabit most church pews. The masses gravitate to these men because they cater to peoples' loose, carnal desires by providing more and more entertainment instead of truth. The religious masses also love them because the gospel pretenders consistently preach tolerance, love, harmony, and unity.

That's just what these evil men specialize in—lots and lots of flashy entertainment and plenty of gooey, syrupy tolerance, love, and harmony. Indeed, they'll provide and fulfill every fleshly want the ravening, laughter-filled, prosperity-mad "Christian" public requests of them. The one thing they *refuse* to do, however, is to preach the hard truth. The wonderful truth. The Whole Gospel. This the gospel pretenders reject. Sometimes, they go on the offensive, attacking the truth with sarcasm, ridicule, and gloating smiles. More often, however, the apostates claim to be above the battle, posing as admirable advocates of tolerance, love, inclusiveness and positivism.

"It's Time to Demote Jesus"

Every day, these men move further and further from that truth, from that *Whole* Gospel. One of these men, theologian Robert Funk, has founded the *Jesus Seminar*. This is an organization of "Christian" seminary professors and clergy, funded by the Rockefellers, who meet annually to proclaim "newfound truths" about Jesus and the scriptures. Jesus, they say, wasn't God and never claimed to be God. He was merely an "itinerant, wandering sage."

Christ did not give *The Lord's Prayer* to his disciples, say the men of the *Jesus Seminar*, nor was Jesus resurrected from the cross, these learned men insist.

"It's time to demote Jesus," Funk proclaims.

From Mary to "Christa"

Would Paul and Jan Crouch, the charismatic, country music promoting heads of TV's Trinity Broadcasting Network (TBN), agree? Well, judging from the couple's newsletter, they might. It's time for Protestants to accept the Catholic reality of the apparitions and visions of Our Lady, Mary, the Mother of God, Paul Crouch suggests. His wife, Jan, says that she recently was visited by the miraculous appearance of Our Lady, the Blessed Mary. In her detailed account, Jan Crouch describes how "Mary" first gave her a perfect rose and then thanked Jan, Paul, and TBN for their magnificent efforts in bringing Catholics and Protestants together in unity.

While TBN enthusiastically promotes the Marian apparitions, others have begun to revere yet another female figure—*"Christa."* At Holy Comforter Episcopal Church in Richmond, Virginia, a rather unusual crucifix has been put on display. The stunning, life-size figure of a naked, crowned woman, dubbed "Christa," is nailed to a crucifix.

"Christa" is described by the Reverend Bruce Gay as an excellent opportunity to help Christians "expand our understanding of Jesus' place in the Church." Earlier, the statue had hung behind the altar in the nation's largest cathedral—St. John the Divine Cathedral, in New York City.

This statue of "Christa" is being put on exhibit at episcopal and other churches across America.

Does Billy Graham Believe in a Father/Mother in Heaven?

Famed evangelist Billy Graham also has joined in celebrating the hyper-feminist revolution within the Christian establishment. First, as a guest on CNN's *The Larry King Show*, Billy

Graham told the host that he was "comfortable" with the teachings and doctrines of Mormons and Jews. The Mormon (LDS) cult officially teaches that, on Earth, Jesus had numerous wives—that Christ was a polygamist. The Mormons also claim that Jesus has multiple eternal wives in heaven (which they say is the planet "Kolub") as well. Thus, we here on earth have many mothers in heaven.

Graham also has stated, on Dr. Robert Schuller's TV program (May 31, 1997), that followers of Hinduism, Islam, and other religions "already have Jesus inside their hearts, whether they know it or not," and therefore do not need to be converted to Christianity to be saved and enter heaven. Of course, Hindus sincerely and fervently believe in untold numbers of goddesses, one of whom ("Kali") is the serpent goddess.

That Graham now accepts the devilish, Mystery Babylon doctrine of a "Father/Mother" in heaven is not surprising. In an issue of the ultra-liberal *Parade* magazine (Oct. 20, 1996), Billy Graham not only admits that he is a registered Democrat (thus helping put in a plug for the November 5th re-election of his pal, Bill Clinton, as President), he also insists that leaders of other religions—Islam, Buddhist, Hindu, Jewish, etc.—be represented at presidential inaugurals.

"Each time a President has asked me to lead the Inaugural Prayer," Graham explains, "I have argued that I should not do it alone, that leaders of other religions should be there, too."

Billy Graham's touchy-feely, ecumenical "love" teachings and his pandering to false religions is monumental. A recognition of the validity of other religions, Graham tells the *Parade* magazine interviewer, will "put our love into action."

Meanwhile, in a separate press release of the Billy Graham Evangelistic Association, Billy Graham lashes out at Southern Baptists who desire to evangelize Jews for Christ. In his pronouncement, Graham makes it clear that he firmly opposes "proselytizing" the Jews.

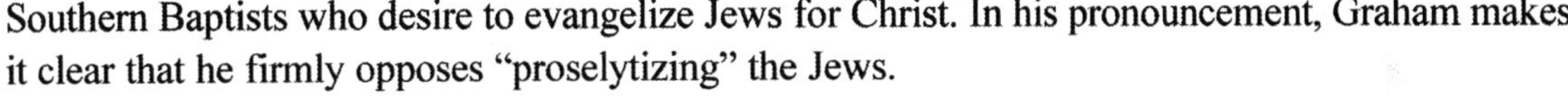

Billy Graham's wicked, unbiblical teaching is that, if you are a Jew, you are already part of the Body of Christ even if you reject Jesus. All Jews "are engrafted into the Christian Church," Graham has stated.

Jack Hayford

African Witch Doctor Dances and Pyramid Prophecies

Billy Graham is the most famous of the apostates, but he is joined by legions of other serpentine deceivers. Indeed, everywhere we turn, atrocities are being mounted in the name of the Lord. At a *Promise Keepers Clergy Conference* in Atlanta, Georgia, heavy metal rock music blared from loudspeakers. Cheerleading yells erupted from the crowd. Then, to wild applause, famed, charismatic pastor Jack Hayford, at the podium, led the audience in performing an "African witch doctor's dance." Hayford said that "the Lord" taught him to dance this way, coming to him in a vision and asking the TBN teacher, "May I have this dance?"

Six hundred Catholic priests, along with 40,000 other

church leaders, were in attendance at the Promise Keepers conclave. The crowd appeared ecstatic with Hayford's demonstration on stage of witch doctor dancing.

In Oklahoma City, Southwest Radio Church's leader, Noah Hutchings, has published his book, *The Great Pyramid: Prophecy in Stone*. Hutchings is, thankfully, a strong King James Bible supporter. Yet, he claims that the secrets found in the Pharaoic pyramids are as reliable as the written prophecies found in the Holy Bible. God has given us the Egyptian Pyramids as a sign, as "prophecy in stone," Hutchings contends.

Southwest Radio Church president, Noah Hutchings, makes the unbiblical and preposterous claim that the Great Pyramid is "prophecy in stone."

Hutchings may have a money-making winner with this new book. After all, pyramidology is a teaching that false Christian teachers, New Age gurus, and Masonic Egyptologists can universally agree on.

Evidently, Hutchings forgets that God told His people to "Come out of Egypt" and, in *Revelation 11,* identifies the world's most contemptible and most wicked, end-times system spiritually as "Sodom and Egypt."

The Pope Believes in Evolution, Dr. Dobson Believes in the Pope

From Rome comes the Pope's fascinating declaration that the biblical account in *Genesis* must be corrected by new findings of the evolutionists.

Protestants may find this a little hard to swallow, but then, are there any Protestant Christian leaders left on the planet to protest the Pope's silliness? Apparently not. From Colorado Springs, Colorado, Christian psychologist and radio superstar, Dr. James Dobson, has accepted an honorary doctorate from a Catholic University in Steubenville, Ohio.

Curiously, Dobson's new ministry headquarters buildings are shaped in the form of Egyptian pyramids. Could there possibly be a connection? Maybe so. You see, Dobson has accepted huge gifts of money from Amway's billionaire founder, Rich DeVos, reportedly a 33° Mason. How appropriate, since Masons preach an Egyptian, pagan religion and Amway's sales methods are basically a "pyramid scheme!"

Reverend Moon Rewards Christian Leaders for Their Support

At a "Moonies" conference September 1993, the Christian Coalition's Ralph Reed joined hands with Concerned Women for America's Bev LaHaye and the Crystal Cathedral's Robert Schuller.

Reverend Sun Myung Moon, Tim and Bev LaHaye, and Robert Schuller.

These and other so-called "Christian" leaders pocketed handsome sums for their services to the Reverend Sun Myung Moon as conference luminaries.

Moon, reportedly in the employ of the Korean Central Intelligence Agency, is an antichrist cult leader who has proclaimed himself the "Messiah." But, if Rev. Moon is Messiah, what does that make Jesus? As Moon explains it, "Christ failed in *his* mission."

Acts of Rebellion Against God

Why have all these famous, high-ranking Christian leaders become so deeply involved in such hideous and monstrous acts of rebellion against God? Is it not because they have forsaken the Lord's inerrant Word, the *King James Bible*, and gone after the strange scriptures found in the grotesque, new "Bible" versions?

"Thy word have I hid in mine heart," wrote the Psalmist, "that I might not sin against thee" *(Psalm 119:11).*

Instead of hiding God's Word in their hearts, many reprobate leaders have opted to fling God's precious, Holy Bible into the trash—to their eternal shame!

Instead of hiding God's Word in their hearts, many reprobate leaders, like Billy Graham, James Dobson, Jerry Falwell, Paul Crouch, Tim and Bev LaHaye, Zola Levitt, and Robert Funk, have opted to fling God's precious, Holy Bible into the trash heap. What a pitiful tragedy! To their eternal shame, these men have blasphemed Truth and embraced a Lie. By their own acts, they condemn themselves as willing, human agents of the Son of Perdition and as stooges of the coming Beast.

Seducing Spirits and Doctrines of Devils Prophesied

How profound, therefore, is this riveting, cutting-edge prophecy, found not in Egypt, not in a Masonic temple, not at a Promise Keepers rally, not at a rock concert, and not at a Moonies conference, but in the majestic and incomparable, perfect Word of God, the King James Bible:

> *"Now the Spirit speaketh expressly, that in the latter times some shall depart from the faith, giving heed to seducing spirits, and doctrines of devils; Speaking lies in hypocrisy; having their conscience seared with a hot iron." (1 Timothy 4:1-2)*

What we are seeing is the Final Seduction of Christianity by a deceitful, rotten, and greedy leadership. Today's Christian establishment is sorrowfully made up of spiritually devoid men and women whose consciences have been seared with a hot iron. Still, I thank God for you reading this who continue, often in the midst of persecution and ridicule, to believe in the simplicity of the Gospel. With you, I cry out in tears, "Please Lord, don't let this go on for long. *Please, come quickly, King Jesus!"*

Billy Graham Says "Pagans Saved Through Nature"

In his fear-mongering, environmentalist propaganda book, *Earth in the Balance*, Vice President Al Gore writes, "Nature, in its fullest, is God." But how many know that the theology of world-acclaimed evangelist Billy Graham fits in well with that of Al Gore, a fellow Southern Baptist?

In *McCall's* magazine (January 1978), Billy Graham told an interviewer that his views on salvation had changed. "I used to believe that pagans in far-off countries were lost—were going to hell," said Graham. "I no longer believe that. I believe that there are *other ways* of recognizing the existence of God—*through nature*, for instance."

New Agers who preach nature worship and who exalt Gaia, the planetary deity, will find great comfort in these words from Billy Graham.

Jews Don't Need Jesus, Either

And there's more. According to Graham, heaven not only awaits earth worshippers but also Christ-rejecting Jews. The popular celebrity told *McCall's* that Jews who reject Jesus may, nevertheless, still go on to heaven.

Graham a Catholic?

"What about Catholics?," the *McCall's* interviewer asked. Yes, said Graham, sincere Catholics will also be saved. Indeed, Billy Graham revealed that his own beliefs "are essentially the same as those of Orthodox Roman Catholics." The evangelist even stated that he would soon go to Rome and preach at a Catholic cathedral. He had been invited to Rome, he revealed, by a top Vatican official.

A Man Loved By the World

Amazingly, these facts—from Billy Graham's own mouth—were revealed almost 20 years ago in *McCall's*, a popular women's magazine read by millions and sold in supermarkets and convenience stores everywhere.

Billy Graham's adoption and promotion of these satanically-inspired philosophies explains why a decadent

Can pagans be saved "through nature?" This is a member of the radical environmentalist group, Earth First! He's decked out as Pan, the horned god of the forest. Pan, an ancient, mystical Greek deity, had a mistress said to be the "Earth Goddess."

and admiring—yet unsaved and sinful—populace holds the Baptist evangelist in such high esteem. If he were to preach the hard truth, like Jeremiah, Elijah, and John the Baptist did, the evangelist would surely be hated and ostracized by the world. But because he speaks the lukewarm, politically correct, unity-in-diversity language of modern *Mystery Babylon*, Billy Graham consistently ranks among "America's Ten Most Admired Men" in opinion polls.

One sure sign of a false prophet is that he is praised by the world. Billy Graham is a man who proudly trumpets his friendship with presidents and prime ministers. He has said, "I no longer believe in a literal hell." He refrains from saying clearly that homosexuality is wickedness. Graham has also stated that he does not complain about abortion because, "No one really knows when life begins."

All this has made him a friend of the world, a man respected and touted even by the liberal media. How stark a contrast with our Lord Jesus who, the Bible records, "made himself of no reputation."

It would be wise for Billy Graham and his legions of supporters to carefully consider these powerful words of the Apostle James:

> *"Ye adulterers and adulteresses, know ye not that friendship of the world is enmity with God? Whosoever therefore will be a friend of the world is the enemy of God." (James 4:4)*

Is He Ushering Men and Women Into Hell?

Obviously, Billy Graham's teaching that men can be saved through nature or by false religion cannot be squared with Scripture. The Bible tells us that only through faith in Jesus Christ and His finished work on the cross can men and women be saved. Not through trees, rocks, and babbling brooks—and not by church traditions as taught by the Pope of Rome and his Catholic minions: *"For there is one God, and one mediator between God and men, the man Christ Jesus." (I Timothy 2:5)*

It cannot be overemphasized that Billy Graham's public statements over the years may have already resulted in untold numbers going to hell. Millions of people believe in Graham. Many place utmost confidence in his every word. If Billy Graham tells them they need not be born again (John 3) through faith in Jesus Christ to go to heaven, they believe him rather than God's word. *Trusting man instead of God, they perish!*

Billy Graham is not alone in his guilt. Isn't it strange and more than a little curious that leaders of the Christian establishment have consistently refused to expose or even to mildly criticize Billy Graham's unscriptural views? Why haven't the editors at *Christianity Today*, *Moody's*, and *Charisma* magazines—and the hundreds of owners and managers of the 1,500 Christian radio stations affiliated with the *National Religious Broadcasters*—spoken out in protest against Billy Graham's heretical statements?

What about the leaders of such powerful denominations as the Southern Baptist Convention, the Assemblies of God, the Lutheran Church, and the Church of God? Why this massive conspiracy of silence?

Seducers Multiply in the End-Times

The answer is found in the Scriptures. There we are told that just before Christ returns, the knowledge of the truth will be in short supply. Men will love the pleasures of this world and the applause of men more than they love God. Thus, "evil men and seducers shall wax worse and worse, deceiving, and being deceived" *(II Timothy 3:13).*

Billy Graham is deceived. That's why he believes that "nature" can save men's souls. That's why he refuses to evangelize lost Jews and Roman Catholics. That's why he arrogantly stands by idly, silently, while millions of precious babies are slaughtered through abortion. Regrettably, in his deceit he is bringing thousands of needy and lost souls down with him. May the one true and merciful God forgive Billy Graham and forgive also the uncaring, lukewarm leaders of the Christian establishment who have long covered up and hidden Billy Graham's great apostasy from the true Gospel.

Billy Graham Says, "Save the Earth, Not Babies!"

Billy Graham has told columnist Cal Thomas that saving babies by fighting abortion is not "a big thing" to him (*World* magazine, Feb. 18, 1995). But, says the famed evangelist, he is concerned about saving Mother Earth. To him, *that's* a big thing. Indeed, Graham is so upset about the environmental harm being done to planet Earth that he recently vowed to begin actively speaking out on this issue.

The Reverend Graham has long maintained that the pro-life movement is irrelevant since "No one really knows when life begins" (*Right to Life of Greater Cincinnati* newsletter, Jan. 1992). Again and again, he has refused to become involved in speaking out against abortion. "It's not an issue I wish to pursue," Graham arrogantly informed CNN talk show host Larry King in 1993. "I try to stay away from these things that are so emotional," Graham told the *Philadelphia Inquirer* newspaper in 1992.

Neither is homosexuality a hot button for Billy Graham. "It's not a big sin," the evangelist recently told startled reporters at a national press conference. On the *Larry King Show* (Dec. 1994), Graham justified this by explaining that homosexuals and lesbians are just "born that way."

But apparently, while the popular North Carolina Baptist evangelist doesn't want to expend his energies battling abortion, homosexuality, pornography, New Ageism in public schools, the New World Order, and other rampant evils, he does not feel the same way about environmentalism. Interviewed recently on Cal Thomas' television program on Cable TV's *CNBC network*, Graham insisted that protecting the environment is more important than protecting the unborn. Here's the exchange between Billy Graham and Cal Thomas (also see *World* magazine, Feb. 18, 1995, p. 10):

Mr. Thomas: "You've been reluctant to speak out on the top social issue of our time, abortion. Why?"

Mr. Graham: "I think the top social issue of our time may be ecology (the environment). I think that's more dangerous... and I'm going to start speaking out on that."

So, to Billy Graham, the murder of 40 million babies through abortion since 1963—in the U.S.A. alone—is not "a big thing" he needs to deal with. Admittedly, Graham is a politically astute liberal. He well knows that fighting abortion is politically incorrect, and he realizes that, were he to support the saving of unborn babies, the famous evangelist would not make the next published list of "America's Ten Most Admired Men."

Graham also knows, however, that saving Mother Earth is politically correct. After all, every good liberal wants to save the environment and kill the unborn babies—all at the same time!

What might God have to say about Graham's pandering to satanic baby-killers? In *Psalm 94:16*, God implores: *"Who will rise up for me against the evildoers? or who will stand up for me against the workers of iniquity?"* Now comes Billy Graham, one of the most liked and most popular men on Earth, to whine and cry out, "Not *me*, Lord, not *me*!"

The hounds of Hell come after you if you dare expose that...

Billy Graham is a Great Deceiver

Every time I expose darkness and subversion *inside* the Christian establishment, the hounds of hell come against me. Every time I unmask Satan's deceptive ministers of unrighteousness within the Christian Church—men who so cleverly disguise themselves as "Angels of Light" but, inside, are ravening wolves—the hounds of hell come against me. They show their ferocious mouths, and lust to tear out my flesh, rip my eyeballs from their sockets—anything to shut out the Truth!

Well, let the hounds come. I am going to tell the whole, unvarnished truth about several of the chief deceivers in our midst. I intend to sound the alarm and to cry aloud: "BEWARE, SAINTS OF GOD! THIS IS THE GREAT FALLING AWAY, PROPHESIED TO COME IN *II THES. 2.*"

But before I begin, I warn you: If you don't want to hear the truth, STOP READING NOW.

No reason to have your comfort zone disturbed with facts, is there? Just throw away this information. Then you can get on with your wooing of the world and your adoration of these big and famous names within the so-called "Christian Community."

Billy Graham Shamelessly Subverts the Faith

I've written about his heretical behavior before. Hundreds of my readers have personally sent him copies of my newsletters revealing his ungodliness. But still, the man the Baptists and others believe to be their sterling and ecumenical "Evangelical Pope," continues down the path of depravity, refusing to repent.

It's bad enough that on NBC television recently, Billy Graham flippantly excused President Bill Clinton's lewd and lascivious sexual sins by declaring that, well, the man just can't help himself. Clinton is handsome and virile, said Graham, and the girls are just "wild" over him.

It's bad enough, too, that in his crusade in October 1998 in San Francisco—Sodom and Gomorrah reborn—Graham announced to the homosexuals, "Whatever your background, whatever your sexual orientation, we welcome you tonight."

Earlier, at a news conference, the famed evangelist thrilled the cockles of the homosexuals' lusty hearts when he snapped to a reporter that he was tired of people trying to get him to criticize gays. "It's not the biggest of sins," Graham said.

Billy followed this up by telling the smiling and happy liberal media: "What I want to preach about in San Francisco is the love of God. People need to know that God loves them no matter what their sexual orientation."

Graham also proudly confided: "I have so many gay friends, and we remain friends."

Billy Graham "brings people together"

They—the gays and Billy Graham—do, indeed, remain friends. According to the *San Francisco*

SUNDAY INTERVIEW

Billy Graham

Superman Of the Cloth

At 78, Billy Graham, confidant to decades of presidents, still looms as an American icon. Protestantism's leading household name reflects on an unparalleled career.

The *San Francisco Chronicle and Examiner* called Billy Graham the "Superman of the Cloth," noting that the evangelist has been friend of Presidents and was awarded the Congressional Gold Medal. It's plainly the case that Graham loves the world. But, what does the Holy Bible say?

Chronicle & Examiner (October 10, 1997), after hearing Graham's latest milktoast sermon, Brian Jackie, a gay San Francisco Catholic, praised the evangelist. "Graham is a man of integrity," said Jackie, adding that Billy Graham always has a "positive message."

Jackie's friend, the Reverend Bill Byrd, homosexual pastor of the San Francisco Evangelical Gay Church, heartily agreed. "I have no problem with Graham's preaching," said the Reverend Byrd, "Billy Graham brings people together."

Brings people together? Yes, Billy Graham does do that—he brings the sinful tares together as one into a huge heap, ready to be burned and destroyed by the dreadful, consuming fire of the Lord at the Great White Throne Judgment. And that's exactly where Billy will be too, unless he repents. He will end up kneeling in fear before his Master, trying to con and bribe God, and bragging, "Look at all the terrific things I did in your name, Lord. I filled stadiums and wowed the public, preaching tolerance and love and Christ all together. Even the lesbians and homos loved me. I was a registered Democrat Party voter. Five Presidents of the United States invited me to stay over at the White House. Lord... Oh Lord, aren't you listening to me? Don't you remember? I was once voted in a poll as the world's most admired man. You know me, don't you? I'm Billy Frank Graham!"

Indeed, Billy Graham *is* possibly the world's most admired man—next to his pals Bill Clinton and Pope John Paul II, that is. And what the popular evangelist taught on May 31, 1997, on the Reverend Robert Schuller's worldwide TV program, has no doubt endeared Mr. Graham even more to people everywhere—especially to Hindus, Buddhist, Moslems, witches, tribalists, and other false religionists.

I have personally obtained from Schuller's Crystal Cathedral Church a video and an audiotape of Billy Graham's interview. Get ready, Christian friends, because you are about to read the exact words of Graham and Schuller, blasphemous and wicked to the hilt.

As you shall see, these are not the words of brokenhearted pastors concerned about saving the souls of the lost and eager to fulfill the Great Commission and preach Jesus crucified and Him alone. These are, instead, the lying words of vile, deceitful devils.

The Infamous May 31, 1997 Interview: Graham and Schuller

Robert Schuller: "Tell me, what do you think of the future of Christianity?"

Billy Graham: "I think everybody who knows Christ, whether they're conscious of it or not, they're members of the Body of Christ...God's purpose is to call out a people for His name, whether they come from the Muslim world, Buddhist world, the Christian world, or the non-believing world, *they are members of the Body of Christ*, because they've been called by God. They may not even know the name of Jesus...and I think they are saved, and that they are going to be in heaven with us."

Robert Schuller (overjoyed): "What I hear you saying is that it's possible for Jesus Christ to come into human hearts and soul and life even if they've been born into darkness and never had exposure to the Bible. Is that a correct interpretation of what you are saying?"

Billy Graham: "Yes it is, because I believe that. I've met people in various parts of the world...that have never seen a Bible or heard about a Bible, and never heard of Jesus, but they've believed in their hearts that there was a God."

So, there you have it. The world's most famous evangelist teaches that *no one needs Jesus to be saved and enter the Kingdom of Heaven.* They're already members of the Body of Christ whether they know it or not! All they have to do is believe in *a* God—like one of the three million Hindu gods; or perhaps the man-god whom many Buddhists worship, the Dalai Lama; or the Moslem's Allah; or perhaps the Cosmic God of the evolutionists; or the witches' horned god, Pan; or perhaps all that people must do is believe in the New Age deity—themselves—as God!

The Reverend Robert Schuller of California's Crystal Cathedral interviewed Billy Graham.

Frankly, if Graham is right, isn't it time we just folded our tents and stopped all this foolishness of preaching? Why print Christian Bibles if the Hindu or Buddhist scriptures will suffice? If Billy Graham is right, we are certainly blowing millions of dollars on missionaries.

In fact, I can't understand why Graham himself is still going on stage to perform. Is it all ego and pretense? Why doesn't Billy just have his aides purchase a blaring, gaudy, and colorful message on thousands of billboards across the globe, declaring: *"Attention Pagans, Heathens, and other Religionists: Whether you know it or not, you already have Christ within. Congratulations—you're on your way to heaven!"—signed, Yours Sincerely, Billy Graham, world-famous Christian evangelist.*

Or maybe this for a billboard message: *"So you don't know Jesus as Lord and have never read the Bible? Big Deal! Don't worry, be happy. You are already a Christian headed for heaven, whether you know it or not! So eat, drink, and be merry. Guess what?—You're already a member of the Body of Christ, just like me. Neat surprise, huh?" signed, With All My Love, Billy Graham.*

How many thousands of sinners are going to split hell wide open, simply because they listened to that velvety-tongued apostle of ecumenicism, Billy Graham, who assures the lost, "Just believe in *a* God, *any* God, and you've made it. Jesus loves and accepts you just as you are, no need to repent and believe in the name of Jesus."

Oh yeah? Well, God's Word begs to differ. The Word says that if you believe in one God, "Thou doest well, the devils also believe and tremble." *(James 2:19)*

That's right. James, the brother of Jesus, told us the devils do even better than Billy Graham, Robert Schuller, and all their associates in lying. The devils actually believe in just *one* God, Jesus Christ! The devils know that the Hindu god, Krishna, the Moslem god, Allah, and all the other false gods have never saved one, single human soul! This is more than Billy Graham knows and teaches.

The Apostle Paul wrote that there is salvation in no other name: *"For there is none other name under heaven, given among men, whereby we must be saved." (Acts 4:12)*

The Bible says that the Buddhist, the Hindu, the Moslem, the African witchdoctor, are not saved because they have never called on His Holy Name: *"For whosoever shall call upon the name of the Lord shall be saved." (Romans 10:13)*

These lost souls need Jesus, but Billy Graham lies to these millions of unsaved people headed for hell. He soothingly tells them they don't need the Bible, and don't need to be born again in Christ. They can continue to bow down to their wooden idols, to their statues and icons, and to their devils made of molten steel and clay. But, hold on: *John 5:12* reveals: *"He that hath the Son hath life, and he that hath not the Son of God hath not life."*

Thus we know that Billy Graham is a walking dead man, and all who believe in his wicked, foul message sadly remain foot soldiers in the legion of the dead. They are of the world and are dead to the Truth. But you, my friends, you who know Jesus Christ, you who contend earnestly for the faith and who refuse to accept a counterfeit Gospel—YOU ARE ALIVE AND CANNOT BE DECEIVED. YOU HAVE OVERCOME THE WORLD THROUGH FAITH IN JESUS OUR LORD: *"Who is he that overcometh the world, but he that believeth that Jesus is the Son of God." (I John 5:12)*

What are we to do about Billy Graham? Be wary now, as you ponder this question, because the hounds of hell are even now at your door. Go against Billy and his foolish fables and abominable heresies, and they'll bare their fangs and pounce on you with full force. Nevertheless, what can a saved, Christian man and woman do but obey the Word of God?

The Word commands us to stay away from he who, like Billy Graham, would pervert the doctrine of Christ Jesus and subvert the Gospel: *"If there come any unto you, and bring not this doctrine, receive him not into your house, neither bid him Godspeed. For he that biddeth him Godspeed is partaker of his evil deeds" (II John vs 10-11).*

Go against Billy Graham and his ilk, and the world will quickly turn against you. Even your pastor and your church friends will probably frown upon and disown you. Some will become as the hounds of hell, and they will seek to tear you to shreds.

Still, Billy Graham, having been admonished repeatedly, yet persisting in his lies, is a proven heretic. Of such, the Word of God commands: *"A man that is a heretic, after the first and second admonition, reject, knowing that he that is such is subverted, and sinneth, being condemned of himself." (Titus 3:10-11)*

Finally, consider this: The Billy Grahams, the Schullers, and other deceivers now are having what they mistakenly think to be their day in the sun. The world hates and despises the truth-tellers but loves and receives its own. Jesus said of false teachers and lovers of the world: *"They have their reward."*

The body of man, however, is corrupt and soon withers like the once lush but brown and crumbling blades of grass. Man's riches and admiration are fleeting, and the pleasures of the flesh are but a phantom of man's unreliable imaginations.

But the Word of the Lord—how exalted, how magnificent, how life-giving! Follow its dictates and its counsel, and you will never be disappointed. The Word of Truth is not corruptible; It builds and grows. The Word was and is: "But the Word of the Lord endureth forever..." *(I Peter 1:25)*. And *Who* is that *Word?* None other than *Jesus*, the name above all other names.

Sorcery and Magic Seduce Many Into the Depths of Satan

Witchcraft Invades Christianity

"Now the works of the flesh are manifest, which are these; adultery, fornication, uncleanness, lasciviousness, idolatry, witchcraft, hatred, variance, emulations, wrath, strife, seditions, heresies, envyings, murders, drunkenness, revellings, and such like..."

—*Galatians 5:19-21*

"Woe to the inhabiters of the earth and of the sea! For the devil is come down unto you, having great wrath, because he knoweth that he hath but a short time."

—*Revelation 12:12*

The seduction is virtually complete. Christianity's top leaders have now gone over to the devil's side. Many today *openly* endorse and embrace witchcraft, magic, and other devilish arts and devices. Most others, by their marked silence, are now acquiescing and joining in on this ghoulish, latter days conspiracy.

I make this accusation boldly and without reservation. Moreover, I have seen this evil day coming for many years. I have preached about it, warned of it, and lamented it. Now, it is here. Today's strong delusion of satanic witchcraft has a fatal, claw-like grasp upon the very heart and soul of stained and rebellious Christianity.

Hated and Reviled for My Faith

Fifteen years ago, my books, *Dark Secrets of the New Age, Ravaged by the New Age*, and others exposed the cancer-like growth of New Age occultism *within* the Christian community. Although these books enjoyed a wide reading, their exposures caused me to become one of the most hated, reviled, and rejected men in the entire Christian world.

I thank God, however, that a tiny remnant of true believers have, through the years, stood by me, encouraging me in my struggle to contend for the faith once delivered to the saints *(Jude, vs. 4)*.

C.S. Lewis Exposed as Pagan Mythologist

In 1987, as one of only a few lone voices in the wilderness, I warned the Christian world of the insidious, unscriptural, satanic, and magical messages and images contained in the books of famous "Christian" author, C.S. Lewis. I wrote particularly of Lewis' *Chronicles of Narnia* series for kids and adults, demonstrating how these works were from the very pit of hell.

And though British author C.S. Lewis was one of the most quoted, admired, and beloved of all "Christian" writers and teachers, I demonstrated that Lewis' own personal and doctrinal life was stigmatized by pagan beliefs, mythological imagery, sexual kinkiness, and adultery.

I showed also C.S. Lewis' mixture and confusion of Hindu and Greek gods with Christian heroes. In one instance, C.S. Lewis even equated Jesus Christ with the ancient Greek sun god Apollo, the son of the mythological Zeus.

C.S. Lewis was most fond of expressing a belief in Jesus, followed by a clarifying exclamation, "Jesus was the fulfillment of myth." According to Lewis, Jesus deserved worship because he was, "the myth that had come true."

As I pointed out in my book, *Ravaged by the New Age*, Lewis also taught in his novels, the *Chronicles of Narnia* series, that all service done by a person on behalf of Lucifer and the dark side was, in fact, also credited by God as service to him!

In Lewis' nonfiction writings, we discover his belief in evolution, in the Catholic version of Mary, and in the odd notion that in our "next lives," Christians may just become planets, stars, or other heavenly objects.

Moreover, Lewis believed the Bible to be flawed, and suggested that Jesus was an ignorant prophet, regrettably tied to the Jewish messianic myth. Lewis further suggested that Jesus' prophecies had failed to come to pass.

Nevertheless, all these things being so, the fantasy books of C.S. Lewis have for decades been super sellers in both Christian *and* New Age occult bookstores. For my efforts in warning Christian parents to keep Lewis' wicked and foul books far from their kids, many a Christian bookstore owner and manager responded by angrily pulling Texe Marrs' books off their shelves and banning them forever from their premises.

Pottermania Invades Christian Homes

Now come the Harry Potter witchcraft books by yet another British author. Ms. J.K. Rowling. The plots of these books are centered around the witchcraft and magical exploits of a young boy, Harry, who goes off to learn his craft at an academy of witchcraft and wizardry after his sorcerer parents are murdered by another sorcerer. As each book is released in this *New York Times* bestseller series, we find the content and theme growing darker and more involved in the deep things of Satan.

***Newsweek's* cover touted Harry Potter, and *Christianity Today* magazine called Harry Potter books "wonderful." Note the "lightning bolt" on Harry Potter's forehead.**

Millions of copies of these Harry Potter books are selling like hotcakes—and Christian children and parents are leading the pack in lusting after them. And why not? These kids have been fed the soul-darkening fantasies of occultist C.S. Lewis, and they have been dumbed down sufficiently by ecumenical pastors and charismatic Word of Faith evangelists. Their hearts and minds are already stained by the filth and degradation viewed daily on TV and by the polluted music and rotten doctrines spouted in their upside-down, pseudo-Christian churches.

So debased have the minds of our children become, they are prone to believe that the 60's Woodstock was a Christian rock festival and that Roman Emperor Nero's wild sexual orgies were, historically, just one more example of a variety of entertaining and flesh-thrilling experiences available to us today.

Far Left: This full page color ad in *Time* magazine (October 23, 2000) by FTD Florist exemplifies how witchcraft has excited the public imagination. In the upper right corner it is indicated that this ad is based on Disney's Winnie the Pooh, a popular kids creation.

Left: A Harry Potter bookstore display. Again. not the satanic symbol, or mark, on Harry's forehead.

Bottom: Most Christian parents are not hesitating to buy Harry Potter sorcery witchcraft books for their kids. Witchcraft has now virtually conquered the whole of the Christian establishment.

A Christian Book Burning?

It was, of course, the apostle Paul who lashed out at the pagan lifestyle and practices rampant in society during the early Christian era. In the book of Acts, we find the encouraging statement that many new Christians who had previously "used curious arts"—that is, sorcery, witchcraft, and magic—*"brought their books together and burned them before all men..."(Acts 19:19).*

Imagine! These Christians took books much like C.S. Lewis' *Chronicles of Narnia* and Rowlings' Harry Potter volumes and had a big, public, book burning!

And what was the end result of such incredibly bold behavior? The very next verse in the book of *Acts* reveals exactly what next happened:

> *"So mightily grew the Word of God and prevailed." (Acts 19:20)*

Please read that inspiring statement again and think about the consequences. The Christians brought out their magical and witchcraft books and publicly burned them, and *"So mightily grew the Word of God and prevailed."*

Now, consider today's results. In our 21st century society, Christians flock to the bookstores to obtain works of the curious arts. Thus, the Word of God is declared null and void in their lives, their children's souls are turned over to Satan, and their tainted churches, hopelessly adrift in a sea of filthiness and uncleanness, cannot possibly prevail.

But where are God's watchmen—the men whom, we are told by the Christian media, the Lord has called to guide us forward into this luminous New Age of 21st century spiritualism? *They are lying right in bed with the sorceress and are eagerly obeying the serpent.* These men, with their pitch-black hearts, are literally embracing Satan's works and promoting them for all they are worth. Our own "Christian" leadership is insuring that America is cursed by God!

Colson and Others Endorse Witchcraft Themes

You say you don't believe me? Well, then, what about Charles Colson, he who is so beloved by the Southern Baptists, by the Catholics, by the Episcopals, by all the Christian world? On his daily *Breakpoint* radio program, Colson recently advised parents to disregard the naysayers. The Harry Potter books are fine examples of good Christian-oriented literature, said the smooth, silver-tongued Colson. They are, he smugly added, highly recommended.

If that were not enough, we also have James Dobson's *Focus on the Family* recommending the Harry Potter books as wholesome. Next, the editors of *Christianity Today*, the magazine founded by Billy Graham, chimed in, calling the Harry Potter series a "Book of Virtues with a pre-adolescent funnybone." The magazine also praised the books as "wonderful examples of compassion, loyalty, courage, friendship, and even self-sacrifice."

These gushing recommendations were made in spite of the blatant and clear witchcraft prevalent in the Harry Potter books. In one scene in the novels, we find a professor whose leg is mangled by a three-headed dog. In another, a mysterious figure drinks blood from a unicorn carcass. In the books we see young Harry lying, breaking rules, making fun of and mocking adults, and seeking revenge. To defeat his foes, Harry uses magic and witchcraft rituals and methods. On his forehead, notably, is the rune symbol of the satanic lightning bolt.

Nevertheless, in response to Christians who write to him complaining, Christian celebrity leader Charles Colson, head of Prison Fellowship, insists that the magic in the Potter books is not really occultic, just "inventive".

White vs. Black Witchcraft

Other Christian leaders try to whitewash their failure to condemn these satanic novels by attempting to portray Harry's magic as *"White Witchcraft,"* which they say is "good magic," versus *Black Witchcraft*, which is "evil magic."

But in his *Satanic Bible*, the late Anton LaVey, High Priest of the Church of Satan, scoffed at such a distinction. "There is no difference in Satanism," sneered LaVey, "between white and black witchcraft or magic."

While the jaded and spiritually bankrupt Christian establishment either promotes the idea of "good magic" and "white witchcraft" or is altogether silent, the true Christian remnant is fighting these evil books. Parents in 28 states have sought to have the Harry Potter books banned at public school libraries.

Yet, few dare mention the fact that the C.S. Lewis books—which are even more vile and more blatantly occultic—continue to be sold in Christian bookstores, endorsed by Hank Hanegraaff, Chuck Colson, Billy Graham, and other leaders, and quoted each Sunday in dozens of "conservative" Southern Baptist and other churches!

This phenomenon is only one striking example of the witchcraft explosion that has erupted and is now ravaging the Christian establishment.

Lucifer is now exalted by some pastors as a "good angel," the goddess "Sophia" is replacing Jesus Christ in some large churches, scholars are denying and debunking the very words of Jesus, the lure of sexual intercourse "entertainment" is being used to entice people to come to church to see sexually oriented theater productions, Charismatic big-wigs have been recruited by the Vatican's Knights of Malta secret society, faith healer Benny Hinn has been caught on camera encouraging gospel singer Steve Brock to smoke a water pipe, famous TBN preacher and bestselling author T.D. Jakes has betrayed the true faith by endorsing for President an avid abortionist/homosexual activist, Vice President Al Gore, Pat Robertson's Masonic connections were made manifest. So-called underground "Christian" churches in the U.S.A. and Great Britain are now performing unholy satanic black masses, with naked women draped over altars.

The horrors are only beginning and will escalate until Jesus returns. Until He does, let us expose the evildoers *(Ephesians 5:11)* and let us take courage knowing that God is still on the throne. He sees, He knows, and His judgement is swift and certain. I thus say to the wicked who seek to despoil Christianity: *"You will not succeed. The remnant shall remain, a righteous, blood-bought church without spot or wrinkle. Even so, come quickly, Lord Jesus!"*

The Scandal of Christian Ghostwriting

"Be not deceived; God is not mocked: for whatsoever a man soweth, that shall he also reap."

—*Galatians 6:7*

Are some of the most cherished books in your personal Christian library written by ghostwriters, some of whom may be homosexuals, atheists, and New Agers? Before you answer "no," please read this article very carefully. A tragic and disreputable hoax is being perpetrated on naive and unsuspecting Christians. And you might just be one of the chief victims.

The Reverend Mel White is a homosexual activist who lives with his male lover, Gary Nixon, in Dallas, Texas. "I am gay, I am proud, and God loves me without reservation," White recently told David Calker, a *Los Angeles Times* reporter.

White, who "pastors" a militantly gay church, is also a writer of many Christian books. But though he's the author, his name doesn't appear on the front covers. Instead, a Christian celebrity's name appears on each of Mel White's books. White is what the book industry fondly calls a "ghostwriter."

Ghostwriting Rampant in "Christian" Publishing

The scandalous practice of an unnamed and concealed person ghostwriting a book for a celebrity is rampant in Christian publishing. Virtually all the larger book publishing firms do it. The question is, is this practice immoral, dishonest, and deceitful? After all, the buyer of these books *thinks* he or she is getting inspired information direct from the hearts and pens of men like Billy Graham and Pat Robertson, each of whom has used ghostwriters.

Billy Graham and Oral Roberts are close associates who have much in common. Both have used ghostwriters for their books. Here are the two in 1967 at the dedication of Oral Roberts University in Tulsa.

The reader pays good money for a beautifully packaged book with the hero celebrity's picture and name on the jacket. Never would the buyer suspect that the book is actually written by a homosexual, an atheist, or a New Ager. Thinking that he or she is taking in digestible spiritual food, the book buyer has no idea the ghostwritten book may contain poisonous and insidious views hostile to Christianity imbedded in its text.

Big Name Personalities Use Ghostwriters

Homosexual activist Mel White has been an influential, behind-the-scenes ghostwriter for many big name personalities. He's written speeches for Lt.Col. Oliver North. White has also authored at least two of evangelist Jerry Falwell's books, including—unbelievable as it may seem—Falwell's autobiography, *Strength for the Journey*. Falwell could well afford White's fee to ghostwrite his books—the Moral Majority preacher was given a *one million dollar* advance by the publisher!

The Reverend Mr. White has also been the secret force behind some of Billy Graham's best known books, including Graham's prophetic bestseller, *The Approaching Hoofbeats*. Indeed, White once even closeted himself in a luxurious condo for weeks with the famed evangelist down in Acapulco, Mexico, writing a book.

However, you'll search in vain to find author Mel White's name on either the cover or the title page of the books he wrote for Billy Graham. Nor is Mel White's name openly connected with Jerry Falwell's books. "It was important," White now reveals, "that Jerry Falwell not be scandalized because his biographer was a queer."

Ghostwriter White also wrote Pat Robertson's book, *America's Dates With Destiny*. But the gay reverend is not the only "ghost" whom the veteran host of TV's *The 700 Club* has used for his chart-topping books. Reportedly, Robertson's recent #1 Christian bestseller, *The New World Order*, was also ghostwritten—by a CBN staffer.

In *The New World Order*, "Pat Robertson" correctly warns readers that Freemasonry is an evil, Luciferian conspiracy. Yet, incredibly, Robertson's Christian Coalition subsequently held a "Road to Victory '93" conference in Washington, D.C., at which high-level Freemasons gave the keynote addresses! Pat Robertson's guest speakers at the conference included Senator Bob Dole, 33° Scottish Rite Mason, and Senator Jesse Helms, yet another 33° Mason.

> ***My investigation of the Christian book world has uncovered the fact that the majority of books supposedly authored by famous Christian personalities are, in fact, the product of ghostwriters.***

Pat Robertson's book, *The New World Order*, also fingered the Council on Foreign Relations (CFR) as a Satan-led, conspiratorial project. But at his "Road to Victory '93" gala, Robertson's keynote speaker was none other than Congressman Newt Gingrich. One worlder Gingrich just happens to be a loyal member of the same group which Pat's book exposes as a devilish front—the CFR! The title of Gingrich's speech for the Christian Coalition conference was "Renewing American Civilization."

We are thus faced with these two alternatives: (1) either Pat Robertson did not even bother to read the bestselling book, *The New World Order*, that sports his celebrity name as author on its glossy cover; *or* (2) he allowed his name to be placed on a book, the contents of which he does not even believe in.

Can We Trust Christian Publishers?

My investigation of the Christian book world has uncovered the disgusting fact that the majority of books supposedly authored by famous Christian personalities are, in fact, the product of ghostwriters. Both novels and nonfiction books are involved. Sometimes, the *real* writer is recognized in the acknowledgments section or elsewhere in the book; but most often, he or she is not.

Some celebrities, such as Chuck Colson, write their books *"with"* an unknown collaborator. In

Left: Chuck Colson's Prison Fellowship paid for this advertisement in *First Things* (August/September 1994), a magazine published by Roman Catholic priest Richard Neuhaus. The ad is seeking a person to write and edit commentaries for Chuck Colson's national radio program, *BreakPoint*. How many people have mistakenly been led to believe that Colson writes his own materials?

Above: You've heard all those stirring patriotic, "Christian" speeches by Oliver North, haven't you? Well, how many of you know that they were ghostwritten for North by Mel White, a devoted and militant homosexual? Here, White and North are pictured delightedly cruising on a private, executive jet. (Photo from White's book, *Stranger at the Gate*.)

such cases, the ghostwriter's name is occasionally shown on the front cover in small, unassuming type. But shouldn't the cover jacket of these books have a warning label or notice revealing what percentage of the book is written by Colson and what percentage is the product of his lesser-known co-writer? *Who* really writes Colson's books—him or his collaborator? *Whose* ideas do his books reflect?

The book buyer also deserves to be told some facts about the ghostwriter or co-writer, so that Mel White-type incidents are minimized. For example, a woman named *Ellen Santilli Vaughn* is listed as the co-writer of many of Chuck Colson's bestselling books, including his ecumenical-oriented book, *The Body*. But just who is "Ellen Santilli Vaughn?" What is her background? Is she a Christian...a Catholic...a Protestant...a New Ager? How much of the contents and philosophy of Chuck Colson's books is Ms. Vaughn responsible for?

Another prime example is prophecy teacher Hal Lindsey. Very few people know that Lindsey's mammoth bestseller, *The Late, Great Planet Earth*, was actually written by a woman, Carla Carlson. To his credit, Lindsey has publicly admitted this. The question remains, however: *Who* is Carla Carlson? *Why* was she involved in writing Lindsey's book? *Why* is her name not highlighted on the cover, in bold letters equally as large as those of Hal Lindsey? And finally: Are *all* of Hal Lindsey's books similarly written by unknown ghostwriters?

It is shameful that such vital and basic information is withheld from the book buyer. Shouldn't truth-in-packaging rules apply to publishing the way they do to other consumer product industries?

There's one thing you *can* count on, however. Every book that lists Texe Marrs as author was *personally written* by Texe Marrs. Every word in his books comes from his pen alone. Every quote is personally selected by me. And that's the way it will always be. Anything less would be a scam on my readers.

How to Make a Bundle from Ghostwritten Books

Now please understand: I do realize that in a few cases, it is perfectly acceptable for a talented professional writer to work with an expert or authority on a technical subject. An engineer, a medical doctor, a dietician or a scientist researcher may find it expedient to work with a writer. But

The unethical practice of ghostwritten books is common among "Christian" celebrities, as these three can attest. They have each made big bucks off books they didn't write.

in such cases, it is the expert who has the original concept for the book. He dictates most of the text, and the book is based solely on his knowledge, ideas, work and research.

This is rarely the case with celebrity Christian authors. Publishers are continually searching for "hot," new topics for books that can make them a lot of money. Usually, they, not the celebrity, choose a title for the book and only then contact and recruit the chosen celebrity. Publishers have been known to hire entire teams of writers and researchers to produce books.

Often, the greedy celebrity author merely gives the finished product a cursory look-over and adds his verbal blessing to the project. The celebrity is pleased because he knows he will make a bundle, with only minimal effort on his part. *His* name goes on the cover, and millions of Christian buyers are deceived into believing the celebrity, inspired by God, personally wrote every word in the book.

The Profit Motive is Paramount

It thus becomes crystal clear why publishers and celebrity authors conspire to produce ghostwritten books. The reason is simple: *money, money, money!* A bestselling, hardcover book with the glittery name of a Graham, Robertson, Colson, or Lindsey on the cover can bring in *five to ten million dollars or more* in income. The celebrity "author" also profits—he can rake in as much as *two million dollars* per book.

No wonder the rush is on by publishers to constantly create new, mostly fluff titles and to line up their ghostwriters with name celebrities known to be guaranteed money-makers in the Christian marketplace.

Truth Telling is in Order

So what's to be done about the lucrative, yet unethical and dishonest, practice of the ghostwriting of Christian books? I believe it is time for some truth telling. Thomas Nelson, Word, and all the other wealthy conglomerates who disguise themselves as "Christian" publishers should step up to the plate and give us a list of which books have been written by "ghosts" and which were really penned by the authors listed on their covers. That's the least they should do to come clean.

Better yet, these greedy publishing houses and their celebrity stablemates should quit trying to fatten their coffers and make bucks off gullible Christian readers. They should cease their publishing of ghostwritten books entirely. It's an unscrupulous and shady practice, and it ought to be stopped *immediately*.

The Scandal of Christian Ghostwriting—An Update

My investigative report, *The Scandal of Christian Ghostwriting*, has caused quite a stir. Some Christian celebrities who use ghostwriters are panic-stricken. Many are wiggling and squirming in discomfort. They are embarrassed that their money-making scam was finally unmasked for what it is: A deception on the buying public. Readers pay exorbitant prices for the books of Christian superstars, never knowing that the volumes are actually written by no-name "ghosts." Among the big names pulling this stunt: Hal Lindsey, Chuck Colson, Jim Bakker, Billy Graham, and Oral Roberts.

After my exposé, several of these men quickly circled their wagons and tried to come up with excuses. Charismatic faith healer Benny Hinn took the direct approach. He went on Paul Crouch's Trinity Broadcasting Network and personally introduced his ghostwriter! Hinn gave the lame excuse that his books were anointed by God, but he just needed help in getting it all into words and into book form.

David Wilkerson phoned me to discuss his situation. "I am responsible for my book, *The Cross and the Switchblade*," insisted the Times Square pastor.

Wilkerson went on to say, "I did go to Sherrill's office almost every day for over a year to work on the book. Together we hammered it out. But he was *not* really a ghostwriter. I personally approved every word, every page."

I do give David Wilkerson credit for at least admitting that someone helped him write his book. And I believe him when he states that he personally approved every word that was written. Moreover, I do not think that David Wilkerson was motivated by money when his book was published.

Wilkerson's book was a biographical

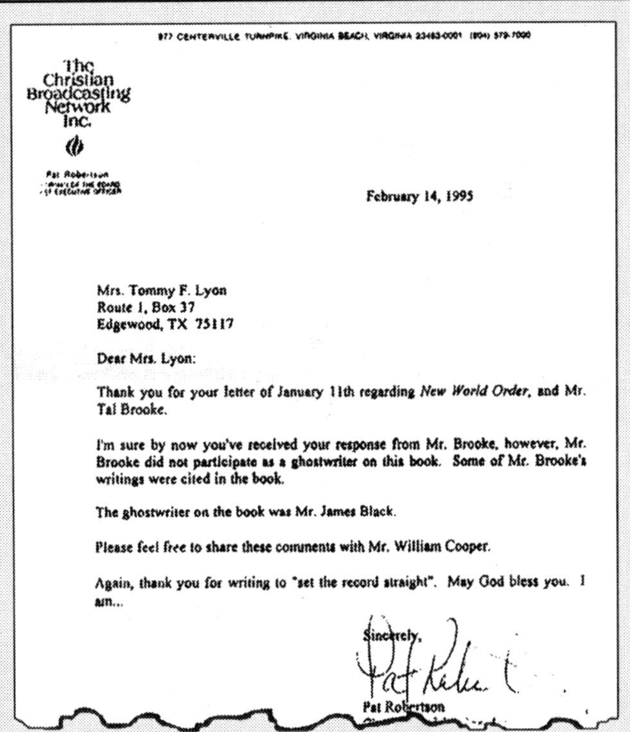

877 CENTERVILLE TURNPIKE, VIRGINIA BEACH, VIRGINIA 23463-0001 (804) 579-7000

The Christian Broadcasting Network Inc.

Pat Robertson

February 14, 1995

Mrs. Tommy F. Lyon
Route 1, Box 37
Edgewood, TX 75117

Dear Mrs. Lyon:

Thank you for your letter of January 11th regarding *New World Order*, and Mr. Tal Brooke.

I'm sure by now you've received your response from Mr. Brooke, however, Mr. Brooke did not participate as a ghostwriter on this book. Some of Mr. Brooke's writings were cited in the book.

The ghostwriter on the book was Mr. James Black.

Please feel free to share these comments with Mr. William Cooper.

Again, thank you for writing to "set the record straight". May God bless you. I am...

Sincerely,

Pat Robertson

Gene Kapp, top *700 Club* official, insisted that Pat Robertson does not use ghostwriters for his books. Too bad he didn't know that his boss had sent out this letter.

account of his true-life experiences in New York City as a street preacher. His justification for obtaining help is that he is not called to be a writer—he's called to be a preacher.

I give Brother Wilkerson the benefit of the doubt. I do wish, though, that he had checked out the beliefs and background of writer-helper, John Sherrill. Sherrill, is, in fact, a rabid ecumenicist who enthusiastically promotes Roman Catholicism and is a member of the apostate, ultra-liberal Episcopal Church (World Council of Churches). Is such a man qualified to "assist" a bible-believing evangelist in writing a book?

Sherrill was also a paid writer on the staff of the late Norman Vincent Peale, a 33° Mason. Peale was the guy who made a mint with his false teachings about "positive thinking." The liberal Reverend Peale promoted spirit channeling and automatic writing. He encouraged communication with the dead. (For proof, see Wanda Marrs' book, *New Age Lies to Women*, and my book, *New Age Cults and Religions*.) I am not implying, of course, that Sherrill has such beliefs, but he was on Peale's staff.

John Sherrill's own book, *They Speak With Other Tongues*, is well known in Charismatic circles—2.5 million copies of the book have been sold over the years to ecumenical-minded charismatics. Yet, the book is devoid of true salvation knowledge and woefully lacks a legitimate, born again Gospel message.

In his book, Sherrill promotes Catholicism; he praises the Popes and gushingly quotes Catholic priests who practice speaking in tongues. In agreement with Vatican doctrine, Sherrill writes that, "The *Eucharist* is at the center of our worship life."

Pat Robertson Admits to Ghostwritten Book

Then we have the case of Gene Kapp, who happens to be "vice president of public relations" for Pat Robertson's *The 700 Club*. In answer to an inquiry by a friend of this ministry, Kapp blatantly misled when he stated: "Pat Robertson does not use 'ghostwriters' for any of his books."

In the very next sentence, however, Kapp contradicts himself. "Mr. Robertson," Kapp writes, "did utilize Mel White as a freelance temporary in 1984, before White publicly announced that he is a homosexual, to assist in the writing of *America's Dates With Destiny*."

Sorry, Mr. Kapp, but your lack of credibility is showing. In my possession and reprinted here is a letter signed by Pat Robertson, Kapp's boss. In the letter, Robertson admits that yes, *he did use a ghostwriter* for his more recent book, *New World Order*. In his letter, Robertson states flat-out: "The ghostwriter on the book was Mr. James Black."

O.K., Pat: Now, that you have finally admitted that you *did* use a ghostwriter—exactly as I reported in my exposé, *The Scandal of Christian Ghostwriting*—don't you think it would be proper to call Mr. Kapp, your VP for public relations, into your office, stand him upright, and plainly tell him: *"Quit misleading people. It's not good public relations!"*

While you're at it, Pat, why don't you just do the right thing yourself: Stop putting your name on books ghostwritten by others. That, in my opinion, is a form of lying.

The same can be said for John Ankerberg, Chuck Colson, Hank Hanegraaff, David Jeremiah, Hal Lindsey, Billy Graham, Jerry Falwell, and all the others who handsomely profit from ghostwritten books.

Rick Warren, Joel Osteen, and A New Generation of "Christian" Leaders

Slumbering Dogs, Greedy Dogs

The Devil comes in many disguises. Quite often, he comes dressed up as a minister of the Gospel. Sometimes it is difficult to spot him. He masquerades as a Pastor, looks so holy, so prosperous, so loving, so helpful. The Devil is sometimes good at using colorful Christian-sounding lingo, hollering out "Praise Jesus!" a few times to his congregation. Words like "Alleluia!" may slide off his tongue like silk.

The Devil knows how to speak in other tongues, too, and he does it often. The Hindu gurus over in India regularly speak in other tongues, as do some witches, and it's been known to happen in Mormon Churches and in Voodoo trance-rituals. But the Devil seems to be most acclaimed and gets the most mileage when he wears the garb of a Charismatic, "spirit-filled" pastor and lets his babbling tongue fly in front of a huge bunch of dancing, jumping up and down, tongue-speaking Charismatic church-goers.

Now understand, I am not doubting for a moment that the Holy Ghost can speak in tongues through a Christian believer. We know that from the scriptures. And, no doubt, that's why the Devil does it, too, to mock, imitate and counterfeit.

The Church from Hell

One Pastor in Louisiana literally turned his church into a hell-house in which members raped and sexually abused as many as 24 children in satanic rituals and devil worship. Neighbors said at night they sometimes heard strange noises coming from the church. *Newsweek* called it, "The Devil's Handiwork."

Such incidents—and they are happening more and more now—boggle the mind. But as sick and monstrous as they are, I believe the Devil is accomplishing much, much more through ministries like that of Rick Warren, Joel Osteen, and Billy Graham than he is through Pastors like the one in Louisiana.

> *His watchmen are blind: they are all ignorant, they are all dumb dogs, they cannot bark; sleeping, lying down, loving to slumber.*
>
> *Yea, they are greedy dogs which can never have enough, and they are shepherds that cannot understand: they all look to their own way, every one for his gain, from his quarter.*
>
> *Come ye, say they, ... to morrow shall be as this day, and much more abundant.*
>
> Isaiah 56: 10-12

Hell is Being Enlarged

You see, the Louisiana Pastor only tainted and brought hell to a very small group of people. What a piker! Slick ministers like Warren, Osteen, and Graham are able to persuade tens of millions of victims to give up Jesus Christ. As a consequence, as the Bible says in *Isaiah 5:14* and *Habakkuk 2:5,* Hell is ever being enlarged, and more and more unsaved

New Age books by lukewarm pastors like Rick Warren and Joel Osteen are all the rage today.

souls are plunging into its depths every day.

Rick Warren, Pastor for the "Me" Generation

Rick Warren, Pastor of Saddleback Community Church in Lake Forest, California, is the hip and trendy, twenty-first century model of Dr. Robert Schuller. In fact, Schuller just happens to be his mentor. Warren's bestselling book, *The Purpose Driven Life*, is vintage New Ageism. The selfish "me" generation loves it, because they are always trying to figure out their "purpose" in life. The Bible, of course, tells us our purpose: Our purpose is to deny ourselves, take up the cross, and follow Jesus. But no one today would buy a book that says that. Today's narcissistic, "party, party, party" generation isn't gonna deny itself. It's looking for a way to affirm self and to deny God.

Jimi Hendrix and "Purple Haze"

What is Rick Warren "driven" to do in his life? In front of a gigantic crowd of some 30,000 people in Los Angeles' baseball stadium, "Pastor Rick" came out in a psychedelic-colored T-shirt and kicked off a rally recently by singing an impersonation of a 60s, hippie-era, Jimi Hendrix' hit song, *"Purple Haze."* The enthusiastic crowd went wild with laughter. Purpose-driven Pastor Rick told them, *"I've always wanted to do that in this stadium."*

Think about it. Jimi Hendrix, a heavy metal guitarist and singer, died of a drug overdose. He was a crackhead and a heroin addict. He would violently smash his guitar, make a fire out of the splinters, and go into a drugged-out voodoo trance. Hendrix said that's when he did his "best" music, when the spirits entered him amidst the "Purple Haze."

Now we have America's Pastor, Rick Warren, soaking up the applause as he goes back to lap up the dead Jimi Hendrix' vomit.

Joel Osteen: Forget About Sin, Judgment and False Religion

Then along comes smiley boy Joel Osteen. He's got a book that's rocketed up to #1 on *The New York Times* bestseller list. He's filling up auditoriums. His happy times prosperity gospel church has even bought up a 60,000 seat stadium for Osteen to do his preaching at.

And what does he preach? Well, Osteen, on CNN's *The Larry King Show*, said he doesn't get into controversial subjects like sin and judgment. False religions such as Islam, Hinduism, and Judaism don't concern him. He doesn't really know who's going to hell and who isn't, says smiley boy Joel.

"God is a good god," he repeats over and over, so Osteen is not into condemnation, hell, fire, and brimstone. If you're a Mormon, a Buddhist, a Mason, a Moslem it's all the same to God. God just wants you to have your "best life, now."

Your Best Life, Now

That's it. That's the Osteen Gospel: The Best Life for Earth's six billion inhabitants, with or without

Jesus. Indeed, with his book they can have it right now, this minute, by thinking positive and staying away from all those unwholesome, negative, Bible believers.

Fornicator-General of the Planet

The twenty-first century ministries of Warren, Osteen, and others of today's up and coming preacher corps dovetail quite nicely with the outgoing crew of Schuller and Graham. At his so-called "final crusade" in Queens, New York, Billy Graham talked about singer Madonna. Then he invited into the pulpit a man who is best described as the *"Fornicator-General of the Planet."* I'm talking about former President Bill Clinton, the big liar who declared, "I did not have sex with that woman, Ms. Lewinsky."

Graham purred and puffed, and praised his pal Bill Clinton, telling the audience in New York and around the world via TV that Clinton was a fine man who should become a Christian evangelist and preach crusades. And as for Hillary—yes, she was there in person, too, invited by Graham—Billy Graham said that while Bill Clinton was out on the road preaching, Hillary should be back at the White House running the country!

Billy Graham Says, "I'm a Lifelong Democrat"

That same week, Billy Graham let everybody know that his pro-Clinton comments were no accident. Interviewed by Katie Couric on NBC's *Today* show, Graham assured the perky little liberal that he has always been a life-long member of the Democrat Party.

Gasp, snort. Billy Graham a Democrat? You mean, Graham is a supporter of that political party that's rabidly pro-abortion, pro-homosexual, pro-globalist, pro-United Nations, pro-Communist? Yep, exactly. Graham says he's *always* been one of those kind of political partisans, always will be.

"Shocked, Shocked"

Anyone who's read Dr. Cathy Burns' documented exposé book of Graham entitled *Billy Graham and His Friends* could have told you. Yet, thousands of Christian evangelicals now say they are "shocked, shocked" to find out Graham is a big, goofy, loopy supporter of Bill and Hillary Clinton and the entire Democrat Party. (Reminds ya of that famous line in the classic Humphrey Bogart movie, *Casablanca,* where the lying, crooked police commissioner protested he was "shocked, shocked," to see gambling going on at a night club in Casablanca.)

Slumbering Dogs, Greedy Dogs

All these things and more I examine in my audiotape exposing the popular new generation of "Christian" leaders. On it, I call them what they are: *Slumbering Dogs, Greedy Dogs*. The Bible uses those words, and I cannot possibly improve on them.

Yes, Pastor Rick and Pastor Joel are, indeed, loved and admired by the world. Everyone loves a nice little dog, especially if it's one of those cute, little lap dogs that have no bark and no bite.

Sadly, that's what the Christian establishment is full of these days: Lazy dogs that eat, consume, luxuriate, sleep, not understanding, believing that this day is prosperous and tomorrow will be even more abundant.

But these men are wrong. By the time these slumbering dogs, greedy dogs and their millions of dumbed-down followers wake up, it will be all over but the shouting and the wailing. And that is why Texe Marrs, and a few like me who subscribe to this newsletter, when we see the ruin caused by apostates like Warren, Osteen, and others, are compelled to drop to our knees and cry out with bitter tears, *"Lord Jesus, please, come quickly."*

TBN's Paul Crouch Pays Homosexual Lover $425,000 Hush Money

In a news story first broken by the *Los Angeles Times*, then reported across the globe by media outlets ranging from Britain's *The Scotsman* newspaper to Russia's *Pravda*, televangelist Paul Crouch has been cited for homosexual and other misconduct.

Crouch, founder of Trinity Broadcasting Network (TBN), the world's largest Christian television network, reportedly carried on a tawdry sexual relationship with a TBN employee, Enoch Lonnie Ford. Ford, an ex-convict, drug user and convicted child molester, had been employed by TBN as a limo driver, telephone receptionist, and also as a photographer, even though he had few job skills and did not know how to operate a camera.

Gay lovers Ford and Crouch evidently had a falling out, and a legal dispute ensued. Ford was given $425,000 in hush money by Crouch, a TBN lawyer says, and he agreed to keep quiet about his and Crouch's sexual relationship.

However, more recently, Ford came back to demand a staggering ten million dollars from Crouch and TBN, or else! Allegedly, TBN and Crouch then offered one million dollars to Ford in exchange for his not publishing a finished book manuscript that Ford had threatened to publish detailing the gay tryst between he and lover Crouch.

In the unpublished manuscript, Ford alleges that Paul Crouch not only had gay sex with him, but forced him to submit to sex to keep his job. Ford also says he and Crouch visited an L.A. area nightclub together and spent two nights at the fancy and luxurious Regent Wilshire Hotel in ritzy Beverly Hills, California.

Paul Crouch's alleged homosexual lover, Enoch Lonnie Ford, as pictured in the *Los Angeles Times*, Sept. 12, 2004, page A29.

TBN and Crouch *admit* that $425,000 hush money was paid Ford, but predictably, deny all other charges. The broadcast network's attorneys are asking a judge to order Ford to keep his end of the hush money bargain by killing the potentially damning manuscript.

According to *L.A.Times* reporter William Lobdell, when Crouch's youngest son, Matt, first learned of his father's sexual transgressions he told TBN lawyer David Middlebrook, *"I am devasted. I am confronted with having to face the fact that my father is a homosexual."*

James Logden, founder of an internet web site promoting the gay lifestyle, told *Power of Prophecy*, "Gay people were not taken by surprise. Many of us had always suspected the flamboyant Paul Crouch was queer. After all, he's married to puffy-lipped, pink-coiffed Jan Crouch, a drag queen if there ever was one."

Does Blessing the Criminal State of Israel Bring Upon the People of America...

The Curse of the Illuminati?

"Then he said unto me, Hast thou seen this, O son of Man? Is it a light thing to the house of Judah that they commit the abominations which they commit here? for they have filled the land with violence, and have returned to provoke me to anger...

Therefore will I also deal in fury: mine eye shall not spare, neither will I have pity: and though they cry in mine ears with a loud voice, yet will I not hear them."

—*Ezekiel 8:17-18*

Has an Illuminati curse fallen on America? Is this God's punishment for America's citizens blessing the nation of Israel, a nation made up of people who despise Jesus Christ, the Son of God?

No nation on Earth has done more for Israel than the United States of America. It was America's President Harry S. Truman, a 33rd degree Freemason, who, in 1948, endorsed the proposal for a nation-state for the Jews to be founded in the Middle East. It was also the U.S.A., under Truman, that was the first country in the world to recognize Israel as an independent nation and sponsor its membership in the United Nations.

Paul Crouch, head of America's largest Christian television network, is an ardent supporter of Israel and the Zionist agenda. He was outed by the *Orange County Register* newspaper for paying $425,000 in hush money to a homosexual lover. Like many other Christian evangelicals, Crouch is a global laughing stock. Is God blessing America by putting this reprobate at the helm of America's largest Christian television network?

Since 1948, United States Presidents and Administrations have favored the theocratic, rabbinical State of Israel among all the nations. We have showered the Jewish State with hundreds of billions of dollars in foreign aid, which they never paid back, and we have armed Israel to the teeth with fighter planes, missiles, tanks, and other military hardware. This year alone, the Bush Administration announced it was giving $30 billion more in military aid to Israel. Our leaders even looked the other way when Israeli spies stole America's

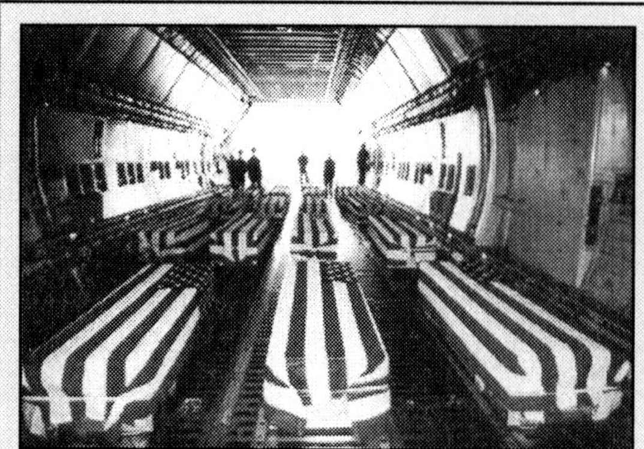

Mainly to further the Israeli agenda, the United States is embroiled in two foreign wars, in Iraq and Afghanistan. As a result, flag-draped coffins of slain U.S. military personnel are regularly brought home by transport aircraft. Is this an example of how much God is blessing America for its support of Israel and the Jewish Zionist Agenda?

most precious military secrets, including the atomic bomb.

That's not all. The United States has consistently used its diplomatic muscle to shield the Jewish thugs in Tel Aviv and Jerusalem from any accountability for their crimes and genocide against the Palestinians, the Lebanese, and other Arab peoples. We also regularly use our veto power at the UN to knock down attempts by that world body to bring Israel to justice for its growing list of murders and global acts of terrorism, as well as the Jews' blatant Zionist racism policies.

Christian Evangelicals Endorse Wicked Nation of Israel

Christian evangelicals have flexed their political biceps repeatedly, causing Congress and the White House to bend to Israel's corrupt foreign aggression and racist conduct. Christian evangelicals, under the leadership of Zionist zealots like Pastor John Hagee, prophecy teacher Hal Lindsey, psychologist James Dobson, the late Reverend Jerry Falwell, prosperity preacher Joyce Meyer, and TV evangelists Paul Crouch and Pat Robertson, actually believe—and teach—that whoever blesses Israel, God will bless, and whoever curses Israel, God will curse. This teaching, they say, requires Christians—indeed, the U.S.A. itself—to refrain from any and all criticism of Israel and the Jews.

Moreover, they claim that America is obligated by God to bless Israel and its people with scads of money, the blood of our young men and women in uniform, and anything else required or desired by the Jews. Remember, they insist, if America blesses Israel, God will bless America.

But what if America "blesses" Israel and instead of blessing America, an angry, unhappy God sends a multitude of evil America's way? Indeed, if that happens, will it not be the case that the Christian evangelicals have all along been dead wrong about this, that they have misread the Bible? What if—think about it—God decides to punish America for helping the corrupt, criminal, antichrist nation of Israel and heaps misfortune after misfortune on America's head?

Sixteen Ways God is Cursing America for Blessing A Corrupt Israel

Well, the fact is that America is the world's greatest benefactor and blesser of Israel. We bless the Jews in countless ways, and yet, consider the many curses that America is now suffering:

1. America is now suffering a staggering economic collapse; with banks and corporations failing, prices skyrocketing, real estate being dumped, jobs being lost, the whole bit. Our federal deficit and national debt are staggering.

2. America is riddled with narcotics, meth, and other illegal drugs.

3. America is saturated to the hilt with pornography and blasphemy against God.

4. America's political leaders consistently lie, cheat, fornicate, kill and otherwise disgrace our once, great country.

5. The whole world thinks of the United States as a rogue, warmongering nation led at the top by a moron, George W. Bush.

6. The United States is now engaged in two foreign wars simultaneously. Over 4,000 of our young people have been slain and tens of thousands maimed with limbs torn off by roadside bombs in far-off Iraq. Thousands more are casualties of the Afghanistan conflict, a war we are losing to the dreaded Taliban. And our crazy, bamboozled leaders, manipulated by the powerful Jewish lobby (ADL, AIPAC, AJC, etc.) are hankering to plunge headlong into yet a third war—against Iran.

7. America is suffering an illegal alien invasion. Some 20 to 40 million illegals are inside our nonexistent borders—no one really knows the real number, but it's huge. Their care and welfare is costing us tens of billions per year, and the illegal aliens are taking millions of jobs away from unemployed and desperate American workers.

8. Our Christian TV evangelists—men like Joel Osteen, Kenneth Copeland, and Paul Crouch—push positive thinking, feel good theology, and a smorgasboard of other nonsense.

9. Our nation's warped children are showing sick effects of having imbibed too much "gangsta" rap and heavy metal rock music and watching too much sorcery and occult TV cartoons. Many youngsters are on Prozac, Ritalin, and other mind-altering drugs.

10. Our nation's teenagers and even many adults idolize and want to be just like their decadent idols—Madonna, Lindsay Lohan, Paris Hilton, Britney Spears and the rest of the Motley Crew of Hollywood. Oh yes, there's also Whoopi Goldberg, Rosie O'Donnell, and similar cretans—all of whom are adored, admired, and paid fabulously for their vulgar, profane jokes, blasphemous conduct, etc.

Black-uniformed, masked police are becoming commonplace in America. Big Brother's apparatus is bearing down on law-abiding citizens more and more everyday. Is this because America is "blessing" Zionist Israel?

11. Crime waves roar not only in American cities, but in small town America. Rapes, murders, kids killing parents, parents killing kids, car jacking, the list goes on and on. Lock your doors, folks, the bad guys are now breaking down doors to rob suburban dwellers, too.

12. The police in America are corrupt, abusive, and often incompetent. Call 911 in many locales and nothing happens. But get on someone's blacklist and a black-uniformed, masked police Swat Team may just show up at your residence, ready to slay your pets, frighten your kids into tears, and take you and the Missus off to jail. Then, they discover, "Whoops, wrong house."

13. Virtually every merchant, every appliance repairman, every auto mechanic in America has become a shyster, ripping consumers off. Identity theft is commonplace.

America is plagued with debauchery. Witness this lesbian kiss between filthy sex-besotten entertainers Madonna and Britney Spears, on public TV airwaves.

14. Bribes and pay-offs are now S.O.P. for city officials and politicians, from lowly city councilmen to the halls of Congress.

15. America is rapidly becoming a Police State, as our liberty and constitutional rights are stripped from us, and Big Brother's high-tech spy apparatus bears down on citizens more each day.

16. We have just handily elected as President a man, Barack Obama, who endorses both gay marriage and the horrors of partial-birth abortion.

READ THIS LIST OF AMERICA'S WOES OVER ONCE AGAIN, AND TELL ME, IS AMERICA REALLY BEING BLESSED BY GOD FOR ITS GENEROSITY, INFLUENCE AND MONEY GIVEN TO ISRAEL AND THE JEWS?

OR INSTEAD—COME ON, TELL THE TRUTH!—HAS AN ANGRY GOD CURSED AMERICA FOR ITS UNGODLY SUPPORT OF THE CHRIST-HATING, SELFISH, RACIST NATION-STATE OF ISRAEL?

Readers are encouraged to order the inspirational CD or audiotape report by Texe Marrs entitled, *The Called, The Chosen, The Faithful.* This scripturally-based report carefully outlines the promises given Abraham and his seed. Its powerful message exposes the false teaching so common in the evangelical church today declaring that we must always favor and bless Israel and the Jews. Discover what the Bible really says and what it means for your future and that of America.

True Christian Believers Not Welcome in Most Churches Today

The Christian Establishment—Greedy, Ignorant, Apostate

"And have no fellowship with the unfruitful works of darkness, but rather reprove them."

—*Ephesians 5:11*

The Christian Establishment is asleep, ignorant, apostate and dead. However, the Christian Church is awake, aware, holy, and alive. There, I've said it, and I meant every word of it. If you are a member of one of the thousands of churches that are part and parcel of the Christian Establishment, I warn you: Get out now...Leave "Sodom and Egypt" far behind and enter the light of true Christianity. Do it today!

It's been over 20 years now that Wanda and I went into Christian ministry full-time, and in these two decades I have, regrettably, become a heart-sickened authority on pastors, ministers, "reverends," theologians and other "priests" of the devil who pretend to be Christian. Tragically, of the hundreds and hundreds of these would-be pillars of the Christian world that I have encountered in my labors, I can probably count on my ten fingers the number of godly men and women I have met in the ranks of today's vast majority of foul-minded, grotesque clergy.

On the other hand, I have been pleased and honored to meet and profit spiritually from fellowship with untold numbers of little known, unheralded, and, often, much despised *true Christian believers*. To my amazement, I have found that rarely are true Christians ordained pastors or theologians. True Christians are never invited to speak at the pulpit of the Establishment churches. *The 700 Club* and *TBN* would not dare to have a true, godly man or woman guest on their milk-toast, silly, hoaxter TV programs.

"You're too old-fashioned"

Almost every day *Power of Prophecy* hears from sincere, faithful, Bible-believing Christians who have been told by new-style pastors that they are no longer welcome at their churches. "You're too old-fashioned," they're told, "too set in your ways."

Anyone who refuses to go along with hip-hop and rock music, who still believes in such a thing as sin or concepts like judgement, heaven, and hell, who sticks with the King James Version, who complains about the modern "God wants you to be rich" dogma, or believes Jesus is the only way to salvation is in jeopardy of being told to "hit the road, you are not our kind of Christian."

What we have today are legions of devilish, politically correct, Establishment pastors and leaders who don't care a plug nickel for Bible truth. These are the goats that Jesus divides from the sheep.

Am I being too hard on these poor, stupid, 21st century so-called "Christian" leaders? No way! These big name liars and pretenders are workers of darkness, masquerading angels of light, ministers of unrighteousness, and we owe them nothing but contempt. They are walking side-by-side with their Master, Satan, and millions of souls are perishing because of their greedy, wicked conduct and stupidity. Why should you and I honor the obedient servants of *Abaddon* and *Apollyon (Revelation 9:11)*.

"New Age? What is that?"

Let me, dear friends, give you just a few examples of the slothful, unseemly, willful ignorance of such men. Several years ago I was invited to dinner at the home of a prominent Austin, Texas physician and his wife, both of whom are Christians. At that dinner was their pastor, a man who led a large evangelical congregation of a Bible Church located in Westlake Hills, one of Austin's most affluent and ritzy suburbs. This pastor had previously been Professor of Theology at Dallas Theological Seminary, an acclaimed training ground for evangelicals and especially for Zionist Judaizer types.

Introduced to this pastor as an author, he asked me what type of books I wrote. "I expose the New Age Movement," I answered.

"New Age? What is that,?" he responded, a puzzled look on his face. Seeking to avoid embarrassing this man, I simply suggested to him, he might find *New Age Lies to Women*, a book by my wife, Wanda, of great interest, particularly since he had taught the Old Testament at Dallas Theological Seminary. The book, I assured him, examines and discusses the unfortunate revival in America of the ancient worship of the Great Goddess.

Seeing once again a bewildered frown on the man's face, I decided once again to try and help him out of his difficulty. I said, "You know, Pastor, remember the goddess, the 'Queen of Heaven' mentioned by the prophet Jeremiah, where the women of Israel angered God by baking cakes as offerings to her, right in the temple." "And of course," I added, "there is the Apostle Paul's controversy over Diana, the great goddess of the Ephesians, as discussed in the book of *Acts*."

"I never heard of those things," the pastor said, "are you sure you are not making this up?"

> *The children gather wood, and the fathers kindle the fire, and the women knead their dough, to make cakes to the queen of heaven, and to pour out drink offerings unto other gods, that they may provoke me to anger.*
>
> *—Jeremiah 7:18*

Friends, I later found out that at that very time, this apostate minister was introducing *"Jewish dance"* into church ritual, and the congregation at his Church was eating it up! And many more abominations were going on in his ecumenical, worldly Church.

A little later, I met up with yet another "learned," would be Christian teacher, a well-known Southern Baptist Pastor from Roswell, Georgia. This guy went on to become the President of the Southern Baptist Convention. He, too, said he didn't know what I was talking about. All this fellow seemed to know about the Christian faith could be found inside the covers of the latest Norman Vincent Peale or Robert Schuller book.

Reading the Bible More Important than Degrees

I can tell you this...I would trust a man or woman with a 3rd grade education who actually reads his or her King James Bible *far more* than I would trust these ignorant men who have PhD, DD, and all the other stupid degree acronyms behind their names and yet have never once read their Holy Bible in its entirety.

In fact, I can't seem to find but a very few pastors today who even believe in the Holy Bible any more! They almost universally claim the Scriptures have errors and mistakes that they and their crummy theologian pals need to fix! I asked one of these lukewarm pastors who called in to complain about me on a talk show in Phoenix, Arizona, which Bible did his professors at his seminary teach from. His answer was: *"None! We never read and studied the Bible. We used books written by learned men; the scholarly."*

> *I know thy works: behold, I have set before thee an open door, and no man can shut it: for thou hast a little strength, and hast kept my word, and hast not denied my name.*
> *—Revelation 3:8*

"Well," I retorted, "there's your problem. You claim to be a minister and preacher of God, and you don't even know God's Word. You only know the words of men!"

Ghostwritten Sermons for Ignorant Men

I have also discovered over the years that not one pastor in a thousand actually prepares his own weekly sermon. They're ghostwritten for him, you see, by unseen and unknown teachers. Apostate publishers put out (sell!) and distribute hundreds of canned, pre-printed "sermons" for dumbed-down pastors. Of course don't ask the apostate pastors who spout all this drivel what it means. They are just "readers"—ignorant, lazy, serpent-following plagiarists of material written and published by other stupid men who also don't read the Scriptures for themselves.

Of course, at most charismatic, misnamed "Full Gospel" churches today, the pastors don't even bother to use the canned, pre-printed sermons. They just come to the pulpit unprepared and depend on the unholy, disorderly confusion and chaos of dozens of people pretending to be super-holy by "speaking in other tongues" all at the same time (a gross violation of the Apostle Paul's admonition in *I Corinthians 14*.) Then the incompetent and slothful pastors pitch-out 15 or 20 minutes of occult psychobabble nonsense about positive confessions and prosperity thinking. They mix in a clamorous, windy bag of jived-up, sensuous rock music and the people then leave the church all emotionally hyped up, imagining they really met God that day. Unbelievable!—also sad and wicked.

> *The faithful people I like to call "The Little People"—men and women who pray and humble themselves before God and who proclaim the power and perfection of His Word—are still out there.*

There is a True Christian Church

But wait! In the midst of all this apostasy, even as the "Congregations of the Dead" continue to spin out the devil's foolishness, there remains a true Christian Church. The wicked and their leaders are greater in number, and the world holds its filthy-lucre pastors in higher esteem. But the faithful people I like to call "The Little People"—men and women who pray and humble themselves before God and who proclaim the power and perfection of His Word—are still out there.

True, the people of the real and authentic Christian Church are hated and despised by the pastors of the bigger "Christian Establishment" churches. Usually, true Christian believers don't even have a church home; at least not a church they go to labeled Baptist, Methodist, Episcopal, Seventh Day Adventist, Lutheran, or Assembly of God. They're not welcome at these places. But then, they do not desire to enter these big and rich sanctuaries of hell!

Regardless of the fall and seduction of the "Christian" establishment, there remains a true and authentic Christian Church made up of faithful men and women.

Instead, they recall and cherish the precious words of Jesus: *"Where two or three are gathered together in my name, there am I in the midst of them."*

Just as vital, the true Christian does not need a popular group of Christian Establishment fun and celebration entertainers, a showman in the pulpit, or an imposing Cathedral of brick or glass and stone. The true Christian has Jesus Christ living in his or her heart. He is drawn nigh to Zion by God's miraculous love. He or she is an overcomer. True Christians know what they are and who He is! They also know who the fakers and pretenders are and are gifted with discernment to understand and appreciate the power of the "mystery of godliness." That's why they don't confuse big numbers and dollars with the spiritual things of God.

Don't be Loved to Death

Today, the world loves it own, and you will be much loved if you are an active member of Sodom and Egypt's big-time tent, the Christian Establishment. Just remember, Satan's Church will love you all right. *It and its people will love a wicked person right to his death.* But Jesus and His Christian Church, though they have no money to give you, no fame and sensual delights to offer, *will love you to life.*

That, dear friends, is the clear choice every person today must make: the choice between the establishment's sure death or Christ's guarantee of eternal life. Have you made your decision yet? Do so quickly. Time may run out very, very soon.

"Come out of her my people, that ye be not partakers of her sins, and that ye receive not of her plagues. For her sins have reached unto heaven and God hath remembered her iniquities." (Revelation 18: 4-5)

Do Wealthy Satanic Jews Secretly Control the Pope and the TV Evangelists?

Smooth Tongues for a Rough Beast

"Now go, write it...that this is a rebellious people, lying children, children that will not hear the law of the Lord: Which say to...the prophets, prophesy not unto us right things, speak unto us smooth things, prophesy deceits..."
—*Isaiah 30:8-10*

It was famous Irish writer William Butler Yeats who wrote the famous, lyrical poem, *The Second Coming*, depicting a rough Beast slouching toward Bethlehem. Today, we find mounting evidence of this horrible, savage, prophetic Beast, slowly and deliberately bypassing Bethlehem and making his way straight toward the Great City, Jerusalem (also known spiritually as "Sodom and Egypt"—see *Revelation 11:8*). Along the way, as he ravenously gobbles up and consumes men's souls, the religious elite are cheering him on, encouraging him and urging the people of the world to follow after and even to love the Beast.

These spiritual con-artists and religious hypesters speak swelling words of deceit which betray their true intentions and gloss over their dark, lying, sorcerous hearts. They are best described by their apostate behavior as SMOOTH TONGUES FOR A ROUGH BEAST. And the gullible masses whom they deceive want it that way! As Isaiah prophesied, the rebellious multitudes of the church-goers now cry out and demand to their religious leaders, *"Speak unto us smooth things, prophesy deceits"* to us.

I have recorded two hours of *Power of Prophecy* radio programs exposing the "Christian" religious elite and their unseemly works and also have a controversial and provocative video exposing this *tower of infamy.*

Tares Among Us

It is a startling fulfillment of Bible prophecy that they do so, for these men are the tares who have grown up among us. Ripe and rich they appear to be; but, beware of the spiritual "nourishment" which these corrupt men promise to feed you with.

One after another, these famous "Christian" teachers prostitute themselves to the Beast. They are helping him to build his earthly kingdom. They must know what they are doing because they do it so well, so convincingly.

They continually utter *lukewarm* words that make the world's citizenry feel warm, fuzzy and good about themselves. Many of these apostates assure Jews, Hindus, even African tribal witchdoctors and voodoo priests that all is well—because all religions have the very same "Father" in heaven. They profess that God loves all religionists equally—Hindu, Moslem, Jew, etc.—and shall save them all, even though many may blaspheme, mock and reject Jesus.

"What a wondrous, compassionate, and nonjudgmental god we all serve," they reassure their blasphemous, idolatrous allies.

One Group They Despise

Frankly, there is only one tiny group of religious people that these *Smooth Tongues* despise. Oh, how they detest the Christian fundamentalists, particularly we who are the troublemaking, "King James Only" believers. They spit with venom in our direction, declaring that there must be a special place in Hell for us reserved by God. Yes, the *Smooth Tongues* brigade hates true Christian Bible-believers with a purple passion. To kill the "outmoded and inflexible" Christian Bible-believers, some suggest, might even be *"doing God service."*

A Global Community of Faith?

The *Smooth Tongues* priesthood says that God has today created a global "Community of Faith," made up of Hindus, Buddhists, Masons, witches, feminists, gays, Jews, and most Christians (as long as they're not old-fashioned, "obsolete" Bible believers). Fundamentalist Moslems are also sometimes hated, because, like true Christians, Moslems teach there is only one God, a doctrine that is anathema to the *Smooth Tongues.*

Billy Graham, Robert Schuller and their mentor, the Pope of Rome, cleverly maintain that the way to salvation is not narrow, but very, very broad indeed. The religionists of the Community of Faith, says the Smooth Tongues priesthood, are diverse in their views, non-doctrinal in their teachings, and nonjudgmental in their attitudes toward others.

The Jews Exalted by the Smooth Tongues Priesthood

But while all faiths, except fundamentalist Christians and Moslems, are claimed to be of equal value, one group, as in George Orwell's *Animal Farm,* is set apart as special. One group is *First Among Equals.* Yes, one particular group is recognized as superior, as *more* spiritual, *more* worthy, *more* Chosen. That would, of course, be the Jews, the religionists who once upon a time cruelly crucified the Lord Jesus and even today reject His teachings.

The Jews, though unrepentant, are forgiven all their evil deeds. The *Smooth Tongues* teachers contend that the Jews are exempt from the requirements laid down by the Apostles as prerequisites for salvation. The collective sins of Jews are said to be automatically blotted out the moment they are committed. Eternally blessed, eternally guiltless, and eternally Chosen—that, say the men of the *Smooth Tongues* priesthood, describes the Jews.

And it doesn't matter, either, whether one is an atheist Jew, an agnostic Jew, a satanist Jew, or an Orthodox Jew. A Jew, by definition, even if his bloodline is Khazar or African or Hispanic or Chinese, is considered to be a blessed Jew for all eternity! Though he may curse Jesus with the foulest and most profane language and threaten to pull God down off his throne and throttle him with a bloody club, a Jew is ...well, Jews are Jews: a superior breed, a god-race, destined to rule this planet. The *Smooth Tongue* brigade will ever shout their praises and lift the Golden Cup in their honor.

A Conspiracy of the High Priests and Wealthy Jews?

In my audiotape exposé *(Smooth Tongues for a Rough Beast,* 2 audiotape or CD set) I reveal the curious connections between wealthy Jewish Illuminati and the top celebrity "Christian" leaders and organizations. Could it be that the Illuminati planned, funded, and set up most of these famous-name preachers and ministries? Do powerful Jews covertly guide and dictate what men like Billy Graham, Paul Crouch, Pat Robertson, James Dobson, Chuck Colson, Oral Roberts, Jerry Falwell,

Texe Marrs' audiotape set, *Smooth Tongues for a Rough Beast*, reveals hidden connections behind the founding of the world's top Christian television networks. Did Illuminist Jewish billionaires secretly set up these big-name TV ministries to promote the corrupt Zionist global agenda? (Note Pat Robertson's Masonic hand signal.)

Pope John Paul II, and Michael Evans say and do?

For example, I reveal that Pat Robertson, (CBN Network) son of an Illuminist father, a U.S. Senator in charge of the Senate's banking and currency committee, was given his initial TV station by none other than CNN founder Ted Turner. Robertson, in turn, gave Jim and Tammy Faye Bakker (PTL Network) their start, and the Bakkers traveled to California and helped Paul and Jan Crouch, of TBN Network get their organization started and going strong. Were Jewish money men behind the establishment of the world's three largest Christian TV networks?

Amazingly, it turned out that when the Bakker sex scandal broke and PTL Network became embroiled in financial difficulty, unknown to all was that an *Orthodox Jewish billionaire from Canada really owned the whole apparatus of PTL, including all its land, buildings, and equipment.* This eye-opening, secret revelation of the Jewish Money Power behind the scenes at the PTL Network came out in federal court.

> *"I consult Rabbi Tannenbaum by phone each and every day for spiritual guidance,"*
>
> *—Billy Graham*

Astonishing, too, is that Billy Graham, perhaps inadvertently, once confided to Larry King, (CNN's *The Larry King Show*) that his closest "spiritual advisor" is Jewish Rabbi Tannenbaum of New York City. *"I consult Rabbi Tannenbaum by phone each and every day for spiritual guidance,"* said Graham.

In my shocking video, *Is the Pope Catholic?,* I show Pope John Paul II speaking at Rome's largest synagogue. His biographers report that the first person that visited John Paul II in his private Vatican apartment immediately after his election to the papacy was a Jewish "friend."

Choosing Between God and Mammon

The hidden Jewish money connection to the celebrity preachers and televangelists is a shock to many, but there's more. When we speak of the *Smooth Tongues* set, we should not forget to mention the *Name It and Claim It*, prosperity gospel preachers. They, too, contribute to the sustenance of the Beast on his journey toward Jerusalem.

Jesus told the Jews they cannot serve two masters. They must choose between God and

Mammon. Mammon is riches. The Jews did, in fact, choose between God and riches. With a little help from their Roman accomplices, the Jews crucified their Master and Messiah, the Son of God, on a crude, wooden cross. Ever since that day, some 2,000 years ago, the vast majority of Jews have warmly embraced Mammon. Even the names of many Jews today are cold testimony to the choice the Jews have made over the centuries: Gold, Goldstein, Goldberg, Ruby, Rubenstein ("ruby stone"), Stein ("stone," as in precious gem), Diamond, Silver, Silverstein, Silversmith, Copperstone, etc., Mammon names all. Even the word "Jewel" comes from the Jewish race, literally meaning the "god of the Jews," or "Jew—El."

Kenneth Copeland, T.D. Jakes, Paul Crouch, John Avanzini, Joyce Meyer, and a score of other smooth-tongued Gentile evangelists have joined the Jews in the pursuit of Mammon. I document this in my video, *The Blind and the Dead.*

Off to See the Wizard

These jaded, last days preachers of money and greed are merrily and obliviously traveling down that Mammon-strewn yellow-brick road, wickedly acting as heralds of the Beast who is pulling up alongside them.

The Billy Grahams, John Hagees, Robert Schullers, Kenneth Copelands, Pat Robertsons, and all the others, figuratively, are also off to see the Wizard. Truly, Toto, the Christian establishment is "not in Kansas anymore."

Once upon a time the leaders of the Christian faith were dangerous threats to Satan's kingdom. They followed the Lamb and refused to budge off that narrow way. They were watchmen, awakened men and women alert and alive with the Spirit of Truth held fast to their breast. These faithful servants ceaselessly fought the Adversary, and he was unable to proceed even one inch toward his endtimes destination, Jerusalem.

Dumb Dogs, Greedy Dogs

Now, the faithful are few. The tares are choking out the wheat. Look around, see, and weep. The mighty watchmen have fallen asleep. Their tongues are smooth; their sentences dark; their eyelids are slowly closing. The future they cannot see, because they are blind and greedy. Slothful servants about to be overtaken by robbers, they now, very quietly, yet ignorantly, await the destruction which surely is at hand.

> *"His watchmen are blind: they are all ignorant, they are all dumb dogs, they cannot bark; sleeping, lying down, loving to slumber.*
>
> *Yea, they are greedy dogs which can never have enough, and they are shepherds that cannot understand: they all look to their own way, every one for his gain.*
>
> *Come ye, say they, I will fetch wine, and we will fill ourselves with strong drink; and tomorrow shall be as this day, and much more abundant...*
>
> *But the wicked are like the troubled sea, when it cannot rest, whose waters cast up mire and dirt. There is no peace, saith my God, to the wicked."*
>
> *—Isaiah 56:10-12, 57:20-21*

The Illuminati, Secret Societies, Reverend Moon, and the Buying and Selling of Televangelists and Other Famous-Name Christian Leaders

Tower of Infamy

Engineered by the Illuminati and led behind the scenes by the initiates of secret societies, a great religious and social movement is sweeping America. Little understood as yet, even by sincere Christians, this movement threatens to change our world in uncommonly evil ways. It is a movement authored by Satan and executed—that is, put into practice—by his devils, as well as their human counterparts.

Already, this radically new religious and social movement has caused volcanic-like eruptions in our daily activities. It has engineered a revolution in man's way of thinking about God and about things of the spirit.

Babylon Reborn

Oddly enough, the new movement, upon close examination, is found to be not so new after all. Indeed, its goals and manifestations can be traced all the way back to ancient Babylon. There, on the banks of the once mighty Euphrates River, Nimrod, the King of Babylon, and his seductive Queen, Semiramis, oversaw the building of a huge and unholy architectural monstrosity, the Tower of Babel. Their aim: Establish a One World Order and unite all peoples in the worship of Lucifer, the solar deity recognized by the ancients under such names as Baal, Marduk, and Nebo.

Today, our planet is experiencing a great revival of the government and worship of Nimrod's Babylon. This was prophesied to occur *(Revelation 17 & 18)*. Now that time is come, and once again, man is building yet another towering edifice of evil, which I call the *Tower of Infamy*. However, this time the Tower has planet-wide underpinnings and is more spiritual than it is bricks and mortar.

In the realm of religion, we see this *Tower of Infamy* go skyward in all its vainglory. America is the global leader in the construction of this massive spiritual monument dedicated to supreme wickedness. The Christian Church, as we once knew it, is dead. Its ghostly bones creak and moan. Its voice is as the voice of ghosts and spirits in chains, screaming from their captivity down in some deep and dark abyss.

Tower of Infamy Built by Liars and Deceivers

At such a cardinal time in human history, we find that the vast majority of men and women who claim to be "Christian" are, in fact, liars and deceivers. They deceive themselves first and then go forth deceiving others. This cycle of deception has continued geometrically until the multitudes have, by now, been brought into *The Lie*.

Look around and what do you find? Pastors and church leaders have sunken to new levels of depravity. Homosexuality and lesbianism are commonplace, witchcraft is rampant, black magic is in vogue, and the sulfurous smell of demons permeates the sanctuaries of churches and cathedrals.

Wiccan (witch) Tom Davis came to a Methodist church in Austin, Texas, as part of a "pulpit swap."

The true Word of God, the King James Version, is despised while a thousand newer versions confuse and disorient readers and leave them clueless as to Christ's gospel and doctrines.

At Trinity United Methodist Church in Austin, Texas, recently, the congregation welcomed into its pulpit, Tom Davis, a Wiccan priest of the Covenant of the Goddess. It was part of a city-wide project called "pulpit swap" in which Native Indian shamans, Buddhist priests, witches, Hindu gurus, and Islamic muftis led Christian congregations in various pagan rituals and ceremonies.

"All are welcome here," said Trinity member Linda Eldredge, *"Everybody's got something to offer."*

Meanwhile, in the nation of Portugal, inside a Catholic Chapel dedicated to Mother Mary who is alleged to visit in apparition at nearby Fatima, the Catholic Bishop was recently given the mark of Shiva in his forehead by a Hindu guru.

Over in Great Britain, the Archbishop of Canterbury, Dr. Rowan Williams, head of the Church of England, issued a declaration that Muslims can go to heaven even though they deny Christ. Dr. Williams, an initiate of the ancient Druidic witchcraft order as well as an Anglican "Christian" priest, chastened Christians for being stubborn in opposing homosexuality. He angrily charged that those who are against the gay lifestyle *"lack grace."*

In Edinburgh, Scotland, top Christian church leaders conducted a "celebration of all the world's religions." Participants passed a resolution that a permanent World Parliament of Religions be set up to work with the United Nations to bring all spiritualities together as one.

Benjamin Crème, the founder of Share International and forerunner to the shadowy Lord Maitreya, the New Age Christ who waits in the wings to emerge and preside over all the world's spiritualities, says a *"Day of Declaration"* is soon approaching. This, he says, will be a glorious day when all the peoples of the planet will simultaneously view Lord Maitreya and miraculously recognize him *enmasse* as their benefactor and Messiah.

Dr. Rowan Williams, Archbishop and head of the Church of England, says that Moslems will go to heaven without Jesus. Williams is a practicing Druid witch.

"May I have this dance?"

The depth of the Apostasy was clearly demonstrated at an Atlanta, Georgia, convention teeming with tens of thousands of *"Promise Keepers."* On the platform of a stadium packed with Christian men excited and shouting and celebrating in unison, Jack Hayford, TBN personality and Pastor of California's Church on the Way, announced that he had heard directly from God. God wants us all to dance for him, said Hayford, just as the tribal witchdoctors dance in Africa to the beat of drums.

The Pastor then began to bounce and dash about the stage, leading the assembled throng of Christian ministers and layman in a voodoo-like dance. Hayford told the cheering crowd that he had heard the very voice of God speaking to him, asking the charismatic preacher, *"May I have this dance?"*

Reverend Moon is Crowned Messiah and Savior of Earth

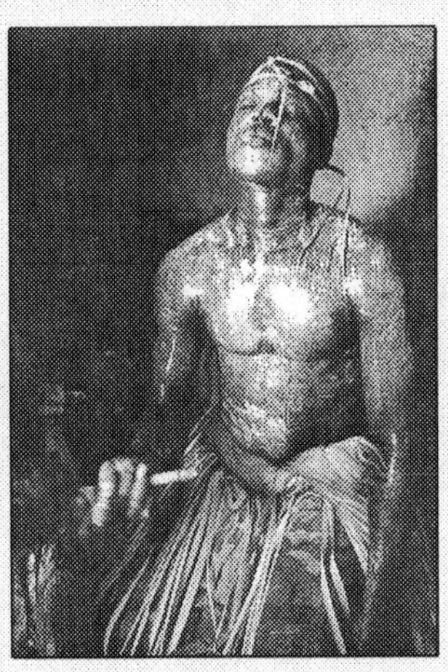

Pastor Jack Hayford, a popular charismatic teacher, led tens of thousands of Promise Keepers in an African witchdoctor tribal dance.

At the Capitol building, the seat of Congress in Washington, D.C. a few months ago, scores of Christian leaders as well as several U.S. Senators and Representatives met for a very special occasion. It was an extravaganza like no other—the victorious crowning of the Messiah, Reverend Sun Myung Moon. Southern Baptist leaders were on hand, as were TBN President Paul Crouch, Reverend Jerry Falwell, Reverend Robert Schuller, Kenneth Copeland, Pat Boone, and many others.

In the ceremony, Congressman Danny Davis (D-Illinois), wearing white gloves, brought forth the royal diadem, the ornate crown, on a white velvet pillow. After his coronation, the Korean cult leader Moon informed Crouch, Falwell, Schuller, Boone and the others that whereas Jesus failed on his mission to earth, he, Reverend Moon, had not. Moon also crowed the good news that, thanks to Moon's teaching in the spiritual dimensions, both Stalin and Hitler had become rehabilitated and renewed.

Reverend Sun Myung Moon claims Jesus failed in His mission on earth.

A New Doctrine of Wideness

Not to be outdone in helping to construct the higher reaches of the fast-rising *Tower of Infamy*, Bishop Carlton Pearson, a friend of Oral Roberts and Paul Crouch who oversees a flock of over 5,000 at Oklahoma's Higher Dimensions Church, announced a new doctrine of Christ. Christ's mercy is wider than Christians have traditionally thought, Pearson told his church and his national radio and TV audience. Indeed, Pearson declared that Christ's mercy is so wide that men and women of any and all religions, from Hindus and Jews to Buddhists and Moslems, were equally loved and accepted *as they are* by Jesus. All religious people qualify for heaven, said the Pastor, and we must stop trying to change and convert them. Let a Hindu be a good Hindu, a Buddhist a good Buddhist etc.

Pearson invited homosexuals as well as the foreign religionists to join his church and boldly said that homosexuals, too, met Jesus' criteria for salvation.

Reverend Carlton Pearson also publicly thanked the wealthy Hindu businessman from Oklahoma who has joined his Christian Church while remaining true to Hindu gods and goddesses. The Hindu businessman is now financially supporting Pearson's work by paying for his national radio show.

A New Spiritual Day

Reverend Carlton Pearson, popular speaker on TBN network and pastor of the 5,000 member Higher Dimensions Church in Oklahoma, teaches that Hindus, Jews, Moslems, and all religious people qualify for heaven.

In an earlier era, when Christians really believed in God's Word and were indwelt by the Holy Ghost, reprobates and pretenders like Pearson, Crouch, Copeland, Falwell, and Moon would have been thrown out on their ears, excommunicated, disgraced, and called upon to repent...or burn. Not so today. It's a new spiritual day, you see, the age of satanic compromise, and the Tower of Infamy must be built.

And so, legions of "Christian" men and women across the globe, from Rome to London, Montreal, Seattle, and Houston busily go about gathering up the spiritual equivalent of bricks and mortar. Some bend over strange plans and mysterious designs furnished them by the Great Architect, the One whom they all secretly adore and privately fear.

They must get on with their Master's business. He is called Lucifer, and he has ordained them precisely for this special mission and cause—the building of the grandest spiritual colossus in the annals of human history—the *Tower of Infamy*.

Yes, the Master of their otherworld lodge, the solar deity, calls them. Some, in ignorance, serve him not recognizing his infernal nature, thinking they do God service. Like the loyal obedient dog on the old RCA Victor logo, when Lucifer beckons, his servants quickly bow and curtsy. They jerkily, but surely, move in unison.

Like their Master, Lucifer, the conspirators must work while there is still night. Somehow, intuitively, they all know that their time is short, and that a horrible, unavoidable destiny awaits them just beyond the colorful but fading New Age rainbow.

Churches and Pastors Gone Wild!

"But these, as natural brute beasts, made to be taken and destroyed, speak evil of the things they understand not; and shall utterly perish in their own corruption; And shall receive the reward of unrighteousness..."

—*II Peter 2:12-13*

Clownish, disgusting, nuts, insane, goofy, sick, sad, idiotic—these are just a few of the adjectives we can use to describe what passes today for the "Christian Establishment." Now notice, I didn't say the "Christian Church." We are talking about a wholly different animal here. We're talking about the huge majority of churches, congregations, ministers, and pastors in America, composed of men and women filled with devils, yet pretending to be sanctimonious and holy. Mouthing the name of Jesus while scheming to do evil deeds. The Bible calls those reprobates "brute beasts." I call them "wild men."

In my exposé videos, *The Blind and the Dead, Tower of Infamy*, and others, I give you a mind-boggling look at some of the antics of the wacky, stupid, and outrageous pastors and evangelists who are leaders of this apostate "Christian Establishment."

These wicked leaders are being hero-worshipped by the average, pew-sitting "Christian." Yet, in truth, scripturally they are undertakers, ministering in vain to the Congregation of the Dead.

For example, there's faith healer Benny Hinn, who is pictured in my video, *The Blind and the Dead*, passing around a hashish pipe. Meanwhile, Hinn's wife is seen preaching to a throng in a crowded auditorium, advising the folks that what they need is a "Holy Ghost enema." (I'm not making this up—you'll actually see all this on my video, *The Blind and the Dead*).

Hush Money and Witchdoctor Dancing

I have informed you in the past about Paul Crouch, wild man and founder of TBN, the world's largest Christian television network, how Crouch gave $425,000 to a black homosexual man he had a sexual affair with, hush money to shut him up. And there is Jack Hayford, who told 60,000 "Christian" men at a massive Promise Keepers rally that God had just whispered in his ear, *"May I have this dance?"* Whereupon, Hayford, a President Bush "spiritual advisor" and authentic wild man, broke out into an African tribal witchdoctor dance.

Now, did the audience all vomit, leave their seats, and depart this unseemly idiotic behavior? No, not at all. Instead, they roared their approval. Crazies all.

At any given time you can take a look across the bow of today's Christian establishment and you'll see a vast sea of unfathomable, bizarre conduct. Wild men and women everywhere, doing their thing, blaspheming God and His Word, partying, frolicking, laughing like hyenas, wild as loons. God must surely be heartsick at what he is seeing.

On CBN's *The 700 Club*, we have evangelist and wanna-be politician Pat Robertson giving the *El Diablo* hand sign and calling publicly for his pal, President Bush, and the federal government to go down to Venezuela and assassinate that country's democratically elected President, Hugo Chavez. Just like Jesus would do, right?

Robertson is a wild man and he's gone wild. So has his viewing audience.

A Condom to Cover the Virgin Mary

Recently, *America*, a popular Catholic magazine published by the Jesuit Order of the Vatican, ran an advertisement for a miniature statue of the Virgin Mary, covered over by a rubber condom! The statuette also showed Mary standing atop a serpent. "I thought the ad was a little odd," explains Reverend James Martin, the magazine's associate editor, "but we accept a lot of strange ads."

Speaking of strange, what about the address given by Billy Graham at Harvard in which he told the assembled students that, "The way to Jesus is expressed by tolerance of other religions." Graham also lauded the Dalai Lama, the Tibetan Buddhist god-man, for being a role model of holiness and peace.

Billy Graham is really a wild man, but instead of wearing animal skins and eating locusts, he wears an expensive, tailor-made suit and is transported around the world in a fleet of executive jets. The media love to depict Graham as a honest, poor, struggling preacher, but, in fact, he spends time in fancy condos in Mexico City and Tokyo, and his books are all ghostwritten for him. Even Graham's autobiography was ghostwritten for him. And one of his chief ghostwriters just happens to be Mel White, a homosexual activist. Now that really is wild! (See *The Scandal of Christian Ghostwriting*, 60-min. exposé audiotape by Texe Marrs, order by phoning toll free 800-234-9673).

Jesus A Marijuana User

Equally wild today are all those alleged "Bible scholars." One of these maniacs recently came up with a novel idea. Dr. Carl Ruck, professor at Boston University, says he believes that Jesus was a regular user of cannabis, or marijuana. Writing in *High Times* magazine, researcher Chris Bennett agrees. Bennet insists that the oils used by Jesus and the disciples to anoint people were "literally drenched" in cannabis, as it can be absorbed through the skin.

Wild men, to be sure, with wild, totally fabricated notions.

But what of Oprah Winfrey, reigning TV talk show queen, whom women have put on a lofty pedestal akin to royalty? Asked about her personal belief in God, Oprah responded:

> "I believe in the FORCE. I call it God. Actually there are many diverse paths leading to what you call God...There couldn't possibly be only one way."

The congregation at St. John's Episcopal Church in Denver, Colorado, would no doubt applaud Oprah's wild New Age theology. That church has just hired a Moslem Imam (clergyman) on their staff. "We hope this sends a message to the community that we don't look upon people of other religions as targets for conversion to Christianity," explained a church spokesman.

Southern Baptist President Quotes Hindu Guru

Along these same lines, we have Ed Young, a wild and crazy guy who is pastor of one of the largest Southern Baptist churches in America, Second Baptist Church, in Houston. Asked to speak to an interfaith group of Moslem imams, Mormon big-wigs, Buddhist monks, Catholic priests, and

Christian clergy last August (*Christianity Today*, Nov. 2005, p.10), Young enthusiastically quoted the late Hindu guru Mahatma Gandhi as once stating, *"You must be the change that you seek in the world."*

Above: **Oprah, most beloved of TV queens, says God is a "FORCE" and is for all religions.**

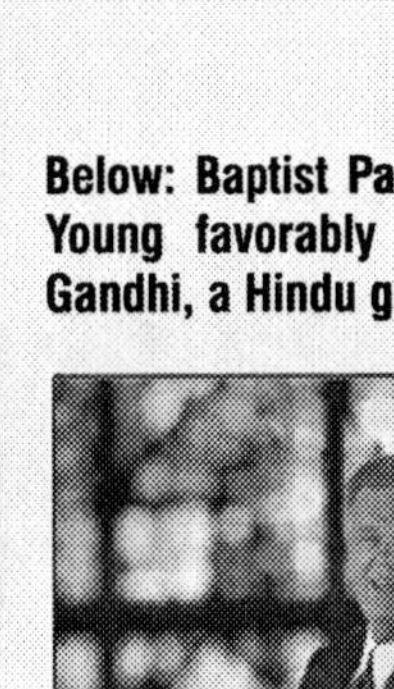

Below: Baptist Pastor Ed Young favorably quotes Gandhi, a Hindu guru.

Impressive, huh? Young, formerly President (yes, the President!) of the entire Southern Baptist Convention, comprising all its alleged 15 million members, seems to have totally forgotten *John 3:16,* and the verses about true change being brought about only by salvation through Jesus Christ.

Commenting on, indeed praising, Young's spiritual adoration of a dead Hindu guru's teachings, Timothy Morgan, editor of *Christianity Today*, gushingly wrote, "A different day is dawning."

Bishop Carlton Pearson, Pastor of a 5,000 member strong church in Tulsa, is evidently part of that different day that is dawning. Pearson now accepts money and sponsorship from wealthy Hindu businessmen for his national radio program. Pearson invites Hindus, Buddhists, Jews, and others to be members of his church. And they can even bring their many gods and goddesses in the door with them. God loves and accepts all gods and religions, Pearson insists, all the while professing he's a bonafide "Christian" Pastor and Bishop.

Elvis & Rock 'n' Roll Churches

At Promiseland Church in Austin, there is rocking in the pews. On Sunday, Pastor Randy Phillips has rock and roll bands bleating out the words and beating on the drums and guitars. "Christian rock 'n' roll moves people," brag members of the large and popular Pentecostal Church.

Not to be outdone, Anglican priest, the Reverend Dorian Baxter, prances about the platform at his church disguised as "ELVIS PRIEST-LEY." Baxter is an Elvis impersonator who sheds his robe and turns on the charisma to woo his congregation. News reports say that, "his wild, sexy performances are driving audiences crazy."

"I love his hip movements," says fan Maggie Hampton, who once tried to climb onstage. "He really rocks. And I just want to dance with him."

"Yes, people are really going berserk for me," says the wild and wooly preacher, Mr. Baxter. "But I do it all for Christ. It's my calling."

Magic, Weight Lifting, and Live Fish Swallowing

While they are waiting for the rock 'n' roll band to warm up, at many churches, congregations can now be entertained by "Christian" magicians and weight lifters. In Florence, Alabama, at the First Assembly of God, the youth minister has been presenting a program called Fear Factor in which youths swallow live fish and lay in a coffin. "Through this ministry, kids are surrendering their lives

Left: Reverend Dorian Baxter is a sexy Elvis impersonator who wows the women in his congregation.

Right: Pastor Kyle Lake, sitting at left, with two associate Pastors, was electrocuted after praying, *"God, surprise me."*

to Jesus and developing a deeper relationship to Jesus," notes youth minister Anthony Martin. Sure they are.

A Shocking Experience

Swallowing live fish and lying in coffins as a new style of "worship" is surprising to those of us who still believe God should be reverenced and honored in dignity. But none of those things are as surprising as what happened last October 30 at the University Baptist Church in Waco, Texas. There, Pastor Kyle Lake, known for his New Age-oriented sermonettes, gave one that day on the subject of living well. He assured the church that they should "Live, and live well. Breathe. Be present. Be now."

"If you are eating and laughing at the same time," Pastor Kyle told his 800-member congregation, "then you might as well laugh until you puke…"

After this brief, but surely inspirational, little sermon, Pastor Lake led the Baptist congregation in an unusual prayer that went this way: *"Surprise me, God."* He then stepped into the baptismal tub to prepare to baptize a candidate when, *zapp!!!* He was electrocuted. Apparently, an electrical wiring malfunction occurred and a deadly voltage rampaged his body. The surprised pastor was pronounced dead by an EMS squad that rushed to the scene.

God does work in mysterious ways, does he not? And truly, he answers prayers. He certainly was prompt in responding to Pastor Kyle's prayers!

Now, would God really wield out instant death to a satan-serving, mocking unbeliever who's pretending to be holy? Perhaps the skeptic might, with wisdom, consider the late Ananias and his wife, Sapphira, and what Peter said straight out to her just moments before she dropped dead in front of the congregation. It's recorded in *Acts 5:9*—

> *"...behold, the feet of them which have buried thy husband are at the door, and shall carry thee out."*

Pastor Kyle, you see, was a wild man, a man drunken in the spirit with demonic excess, sated by the world's pleasures, devoid of the cleansing spirit of God. Kyle was a rebel, a revolutionary opponent to the true Christian faith. And he was a leader of a Christian establishment made up of tens of millions of soul-dead church-goers gone wild with hedonism and sin.

Let Kyle's sudden death be a warning to all the wild men and wild women who today darken the doors of so-called Christian Churches: *God is not mocked (Galatians 6:7). He will in due time reward all men for their works. Of that you can be sure.*

Greedy Evangelists and Religious Charlatans Leading the World into a Spiritual Wasteland

The Blind and the Dead

"Woe unto ye, ye blind guides..."

—*Matthew 23:16*

"...clouds they are without water, carried about of winds; trees whose fruit withereth, without fruit, twice dead, plucked up by the roots...to whom is reserved the blackness of darkness forever."

—*Jude 12-13*

They're flamboyant. They're colorful. And they're deceiving and leading millions of unsuspecting victims with all deliberate speed straight down to the very core of hell!

I call them *the blind and the dead.* They're today's most popular televangelists and ministers. Practicing their money-making craft with smooth tongues, corrupt personalities, and captivating charm, they have already delivered untold millions of souls into the waiting arms of their master, a rough beast whom the Bible calls Satan, the devil, the adversary, the deceiver.

For years now in tears I have warned people to stay away from the horrendously defective ministries of these pretenders of the Gospel. I have frequently named the worst offenders and cited in print examples of their heresies and horrors.

Texe Marrs' shocking video exposes the pretenders of the Gospel.

Invariably, each time I exposed such men and women in my newsletter or on my radio program, I would be besieged by a slew of angry letters and phone calls from their legions of fans and groupies. These zealots would caution me not to "touch God's anointed." They sometimes threatened me, warning that God would severely punish me for reporting anything negative or derogatory about their favorite TV preacher, evangelist, or faith healer.

"If the blind lead the blind..."

The fervent, almost mesmerized fans of the false teachers insisted that I was wrong; they alleged I had made a mistake, that I had misquoted their hero. Some of these deluded, pitiful, blind people angrily and blatantly called me terrible names.

Paul Crouch

Tired of "doctrinal doo-doo."

Jan Crouch

Says Jesus was tortured in hell.

Rodney Howard-Browne

"Holy Ghost Bartender"

"Texe Marrs," they would typically exclaim, "you are a rotten liar. Repent, my friend, of what you have said about God's great, anointed servant, Mr. Wonderful, or you will burn in hell!"

As our Lord so sagely put it, "If the blind lead the blind, both shall fall into the ditch" (Matthew 15:14). And fall these blind victims did, one after another, into the mud and mire of apostasy and heresy.

What has always broken my heart is that these folks are often so very sincere. They genuinely want to believe in the fabrications and false teachings indulged in by their particular hero. Regrettably, the followers of these deceitful religious leaders are devoid of discernment, and either are unable or are unwilling to render righteous judgement. Most refuse to judge anyone or anything. Politically correct, they proudly boast they are *nonjudgemental and unprejudiced.* Yet, oddly, they are quick to harshly criticize and judge those of us who expose their hero's falsehoods.

Casting Pearls Before Swine

These misguided people love to quote (out of context, to be sure) *Matthew 7:4, "Judge not, that ye be not judged."* Of course, they fail to note that in that same chapter, in verse 6, our Lord Jesus admonishes Christians, *"neither cast ye your pearls before swine."* Naturally, to obey this admonition, we must first *judge* who is swine and who isn't. But that fact simply escapes the nonjudgemental crowd.

It is mainly due to the gullibility of those deceived multitudes of followers that I decided to produce a definitive new video on this important topic. The result is *The Blind and The Dead*, a bombshell video exposé that accurately documents the tragic and monstrously harmful works of these evil men and women in high religious places.

In *The Blind and The Dead* you will see some of the world's top televangelists and teachers as they really are. I know that after viewing this eye-opening documentary you will conclude, as have I, that finally, "The Emperor has no clothes!" What these deceitful teachers from hell are feeding to millions of duped followers is so stunningly different than what the Word of God teaches, you will marvel that *anyone* could believe such terrible garbage as these men and women are spreading over the airwaves.

Men on Dog Leashes, Women Howling like Wolves

For example, on this video, you'll actually see popular charismatic Benny Hinn, who fills auditoriums with his healing crusades, declaring that he doesn't want to wait till he gets to heaven to acquire heaps of money and riches, he wants them *right now, here on earth!*

You'll marvel, too, as you see TBN's big-wig Paul Crouch scream that he doesn't want to hear about *"doctrinal doo-doo."* Then, you'll see Crouch angrily tell people that if they want to complain to him about false teachings, they are simply wasting their time. *"Get out of my sight,"* he screams, *"I don't want to see your ugly faces!"*

On this video you'll see such bizarre happenings you'll scarcely believe your eyes: men barking and crawling around church platforms on all fours, being led on dog leashes...women howling from the pulpit like wild wolves...crowded auditoriums erupting in crazed laughter, with people going bonkers and running around whooping and hollering like chickens with their heads cut off.

Your jaw will especially drop when you see famous Word of Faith prosperity teachers Kenneth Copeland and Kenneth Hagin laughing like lunatics and speaking in mocking, unseemly tongues that certainly are not of God.

God's Holy Bartender

You'll see popular, foreign-based evangelist Rodney Howard-Browne proclaiming himself to be God's *"Holy Bartender,"* and you'll see TBN's Jan Crouch insisting that Jesus was taken captive by the devil down in hell and tortured and tormented in the flames.

You'll also witness the grotesque fruits of the Brownsville and Toronto Revivals—people laughing hysterically, dancing and prancing about, some struck dumb, others jerking and shaking violently and falling down, still others slithering around the floor like serpents. And all giving God the "credit" for their ungodly performances.

You'll be disgusted as you watch a private video clip of Benny Hinn passing around to associates, as well as a big-name gospel singer, a "hookah," a Turkish smoking pipe. Then, you'll find out that, shortly afterwards, two of Benny Hinn's top lieutenants died of heroin overdoses.

Lewd, Crude, and Vulgar

But as bad as this is, it doesn't even compare with what you'll see on this video as Benny Hinn's wife takes the stage. What she says and does before a huge throng of admiring people at one of Hinn's crusades is so unbelievably lewd, crude, and vulgar, I am reluctant to describe it here. But, believe me, you'll fall off your chair when you see it. I know I did. In fact, I am still in a state of shock over what I witnessed on this video.

You will be appalled to see Benny Hinn and Paul Crouch declare themselves "little gods," watch as Kenneth Copeland says he is the "I AM," and hear evangelist Dwight Thompson spinning a tall tale about pianos that supernaturally play in churches with no pianist around.

You'll also see Marjoe, once a famous, tongue-speaking evangelist, brag about and detail how he ripped so many people off for filthy lucre's sake, and you'll hear faith healer Kenneth Hagin explain that he doesn't pray anymore, he just commands the spirits, *"Go get me money."*

Kenneth Copeland

Proclaims himself a "little god."

Kenneth Hagin

Commands spirits, "Go get me money."

Benny Hinn

Wants riches and treasures now!

Inventors of Evil Things

My friends, this is the shocker of all shocker videos. The scriptures speak of *"inventors of evil things" (Romans 1:30).* Well, after seeing this video, I know you will agree with me that these deceitful men and women, slick as they are with their covetous promises of prosperity and lying signs and wonders on unholy display, are not mere religious charlatans. They are, in fact, truly *"inventors of evil things."*

Finally, after you personally view this video, my prayer is that you will invite some of the more zealous fans of these deceivers over to your house—or to your church—and *present the video to them.* Then, they will have no excuse.

Here is enough evidence to convince even the most dull and insensitive of believers in Christ that we are all in the chaotic midst of a rampaging pack of apostate wolves.

These wolves, unfortunately, have up to now fooled untold millions into accepting as valid their black, black behavior and conduct.

Cleaning Up the Spiritual Wasteland

These famous, yet greedy, charlatans must be exposed, otherwise, countless more victims will suffer loss. I'm counting on each of you who are friends of *Power of Prophecy*. Please, obtain your own personal copy of this powerful video, *The Blind and the Dead*, and, together, let's broadcast the truth far and wide before it's too late.

Together, let's work to clean up this spiritual wasteland and light a candle so that God's great light of righteousness will shine through the prevailing darkness of deceit and folly.

Billy Graham and Al Gore Team Up to Save the Earth

Vice President Al Gore has a powerful, new ally in his campaign to save Mother Earth—Billy Graham. Alicia Shepard, reporter for the Religious News Service (RNS), reports that Billy Graham has decided to join Gore's ecology, nature effort. In her curiously titled article, "Billy Graham Goes Global in 'Capstone' of His Career" (Feb. 6, 1995), she writes:

> Graham had a two-hour candlelight dinner with Vice President Al Gore, spending a third of the session talking about the environment—Gore's signature issue. Afterwards, Graham said he would speak publicly on "ecology and our responsibility to the environment" after meeting with environmental experts.

Shepard says that Billy Graham's support could be critical to Gore's campaign. She notes that Graham "is a powerful, behind the scenes player" in politics and national affairs. She reports, too, that the evangelist "talks often of his friendship with religious leaders such as Pope John Paul II and the Rev. Martin Luther King and with political leaders such as Nixon, Clinton, Gorbachev, and Rabin."

Alchemy, Mind Control, and Black Science

Mind Control and the Processing of Humanity

In every area of our lives, the *invisible powers* are staging furious, pile-driver assaults against us. Their goal: to demolish the individual human mind and condition all of humanity for the coming, final takeover of America and the whole earth. This is what I conclude in my incredible book: *DARK MAJESTY: The Secret Brotherhood and the Magic of a Thousand Points of Light.*

Dark Majesty is the first book to fully unmask the fantastic—yet diabolical—method used by The Order to mesmerize and control human minds. That method can accurately be described as the Processing of Humanity.

Evidence that our minds and souls are being processed and that man has become like sheep led to slaughter can be amply found in the following mind-boggling example. I call this the true-life story of the school program designed in hell.

Goodbye Christmas, Hello Devil's Day

The kids at a public elementary school in Portland, Oregon, were not allowed to celebrate a traditional Christmas this last year. School authorities decided that would be wrong. Religion is not permissible in the classroom. Church and state must be kept separate. Right?

Since Christmas is a *Christian* holiday, school officials decided that the very word "Christmas" must be forbidden to be spoken. And in place of the annual Christmas event, the school's kids would be required instead to participate in a *Winter Solstice Program.*

On December 19, 1991, the *Winter Solstice* was celebrated in the school's auditorium. The theme: *"To celebrate the return of light."* The cover of the official printed program handed out to students and their parents was revealing. It depicted the Sun God (Lucifer, god of light) and the Moon Goddess (see *Revelation 17*—Mystery Babylon).

Inside the printed program, sent to me by a friend of the ministry, is found this description of the Winter Solstice Program:

Cover for the Program of the Winter Solstice celebration at a Portland, Oregon public school.

"Each child will partake of the sun and moon cake before

> entering the auditorium, where they will seat themselves according to their astrological signs…Chanting will begin on entering the auditorium…
>
> The Sun God and Moon Goddess will enter with attendants."

A Witchcraft and Satanism Ceremony

So what we have here is a Solstice celebration (historically a witchcraft and satanic holiday) in which occult astrology and chanting are employed and the Sun God and Moon Goddess of paganism are worshipped.

The cakes to be eaten are the same ones devoured by the heathen worshippers of the god Baal (Sun God) and the goddess Ashtoreth (the Moon Goddess) in the ritual denounced as an abomination by God in our Bible (see the books of Ezekiel, Jeremiah, and I Kings).

But wait, there's more! The Solstice program included New Age dancing and pagan drumming. A number of children came dressed-up as "trees and animal spirits" (coyotes, hawks, frogs, etc.). Songs like *This Little Light of Mine* and *Bye, Bye Blackbird* were sung and birds were released to "fly into the universe."

Other ritual practices observed: "a burning of bad experiences," a blessing of the kids by the school staff, and finally, dancing in a circle to close out the celebration, followed by "whooping and hugs all around."

The Taking of The Mark

In one segment of the school's *Solstice* program, kids came in with *bar codes* stamped on their foreheads. The bar code of some was read and accepted. But other children, *who did not have the proper mark*, were rejected. Only those who had the *chosen mark* were deemed "good and worthy." To understand the significance of this, simply turn to *Revelation 13*, where we find prophesied that in the last days, all shall receive a *mark*, either in the forehead or in the right hand, indicating allegiance to the antichrist.

Now again, keep in mind, this program replaced the school's traditional Christmas event, with the excuse given that observance of a Christmas "religious" event, is unlawful. *So instead, the kids were treated to one of the most pagan, witchcraft, occultic, satanic, and New Age religious rituals imaginable.* In other words, it is only the *Christian* religion that is now banned from our schools, not the *pagan religions* of the devil!

The Technique of Double-speak

This type of double-standard and double-speak is a common technique employed in the *Processing of Humanity*. Pronouncing themselves tolerant and broadminded, the "experts" who run our schools and other cultural institutions consistently favor other religions while scornfully rejecting Biblical Christianity.

Thus, the mind controllers don't really object to *prayer* in our public schools. They just don't want *Christian* prayers. The mind controllers are also not opposed to the teaching and practice of *religion* in the classroom. But they *are* violently opposed to the teaching and practice of anything faintly related to the *Christian* religion.

This is all a part of the ingenious mind control methodology known as the *Processing of Humanity* now being employed against all of us.

Someday, this processing will be complete. And if what I see that is now being taught to our kids in Portland, Oregon and in 99% of the other school districts in America is any indication. I shudder to think of the monstrous end result.

International Pedophile Ring of Sexual Predators Abuses and Tortures Children

Satanism, Sex Crimes, and Consequences

"But whoso shall offend one of these little ones which believe in me, it were better for him that a millstone were hanged about his neck, and that he were drowned in the depth of the sea."

—Matthew 18:6

Imagine an elite group of evil child molesters meeting privately in an undisclosed location. Imagine, too, these wicked sexual predators making plans to conduct grotesque, real-life experiments on innocent little boys and girls. In these experiments, the children will be systematically raped, sodomized, and physically violated. Detailed records will be kept of the children's reactions so that pedophiles worldwide can "enjoy" seeing the results.

Satanic Doctor to Conduct Experiment

Next, imagine this elite group deciding that these horrendous sexual experiments are to be supervised by a well known professor, or "doctor," of zoology. The chosen doctor happens to be an admirer of the infamous British satanist, Aleister Crowley (the Beast), and is himself a pedophile and homosexual. He will be given millions of dollars to set up a sexual laboratory and institute at a public university somewhere in Middle America.

After this doctor's depraved team completes its abominable research, the mass media will be employed. The nation's newspapers, television, and radio, along with educational organizations, will join in congratulating the pedophile research doctor on a job well done. His name as a great thinker and scientist will go up in lights. The whole world shall sing his praises and be joyful for what this man has done to these little children, all in the name of science.

Kinsey is shown here visiting satanic High Priest Aleister Crowley's temple at Thelema, in Sicily, with occult porno film maker Kenneth Anger. This photograph was obviously posed to create deeply occult symbols and images.

The Work is Begun and is Successful

And so it is that the doctor of zoology and his helpers go about their grim business of sexual molestation. Thousands of children are thrown into beds. Pedophile molesters described as supposed "research associates" repugnantly and with wicked abandon ravage their cringing, young bodies. Some infants molested are only five months of age. The abused children are counted as statistics and labeled as "scientific subjects."

All goes according to plan. The satanist doctor's name becomes a household word. Educators toast his brilliance. Commendatory books are published examining his work and touting his findings. Clergymen and readers of mass circulation magazines—including family-oriented publications—agree with his conclusions and change their attitudes and behaviors accordingly.

No one seems upset. No one is alarmed. Yet, thousands of children are systematically tortured and raped. The majority of people rejoice that a stunning sexual revolution has taken place. Somehow, though, God's born again believers suspect that the world will never again be the same. Never.

A Horror Movie...or Real?

Could what I have just described be the makings of a raw and explicit horror movie? Or could it be real? Did these monstrously sordid events and acts actually take place, and in America no less, home of the brave and the free—a country where the President almost daily claims he has done this or that "for the good of our children?"

In fact, the scenes I have described are real. This vile plot and activity did take place—and not in Nazi Germany either. Not in Soviet Russia, not in Asia or in South America. These things happened in America in the lifetime of most of us. Furthermore, I believe they are still happening today as you read this. Hundreds, even thousands of little boys and girls are being offered up on the altar of pedophile sex magick. They are being abused regularly and often, and the authorities know about it and are doing nothing to prevent these filthy and ungodly crimes from occurring.

In a mind-absorbing book, *Kinsey: Crimes and Consequences—The Red Queen and the Grand Scheme*, Dr. Judith Reisman explodes the strange and malevolent myth of Albert Kinsey, the world-acclaimed satanic doctor responsible for this outrageous criminal atrocity. It was Kinsey who burst on the scene in the early 50s with his widely admired but shocking *The Kinsey Report*. The findings in this report were based on Kinsey's book, *Sexual Behavior in the Adult Male*. In it, the now famous Indiana University sex researcher claimed that homosexuality—as well as almost any other deviant and perverted sexual activity—is natural and normal. Children, said Kinsey, are sexual from birth, even in the crib. Kids just a year or two old were claimed to want "positive" sex and said to enjoy pleasurable feelings from sexual activity.

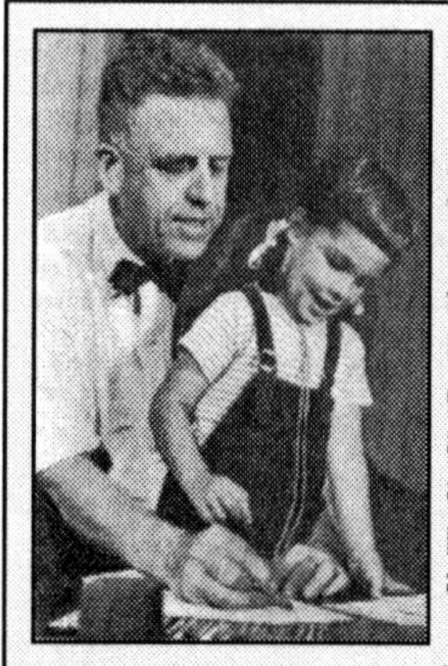

As this staged photo illustrates, the Illuminati's public relations machine, with Rockefeller funding, created an image of Kinsey as a nice, caring, family-oriented researcher. In fact, he and his associates were part of an international ring of sadistic, pedophile child torturers and abusers.

Children Strapped Down and Abused

Reisman's astonishing book documents some of the fiendish ways in which Dr. Kinsey and his institute carried out much of their research. For example, children three to seven years in age were regularly strapped or held down while grotesque sexual acts were performed on them. Stop watches were often used to time the children's physical responses.

Judith Reisman appropriately asks: "Where were the police and law enforcement authorities when these disgraceful and outrageous criminal acts were being committed? Where is the outrage in the academic community and the mass media today? Why, seemingly, is no one disturbed or alarmed at these atrocities committed in the name of science?"

Adult Sex with Children Normal

Kinsey's research findings were that adults who used children for "sex outlets" were quite normal. One Kinsey research associate, who was reported to have had various forms of sexual activity with 800 children, was deemed by Kinsey to be a "refined gentleman" and a "scientific hero." Government funds were used to help compensate this serial child molester for his contributions to science!

From Kinsey's flawed research conclusions a new generation built an entire, new working theory of sexual freedom and license. Kinsey was described by the press and the academic world as the "Father of the Sexual Revolution." Author and novelist Gore Vidal, himself a notorious homosexual, candidly stated that Kinsey was "the most famous man in America, in the world."

Dr. Judith Reisman, whose sensational book, *Kinsey: Crimes and Consequences*, fully documents the grotesque, sexual crimes of Kinsey and the elite. This powerful book indicts virtually the entire political, media, and academic establishments of America.

Rockefeller, Kinsey, and the Grand Scheme

In her revealing book, Dr. Judith Reisman for the first time exposes Kinsey's satanist connections. She also unmasks the fact that it was the Rockefeller Foundation that gave the wicked Dr. Kinsey the money to conduct his sin-laden, genocidal, child soul-killing research.

At the heart of it all was a "Grand Scheme" by the late Kinsey and his associates to destroy the very building blocks of society. Their goal was to create a New Civilization. The decadent dream of the surviving conspirators remains. They are determined to create a nonjudgmental, anti-God world where homosexual pedophiles can treat children like slabs of meat at a neighborhood flesh market—plundering them in the name of "loving and caring for their needs."

In effect, the release of the *Kinsey Report* was a planned and staged event, carefully and meticulously crafted in minute detail, intended to dissolve morality and to manipulate and catapult the entirety of humanity into a New Age of sexual and social slavery. As such, the Grand Scheme worked beautifully.

Our Twisted and Sick Culture

Look around you, kind readers, and ask yourself: Why is our twisted and sick culture the way it is today? Why have even the youngest of our kids become sexual barbarians and menacing satanic warriors? Why is the MTV generation so devoid of a conscience? And what of their parents—the drug-crazed, sexually liberated, 60s New Age generation? This was an entire generation made into zombies by marijuana, cocaine, heavy metal music, and Hindu gurus. Between the mixed-up kids and their demented parents, America has become a dumbed-down nation of unthinking feelies and sexually weird immorals.

America is now so far gone that no sooner is the President of the United States exposed as a sexual molester of a 21-year old intern, engaging in oral sex or possibly worse things in the very bowels of the oval office in the White House. Then—lo and behold—his popularity ratings soar.

The majority of Americans cry out in unison to would-be accusers: "Leave our great President alone! So what if he *is* a sexual predator? So what if he, being a married man, *has* done these things to women, young and old alike, in the oval office? Who cares? Our economy is strong. We have money in our purses and billfolds. Anyway, Bill Clinton is only an anointed reflection of us all. We're all sexually free and liberated. *America is Bill Clinton and he is us!"*

Was it not Albert Kinsey, agent of the Illuminati and its Grand Scheme, who began this wicked era of sexual confusion and chaos? Why were he and his pedophile ring of child molesting collaborators allowed to go unpunished? Why have their sins been hidden from view for so long? And why has the courageous Dr. Judith Reisman become so hated and despised by the academic world since she first came out with her eye-opening revelations about the sex crimes committed by this elite group of international conspirators?

"The Wise Shall Understand"

As Reisman argues in her book, *Kinsey: Crimes and Consequences—The Red Queen and The Grand Scheme,* it is time that Americans discover how their way of life has been so dramatically changed by an unheralded, little known cadre of evil sexual perverts and their financial backers. It is time that Americans learn of how monied "special interests" shut down the lone Congressional Committee that dared investigate. It is time for the truth to come out and be told. As Jesus our Lord promised us in His Word, in the last days many hidden secrets shall be uncovered, and the wise shall understand:

> *"And he said, Go thy way, Daniel: for the words are closed up and sealed till the time of the end. Many shall be purified, and made white, and tried; but the wicked shall do wickedly: and none of the wicked shall understand; but the wise shall understand." (Daniel 12:9-10)*

The Deluded, Mind-Sapped Masses

Walter Bowart, in his classic exposé *Operation Mind Control*, asserts that the true purpose of intelligence agencies is "to take human beings... and transform them into unthinking, subconsciously programmed zombies." This is accomplished, he says, "through the use of various techniques... including brainwashing, thought reform, behavior modification, hypnosis, and conditioned reflex therapy."

Affirming Bowart's conclusions, the astute Jim Keith, in *Saucers of the Illuminati*, explains that, "The advent of television in the late 1940s has provided a potent mind drug administered to the vast majority of the population." Studies have shown, says Keith, that, "television actually induces a trance state."

Moreover, newer technologies empower government intelligence agencies and Illuminati-funded black operations groups to subject entire populations to electromagnetic radiation. Eldon Byrd, researcher with the U.S. Navy's Office of Non-Lethal Weapons, states that this beam radiation causes a "drastic degradation of intelligence" and results in "a very definite and irreversible damage to the central nervous system."

Power of Prophecy believes that given this vast array of mind control weaponry, only the power of the Living God can shield and protect human beings. Unfortunately, the deluded masses do not believe in either God or in His protective powers.

The 911, Israeli, and Satanism Connection

The Mysterious Riddle of Chandra Levy

In all the horror and psychodrama that ensued after the September 11th terrorist attack on America, the scandal involving Congressman Gary Condit and the missing intern, Chandra Levy, was swept under the rug. However, strange as it may be, the mystery of the Chandra Levy disappearance is intimately connected with the war on terrorism and especially with the September 11th hijackings and mass murders.

Just two months prior to her disappearance, Chandra and her mother, Susan, flew to Israel where Chandra was photographed in odd, but revealing, esoteric poses amid ancient ruins. These pictures were later published in *Talk* magazine (Aug. 8, 2001) and elsewhere.

The Tribe of Levi

Keep in mind that Chandra's Jewish name, "Levy," comes from the tribe of Levi. In the Bible in Numbers 1:48-51 the Lord spoke to Moses commanding that the Levites be appointed over the tabernacle of God and be ministers. Only the Levitical priests were ordained to offer a holy sacrifice unto the Lord. The Levites kept the law.

Did the notorious men of Satan's Washington, D.C. Illuminati brotherhood endeavor to commit the obscene abomination of *sacrificing* a young Jewish woman named "Levy" on their high holy day, the day revered in the occult netherworld as the day of *Grand Sacrifice?* Did Chandra Levy's murder symbolize for them their liberty to be free of God and God's law?

Chandra Levy a Mossad Agent?

An accumulation of evidence indicates that the 24-year old Levy was a youthful recruit of the Israeli Mossad, that nation's premier spy agency. In that capacity, she had served as an intern in the executive offices of California Governor Gray Davis, an Illuminati initiate, and that is where she first met Mr. Condit, also an Illuminati servant.

In Washington, D.C., Ms. Levy not only began a relationship and affair with Gary Condit, she also was introduced to the perverted inner sex lives of numbers of other congressmen, all of whom are part of D.C.'s exclusive satanic brotherhood.

Working at the top level of the Federal Bureau of Prisons, the ingenious Chandra was able to obtain highly classified information pertaining to Timothy McVeigh, then awaiting execution in a federal penitentiary. She came upon documents linking McVeigh to a broad, Illuminati-U.S. intelligence operation involving FBI

Did Chandra Levy have advance knowledge of the September 11th horror?

and CIA-sponsored domestic "pseudo terrorists" (McVeigh, Nichols, et. al), Arab Islamic agents, and foreign intelligence services (Germany, Britain, and Israel).

Gary Condit is himself a senior member of the House Select Committee on Intelligence, a fact that Chandra Levy used to good advantage in her role as a Mossad agent. It has been suggested that Ms. Levy requested Condit obtain for her a position at CIA headquarters, suggesting that if he did not, certain "private things" about Condit's intelligence connections and his grotesquely satanic, sexual misconduct might be made public.

I believe that at that point Chandra Levy had somehow stumbled onto the most shocking intelligence secret of the last few decades—the horrific Illuminati plot to manipulate so-called Arab Islamic terrorists to smash airliners into the World Trade Center Towers and the Pentagon.

Death in Baphomet's Rock Creek Park

This unauthorized disclosure sealed Chandra Levy's doom. On May 1st, a date numerologically and occultly significant in the Illuminati's witchcraft and satanic calendar, she was disposed of during a ritual at D.C.'s mysteriously gothic Rock Creek Park, a large, forested area which is shaped like a goat's head—the hideous head of Baphomet, the Masonic goat-god, representative of the coming antichrist.

Israeli Spies and Commandos in New York City

According to *Ha'aretz*, the largest circulation daily newspaper in Israel, on the day the two hijacked aircraft exploded the twin towers of the World Trade Center in New York City, five Israelis were sighted atop a New York Manhattan building. They were working a video camera. This Israeli spy team videotaped the entire terrorist incident from start to finish. Nearby observers who clandestinely saw them were astonished to see the five men shouting joyously and jumping up and down as the explosions ripped the towers and each building collapsed.

These nearby witnesses phoned the NYC police and the FBI. The FBI came and arrested the five, who turned out to be Israelis carrying false visa papers. The *Ha'aretz* article said the five were stripped of their clothes, incarcerated in dark jail cells, and interrogated nonstop for 13 solid hours by FBI agents. The FBI interrogators accused the five of being Israeli Mossad spy agents.

Their arrest alerted the FBI to the existence of some 200 Israeli "commandos" training at a warehouse in New Jersey. They and the five arrested were "employed" by a bogus moving company owned by an Israeli.

After diplomatic intervention at the highest levels of the Israeli and U.S. governments, the NYC FBI squad was ordered to cease their investigation, release the five suspects, and turn them over to the Israeli Consul. They were immediately flown to Israel.

Did these bizarre events have anything to do with advance intelligence information obtained by Chandra Levy and passed on to Israel prior to her May 1st abduction?

Congressman Gary Condit Promoted by Elite

Our eyes are further opened when we discover what has happened in the past few weeks since September 11th, to the disgraced Congressman Gary Condit. Thought to be on the ropes, his career finished, Condit's Illuminati friends have now come to his rescue.

House Speaker Dennis Hastert (R-IL) and House Minority Leader Richard Gephardt (D-MO) on September 16 moved to elevate and promote Condit, naming him to sit on the just-created, influential new *House Committee on Homeland Defense and Terrorism.* Meanwhile, Democratic Party big-wigs, working behind-the-scenes, promised Condit their full support—and all the money he needs—to run for re-election next year.

Amazingly, even though he has been outed to all of America as a vicious, unfeeling, immoral viper, Condit remains the Illuminati's reigning, California "Pretty Boy," if you get my drift.

Star Magazine Punished with Anthrax

It was the surprisingly reliable *Star*, a tabloid, that first broke the Bill Clinton/Gennifer Flowers sex scandal. It was also the *Star* that, back in July, broke the stunning, eye-opening story and revelation that *Gary Condit is a sick sex pervert into bizarre ritual.* Guess which magazine in Boca Raton, Florida was punished by "terrorists" with an anthrax attack in September? That's right—*Star!*

It was a *Star* company employee who died of anthrax infection, and the germ was found on a *Star* keyboard. The U.S. Justice Department then ordered the entire building owned by the 300-employee corporation that publishes *Star* and two other tabloids to be closed and sealed. This was a lesson that the Illuminati elite would no longer allow independent "rogue" media to "out" its political servants.

Star magazine has long been a thorn in the side of the elite, bravely exposing their plots and murders. Payback came with a vicious anthrax germ disease attack against the magazine and its employees.

Orwellian Illusion and the Morning of the Magicians

These astonishing things amply prove that few things in Washington, D.C. (or Florida!) are what they seem. Orwellian Illusion is rampant as the Illuminist, global psychodrama continues unabated. Neither should we make the mistake of thinking that September 11 occurred precisely the way it has been described in the media.

It is but morning and the magicians are already fast at work, deceiving and gulling the masses. Soon, however, "night cometh" when, as our Lord and Saviour Jesus Christ testified, "no man can work." Even so, come quickly, Lord Jesus!

"For there is nothing covered, that shall not be revealed; neither hid, that shall not be known." (Luke 12:2-3) 

Chandra Levy Update: In this exclusive article published in *Power of Prophecy* newsletter, I detailed the hideous fate which befell the missing young intern, Chandra Levy, stating that she had been murdered at Rock Creek Park in Washington, D.C. Almost a *year* after I reported this, the remains of the dead Chandra Levy were discovered, exactly where I had said the murder/ritual occurred—in Rock Creek Park! As for Congressman Gary Condit, he was eventually forced to resign from office after he botched interviews with the media.

Flesh-crunching mini-robots to be injected in human bodies...Transmitters for global electronic control system disguised as stadiums.

The World Cup Conspiracy

What if every man, woman, and child on earth were injected with a "vaccine," a vaccine which, unbeknownst to the recipient, contained thousands of miniscule bioflesh robot machines? Robot machines so tiny, so virtually undetectable, that each is only about one 50,000th the width of a single human hair.

What if multitudes of these robot machines, each so small they cannot be seen with the naked eye, travel about in the person's blood stream, lodge themselves, and furiously begin their amazing work, all at the direction of powerful remote computer terminals? Computer terminals which send their signals via invisible ELF waves directly into the programmable "nanotransistor brains" of these incredible robotic devices?

What if these invisible ELF waves were produced, generated, and distributed by gigantic, antennae-like structures cleverly built to resemble 21st century athletic stadiums? Stadiums erected in scores of cities around the globe, linking their signals up with an array of satellites overhead, the whole system being superintended and run by secret intelligence services from computer correlation centers in the United States, Europe, and elsewhere?

What if you, having voluntarily been vaccinated to ward off anthrax, ebola virus, smallpox, and various other dread toxins, are blissfully unaware that the substances injected into your blood stream, while containing preventive vaccines, also contain legions of tiny, but efficient, programmable robot machines? Nano-transistor robot machines which silently lie in your blood stream, passive and inert, but ready to spring into action when the signal is given and received.

"We need a program of psychosurgery for political control of our society. The purpose is physical control of the mind. Everyone who deviates from the given norm can be surgically mutilated.

The individual may think that the most important reality is his own existence, but this is only his personal point of view... Man does not have the right to develop his own mind....

We must electronically control the brain. Someday armies and generals will be controlled by electronic stimulation of the brain."

– Dr. Jose M.R. Delgado
Director of Neuropsychiatry
Yale University Medical School
Congressional Record, No. 26,
Vol. 118, February 24, 1974

A Threat to Society

What if the men who run the master computers that control these nanotransmitter robot machines someday are notified that you are a "threat" to society, to the New World Order? Why? Well, perhaps it's because of your unorthodox, pro-constitutionalist views, your fundamentalist Bible-beliefs, or possibly your failure to fit in with Big Brother's carefully planned New Age Society.

What if some faceless bureaucrat sitting

Twenty New World Cup Stadiums In 2002 Twenty More by 2006

A gigantic new World Cup stadium goes up in Seoul, Korea. Note the huge, metal, antennae-like internal super-structure. Ten of these ultra-modern stadiums have recently been erected in Korea, and ten in Japan, all in readiness, we are told, for the 2002 World Cup soccer (futbol) sports championship games. These 20 stadiums cost untold billions of American dollars to build. Yet, even as they rise, both Korea and Japan are suffering staggering economic depressions.

By 2006, some twenty more World Cup stadiums are planned for Europe and Africa. Who is providing the funding? Are these colossal new stadiums, in reality, designed to operate as advanced over-the-horizon ELF (electromagnetic low frequency) wave transmitters, linking space platforms, satellites overhead, U.S. Naval vessels at sea, and HAARP systems in Alaska with CIA and NSA "Echelon" computer centers in the U.S.A., Great Britain, Greenland, Australia, New Zealand, South Africa, and Russia?

Will this astonishing new global surveillance and human control system be unleashed in the year 2006 to establish iron-clad control by antichrist and his 666 world government? Will the earth's inhabitants be required, unwittingly, to take into their bodies, through mass medical vaccination campaigns, robotic devices made possible through fabulous advances in miniaturized nanotransistor technology?

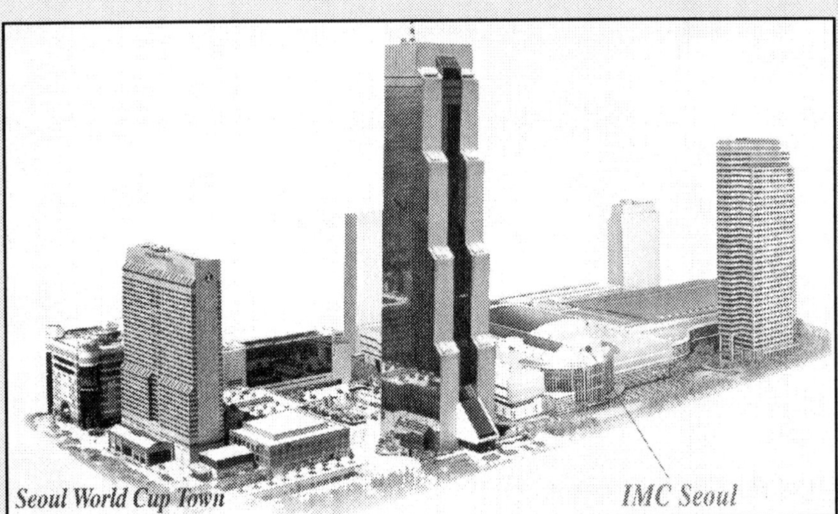

This is World Cup Town, established in Seoul, Korea. IMC Seoul is the nerve center for global broadcast and print media coverage. Public Relations representatives say that this "town" will bring together the "best technology and maximum efficiency."

somewhere decides that you believe—or worse, preach to others—the dangerously outmoded view that God, truth, family, individual rights, country are more important than the universalist-promoted tenet that the socialist *collective consciousness* of the global village is all that exists and all that matters.

And what if, having been duly notified by cyberspace message of your worthlessness and uselessness to the cause of the Illuminati's *Great Work*, the computer operator takes immediate action. He calls up your social security number, by which you are identified and tracked each moment of the day, and assigns you *"Code Red"* classification.

Psychosurgery: Robots Rip You to Shreds

Instantly, the insidious, once latent, but now fast moving, now fully orchestrated, armies of nanotransmitter robots inside your body crank up and go straight to work. They tear into their targets, chomping, gouging, drilling, and demolishing your human tissue. Steadily, they destroy life-giving arteries to the heart; they eat away at the brain and liver cells, and tear off bits of plaque and cholesterol which dislodge, travel to the brain, heart, and kidneys, and induce strokes and hemorrhaging.

In minutes, or less, you are dead. The official autopsy and death certificate says that you died of cardiac arrest, or stroke, aneurysm, or perhaps cancer or bacterial infection. No one—not your doctor, not the coroner, not the members of your family—are even minutely aware of the real cause of your demise. How could they be?

The monstrous robots are now turned off, their mission accomplished. Too small to be seen—so infinitesimal in size they are dwarfed by bacteria and viruses—they have proven to be hidden killers, smart machines without souls, directed in their foul and deadly work by human killers from afar, men without souls.

A Change in Attitude

If, however, the powers that be wish to keep you alive but simply change you, they might computer-instruct some of the robots stealthily residing in your body to "correct" only a specified, surgically precise section of your brain's cortex—the area that controls certain feelings, emotions, and cognitive knowledge. Other robots on stand-by in your blood stream will then be instructed to insert new "knowledge modules" in place of those destroyed and removed.

The psychosurgery procedure having been successful, suddenly your bedside doctors and nurses notice that your attitude has improved. Now, you no longer oppose the government's "public policy." Miraculously, you have an entirely new attitude. Why, you even admire and respect Big Brother, and you possess a strong desire to serve him at all cost.

You begin to feel tears welling up. You just can't help yourself. Slowly, your lips form the words. "Yes....Yes," you hear yourself moaning, *"Yes, I do love Big Brother."*

Science Fiction Becomes Reality

What if everything I have written here is true? *What if* early models of these horrific nanotransistor robots have already been built? *What if* a network of metallic and concrete, antennae-like structures, operating as giant transmitters and disguised as athletic stadiums, have already been built? And *what if* intricate plans for a universal, high tech, Big Brother identification and tracking system already exist and, even now, await implementation?

You'll recall that *Power of Prophecy* was the first to warn men with eyes to see and ears to hear of the coming Age of *Frankenfoods*, genetically engineered food produced by industrial corporations. Now, this food is here. Advanced new biotechnology has made it possible, and our farmers no longer control their own destiny.

Power of Prophecy was the first to alert discerning Christians to the development of the implantable biochip. Now, it's here, and many people have already been "chipped," some at their request!

Power of Prophecy was also the first to make you aware of Project L.U.C.I.D., the hellish project to create the Beast 666 Universal Human Control System, linking all the world's computers and making possible the issuance to all mankind of a trackable, biometrics I.D. card.

We further told you of the Illuminati's scheme to take advantage of a coming horrible crisis, brought about by "terrorists," which would cause people everywhere to cry out and demand that Big Brother issue this card for our own good, for security, safety, and control.

On September 11, 2001, that crisis which so frightened the masses came about.

Now, post 9/11, there are few that would resist the pre-planned, privacy-destroying L.U.C.I.D. system. Most will thank Big Brother for his love and generosity in providing for their safety.

Now, *Power of Prophecy* is the first to unmask this broad scheme for total human control which we call *"The World Cup Conspiracy."*

Scoffers and skeptics, no doubt, will be in denial. "It can't be," they will protest, "It just can't be!" But as our investigation has discovered and my latest audiotapes demonstrate, this monstrous project—*The World Cup Conspiracy*—has gone far beyond the what if stage.

The capability to commit maximum ultimate evil is here. The technology genie is out of the bottle. And the world will never be the same.

"Incredible shrinking doctors" is what the editors of *Popular Science* magazine called nanorobots. Here are mythical pictures of what some of these microscopic machines will look like. *Popular Science* (July 2000, p. 63) says, "Nanorobots will be mass produced in such miniscule size, far less than the diameter of a human hair—they will be able to travel through capillaries without being rejected by the body's immune system." The nanorobots will be "smaller than bacteria," says Dr. Carlo Montemagno, research professor of biological engineering at prestigious Cornell University.

What do glamorous new stadiums, fabulous new nanotransistor robots, Microsoft founder Bill Gates' billions, and Project L.U.C.I.D. have in common?

The World Cup Conspiracy (Part 2)

The greatest sports spectacular on earth is not America's football Superbowl or baseball World Series. It is the *World Cup*, the trophy and award given to the winner of championship competition soccer after a feverish playoff among teams from all nations on earth. In 2002 the World Cup finals are being held in Japan and Korea. Twenty fabulous new stadiums have been constructed especially for the games, as well as a World Cup Town in Korea. In 2006, twenty more new stadiums are to be built in Europe and Africa.

Where does the money come from to build these luxuriously modern and super expensive stadiums? Are these architectural marvels really athletic stadiums, or—could it be?—that these monolithic sports structures are huge, high tech transmitter antennas which produce and beam electromagnetic waves across the globe? Do they, in fact, link up with the HAARP fields in Alaska, and are they connected with CIA, DIA, and NSA computer centers in Wyoming, Nebraska, Colorado, Virginia, and Washington, D.C.?

Nanorobots—The Amazing New Technology

There is also growing evidence that a mind-warping new technology, *nanorobotics*, the mass production of thousands of miniature robot machines, nanotransistor powered, smaller than the size of bacteria, could soon be linked with the new, global, electromagnetic transmission system.

Scientists say that nanorobots will soon be able to be injected into the bodies of every person on earth. The nanorobots could be programmed by remote computers, and signals sent via World Cup stadium transmitters. These nanorobots would then become deadly and murderous. They could be remotely directed to traverse the human body, traveling through it's blood circulatory system and then attacking targets such as the vital organs of the heart and brain.

It is even possible that *Project L.U.C.I.D.*, the Beast 666 Universal Human Control System first revealed in my prophetic book of the same title, could be directed through the World Cup transmitter and computer network. This new technology will employ biometrics and biochips to identify and track every person on earth.

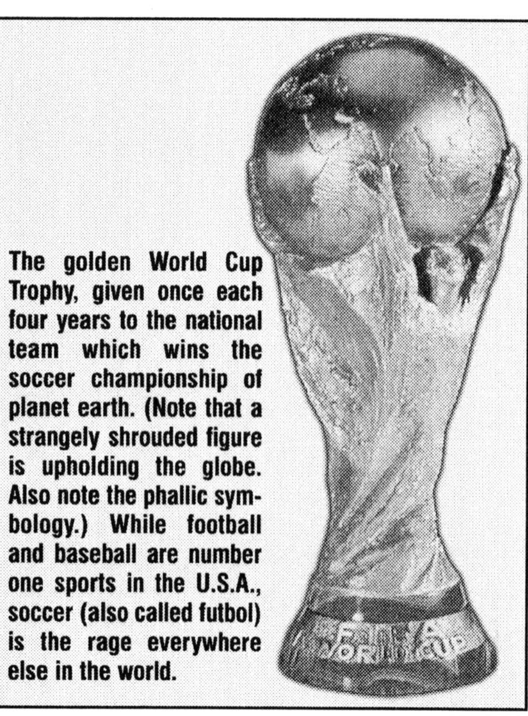

The golden World Cup Trophy, given once each four years to the national team which wins the soccer championship of planet earth. (Note that a strangely shrouded figure is upholding the globe. Also note the phallic symbology.) While football and baseball are number one sports in the U.S.A., soccer (also called futbol) is the rage everywhere else in the world.

Bill Gates — The Vaccine Connection

Some believe that Microsoft founder Bill Gates, one of the richest men in the world, is playing an important role in creating this fantastic human control system. Gates is donating money from his $24 billion Gates Foundation to develop vaccines to be used to vaccinate every person on earth. Will the undetectable nanorobots be hidden in the vaccine? Why is Gates researching his new vaccines in India and Korea and not in the U.S.A.?

> *Microsoft founder Bill Gates, one of the richest men in the world, is donating money from his $24 billion Gates Foundation to develop vaccines to vaccinate every person on earth.*

Enron and Global Crossing

We should also question the role that the once prosperous and mighty global corporations *Enron* and *Global Crossing* play in the World Cup conspiracy? Why was Europe's *UBS Warburg*, an Illuminati held firm, allowed to take control of Enron's oil transmission pipeline trading system? Why is Red China being allowed to merge the hundreds of thousands of miles of Global Crossing fiber optic lines, spread across oceans, with it's secretive, gigantic, state-owned company, Whampoa-Hutchinson Limited?

Satan's Mascots Ride the Air

Mascots for the World Cup are these three computer-generated creatures, named "Kaz," "Ato," and "Nik." In an animated film promoting the tournament, it is explained that the three characters "live high in the sky in a place called Atmozone." The mascots, we are told, have numerous adventures which lead to chaos. But in the end, they convey "the lesson that harmony is the key to success."

A fascinating aspect is that the wealthy sponsors of the World Cup have adopted three strange creatures to be its mascots. The World Cup promoters say in a promotion video that these three mascots "ride the air" and live in another dimension. Look closely at the picture we provide of the three mascots, and you will observe what I believe is their satanic nature.

One of the mascots is a sun-flame creature with horns and a goatee. He carries a crystal globe containing light. Is this not representative of the New Age's solar angel, the "Prince of the Power of the Air," in other words—Lucifer?

The Golden Cup of Mystery Babylon

Truly, the Holy Bible was on target when it depicted the last days world system as a prostitute who sits astride the beast, controlling all peoples, languages, and nations, Revealing, too, is the prophecy of John in which the Apostle described the last days *Whore of Babylon*, symbol of a global system of maximum evil, as having *"a golden cup* in her hand full of abominations and filthiness of her fornication." *(Revelation 17:4)*

THE WORLD CUP CONSPIRACY

Ten World Cup stadiums went up in Korea in 2002...

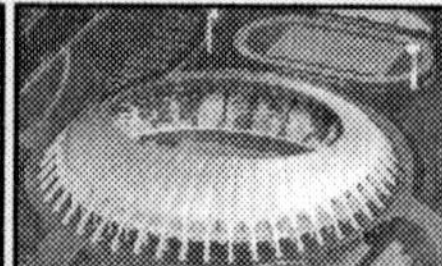

Ten more World Cup stadiums raised in Japan in 2002...

And twenty more new World Cup stadiums for Africa and Europe in 2006!... Who's behind it all and why?

Nanotransistors Readied for Humans

Following the lead of American researchers, scientists in Korea have moved from the realm of science fiction and developed the worlds smallest transistor (the nanotransistor) using a single molecule. Dr. Eric Drexton, a leading proponent of nanotechnology, says that nanomachines, or biological robots, injected in human bodies, can be programmed to recognize and kill diseased or defective cells. "Intelligent nano-scale devices will, in a few years, be injected into the human body," says Phil Kuekes, a computer scientist at Hewlett-Packard Labs.

Bill Gates, founder of Microsoft, is reputed to be leading a massive nanorobot research effort headquartered in India and Korea. Could this research effort involve the injection of nanorobots into humans via vaccines?

Meanwhile, at IBM, a scientific team expects to have a nanomachine called Blue Gene built and in use by 2003. Other advanced biotech teams are working on similar projects. In January 2000, President Clinton even declared a National Nanotechnology Initiative, promising $500 million for the effort.

Physicists at Harvard, Yale, Berkeley, and other universities believe that nanotechnology will be for the 21st century what computers, aircraft, autos, atomic power, and electricity were for the 20th century. Scientists believe that, eventually, tiny nanotechnology robots will rebuild all of society and even fabricate new baby humans!

Scientists make transistor with single molecule

By Hwang Jang-jin
Staff reporter

Scientists have developed the world's smallest transistor using a single molecule, which some day could be used to put the processing power of a desktop computer into a device as small ...

from gate electrode.

When they applied a positively charged current, the material gripped the electron blocking it from migrating from one electrode to another.

But when they excited it with a negatively charged current, the material began to os-...

for their findings.

This marks an important breakthrough in scientific efforts to shrink the size of transistors and find an alternative to silicon-based chips.

Much effort has been directed towards extending studies of electron transport to chemical nano-structures.

Most recently, Prof. Ihm Ji- ... Seoul National ...

Bill Gates to Donate $40 Million to Seoul-Based Vaccine Institute

By Son Key-young
Staff Reporter

Microsoft chairman Bill Gates has decided to donate $40 million to the Seoul-based International Vaccine Institute to help fight cholera and other diseases hitting the world's most impoverished regions, a Foreign Affairs-Trade Ministry official said yesterday.

The institute, an intergovernmental organization based on the campus of Seoul National University, ...

Program aimed at conducting research and development of a number of promising vaccine candidates against the three target diseases: cholera, dysentery and typhoid.

DOMI will be carried out in collaboration with Harvard University, the University of Gothenburg, the University of Maryland, the Pasteur Institute, and the London School of Hygiene and Tropical Medicine.

"We are pleased to have this opportunity to help develop these desperately needed vaccines. We first became aware of the International Vaccine ... while helping to ...

NANO: Creation of Tiny Transistor Next Step to Smaller Smart Devices

Continued from C1

Transistors are the building blocks of today's integrated circuits. Their ability to register an on or off state—"0" or "1" in the lingo of computer scientists—produces the basic structure of digital data. Millions of transistors operate in tandem within microprocessors to perform all manner of computations. The smaller the transistors, the more powerful the processor and the less energy required to operate it.

For decades, conventional microcircuits have been manufactured using photolithography, which uses light to etch circuits on a photosensitive film covering silicon chips. ...

tion of superintelligent, microscopic devices that will push computing into futuristic realms. A multitude of micro devices might solve the toxic waste problem by disassembling poisonous molecules, such as dioxin, into the innocuous atoms that compose them, for example.

Eric Drexler, a leading proponent of nanotechnology, has suggested that nanomachines will eventually be injected into cancer victims. The tiny robots would be programmed to recognize and kill malignant cells—much as an antibody can kill a disease-causing virus.

bending a molecule known as a carbon nanotube—a hollow cylinder that resembles a drinking straw. Using an atomic force microscope—an instrument capable of moving individual atoms—researchers pushed on the tube, causing it to buckle in two places. Like a bent straw restricting the volume of water passing through it, the bent nanotube enables one electron to move through at a time.

"The next thing will be developing strategies to assemble such devices into processors—a chip that can do ...

High Tech Magic of World Cup—Conspiracy to Produce Image of the Beast?

Will the transmitting antennas disguised and built as World Cup stadiums link up with those of the U.S. Air Force's HAARP (High Frequency Active Auroral Research Program) system? HAARP goes on line this year—the same month as the grand opening of the World Cup stadiums. Based in Alaska, HAARP comprises 180 antennas. Together, these smaller antennae heat a patch of the sky's ionosphere to make it act like single giant antenna hundreds of miles long.

Project Freedom, a study group in Great Britain, is warning that the ELF electronic waves thus created can easily be used as a *psy-electronic* weapon, with devastating effects.

But the ultimate use for the combined World Cup stadium/HAARP technology system may be to create virtual images in space, in the sky, or on-ground below. Fantastic new optical holographic technology can produce computer graphics (pictures and images) designed to appear as life-like, 3-D images that float on air.

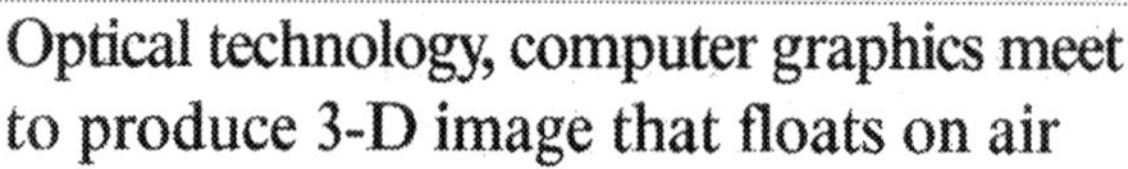

Optical technology, computer graphics meet to produce 3-D image that floats on air

By Hwang Jang-jin
Staff reporter

Looking like an ordinary TV, a display screen shows a recent news clip in which a North Korean military leader shakes hands with U.S. officials. With a simple push of a button, the characters suddenly leap up forming a three-dimensional image 50 cm from the screen. It almost looks like the real thing so much that, unless you touch it, it's hard to tell it is an illusion assembled from computer data.

A hybrid computer graphics and optical image processing has brought to reality what has only been seen so far in futuristic sci-fi flicks.

"Everything on the screen from beverage cans to new cars, from geology guides to animated characters can be converted to 3-D images," said Kim Yong-min, 29, chief executive of Korbis Co. Ltd. at a

A computer graphic image floats on the air using the 3-D visualization technology by Korbis Co.

vided into foreground and background images, which are then synchronized as a coherent 3-D image floating in the air.

Core technology was provided by Optical Products

image in the air and is too expensive for commercial applications. What 3-D computer graphics offer is actually just 2-D images that have a 3-D feel.

"The device gets around

signboards for advertising, allowing vendors to visualize features of their products more effectively.

"Almost any communication or media delivery application can be greatly enhanced with the 3-D visualization techuology," Kim said.

"Imagine that vivid image of objects float in space at your store, offering clients a closer look of them in every color, pattern and from various angles."

Kim is optimistic about the commercial prospects as "the advantages will be simply irresistible."

The merits have already succeeded in persuading some domestic corporations.

The company, founded in March with a capital of 700 million won, has signed with SK Telecom to install the device in mobile phone stores. It will also be deployed at an exhibition hall of the Convention

The net result will be that onlookers are totally deceived by *programmed illusions* of color and light scenes assembled from computer data. Entire armies of moving, military-action troops can be created, appearing to be real unless you touch them.

A report in Korea's *Herald News* says that holography-based TV shows are expected to debut this year. According to the news report, "Broadcasters plan to air the World Cup soccer finals in hologram."

In *Revelation 13* is found the astounding prophecy of the image of the beast. This image is said to be able to talk and walk, and deceive the masses. The technology for this image is here, now!

And I beheld another beast coming up out of the earth; and he had two horns like a lamb, and he spake as a dragon.

And he had power to give life unto the image of the beast, that the image of the beast should both speak, and cause that as many as would not worship the image of the beast should be killed. (Revelation 13: 11,15)

A Psychological and Economic War on the People is Being Waged

Contrived Shortages and the New Reality

"Though hand join in hand, the wicked shall not be unpunished: but the seed of the righteous shall be delivered."

—*Proverbs 11:21*

Never before have the American people been in such terrible danger as they are now. On every side, the elite have created fire-breathing dragons that are steadily advancing and threatening to destroy us.

First, there is the hocus-pocus, contrived energy crisis. The establishment story is that we are fast running out of oil. The earth's petroleum stores are almost depleted—supplies are peaking and now economic and human tragedy is at our doorstep. Predictably, the price of gasoline has rocketed into the stratosphere, leaving the ordinary working public terribly depleted of income and financially up against the wall.

Are we really running out of oil? No! Of course not. In fact, the planet is awash with the gooey black stuff. Earth is truly *Planet Petroleum.* Recent drilling successes in Brazilian waters, in the Gulf of Mexico, in the Bakken oil region of North and South Dakota, in Canada and Alaska, and around the globe prove that mankind will never run out of oil. *Never!—Never!—Never!*

The unscientific theories of "fossil" fuel depletion and hoax of "Peak Oil" are absurd nonsense, lies designed by oil corporation hucksters and their paid shills to justify their highway robbery of the American and world consumer.

And More Contrived Crises

The contrived crises of *"Global Warming"* and *"Climate Change"* are similar scams. The entire environmentalist movement was founded—and funded—by the huge multinational oil corporations: Exxon, Mobil, Shell, etc. They *want* the Mother Earth crazies to act-up. It gives the greedy oil potentates an excuse to

The planet is awash in oil, but the elite have fabricated lies of "scarcity" to drive prices skyward to astronomical levels.

Agribusiness corporations now own over 90% of farm capacity. To gouge consumers, they lie and contend that food is scarce. Thus, prices are escalating fast.

shelve most of the world's oil that is discovered and cap-off tens of thousands of producing oil wells. It also provides the elite an excuse for their failure to build new gasoline refineries and pipelines.

Remember: It was President Richard Nixon, a supposedly "conservative" Republican, who created Big Brother's energy bureaucracy in Washington that today is in bed with the oil companies. It was Nixon who gave us the unconstitutional *Endangered Species Act* and *Environmental Protection Act* with their goal of taking away the citizen's private property rights. And it was during Nixon's ill-fated presidency that we had our first taste of long lines of autos waiting desperately at gas station pumps for "limited" and expensive gasoline for their tanks.

Regrettably, we now have con-artists like former Vice President Al Gore out on the hustings, pimping for the oil companies with his pretentious, undocumented and preposterous claims of "Global Warming." The Gore family—Al, Jr. and his corrupt father before him, Albert Gore, Sr.—were and are shills for Occidental Petroleum, owned by Communist/Capitalist (I know it sounds like an oxymoron, but it's the truth!) greedster, Armand Hammer. Gore's ambition is to become a billionaire and he doesn't intend to let a little thing like "truth" hold him back from achieving that aim.

Everyone Will Go Hungry

There is now also the new "scare"—the global shortage of food and the outrageous runup in the prices of commodities such as corn, wheat, rice, and other staples. Again, this is a contrived crisis designed to line the pocketbooks of corporate Mafia. Yes, the food riots by angry and hungry mobs of starving people in countries like Somalia, Ethiopia, Haiti, Bangladesh, and Indonesia are real. And the pictures of hungry emaciated children in Africa are, too. There is a food crisis—but it's an artificial crisis.

The fact is, new technologies in agriculture have increased production potential 100-fold in the past quarter of a century. Like the oil situation, the planet is awash in food. Thus, while the poverty-stricken masses overseas are begging for crumbs and some shortages are beginning to rear up even in the U.S.A. and developed nations, the distribution warehouses of the agribusiness corporations are bursting at the seams with surplus grains and other foodstocks. No one, anywhere, should be going hungry.

So, why the crisis? Look, at what has been happening on the commodity markets in Chicago and you'll find the answer. The well-fed Illuminati billionaires have bid up the *"futures"* prices for soybeans, wheat, rice, corn, cattle and every other product to ridiculously high levels. Now, to get their market manipulation to pay off, they must engineer global food shortages to drive prices through the roof. The fat cats are getting more and more wealthy off the misery of the hungry, fear-filled masses.

The Coming Great Thirst

Water is also an area where the rich are scamming the citizenry. There is a reason why Maurice Strong, former head of the UN's Environmental Program, owns most of the underground water reservoirs in Colorado and New Mexico, and has water interests in Canada, and why billionaires like T. Boone Pickens are investors in water supplies. Water is going to join oil and food as scarce resources so that, once again, the average person is scalped. I predict that within a few short years the price of water will escalate so much and shortages will be so severe that convenience stores won't even have bottled water to sell and restaurants will start charging customers $2, $3, or more for a small glass of H_2O!

And when the water crunch comes, don't even think about watering your lawn or using scarce water supplies to grow your home garden. Satellites overhead will be monitoring backyards to catch "violators" of new water regulations that are already on the drawing boards.

Schemes to Soak the Public

In the State of Texas, they've been working on a plan to tax citizens according to the amount of *rain* that annually falls on a person's property. That's right, if it is a wet year and you own even a postage stamp-sized suburban home, you could get socked with a new "rain use" tax of hundreds or thousands of dollars. That'll teach you to have the audacity to build your home in a place where it rains.

Taxing for the rain that falls on a person's property is only one of countless sinister methods being cooked up by the elite to plunder individual citizens of their hard-earned income and drive the masses into abject screaming poverty.

The United Nations has a scheme to charge every person who operates a tractor, a lawn mower, auto, power tool, or any other energy-using device a "carbon tax." A punishing tax will also hit homeowners and businesses that have air conditioning systems. Meanwhile, a global pollution tax will be placed on every gallon of gas you buy for vehicles.

The contrived food crisis gives the elite many golden opportunities to rip us off financially and consolidate their Big Brother police state control of the people.

Illuminist billionaires like T. Boone Pickens (left) and Maurice Strong (right) now control water rights to underground aquifers throughout the U.S.A. and Canada. Look for prices of water to go through the roof in coming years and for the media to print more absurd lies about how the world is running out of drinkable water.

The UN has erected a gigantic building in Europe to house its new globalist agency, the World Agriculture and Food Organization. From this gargantuan complex, bureaucrats will tell farmers in the U.S.A. and around the world what and when to plant. No one will be able to buy or sell food not approved by the global organization. This is the reason why the U.S. Department of Agriculture is demanding that every farm animal—horses, cows, sheep, goats—be microchipped and tagged and that ranchers and farmers maintain exhaustive records of the birth, death, and life of each and every animal. Soon, you will not be able to own livestock or any other farm animal without obtaining a government permit. Not even a single cow.

This is similar to what the oil industry is doing to keep mavericks and independents from drilling for and producing oil. Anyone who tries finds that they must first obtain a thousand permits from the "authorities" and face a blizzard of environmental and energy regulations. Only the multinationals—the Exxons and Mobils—are allowed to make money by bilking the public.

***Days of Hunger, Days of Chaos* by Texe Marrs, was the first book to reveal the "Terminator Gene" seed technology invented by elite-controlled scientists. The plan is eventually to starve the planet's teeming masses into submission.**

The New Reality

The Illuminati elite are processing and pushing humanity psychologically into a New Reality. Their goal is to force us all to accept this New Reality and to willingly enter their artificially created, new *Age of Scarcity*. Naturally, they, the High Priests, claim to have the solutions necessary to fix each and every crisis. If, however, we do not accept their prefabricated solutions, we will be crushed—the whole world will grind to a halt due to lack of oil, and we will all starve and thirst to death. What monstrous beasts and liars these elitist human devils are!

What You and I Can Do

I encourage you to obtain some of the resources—books, audios, and videos—we offer. My pivotal book, *Days of Hunger, Days of Chaos*, remains the classic text exposing the plot of the globalist elite and the government to control our food and bring forth panic and food chaos. My video and audio, *The Coming Great Thirst*, predicted the current squeeze and contrived crisis in water supplies, and my recent audiotapes/CDs, *Planet Petroleum* and *Everyone Will Go Hungry*, provide extensive facts about our current predicament.

Please order these resources, stay informed, then go forth and educate others. Only by spreading the truth far and wide do we have any hope at all of defeating the sick, disastrous schemes of the elite and their media cohorts who are Satan's allies. With God's help, we will prevail.

Genocide, Depopulation of the Earth, and Environmental Extremism

Masonic Jews Plot to Kill Followers of Jesus in New Holocaust

A Sea of Blood

"And the second angel poured out his vial upon the sea; and it became as the blood of a dead man: and every living soul died in the sea. And the third angel poured out his vial upon the rivers and fountains of waters; and they became blood. And I heard the angel of the waters say, Thou art righteous, O Lord, which art, and wast, and shalt be, because thou has judged thus. For they have shed the blood of saints and prophets..."

—*Revelation 16:3-6*

Surveying all the prophecies of the Holy Bible, we might well conclude that one of the most startling of all prophecies is the horrifying image of a *Sea of Blood.* Throughout the 20th century mankind experienced savage atrocities and bloodshed on a breathtakingly brutal magnitude.

Reviewing the ages of man, we see that there have, of course, always been massacres and genocide. But, the 20th century stands out because of the growth of the totalitarian nature of governments. True, in past eras, we had our Alexander the Greats, our Genghis Khans, and our Attila the Hun types who killed and rampaged with impunity. But, with the explosion of the ideological "isms"—fascism, communism, socialism, nazism, zionism—and the rise of Big Brother tools, concentration camps and gulags, the butchery and black evil of genocide and mass killings seemed to take a quantum leap. Worse, the 20th century may prove to be a harbinger of even greater bloodshed and horror to come in the 21st century.

In 1915, Masonic Jewish socialists overthrew the Islamic Ottoman government of Turkey and commenced the genocidal murder of two million Christian Armenians. "Butcher Brigades" of criminals cut off so many hands of Christian victims, the British Consul reported, that, if placed side-by-side, a highway could have been built of severed human hands. This severed hand of a Christian Armenian woman slain in the massacre was dried and kept as a souvenir and talisman by a Jewish Mason in the town of Salonika.

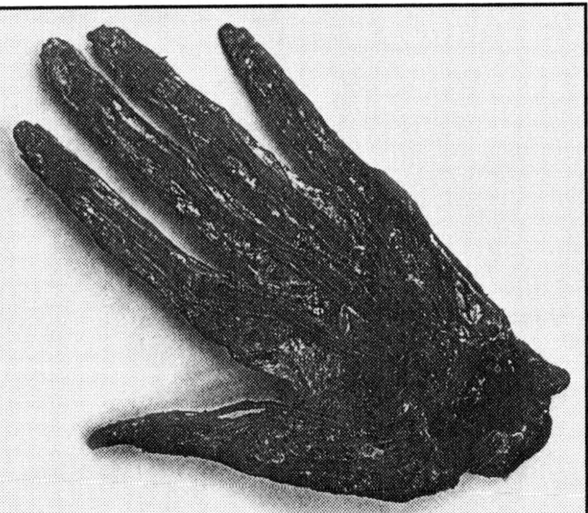

Interestingly, the mass media has focused most all its attention on just one great genocide and massacre: The alleged Nazi holocaust. Ask the average person to describe the carnage and holocausts of Armenia, Rwanda, Nigeria, Cambodia, Red China, or Soviet Russia and you will receive a blank stare. Due to media brainwashing, as far as the public is concerned, there has only been one holocaust, one genocide—that of the Nazi Germans who, we are reminded over and over, singled out the Jews for victimhood.

My Investigation Into Genocides

For years, I have poured over thousands of books and papers to ascertain the truth about genocides and holocausts throughout human history, during the 20th century and prior. Few people have done as much research and investigation on these monstrous events. In so doing, I have been able, with God's help, to gain a clear understanding of what really happened during the centuries after Christ when the Romans put hundreds of thousands of Christians to death. I know of the intrigue surrounding the Inquisition, of the murderous intentions of the Illuminati who massacred thousands in the bloody French Revolution, of the horrors and crimes of the men who invented the Soviet Gulags, and of the countless dead bodies stacked into pyramids of bones by the Khmer Rouge of Cambodia.

My most shocking discovery is this: That the greatest murderers of all times were not the Romans, nor the French revolutionaries. No, it was not even the Red Chinese Maoists or the Nazi overlords who were the most bloodthirsty. *In fact, it is undisputed that the greatest murderers of all time have been Zionist Jews.*

I know. You have never heard such a thing before. So what? That is simply proof that one cannot trust the establishment media to tell us the whole truth. Nor can we believe in the falsification of history foisted on us by establishment historians and scholars—men and women who have sold their souls for a bacteria-infested bowl of porridge.

The past is truly a prelude to tomorrow's events. The prophetic scriptures warn us that a sea of blood is revealed in our future. Genocide is a continuing project of evildoers. What we must realize is that one particular group has clearly been designated as the next to be butchered. That group is made up of all those who refuse to pledge allegiance to the fledgling Zionist New World Order, as well as those who get in the way of its march to fulfillment.

Symbolic Snake of Zionism

Across the globe, the symbolic snake of Zionism has slowly and inexorably worked its way across the continents of earth, conquering and gorging on spoils. The snake was made fat with the blood of Armenian Christians in 1915. The snake gorged itself with Russian, Ukrainian, and Polish blood in the 1920s, 30s, 40s, and 50s, with Lenin, Trotsky, Stalin, Beria, and Khruschev over-seeing the dismemberment of victims. Innocent German men, women, and children were devoured beginning in 1945 in gulags ruled by Jewish Commissars like Solomon Morel. In Cambodia, Pol Pot and other Jewish-trained agents of Paris' Grand Orient Masonic Lodge stacked corpses up like cordwood.

All-in-all, Masonic Jews, often pretending to be Russian, Polish, Turkish, and other nationalities, massacred well over 100 million innocents. And that is only in one century.

Today, the all-seeing eyed snake, led by Zionist masters, has dual headquarters in the United States/Europe and in Israel.

Jews Loyal Only to Themselves

Some 18 million Jews are on this planet. Most are more loyal to Israel and to the global "Jewish Nation" than they are to the country in which they reside. Only a few of them are actively assisting the global Illuminati conspiracy. Most have little or no knowledge of the conspiracy, but because most Jews continually "feed," encourage, and support the goals of the Zionist elite and promote Israel's brutal imperialistic ambitions, almost all Jews are complicit—that is, are guilty.

Because most Jews boastfully tout themselves as a *superior race, "God's Chosen," rulers and judges of earth,* they must share the blame, excepting the few who have repented. The evil and poisonous doctrine of Jewish supremacy has infected almost all the Jews on earth. It causes many Jews to be arrogant and hateful. After all, their most holy religious book, The Talmud, instructs them that even the best of Christians should be killed and that the goyim (gentiles) are but cattle, slaves destined to serve Jewish masters. This religious doctrine is a recipe for satanic mayhem and destruction.

Through secret societies and their many evil organizations—the Jerusalem government, the ACLU, the ADL, the B'nai B'rith, the American Jewish Committee, People for the American Way, etc.—the majority of Jews have incited, encouraged, and sanctioned the commission of grievous crimes against humanity and against God.

Filling Up the Sea with Blood

These worldwide Jews are helping the few at the top to fill up the sea with blood. As Zionists, their aim is to rule over mankind. Sadly, what the majority of Jews cannot understand, because they are carnal and have not the spirit of Christ in their hearts, is that they will, themselves, someday become victims of their own avarice, greed, and racial pride. Pride goeth before a fall, and that fall is surely coming. Throughout the centuries, Zionists Jews have butchered and killed Christians. The Bible says they have "shed the blood of saints and prophets" *(Matthew 23:27-39 Revelation 18:23-24).* God surely will not allow this situation to continue.

Still, it is not our task as Christians to get revenge on the Jews no matter how vile and criminal they are in their conduct and behavior toward us. "Vengeance is mine, saith the Lord."

What, Then, Must Christians Do?

Every Christian who reads this—and I define a Christian as only those who insist that Jesus alone is the way, the truth, and the life—needs to educate himself on the past genocidal crimes of the Jewish Zionists. Unless you understand that over 100 million Christians have already been massacred by the Zionist Jewish leadership in the past, you will not understand that their evil leadership plan targets you and me to become victims in the near future. That is why I offer a vital, 3-part audiotape or CD series on this topic, *A Sea of Blood.* Obtain and listen to the voluminous evidence I present in *A Sea of Blood,* and I guarantee, you will understand not only what has happened, but more important, what is coming.

> *"The thing that hath been, it is that which shall be; and that which is done is that which shall be done: and there is no new thing under the sun."*
>
> —*Ecclesiastes 1:9*

> *"And when he had opened the fifth seal, I saw under the altar the souls of them that were slain for the word of God, and for the testimony which they held: And they cried with a loud voice, saying, How long, O Lord, holy and true, dost thou not judge and avenge our blood on them that dwell on the earth? And white robes were given unto every one of them...that they should rest yet for a little season, until their fellowservants also and their brethren, that should be killed as they were, should be fulfilled."*
>
> —*Revelation 6:9-11*

Filling the World with Terror...

Long Night of the Black Marias

The Communists wasted no time after seizing the organs of government in Soviet Russia. Almost immediately the arrests began. The Gulag began to overflow with prisoners. The pain grew and grew. Torrents of blood were spilled. Only the Jews were exempt, and even a few of them were taken away:

> "And so in Moscow they began a systematic search, block by block. Someone had to be arrested everywhere. The slogan was: "We are going to bang our fist on the table so hard the world will shake with terror!"...
>
> The Black Marias, the passenger cars, the enclosed trucks, the open hansom cabs, kept moving...The Gulag Archipelago had already begun its malignant life and would shortly metastasize throughout the whole body of the nation." (Aleksandr Solzhenitsyn, *The Gulag Archipelago*, pp. 42-43).

The persons most hated and reviled by the Communist Jews who ran the Gulag prisons were the Christians, the Bible-believers, the faithful Gentiles. Lenin, the Jewish Commissar who had become the Kremlin's new master, demanded *"merciless suppression" of the "counterrevolutionaries and other persons."* Christians, no matter how meek, gentle, and nonviolent, certainly fit into that broad, all-encompassing category of "other persons!"

Harmful Insects to be Purged

In his essay, "How to Organize the Competition" (January 7 and 10, 1918), Lenin proclaimed the common, united purpose of *"purging the Russian land of all kinds of harmful insects."*

The Jewish overlords, led by Lenin and Trotsky, (later, Kaganovich, and Beria) were self-appointed exterminators. Some 66 million "insects" (people, many of whom were Christians) were the vermin who had to be exterminated. The "parasites" must vanish. It was all for the good of building the new Jewish Utopia, a global-wide One World Order to be ruled by the Jewish clique, which euphemistically called itself the *"Vanguard."*

Leon Trotsky, a Communist Jew from the Bronx, New York City, whose real name was "Bronstein," was sent by the Jewish Illuminati to Moscow to help overthow the government and set up a Jewish-run dictatorship. Trotsky was a principal architect of the "Red Terror."

Solzhenitsyn, in his classic book, *Gulag Archipelago*, writes that all those active in Christian churches were deemed *"insects"* and *"parasites,"* even those who sang in church choirs. But, of course, there were also many other groups considered too dangerous to be allowed to exist. And so, factory workers, artists, teachers, youth, farmers, engineers—millions of people from just about every social category—were culled out and taken away to prison labor camps. Many of these hapless victims were driven to the fateful kangaroo courts in the despised and feared Black Marias.

Taking power in Russia, Jewish Communist leaders took delight in demolishing Christian churches. Some were converted into barns and stables, others into factories and warehouses.

The Black Marias Came Out At Night

Ah, yes, the Black Marias. They usually came at night. They found their victims at home, in their apartments and flats, or on the street, in bars and in theatres. They worked off lists, and oh, how lengthy some lists were. Resisters were pummeled, beaten, sometimes bayoneted and dragged into the long, black, box-car, limo-like automobiles that came to be called the *"Black Marias."*

In a typical night's work in a city, the Communist thugs would round up fourteen to sixteen victims and crowd them like sardines into the austere compartments of the Black Marias.

Solzhenitsyn tells the sad story of one young woman, a secretary, dragged into a Black Maria car. Innocent and a virgin, guilty of nothing more than the fact that she had refused to give in to the sexual demands of a Communist bureaucrat, the naive girl was attacked inside the crowded cab by a half dozen filthy gangsters. They stripped her of her purse and shoes, ripped her dress, and their hands went all over her body. Raped and battered, the girl was a physical and emotional wreck by the time the Black Maria rolled into the police courtyard where she and the others were ordered out.

The girl began to whimper, cry, and complain about her treatment, but the guard simply shrugged his shoulders and told her to move on. He knew that what awaited the girl in the gulag prison was even more hellish than the savage pounding she had just taken. In any event, these things happened every night, seven nights a week. It was the nature of the beast. The beast demanded victims.

The innocence of the arrested was no excuse. Chance, randomness, also had its premium in the lives—and deaths—of the millions of "selectees" chosen to be human chattel, slaves of the beast and its Gulag.

An Eye For An Eye

It was not only in Soviet Russia and its conquered republics that the prisons filled up with slaves. In occupied Eastern Europe, too, the Jews who ran Poland, Czechoslovakia, Hungary, Romania, and other nations that had fallen under the jackboots of the Soviets, set up concentration camps. In *An Eye For An Eye*, heartsick, prize-winning Jewish reporter Jonathan Sack documents the cruel fate of thousands of men, women, and children whose only "crime" was that they had the misfortune to have a German surname. The Jews were determined to get their revenge for Nazi crimes, and these poor souls, even little children, babies, and old men and women who had had nothing at all to do with the Nazis—many of them had even suffered themselves under Nazi occupation—would

Below: An isolated slave camp in the icy region of Siberia. Inmates worked and shivered in frigid conditions, and untold millions perished. Today, Jewish controlled government media in Russia and the U.S.A. allow no-one to tell their pitiful story of suffering, pain, and death.

Communist Gulag camps were hell on earth. Above: Entrance to a Russian slave labor camp. The sign reads: "Work in the Soviet Union is a Matter of Honor and Glory."

just have to serve as scapegoats.

And so, the arrests, the torture, and the slaughter began in earnest. Women were raped and brutalized by the vicious Jewish guards who ran the Communist camps, boys were sodomized, and children molested and ritually sacrificed in what can only be described as some type of medieval Jewish, satanic, kabbalistic rites.

"You Have Come Here to Die"

Sack's stunning reports even introduce us to a Jewish woman prison camp commandant, but especially distressing is Sack's numbing account of the genocidal savagery of Solomon "Schlomo" Morel. Morel, a Polish Jew, was surely the inhuman equal of Ivan the Terrible or, say, Joseph Mengele. Morel liked to greet each new trainload or truckload of German-surnamed prisoners. *"You have come here to die,"* the strutting, military-uniformed, polished boot-wearing Morel would announce to the heart-fallen men, women, and children, *"and I shall be your executioner!"*

The Past as a Picture of an Ominous Future?

Why, some might ask, is it necessary for me to remind you, dear reader, of these tragic and awful things? Why not just forget the past? Let bygones be bygones.

It has often been said that he who forgets the past is doomed to repeat it. The past is prologue to the future. The Old Testament tells us there is nothing new under the sun. What has happened before could—and does—happen again.

This, then, is a warning. Already, we can see the storm clouds gathering.

Solomon "Schlomo" Morel, a murderous Jewish Commandant who imprisoned, tortured, and killed so many innocent German men, women, and children. Morel loved to physically beat Germans to death. He once grabbed a German Mother's baby from her arms. Holding the baby by its legs, he swung and smashed its head into a wall, killing it instantly. Today, this genocidal monster, indicted and wanted for murder by the Polish government, is living in Israel, shielded from prosecution by the Israeli government of Prime Minister Benjamin Netanyahu.

Lightning is flashing. America has become the destined New Rome and Israel is the driver of that destiny. Around the world, America is the proxy Rottweiler for the Jews, their attack dog. Zionist Jews covertly rule behind the scenes in Washington, D.C. They control our media and news, our entertainment industries, our education establishment, and our book and magazine publishing. They own our computer and high tech corporations. With the assistance of the CIA and FBI, the Israeli Mossad and its ADL cohorts are now monitoring what we say on the internet.

Again, there is talk of a Zionist Kingdom on planet earth, and the buzz among high-level Jews is their plot to rid the earth of the *goyim* (Gentiles), the inferior "insects"—first, the Palestinians and Arabs and, next, the Christians. Not the average "Christian," mind you—only the Bible-believer who understands *(Daniel 12:10)*. The other "Christians" the Zionist Jewish elite already have in their back pocket.

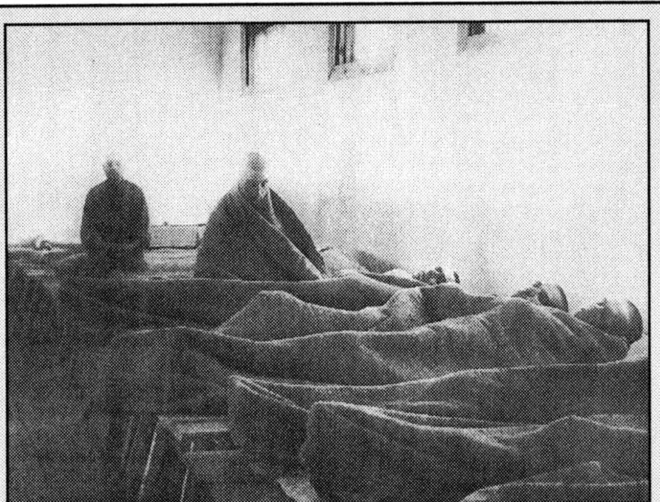

Many of the Communist Gulag prisoners died of malnutrition. Their meager daily diet consisted of a filthy, rat feces-infested bowl of gruel and occasionally a tiny bit of hard black bread.

These dark forces have worked diligently for centuries to usher in a New World Zionist Order. With their iron grip on the world's media and banking and by using the armed might and diplomatic influence of their powerful proxy, America *(Revelation 17),* they intend to conquer and seize total global domination. Amazingly, they are on the threshold of accomplishing this incredible feat.

A Special Message to Zionists and to All Jews

But, I warn these dark forces: In attacking God's people, true Christian believers, and in working to destroy all vestiges of freedom and liberty in America and the world, you are unwittingly undoing yourself. Be assured: God will avenge crimes committed against His people.

Please, I beg you: Think about what you are doing. Do not feed the *curse* that is already upon you. In Illuminist Revolutionary France, in Communist Russia, and elsewhere, your Protocols have been wildly successful. They have vaulted you into the upper echelons of power. Now, you believe yourself to be gods on earth. But you are mistaken. You are mere men, born sinners as are all men.

My message, then, to Zionist Jews, is: Do not lie to yourself. Only the Truth will save you. And only Jesus Christ is that Truth. He has set before you Death and Life. Therefore, choose Life through Him! If you refuse, then do not be surprised when someday, in a future, long night of the Black Marias, the Black Marias come for YOU.

But you, as an individual Jewish man or woman, do not have to be a victim. You do not have to participate in The Lie. You do not have to join in the unholy, ages-old plot and scheme of your Zionist leaders. You can put an end to the long night. We, Gentiles and, yes, some Jews, who know Christ Jesus are your only true friends. Call on us before it is too late, and believe in our Savior, Jesus. He is able to deliver you and us. We promise: He will not fail you!

Media Keep Lid on Worst Holocaust in Human History

Jewish Killers Massacre 66 Million in Soviet Gulag

"I love strong opponents! It's such fun to break their backs! said the Leningrad interrogator Shitov. And if your opponent (e.g. your prisoner) is so strong that he refuses to give in, all your methods have failed and you are in a rage? Then, don't control your fury! It's tremendously satisfying, that outburst! Let your anger have its way; don't set any bounds to it. Don't hold yourself back! That's when interrogators spit in the open mouth of the accused! And shove his face into a full toilet! That's the state of mind in which they drag Christian believers around by their hair. Or urinate in a kneeling prisoner's face! After such a storm of fury you feel yourself a real honest-to-God man!"

— Aleksandr Solzhenitsyn
The Gulag Archipelago

It's been all over the press, on TV and in newspapers. Mel Gibson, the famous movie actor and director, has been horribly slandered, defamed, and verbally mauled by the Jewish elite who uniformly hate and despise Gibson's powerful film, *The Passion of The Christ*. The ADL, the Simon Wiesenthal Center, and other racist anti-Christian hate groups have made Gibson their whipping boy now for over a year.

But, hold on! You think Gibson has been treated unfairly, you haven't seen anything yet. Consider the case of Nobel Prize-winning historian and writer Aleksandr Solzhenitsyn. The Jews have been ripping into, slandering and otherwise savaging the reputation of the solidly Christian Solzhenitsyn for some four years now. But unlike the Gibson affair, the controlled media disingenuously refuse to report it. Solzhenitsyn is the hapless victim whose brutal mental whipping and emotional beating the world knows nothing about.

It now seems aeons ago that the stoic Russian author was celebrated for his insightful, poignant accounts of the horrible, subhuman treatment of the victims of the Soviet Communist Gulag, an interlocking system of thousands of concentration and slave labor camps. Solzhenitsyn

The brave Aleksandr Solzhenitsyn, the famous Russian writer who has been called the "Conscience of the 20th Century," served eight long years in the Soviet Gulag prison system. Today, he is hated by top-level Jews in America and around the world because he exposed the Jewish leadership of the genocide of 66 million Communist Gulag victims. Many victims were Christians.

himself had been a prisoner of the Gulag for a decade, preventively jailed for nothing more than the fear of the communist overlords that he might someday write something the Kremlin masters might find offensive to the state.

Solzhenitsyn: The "Conscience of the 20th Century"

Historian Solzhenitsyn's gut-wrenching book, *Gulag Archipelago*, went through countless printings—in over 50 languages—and touched the hearts of westerners. Expelled by the Kremlin for telling the awful truth, this great man was honored by freedom-loving people both in the United States and in Europe. He was often called the *"Conscience of the 20th Century"* and recognized universally as one of the globe's prime examples of bold courage and moral conviction. Even the liberal press initially had nice things to say about Solzhenitsyn. They were reluctant to go up against a man so honored for high moral stature, and recognized by so many as a truthteller of the highest character.

Karl Marx, the Jewish radical who inspired Lenin and Trotsky with his communist theories, was secretly a High Priest of Satan (see Richard Wurmbrand's book, *Marx and Satan*). Shown here in his official portrait, Marx is giving an enigmatic Masonic hand sign (see *Richardson's Monitor of Freemasonry*, p. 74).

Then, the historian and truthteller Solzhenitsyn made what was, to liberals and communists, a grave error. Asked at a press conference his opinion on why the terrible events behind the Iron Curtain had occurred, why millions were carted away, tortured, starved and worked to death in Gulag slave camps, Solzhenitsyn gave this simple, yet startling, response: *"Man has forgotten God."*

"Outrageous," the Critics Roared

"What did you say? God? Outrageous!" the critics roared. Immediately, the world's press began a reversal of opinion about this man they once had lionized. Some called him a *"Christian fanatic."* Others said Solzhenitsyn was *"reactionary...right wing...a religious nut."*

Then, in 2000, Solzhenitsyn released a blockbuster new book he had penned entitled *Together For Two Hundred Years*. The new book was a lengthy treatise, a thorough and far-reaching compilation of several decades of research by Aleksandr Solzhenitsyn into the machinations for two centuries of Jews inside Russia and the Soviet Empire.

Accurate in every detail, painstakingly documented, the author showed how, over the centuries, a small band of revolutionary Jews had conspired and plotted to overthrow the Russian Czars. Their aim: seize control of Czarist Russia and establish a beachhead for a Jewish utopia on planet earth—the long sought after Kingdom of the Jews.

The Gulags of the Jewish Revolutionaries

With staggering implications, *Together For Two Hundred Years* showed how Lenin, Trotsky and other Jewish conspirators had overthrown the Romanov dynasty in 1917 and set up their own Bolshevik totalitarian system. The result: The nightly assassination and roundup of thousands of innocent men, women, and children, most of whom were herded by black-hearted Big Brother secret police into thousands of monstrously evil Gulag concentration camps.

The largest number of victims, Solzhenitsyn reports, were Christian believers, understandable since the revolutionary Jews despised and hated Jesus and His Chosen People, the Christians. All-in-all, about *66 million* innocent people were kidnapped and eventually died a hideous death at the

Four Gulag camp commandants. Note that all four are giving the secret sign of Jewish Freemasonry, just as did Communism's founding father, the Jewish Mason, Karl Marx.

hands of the Jewish "Ivan the Terrible" corps.

66 million murdered by mostly Jewish Gulag overlords! That's over ten times the number of Jews claimed to have been slain in Nazi concentration camps.

Obviously, such a powerful—and truthful—book as *Together For Two Hundred Years* must be suppressed. And it has been. No English-speaking publisher, either in Britain or in the U.S.A. has dared to publish it. So far, Solzhenitsyn's book has only been issued in the Russian language.

"Crush This Insolent Wretch"

Shamelessly, yet quietly and without a lot of fanfare, Jewish organizations have put out the word: *"Crush this insolent wretch, Aleksandr Solzhenitsyn. Give his works, his voice no forum, kill him with neglect. If you must mention his name, say it with scorn and with taunts and ridicule. Punish him severely for attempting to reveal our secrets to the world. Let him be an example of what the Jewish Power can do to a man who stubbornly refuses to tow the Zionist party line."*

I have seen what they have done to Solzhenitsyn. I have read their biased and spiteful reviews of his book in the controlled media and witnessed their revengeful hatred of him in countless Jewish magazines, websites, and journals influential but relatively unknown to the public at large. The ruthless Jewish Power clique works to kill men in a variety of ways. With Mel Gibson, it was more public. With Solzhenitsyn, it is more personal and private. Clearly, Solzhenitsyn's writings about the Jewish leadership of the Soviet Holocaust is viewed as a grave threat to the Jewish Plan for global supremacy.

> *Fascinating, isn't it, how much fury, venom, and wrath just a touch of truth can whip up among the Jewish overlords and their Gentile accomplices who today guide Western culture.*

In Russia, millions of people—many of them survivors of the Gulag—still love and respect the aging man of God, Aleksandr Solzhenitsyn. They have read his newest book, and they know it is true. They lived it! They also well understand why such a book is being kept from the American people. The Talmudic Jews are fiercely determined that the whole truth about their repugnant, genocidal crimes be covered up. Solzhenitsyn's reputation must be progressively tarnished and his writings buried forever.

So now, the man, Solzhenitsyn, who suffered under the Jewish Gulag tormentors for so long, must now be tortured once again, and for the same purported "crime," the offense of using "words."

"Words Are More Deadly Than Bullets"

It was Lenin who once said, *"Words are more deadly than bullets."* Leninist ideology is truly an exemplar of the poisonous Talmudic Jewish mindset. Today, in America, there are, consequently, many things a man cannot say, cannot write about, and cannot publish. I know. I have, myself, faithfully followed God's calling and done my best to follow in Solzhenitsyn's footsteps. The Jewish holocaust revisionists have punished me, too, and they continue today to threaten and bully whip me and *Power of Prophecy* ministries.

Like Mel Gibson and Aleksandr Solzhenitsyn, Texe Marrs is now being falsely and cruelly branded an "anti-Semite," a "Jew-hater" and worse, on all seven continents.

Fascinating, isn't it, how much fury, venom, and wrath just a touch of truth can whip up among the Jewish overlords and their Gentile accomplices, who today guide Western culture and minutely monitor and control every aspect of media reporting on politics, economics, and religion.

The Fearless Few Are Hated

Their greatest hatred, their most vicious spewing of venom, is reserved for the fearless few who dare to reveal to the world the heinous crimes committed by the Jewish Power in the Communist Gulag, especially the Zionist murder of 66 million men, women, and children, many of them Bible-believing Christians.

Equally hated are men like Ernst Zundel of Canada, who have questioned whether six million Jews actually died in a Nazi Holocaust. But even if six million died in a Nazi Holocaust, what of the *sixty-six million* who perished in the Jewish Gulag? And remember: Thousands of Nazis have been tracked down and punished for their reported crimes against humanity. Why is it that *not even one Zionist Jew* has ever been brought to justice for the heinous crimes committed in the Jewish Communist Gulag? Why?

For almost six decades, America and the planet have been preaching to the Germans, reminding them of the terrible crimes of their Nazi ancestors. It is only fair and just that we all now turn our attention to the Communist Gulag Holocaust, that we expose the Jews' role in its monstrous crimes and remind the Jews of what *their* criminal ancestors did to these sixty-six million innocent victims, most of whom were Christians.

This official postcard, widely circulated by the Communist government in Russia following the Jewish Bolshevik takeover, is entitled "Leaders of the Proletarian Revolution." The postcard reveals the Jewishness of these original leaders of the Communist Party. All six shown, including Lenin and Trotsky, are Jews!

Time For a Christian Holocaust Museum?

Isn't it also time we demand construction of a Christian Holocaust Museum in Washington, D.C., to be erected next door to the existing taxpayer-funded Jewish Holocaust Museum? Is only the suffering of Jews worthy of being memorialized? What about the pain and suffering endured by so many other ethnic and religious groups, including that of Russian and Eastern European Christians during the Jewish Bolshevik era? Don't these tens of millions of Gentiles killed and tortured deserve to be remembered as well?

Today's Stalins, Hitlers, and Pol Pots—be advised...

He That Killed With The Sword Must Be Killed With The Sword

"Some men are of so cruel a nature as to take a delight in killing men more than you should to kill a bird."

— Thomas Hobbes
Brief Lives (1949)

"We were not allowed to cry or show any grief when they took away our loved ones. A man would be killed if he lost an ox he was assigned to tend. A woman would be killed if she were too tired and exhausted to work. Human life was not even worth a bullet. They clubbed the backs of our necks and pushed us down to smother us and let us die in a deep hole with hundreds of other bodies."

These are the sorrowful words of Teeda Mam, victim and survivor of a Cambodian death camp, as reported in Dith Pran's book, *Children of Cambodia's Killing Fields.*

In the 1970s, the Communist regime in Cambodia methodically and without the smallest tinge of human sympathy or compassion saw to the abduction, torture, incarceration and death of up to three and a half million of its own citizens. Men, women, and children suffered unfathomable cruelty and deprivation. Numerous torture centers were set up and prisoners were duly numbered and "processed." Beatings, starvation, rapes, and the most savage tortures were inflicted. It was as if all the hounds and beasts of hell were unleashed in one place at the same time.

Amazingly, until this time, the Cambodians had gained a reputation as being a gentle people, occupying a land of smiles: friendly, humble city dwellers and peasants eager to demonstrate kind acts. Almost in a moment, many of these same "good" people were inspired to commit repugnant,

Meticulous records of Cambodians taken to torture and death camps were kept by their Communist captors, and their pictures and dossiers kept in files. All of those shown here perished.

bloody crimes of utter horror, of unspeakable dimensions. Had Satan turned on a switch inside their brains? What insanity possessed these schizophrenic killers to cause them to launch such monstrous acts against innocent neighbors and countrymen?

Barbarism and Cruelty are Universal Traits

Is it possible that Americans, too, can somehow be led to commit such horrors? Many in our nation imagine that America is immune from such evil, and that Americans are of a different mental set. But, in fact, as I document in my revealing video, *Gulag USA—Concentration Camps in America*, historical evidence of American genocide and barbarism can easily be traced. During the Civil War (1861-1865), horrific acts of cruelty and murderous barbarity were common in POW camps run by both the North and South. During World War II, Japanese-Americans were forcibly rounded up and imprisoned in U.S. government "internment camps."

In Vietnam in the 1960s, under its hellish, Top Secret *Phoenix* program, the American CIA and U.S. Army helpers abducted, murdered, and unmercifully tortured tens of thousands of victims. Many were thrown into inhuman cages, starved into submission and finally bludgeoned or shot to death. Some were drowned, others thrown out of helicopters. Young women and children were not spared by the "gods" of the American CIA and military.

America's leaders, including Presidents Johnson and Nixon, were never called to account for these grotesque crimes against humanity. Nor were the Communist butchers who ran the thousands of gulags in the former USSR and Mao's Red China ever punished for their demonic, terror-filled crimes.

Top: "Uncooperative" Japanese-American at a U.S. government internment camp is led away to a prison cell.

Middle: Two inmates at the U.S. government's Tule Lake concentration camp for Japanese-Americans are caught by guards trying to escape. Notice the guard tower in the background.

Bottom: Inmates at a U.S. "internment camp" for Japanese-Americans were forced to post this welcoming sign when D.S. Myer, government official from Washington, D.C. visited their camp.

"This animal is very wicked"

A hundred and one movies or more have been made by Hollywood depicting alleged Nazi concentration camp horrors. But strangely, not one film has every been made accurately portraying the fiendish genocidal death camps approved and supervised by Roosevelt, Johnson, Nixon, Helms, Komer, Colby, Stalin, Lenin, Mao, Pol Pot and their associates.

David Carlin, writing in *First Things* magazine (November 1994), noted: "While Stalin was running one of the two worst dictatorships in the history of the human race (the other having been presided over by his sometimes ally, Hitler), murdering tens of millions of human beings, here in America great numbers of privileged and influential citizens either supported Communism or admired it."

As Carlin lamented, those who consider themselves to be "sophisticated" (political socialists like FDR, Bill and Hillary Clinton, the FBI's former head Louis Freeh, Attorney Generals Reno and Ashcroft, as well as Hollywood's movie and New York's Broadway cliques) are firmly convinced that the commandment, "Thou shalt not murder," is intended (as Leona Helmsley said about taxes) only for the little people, whereas mass murder, though admittedly a nasty business, is virtuous

Unmarked military trucks at what appears to be a FEMA/CIA facility. Are these strangely configured vehicles designed to transport people to concentration camps? A sign on the barbed wire fence announces: "WARNING: This is a U.S. Customs Bonded Warehouse."

when done by the right people for the right reasons.

Judging from what happened at Ruby Ridge and at Waco, there is no doubt that the philosophy of many in high leadership positions in America today toward the downtrodden is best described by the old French witticism—*"Cet animal est tres méchant; quand on láttaque, il se défend."* ("This animal is very wicked; when you attack it, it defends itself.")

Hollywood and the Jews who control the media want us to believe that only the Germans are so wicked and vile as to be capable of committing such horrific crimes. In any case, the message is: "Don't worry; forget about what the Communists did. It is irrelevant. Your great American leaders will never let this be repeated over here, inside the good, old U.S.A."

Death by Design

Wrong. Once you view *Gulag USA—Concentration Camps in America*, you will know for sure it can happen here. And it is going to happen, *by design*. The *Phoenix Program* is alive! The U.S. death camps already exist, and soon they will be filled with prisoners. And the President and his associates will tell us they are needed for our safety and protection, to end the threat of terrorism.

Today, our future tormentors calmly walk the halls of the Pentagon, the U.S. Congress, the Justice Department, and the White House, nattily dressed in tailored suits or in crisply starched military green.

American children have long been fed a steady cultural diet of sorcery, death and violence. From an early age, they were immersed in gruesome, cannibalistic movies like *The Texas Chainsaw Massacre* and *Silence of the Lambs*. They are primed to kill. Ready to inflict pain. Tomorrow, you will see them face to face, emotionless, in their blood-spattered fatigues, as they systematically torture and humiliate you. They will be your captors, your executioners, your nightmares. It is what they have been taught to do, by society, by our schools, with the acquiescence of their parents and guardians. And now they are in charge.

> *And when he had opened the fifth seal, I saw under the altar the souls of them that were slain for the word of God, and for the testimony which they held: And they cried with a loud voice, saying, How long, O Lord, holy and true, dost thou not judge and avenge our blood on them that dwell on the earth?*
>
> *—Revelation 6:9-10*

> *He that leadeth into captivity shall go into captivity: he that killeth with the sword must be killed with the sword. Here is the patience and the faith of the saints.*
>
> *—Revelation 13:10*

Real Life Blood Games...

The Report From Iron Mountain

Was the Oklahoma City atrocity plotted out in advance as part of a *"Blood Games"* agenda? How about other recent historical "terrorist acts" and the whole array of bloody movies and popular modern entertainment brimful of violent, blood-soaked, sadistic acts, death and destruction? Are these, too, part and parcel of the Illuminati's *Blood Games* agenda?

In fact, there is such an agenda, deadly in nature, that has been foisted on the American people and, indeed, on the inhabitants of the entire planet.

In 1963 a special Top Secret commission of government experts met secretly underground in a place called Iron Mountain, a highly protected and shielded defense installation deep inside the earth in New York state. Its mission: To devise goals for the worlds' governments to pursue to insure *continuing control of the people of Earth*, once the Cold War of the two superpowers was ended and global peace enforced.

It was believed by our hidden rulers that wars had been tremendously effective in channeling the peoples' energies and permitting governments to establish and maintain social control. The masses were told that war is necessary for state security and defense needs, to present a common front against the enemy, protect the people's way of life, etc.

If however, wars were abolished, the committee's task was to come up with *alternative* mechanisms and methods of social control.

In its final report to the President of the United States, informally entitled The Report From Iron Mountain, the distinguished men of this committee presented five substitutes for war in the event the worlds rulers chose to end the Cold War and to establish a New World Order based on peace and cooperation among the world's superpowers. The substitute for war which stands out from among the others is: "Blood Games."

A "Blood Price" Must Be Paid

I have in my files a copy of *The Report From Iron Mountain*, and I am astonished at the blunt proposals of this Top Secret committee. Obviously, the government and its hidden rulers never thought for a moment you and I would have access to this classified information, but here it is, from pages 70 and 71:

> "When it comes to postulating a credible substitute for war capable of directing human behavior patterns in behalf of social organization...the motivational function of war requires the existence of a genuinely menacing social

REPORT FROM IRON MOUNTAIN ON THE POSSIBILITY AND DESIRABILITY OF PEACE

WITH INTRODUCTORY MATERIAL BY LEONARD C. LEWIN

"The unwillingness of [The Special Study Group] to publicize their findings [is] readily understandable.... They concluded [that] lasting peace, while not theoretically impossible, is probably unattainable; even if it could be achieved it would almost certainly not be in the best interests of a stable society to achieve it...."

> enemy... The "alternate enemy" must imply a more immediate, tangible, and directly felt threat of destruction. It must justify the need for taking and paying a "blood price" in wide areas of human concern...
>
> Games theorists have suggested, in other contexts, the development of "blood games" for effective control of individual aggressive impulses... It was left not to scientists but to the makers of a commercial film to develop a model for this... on the implausible level of popular melodrama, as a ritualized manhunt.
>
> More realistically, such a (Blood Games) ritual might be socialized, in the manner of the Spanish Inquisition and the less formal witch trials of other periods, for purposes of "social purification," "state security," or other rationale both acceptable and credible to postwar societies."

Real Life Blood Games

The high-level government intelligence operatives who gave us *The Report From Iron Mountain* proposed a plan to carry out popularly accepted, new forms of ritualized Blood Games:

> Combining this function (blood games) with sophisticated, modern forms of human slavery, based on the precedent of organized ethnic repression, warrants careful consideration.

He whom the elite rulers have chosen to be sacrificed must first be smeared and demonized.

The United States has recently conducted a series of popular, real-life Blood Games—each of which was watched by the cheering, bloodlusty masses who observed the Games on big-screen televisions from the comfort of their living rooms. First, there were the smart bombs and missiles rained down on the Third World nation of Iraq. Our destruction of Iraqi forces was delivered with deafening blows by American military "gladiators" from the relative safety of high tech tanks, armored vehicles, jet aircraft, and computer-run ships.

Next on the Blood Game schedule was the U.S. initiated aggression against the Serb nation in Bosnia/Yugoslavia. Americans and Europeans saw on television the visual feast of U.S. air strikes raining fire and death down on civilian skyscrapers, passenger trains, once tranquil neighborhoods, even fleeing flocks of refugees. We massacred tens of thousands supposedly to get at one man, Mr. Slobodan Milosevic, who happened to be this poor nation's sitting political leader. A Roman Emperor Commodus for a new era—that's what Milosevic was.

Saddam Hussein, Osama Bin Laden—each has been portrayed as a type of Commodus, worthy of death—but first, the Blood Games must be conducted. Call forth the American Gladiators!

He whom the elite rulers have chosen to be sacrificed must first be smeared and demonized. Randy Weaver?—he and his family were branded by the media as "white separatists." So—away with them. Off with their heads. Call in the gladiators!

David Koresh and his peaceful, if confused, congregation? "Cultists... weapons possessors." Oh my!—Kill them! Bring in the heavy artillery! Let the gladiators do their bloodwork!

Death and Blood Games as Entertainment

What we are seeing in the U.S.A., then, is a fascinating, if gruesome, updated reenactment of the ancient Blood Games of Rome but with a new, internet and television age, high tech slice of favor. In ancient Rome, Christians were seen as dangerous criminals. These "criminals" were executed, and their executions became a vehicle for mass public entertainment.

Today, American audiences are clamoring to watch on television convicts be put to death by lethal injection, by firing squad, and by electric chair. Better yet, public bloodlust demands that entire classes and groups of designated public enemies—even rogue nations!—be killed, with the TV-wired public viewing the action live, staged as huge entertainment.

It was only natural that public lasciviousness progress in its debauchery from movie dramas like the *Texas Chainsaw Massacre* and *Scream* to greater, more jaw dropping realism. Even thrills and chills television shows like the "reality-based" *Survivor, Fear Factor, Spy TV, Jackass, Cops,* and others soon lose their ability to titillate. The desensitized masses will always want more and more. Shock value is fleeting. Bloodlust never diminishing.

Returning to *Gladiator*, my friend, Allen Woodham, director of South East Christian Witness, in Australia, observes:

> I have read reviews of the new blockbuster movie recently released called *Gladiator*. The fact that so many are going to see it proves that the same perverted bloodlust now exists in people that was present in the early Romans. Soon, they will grow weary of high tech "special effects" and demand something more "in your face" to obtain the same thrill...
>
> The deranged butchery of those early Roman days (when Christians were persecuted) should cause everyone to see where worldly entertainment is truly headed... The day could soon arrive when people will be in the bleachers watching Christians die.
>
> That might appear to be an over-reactionary statement to some. If you think this, it is only solid proof that your mind has already been satanically brainwashed by Hollywood. (*South East Christian Witness*, April-May 2000, p. 14).

The Designated Enemy

The Holy Bible says that near the end of time, one, very special group shall be cast as the designated enemy—as the villains of society, as a collection of dangerous misfits. The Bible-believer who refuses to compromise his or her faith, who clings to Jesus, who says *no* to false Bible versions, *no* to homosexual perversion, *no* to murder of little babies through abortion, *no* to other gods and other religions—he or she shall become the publicly despised sacrifice of the prophesied Blood Games of *Revelation*. Jesus said, "They will kill you and thinketh they do God service."

This, then, is how we as Christians should view the current mania for bloodlust. This is how we must understand and interpret the flood of fiendishness so prevalent in today's popular culture. The devil is now preparing and training the final generation of killers—desensitized and unfeeling, modern-day gladiators.

The ultimate Blood Games are about to begin. The lions are hungry and in their cages. The new Emperor is about to take his throne and will oversee the bloodletting. Let the Games begin!

Even so, come quickly, Lord Jesus!

God's Warning to the Green Barbarians: He Shall...

"Destroy Them Which Destroy the Earth"

"And the seventh angel sounded; and there were great voices in heaven, saying, The kingdoms of this world are become the kingdoms of our Lord, and of His Christ; and he shall reign for ever and ever...and thy wrath is come, and the time of the dead, that they shall be judged, and that thou...shouldest destroy them which destroy the earth."

—*Revelation 11:15,18*

They claim to be lovers and friends of the earth, admirers of nature and protectors of its bounties. But then, Satan, their hellish director, is justly accused by Jesus our Lord as being the father and inventor of lies. Thus it is that, far from being benefactors and nurturers of nature, environmentalist fanatics are in fact DESTROYERS.

Yes, environmentalist true believers must be unmasked and exposed for what they truly are: "DESTROYERS OF THE EARTH."

The Reign of the Green Gestapo

In a recent issue of *Freedom Network News*, Jarret Wollstein chronicles the frightening belief system of the environmentalists. He calls them the "Green Gestapo" and describes their behavior as "insane."

Wollstein recounts the horrifying true tale of Mr. John Pogasi, a self-employed truck mechanic from Morristown, Pennsylvania. Mr. Pogasi fled the tyranny of Communist Hungary in 1956 and proudly became an U.S. citizen. He told one and all that only in America could a man breathe free. But that was before the Green Gestapo began its terror campaign.

You see, John Pogasi believed in conservation and beautifying his surroundings. He bought an abandoned, filthy, unsanitary lot and improved

dam comes tumbling down

Destruction began last week on the 162-year-old Edwards Dam on the Kennebec River in Augusta, Maine. Federal authorities ordered the dam destroyed because its hydroelectric benefits did not offset the environmental damage it caused. The state plans a fisheries restoration program for the river.

Federal authorities ordered the 162-year old Edwards Dam in Maine destroyed at the insistence of environmentalists. Environmental leaders want the demolition of all of America's 600 dams, including the behemoth Hoover Dam, the Grand Coulee, and Glen Canyon Dam. They have expressed no sorrow for the many thousands of animals and other forms of wildlife that will be killed by resulting floods and raging waters. In Proverbs, God says, "All they that hate me love death."

it by removing over 7000 mosquito-breeding, used tires. He cleaned up old rusting auto parts and other trash and debris on the lot and filled dirty, sewage-filled ditches.

The environmentalists couldn't stand it. They were furious that anyone would clean up and beautify that lot. They reported Mr. John Pogasi to the Environmental Police—the federal EPA bureaucrats.

Mr. Pogasi was indicted and convicted by a jury and judge of 41 violations of the Clean Water Act and sentenced to three years in a federal prison. A man who had escaped the ravages of the Communists in Eastern Europe had fallen into the hands of the Communists in the Eastern region of the United States.

Turning the Truth End on End

Now imagine: The federal law by which this poor man was unjustly imprisoned is amazingly called the *Clean Water Act*. What a misnomer! Proving once again that Satan and his earthly minions love to turn the truth end on end. In satanic circles, language is reversed. Black is white and vice versa, good is bad, unclean is clean, and death is life. That is why, in the satanic black mass, the Lord's Prayer is recited backwards. And the cross, or crucifix, is blasphemously displayed upside down.

FEATURES

*Plans are to kill most of the Kaimanawa wild horses in the next few weeks. **Alan Samson** examines a*

Horses stir unbridled emotions

In Australia, these beautiful wild horses were unmercifully massacred by the government after environmentalists claimed the horses were injuring "flora and fauna" (grasses). Environmentalists sneered at citizen groups who begged the horses be spared and not shot. Are these victimized horses blood sacrifices for Satan-worshipping environmentalists?

"Come, Let Us Kill the Children!

Environmentalist barbarians profess to love the earth and all life, but they deceive, converting dark falsehoods into politically correct "truth." For example, they have no sympathy for unborn babies, demanding cruel abortions, even partial birth abortions, of live, fully-formed little babies.

That's not all. They get perverse satisfaction from wolves, mountain lions, grizzly bears, and other wild beasts they release in densely populated areas that attack, maim, and kill innocent children and adults. Environmentalists justify the carnage by pointing out that people are plentiful and can be spared, while the animals are "endangered species."

"Come, Let us Destroy Homes and Extinguish Living Things"

Wollstein reports that in Riverside, California, in 1993, dozens of homes were destroyed as wildfires erupted in the area. But desperate homeowners were threatened with prison and fines if they cleared dry, overgrown brush. Reason: endangered rats, vermin, inhabited the brush. Net result: The homes, the brush, and the rats alike went up in flames. DESTROYERS OF THE EARTH.

In towns and cities across America, federal, state, and local environmental police and bureaucrats are bullying citizens—and destroying their property. In Galveston, Texas, a 67 year-old retired couple wept as their tiny home was bulldozed into ruins. The defeated husband was branded an eco-criminal by a federal judge and castigated in local newspapers. His crime: The couple's house had been built in an area the environmentalists said was *once* (not now—but in eons past) a "wetland."

When the old man complained there was no water on his quarter-acre lot or anywhere else in the subdivision, so it couldn't possibly be a "wetland," angry environmentalist bureaucrats snarled and said, "For regulatory purposes, a wetland is whatever we decide it is."

Louise and Fred Williams of Little Compton, Rhode Island also lost their home, after the EPA ordered them to tear it down. DESTROYERS OF THE EARTH.

"Come, Let Us Hack Down the Trees"

In Chicago's suburbs, environmentalists are now demanding that 80,000 trees be uprooted and destroyed. These DESTROYERS OF THE EARTH explain that the "native habitat" of the midwest United States was once plains and grass. No trees. Let us, they demand, "restore the land to its primitive wild state."

Scientists, of course, maintain that in the far distant past the entire North American continent was ice. Grasses came later. So, there is no real logic to the environmentalists' demands. Just an insatiable appetite to destroy green things—trees. (And to think we are constantly told by the media that environmentalists are lovers of trees—tree huggers!)

"Come, Let us Firebomb and Destroy Private Property"

Across the U.S.A., evil, crazed environmental terrorists are inspired by Satan to DESTROY AND KILL. In Vail, Colorado, they fire-bombed the Two Elks Restaurant and a ski lodge. Environmentalists said they did it to "save" the endangered lynx, a wildcat. The BATF and FBI didn't bother to investigate—they were too busy tracking down leads about potentially dangerous (though nonexistent!) right-wing terrorists.

In Lincoln, Montana, gun-toting warrior-thugs, wearing khaki uniforms and calling themselves "Environmental Rangers," tell their pals in the media (*Los Angeles Times*, Jan 11, 1990), "It's time to take up arms to defend the environment." "It's war," shouts environmental wacko leader Ric Valois. Predictably, again their friends, the FBI and BATF, have no problem with the threats of the environmentalist militia. DESTROYERS OF THE EARTH.

> *"If I were reincarnated, I would wish to be returned to the earth as a killer-virus to lower human population levels."*
>
> *—Prince Phillip of Great Britain*
> *President, World Wildlife Fund*

Timothy McVeigh, we are told, bombs and kills people in Oklahoma. He's promptly labeled by the feds as "another" vicious, right-wing, ignorant militia type. Meanwhile, environmentalist Ted Kaczynski, the unabomber, bombs and kills people. He's lionized by the press. Time magazine calls him a "Mad Genius." *U.S. News and World Report* also used the term, genius, in referring to Kaczynski's rantings and ravings. Other liberal groups described the writings of the unabomber as a "philosophical masterpiece."

Oh, I forgot to add: when the cops searched Kaczynski's isolated mountain shack, they found lying on a crude table a dog-eared copy of Vice President Gore's bestselling book, now an environmentalist "bible," *Earth in the Balance.*

"Come, Let Us Commit Genocide by Massacring Billions of Innocents"

Environmentalist "geniuses" like the unabomber are regularly praised by our earth-adoring media. Jacques Cousteau, the oceanographer, was warmly cheered after he announced that to save and make the earth sustainable, over 350,000 of its human inhabitants would have to be eliminated each day. DESTROYERS OF THE EARTH.

In addition to calling Christianity "A religion for losers and bozos," CNN founder Ted Turner received applause from environmentalists by agreeing with Cousteau. "The earth can sustain only 500 million people." Turner has repeated. That would mean some five and one-half billion would have to be eliminated. Presumably, Mr. Turner did not volunteer to be one of the hapless five and one-half billion to die.

In Britain, Prince Philip, Queen Elizabeth's environmentalist wacko husband, despises human life so much he has declared that, if he is reincarnated, he wants to come back as a deadly virus to kill off most of the Earth's human population. DESTROYERS OF THE EARTH.

In community after community, in state after state, environmentalists have recently selected shocking, new targets for destruction: dams and levees. They say that all dams and levees must come down and stay down. Homes and communities must be flooded. All land must be returned to wildland. To hell with the devastated people who lose their homes and businesses and to hell with all the suffering animals that will be flooded out and drowned, their habitats destroyed by the raging waters. DESTROYERS OF THE EARTH.

Austin American-Statesman

Smoke rises Tuesday from wildfires in the Everglades, which have consumed 160,000 acres, charring the dry sawgrass home of the alligator, the egret and the whitetail deer. Firefighters had the blaze contained within a perimeter of wet areas, levees and Interstate 75.

Walter Michot/ Miami Herald

Everglades fire expected to help nourish ecosystem

By Ian James
Associated Press

FLORIDA EVERGLADES — The flames that have roared through the Everglades, cutting

sprout quickly, and wildlife will flourish in the area that is burning, he said.

Even though the fire will help the ecosystem, forestry officials said, containing it is important because

Explorer was spotted in the area.

The primary fire began in the eastern Everglades late last week and may have been ignited by heat from a vehicle's catalytic converter. Aided by swirling winds, it

Bizarre and deadly, in Florida and across the U.S.A, federal environmental authorities are intentionally setting fires wasting millions of acres of timber and natural habitat, torturously burning to death and suffocating countless trapped animals. The feds say they are doing it to clear old growth and "nourish the ecosystem," but they refuse to allow loggers to first cut down and haul away the trees to be burnt. They also refuse the plea of citizen groups to rescue and save the animals. Are these massive fires a form of occult, pagan ritual and sacrifice?

Their Chief Enemy Identified

Pity the man or woman who opposes the Green Barbarians. Interior Secretary Bruce Babbitt, Bill Clinton's point man in killing off living things and destroying roads, dams, and forests, bluntly states, *"We must identify our enemies and drive them into oblivion."*

Uh ohh...You've got a real problem there, Mr. Babbitt. Your chief enemy, judging by the Scriptures, is not man—or dams and levees, animals, or trees. *Your principal enemy is God.* He put man on earth and, as recorded in *Genesis 1:28,* commanded him to *subdue and dominate the earth.* You and your fellow murderers, Mr. Babbit, have turned this scriptural truth end on end by having the government and its green gestapo subdue and dominate man, created in God's image. Moreover, though you and other environmentalists, like Satan and his devils, come disguised as "angels of light," God reveals your true, hidden secrets. Instead of saving the earth, your evil objective is really to plunder, wreck and destroy this planet and to bloodily kill off and extinguish people and living things as occult sacrifices to your pagan gods and philosophies.

Beware, all ye Green Barbarians! Now comes the Truth, upright and unyielding, to warn these would-be saviors of the cosmos: Surely, God will do all that he has prophesied. He shall, indeed, "DESTROY THEM WHICH DESTROY THE EARTH."

Deadly Vaccines of the New World Order

There is no doubt that vaccines have miraculously been used to save tens of millions of human lives and to prevent horrible forms of human suffering from diseases. The polio and smallpox vaccines are only two examples of life-giving vaccines. But the same medical achievement that saves lives, in the hands of evil men, may be used to abuse and harm.

Illuminati Establishes Vaccine Task Force

The Illuminati's most pre-eminent leaders have recently taken a keen interest in the field of vaccines. They have established a special task force to oversee the administration of vaccines to children and adults throughout the world, called the Global Alliance for Vaccines and Immunization (GAVI).

The first meeting of this eerie and ominous GAVI task force was held in Davos, Switzerland, in 2000. Its members include Microsoft's Bill and Melinda Gates, the United Nations World Health Organization (WHO), the Rockefeller Foundation, and the World Bank. The national governments of Russia and the U.S.A. are also involved. Bill Gates, for now, seems to be the principal force behind the work of GAVI.

Gates, whose Microsoft is at the forefront of developing new nanotransistor technology, says he has 24 billion dollars of his own money to give away. A lot of this money is going to go toward the development of new vaccines, which the United Nations World Health Organization (WHO) will administer by injections of the world's poor.

Microsoft founder, Bill Gates, reputed to be the world's richest man, is helping to fund the United Nations vaccine programs. Gates, a secular Jew, has said he does not believe in God. He regularly attends former Communist party boss Mikhail Gorbachev's annual State of the World Forum held at the former Presidio Army base in California.

Secret Vaccine Ingredient Kills Unborn Babies

Gates, said to be the richest man on earth, and his wife, Melinda, are also known to support Planned Parenthood and other pro-abortion and global depopulation causes. According to reliable sources, some of the new vaccines being developed by the United Nations (WHO) with Gates' money secretly contain poisonous chemicals—chemicals which act to kill unborn babies inside the mothers' womb.

In 1999, the American Life League was horrified to discover that UN vaccines were being used as hidden depopulation "bombs." The pro-life group went straight to Bill Gates with its discovery and confronted him, as the following news report indicates:

Gates-Sponsored Vaccine Program a Depopulation Measure?

> Washington, Dec. 14 (LSN.ca)—The American Life League, a pro-life organization, confronted software mogul Bill Gates last week, telling him that a World Health Organization (WHO) tetanus vaccination program undertaken with Gates' sponsorship bears striking resemblance to a similar WHO program which was exposed as a measure to involuntarily sterilize young women in the Philippines. Gates has donated $26 million to a WHO tetanus program in several developing countries.

In its press release, the American Life League notes that a previous tetanus program, conducted in the Philippines in 1995, aroused suspicion from Catholic health workers since it involved only women in their child-bearing years, an oddity since tetanus effects men and women, old and young alike. An investigation revealed that the women were given the tetanus vaccine combined with a chemical called Human Chorionic Gonadotrophin (HCG) to create an anti-pregnancy agent. The BBC, in conjunction with the Philippine Department of Health and the Philippine Medical Association, reported that many Filipino women suffered spontaneous abortions due to the vaccine, which creates an immune response to pregnancy in the mother's body.

"The current Gates funded program, involving the WHO in several developing countries, is once again aimed only at women in their child-bearing years. This is the world of population elimination," said the American Life League. "Most likely, Gates believes his funds are helping sick women and children, but in reality they're creating unimaginable suffering."

New Israeli Virus Bioweapon Targets Arabs Only

Nexus, an Australian magazine, has done terrific work in exposing yet another aspect of the use of vaccines for deadly purposes—the development of bioweapons designed to kill only designated races and ethnic groups. It was reported in the *London Sunday Times* in 1997 that Israel is working on a biological weapon which is genetically targeted against Arabs. The highly respected *Foreign Report*, a *Jane's* publication which monitors security and defense matters, reported that Israeli scientists have used South African genetic warfare research in an attempt to develop an "ethnic bullet."

Israeli scientists at the super-secret Nes Tziyona biowarfare laboratory near Tel Aviv have engineered deadly microorganisms that only attack DNA within the cells of victims with distinctive Arab genes. Nes Tziyona produces a wide range of chemical and biological weapons and is reportedly larger than all Arab and Iranian biowarfare laboratories combined.

The Israeli research mirrors biological studies conducted by South African scientists during the apartheid era and disclosed in testimony before the Truth and Reconciliation Commission.

Daan Goosen, head of a South African chemical and biological warfare facility, said his team was ordered in the 1980s to develop a "pigmentation weapon" to target only black people.

The British Medical Association has become so concerned about the lethal potential of genetically based biological weapons that it has opened an investigation.

(Sources: *Nexus*, February-March 1999; *The Sunday Times*, London, 15 Nov. 1998; *The Australian*, 16 Nov. 1998).

A Dark, Dark Future

If we did not know Jesus Christ as Lord, these strange and ominous developments in vaccines and genetic engineering would fill us with dread and alarm. Combined with amazing new discoveries in nanotechnology robots, we now see how dramatically effective The World Cup Conspiracy could be in depopulating earth and establishing global systems of electronic, "Big Brother" control.

The evidence is conclusive. Preparations are in high gear for...

Concentration Camps in America

"The police state has become a work of art."

—Marshall McLuhan

Some nine years ago a French-Canadian reporter named Serge Monast called the ministry, desperate to speak with me personally. Mr. Monast stated he had come into possession of documents which proved the existence of a secret plan for a concentration camp system throughout North America. He sent them to me and, after a parallel investigation of my own, I became convinced the documents were authentic. Serge Monast was telling the truth. The horrible, horrible truth.

Not too long afterward, Serge Monast, a vigorous man in his 40s, died unexpectedly of a brief and mysterious illness. His friends suspected foul play, but there was no definite proof he was murdered. Just before he died, Serge wrote to tell me he would be contacting me soon to give me details of stunning new information he had discovered about the concentration camps, including a map pinpointing locations. Information which, Serge assured me, *"will blow your mind."*

I never received that information. Serge Monast died before he could get it to me. I made a promise back then that I would get to the bottom of this matter and report the truth to you, the dear readers of *Power of Prophecy* newsletter, who truly care for humanity and are concerned about the rapid growth of the Police State.

This is believed to be a U.S. government concentration camp in Arizona.

After years of intensive research and investigation, I released my video, *Gulag USA—Concentration Camps in America*. In this jaw-dropping video, I present a mountain of new evidence and facts with many photographic materials. I encourage you to obtain a copy of this revealing and documented video. Judge the facts for yourself—and then act accordingly.

In *Gulag USA*, I examine and review the bloody and deadly historical record of concentration camps. Many believe the Nazis in the 1930s and 40s were the first to develop the systematic use of such camps. In fact, for over 150 years, genocidal concentration camps have been used to roundup, incarcerate, torture, and methodically massacre targeted "enemies of the state," "inferior races," or "class enemies."

Harbinger of things to come? Victims' bones of Cambodia's incredible genocide are stacked behind a monk. The Khmer Rouge communists of the 1970s learned their gruesome techniques of concentration camp "science" from a study of Stalin's and Mao's death camps.

"Exterminate all the brutes"

In the colonial era in Africa, the British became experts at genocide. This was justified, wrote the great liberal philosopher Herbert Spencer, insisting that "imperialism has served civilization by clearing the inferior races off the earth."

The blacks, the European conquerors concluded, were "like unto brute beasts," worthy of slavery, isolation, banishment and death. As the bloodthirsty character Kurtz, in Conrad's apocalyptic novel, *Heart of Darkness*, remarked, "*Exterminate all the brutes.*"

Later, the Bolshevik Communists, international Jews under the leadership of Lenin and Stalin, further refined the genocidal goals of concentration camps. While some ethnic and racial groups, such as the Kulaks, were chosen for extinction by Soviet gulag, the Communists mostly chose as their victims those whom they believed to be enemies, or "potential" enemies, of their peculiar Illuminist philosophy. In this category, enforcing section 58 of the USSR's criminal code, the Soviets rounded up people adjudged guilty of "thought crimes."

Then, of course, there were the millions who were abducted and taken away, not for anything they had said or done, but simply as a means of raising fear and terror in the hearts and minds of the remaining populace.

"What we need," raged the insane Lenin, is "more Red terror. More and more and more."

The Nazis ran dozens of concentration camps. The Soviets had thousands.

The Theory and Practice of Hell

I recently reread Eugen Kogon's thought provoking book, *The Theory and Practice of Hell*, which claims to be a description of the hellishness of Nazi concentration camps like Auschwitz, Buchenwald, and Lublin. In a postnote to his book, Kogon shows how, in the post World War II period, after helping to conquer the Germans, the Russians conveniently seized and kept in operation all the Nazi concentration camps. In places like Ravensbruch and Sachsenhausen, the Communists built up prisoner populations of up to 250,000 inmates per concentration camp.

In the investigative exposé book, *An Eye for an Eye*, Jonathan Sack, himself a Jew, sadly notes that the Soviet regime installed ruthless Communist Jews as commandants of these brutal horror camps.

Their victims included forbidden "class enemies," certain categories of "intellectuals," hapless women and children driven off their lands and out of their apartments simply because they looked "too German," and American POWs captured by the Nazis. (The Russians never released these

American POWs. After the war, they either killed them or shipped them as slaves to Siberia to die of overwork and starvation.)

The Japanese, too, were busy in the 30s and 40s building concentration camps in China, Korea, and Southeast Asia. And in the United States, 33rd degree Mason President Franklin D. Roosevelt, his FBI Masonic crony, J. Edgar Hoover, and other bureaucratic pals built America's own version of such gulags—"internment camps" for Japanese Americans. Japanese who refused to voluntarily climb into the crude cattle trucks to be hauled off to the camps were often beaten and forcibly hauled away in handcuffs.

Most of the American people applauded. After all, anything that insures our security from potential terrorists is a good thing, right?

The Deadly "Operation Phoenix"

In Vietnam, in the 60s and 70s, the United States really got its concentration camp program in high gear. The CIA and U.S. Army special units set up a string of torture and death camps throughout South Vietnam. The program was called *"Operation Phoenix."* Sometimes, entire villages and towns were targeted for extinction. My Lai was one such village, and U.S. Army Lt. William Calley and his soldiers carried out orders and wiped out hundreds of men, women and children at My Lai.

Just like in Nazi Germany and Stalinist Russia, the genocidal butchers of the U.S.A. used the best of statistical and high tech methods in their Vietnamese concentration camp program. Death quotas had to be fulfilled by village chiefs, local political bureaucrats and lower-level commanders.

As Doug Valentine points out in his powerfully documented book, *The Phoenix Program*, "neutralization quotas put on them meant they had to sentence so many people a month regardless. And God, if you ever saw those prisons!"

This is the carnage of Jim Jones' Peoples Temple in Guyana, South America.

Independent investigators now believe this to have been an experimental death, torture, and brainwashing camp clandestinely run by the CIA.

To cover up their atrocities, the CIA ordered an assassin team to go in and kill Jones and his followers. The Guyana coroner reported that most died of gunshot wounds, not the so-called cyanide poisoning.

In *Hostages of War*, Don Luce also examines the perverse Phoenix Program, recounting its massive and unjustifiable use of torture, repression, and assassination. Most victims, he notes, were innocent, brought in only after a nosey neighbor, village gossiper, or family enemy falsely reported them to authorities as a potential threat to security. Many were accused of saying something they shouldn't have said, or of "insufficient support" for the political system.

Both Valentine and Luce say this demented brainchild system came straight out of The Company (the CIA) in Langley, Virginia. Computers were used by the thugs that ran it, and everyone in authority, from the military officials, to the U.S. Ambassador, the bureaucrats of the State Department, and the occupants of the White House, knew of *Phoenix*.

But—consider this—the American people knew little or nothing about Phoenix. And to this day, over three decades later, the press (CBS, NBC, ABC, Washington Post, etc.) still refuse to report the facts.

Those who scoff at the very word, "conspiracy," better rethink things. How often have you heard the faulty rhetoric, "Oh, I don't believe in conspiracies. If that was true, why don't I read about it in the newspaper or see it exposed on the TV news?"

Sure, just the way *Phoenix* was so courageously exposed by our bold journalists, huh?

Investigators found this rail car, equipped with shackles, parked in an isolated area on the train tracks. It appears to be designed to transport prisoners.

"Everything Must Change"

In my video, *Gulag USA*, you will see just how close we are to that scary night when the jackbooted thugs of America's ruthless new Special Forces Gestapo will begin breaking down doors and hauling Christians and patriots off to the camps. These gulag camps are already built. They are being furnished with the most heinous of torture devices. Some will be equipped with guillotines and crematoria. Thumbscrews, cattle prods, branding irons, skull crushers, tongue clamps, and microchip implantation devices will be used in dark dungeons of torture and death.

Bush, Ashcroft, Tenet and the boys are preparing the way, conditioning the mass public, rousing fear and alarm, declaring that cell after cell of domestic and foreign terrorists are out there, "plotting more crimes of infamy." If necessary, Washington, D.C. tells us, the Constitution must be shelved. The need for the peoples' security and safety make the Bill of Rights antiquated and obsolete. Torture, also, must be made acceptable say Jewish lawyers like New York's Alan Dershowitz and associates.

During the French Revolution, as the Masonic/Illuminist plotters ominously rounded up frightened legions of bewildered men, women, and children targeted for rape, torture, mass drownings, and the guillotine, the revolutionary leaders of the government in Paris, led by Robespierre, Voltaire, and other Illuminists, cried out *"Everything now is different. Everything has changed. Liberty requires action. Carpe Diem!" (Seize the day!)* Listen closely, my friends, for that same, fatal cry is being loudly cried out, even today, in the U.S.A. And the same devils are behind it.

Violence and Disease Are Only the Beginning of Woes For the World's #1 Superpower

Hunger, Thirst, and Concentration Camps

Pax Americana is the name coined by the neocons who preside over the Rumsfeld Pentagon and the Bush White House. It stands for the global reign of the United States of America. After all, they boast, we are the only superpower, the New Rome. On behalf of the Zionist cause (spreading a fascist style of "Democracy" around the world) the neocons propose that America threaten to bludgeon all who oppose their elitist goal of global supremacy.

The Bible warns, however, that God hates a haughty spirit. He despises the proud and will eventually bring them low. Pride goeth before the fall.

I am persuaded that America is on the very threshold of exactly that: A great fall. The resounding fall of American power will be so dramatic, so sudden, that it will take the citizenry by complete surprise. Indeed, when the American Goliath comes crashing down to earth with a loud thud, the people and nations of the whole world will be shaken.

Revelation 18:7-11 records the torment to befall an unholy, decadent American nation that, today, glorifies herself and lives deliciously while leading the world in wealth and commerce:

> *"How much she hath glorified herself, and lived deliciously...for she saith in her heart, I sit a queen, and am no widow, and shall see no sorrow.*

The National Animal Identification System requires every farm animal to be "tagged" with a computer chip and registered in a federal database.

Therefore shall her plagues come in one day, death, and mourning, and famine...

Alas, alas, that great city, Babylon, that mighty city! for in one hour is thy judgment come.

And the merchants of the earth shall weep and mourn over her; for no man buyeth their merchandise any more."

In the coming time of plague, hunger, pestilence, disease, and confusion, America's vast wealth will be of no use to its people: *"For in one hour so great riches is come to naught." (Revelation 18:17)*

It is a firm biblical principle that *"He who lives by the sword shall die by the sword."* America is a warfaring nation that readily exports violence to foreign shores and does not hesitate to threaten its perceived enemies with death and destruction. However, the horror and bloodshed we visit on others will surely be visited on us in due time. The prophetic Scriptures speak of unparalleled violence to come. There will be plagues, disease, pestilence, hunger, and natural disasters. The weapons stored in God's arsenal of wrath are many.

The Gathering Storm

He who hath eyes to see and ears to hear take note of the gathering storm that is at our doorstep:

- Pandemic bird flu and a revival of the terror-wreaking ravages of the 1918 Spanish flu and the 1950s Asian flu. If bird flu hits America, the billions of chickens we produce annually must be rapidly slaughtered, severely reducing our food supply.

- Mad-cow disease and the potential destruction of America's huge livestock/cattle population. This means no more beef available.

- Wasting disease, now threatening the entire deer population of the U.S.A.

- Anthrax, the stealthy dreaded killer, still waiting in the wings, a disease that attacks farm animals and people alike.

- The "Terminator Gene" that some biological experts warn may devastate America's farm crops, caused by genetically engineered seed produced by profit-mad chemical and pharmaceutical corporations.

- Wild and erratic extreme weather, producing historic droughts in some areas of the country, epic rains and floods in others, ruining crops and destroying homesteads.

Desperate Survivors and Explosive Times

The devastation in New Orleans and the Gulf Coast from Hurricane Katrina we all saw on TV dredges up memories we'd all just as soon forget—filthy water everywhere, but not a drop to drink, Starving, thirsty throngs of desperate survivors at the New Orleans Superdome, hospital patients euthanized because they had no food and no medicine. Rapes, crime, violence, looting.

Think about it...when hunger and thirst hits everywhere at once in America, in all 50 states, what do you think will happen?

Do you think the 25 million illegal aliens in our midst will just sit idly by and watch as long-

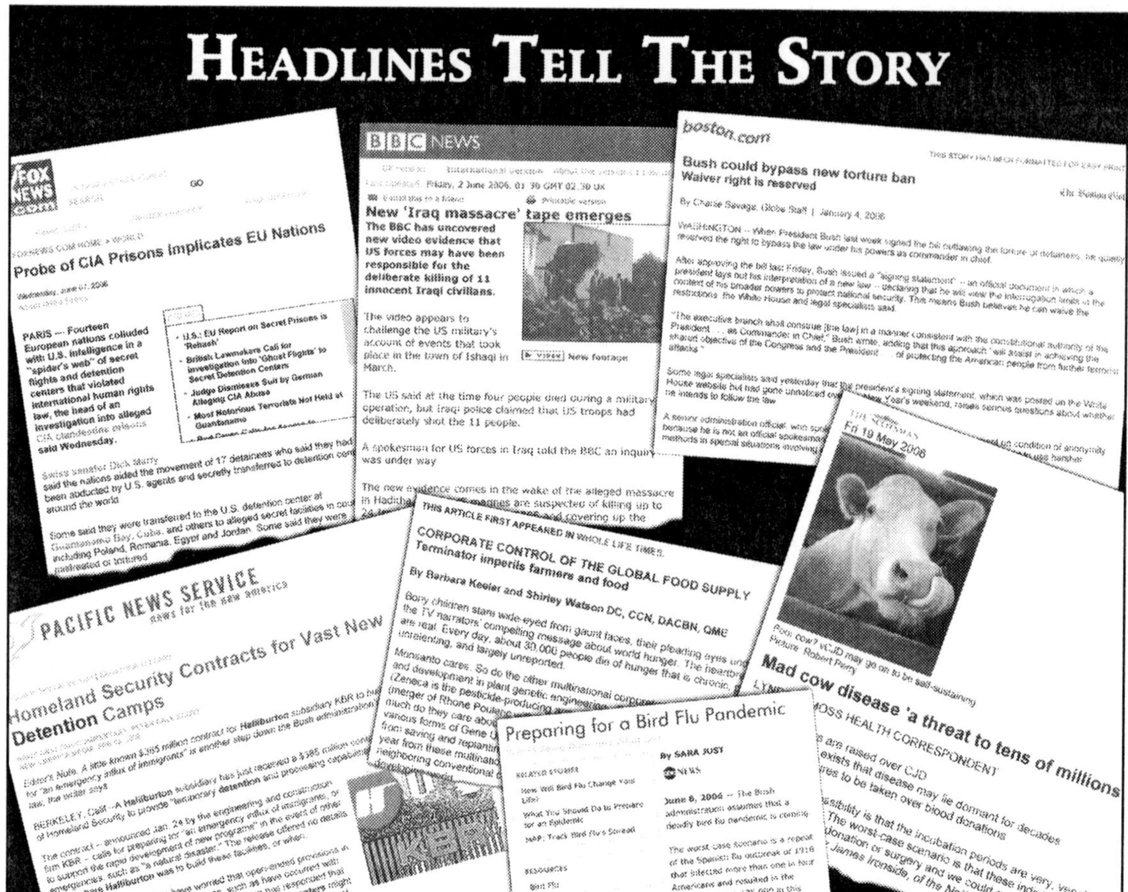

time American citizens enjoy what is left of the scarce food, water, and shelter? Will heavily armed criminal elements and drug dealers among the blacks in the ghettos and the meth-crazed white population happily endure the empty shelves in their convenience and food stores? What happens when their welfare checks don't arrive? How much rage will they express when disease and famine strike their neighborhood slums?

Ordo Ab Chao of Illuminati

The Illuminati elite know exactly what is going to happen. It's been pre-planned and strategized in advance. Remember, their motto is *"Ordo Ab Chao"*—Order Out of Chaos. Hellish conditions, rioting, killing and desperation all bring opportunity for their Great Plan to work out.

When the evil times explode around us, the United Nations World Food and Agriculture Organization will quickly assume power. The World Health Organization has its quarantine power ready, too.

Those scary, dictatorial presidential executive orders I describe in my book, *Days of Hunger, Days of Chaos* will be rushed into effect. Like the executive order prohibiting *"hoarding"* of water and food by citizens and the executive orders requiring ration cards and the use of biochips, RFIDs or smart ID cards to identify all citizens. Then, no man may buy or sell, without the mark, a name, or number assigned by the Police State.

Millions for "Detention Centers"

In February 2006, *The New York Times* reported that Halliburton Corporation subsidiary Kellogg, Brown & Root was given a $385 million contract by Bush's Homeland Security Department to build detention centers on American soil. These will be in *addition* to the hundreds of camps already built for the American gulag system.

Meanwhile, America's global gulag continues under construction, as fleets of 737 and 757 aircraft ferry so-called potential "terrorists" to torture centers in Romania, Egypt, Belarus, and other countries. The savage dictators and cruel police in these countries do not hesitate to apply medieval-style torture and mete out death and punishment without limitations.

Using Orwellian language, America's insane Attorney General Alberto Gonzales and Homeland Security Czar Michael Chertoff call this abduction and transport of terror suspects and government resisters *"renditions."* A new word for a New Age of horror.

In fact, the Geneva Convention and over 225 years of American tradition forbidding the torture, humiliation, and degrading of prisoners of war has been hastily thrown out the window by the jack-booted thugs of the Bush Administration.

Other Police State innovations have also recently been introduced by Bush's "Himmler Corps." Like the mind-boggling National Animal Identification System. Under new federal rules, in a few more years, owners of even one pig, one goat, one chicken, one cow, or one sheep must obtain a 7 digit I.D. number and register the birth, health, whereabouts, and death of each of their animals in a newly created federal government database, at a cost of $3 to $20 per animal.

The Coming Great Thirst—A Bonanza for the Elite

New water rules are also taking effect. Many states now require licenses before citizens can store even small quantities of water. In other states, rural families who have water wells must put a meter on their wells so the authorities can monitor how much water they use. Some locales now forbid cattle drinking from creeks, rivers, and streams.

Multimillionaire Texas Oilman T. Boone Pickens has gone into the water business.

Meanwhile, multimillionaire investors like Texas Oil man T. Boone Pickens and UN environmentalist Maurice Strong have shrewdly bought up the underground water rights to millions of acres in Colorado, New Mexico, and the West, as well as in Canada. According to *Newsweek* (Sept. 2, 2002), Pickens owns 150 years worth of water, and he's just waiting for the day when the parched, thirsting masses come begging him for a drink. He'll have the water, he says, but it's gonna cost them, and plenty!

Thus, the far-sighted men of the Illuminati are braced and ready for the Last Days onslaught. Detention centers, foreign troops, water rights, vaccines, emergency medicines—all are in hand. The elite have what we need to survive, but it's gonna cost us plenty: our freedom, our honor, our dignity, maybe our lives. Pride surely goeth before a fall.

Days of Hunger, Days of Chaos

"...and there shall be famines, and pestilences...All these are the beginning of sorrows."

—*Matthew 24:7-8*
Prophecy of Jesus

There is coming a brutish time of severe food shortages in America. Each of us will be dramatically affected. There will be little or no food at any price. What limited food supplies do remain will be strictly controlled by government authorities. Food will be rationed by law, and you and I will be allowed to purchase only our meager portion. Moreover, your cries and earnest plea to buy food will be refused by the authorities unless your name and number are found in the *World Food Authority's* central computer database.

I repeat: Food shortages are soon to become painfully evident in America. The specter of famine will loom large in our lives. The Bible prophesies it. How will this frightening catastrophe transpire? What forces will be set in motion to accomplish it? Will the coming days of hunger be the result of monumental acts of God—like killer hurricanes, floods, and droughts? Will mass starvation be caused by deadly viruses and natural pestilences attacking our crops? Could this drama of unheralded human misery unfold as a byproduct of general nuclear war?...or of an unexpected, deadly comet or meteor smashing into Earth from outer space?

Planned Acts of Selfish and Greedy Men

Certainly, God can cause shattering types of Earth-changing events to occur. But based upon careful analysis and years of meticulous research, I believe that the ravaging hunger will come about primarily because of the planned acts of selfish and greedy men. Yes, evil, devilish men.

It is the plan of these super-rich plotters to gain total world power through their control of the production, storage, distribution, and sale of food. Food, they are convinced, translates into empire and is the ultimate weapon in the seduction of mankind.

"Food is Power!"—They Shall Control Food, Life, and Death

"Food is Power! We use it to change behavior. Some may call that bribery. We do not apologize." These were the threatening, blustery words of the stern-faced Catherine Bertini at the recent United Nations World Food Summit. Ms. Bertini is executive director of the UN's World Food Program. Her threat is real. In a world that has become, in the words of a rather notorious First Lady, a "Global Village," it is food that the people of the village must have to survive. And it is the control of food—it's production and distribution—that rogue agents of global evil will use as a battering

ram to drive a desperate and starving people of America into submission.

I document in my revealing book, *Days of Hunger, Days of Chaos*, the staggering facts of what is planned for our future. Secret units of our own federal government have already set up a structure of control over the food production and supply system. Their spy satellites overhead in the sky are now monitoring what farmers are planting. Weather modification weapons are being employed to cause intermittent floods and droughts. The World Trade Organization is establishing quotas and new guidelines for farmers.

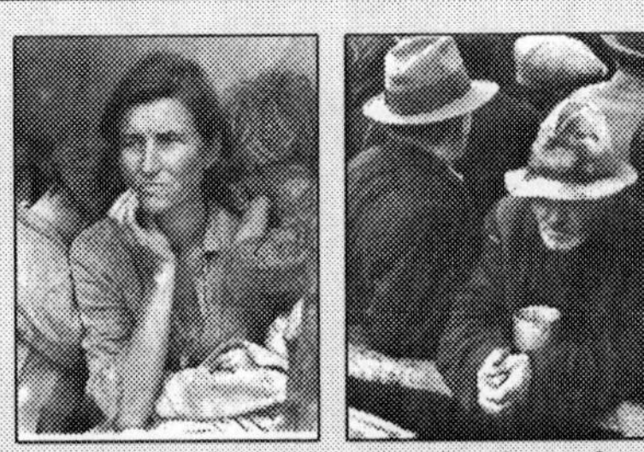
The 1930s Great Depression brought untold human suffering and misery to tens of millions of Americans. Soup lines were set up in major cities to feed the unemployed. The superrich, however, became immensely wealthier and were able to further their ultimate aim of total economic domination via government socialism. Today, the elite see food as the ultimate weapon for control. They intend to frighten a starving populace into relinquishing its freedoms. As one UN official stated, *"Food is Power. We use it to change behavior."*

The conspiratorial elite have bought up vast land holdings and have locked up agricultural resources in America. They have driven out of business and financially strangled to death the small family farmer. Farming is now a mega-business run by the super-rich. Their multinational, corporate conglomerates own beef, pork, and chicken processing plants and hold iron-clad, exclusive patents on seeds. They also own the chemical plants that manufacture commercial fertilizer.

The elite run the money center banks that can make or break the small farmer through the debt process, and they have their men in the White House and in the Congress as chairmen of the appropriate congressional committees overseeing banking, trade, commerce, and agriculture.

"Behold a Pale Horse"

Frankly, the coming events I chronicle in my shocking new book, *Days of Hunger, Days of Chaos*, are so horrific that were it not for the knowledge of God's divine protection, I would myself be filled with terror. Bible prophecy says that God has determined a furious and grim period of intense, overwhelming hunger and death to be visited upon mankind. This will be a breathtaking panorama of destruction and suffering like nothing you and I have ever witnessed or, possibly, can even imagine. Men and women will become so desperate for food they will kill their fellow man and eat his flesh. Some will even cut off their own limbs and eat them *(Isaiah 9:20)*.

The coming time of danger is pictured in *Revelation 6* as a brief, but savage era of bloodshed, carnage, famine, hunger, and disease. In breathtaking succession we envision the image of the rider of the white horse, the red, the black, and, finally, the pale horse. The rider of the pale horse is surely the most terrifying of the four. His very name is Death, spelled with a capital letter "D"!—

> *And I looked, and behold a pale horse: and his name that sat on him was Death, and Hell followed with him.*
>
> *And power was given unto them over the fourth part of the earth, to kill with sword, and with hunger, and with death..." (Revelation 6:8)*

The toll of death prophesied to occur translates into a mind-boggling *one and a half billion unfortunate men, women, and children* who are soon to meet their maker.

These victims, as well as you and I, have a rendezvous and appointment with destiny. None of us can avoid this time of destiny. From the beginning of time, God preordained all things and wrote in His book a detailed plan and roadmap for your life and mine.

Financial Collapse Leads to Panic and Fear

This gruesome time of hunger and bloodcurdling physical devastation will be preceded by graphic developments of monumental scale in the financial world. The world economy will collapse, leaving the stock markets in tatters, banks in total ruin, American currency worthless, and hundreds of millions of people in dire straits—demoralized, shocked, hungry, sick, and frightened.

The rapid decline of the dollar and devaluation of foreign currencies will cause stocks of food and other consumer goods to plummet and fall. Bread, milk, meat, cereals, and other staples will be controlled. All foodstuffs will be stored at central distribution points and rationed. Doors of local grocery stores and supermarkets will be padlocked, and shelves left stark and empty.

Meanwhile; in a strange and ghastly contradiction, farmers who attempt to harvest their fields will be harshly punished by the authorities. Crops that could be used to feed starving children and adults will either be allowed to rot or will be plowed under.

Panic will seize the hearts of peoples everywhere. Money gone, no food to eat, the world will be brought to its knees. After a brief denial of economic collapse will come the all-consuming specter of famine, disease, and homelessness. The grim future will fill men and women with fear and dread. Quickly, anger and frustration will break out. Formerly law-abiding citizens will turn on one another, even brother against brother, in a violent rampage and scramble for food and survival.

"He Who Has the Food Wins"

The super-rich elite have always despised the middle class, and now, at last, they have discovered the ultimate means to suppress and dominate the less fortunate. The elite conspirators have developed a fantastically multifaceted plan to take over and manage the food supply for planet Earth. The final struggle, the final war, will be fought not with aircraft, bombs, and bullets, but with food. "He who has the food wins"—that is the new motto of the Illuminati.

There is Hope!

Still, there is hope. Marvelous hope. Christians who trust in the Lord need fear man nor devil. And because of their faith and hope, they shall be amply and magnificently rewarded by He who holds the key to life and death. His eye is upon them and in perilous time of famine and death, they shall live and prosper:

> *Behold, the eye of the Lord is upon them that fear him, upon them that hope in his mercy; To deliver their soul from death, and to keep them alive in famine. (Psalms 33:18-19)*
>
> *They shall not be ashamed in the evil time: and in the days of famine they shall be satisfied. (Psalms 37:19)*
>
> *But the salvation of the righteous is of the Lord: he is their strength in the time of trouble. And the Lord shall help them, and deliver them: he shall deliver them from the wicked, and save them, because they trust in him. (Psalms 37:39-40)*

Are you prepared for the long prophesied and now emergent *Days of Hunger, Days of Chaos*? If you desire refuge, you must rely on the Lord of glory. You must believe in Him and come to the cross. In the savage days just ahead, he who attempts to save his life will lose it, while he who trusts in Him and turns his life over to God will save it. Whoever does not have Jesus will lose everything. But he who has Jesus will possess the riches of ages past and of all ages to come.

Questions Answered in *Days of Hunger, Days of Chaos*

Here are just some of the probing questions this groundbreaking book answers in its investigation into the coming, great food crisis:

- ❒ Does the Illuminati's Rockefeller Foundation now control the seeds of 95 percent of the Earth's major cereal crops—wheat, barley, and corn? (page 69)
- ❒ Is there a "Global Seeds Conspiracy" to place total ownership of the world's seeds—and ultimately the survival of mankind itself—in the hands of an elite cartel of multinational corporations? (page 83)
- ❒ Why are spy satellites now being used to monitor and control the crop production of farmers? (page 75)
- ❒ Will the United Nations Biodiversity Treaty force farmers and small property owners to abandon their homes and lands and "resettle" in approved government metro areas? (page 66)
- ❒ What top secret government projects are designed to use weather, viruses, bacterial pestilences, and other scientific tools to manipulate and diminish the Earth's food crops? (page 38)
- ❒ Are the police powers of the federal government—FBI, USDA, EPA, FDA, CIA, BATF, U.S. Fish and Wildlife Service, IRS, BLM, etc.—being used to taunt, harass, intimidate, frighten, impoverish, imprison and sometimes kill farmers, ranchers, and small land owners who oppose the takeover of our food supply? (page 123)
- ❒ What Executive Orders have recently been issued in advance of the coming, great food crisis to pave the way for a police state in America? (page 177)
- ❒ Are pre-planned and contrived food shortages on the way, with small farmers being purposely driven out of business? Will a starving and desperate American populace be left begging for federal government "saviors" to solve the crisis? (page 13)
- ❒ Is there a plan for a powerful, new United Nations agency, the World Food Authority, to control the production and distribution of food? (page 189)
- ❒ Were the recent famines in Somalia, Liberia, North Korea and elsewhere dress rehearsals for the great hunger soon to plague America? (page 205)
- ❒ During the coming deadly food shortages, who will be allowed the privilege of buying sufficient food to feed themselves...and who will be denied? (page 194)
- ❒ Should Christians and patriots immediately begin in earnest to acquire and store a year or more's supply of food? (page 219)
- ❒ What little known federal law makes it a heinous crime, punishable by imprisonment, for American citizens to hoard food, water, or fuels? (page 190)
- ❒ Will anger and chaos soon grip the world as desperately hungry masses of people panic, riot and storm grocery stores and supermarkets, only to find shelves cleaned out and empty? (page 195)
- ❒ What can you and I do now, before it is too late, to prepare for the coming, severe food shortages? Is it possible that you, I, and our families can not only stay healthy, well fed, and safe, but also prosper during the coming hard times? (page 209)

While the Rich Reap Huge Profits, Millions Will Die from Water Shortages and Waterborne Illnesses

The Coming Great Thirst

Son of man, eat thy bread with quaking, and drink thy water with trembling and with carefulness."

—*Ezekiel 12:18*

Grim reports about our water supplies and sources have been much in the news lately. A crisis of biblical proportions is at hand.

USA Today newspaper, in an eye-opening special supplement (Oct. 21, 1998) titled *"Drinking Water's Hidden Dangers,"* listed a growing number of threats to America's water supply. The report also described a rash of waterborne illnesses plaguing America's citizens, including severe nausea, diarrhea, fevers, and deaths.

The newspaper further noted that in Milwaukee, Wisconsin, in 1993, a devastating parasite infecting the city's water system actually killed 111 people and made a staggering 403,000 more violently sick.

"River Blindness" Plagues Africa

As bad as was the situation in Milwaukee, in Africa, things are tragically worse. News reports tell us that up to *ten million* Nigerians are currently afflicted with onchocerciosis, a horrible disease known as "river blindness." Overall, over 150,000 victims have been left permanently blind from this disease, which is now rampant in 16 African countries. Health authorities fear that a similar outbreak of "river blindness" might soon erupt in the United States.

In Israel, A National Catastrophe

In the nation of Israel, authorities announced that a *"national catastrophe"* exists because the whole country's water supply is found to be packed with dangerous, parasitic bacteria. Declaring the water system "on the edge of collapse," Environmental Minister Dalia Itzik requested that the Israeli Knesset (Parliament) set up an "emergency water regime." The damage, said Itzik, is "irreversible." (*Jerusalem Report*, July 20, 1999, Page 1)

Bloody Wars to be Fought Over Water, Says UN

In New York City, at the headquarters of the United Nations, a new study just published suggests that in coming years, nation will take up arms against nation in bloody wars and conflicts fought over water rights. Drinkable water, said the UN report, is a globally diminishing resource, and world peace is definitely at stake as thirsty nations are expected to bicker furiously over dwindling supplies.

The United Nations declared the year 1998 as the "International Year of the Oceans." This emphasized the importance that the globalist community attributes to the Earth's oceanic stores of water. Yes, undoubtedly, UN officials—and their overseers, the Illuminati elite—recognize the vast significance of man's competition for the scarce and quickly vanishing water supply of this planet. They well know that disastrous water shortages are imminent

What Lies Ahead?

But, one might object, water is everywhere, everywhere. Great rivers and their tributaries still seem to flow unimpeded, emptying into gargantuan seas. Lakes and streams are not totally empty, and after all, Americans have always been able to simply turn on a water tap and—voila!—a clear, amply flowing supply of life-enriching water has unfailingly been produced.

However, dramatic changes lie just ahead. The question becomes: *What will happen to our water in the days soon to come? Can we continue to depend on our governmental authorities providing us with never-ending flows of safe water?*

Bible Prophecy Has the Answer

Bible prophecy provides the answer. Read the Scriptures and you will readily know why the UN and the Illuminati are now beginning to focus maximum effort and energy to the issue of preparing for coming, severe water shortages.

Take *Revelation 8:10-12*, for example. There, we are told of a spectacular event to come in which waters and oceans become poisonously toxic as a burning star, called "Wormwood," falls upon the third part of the rivers, and upon the fountains of water: *"And many men died of the waters, because they were made bitter."*

Might this vivid image of a burning star called "Wormwood" be a picture of a fiery meteor plunging into the sea from outer space? Or is this the image of flaming, Russian intercontinental and sea-launched missiles bearing chemical or biological toxins which crash into oceans and rivers, making the waters bitter and poisonous?

Waters Contaminated by Nuclear Radiation

Former high-ranking Soviet military men, such as General Alexander Lebed and Colonel Stanislav Lunev, have been warning of miniature bombs so tiny they can be fitted in briefcases. Such devices are now reported missing from Soviet Army inventories.

Could the fiery explosions of these transportable nuclear devices cast a mega-tonnage of poisonous and deadly radiation contamination into the water supplies and reservoirs of our cities?

Could such a ruination of water supplies by suitcase bomb-carrying terrorists be the fulfillment of the prophecies in *Ezekiel 12:19?* These prophecies grimly reveal that, in the last days, people will *"drink their water with astonishment...because of the violence of all them that dwell therein."*

"And the Water Turned Into Blood"

There's also the dramatic finding by scientists that a number of America's rivers and sea beds are fast being polluted by deadly *pfeisteria* bacteria, which literally turn the waters blood-red! Many people in North Carolina and other eastern states have lately been hospitalized after eating fish infected by this mysterious bacteria.

What an amazing thing, for the Holy Scriptures speak of the sea turning to *blood* in the last days. *(Revelation 8:8)* The Bible says that when this occurs, one-third of all living things in the oceans are destroyed—and a third of all ships.

Illuminati chieftains like billionaire Maurice Strong intend to get even richer from the sale of water to the desperate, thirsty masses.

Illuminati Eye Big Profits

The devil is preparing his filthy legions of dark angels and wicked human disciples for the coming, brutish times. The devil and his agents well know of the prophesied, scorched-earth droughts, seas of blood, and life-destroying water shortages to come. Indeed, Satan and his human helpers are the "change agents" who have planned and are now engineering most of these catastrophic water disasters!

As I uncover and expose in my video, *The Coming Great Thirst*, the super-rich of the Illuminati have quietly been buying up shares of stock in water companies. They have also been acquiring huge expanses of raw land in Colorado and other states, under which flow billions of barrels of water through underground aquifers. They intend to haul in truckloads of cash on the back of the miserable masses who will be willing to pay anything—exorbitant sums—to stay alive by buying scarce water to drink.

One such Illuminatus, billionaire Maurice Strong, former Chairman of the UN's Environmental Program, is now the chief shareholder and the managing director of Ontario Hydro, Canada's largest water corporation.

Strong also has acquired thousands of acres of land in the thinly populated, but expansive, *Baca Grande* region of America's West. As a result, Strong and his rich pals now own aquifer water rights affecting almost the whole of Colorado as well as several other western states. When the crunch hits and people in those states are dying for lack of water, it is to Maurice Strong and his associates they must turn. They will be forced to grovel before the former United Nations bigwig on bended knees, begging for a few drops of the world's most precious, but rare, resource: *pure, clear, water!*

UFOs Spotted Over Waters

Even UFOs and extraterrestrials are getting into the mix of coming events. More and more UFOs are being spotted rising up out of the oceans and out of rivers and other bodies of water. Are these UFOs of demonic origins?

God's Advance Warning to the Saints

I believe that God wants His people to know of *The Coming Great Thirst*. He never leaves His children in the lurch. We perish without knowledge, but God promises us (see *Daniel 12:10*) that we will know in advance of the momentous disasters to overtake the world.

My video, *The Coming Great Thirst*, is God's warning to His saints. He is saying to us, *"Know now. Get ready. Prepare yourselves and your loved ones for that astonishing day just ahead when water shall be no more."*

Index

More Resources For You

Books:

Circle of Intrigue—The Hidden Inner Circle of the Global Illuminati Conspiracy, by Texe Marrs (304 pages) $24.00

Codex Magica—Secret Signs, Mysterious Symbols, and Hidden Codes of the Illuminati, by Texe Marrs (624 pages) $39.00

Dark Majesty—The Secret Brotherhood and the Magic of a Thousand Points of Light, by Texe Marrs (304 pages) $22.00

Mysterious Monuments—Encyclopedia of Secret Illuminati Designs, Masonic Architecture, and Occult Places, by Texe Marrs (624 pages) $39.00

Mystery Mark of the New Age—Satan's Design for World Domination, by Texe Marrs (288 pages) $19.00

Project L.U.C.I.D.—The Beast 666 Universal Human Control System, by Texe Marrs (224 pages) $22.00

Letters on Freemasonry, by John Quincy Adams (334pages) $24.00

Masonic and Occult Symbols Illustrated and Exposed, by Dr. Cathy Burns (553 pages) $24.00

Hidden Secrets of the Eastern Star—The Masonic Connection, by Dr. Cathy Burns (491 pages) $22.00

Secret Societies and Psychological Warfare, by Michael Hoffman (215 pages) $22.00

Videos:

Rothschild's Choice—Barack Obama and the Hidden Cabal Behind the Plot to Murder America (DVD) $29.00

Architectural Colossus—Mysterious Monuments Enshroud the World With Magic and Seduction (VHS or DVD) $29.00

Face to Face With the Devil—Close Encounters With Unexpected Evil (DVD) $29.00

The Sun at Midnight—Pyramids of Mystery, Temples of Blood (DVD) $29.00

Where the Rich and Famous Dwell—Architectural Secrets of the Rothschilds, the Vanderbilts, the Rockefellers, the Astors, and Other Storied Bloodlines and Dynasties (DVD) $29.00

Baal's Shaft and Cleopatra's Needle—Phallic Architecture and Sex Monuments of the Illuminati (DVD) $29.00

Cauldron of Abaddon—"From Jerusalem and Israel Flow a Torrent of Satanic Evil and Mischief Endangering the Whole World" (DVD) $29.00

Is the Pope Catholic? Shocking New Revelations About the World's Most Powerful Religious Leader (VHS or DVD) $24.00

The Sun at Midnight—Pyramids of Mystery, Temples of Blood (DVD) $29.00

Thunder Over Zion—Illuminati Bloodlines and the Secret Plan for A Jewish Utopia and a New World Messiah (VHS or DVD) $29.00

The Blind and The Dead—Greedy Evangelists and Religious Charlatans Leading the World Into a Spiritual Wasteland, by Texe Marrs (VHS or DVD) $29.00

Tower of Infamy—The Illuminati, Secret Societies, and the Buying and Selling of Televangelists and Other Famous-Name Christian Leaders, by Texe Marrs (DVD) $29.00

"The Eagle Has Landed!"—Magic, Alchemy and the Illuminati Conquest of Outer Space (VHS or DVD) $29.00

Illuminati Mystery Babylon—The Hidden Elite of Israel, America, and Russia, and Their Quest for Global Dominion (VHS or DVD) $29.00

Leviathan In Space—Strange Mysteries, Oddities, and Monstrosities of the U.S. Space Program (VHS or DVD) $29.00

About the Author

Well-known author of the #1 national bestseller, *Dark Secrets of The New Age*, Texe Marrs has written 40 books for such major publishers as Simon & Schuster, John Wiley, Prentice Hall/Arco, McGraw-Hill, and Dow Jones-Irwin. His books have sold millions of copies. He is one of the world's foremost symbologists and is a first-rate scholar of ancient history and Mystery religions.

Texe Marrs was assistant professor of aerospace studies, teaching American defense policy, strategic weapons systems, and related subjects at the University of Texas at Austin for five years. He has also taught international affairs, political science, and psychology for two other universities. A graduate *summa cum laude* from Park College, Kansas City, Missouri, he earned his Master's degree at North Carolina State University.

As a career USAF officer (now retired), he commanded communications-electronics and engineering units. He holds a number of military decorations including the Vietnam Service Medal and Presidential Unit Citation, and has served in Germany, Italy, and throughout Asia.

President of RiverCrest Publishing in Austin, Texas, Texe Marrs is a frequent guest on radio and TV talk shows throughout the U.S.A. and Canada. His monthly newsletter, *Power of Prophecy*, is distributed around the world, and he is heard globally on his popular, international shortwave and internet radio program, *Power of Prophecy*. His articles and research are published regularly on his exclusive websites: *powerofprophecy.com* and *conspiracyworld.com.*

For Our Newsletter

For a *free* sample copy of the *Power of Prophecy* newsletter revealing the innermost secrets of the Illuminati, unraveling globalist conspiracies, and focusing on world events, secret societies, cults, and the occult challenge to Christianity. If you would like to receive this newsletter, please write to:

Power of Prophecy
4819 R.O. Drive, Suite 102
Spicewood, Texas 78669

You may also e-mail your request to:
customerservice1@powerofprophecy.com

For Our Website

Power of Prophecy's newsletter is published free monthly on our websites. These websites have descriptions of all Texe Marrs' and other informative authors' books, and are packed with interesting, insight-filled articles, videos, breaking news, and other information unraveling illuminist secrets, delving into conspiracies and coverups, and exposing the elite agenda in opposition to American freedom. You also have the opportunity to order an exciting array of books, tapes, and videos through our online *Catalog and Sales Stores*. Visit our websites at:

www.powerofprophecy.com
www.conspiracyworld.com

Our Shortwave Radio Program

The international radio program, *Power of Prophecy*, is broadcast weekly on shortwave radio throughout the United States and the world. *Power of Prophecy* can be heard on WWCR at 4.840 on Sunday nights at 9:00 p.m. Central Time. You may also listen to *Power of Prophecy* 24/7 on websites *powerofprophecy.com* and *conspiracyworld.com.*